Come with us to the Spanish-speaking world!

¡Ven conmigo!

—a fully integrated Spanish program—makes it possible for you to accomplish all your teaching objectives as never before! *¡Ven conmigo!* ensures development of language proficiency in Spanish and builds students' language skills, so they can communicate effectively and express themselves with confidence.

- The FOUR LANGUAGE SKILLS—listening, speaking, reading, and writing—plus CULTURE, are all interwoven throughout the program.
- Strong GRAMMAR support lays an invaluable foundation for proficiency.
- All three levels of *¡Ven conmigo!* are PACED so that you can finish each text within the year. And because the first two chapters of the Levels 2 and 3 *Pupil's Editions* are review, the program provides an easy transition from level to level.
- Designed for LEARNERS OF ALL TYPES, *¡Ven conmigo!* is the program of choice for every one of your students.
- VIDEO CORRELATIONS and ON-PAGE BARCODES let you easily integrate video and videodisc segments into your instruction.
- A COMPLETE AUDIO PROGRAM—available on audiocassettes or compact discs—reinforces the text material and gives students another learning option.
- Constant SPIRALING and RE-ENTRY of material from earlier chapters provide consistent reinforcement and review.

See and hear native speakers in authentic locations around the Spanish-speaking world!

Where Will We Go?

Each Location Opener introduces your students to the diversity of Spanish-speaking countries. The *Video Program, Expanded Video Program*, and *Videodisc Program* target the same locations so your students see, hear, understand—and use—the language and culture.

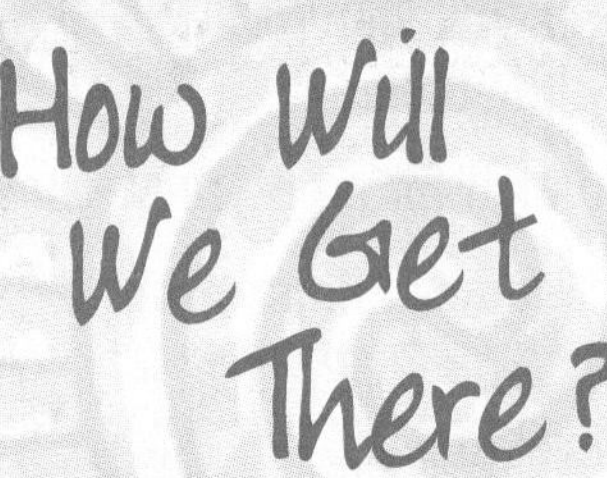

How Will We Get There?

Chapter Openers serve as advance organizers, identifying learner outcomes and stimulating interest.

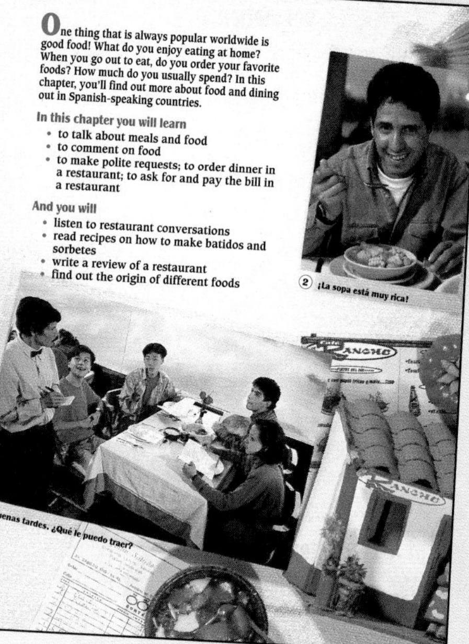

Authentic Locations & Language

De antemano features introduce the functions, vocabulary, and grammar targeted in the chapter and are reproduced in both the video and audio programs.

Your Building Blocks to Proficiency

The function, grammar, and vocabulary features in each chapter of *¡Ven conmigo!* are linked to give your students the building blocks they need to develop complete language proficiency.

In this function-driven program, each *Así se dice* presentation equips your students for specific language tasks appropriate to the chapter theme.

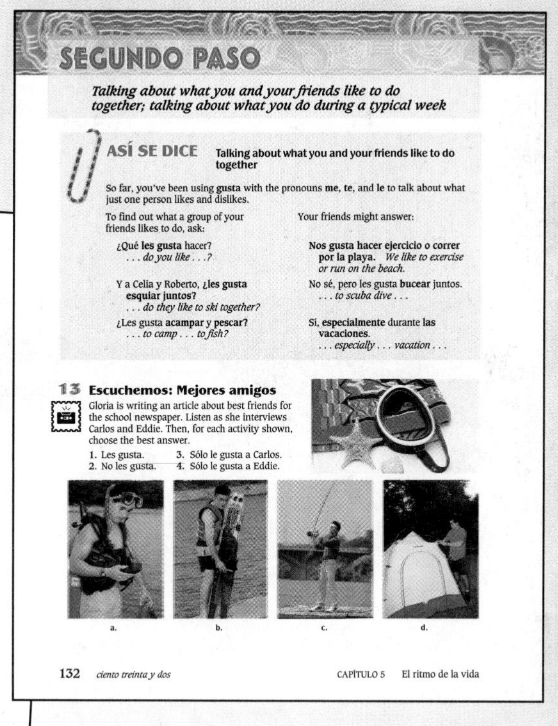
SEGUNDO PASO

Talking about what you and your friends like to do together; talking about what you do during a typical week

ASÍ SE DICE Talking about what you and your friends like to do together

So far, you've been using **gusta** with the pronouns **me**, **te**, and **le** to talk about what just one person likes and dislikes.

To find out what a group of your friends likes to do, ask:

¿Qué **les gusta** hacer?
. . . do you like . . .?

Y a Celia y Roberto, ¿**les gusta esquiar juntos**?
. . . do they like to ski together?

¿**Les gusta acampar y pescar**?
. . . to camp . . . to fish?

Your friends might answer:

Nos gusta hacer ejercicio o correr por la playa. *We like to exercise or run on the beach.*

No sé, pero les gusta **bucear** juntos.
. . . to scuba dive . . .

Sí, **especialmente** durante las **vacaciones**.
. . . especially . . . vacation . . .

13 Escuchemos: Mejores amigos

Gloria is writing an article about best friends for the school newspaper. Listen as she interviews Carlos and Eddie. Then, for each activity shown, choose the best answer.

1. Les gusta.
2. No les gusta.
3. Sólo le gusta a Carlos.
4. Sólo le gusta a Eddie.

a. b. c. d.

132 *ciento treinta y dos* CAPÍTULO 5 El ritmo de la vida

The *Gramática* presentation provides strong grammar support for the function-driven base of *¡Ven conmigo!*, the perfect combination to help your students develop their Spanish proficiency.

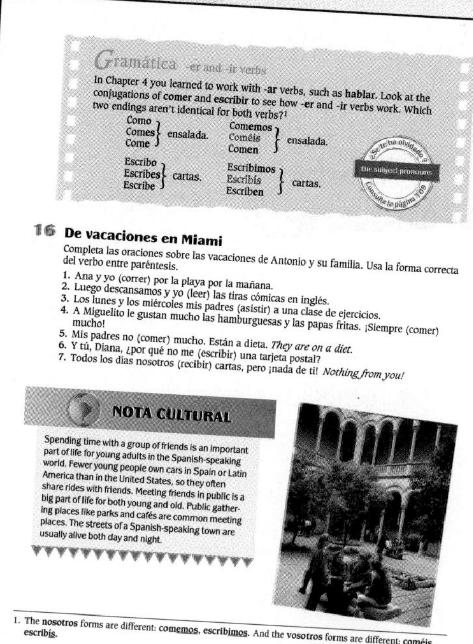
Gramática -er and -ir verbs

In Chapter 4 you learned to work with **-ar** verbs, such as **hablar**. Look at the conjugations of **comer** and **escribir** to see how **-er** and **-ir** verbs work. Which two endings aren't identical for both verbs?[1]

Como / Comes / Come } ensalada. Comemos / Coméis / Comen } ensalada.

Escribo / Escribes / Escribe } cartas. Escribimos / Escribís / Escriben } cartas.

¿Se te ha olvidado? the subject pronouns Consulta la página 199

16 De vacaciones en Miami

Completa las oraciones sobre las vacaciones de Antonio y su familia. Usa la forma correcta del verbo entre paréntesis.

1. Ana y yo (correr) por la playa por la mañana.
2. Luego descansamos y yo (leer) las tiras cómicas en inglés.
3. Los lunes y los miércoles mis padres (asistir) a una clase de ejercicios.
4. A Miguelito le gustan mucho las hamburguesas y las papas fritas. ¡Siempre (comer) mucho!
5. Mis padres no (comer) mucho. Están a dieta. *They are on a diet.*
6. Y tú, Diana, ¿por qué no me (escribir) una tarjeta postal?
7. Todos los días nosotros (recibir) cartas, pero ¡nada de ti! *Nothing from you!*

NOTA CULTURAL

Spending time with a group of friends is an important part of life for young adults in the Spanish-speaking world. Fewer young people own cars in Spain or Latin America than in the United States, so they often share rides with friends. Meeting friends in public is a big part of life for both young and old. Public gathering places like parks and cafés are common meeting places. The streets of a Spanish-speaking town are usually alive both day and night.

1. The **nosotros** forms are different: **comemos**, **escribimos**. And the **vosotros** forms are different: **coméis**, **escribís**.

134 *ciento treinta y cuatro*

The *Vocabulario* found in each chapter relates to the theme and language function, and is presented visually whenever possible.

VOCABULARIO

pasar el rato con amigos — caminar con el perro — montar en bicicleta

trabajar en un restaurante — tomar un refresco/un helado — preparar la cena

También se puede decir...
In many Spanish-speaking countries, you'll also hear **andar en bicicleta** or **dar un paseo en bicicleta** in addition to **montar en bicicleta**.

NOTA CULTURAL

Soccer, cycling, tennis, and baseball are popular sports in Spanish-speaking countries. Fans in these countries have had a lot to cheer about! In 1993 and 1994, Sergi Bruguera of Spain won the French Open, one of the four grand slam events in professional tennis. In 1994, Conchita Martínez became the first Spanish woman to win the Wimbledon crown, tennis's premier tournament. In the United States, Spanish-speaking athletes have contributed greatly, especially to the sport of baseball.

9 Hacemos un poco de todo

Tell Mariana, your new classmate, what these people do in their free time. Write complete sentences using the information provided.

1. Yo/tocar/la guitarra en el tiempo libre
2. Mi hermana/trabajar/después de clases
3. Mi padre/caminar con el perro en el parque a las cinco
4. Beto y Shoji/hablar por teléfono después de clases
5. Maya y yo/nadar en la piscina antes de regresar a casa
6. Ellas/escuchar la radio antes de clases

PRIMER PASO *ciento tres* 103

An Abundance of Activities

Throughout *¡Ven conmigo!*, activities flow from controlled and structured through transitional to open-ended and communicative activities. Plenty of activities are contained within the program to build competency in each of the four language skills. Types of activities included in each chapter are:

- Contextualized listening activities
- Pair and group work
- Journal writing activities (can be used as portfolio assessment activities)
- Reading, writing, and role-playing activities
- Discovery questions and discussions of culture topics

Critical Thinking Through Multicultural Awareness

¿Cómo es una semana típica?

In this chapter, we asked some students what they usually do during the week and on weekends.

PANORAMA CULTURAL

María Luisa
Quito, Ecuador
"Vengo al colegio y del colegio a la casa, y de ahí no hago nada más".
¿Y los fines de semana?
"Salgo a comer con mis amigas, me voy a casa de ellas o ellas vienen a mi casa".

Maikel
Caracas, Venezuela
"Ir al liceo, llegar a casa en la tarde, hacer mis tareas y descansar".
¿Y los fines de semana?
"Bueno, quedarme en mi casa o si no, salgo con mis padres".

Matías
Buenos Aires, Argentina
"Vengo al colegio a las ocho y cuarto; salgo doce y cuarto para irme a comer, vuelvo a la una y media y salgo de nuevo a las cuatro y cuarto, llego a mi casa, veo tele y como, y voy a dormir."
¿Y los fines de semana?
"Voy a andar en velero al club náutico, y después vuelvo tarde a eso de las ocho y vuelvo a mi casa directo a dormir".

Para pensar y hablar...

A. Read the interviews carefully. Whose weekday routine is most like yours? Whose weekend routine is similar to yours?

B. What you do says a lot about you. What do you think María Luisa, Matías, and Maikel are like?

The *Panorama cultural* is designed to give your students a chance to meet people from around the Spanish-speaking world who share their views, opinions, and thoughts on a variety of topics that are thematically related to the chapters in *¡Ven conmigo!*. Filmed on location, authentic interviews with native speakers can be found in the text, on the *Video Program*, the *Expanded Video Program*, the *Audio Program*, and the *Videodisc Program*. The result: total video, audio, and text integration for complete language development. The *Panorama cultural* also contains critical-thinking activities that expand upon what students learn from the interviews.

An Encounter of Cultures

Do you ever wonder how you can make your students "walk in someone else's shoes?" With *¡Ven conmigo!*'s *Encuentro cultural*, you can do just that! This unique presentation introduces your students to customs in Spanish-speaking cultures that may be unfamiliar to them, but are a way of life in that culture. They'll also learn what people in the target culture may find unfamiliar about Americans, and follow up what they've learned with critical-thinking questions. This expands your students' horizons beyond their own backyard. They'll realize that diverse viewpoints and different ways of doing similar things enrich our global community.

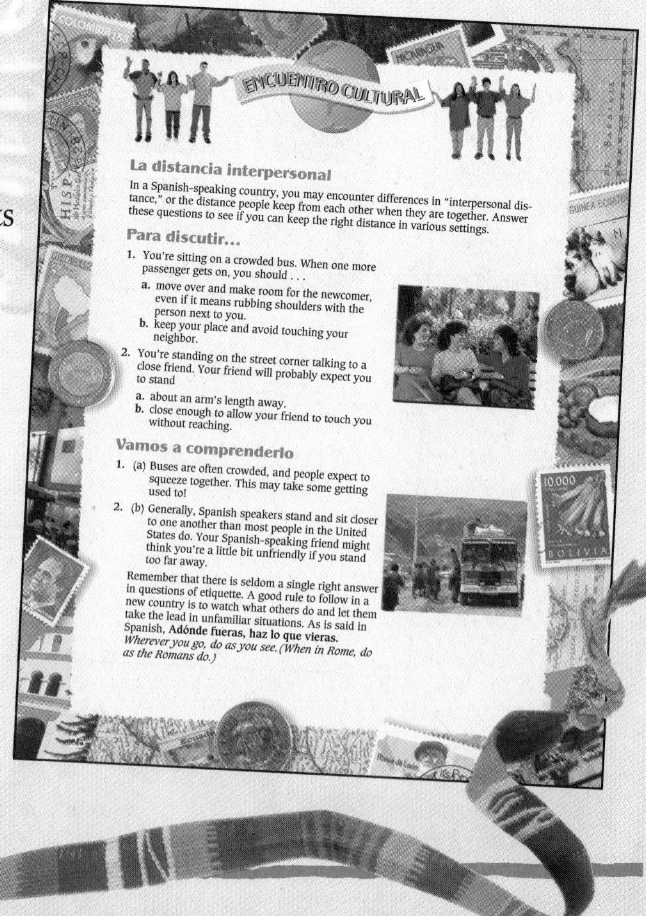

ENCUENTRO CULTURAL

La distancia interpersonal

In a Spanish-speaking country, you may encounter differences in "interpersonal distance," or the distance people keep from each other when they are together. Answer these questions to see if you can keep the right distance in various settings.

Para discutir...

1. You're sitting on a crowded bus. When one more passenger gets on, you should . . .
   a. move over and make room for the newcomer, even if it means rubbing shoulders with the person next to you.
   b. keep your place and avoid touching your neighbor.
2. You're standing on the street corner talking to a close friend. Your friend will probably expect you to stand
   a. about an arm's length away.
   b. close enough to allow your friend to touch you without reaching.

Vamos a comprenderlo

1. (a) Buses are often crowded, and people expect to squeeze together. This may take some getting used to!
2. (b) Generally, Spanish speakers stand and sit closer to one another than most people in the United States do. Your Spanish-speaking friend might think you're a little bit unfriendly if you stand too far away.

Remember that there is seldom a single right answer in questions of etiquette. A good rule to follow in a new country is to watch what others do and let them take the lead in unfamiliar situations. As is said in Spanish, **Adónde fueras, haz lo que vieras.** *Wherever you go, do as you see. (When in Rome, do as the Romans do.)*

Holt Spanish

Level 1

Annotated Teacher's Edition

HOLT, RINEHART AND WINSTON

Harcourt Brace & Company

Austin • New York • Orlando • Chicago • Atlanta • San Francisco • Boston • Dallas •Toronto • London

Printed in the United States of America

ISBN 0-03-096523-3

1 2 3 4 5 6 7 032 99 98 97 96 95

Acknowledgments

Abbreviations used: (t) top, (c) center, (b) bottom, (l) left, (r) right, (bckgd) background, (bdr) border.

For permission to reprint copyrighted material, grateful acknowledgment is made to the following sources:

In the *Annotated Teacher's Edition:*

Front Matter: Page T34(br), HRW Photo/Michelle Bridwell; T41(br), HRW Photo/Marty Granger/Edge Production; T47(bl), HRW Photo/Marty Granger/Edge Production; T49(bl), HRW Photo/Marty Granger/Edge Production; T55(bl, bc, br), HRW Photo/Marty Granger/Edge Production. **Preliminary Chapter:** Page T64(bl), Bettman Archives; (bc), HRW Photo/Marty Granger/Edge Production; (br), S. Howell/Gamma Liaison; T67(tr), (br), HRW Photo/Michelle Bridwell. **Chapter One:** Page 15E(b), Manuel García. **Chapter Two:** 41D (c), Mario Mistriano; 41E, Michelle Bridwell/Frontera Fotos. **Chapter Three:** Page 69E, HRW Photo/Marty Granger/Edge Production. **Chapter Four:** 95C (br), Eva Vagreti Cockrille; 95C, 95D, HRW Photo/Marty Granger/Edge Production; 95F (br), Gary Undercuffler. **Chapter Five:** 123D(b), Edson Campos; 123F(b), Eva Vagreti Cockrille. **Chapter Six:** Page 147C(bl), (blc), Michelle Bridwell/Frontera Fotos; (brc) HRW Photo; (br), Robert Frerck/ Woodfin Camp & Associates; 147D(l), (c), (r), Michelle Bridwell/ Frontera Fotos. **Chapter Seven:** Page 177D, HRW Photo/Marty Granger/Edge Productions. **Chapter Twelve:** 311D(b), Ignacio Gómez; 311E(b), Meryl Henderson.

In the *Pupil's Edition:*

American Express Publishing Corporation: Excerpt from "Festival of the Masks" from *Puerto Rico,* a supplement to *Travel & Leisure,* December 1992. Translated into Spanish by Holt, Rinehart and Winston, Inc.

Banco Central de Cuenca: Excerpts and illustrations from "Calendario de Eventos" from *60 Aniversario de la Fundación del Banco Central de Cuenca, Antiguo Hospital San Vicente de Paul,* June-July 1988.

La Choza: Advertisement for "La Choza: El palacio de la cocina Ecuatoriana" from brochure, *Viajes y entretenimientos: Guía de establecimientos Diners Club del Ecuador.*

Cines Lumiere: Advertisement for "Cines Lumiere" from *Guía El País,* no. 57, December 27, 1990.

Club de Tenis Las Lomas: Advertisement for "Club de Tenis Las Lomas" from *Guía El País,* no. 57, December 27, 1990.

Colsanitas: Adaptation from "17 Claves para manejar el Estrés" (Retitled: "7 Claves para manejar el Estrés") from *Bienestar,* no. 9. Copyright © by Colsanitas.

Compañia de Turismo, Estado Libre Asociado de Puerto Rico: Excerpts and symbols from brochure, "Descubre los Paradores de Puerto Rico."

Desarrollo Internacional de Medios S.A. de C.V.: Excerpts from "A Bajio Octoberfest" by Leon Lazaroff from *México Journal,* vol. II, no. 50, September 25, 1989. Copyright © 1989 by Desarrollo Internacional de Medios S.A. de C.V.

Diario El Comercio: Advertisement for "Teatro Republica" from the "Deportes" section from *El Comercio,* August 22, 1993. Advertisement for "El mimo José Vacas" and "Cafelibro," and the header "Caleidoscopio" from the "Caleidoscopio" section from *El Comercio,* September 4, 1993. Advertisement for "Circo Rolan" from the "Especial" section and advertisement for "En el Museo de Arte Moderno de la Casa de la Cultura Ecuatoriana" from the "Registro Cultural" section from *El Comercio,* September 6, 1993.

Diario Hoy: Advertisement for "El Cafélibro" from the "Ruta del lector" section from *Hoy,* February 11, 1994.

ACKNOWLEDGMENTS continued on page 372, which is an extension of the copyright page.

Annotated Teacher's Edition Credits

CONTRIBUTING WRITERS

Marjorie E. Artzer
Northern Kentucky University
Highland Heights, KY

Dr. Artzer was the principal writer for Level One.

Jackie Moase-Burke
Language Arts Oakland Schools
Clinton Township, MI

Jo Anne Wilson
J. Wilson Associates
Glen Arbor, MI

Ms. Moase-Burke and Ms. Wilson contributed Teaching Suggestions and notes.

CONTRIBUTING EDITORS

Letitia Blalock
Austin, TX

Peggy Patterson
The University of Texas
Austin, TX

CONSULTANTS

Audrey L. Heining-Boynton
The University of North Carolina
Chapel Hill, NC

JoAnne Wilson
J. Wilson Associates
Glen Arbor, MI

FIELD TEST PARTICIPANTS

Bill Braden
South Junior High School
Boise, ID

Paula Critchlow
Indian Hills Middle School
Sandy, UT

Frances Cutter
Convent of the Visitation School
St. Paul, MN

Carlos Fernández
Sandy Creek High School
Tyrone, GA

Jan Holland
Lovejoy High School
Lovejoy, GA

Gloria Holstrom
Emerson Jr. High School
Yonkers, NY

K. A. Laguna
Ponus Ridge Middle School
Norwalk, CT

Michelle Mistric
Iowa High School
Iowa, LA

Rubén Moreno
Aycock Middle School
Greensboro, NC

Fred Pratt
San Marcos High School
San Marcos, TX

Regina Salvi
Museum Jr. High School
Yonkers, NY

Lorraine Walsh
Lincoln Southeast High School
Lincoln, NE

REVIEWERS

Edward D. Allen
Ohio State University
Columbus, OH

Daniel Bender
Adlai Stevenson High School
Lincolnshire, IL

O. Lynn Bolton
Nathan Hale High School
West Allis, WI

June Carter
The University of Texas
Austin, TX

Marie Carrera Lambert
Iona College
New Rochelle, NY

Myrtress G. Eddleman
Carver High School
Birmingham, AL

Rubén Garza
James Bowie High School
Austin, TX

Joseph N. Harris
Poudre School District
Fort Collins, CO

Nancy Holmes
Marian Catholic High School
Chicago Heights, IL

Stephen L. Levy
Roslyn Public Schools
Roslyn, NY

Maureen Nelligan
Marian Catholic High School
Chicago Heights, IL

Laura Olson
Austin Waldorf School
Austin, TX

Carmen Reyes
Jonesboro High School
Jonesboro, GA

Dr. Yolanda Russinovich Solé
The University of Texas
Austin, TX

Elena Steele
Clark County School District
Las Vegas, NV

Brian A. Souza
Plymouth South High School
Plymouth, MA

Dora Villani
John F. Kennedy High School
Bronx, NY

PROFESSIONAL ESSAYS

Standards for Foreign Language Education
Robert LaBouve
Board of National Standards in Foreign Language Education
Austin, TX

Teaching Culture
Nancy A. Humbach
The Miami University
Oxford, OH

Dorothea Bruschke
Parkway School District
Chesterfield, MO

Learning Styles and Multi-Modality Teaching
Mary B. McGehee
Louisiana State University
Baton Rouge, LA

Higher-Order Thinking Skills
Audrey L. Heining-Boynton
The University of North Carolina
Chapel Hill, NC

Using Portfolios in the Foreign Language Classroom
JoAnne Wilson
J. Wilson Associates
Glen Arbor, MI

New Perspectives for Native Speakers
Cecilia Rodríguez-Pino
New Mexico State University
Las Cruces, NM

Pupil's Edition Credits

Authors

Nancy A. Humbach
Miami University
Cincinnati, OH

Ms. Humbach collaborated in the development of the scope and sequence and video material, and created activities and culture features.

Oscar Ozete
University of Southern Indiana
Evansville, IN

Mr. Ozete collaborated in the development of the scope and sequence, reviewed all Pupil's Edition material, and wrote grammar explanations.

Contributing Writers

Charles J. Bruno
The University of Texas at Austin

Mr. Bruno wrote video materials.

Michael A. García
The University of Texas at Austin

Mr. García researched and wrote the Location Openers.

Jean R. Miller
The University of Texas at Austin

Ms. Miller wrote the **Sugerencias.**

Susan Peterson
The Ohio State University
Columbus, OH

Mrs. Peterson selected realia for readings and developed reading activities.

The following people researched and wrote culture features:

Dolores Brown
Tucson, AZ

Mariana Colten
Frankfort, KY

Lisa Contreras
Lexington, KY

Melinda Gale
Portland, OR

Mary Maggi
Austin, TX

Jaime Ugaz
Austin, TX

Consultants

John DeMado
John DeMado Language Seminars
Washington, CT

Ingeborg R. McCoy
Southwest Texas State University
San Marcos, TX

JoAnne S. Wilson
J. Wilson Associates
Glen Arbor, MI

Reviewers

These educators reviewed one or more chapters of the Pupil's Edition.

Edward David Allen
The Ohio State University
Columbus, OH

Dr. Marjorie E. Artzer
Northern Kentucky University
Highland Heights, KY

Daniel J. Bender
Adlai Stevenson High School
Prairie View, IL

O. Lynn Bolton
Nathan Hale High School
West Allis, WI

Juanita Carfora
Central Regional High School
Bayville, NJ

Lolita Carfora
Central Regional High School
Bayville, NJ

Dr. June Carter
The University of Texas at Austin

Renato Cervantes
Pacific High School
San Bernadino, CA

Lucila Dorsett
Austin, TX

Myrtress G. Eddleman
Carver High School
Birmingham, AL

Maureen Fischer
Marian Catholic High School
Chicago Heights, IL

Rubén Garza
James Bowie High School
Austin, TX

Dr. Gail Guntermann
Arizona State University
Tempe, AZ

Joe Harris
Poudre School District
Ft. Collins, CO

Audrey L. Heining-Boynton
The University of North Carolina at Chapel Hill

Nancy Holmes
Marian Catholic High School
Chicago Heights, IL

Stephen L. Levy
Roslyn Public Schools
Roslyn, NY

Marcela Malo
Cuenca, Ecuador

Carmen Reyes
Jonesboro High School
Jonesboro, GA

Dr. Yolanda Russinovich Solé
The University of Texas at Austin

Elena Steele
Clark County School District
Las Vegas, NV

Christina Suárez
Madrid, Spain

Carol A. Villalobos
Hazelwood Central High School
St. Louis, MO

Field Test Participants

We express our appreciation to the teachers and students who participated in the field test. Their comments were instrumental in the development of this program.

Bill Braden
South Junior High School
Boise, ID

Paula Critchlow
Indian Hills Middle School
Sandy, UT

Frances Cutter
Convent of the Visitation School
St. Paul, MN

Carlos Fernández
Sandy Creek High School
Tyrone, GA

Jan Holland
Lovejoy High School
Lovejoy, GA

Gloria Holstrom
Emerson Jr. High School
Yonkers, NY

K.A. Laguna
Ponus Ridge Middle School
Norwalk, CT

Michelle Mistric
Iowa High School
Iowa, LA

Rubén Moreno
Aycock Middle School
Greensboro, NC

Fred Pratt
San Marcos High School
San Marcos, TX

Regina Salvi
Museum Jr. High School
Yonkers, NY

Lorraine Walsh
Lincoln Southeast High School
Lincoln, NE

To the Student

Some people have the opportunity to learn a new language by living in another country. Most of us, however, begin learning another language and getting acquainted with a foreign culture in a classroom with the help of a teacher, classmates, and a book. To use your book effectively, you need to know how it works.

¡Ven conmigo! (*Come along!*) takes you to six different Spanish-speaking locations. Each location is introduced with photos and information on four special pages called Location Openers.

There are twelve chapters in the book, and each one follows the same pattern.

The two Chapter Opener pages announce the chapter theme and list the objectives. These objectives set goals that you can achieve by the end of the chapter.

De Antemano (*Beforehand*) The next part of the chapter is an illustrated story that shows you Spanish-speaking people in real-life situations, using the language you'll be learning in the chapter. You'll also have fun watching this story on video.

Primer, Segundo, Tercer paso (*First, Second, Third Part*) Following the opening story, the chapter is divided into three parts, called **Pasos.** At the beginning of each **Paso** there's a reminder of the objective(s) you'll be aiming for in this part. Spanish expressions you'll need to communicate are summarized in boxes called **Así se dice** (*Here's how to say it*). You'll also need vocabulary; look for new words under the heading **Vocabulario.** You won't have trouble finding grammar, for you're sure to recognize the headings **Gramática** and **Nota gramatical.** Now all you need is plenty of practice. In each **Paso** there are listening, speaking, reading, and writing activities for you to do individually, with a partner, or in groups. By the end of the **Paso,** you'll have achieved your objective(s).

This book will also help you get to know the cultures of the people who speak Spanish.

Panorama cultural (*Cultural Panorama*) On this page of the chapter you'll read interviews with Spanish-speaking people around the world. They'll talk about themselves and their lives, and you can compare their cultures to yours. You'll watch these interviews on video or listen to them on audiocassette.

Nota cultural (*Culture Note*) These notes provide a lot of interesting cultural information.

Encuentro cultural (*Cultural Encounter*) This page in six of the chapters offers a firsthand encounter with Spanish-speaking cultures.

Vamos a leer (*Let's read*) After the three **pasos,** one or more reading selections related to the chapter theme will help you develop your reading skills in Spanish.

Repaso (*Review*) A variety of activities gives you opportunities to put into practice what you've learned in the chapter in new situations. You'll improve your listening skills and practice communicating with others orally and in writing.

A ver si puedo... (*Let's see if I can . . .*) Here's a chance to check yourself at the end of the chapter. On this page a series of questions, followed by short activities, will help you decide how well you can do on your own.

Vocabulario (*Vocabulary*) On the last page of the chapter, you'll find a Spanish-English vocabulary list. The words are grouped by **paso** and listed under the objectives they support. You'll need to know these words and expressions for the Chapter Test!

Sugerencia (*Suggestion*) Check out the helpful study hints scattered throughout the book.

¿Te acuerdas? (*Do you remember?*) and **¿Se te ha olvidado?** (*Have you forgotten?*) Along the way, these notes and stamps will remind you of things you might have forgotten.

A lo nuestro (*The Spanish way*) Be on the lookout for these boxes, too. They'll give you additional Spanish expressions to add more color to your speech.

Un poco más... (*A little more . . .*) From these lists, you'll be able to choose extra words and expressions you might want to use when you talk about yourself and your interests.

At the end of your book, you'll find more helpful material, including a list of the communicative expressions you'll need, a summary of the grammar you've studied, supplementary vocabulary, and Spanish-English, English-Spanish vocabulary lists the words you'll need to know for the tests in bold type.

¡Ven conmigo! Come along on an exciting trip to a new culture and a new language.

¡Buen viaje!

ANNOTATED TEACHER'S EDITION

¡Ven conmigo! Contents

Come along— to a world of new experiences!

*¡**Ven conmigo!** offers you the opportunity to learn the language spoken by millions of people in the many Spanish-speaking countries around the world. Let's find out about the countries, the people, and the Spanish language.*

Capítulo Preliminar

¡Ven conmigo a España!

VISIT THE COSMOPOLITAN CITY OF MADRID WITH FOUR SPANISH TEENAGERS AND—

Introduce yourself to some Spanish-speaking students • **CAPÍTULO 1**

Talk about what you need and want to do • **CAPÍTULO 2**

CAPÍTULO 1

¡Mucho gusto! 16

Capítulo 2

¡Organízate! 42

¡Ven conmigo a México!

VISIT THE HISTORIC CITIES OF CUERNAVACA AND MEXICO CITY WITH FOUR MEXICAN TEENAGERS AND—

Talk about things you like and explain why • CAPÍTULO 3

Discuss what you and others do during free time • CAPÍTULO 4

CAPÍTULO 3

CAPÍTULO 4

¿Qué haces esta tarde? 96

¡Ven conmigo a la Florida!

VISIT THE LIVELY CITY OF MIAMI WITH FIVE HISPANIC TEENAGERS AND—

Talk about what you do during a typical week • **CAPÍTULO 5**

Describe a family • **CAPÍTULO 6**

CAPÍTULO 5

El ritmo de la vida 124

Capítulo 6

Entre familia 148

¡Ven conmigo a Ecuador!

VISIT THE ENCHANTING CITIES OF QUITO AND OTAVALO WITH FIVE ECUADOREAN TEENAGERS AND–

Make plans • **CAPÍTULO 7**

Talk about meals and food • **CAPÍTULO 8**

CAPÍTULO 7

¿Qué te gustaría hacer? 178

CAPÍTULO 8

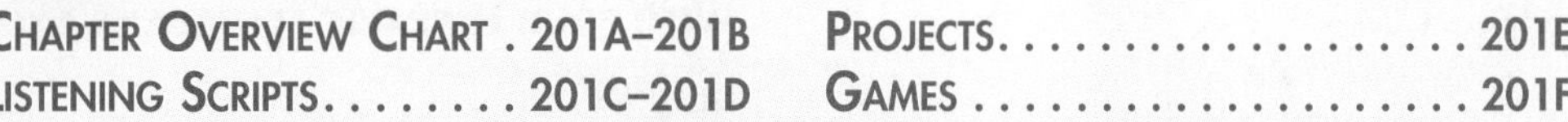

¡A comer!............202

¡Ven conmigo a Texas!

VISIT THE EXCITING CITY OF SAN ANTONIO WITH FOUR HISPANIC TEENAGERS AND–

Discuss gift suggestions and comment on clothes • **CAPÍTULO 9**

Ask for help and respond to requests • **CAPÍTULO 10**

CAPÍTULO 9

Capítulo 10

Celebraciones......256

¡Ven conmigo a Puerto Rico!

VISIT THE COLORFUL CITY OF SAN JUAN, PUERTO RICO WITH SOME HISPANIC TEENAGERS AND–

Make suggestions and express feelings • CAPÍTULO 11

Say where you went and what you did on vacation • CAPÍTULO 12

CAPÍTULO 11

Capítulo 12

Las vacaciones ideales............312

Reference Section..336

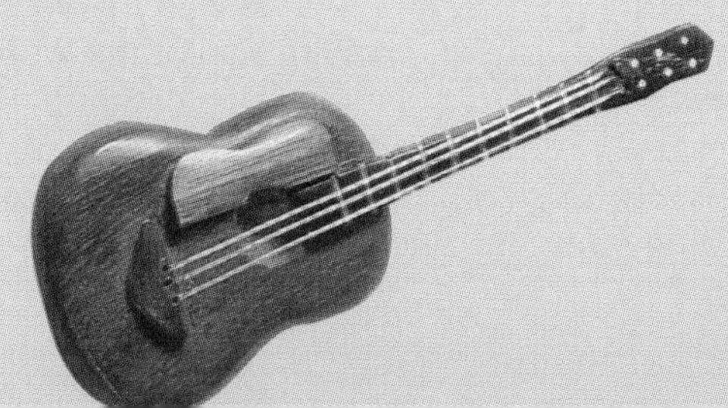

Cultural References

Numbers in **boldface type** *indicate material referenced in the* ***Annotated Teacher's Edition.*** *Culture Notes, Multicultural Links, and other Links refer to information in the* ***Annotated Teacher's Edition.*** *Many additional cultural topics are included in the* ***Video Program.***

▶ HOME AND FAMILY LIFE

▶ MONEY

▶ NAMES

▶ NUMBERS

▶ PARKS

▶ PEOPLE

▶ POINTS OF INTEREST

▶ RECIPES

▶ RESTAURANTS AND CAFES

▶ SCHOOL LIFE

▶ SEASONS, WEATHER, AND TIME

▶ SHOPPING

▶ SOCIAL CUSTOMS

▶ SPORTS AND FITNESS

▶ TELEPHONE

▶ TRANSPORTATION

▶ VACATIONS

La península ibérica

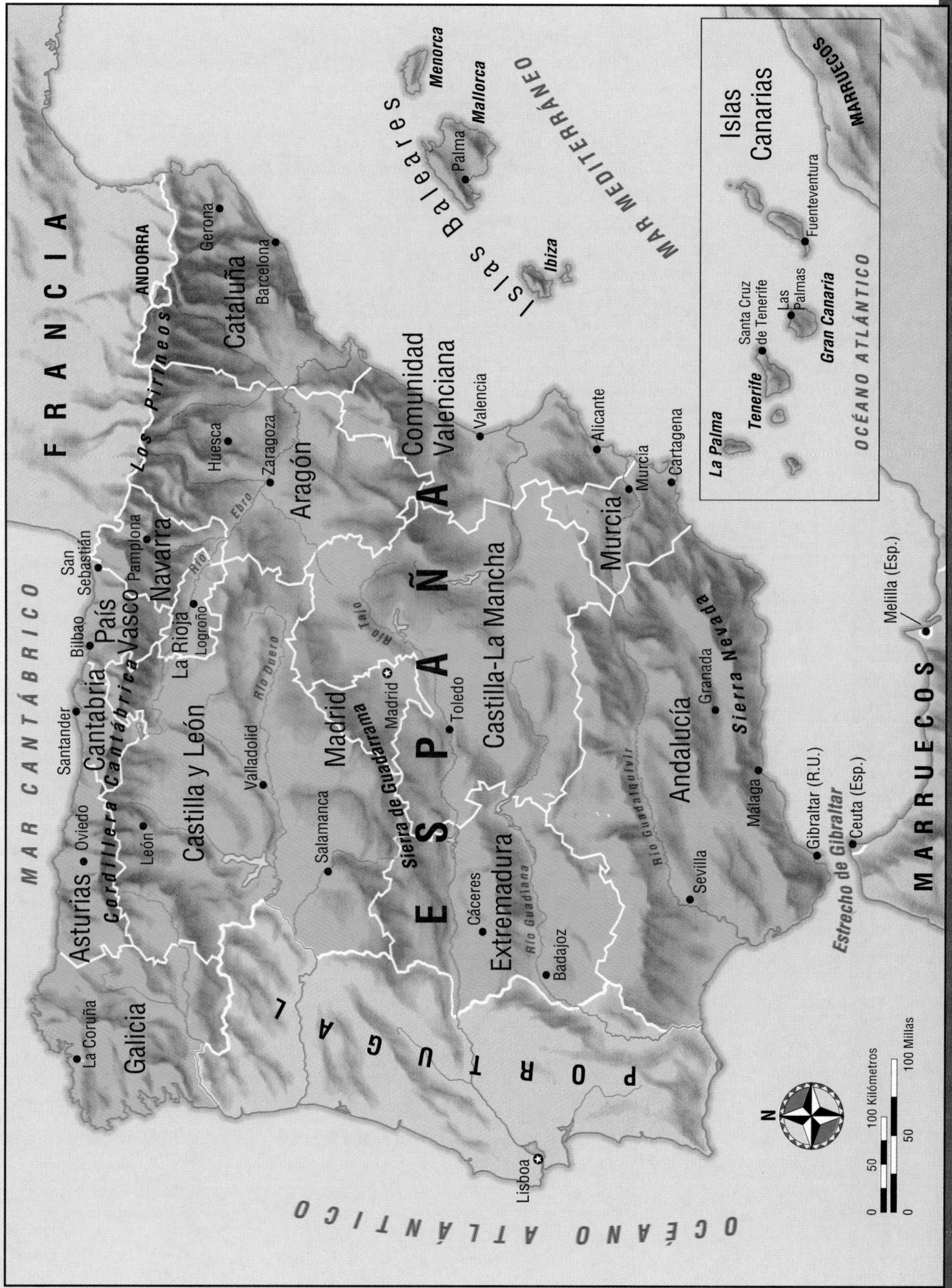

FRANCIA
ANDORRA
MAR CANTÁBRICO
OCÉANO ATLÁNTICO
PORTUGAL
ESPAÑA
MARRUECOS
MAR MEDITERRÁNEO
Islas Baleares
Menorca
Mallorca
Palma
Ibiza
Los Pirineos
Cordillera Cantábrica
Sierra de Guadarrama
Sierra Nevada
Río Ebro
Río Duero
Río Tajo
Río Guadiana
Río Guadalquivir
Estrecho de Gibraltar
Galicia
La Coruña
Asturias
Oviedo
León
Cantabria
Santander
País Vasco
Bilbao
San Sebastián
Navarra
Pamplona
La Rioja
Logroño
Castilla y León
Valladolid
Salamanca
Aragón
Huesca
Zaragoza
Cataluña
Gerona
Barcelona
Madrid
Castilla-La Mancha
Toledo
Comunidad Valenciana
Valencia
Alicante
Murcia
Cartagena
Extremadura
Cáceres
Badajoz
Andalucía
Sevilla
Málaga
Granada
Gibraltar (R.U.)
Ceuta (Esp.)
Melilla (Esp.)
Lisboa
Islas Canarias
La Palma
Tenerife
Santa Cruz de Tenerife
Gran Canaria
Las Palmas
Fuenteventura
OCÉANO ATLÁNTICO
MARRUECOS
N
0 50 100 Kilómetros
0 50 100 Millas

xxi

El mundo

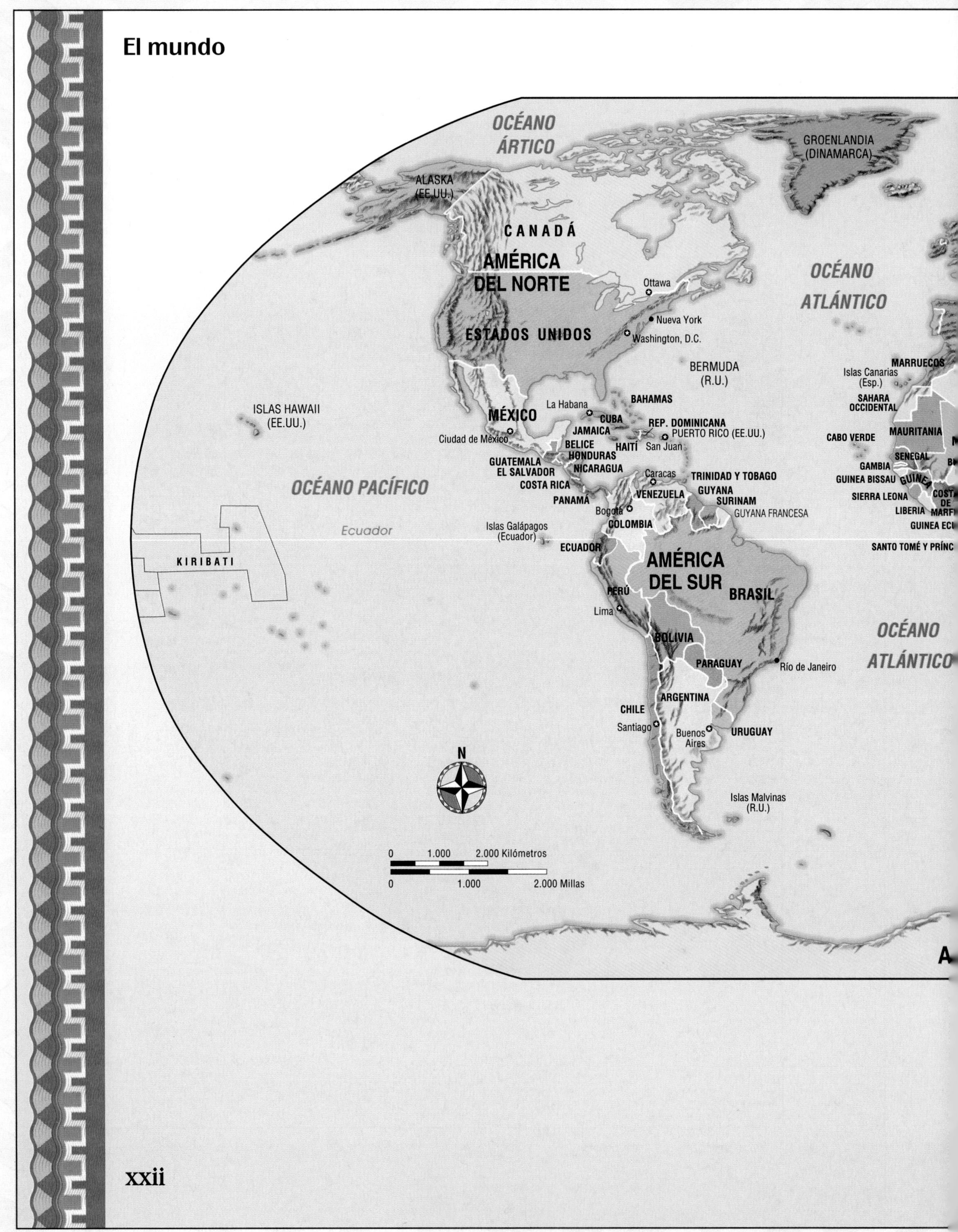

OCÉANO ÁRTICO
GROENLANDIA (DINAMARCA)
ALASKA (EE.UU.)
CANADÁ
AMÉRICA DEL NORTE
Ottawa
OCÉANO ATLÁNTICO
Nueva York
ESTADOS UNIDOS
Washington, D.C.
BERMUDA (R.U.)
MARRUECOS
Islas Canarias (Esp.)
SAHARA OCCIDENTAL
ISLAS HAWAII (EE.UU.)
La Habana
BAHAMAS
MÉXICO
CUBA
REP. DOMINICANA
JAMAICA
PUERTO RICO (EE.UU.)
CABO VERDE
MAURITANIA
Ciudad de México
BELICE
HAITÍ
San Juan
HONDURAS
SENEGAL
GAMBIA
GUATEMALA
EL SALVADOR
NICARAGUA
COSTA RICA
Caracas
TRINIDAD Y TOBAGO
GUINEA BISSAU
GUINEA
OCÉANO PACÍFICO
PANAMÁ
VENEZUELA
GUYANA
SURINAM
SIERRA LEONA
LIBERIA
Bogotá
GUYANA FRANCESA
Ecuador
Islas Galápagos (Ecuador)
COLOMBIA
KIRIBATI
ECUADOR
AMÉRICA DEL SUR
PERÚ
BRASIL
Lima
BOLIVIA
OCÉANO ATLÁNTICO
PARAGUAY
Río de Janeiro
ARGENTINA
CHILE
Santiago
Buenos Aires
URUGUAY
N
Islas Malvinas (R.U.)
0 1.000 2.000 Kilómetros
0 1.000 2.000 Millas

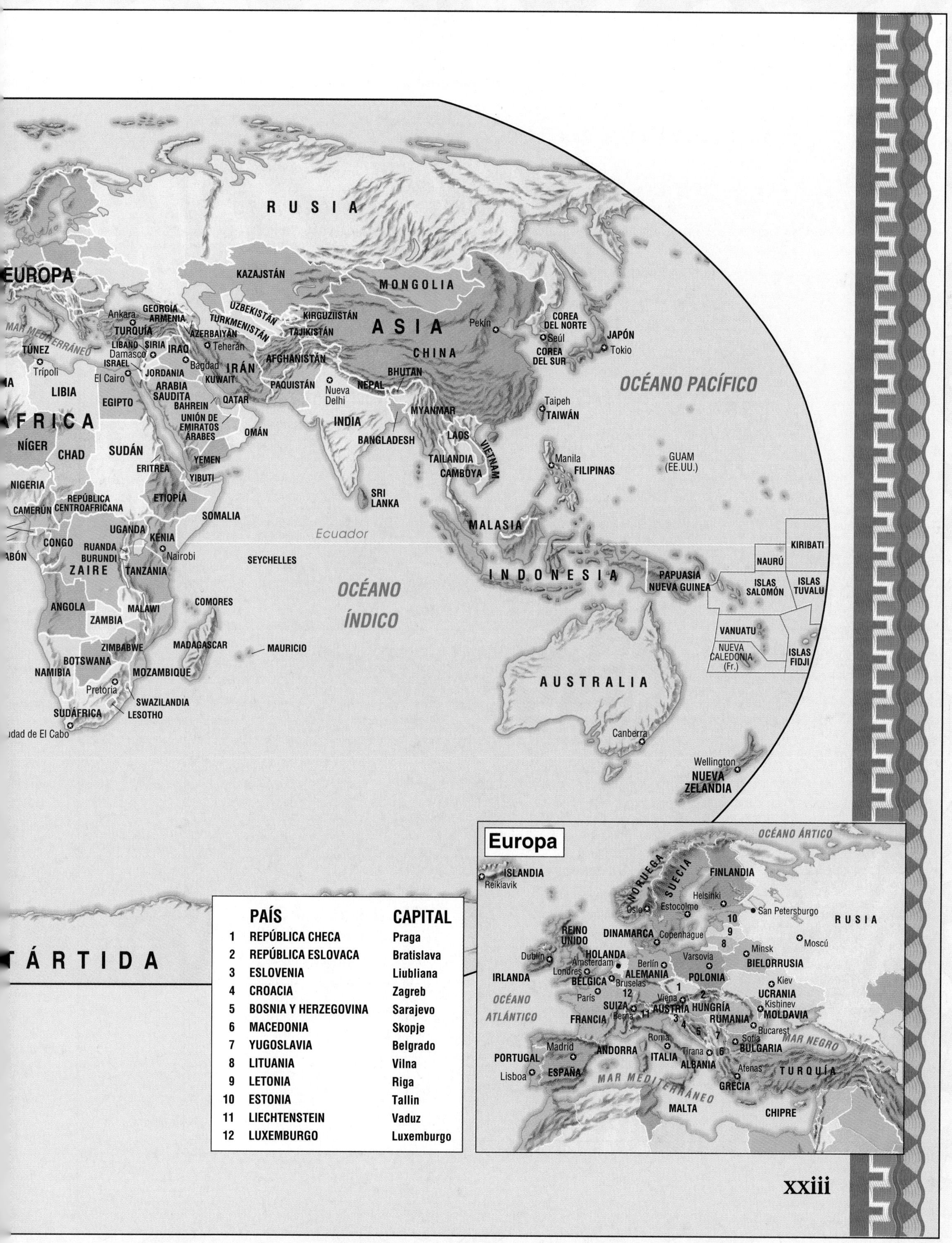

	PAÍS	CAPITAL
1	REPÚBLICA CHECA	Praga
2	REPÚBLICA ESLOVACA	Bratislava
3	ESLOVENIA	Liubliana
4	CROACIA	Zagreb
5	BOSNIA Y HERZEGOVINA	Sarajevo
6	MACEDONIA	Skopje
7	YUGOSLAVIA	Belgrado
8	LITUANIA	Vilna
9	LETONIA	Riga
10	ESTONIA	Tallin
11	LIECHTENSTEIN	Vaduz
12	LUXEMBURGO	Luxemburgo

América del Sur

América Central y las Antillas

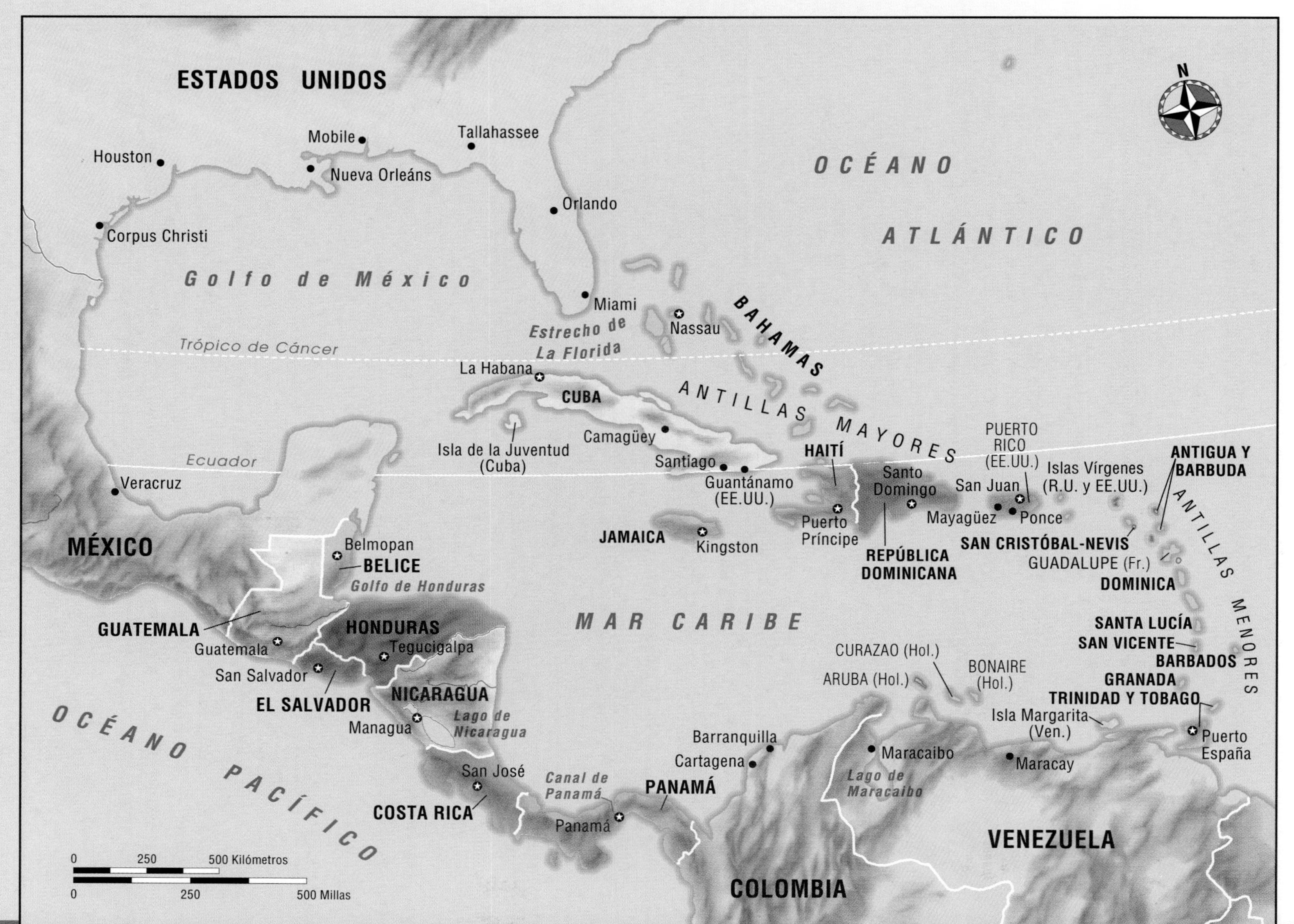

México

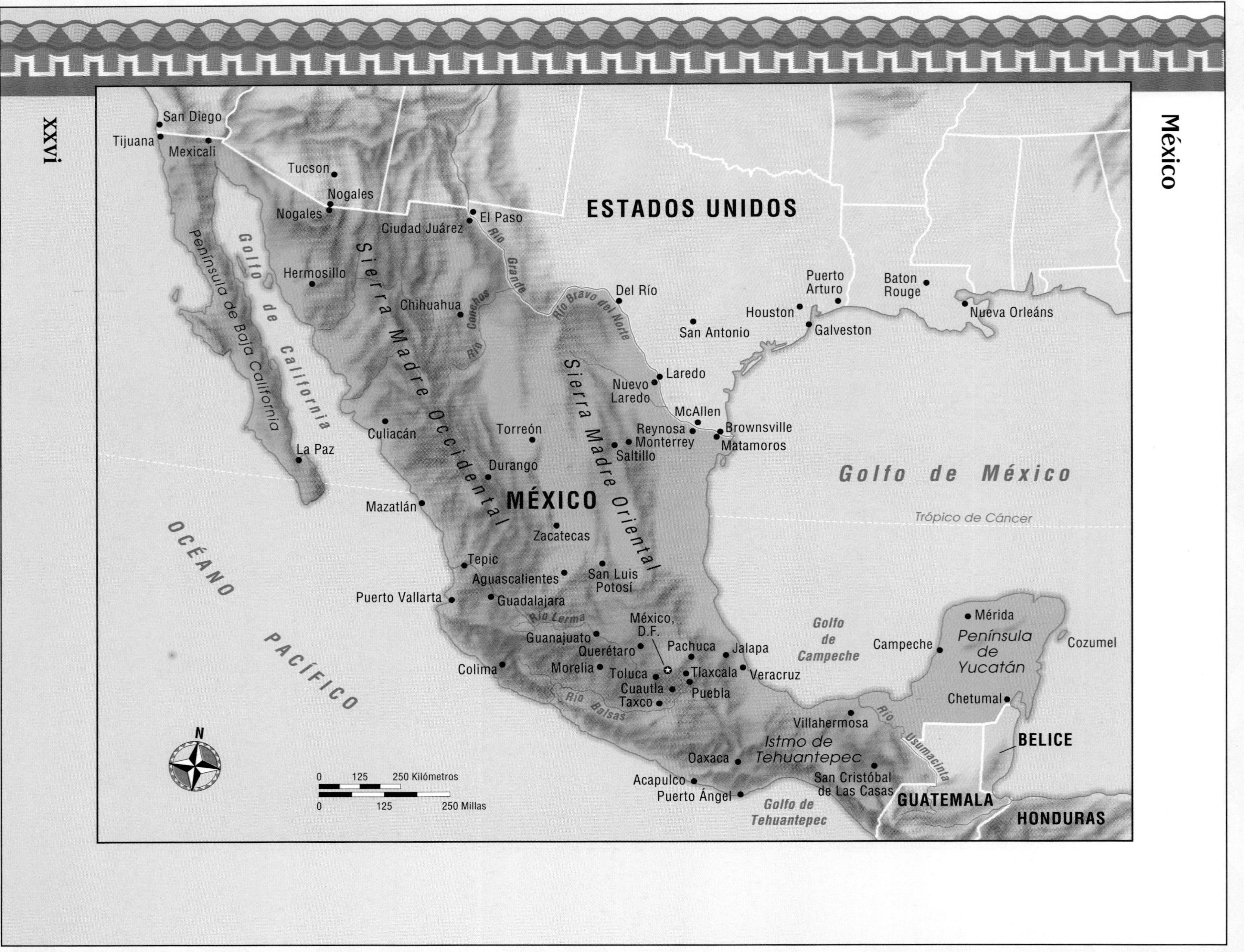

ESTADOS UNIDOS
MÉXICO
BELICE
GUATEMALA
HONDURAS
Golfo de México
Golfo de Campeche
Golfo de California
Golfo de Tehuantepec
OCÉANO PACÍFICO
Trópico de Cáncer
Península de Yucatán
Península de Baja California
Istmo de Tehuantepec
Sierra Madre Oriental
Sierra Madre Occidental
Río Grande
Río Bravo del Norte
Río Conchos
Río Lerma
Río Balsas
Río Usumacinta
San Diego
Tijuana
Mexicali
Tucson
Nogales
Nogales
Hermosillo
Ciudad Juárez
El Paso
Chihuahua
Culiacán
La Paz
Mazatlán
Torreón
Durango
Del Río
Nuevo Laredo
Laredo
San Antonio
Houston
Puerto Arturo
Galveston
Baton Rouge
Nueva Orleáns
McAllen
Reynosa
Brownsville
Matamoros
Monterrey
Saltillo
Zacatecas
San Luis Potosí
Tepic
Aguascalientes
Guadalajara
Puerto Vallarta
Colima
Guanajuato
Querétaro
Morelia
Toluca
México, D.F.
Pachuca
Tlaxcala
Puebla
Cuautla
Taxco
Jalapa
Veracruz
Acapulco
Oaxaca
Puerto Ángel
Villahermosa
San Cristóbal de Las Casas
Campeche
Mérida
Cozumel
Chetumal
0 125 250 Kilómetros
0 125 250 Millas
N

Estados Unidos de Norteamérica

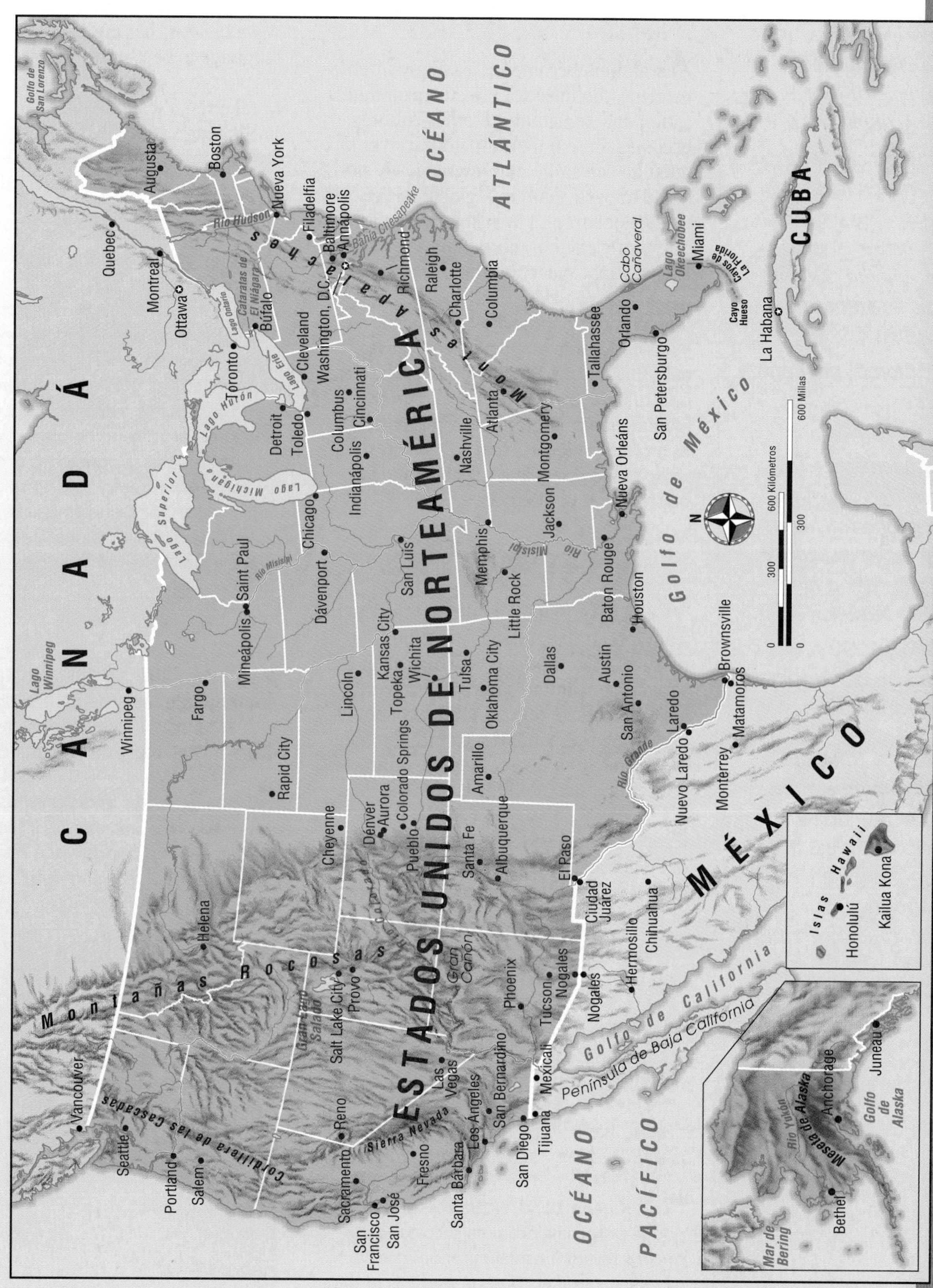

To the Teacher

Since the early eighties, we have seen significant advances in modern foreign language curriculum practice:

(1) a redefinition of the objectives of foreign language study involving a commitment to the development of proficiency in the four skills and in cultural awareness;

(2) a recognition of the need for longer sequences of study;

(3) a new student-centered approach that redefines the role of the teacher as facilitator and encourages students to take a more active role in their learning;

(4) the inclusion of students of all learning abilities.

The new Holt, Rinehart and Winston foreign language programs take into account not only these advances in the field of foreign language education but also the input of teachers and students around the country. ◆

Principles and Practices

As nations become increasingly interdependent, the need for effective communication and sensitivity to other cultures becomes more important. Today's youth must be culturally and linguistically prepared to participate in a global society. At Holt, Rinehart and Winston, we believe that proficiency in more than one language is essential to meeting this need.

The primary goal of the Holt, Rinehart and Winston foreign language programs is to help students develop linguistic proficiency and cultural sensitivity. By interweaving language and culture, our programs seek to broaden students' communication skills while at the same time deepening their appreciation of other cultures.

◆◆

We believe that all students can benefit from foreign language instruction. We recognize that not everyone learns at the same rate or in the same way; nevertheless, we believe that all students should have the opportunity to acquire language proficiency to a degree commensurate with their individual abilities.

Holt, Rinehart and Winston's foreign language programs are designed to accommodate all students by appealing to a variety of learning styles.

◆◆

We believe that effective language programs should motivate students. Students deserve an answer to the question they often ask: "Why are we doing this?" They need to have goals that are interesting, practical, clearly stated, and attainable.

Holt, Rinehart and Winston's foreign language programs promote success. They present relevant content in manageable increments that encourage students to attain achievable functional objectives.

We believe that proficiency in a foreign language is best nurtured by programs that encourage students to think critically and to take risks when expressing themselves in the language. We also recognize that students should strive for accuracy in communication. While it is imperative that students have a knowledge of the basic structures of the language, it is also important that they go beyond the simple manipulation of forms.

Holt, Rinehart and Winston's foreign language program reflects a careful progression of activities that guides students from comprehensible input of authentic language through structured practice to creative, personalized expression. This progression, accompanied by consistent re-entry and spiraling of functions, vocabulary, and structures, provides students with the tools and the confidence to express themselves in their new language.

◆◆

Finally, we believe that a complete program of language instruction should take into account the needs of teachers in today's increasingly demanding classrooms.

At Holt, Rinehart and Winston, we have designed programs that offer practical teacher support and provide resources to meet individual learning and teaching styles.

Using the Pupil's Edition of ¡Ven conmigo!

***¡Ven conmigo!** offers an integrated approach to language learning. Presentation and practice of functional expressions, vocabulary, and grammar structures are interwoven with cultural information, language learning tips, and realia to facilitate both learning and teaching. The technology, audiovisual materials, and additional print resources integrated throughout each chapter allow instruction to be adapted to a variety of teaching and learning styles.* ◆

¡VEN CONMIGO! LEVEL 1

¡Ven conmigo! Level 1 consists of a preliminary chapter that introduces students to Spanish and the Spanish-speaking world followed by twelve instructional chapters. To ensure successful completion of the book and to facilitate articulation from one level to the next, Chapter 11 introduces minimal new material and Chapter 12 is a review chapter.

Following is a description of the various features in *¡Ven conmigo!* and suggestions on how to use them in the classroom. While it is not crucial for students to cover all material and do all activities to achieve the goals listed at the beginning of each chapter, the material within each chapter has been carefully sequenced to enable students to progress steadily at a realistic pace to the ultimate goal of linguistic and cultural proficiency. You, the teacher, as presenter, facilitator, and guide, will determine the precise depth of coverage, taking into account the individual needs of each class and the amount and type of alternative instructional material to be used from the *¡Ven conmigo!* program.

STARTING OUT...

In *¡Ven conmigo!* chapters are arranged in groups of two, with each pair of chapters set in a different Spanish-speaking location. Each new location is introduced by a **Location Opener,** four pages of colorful photos and background information that can be used to introduce the region and help motivate students.

The two-page **Chapter Opener** is intended to pique students' interest and focus their attention on the task at hand. It is a visual introduction to the theme of the chapter and includes a brief description of the topic and situations students will encounter, as well as a list of objectives they will be expected to achieve.

SETTING THE SCENE...

Language instruction begins with **De antemano,** the comprehensible input that models language in a culturally authentic setting. Whether presented on video or as a reading accompanied by the audiocassette or compact disc recording, the highly visual presentation—frequently in **fotonovela** format in the textbook—ensures success as students practice their receptive skills and begin to recognize some of the new functions and vocabulary they will encounter in the chapter. Following **De antemano** is a series of activities that can be used to help guide students through the story and check comprehension.

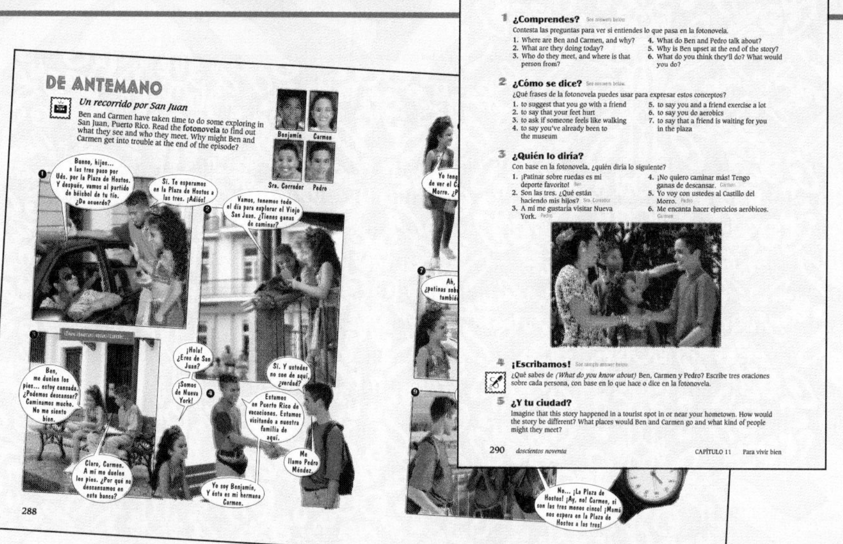
DE ANTEMANO

Un recorrido por San Juan

Ben and Carmen have taken time to do some exploring in San Juan, Puerto Rico. Read the **fotonovela** to find out what they see and who they meet. Why might Ben and Carmen get into trouble at the end of the episode?

288

1 **¿Comprendes?** See answers below.

Contesta las preguntas para ver si entiendes lo que pasa en la fotonovela.

1. Where are Ben and Carmen, and why?
2. What are they doing today?
3. Who do they meet, and where is that person from?
4. What do Ben and Pedro talk about?
5. Why is Ben upset at the end of the story?
6. What do you think they'll do? What would you do?

2 **¿Cómo se dice?** See answers below.

¿Qué frases de la fotonovela puedes usar para expresar estos conceptos?

1. to suggest that you go with a friend
2. to say that your feet hurt
3. to ask if someone feels like walking
4. to say you've already been to the museum
5. to say you and a friend exercise a lot
6. to say you do aerobics
7. to say that a friend is waiting for you in the plaza

3 **¿Quién lo diría?**

Con base en la fotonovela, ¿quién diría lo siguiente?

1. ¡Patinar sobre ruedas es mi deporte favorito! Ben
2. Son las tres. ¿Qué están haciendo mis hijos? Sra. Corredor
3. A mí me gustaría visitar Nueva York. Pedro
4. ¡No quiero caminar más! Tengo ganas de descansar. Carmen
5. Yo voy con ustedes al Castillo del Morro. Pedro
6. Me encanta hacer ejercicios aeróbicos. Carmen

4 **¡Escribamos!** See sample answer below.

¿Qué sabes de *(What do you know about)* Ben, Carmen y Pedro? Escribe tres oraciones sobre cada persona, con base en lo que hace o dice en la fotonovela.

5 **¿Y tu ciudad?**

Imagine that this story happened in a tourist spot in or near your hometown. How would the story be different? What places would Ben and Carmen go and what kind of people might they meet?

290 *doscientos noventa* CAPÍTULO 11 Para vivir bien

289

BUILDING PROFICIENCY STEP BY STEP...

Primer, Segundo, and **Tercer paso** are the three core instructional sections where the greater part of language acquisition will take place. The communicative goals in each chapter center on the functional expressions presented in **Así se dice** boxes. These expressions are supported and expanded by material in the **Vocabulario, Gramática,** and **Nota gramatical** sections. Activities immediately following the above features are designed to practice recognition or to provide closed-ended practice with the new material. Activities then progress from controlled to open-ended practice where students are able to express themselves in meaningful communication. Depending on class size, general ability level, and class dynamics, you may wish to proceed sequentially through all activities in a chapter, supplementing presentation or practice at various points with additional materials from ***¡Ven conmigo!,*** or to proceed more quickly to open-ended pair and group work.

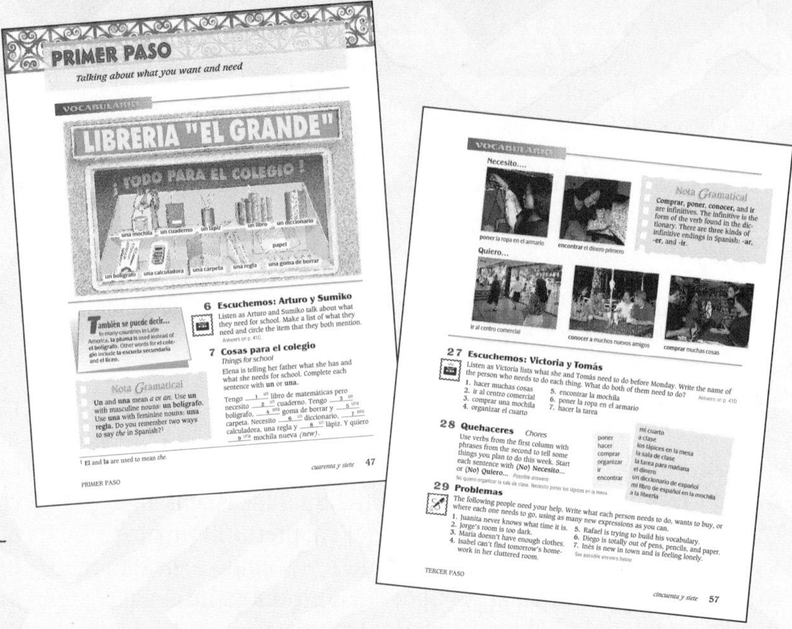

DISCOVERING THE PEOPLE AND THE CULTURE...

Cultural information has been incorporated into activities wherever possible. There are also two major cultural features to help students develop an appreciation and understanding of the cultures of Spanish-speaking countries.

Panorama cultural presents spontaneous interviews conducted in various countries in the Spanish-speaking world on a topic related to the chapter theme. The interviews may be presented on video or done as a reading supplemented by the audiocassette or compact disc recording. Culminating activities on this page may be used to verify comprehension and encourage students to think critically about the target culture as well as their own.

Encuentro cultural presents a cultural encounter that invites students to compare and contrast the foreign culture with their own.

> **NOTA CULTURAL**
>
> Soccer, cycling, tennis, and baseball are popular sports in Spanish-speaking countries. Fans in these countries have had a lot to cheer about! In 1993 and 1994, Sergi Bruguera of Spain won the French Open, one of the four grand slam events in professional tennis. In 1994, Conchita Martínez became the first Spanish woman to win the Wimbledon crown, tennis's premier tournament. In the United States, Spanish-speaking athletes have contributed greatly, especially to the sport of baseball.

> **También se puede decir...**
>
> In many Spanish-speaking countries, you'll also hear **andar en bicicleta** or **dar un paseo en bicicleta** in addition to **montar en bicicleta**.

Nota cultural provides tidbits of both "big C" and "little c" culture that can be used to enrich and enliven activities and presentations at various places throughout each chapter.

También se puede decir... presents regional alternatives for the vocabulary introduced in the chapter. This feature helps students become familiar with the linguistic richness and variety of the Spanish-speaking world.

UNDERSTANDING AUTHENTIC DOCUMENTS...

Vamos a leer presents reading strategies that help students understand authentic Spanish documents and literature. The reading selections vary from advertisements to letters to short stories or poems in order to accommodate different interests and familiarize the students with different styles and formats. The accompanying activities progress from prereading to reading to postreading tasks and are designed to develop students' overall reading skills and challenge their critical thinking abilities.

TARGETING STUDENTS' NEEDS...

In each **Paso** several special features may be used to enhance language learning and cultural appreciation.

Sugerencia suggests effective ways for students to learn a foreign language.

A lo nuestro provides students with tips for speaking more natural-sounding Spanish.

Un poco más... presents optional vocabulary related to the chapter theme. These words are provided to help students personalize activities; students will not be required to produce this vocabulary on the Chapter Quizzes and Test.

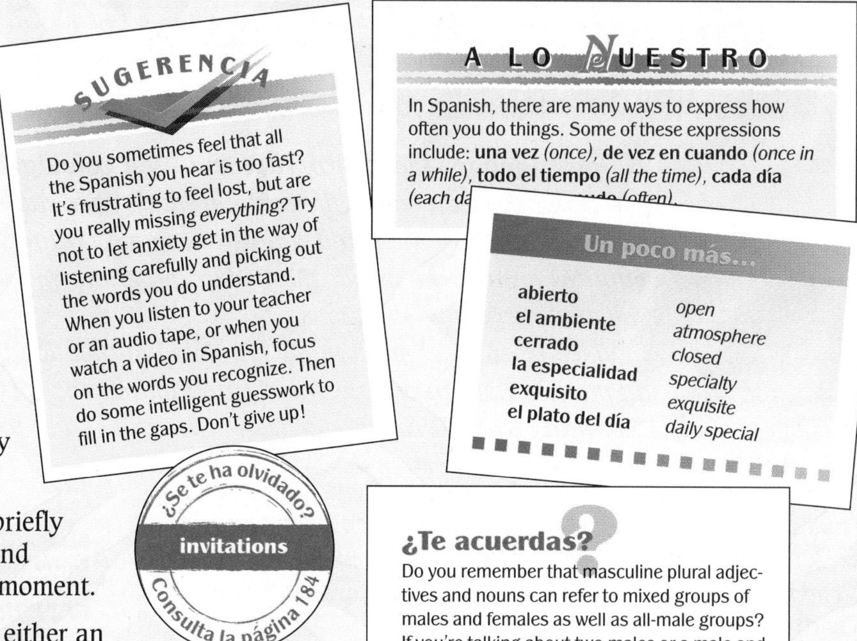

¿Te acuerdas? is a re-entry feature that lists and briefly explains previously learned vocabulary, functions, and grammar that students might need to review at the moment.

¿Se te ha olvidado? is a handy page reference to either an earlier chapter where material was presented or to a reference section in the back of the book that includes such aids as the Summary of Functions and the Grammar Summary.

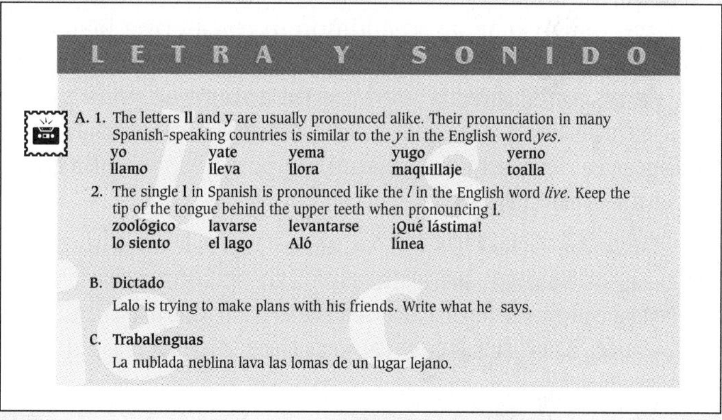

LETRA Y SONIDO

At the end of each **Tercer paso** is **Letra y sonido,** a pronunciation feature where certain sounds and spelling rules are explained. Pronunciation is practiced using vocabulary words that contain the targeted sounds. In a dictation exercise that follows, students hear and write sentences using the targeted sounds and letters. The last part of this feature, the **trabalenguas,** gives students an additional opportunity to practice the targeted sounds in amusing and challenging tongue-twisters.

LETRA Y SONIDO

A. 1. The letters ll and y are usually pronounced alike. Their pronunciation in many Spanish-speaking countries is similar to the *y* in the English word *yes*.

yo	**yate**	**yema**	**yugo**	**yerno**
llamo	**lleva**	**llora**	**maquillaje**	**toalla**

2. The single l in Spanish is pronounced like the *l* in the English word *live*. Keep the tip of the tongue behind the upper teeth when pronouncing l.

zoológico	**lavarse**	**levantarse**	**¡Qué lástima!**
lo siento	**el lago**	**Aló**	**línea**

B. **Dictado**

Lalo is trying to make plans with his friends. Write what he says.

C. **Trabalenguas**

La nublada neblina lava las lomas de un lugar lejano.

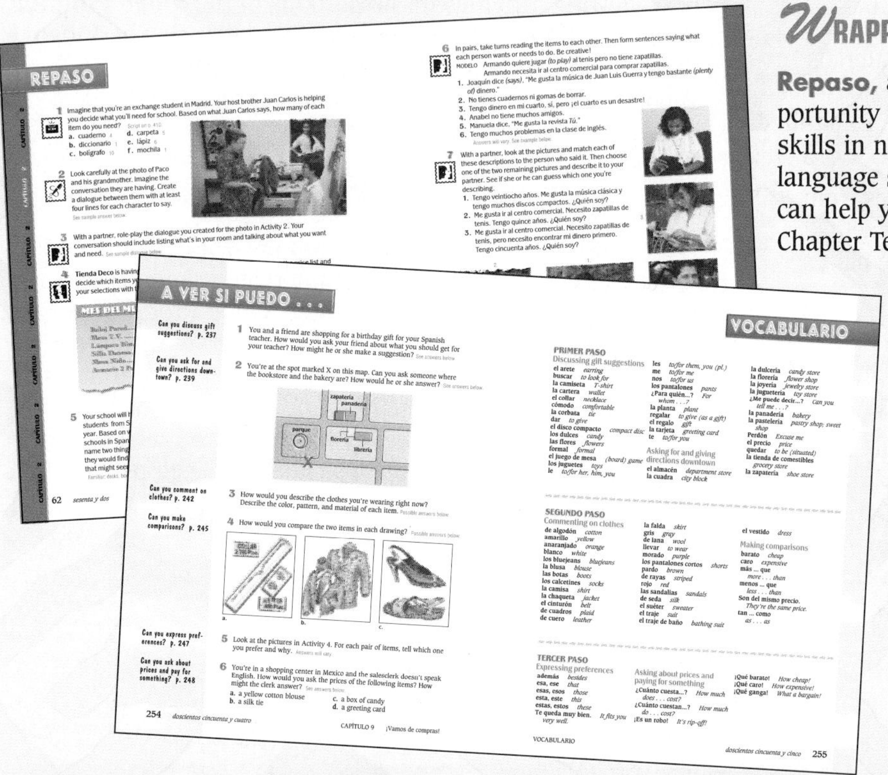

WRAPPING IT ALL UP...

Repaso, at the end of each chapter, gives students the opportunity to review what they have learned and to apply their skills in new communicative contexts. Focusing on all four language skills as well as cultural awareness, the **Repaso** can help you determine whether students are ready for the Chapter Test.

A ver si puedo... follows the **Repaso** and is a checklist that students can use on their own to see if they have achieved the goals stated on the Chapter Opener. Each communicative function is paired with one or more activities for students to use as a self-check. Page references are given for students who need to return to the chapter for review.

Vocabulario presents the chapter vocabulary grouped by **Paso** and arranged according to communicative function or theme. This list represents the active words and expressions that students will be expected to know for the Chapter Quizzes and Test.

¡Ven conmigo! *Video*

¡Ven conmigo! ***Video Program*** *and* **¡Ven conmigo!** ***Expanded Video Program*** *bring the textbook to life and introduce your students to people they will encounter in every chapter of the* ***Pupil's Edition.*** *Filmed entirely on location in Spanish-speaking countries around the world, these video programs feature native speakers of Spanish in realistic, interesting situations.*

Video is an ideal medium for providing authentic input needed to increase proficiency in Spanish. Both informative and entertaining, the episodes of the ***Video Program*** *and* ***Expanded Video Program*** *provide rich visual clues to aid comprehension and motivate students to learn more.* ◆

¡VEN CONMIGO! VIDEO PROGRAM

The video program is fully integrated and correlates directly with the ***¡Ven conmigo!*** *Pupil's Edition:*

DE ANTEMANO The introductory dialogue or story in each chapter is a videotaped dramatic episode based on the chapter theme. It introduces the targeted functions, vocabulary, and grammar of the chapter, in addition to re-entering material from previous chapters in new contexts. Since this video episode corresponds directly with the **De antemano** and the chapter, it can be used as a general introduction to the chapter, as a chapter review, and as a visual support for presenting the elements of the lesson.

PANORAMA CULTURAL Authentic interviews with native speakers of Spanish bring the Spanish-speaking world to life as real people talk about themselves, their country, and their way of life. Each interview topic is thematically related to the chapter.

¡VEN CONMIGO! EXPANDED VIDEO PROGRAM

The **Expanded Video Program** includes all of the material provided in the **Video Program,** plus additional materials designed to extend and enrich students' learning experience through additional authentic input. Included in the **Expanded Video Program** are the following:

LOCATION OPENER A narrated collage of images from regions of Spanish-speaking countries expands students' acquaintance with the geography and people of the places presented in each Location Opener.

DE ANTEMANO (see Video Program)

A CONTINUACIÓN These continuations of the dramatic episodes provide high-interest input that helps motivate students and offers additional opportunities to expand on what they've learned. **A continuación** continues the story and resolves the dramatic conflict that was created in **De antemano.** Designed to facilitate proficiency by providing additional comprehensible input, this episode offers an extended presentation of the chapter material as well as re-entering functions, vocabulary, and structures from previous chapters.

PANORAMA CULTURAL Additional authentic interviews are offered in the **Expanded Video Program.** They feature a wide variety of native speakers from around the world and introduce students to regional variations in speech, cultural diversity, and varying points of view. This assortment of interviews from around the Spanish-speaking world enriches students' appreciation of Spanish-speaking cultures and helps them better understand their own.

VIDEOCLIPS Students will enjoy the authentic footage from Spanish and Latin Amerian television: music videos, commercials, and more. These short segments of video give students confidence as they realize that they can understand and enjoy material that was produced for native speakers of Spanish!

¡VEN CONMIGO! VIDEO GUIDE

¡Ven conmigo! **Video Guide** provides background information together with suggestions for presentation and pre- and post-viewing activities for all portions of the **Video Program** and the **Expanded Video Program.** In addition, the **Video Guide** contains a transcript and synopsis of each episode, supplementary vocabulary lists, and reproducible student activity sheets.

¡VEN CONMIGO! VIDEODISC PROGRAM AND GUIDE

¡Ven conmigo! **Videodisc Program** presents in videodisc format all the authentic footage, interviews, and dramatic episodes presented in the **Expanded Video Program** plus additional cultural and geographic material to further enrich your students' experience. Barcodes provide instant access to all material and facilitate efficient integration of video resources into each lesson. Key barcodes are provided in the *Annotated Teacher's Edition.* Teaching suggestions, activity masters, and a complete barcode directory are provided in the **Videodisc Guide.**

¡Ven conmigo! *Ancillaries*

The **¡Ven conmigo!** *Spanish program offers a state-of-the-art ancillary package that addresses the concerns of today's teachers. Because foreign language teachers are working with all types of students, the activities in our ancillaries accommodate all learning styles. The variety of activities provided in the* **¡Ven conmigo!** *ancillary materials are both innovative and relevant to students' experiences.* ◆

TEACHING RESOURCES WITH PROFESSIONAL ORGANIZER

Holt, Rinehart and Winston has taken an innovative approach to organizing our teaching resources. The ***¡Ven conmigo!*** ancillaries are conveniently packaged in time-saving **Chapter Teaching Resources** booklets with a tri-fold **Professional Organizer.** Each **Chapter Teaching Resources** booklet puts a wealth of resources at your fingertips!

CHAPTER TEACHING RESOURCES, BOOKS 1-3

Oral communication is the language skill that is most challenging to develop and test. The ***¡Ven conmigo!*** **Situation Cards** and **Communicative Activities** help students develop their speaking skills and give them opportunities to communicate in a variety of situations.

Additional Listening Activities, in combination with the **Audiocassette** and **Audio CD Program,** provide students with a unique opportunity to actively develop their listening skills in a variety of authentic contexts.

The ***¡Ven conmigo!*** **Realia** reproduce real documents to provide your students with additional reading and language practice using culturally authentic material. Included with the **Realia** are teacher suggestions and student activities.

The **Student Response Forms** are provided for your convenience. These copying masters can be reproduced and used as answer forms for all the textbook listening activities.

The **Assessment Program** responds to your requests for a method of evaluation that is fair to all students and that encourages students to work towards realistic, communicative goals. The **Assessment Program** includes the following components:

- Three **Quizzes** per chapter (one per **Paso**)
- One **Chapter Test** per chapter; each **Chapter Test** includes listening, reading, writing, and culture sections and a score sheet for easy grading. Part of each test can be corrected on ScanTron®.
- **Speaking tests,** provided in the **Assessment Guide.**

Also included in the **Chapter Teaching Resources:**

- **Answer Key** for the **Practice and Activity Book**
- **Teaching Transparency Masters** and suggestions for use in a variety of activities
- **Listening Scripts** for the **Additional Listening Activities, Quizzes,** and **Chapter Tests.**

ASSESSMENT GUIDE

The **Assessment Guide** describes various testing and scoring methods. This guide also includes:

- **Portfolio Assessment** suggestions and rubrics
- **Speaking Tests** to be used separately or as part of the **Chapter Test**
- A cumulative **Midterm Exam** with scripts and answers
- A comprehensive **Final Exam** with scripts and answers.

PROFESSIONAL ORGANIZER

A tri-fold binder helps you organize the ancillaries for each chapter.

TEACHING TRANSPARENCIES

The **Teaching Transparencies** benefit all students, and the visual learner in particular. These colorful transparencies add variety and focus to your daily lesson plans. Suggestions for using the transparencies can be found in the **Chapter Teaching Resources.**

AUDIO PROGRAM

All recorded material is available in either the **Audiocassette Program** or the **Audio CD Program.** The listening activities, pronunciation activities, and dialogues help students further develop their listening and pronunciation skills by providing opportunities to hear native speakers in a variety of authentic situations.

PRACTICE AND ACTIVITY BOOK

The **Practice and Activity Book** is filled with a variety of activities that provide further practice with the functions, grammar, and vocabulary presented in each **Paso.** Additional reading, culture, and journal activities for each chapter give students the opportunity to apply the reading and writing strategies they've learned in relevant, personalized contexts.

The **Native Speaker Activity Book** includes suggestions and activities designed to address the native speakers in your Spanish class. It includes reading, writing, and speaking tasks for native speakers to complete, rounding out their Spanish language learning.

TEST GENERATOR

The **Test Generator** is a user-friendly software program that enables you to create customized worksheets, quizzes, and tests for each chapter in ***¡Ven conmigo!*** The **Test Generator** is available for IBM® PC and Compatibles and Macintosh® computers.

The Annotated Teacher's Edition

The **¡Ven conmigo!** Annotated Teacher's Edition *is designed to help you meet the increasingly varied needs of today's students by providing an abundance of suggestions and strategies. The* Annotated Teacher's Edition *includes the reduced pages of the* Pupil's Edition *with teacher annotation, wrap-around teacher text with video references and barcodes, notes, suggestions, answers, and additional activities, as well as interleafed pages of scripts, projects, and games before each chapter.* ◆

Using the Location Opener

Each reduced student page is wrapped with background information for you about the photographs and settings. In addition, teaching suggestions help you motivate students to learn more about the history, geography, and culture of Spanish-speaking countries.

Using the Chapter Interleaf

The chapter interleaf includes a chapter overview correlation chart for teaching resources, *Pupil's Edition* listening scripts, and suggestions for projects and games.

The **Chapter Overview** chart outlines at a glance the functions, grammar, culture and re-entry items featured in each **Paso.** A list of corresponding print and audiovisual resource materials for each section of the chapter is provided to help integrate video and ancillaries into your lessons. The pronunciation, reading, and review features for each chapter are also referenced, as well as a variety of assessment and portfolio options.

Textbook Listening Activities Scripts provide the scripts of the chapter listening activities for reference or for use in class. The answers to each activity are provided below each script for easy reference.

Projects propose extended four-skills activities based on the chapter theme and content. **Projects** suggestions are provided to give students the opportunity to personalize the information they've learned in the chapter. Individual projects offer students the chance to explore topics related to the chapter theme that are of personal interest to them. Group and cooperative learning projects encourage students to work together to apply what they've learned in the chapter by creating a poster, brochure, or report, often accompanied by an oral presentation.

Games provide students with informal, entertaining activities in which they can apply and reinforce the functions, structures, vocabulary, and culture of the chapter. **Games** appeal to a variety of learners and encourage teamwork and cooperation among students of different levels and learning styles.

Using the Wrap-Around Teacher Text

Wrap-around teacher text gives point-of-use suggestions and information to hep you make the most of class time. The wrap-around style of the *Annotated Teacher's Edition* conveniently presents barcodes, video references, teacher notes, suggestions, and activity answers together on the same page with the reduced *Pupil's Edition* page.

Teaching Cycle

For each **Paso**, a logical instructional sequence includes the following steps to enable you to:

- **Jump Start!** your students with an individual writing activity that focuses their attention on previously-learned material while they wait for class to begin.
- **Motivate** students by introducing the topic in a personalized and contextualized way.
- **Teach** the functions, vocabulary, structures, and culture with a variety of approaches.
- **Close** each **Paso** with activities that review and confirm the communicative goals.
- **Assess** students' progress with a quiz and/or performance assessment activity. **Performance Assessment** suggestions provide an alternative to pen and paper tests and give you the option of evaluating students' progress by having them perform communicative, competency-based tasks. These may include teacher-student interviews, conversations, dialogues, or skits that students perform for the entire class. These tasks can also be recorded or videotaped for evaluation at a later time.
- **Portfolio** icons signal activities that are appropriate for students' oral or written portfolios. They may include lists, posters, letters, journal entries, or taped conversations or skits. A variety of suggestions are provided within each chapter so that you can work with your students to select the activities that would best document their strengths and progress in the language. Portfolio information, including checklists and suggestions for evaluation, are provided in the *Assessment Guide,* pages 2–13. On pages 14–25 of the *Assessment Guide,* there are suggestions for the expansion of the two designated portfolio activities from the *Pupil's Edition.* In each chapter overview, these two activities are listed under "Portfolio Assessment" (one written and one oral). The portfolio suggestions will help students to further develop their oral and written language skills, often in the context of real-life situations. For a discussion of portfolio creation and use, see *Using Portfolios in the Foreign Language Classroom,* page T52.

For Individual Needs

Suggestions under the following categories provide alternate approaches to help you address students' diverse learning styles.

Visual, Auditory, Tactile, and Kinesthetic Learners benefit from activities that accommodate their unique learning styles.

- **Slower Pace** provides ideas for presenting material in smaller steps to facilitate comprehension.
- **Challenge** extends activities into more challenging tasks that encourage students to expand their communicative skills.

Native Speakers

Native speakers benefit from the various projects and activities that validate their individual culture and language. They are encouraged to share their knowledge of Spanish regionalisms and culture with non-native students. Native speaker activities are designed to highlight the skills and culture of native speakers and to channel their input to the advantage of the entire class. The in-class activities and out-of-class assignments for native speakers often integrate family and community into the students' learning experience. Native speaker work lends authenticity to Spanish language instruction and guides students toward a comprehensive understanding of the Spanish-speaking world. For more information on native speakers, see the essay *New Perspectives for Native Speakers* by Cecilia Rodríguez-Pino on pages T54–55 of the *Annotated Teacher's Edition.*

Making Connections

To help students appreciate their membership in a global society, suggestions for linking Spanish with other disciplines, their community, and other cultures appear under the following categories:

- **Math...Geography...Health...Science ...History...Language Arts Links** relate the chapter topic to other subject areas, making Spanish relevant to the students' overall academic experience.
- **Multicultural Link** provides students the opportunity to compare and contrast their language and culture with those of Spanish-speaking countries and other parts of the world.
- **Community...Family Link** encourages students to seek opportunities for learning outside of the classroom by interacting with neighbors and family members. These suggestions also call on students to share their learning with their family and community.

Developing Thinking Skills

Thinking Critically helps students develop their higher-order thinking skills.

Drawing Inferences, Comparing and Contrasting, Analyzing, Observing, and Synthesizing are suggestions to extend activities beyond an informational level. They increase comprehension of language and cultures, and they help students exercise and develop higher order thinking skills.

Establishing Collaborative Learning

Cooperative Learning allows students to work together in small groups to attain common goals by sharing responsibilities. Students are accountable for setting the group objectives, completing the assignment, and ensuring that all group members master the material. Working together in cooperative groups allows students to take an active role in the classroom, to develop more self-esteem as they to contribute to the success of the group, and to experience less anxiety by working in small groups. Cooperative learning enables students to improve interpersonal communication skills by encouraging them to listen to, share, and respect other opinions.

Total Physical Response (TPR) techniques visually and kinesthetically reinforce structures and vocabulary. They are active-learning exercises that encourage students to focus on class interaction while learning Spanish.

Teaching Vamos a leer

Teacher's notes and suggestions in **Vamos a leer** offer prereading, reading, and postreading activities to help students develop reading skills. Background information and useful terms related to the reading are provided as well.

Chapter 4 Sample Lesson Plan

The following lesson plan suggests how the material in Chapter 4 may be distributed over twelve days. You may wish to prepare similar plans to guide you through the other chapters of **¡Ven conmigo!**, *adjusting the daily schedule and selecting appropriate activities and ancillary material that best suit your individual needs and those of your students. (Page numbers set in* ***boldface type*** *refer to activities in the* Annotated Teacher's Edition.*)* ◆

DAILY PLANS	RESOURCES
DAY 1 **OBJECTIVE:** To find out what some Spanish-speaking students do on the weekend	
Chapter Opener, pp. 96–97 **De antemano,** pp. 98–100 Presentation: **¿Dónde está María Inés?, p. 98** Activities 1–3, p. 100 Close: Activity 5, p. 100 Assignment: Activity 4, p. 100	*Textbook Audiocassette 2B/Audio CD 4* *Practice and Activity Book, p. 37* *Video Program OR Expanded Video Program, Videocassette 1* *Videodisc Program, Videodisc 2B*
DAY 2 **OBJECTIVE:** To talk about what you like to do	
Review assignment from Day 1 **Primer paso,** p. 101 Jump Start!, **p. 101** Motivating Activity, **p. 101** Presentation: **Así se dice, Vocabulario, p. 101** Activity 6, p. 101, Listening Script on **p. 95C** Activity 7, p. 101 Presentation: **Gramática, p. 102** Activity 3, *Practice and Activity Book*, p. 38 Assignment: Activities 4 and 5, *Practice and Activity Book*, p. 38	*Textbook Audiocassette 2B/Audio CD 4* *Practice and Activity Book, pp. 38–40* *Chapter Teaching Resources, Book 1* *Teaching Transparency 4-1, pp. 181, 184* *Videodisc Program, Videodisc 2B*
DAY 3 **OBJECTIVE:** To discuss what you and others do during free time	
Review assignment from Day 2 Presentation: **Así se dice, p. 102** Activity 8, p. 102, Listening Script on **p. 95C** Presentation: **Vocabulario, p. 103** For Individual Needs, **p. 103** Activity 10, p. 104 Activities 11 and 12; Optional: Activity 13, p. 104 Close, **p. 105** Assignment: Activities 9, p. 103; 14 and 15, p. 105	*Textbook Audiocassette 2B/Audio CD 4* *Practice and Activity Book, pp. 38–40* *Chapter Teaching Resources, Book 1* *Teaching Transparency 4-1, pp. 181, 184* *Videodisc Program, Videodisc 2B*
DAY 4 **OBJECTIVE:** To tell where people and things are	
Review assignment from Day 3 Quiz 4-1 Assessment: Performance Assessment, **p. 105** **Segundo paso,** p. 106 Jump Start!, **p. 106** Activity 16 or 17, p. 105 Presentation: **Así se dice, Nota gramatical, p. 106** Activities 18, p. 106, Listening Script on **p. 95C** Assignment: Activities 19, p. 106; 20, p. 108	*Chapter Teaching Resources, Book 1, pp. 197–198* *Teaching Transparency 4-2, pp. 182, 184* *Assessment Items* *Audiocassette 7B/Audio CD 4* *Textbook Audiocassette 2B/Audio CD 4* *Practice and Activity Book, pp. 41–43*
DAY 5 **OBJECTIVE:** To use subject pronouns to talk about what you and others do	
Review assignment from Day 4 Presentation: **Vocabulario, p. 107** Option: Additional Practice, **p. 107** Activity 21, p. 108, Listening Script on **p. 95C** Activity 22 or 23, p. 108 Option: Activity 24, p. 109 Assignment: Activity 25, p. 109	*Textbook Audiocassette 2B/Audio CD 4* *Chapter Teaching Resources, Book 1* *Teaching Transparency 4-2, pp. 182, 184* *Practice and Activity Book, pp. 41–43* *Video Program OR Expanded Video Program, Videocassette 1* *Videodisc Program, Videodisc 2B*

DAILY PLANS	RESOURCES
DAY 6 **OBJECTIVE:** To talk about where you and others go during free time	
Review assignment from Day 5 Presentation: **Gramática, p. 109** Activity 16, *Practice and Activity Book,* p. 46 Close, **p. 109** Quiz 4-2 Assessment: Performance Assessment, **p. 109** **Panorama cultural,** p. 110 Assignment: Activity 12, *Practice and Activity Book,* p. 44	*Chapter Teaching Resources, Book 1, pp. 199–200* *Teaching Transparency 4-2, pp. 182, 184* *Assessment Items* *Audiocassette 7B/Audio CD 4* *Textbook Audiocassette 2B/Audio CD 4* *Practice and Activity Book, pp. 41–43*
DAY 7 **OBJECTIVE:** To use the verb *ir* to talk about activities	
Review assignment from Day 6 **Tercer paso,** p. 111 Jump Start!, **p. 111** Presentation: **Así se dice, p. 111** Activity 26, p. 111, Listening Script on **p. 95D** Presentation: **Nota gramatical, p. 111** Activity 27, p. 111 Activity 28 or 29, p. 112 Assignment: Activity 11, *Practice and Activity Book,* p. 44	*Textbook Audiocassette 2B/Audio CD 4* *Practice and Activity Book, pp. 44–46* *Chapter Teaching Resources, Book 1* *Teaching Transparency 4-3,* pp. 183, 184 *Videodisc Program, Videodisc 2B*
DAY 8 **OBJECTIVE:** To talk about what you do during the week and on weekends	
Review assignment from Day 7 Presentation: **Vocabulario, Nota gramatical, p. 112** Activity 15, *Practice and Activity Book,* p. 46 For Individual Needs, **p. 112** Activity 30 or 31, p. 113 Assignment: Activity 13, *Practice and Activity Book,* p. 45	*Textbook Audiocassette 2B/Audio CD 4* *Practice and Activity Book, pp. 44–46* *Chapter Teaching Resources, Book 1* *Teaching Transparency 4-3,* pp. 183, 184 *Videodisc Program, Videodisc 2B*
DAY 9 **OBJECTIVE:** To describe where you go and when you do things	
Review assignment from Day 8 Presentation: **Letra y sonido,** p. 113 **Dictado,** p. 113, Listening Script on **p. 95D** Cooperative Learning, **p. 108** Close, **p. 113** Assessment: Performance Assessment, **p. 113** Assignment: Activity 32, p. 113	*Textbook Audiocassette 2B/Audio CD 4* *Practice and Activity Book, pp. 44–46* *Chapter Teaching Resources, Book 1* *Teaching Transparency 4-3,* pp. 183, 184 *Videodisc Program, Videodisc 2B*
DAY 10 **OBJECTIVE:** To read Spanish classified ads	
Review assignment from Day 9 Quiz 4-3 Presentation: **Vamos a leer, pp. 114–115** Motivating Activity, **p. 114** Activities A–D, pp. 114–115 Assignment: Activity E, p. 115	*Chapter Teaching Resources, Book 1,* pp. 201–202 *Assessment Items* *Audiocassette 7B/Audio CD 4* *Textbook Audiocassette 2B/Audio CD 4* *Practice and Activity Book, p. 47*
DAY 11 **OBJECTIVE:** To use what you have learned, to prepare for the Chapter Test	
Review assignment from Day 10 **Repaso,** pp. 116–117 Activity 1, p. 116, Listening Script on **p. 95D** Activities 2–4, p. 116 Activities 5–8, p. 117 **Situación,** p. 117 **A ver si puedo...** p. 118 Activities 1–6, p. 118 Assignment: **Vocabulario**	*Textbook Audiocassette 2B/Audio CD 4* *Chapter Teaching Resources, Book 1* *Video Program* OR *Expanded Video Program, Videocassette 1* *Videodisc Program, Videodisc 2B*
DAY 12 **OBJECTIVE:** To assess progress	
Capítulo 4 Chapter Test Games, **pp. 119, 95E**	*Chapter Teaching Resources, Book 1,* p. 203–210 *Assessment Guide* Speaking Test, p. 29 Portfolio Assessment, pp. 10–13, 17 *Assessment Items* *Audiocassette 7B/Audio CD 4*

Standards for Foreign Language Education

BY ROBERT LABOUVE

NATIONAL STANDARDS AND SCHOOL REFORM

In 1989 educational reform in the United States took on an entirely different look when state and national leaders reached consensus on six national educational goals for public schools. In 1994 a new law, *Goals 2000: Educate America Act,* endorsed these six goals and added two more. The most important national goal in the law for foreign language educators is Goal Three, which establishes a core curriculum and places foreign languages in that core. As a result of this consensus on national goals, the Federal government encouraged the development of high standards in the core disciplines. While the Federal government does not have the authority to mandate the implementation of foreign language standards locally, it will encourage their use through leadership and projects funded by the U.S. Department of Education.

We must first define "standards" in order to fully understand the rationale for their development. Content standards ask: What should students know and be able to do? Content standards are currently under development by foreign language professionals. Performance standards ask: How good is good enough? Opportunity-to-learn standards ask: Did the school prepare all students to perform well? There is a growing consensus that states and local districts should address the last two types of standards.

PROGRESS TOWARD NATIONAL FOREIGN LANGUAGE STANDARDS

A task force of foreign language educators began work on the standards in 1993 by establishing specific foreign language goals. They then set content standards for each goal. The task force sought feedback from the foreign language profession through an extensive dissemination program and produced a draft of the standards document for introduction at a number of sites around the United States during the 1994-1995 school year.

The target publication date for a final document is late 1995. The final version will incorporate suggestions from the sites where the standards were introduced and reaction from volunteer reviewers and the field in general. While the standards should be world class, they must also be realistic and attainable by most students. The task force also realizes that the general set of goals and standards will have to be made language specific in a curriculum development process and that

PROPOSED FOREIGN LANGUAGE STANDARDS			
Goal One	Communicate in languages other than English	**Standard 1.1**	Students will use the target language to participate in social interactions and to establish and maintain personal relationships in a variety of settings and contexts.
		Standard 1.2	Students will use the target language to obtain, process, and provide information in spoken or written form on a variety of topics of academic, personal, cultural, and historic interest.
		Standard 1.3	Students will use language for leisure and personal enrichment.
Goal Two	Gain knowledge of other cultures	**Standard 2.1**	Students will demonstrate knowledge of the components of the target culture.
Goal Three	Acquire information and connect with other disciplines	**Standard 3.1**	Students will use the target language to gain access to information and perspectives that are only available through the target language or within the target culture.
		Standard 3.2	Students will use the target language to reinforce and further their knowledge of other cultures.
Goal Four	Develop insight into own language and culture	**Standard 4.1**	Students will recognize that different languages use different patterns to communicate.
		Standard 4.2	Students will recognize that cultures view situations from varying perspectives and evolve different patterns of interaction.
Goal Five	Participate in multilingual communities and global society	**Standard 5.1**	Students will use the language both within and beyond the school setting with representatives of the target culture in a variety of ways.

continuing staff development will be essential.

Proposed National Foreign Language Goals and Standards

The proposed goals and standards in the draft document describe a K–12 foreign language program for *all* students, presenting languages, both modern and classical, as part of the core curriculum for every student, including those whose native language is not English. Broad goals establish the basic framework of the language program. The proposed content standards set for these goals describe what students should know and be able to do in a language. The chart on p. T44 shows how the standards are arrayed alongside the goals.

The first two goals in this expanded language program describe today's typical school language program. The last three are often identified by teachers as important, but are not always implemented. The standards-based program moves beyond an emphasis on skills to a redefinition of the content of a language program itself.

Sample benchmark tasks will be provided for Grades 4, 8, and 12 as examples of what students can do to meet the standards and accomplish the goals of the language program. A higher level of performance will be expected as students progress from one benchmark grade to another. For example, Standard 1.1 at Grade 4 expects students "to give and follow simple instructions by participating in various games or other activities with partners or groups," but Standard 1.1 at Grade 12 expects the students to "communicate (orally or in writing) with a speaker of the target language regarding a future event."

Impact of the Standards

While there is an assumption that national foreign language goals and standards will have a great impact upon the states and local districts, the standards themselves are voluntary. Clearly, standards will influence instruction and curriculum development in districts that choose to align their language programs with the national standards. Assessment programs will most likely begin to reflect the influence of the standards. The standards will also have an impact on the preparation of future teachers and on staff development for teachers now in the classroom.

A curriculum based on the standards will encourage students to take responsibility for their learning by making the language curriculum coherent and transparent to them. Students will know from the beginning what they should be able to do when they exit the program and they will be able to judge for themselves how they are progressing, especially at established benchmarks, i.e., Grades 4, 8, and 12.

The standards will direct instruction in the classroom by providing curriculum developers and teachers with a broad framework upon which to construct the expanded language program. Standards for each goal will ensure that no goal is treated informally or left to chance. Teachers who use the content standards should play a critical role in their district by deciding how good is good enough for students who exit the program.

The standards will also have a significant impact on the demand for sequential, cross-disciplinary instructional materials for a K–12 language program. Another challenge will be the development of new technologies that increase learning in order to meet high standards.

Probably the greatest benefit that national standards may bring will be in the area of making possible articulation that is horizontal (linking languages to other disciplines) and vertical (grade to grade, school to school, and school to college). Language teachers will join their English and social studies colleagues in helping students become language competent, literate citizens of the world. A language program that is at once coherent and transparent to students and others will provide all language educators a basis to reach consensus about their expectations on what students should know and do. To those of us who feel that foreign language education is basic education for all students, the national standards document will become a strong advocate for languages in the curriculum of every school and for the extended sequences of study presented by the goals and standards. The standards document will make it easier for language educators to present a solid rationale for foreign languages in the curriculum.

The standards document is still in draft form and some changes are expected before the official document is published. To receive the most up-to-date version, please contact the project office:

National Standards Project,
c/o ACTFL,
6 Executive Plaza,
Yonkers, NY 10701,
(914) 963-8830.

¡Ven conmigo!

supports the proposed National Foreign Language Goals and Standards in the following ways:

THE PUPIL'S EDITION

- Encourages students to take responsibility for their learning by providing clearly defined objectives at the beginning of each chapter.
- Provides a variety of pair- and group-work activities to give students an opportunity to use the target language in a wide range of settings and contexts.
- Offers culture-related activities and poses questions that develop students' insight and encourage them to develop observational and analytical skills.

THE ANNOTATED TEACHER'S EDITION

- Provides a broad framework for developing a foreign language program and offers specific classroom suggestions for reaching students with various learning styles.
- Offers ideas for multicultural and multidisciplinary projects as well as community and family links that encourage students to gain access to information both at school and in the community.

THE ANCILLARY PROGRAM

- Provides students with on-location video footage of native speakers interacting in their own cultural and geographic context.
- Includes multiple options for practicing and assessing performance, including situation cards, portfolio suggestions, speaking tests, and other alternatives.
- Familiarizes students with the types of tasks they will be expected to perform on exit exams.

Teaching Culture

BY NANCY HUMBACH AND DOROTHEA BRUSCHKE

Ask students what they like best about studying a foreign language. Chances are that learning about culture, the way people live, is one of their favorite aspects. Years after language study has ended, adults remember with fondness the customs of the target culture, even pictures in their language texts. It is this interest in the people and their way of life that is the great motivator and helps us sustain students' interest in language study.

We must integrate culture and language in a way that encourages curiosity, stimulates analysis, and teaches students to hypothesize and seek answers to questions about the people whose language they are studying. Teaching isolated facts about how people in other cultures live is not enough. This information is soon dated and quickly forgotten. We must go a step beyond and teach students that all behavior, values, and traditions exist because of certain aspects of history, geography, and socio-economic conditions.

There are many ways to help students become culturally knowledgeable and to assist them in developing an awareness of differences and similarities between the target culture and their own. Two of these approaches involve critical thinking, that is, trying to find reasons for a certain behavior through observation and analysis, and putting individual observations into larger cultural patterns. ◆

We must integrate culture and language in a way that encourages curiosity, stimulates analysis, and teaches students to hypothesize.

FIRST APPROACH: QUESTIONING

The first approach involves questioning as the key strategy. At the earliest stages of language learning, students begin to learn ways to greet peers, elders, and strangers, as well as the use of **tú** and **usted.** Students need to consider questions such as: "How do Spanish-speaking people greet each other? Are there different levels of formality? Who initiates a handshake? What's considered a good handshake?" Each of these questions leads students to think about the values that are expressed through word and gesture. They start to "feel" the other culture and, at the same time, understand how much of their own behavior is rooted in their cultural background.

Magazines, newspapers, advertisements, and television commercials are all excellent sources of cultural material. For example, browsing through a Spanish magazine, one finds an extraordinary number of advertisements for health-related products. Could this indicate a great interest in staying healthy? Reading advertisements can be followed up with viewing videos and films, or with interviewing native speakers or people who have lived in Spanish-speaking countries to learn about customs involving health. Students might want to find answers to questions such as: "How do Spanish speakers treat a cold? What is their attitude toward fresh air? toward exercise?" This type of questioning might lead students to discover that we view health matters, and the curative properties of food and exercises differently. As in this country, many of the concepts have their roots in the traditions of the past.

An advertisement for a refrigerator or a picture of a Spanish or Latin American kitchen can provide an insight into practices of shopping for food. Students first need to think about the refrigerator at home, take an inventory of what is kept in it, and consider when and where their family shops. Next, students should look closely at a Spanish or Latin American refrigerator. What is its size? What could that mean? (Shopping takes place more often, stores are within walking distance, and people eat more fresh foods.)

Food wrappers and containers also provide good clues to cultural insight. For example, laundry detergent is packaged in small plastic bags in many Spanish-speaking countries. Further, instead of "blue-white" cleaning properties, a "red-white" is preferred and considered the epitome of clean. Because of the lack of paper board for boxes, the humidity in many areas, the use for hand laundry, and shopping habits, plastic bags are a more practical form of packaging.

SECOND APPROACH: ASSOCIATING WORDS WITH IMAGES

The second approach for developing cultural understanding involves forming associations of words with the cultural images they suggest. Language and culture are so closely related that one might actually say that language *is* culture. Most words, especially nouns, carry a cultural connotation. Knowing the literal equivalent of a word in another language is of little use to students in understanding this connotation. For example, **relación** cannot be translated simply as relationship, **comida** as food, or **paseo** as walk. The Spanish phrase **dar un paseo,** for instance, carries with it such social images as people out walking with friends or family, sitting in a sidewalk café, seeing people and being seen by others. In Spanish-speaking countries, "to go for a walk" often means something entirely different than it does for North Americans.

When students have acquired some sense of the cultural connotation of words —not only through teachers' explanations but, more importantly, through observation of visual images—they start to discover the larger underlying cultural themes, or what is often called deep culture.

These larger cultural themes serve as organizing categories into which individual cultural phenomena fit to form a pattern. Students might discover, for example, that Spanish speakers, because they live in much more crowded conditions, have a great need for privacy (cultural theme), as reflected in such phenomena as closed doors, fences or walls around property, and sheers on windows. Students might also discover that love of nature and the outdoors is an important cultural theme, as indicated by such phenomena as flower boxes and planters in public places—even on small traffic islands—well-kept public parks in every town, and people going for a walk or going hiking.

As we teach culture, students learn not only to recognize elements of the target culture but also of their American cultural heritage. They see how elements of culture reflect larger themes or patterns. Learning what constitutes American culture and how that information relates to other people throughout the world can be an exciting journey for a young person.

As language teachers, we are able to facilitate that journey into another culture and into our own, to find our similarities as well as our differences from others. We do not encourage value judgments about others and their culture, nor do we recommend adopting other ways. We simply say to students, "Other ways exist. They exist for many reasons, just as our ways exist due to what our ancestors have bequeathed us through history, traditions, values, and geography."

¡Ven conmigo!

develops cultural understanding and awareness in the following ways:

THE PUPIL'S EDITION

- Informs students about Spanish-speaking countries through photo essays, maps, almanac boxes, and **Notas culturales** that invite comparison with the students' own cultural experiences.
- Engages students in analysis and comparison of live, personal interviews with native speakers in the **Panorama cultural** sections.
- Uses the **Encuentro cultural** section to expose students to cross-cultural situations that require observation, analysis, and problem-solving.
- Helps students integrate the language with its cultural connotations through a wealth of authentic art, documents, and literature.

THE ANNOTATED TEACHER'S EDITION

- Provides teacher with additional culture, history, and language notes, background information on photos and almanac boxes, and multicultural links.
- Suggests problem-solving activities and critical thinking questions that allow students to hypothesize, analyze, and discover larger underlying cultural themes.

THE ANCILLARY PROGRAM

- Includes additional realia to develop cultural insight by serving as a catalyst for questioning and direct discovery.
- Offers activities that require students to compare and contrast cultures.
- Provides songs, short readings, and poems as well as many opportunities for students to experience regional variation and idioms in the video and audio programs.

Learning Styles and Multi-Modality Teaching

BY MARY B. MCGEHEE

The larger and broader population of students who are enrolling in foreign language classes brings a new challenge to foreign language educators, calling forth an evolution in teaching methods to enhance learning for all our students. Educational experts now recognize that every student has a preferred sense for learning and retrieving information: visual, auditory, or kinesthetic. Incorporating a greater variety of activities to accommo-date the learning styles of all students can make the difference between struggle and pleasure in the foreign language classroom. ◆

Incorporating a greater variety of activities to accommodate the learning styles of all students can make the difference between struggle and pleasure in the foreign language classroom.

ACCOMMODATING DIFFERENT LEARNING STYLES

A modified arrangement of the classroom is one way to provide more effective and enjoyable learning for all students. Rows of chairs and desks must give way at times to circles, semicircles, or small clusters. Students may be grouped in fours or in pairs for cooperative work or peer teaching. It is important to find a balance of arrangements, thereby providing the most comfort in varied situations.

Since visual, auditory, and kinesthetic learners will be in the class, and because every student's learning will be enhanced by a multi-sensory approach, lessons must be directed toward all three learning styles. Any language lesson content may be presented visually, aurally, and kinesthetically.

Visual presentations and practice may include the chalkboard, charts, posters, television, overhead projectors, books, magazines, picture diagrams, flash cards, bulletin boards, films, slides, or videos. Visual learners need to see what they are to learn. Lest the teacher think he or she will never have the time to prepare all those visuals, Dickel and Slak (1983) found that visual aids generated by students are more effective than ready-made ones.

Auditory presentations and practice may include stating aloud the requirements of the lesson, oral questions and answers, paired or group work on a progression of oral exercises from repetition to communication, tapes, CDs, dialogues, and role-playing. Jingles, catchy stories, and memory devices using songs and rhymes are good learning aids. Having students record themselves and then listen as they play back the cassette allows them to practice in the auditory mode.

Kinesthetic presentations entail the students' use of manipulatives, chart materials, gestures, signals, typing, songs, games, and role-playing. These lead the students to associate sentence constructions with meaningful movements.

A SAMPLE LESSON USING MULTI-MODALITY TEACHING

A multi-sensory presentation on greetings might proceed as follows.

FOR VISUAL LEARNERS

As the teacher begins oral presentation of greetings and introductions, he or she simultaneously shows the written forms on transparencies, with the formal expressions marked with an adult's hat, and the informal expressions marked with a baseball cap.

The teacher then distributes cards with the hat and cap symbols representing the formal or informal expressions. As the students hear taped mini-dialogues, they hold up the appropriate card to indicate whether the dialogues are formal or informal. On the next listening, the students repeat the sentences they hear.

FOR AUDITORY LEARNERS

A longer taped dialogue follows, allowing the students to hear the new expressions a number of times. They write from dictation several sentences containing the new expressions. They may work in pairs, correcting each other's work as they "test" their own understanding of the lesson at hand. Finally, students respond to simple questions using the appropriate formal and informal responses cued by the cards they hold.

FOR KINESTHETIC LEARNERS

For additional kinesthetic input, members of the class come to the front of the room, each holding a hat or cap symbol. As the teacher calls out situations, the students play the roles, using gestures and props appropriate to the age group they are portraying. Non-cued, communicative role-playing with props further enables the students to "feel" the differences between formal and informal expressions.

HELPING STUDENTS LEARN HOW TO USE THEIR PREFERRED MODE

Since we require all students to perform in all language skills, part of the assistance we must render is to help them develop strategies within their preferred learning modes to carry out an assignment in another mode. For example, visual students hear the teacher assign an oral exercise and visualize what they must do. They must see themselves carrying out the assignment, in effect watching themselves as if there were a movie going on in their heads. Only then can they also hear themselves saying the right things. Thus, this assignment will be much easier for the visual learners who have been taught this process, if they have not already figured it out for themselves. Likewise, true auditory students, confronted with a reading/writing assignment, must talk themselves through it, converting the entire process into sound as they plan and prepare their work. Kinesthetic students presented with a visual or auditory task must first break the assignment into tasks and then work their way through them.

Students who experience difficulty because of a strong preference for one mode of learning are often unaware of the degree of preference. In working with these students, I prefer the simple and direct assessment of learning styles offered by Richard Bandler and John Grinder in their book *Frogs into Princes*, which allows the teacher and student to quickly determine how the student learns. In an interview with the student, I follow the assessment with certain specific recommendations of techniques to make the student's study time more effective.

It is important to note here that teaching students to maximize their study does not require that the teacher give each student an individualized assignment. It does require that each student who needs it be taught how to prepare the assignment using his or her own talents and strengths. This communication between teacher and student, combined with teaching techniques that reinforce learning in all modes, can only maximize pleasure and success in learning a foreign language.

▶ REFERENCES

Dickel, M.J. and S. Slak. "Imaging Vividness and Memory for Verbal Material." *Journal of Mental Imagery* 7, i (1983):121–6.

Bandler, Richard, and John Grinder. *Frogs into Princes*. Real People Press, Moab, UT. 1978.

¡Ven conmigo!

accommodates different learning styles in the following ways:

THE PUPIL'S EDITION

- Presents basic material in audio, video, and print formats.
- Includes role-playing activities and a variety of multi-modal activities, including an extensive listening strand and many art-based activities.

THE ANNOTATED TEACHER'S EDITION

- Provides suggested activities for visual, auditory, and kinesthetic learners as well as suggestions for slower-paced learning and challenge activities.
- Includes Total Physical Response activities.

THE ANCILLARY PROGRAM

- Provides additional reinforcement activites for a variety of learning styles.
- Presents a rich blend of audiovisual input through the video program, audio program, transparencies, and blackline masters.

Higher-Order Thinking Skills

BY AUDREY L. HEINING-BOYNTON

*Our profession loves acronyms! TPR, ALM, OBI and now the HOTS! HOTS stands for **h**igher-**o**rder **t**hinking **s**kills. These thinking skills help our students listen, speak, write, and learn about culture in a creative, meaningful way, while providing them with necessary life skills.* ◆

Introduce students to the life skills they need to become successful, productive citizens in our society.

What are higher-order thinking skills?

Higher-order thinking skills are not a new phenomenon on the educational scene. In 1956, Benjamin Bloom published a book that listed a taxonomy of educational objectives in the form of a pyramid similar to the one in the following illustration:

Bloom's Taxonomy of Educational Objectives

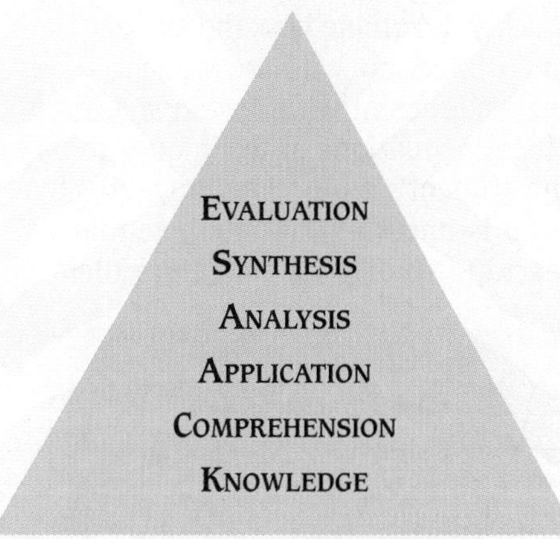

Knowledge is the simplest level of educational objectives, and is not considered a higher-order thinking skill. It requires the learner to remember information without having to fully understand it. Tasks that students perform to demonstrate knowledge are recalling, identifying, recognizing, citing, labeling, listing, reciting, and stating.

Comprehension is not considered a higher-order thinking skill either. Learners demonstrate comprehension when they paraphrase, describe, summarize, illustrate, restate, or translate.

Foreign language teachers tend to focus the most on knowledge and comprehension. The tasks performed in these levels are important because they provide a solid foundation for the more complex tasks at the higher levels of Bloom's pyramid. However, offering our students the opportunity to perform at still higher cognitive levels provides them with more meaningful contexts in which to use the target language.

When teachers incorporate **application, analysis, synthesis,** and **evaluation** as objectives, they allow students to utilize **higher-order thinking skills.**

- **Application** involves solving, transforming, determining, demonstrating, and preparing.
- **Analysis** includes classifying, comparing, making associations, verifying, seeing cause and effect relationships, and determining sequences, patterns, and consequences.
- **Synthesis** requires generalizing, predicting, imagining, creating, making inferences, hypothesizing, making decisions, and drawing conclusions.
- Finally, **evaluation** involves assessing, persuading, determining value, judging, validating, and solving problems.

Most foreign language classes focus little on higher-order thinking skills. Some foreign language educators mistakenly think that all higher-order thinking skills require an advanced level of language ability. Not so! Students can demonstrate these skills by using very simple language available even to beginning students. Also, higher-order thinking tasks about the target culture or language can be conducted in English. The use of some English in the foreign language class in order to utilize higher cognitive skills does not jeopardize progress in the target language.

Higher-order thinking skills prepare our students for more than using a foreign language. They introduce students to the life skills they need to become successful, productive citizens in our society. When we think about it, that *is* the underlying purpose of education.

WHY TEACH HIGHER-ORDER THINKING SKILLS?

There is already so much to cover and so little time that some teachers may question the worth of adding this type of activities to an already full schedule. Yet we know from experience that simply "covering" the material does not help our students acquire another language. Incorporating higher-order thinking skills in the foreign language classroom can help guide students toward language acquisition by providing meaningful experiences in a setting that can otherwise often feel artificial.

Also, we now know that employing higher-order thinking skills assists all students, including those who are at risk of failing. In the past, we felt that at-risk students were incapable of higher-order thinking, but we have since discovered that we have been denying them the opportunity to experience what they are capable of doing and what they need to do in order to be successful adults.

SAMPLE ACTIVITIES EMPLOYING HIGHER-ORDER THINKING SKILLS

There are no limitations to incorporating higher-order thinking skills in the foreign language classroom. What follows are a few sample activities, some of which you might already be familiar with. Use *your* higher-order thinking skills to develop other possibilities!

▶ LISTENING

HOTS:	Analysis
TASKS:	Patterning and sequencing
VOCABULARY NEEDED:	Three colors
MATERIALS REQUIRED:	Three colored-paper squares for each student

After reviewing the colors, call out a pattern of colors and have the students show their comprehension by arranging their colored pieces of paper from left to right in the order you give. Then have them finish the pattern for you. For example, you say: **rojo, verde, azul, rojo, verde, azul, rojo, verde, azul...** now what color follows? And then what color?

This is not only a HOTS activity; it also crosses disciplines. It reviews the mathematical concept of patterning and sequencing. You can have the students form patterns and sequences using any type of vocabulary.

▶ READING

HOTS:	Synthesis
TASKS:	Hypothesizing and imagining
VOCABULARY NEEDED:	Determined by level of students
MATERIALS REQUIRED:	Legend or short story

After the students have read the first part of the story, have them imagine how the story would end, based on the values of the target culture.

▶ SPEAKING

HOTS:	Evaluation
TASKS:	Assessing and determining value
VOCABULARY NEEDED:	Numbers 0-25, five objects students would need for school
MATERIALS REQUIRED:	Visuals of five school-related objects with prices beneath them

Tell students that they each have twenty-five dollars to spend on back-to-school supplies. They each need to tell you what they would buy with their money.

▶ WRITING

HOTS:	Analysis
TASKS:	Classifying
VOCABULARY NEEDED:	Leisure activities
MATERIALS REQUIRED:	Drawings of leisure activities on a handout

From the list of activities they have before them, students should write the ones that they like to do on the weekend. Then they should write those that a family member likes to do. Finally, students should write a comparison of the two lists.

COMMITMENT TO HIGHER-ORDER THINKING SKILLS

Teaching higher-order thinking skills takes no extra time from classroom instruction since language skills are reinforced during thinking skills activities. What teaching higher-order thinking skills does require of teachers is a commitment to classroom activities that go beyond the objectives of Bloom's knowledge and comprehension levels. Having students name objects and recite verb forms is not enough. Employing HOTS gives students the opportunity to experience a second language as a useful device for meaningful communication.

¡Ven conmigo!

encourages higher-order thinking skills in the following ways:

THE PUPIL'S EDITION

- Develops critical thinking skills through a variety of activities, including interpretation of the visually-presented **De antemano**, journal writing, interviews, **Encuentro cultural** presentations, application of reading strategies, and situational role-plays.

THE ANNOTATED TEACHER'S EDITION

- Includes Thinking Critically and Multicultural Links features that provides the teacher with suggestions for activities requiring students to draw inferences, compare and contrast, evaluate, and synthesize.

THE ANCILLARY PROGRAM

- Incorporates higher-order thinking skills, such as in Communicative Activities, the Additional Listening Activities, and the chapter-related realia. In the *Practice and Activity Book,* students are guided carefully from structured practice to open-ended tasks that require higher-order thinking.

Using Portfolios in the Foreign Language Classroom

BY JO ANNE S. WILSON

The communicative, whole-language approach of today's foreign language instruction requires assessment methods that parallel the teaching and learning strategies in the proficiency-oriented classroom. We know that language acquisition is a process. Portfolios are designed to assess the steps in that process. ◆

Portfolios offer a more realistic and accurate way to assess the process of language teaching and learning.

WHAT IS A PORTFOLIO?

A portfolio is a purposeful, systematic collection of a student's work. A useful tool in developing a student profile, the portfolio shows the student's efforts, progress, and achievements for a given period of time. It may be used for periodic evaluation, as the basis for overall evaluation, or for placement. It may also be used to enhance or provide alternatives to traditional assessment measures, such as formal tests, quizzes, class participation, and homework.

WHY USE PORTFOLIOS?

Portfolios benefit both students and teachers because they

- **Are ongoing and systematic.** A portfolio reflects the real-world process of production, assessment, revision, and reassessment. It parallels the natural rhythm of learning.
- **Offer an incentive to learn**. Students have a vested interest in creating the portfolios through which they can showcase their ongoing efforts and tangible achievements. Students select the works to be included and have a chance to revise, improve, evaluate, and explain the contents.
- **Are sensitive to individual needs**. Language learners bring varied abilities to the classroom and do not acquire skills in a uniformly neat and orderly fashion. The personalized, individualized assessment offered by portfolios responds to this diversity.
- **Provide documentation of language development.** The material in a portfolio is evidence of student progress in the language learning process. The contents of the portfolio make it easier to discuss student progress with the students as well as with parents and others interested in the student's progress.
- **Offer multiple sources of information.** A portfolio presents a way to collect and analyze information from multiple sources that reflect a student's efforts, progress, and achievements in the language.

PORTFOLIO COMPONENTS

The foreign language portfolio should include both oral and written work, student self-evaluation, and teacher observation, usually in the form of brief, nonevaluative comments about various aspects of the student's performance.

THE ORAL COMPONENT

The oral component of a portfolio might be an audio- or videocassette. It may contain both rehearsed and extemporaneous monologues and conversations. For a rehearsed speaking activity, give a specific communicative task that students can personalize according to their individual interests (for example, ordering a favorite meal in a restaurant). If the speaking activity is extemporaneous, first acquaint students with possible topics for discussion or even the specific task they will be expected to perform. (For example, tell them they will be asked to discuss a picture showing a sports activity or a restaurant scene.)

THE WRITTEN COMPONENT

Portfolios are excellent tools for incorporating process writing strategies into the foreign language classroom. Documentation of various stages of the writing process—brainstorming, multiple drafts, and peer comments—may be included with the finished product.

Involve students in selecting writing tasks for the portfolio. At the beginning levels, the tasks might include some structured writing, such as labeling or listing. As students become more proficient, journals, letters, and other more complicated writing tasks are valuable ways for them to monitor their progress in using the written language.

STUDENT SELF-EVALUATION

Students should be actively involved in critiquing and evaluating their portfolios and monitoring their own progress. The process and procedure for student self-evaluation should be considered in planning the contents of the portfolio. Students should work with you and their peers to design the exact format. Self-evaluation encourages them to think about what they are learning (content), how they learn (process), why they are learning (purpose), and where they are going in their learning (goals).

TEACHER OBSERVATION

Systematic, regular, and ongoing observations should be placed in the portfolio after they have been discussed with the student. These observations provide feedback on the student's progress in the language learning process.

Teacher observations should be based on an established set of criteria that has been developed earlier with input from the student. Observation techniques may include the following:

- Jotting notes in a journal to be discussed with the student and then placed in the portfolio
- Using a checklist of observable behaviors, such as the willingness to take risks when using the target language or staying on task during the lesson
- Making observations on adhesive notes that can be placed in folders
- Recording anecdotal comments, during or after class, using a cassette recorder.

Knowledge of the criteria you use in your observations gives students a framework for their performance.

HOW ARE PORTFOLIOS EVALUATED?

The portfolio should reflect the process of student learning over a specific period of time. At the beginning of that time period, determine the criteria by which you will assess the final product and convey them to the students. Make this evaluation a collaborative effort by seeking students' input as you formulate these criteria and your instructional goals.

Students need to understand that evaluation based on a predetermined standard is but one phase of the assessment process; demonstrated effort and growth are just as important. As you consider correctness and accuracy in both oral and written work, also consider the organization, creativity, and improvement revealed by the student's portfolio over the time period. The portfolio provides a way to monitor the growth of a student's knowledge, skills, and attitudes and shows the student's efforts, progress, and achievements.

HOW TO IMPLEMENT PORTFOLIOS

Teacher/teacher collaboration is as important to the implementation of portfolios as teacher/student collaboration. Confer with your colleagues to determine, for example, what kinds of information you want to see in the student portfolio, how the information will be presented, the purpose of the portfolio, the intended purposes (grading, placement, or a combination of the two), and criteria for evaluating the portfolio. Conferring among colleagues helps foster a departmental cohesiveness and consistency that will ultimately benefit the students.

THE PROMISE OF PORTFOLIOS

The high degree of student involvement in developing portfolios and deciding how they will be used generally results in renewed student enthusiasm for learning and improved achievement. As students compare portfolio pieces done early in the year with work produced later, they can take pride in the progress as well as reassess their motivation and work habits.

Portfolios also provide a framework for periodic assessment of teaching strategies, programs, and instruction. They offer schools a tool to help solve the problem of vertical articulation and accurate student placement. The more realistic and accurate assessment of the language learning process that is provided by portfolios is congruent with the strategies that should be used in the proficiency-oriented classroom.

¡Ven conmigo!

supports the use of portfolios in the following ways:

THE PUPIL'S EDITION

- Includes numerous oral and written activities that can be easily adapted for student portfolios, such as **En mi cuaderno** and the more global review activities in **Repaso.**

THE ANNOTATED TEACHER'S EDITION

- Suggests activities in the Portfolio Assessment feature that may serve as portfolio items.

THE ANCILLARY PROGRAM

- Includes criteria in the *Assessment Guide* for evaluating portfolios, as well as Speaking Tests for each chapter that can be adapted for use as portfolio assessment items.

New Perspectives for Native Speakers

BY CECILIA RODRÍGUEZ-PINO

Spanish teachers often simultaneously teach two groups of students whose learning needs are markedly different. The first group, the majority, for whom most curricula are developed, are English-proficient but at a beginner's level in Spanish. The second group consists of students whose proficiency in English varies but who already speak Spanish, often quite proficiently. From their own experience they already understand a great deal about Spanish language and the cultures of Spanish speakers. Many schools have not yet set up Spanish for Native Speakers (SNS) sections with specialized curricula that would build on these students' linguistic and cultural strengths. As a result, in some schools native speakers who want to study Spanish are enrolled in courses where Spanish is taught as a foreign language. Addressing their learning needs thus becomes the particular challenge of the teacher, who must create and implement supplemental classroom materials. ◆

TYPES OF NATIVE SPANISH SPEAKERS

The greatest number of native Spanish speakers in the classroom are Spanish-speaking immigrants and American students of Hispanic descent. Many immigrants have been uprooted from their native countries and find themselves in a new and foreign environment without the skills to communicate. Often they must struggle to adapt to mainstream sociocultural norms and values. Psychological adjustment, cultural integration, and the acquisition of new communicative skills are daily concerns for them. Building teacher-student and peer-peer learning relationships may be harder for such students.

American students of Hispanic descent are often bilingual. Some are highly proficient in both written and oral Spanish, but many are proficient to varying degrees, depending on the curcumstances, topics, tasks, and informal situations. These students reflect the various socioeconomic classes of society and speak a wide range of Spanish dialects. Research indicates that the dialect they speak affects how they are viewed at school. When they speak a "standard" variety of Spanish and are from an educated class, such as many Cuban Americans in Florida, reactions to them are usually positive. But when Spanish speakers are from a rural background, speak a "nonstandard" dialect, or come from a nonliterate background, reactions in school are often negative. Attempting to modify their dialect can be detrimental to their linguistic and social development.

LINGUISTIC NEEDS

Native Spanish speakers need to retrieve any Spanish they may have lost, maintain the competency they already have, and expand their knowledge and skills in Spanish.

The problem of native language loss is receiving much attention in the profession. Children appear to lose production skills more quickly than they lose comprehension ability. Thus retrieval efforts should focus on production. Rapid changes in society and in the patterns by which Spanish is transmitted from one generation to the next account for much of students' language loss. Word borrowing and code switching to English may also account for language loss. These practices are not unique to bilingual students in the United States; they are common linguistic phenomena, observed wherever languages are in contact. A native speaker may switch from Spanish to English when referring to activities generally associated with the dominant culture—even when the speaker is perfectly familiar with the relevant Spanish vocabulary. Efforts to eradicate code switching may harm students' linguistic and social development.

AFFECTIVE NEEDS

Native Spanish-speaking students bring to class much valuable cultural and linguistic experience. Cultural opportunities need to be provided for them through which they can express their knowledge of their own particular Spanish-speaking culture and gain a greater overview of other Spanish-speaking communities and countries. They need to understand that their heritage, language, culture, dialect, and individual abilities are valuable to society. As teachers we must respect and value the different languages and dialects our students speak, and we must create an instructional context in which students will develop positive attitudes toward their own ethnic group and their own ethnic identity.

AN SNS PROGRAM APPROACH

A task-based, whole-language approach is recommended. Receptive and productive skills can be developed through culturally meaningful activities whose contexts are community, school, home, and self. These activities can be carried out in conjunction with textbook thematic units. Such an approach creates a student-centered classroom in which the teacher acts as a facilitator connecting students to the bilingual community.

EXPANDING RECEPTIVE SKILLS

Students should perform activities in which they listen to their native language in a broad range of formal and informal contexts, from simple topics to complex ones. Audio- or videotaped versions of stories, songs, documentaries, speeches, or debates can be adapted for class assignments. Guest speakers from the community are extremely valuable resources for presentations or interviews on the chapter topic.

Students should have access to diverse, authentic reading materials from the popular culture as well as from more formal subject areas. Chicano, Cuban, Dominican, Colombian, Nicaraguan, Honduran, Panamanian, and Puerto Rican literature—which are underrepresented in the mainstream literary canon—can play an important role in instilling in students a sense of pride and awareness of their cultural heritage. Students relate well to literature written by contemporary Hispanic authors who have had experiences similar to the students' in the United States. For example, they might read the short story "Desde que se fue," from the collection *Madreselvas en flor* by literary prize-winning Chicano author Ricardo Aguilar-Melantzón, about growing up in a bilingual setting.

Developing Productive Skills

Oral history projects, ethnographic interviews, and sociolinguistic surveys, dialogue journals, letter writing, and other purposeful authentic activities are effective techniques that focus on interactions among students, teacher, and community. These kinds of activities give students the opportunity to develop individual strengths and to explore their language and culture in a community context.

Classroom Environment

We can change the classroom space itself to create an environment that recognizes the prestige of the students' language and cultural heritage. Using a brief questionnaire, the teacher can find out the students' backgrounds and then display relevant posters, travel brochures, art, literature, or historical information. Students can contribute captioned photographs depicting cultural events and family traditions, so that the bulletin board reflects their personal view of the Spanish-speaking world rather than just the teacher's perspective.

Individual Assessment and Evaluation

Individual assessment at the beginning of the year should be based primarily on content so that students' errors are not the main focus. Use content, organization, and language as criteria for evaluating speaking and writing. In evaluating students' work for the year, the teacher should take into account how students have broadened their functional range. This requires students to be responsible for the concepts that are essential to comprehension and production. A writing portfolio is a valuable component of the evaluation process. Oral presentations of ethnographic and sociolinguistic projects are contextualized activities for evaluating speaking.

¡Ven conmigo!

supports native speakers' continued development of Spanish in the following ways:

THE PUPIL'S EDITION

- Promotes pride and awareness of cultural heritage through location openers on U.S. Spanish-speaking areas, as well as cultural features, interviews with native speakers, and literary selections by U.S. and non-U.S. native speakers.
- Validates the use of regionally-specific vocabulary and authentic expression in the **También se puede decir** and **A lo nuestro** features.
- Fosters the student's self-concept by encouraging individual expression in journal entries and other authentic tasks, such as letter writing.

THE ANNOTATED TEACHER'S EDITION

- Includes specific suggestions for activities to be performed by native speakers, both independently and with other students.
- Provides the teacher with additional vocabulary suggestions and language notes that validate regional variants.
- Suggests family and community links that strengthen students' ties to the wider bilingual community via family and community interviews and ethnographic reports.

THE ANCILLARY PROGRAM

- Offers a *Native Speaker Activity Book* with a diagnostic instrument and, chapter by chapter, additional reading practice based on authentic literature on topics of interest to native speakers. In addition, this book addresses issues of formal usage and pronunciation and provides additional writing and speaking practice.

Professional References

This section provides information about resources that can enrich your Spanish class. Included are addresses of Spanish and Latin American government offices, pen pal organizations, subscription agencies, and many others. Since addresses change frequently, you may want to verify them before you send your requests. ◆

Pen Pal Organizations

For the names of pen pal groups other than those listed below, contact your local chapter of AATSP. There are fees involved, so be sure to write for information.

Student Letter Exchange (League of Friendship)
630 Third Avenue
New York, NY 10017
(212) 557-3312

World Pen Pals
1694 Como Avenue
St. Paul, MN 55108
(612) 647-0191

Embassies and Consulates

Addresses and phone numbers of embassies and consulates for Spanish-speaking countries are available in most U.S. city telephone directories. All are available in the directory for Washington, D.C.

Periodicals

Subscriptions to the following cultural materials are available through jobbers or directly from the publishers. See also the section on Subscription Services.

- **Blanco y negro**, a general interest weekly magazine in Spain.
- **Eres**, a Mexican magazine for teens.
- **El País**, a major daily newspaper in Spain.
- **Hispanic**, an English-language magazine about Hispanics in the U.S.
- **La Prensa**, a major daily paper in Argentina.
- **Tú internacional**, a magazine for teens published in several Spanish-speaking countries.
- **México desconocido**, a cultural and environmental magazine about Mexico.

Cultural Agencies

For historic and tourist information about Spanish-speaking countries, contact:

Mexican Government Tourism Office
2707 N. Loop West, Suite 450
Houston, TX 77008
(713) 880–5153

Tourist Office of Spain
665 Fifth Avenue
New York, NY 10022
(212) 759–8822

Intercultural Exchange

CIEE Student Travel Services
205 East 42nd St.
New York, NY 10017
(212) 661–1414

American Field Service
220 East 42nd St., 3rd Floor
New York, NY 10017
(212) 949–4242

Professional Organizations

The American Council on the Teaching of Foreign Languages (ACTFL)
6 Executive Plaza
Yonkers, NY 10701
(914) 963–8830

American Association of Teachers of Spanish and Portuguese (AATSP)
Gunter Hall, Room 106
University of Northern Colorado
Greeley, CO 80639
(303) 351–1090

Subscription Services

Spanish-language magazines can be obtained through subscription agencies in the United States. The following companies are among the many which can provide your school with subscriptions:

EBSCO Subscription Services
P.O. Box 1943
Birmingham, AL 35201-1943
(205) 991–6600

Continental Book Company
8000 Cooper Ave., Bldg. 29
Glendale, NY 11385
(718) 326–0572

Miscellaneous

Gessler Publishing Company, Inc.
55 West 13th St.
New York, NY 10011
(212) 627–0099
- Foreign language periodicals.

The International Film Bureau
332 South Michigan Ave.
Chicago, IL 60604-4382
(312) 427–4545
- Foreign language videos for sale and/or rent.

A Bibliography for the Spanish Teacher

This bibliography is a compilation of resources available for professional enrichment. ◆

SELECTED AND ANNOTATED LIST OF READINGS

▶ I. METHODS AND APPROACHES

Cohen, Andrew D. ***Assessing Language Ability in the Classroom,*** **2/e. Boston, MA: Heinle, 1994.**
- Assessment processes, oral interviews, role-playing situations, dictation, and portfolio assessment.

Hadley, Alice Omaggio. ***Teaching Language in Context,*** **2/e.** Boston, MA: Heinle, 1993.
- Language acquisition theories and models and adult second language proficiency.

Krashen, Stephen, and Tracy D. Terrell. ***The Natural Approach: Language Acquisition in the Classroom.*** New York: Pergamon, 1983.
- Optimal Input Theory: listening, oral communication development, and testing.

Oller, John W., Jr. ***Methods That Work: Ideas for Language Teachers,*** **2/e.** Boston, MA: Heinle, 1993.
- Literacy in multicultural settings, cooperative learning, peer teaching, and CAI.

Shrum, Judith L., and Eileen W. Glisan. ***Teacher's Handbook: Contextualized Language Instruction.*** Boston, MA: Heinle, 1993.
- Grammar, testing, using video texts, microteaching, case studies and daily plans.

▶ II. SECOND LANGUAGE THEORY

Krashen, Stephen. ***The Power of Reading.*** New York: McGraw, 1994.
- Updates Optimal Input Theory by incorporating the reading of authentic texts.

Liskin-Gasparro, Judith. ***A Guide to Testing and Teaching for Oral Proficiency.*** Boston, MA: Heinle, 1990.
- Oral proficiency through interview techniques and speech samples.

Rubin, Joan, and Irene Thompson. ***How To Be a More Successful Language Learner,*** **2/e.** Boston, MA: Heinle, 1993.
- Psychological, linguistic, and practical matters of second language learning.

▶ III. VIDEO AND CAI

Altmann, Rick. ***The Video Connection: Integrating Video into Language Teaching.*** Boston, MA: Houghton, 1989.
- Diverse strategies for using video texts to support second language learning.

Dunkel, Patricia A. ***Computer-Assisted Language Learning and Testing.*** Boston, MA: Heinle, 1992.
- CAI and computer-assisted language learning (CALL) in the foreign language classroom.

Kenning, M. J., and M.M. Kenning. ***Computers and Language Learning: Current Theory and Practice.*** New York, NY: E. Horwood, 1990.
- Theoretical discussions and practical suggestions for CAI in second language development.

▶ IV. TEACHING NATIVE SPEAKERS

Aguilar-Melantzón, Ricardo. "Desde que se fue."
- Produced for Teaching Spanish to Southwest Hispanic Students, National Endowment for the Humanities Summer Conference, Cecilia Rodríguez-Pino, project director. Las Cruces: New Mexico State University, 1993. Available through Spanish for Native Speakers Program, New Mexico State University. Audiotape of short story narrated by author.

Merino, Barbara J., Henry T. Trueba, and Fabián A. Samaniego. ***Language and Culture in Learning: Teaching Spanish to Native Speakers of Spanish.*** London, England: Falmer Press, 1993.

Rodríguez-Pino, Cecilia, and Daniel Villa. "A Student-Centered Spanish for Native Speakers Program: Theory, Curriculum Design and Outcome Assessment." In *Faces in a Crowd: The Individual Learner in Multisection Courses.* Edited by Carol A. Klee. American Association of University Supervisors Series. Boston: Heinle and Heinle, 1994.

Valdés, Guadalupe. "The Role of the Foreign Language Teaching Profession in Maintaining Non-English Languages in the United States." In *Northeast Conference Reports: Languages for a Multicultural World in Transition.* Edited by Heidi Byrnes. Lincolnwood, IL: National Textbook, 1992.

Scope and Sequence: Spanish Level 1

¡ADELANTE!

Getting acquainted with the Spanish-speaking countries:
- **Map of the Spanish-speaking world**
- **El español—¿Por qué?**
- **¿Sabías...?**
- **¿Los conoces?**

Getting started with Spanish:
- **Nombres comunes**
- **El alfabeto**
- **Frases útiles**
- **Colores y números**
- **Para mejor aprender**

CAPÍTULO 1: ¡MUCHO GUSTO!

Functions:
- Saying hello and goodbye
- Introducing people and responding to an introduction
- Asking how someone is and saying how you are
- Asking and saying how old someone is
- Asking where someone is from and saying where you're from
- Talking about likes and dislikes

Grammar:
- Spanish punctuation marks
- Pronouns **yo** and **tú**
- Use of **ser** for origin
- Forming questions with **cómo, cuántos, de dónde**
- Singular definite articles: **el, la**
- Noun gender and agreement

Culture:
- Greetings
- First names and Saint's days
- **¿De dónde eres?**
- **La distancia personal**

Re-entry:
- Accent marks
- Number 0–30

CAPÍTULO 2: ¡ORGANÍZATE!

Functions:
- Talking about what you want and need
- Describing the contents of your room
- Talking about what you need and want to do

Grammar:
- Indefinite articles **un, una, unos, unas**
- Making nouns plural
- Agreement of **mucho** and **cuánto** with nouns
- Subject pronouns **él** and **ella**
- The three types of infinitives: **-ar, -er, -ir**

Culture:
- The school day in Spain and Latin America
- **¿Qué necesitas para el colegio?**
- Apartments in Spain
- Spanish currency

Re-entry:
- Subject pronouns **yo** and **tú**
- Talking about likes and dislikes
- Numbers 0–30
- Forming questions with **cuántos**

CAPÍTULO 3: NUEVAS CLASES, NUEVOS AMIGOS

Functions:
- Talking about class schedules and sequencing events
- Telling time
- Telling at what time something happens
- Talking about being late or in a hurry
- Describing people and things
- Talking about things you like and explaining why

Grammar:
- Plural definite articles **los, las**
- Using **ser** to tell time
- Forms of **ser**
- Adjective agreement
- Tag questions
- Possession with **de**

Culture:
- Grade scales
- **¿Cómo es un día escolar típico?**
- Student course loads
- **Hora latina**
- Mexican TV listing
- Entertainment guide

Re-entry:
- Present tense of **tener**
- Numbers 0–199
- School supplies
- Forming questions
- Noun-adjective agreement
- Forms of **necesitar, querer**
- Talking about likes and dislikes

CAPÍTULO 4: ¿QUÉ HACES ESTA TARDE?

Functions:
- Talking about what you like to do
- Discussing what you and others do during free time
- Telling where people and things are
- Talking about where you and others go during free time

Grammar:
- Present tense of regular verbs **-ar**
- **Con, conmigo, contigo**
- Use of **que**
- Present tense of **estar**
- Subject pronouns
- Present tense of **ir**
- Use of **el** and **los** with days of the week

Culture:
- Popular sports in Spanish-speaking countries
- Use of **tú** and **usted**
- **El paseo**
- School-sponsored extracurricular activities

Re-entry:
- Subject pronouns: **yo, tú, él, ella**
- Present tense of **ser** and **tener**

CAPÍTULO 5: EL RITMO DE LA VIDA

Functions:
- Discussing how often you do things
- Talking about what you and your friends like to do together
- Talking about what you do during a typical week
- Giving today's date
- Talking about the weather

Grammar:
- Negation
- **¿Quién?** and **¿Quiénes?**
- **les** and **a ustedes, a ellos, a ellas**
- Regular **-er** and **-ir** verbs
- Giving the date in Spanish

Culture:
- Getting together with friends
- **¿Cómo es una semana típica?**
- Seasons in South America

Re-entry:
- Gender
- Subject pronouns with **-er** and **-ir** verbs
- Days of the week

CAPÍTULO 6: ENTRE FAMILIA

Functions:
- Describing a family
- Describing people
- Discussing things a family does together
- Discussing problems and giving advice

Grammar:
- Possessive adjectives
- Present tense of **hacer** and **salir**
- Present tense of **deber**
- Present tense of **poner**
- Understanding "personal **a**"

Culture:
- **El compadrazgo**
- Privacy in Hispanic culture
- **La familia**
- Diminutives

Re-entry:
- **Hay**
- Possessive adjectives
- Demonstrative adjectives
- Colors
- Descriptions of people
- Pastimes/hobbies
- **¿Con qué frequencia?**
- Forming questions with **¿Cómo?** and **¿Cuántos?**

CAPÍTULO 7: ¿QUÉ TE GUSTARÍA HACER?

Functions:
- Talking on the telephone
- Extending and accepting invitations
- Making plans
- Talking about getting ready
- Turning down an invitation and making an excuse

Grammar:
- **e** to **ie** stem-changing verbs
- **pensar** + infinitive
- **ir + a** + infinitive
- Reflexive verbs
- Expressions with **tener**

Culture:
- Common telephone expressions
- Getting around without a car
- **¿Qué haces para conocer a una persona?**
- **Tira cómica**
- Party invitation

Re-entry:
- Invitations
- **gustar**
- Days of the week
- **pensar** and **ir**
- Future expressions
- Expressions of frequency

CAPÍTULO 8: ¡A COMER!

Functions:
- Talking about meals and food
- Commenting on food
- Making polite requests
- Ordering dinner in a restaurant
- Asking for and paying the bill in a restaurant

Grammar:
- Present tense of **encantar** and indirect object pronouns
- Use of **estar** to talk about how things taste
- **ser** vs. **estar**
- **o** to **ue** stem-changing verbs
- Expressions with **tener**
- The forms of **otro**

Culture:
- **La comida de las Américas**
- Breakfast in Spanish-speaking countries
- Lunch in Spanish-speaking countries
- Dinner in Spanish-speaking countries
- **¿Cual es un plato típico de tu país?**
- Table manners in Spanish-speaking countries

Re-entry:
- **e** to **ie** stem-changing verbs
- Numbers 200–100,000
- Expressing likes and dislikes
- Expressions with **tener**

CAPÍTULO 9: ¡VAMOS DE COMPRAS!

Functions:
- Discussing gift suggestions
- Asking for and giving directions downtown
- Commenting on clothes
- Making comparisons
- Expressing preferences
- Asking about prices and paying for something

Grammar:
- Indirect object pronouns: **le, les**
- **es/son + de** + material or pattern
- Comparisons: **más... que, menos... que, tan... como**
- Demonstrative adjectives

Culture:
- Specialty stores in Spain
- **¿Estás a la moda?**
- Catalogue page with clothing
- ***Tamalada***
- Currency in some Spanish-speaking countries

Re-entry:
- **ir + a** + infinitive
- Describing family
- Present tense of **ser**
- Numbers 0–100,000

CAPÍTULO 10: CELEBRACIONES

Functions:
- Talking about what you're doing right now
- Asking for and giving an opinion
- Asking for help and responding to requests
- Telling a friend what to do
- Talking about past events

Grammar:
- Present progressive
- Informal commands
- Preterite tense of regular **-ar** verbs
- Direct object pronouns **lo** and **la**

Culture:
- **Día del Santo**
- **¿Qué hacen ustedes para celebrar?**
- **La quinceañera**
- **¿Cómo se celebra una boda?**
- **Agenda**

Re-entry:
- **estar**
- **tú** versus **usted**
- Dates, months, seasons
- Extending and turning down invitations
- Household chores
- Days of the week
- **¿quién?, ¿quiénes?**
- Free-time activites

CAPÍTULO 11: PARA VIVIR BIEN

Functions:
- Making suggestions and expressing feelings
- Talking about moods and physical condition
- Saying what you did
- Talking about where you went and when

Grammar:
- **o** to **ue** stem-changing verbs
- The verb **sentirse**
- The verb **doler** with **me, te, le**
- The verbs **ir** and **jugar** in the preterite

Culture:
- **Drogas no y cuestionario**
- Questionnaire about living well
- Baseball players from Spanish-speaking countries
- **¿Qué deporte practicas?**
- Soccer
- **Remedios caseros**

Re-entry:
- **estar** + condition
- Expressions of frequency
- Stem-changing verbs
- The preterite
- Food vocabulary
- Sports

CAPÍTULO 12: LAS VACACIONES IDEALES

Functions:
- Talking about what you do and like to do every day
- Making future plans
- Discussing what you would like to do on vacation
- Saying where you went and what you did on vacation

Grammar:
- **e** to **ie** and **o** to **ue** stem-changing verbs
- Verbs followed by an infinitive
- Uses of verbs **ser** and **estar**
- Uses of the preterite

Culture:
- **¿Adónde vas y qué haces en las vacaciones?**
- Spain's **paradores**
- Spanish colloquialisms

Re-entry:
- Chapter 12 is a global review of Chapters 1–11.

Scope and Sequence: Spanish Level 2

CAPÍTULO 1: MIS AMIGOS Y YO

Functions:
- Introducing yourself and others
- Describing people
- Talking about what you and others do
- Saying what you like and don't like

Grammar:
- Present tense of **tener**
- Adjective agreement with **ser**
- Present tense of regular -**ar**, -**er**, -**ir** verbs

Culture:
- **¿Cuáles son las cualidades de un buen amigo?**
- Planning evening activities in Spain
- **¿Quién es americano?**

Re-entry:
- Chapter 1 reviews Spanish taught in *¡Ven conmigo! Level 1.*

CAPÍTULO 2: UN VIAJE AL EXTRANJERO

Functions:
- Talking about how you're feeling
- Making suggestions and responding to them
- Saying if something has already been done
- Asking for and offering help
- Describing your city or town

Grammar:
- Preterite of -**ar** verbs
- Present tense of **querer** and **poder**

Culture:
- Many generations living together
- **¿En dónde te gustaría vivir?**
- Celsius versus Fahrenheit

Re-entry:
- Chapter 2 reviews Spanish taught in *¡Ven conmigo! Level 1.*

CAPÍTULO 3: LA VIDA COTIDIANA

Functions:
- Talking about your daily routine
- Talking about responsibilities
- Complaining
- Talking about hobbies and pastimes
- Saying how long something has been going on

Grammar:
- Stem-changing verb **e** to **i**: **vestirse**
- Adverbs + -**mente** to express how things are done
- Direct object pronouns: **lo, la, los, las**
- **hace** + quantity of time + **que** + present tense
- Reflexive verbs and pronouns to talk about things you do

Culture:
- **¿Cuál es tu profesión?**
- Household chores
- Popular free-time activities among teenagers

Re-entry:
- Discussing how often you do things
- Talking about what you do during a typical week
- Present tense of the regular verbs
- Reflexive verbs

CAPÍTULO 4: ¡ADELANTE CON LOS ESTUDIOS!

Functions:
- Asking for and giving opinions
- Giving advice
- Talking about things and people you know
- Making comparisons
- Making plans

Grammar:
- **deberías** versus **debes**
- **ser** + adjective to describe people
- **estar** + adjective to describe location
- Present tense of the verb **conocer**
- Direct object pronouns

Culture:
- School levels in Mexico
- **¿Qué haces después del colegio?**
- School schedules

Re-entry:
- **ser** versus **estar**
- Comparisons: **más... que**
- **ir + a** + infinitive
- School subjects
- **para** (in order to) + infinitive

CAPÍTULO 5: ¡PONTE EN FORMA!

Functions:
- Talking about staying fit and healthy
- Telling someone what to do and not to do
- Making excuses

Grammar:
- Preterite of the verb **dormir**
- Preterite of regular -**er** and -**ir** verbs
- Informal commands
- Irregular informal commands
- Preterite of **poder**
- Reflexive verbs to express feelings

Culture:
- Vending machines in high schools
- **¿Qué haces para mantenerte en forma?**
- Fast foods

Re-entry:
- Preterite of regular verbs -**ar**
- **tú** commands
- **deber** versus **deberías**
- **para** + infinitive
- Parts of the body

CAPÍTULO 6: DE VISITA EN LA CIUDAD

Functions:
- Asking for and giving information
- Relating a series of events
- Ordering in a restaurant

Grammar:
- Present tense of **saber**
- **saber** versus **conocer**
- Preterite forms of **pedir, servir, traer**

Culture:
- San Antonio
- **¿Cómo llegas al colegio?**
- Birthday customs

Re-entry:
- The preterite for listing events
- Direct object pronouns
- **Poder**
- Forming questions with **¿cómo?** and **¿cuántos?**
- Food vocabulary

CAPÍTULO 7: ¿CONOCES BIEN TU PASADO?

Functions:
- Talking about what you used to do
- Saying what you used to like and dislike
- Describing what people and things were like
- Using comparisons to describe people

Grammar:
- The imperfect tense of -**ar**, -**er**, -**ir** verbs
- The imperfect tense of **ir** and **ver**
- Imperfect of **ser** to describe people and things
- The imperfect of **hay**
- **tan** + adjective/adverb + **como**

Culture:
- **¿De quién es esta estatua?**
- Last names of all origins

- Old cities in Latin America and Spain
- Public services

Re-entry:
- Comparisons: **más/menos** + adjective + **que**
- Complaining
- The preterite
- Talking about likes and dislikes using the preterite
- Descriptive adjectives

CAPÍTULO 8: DIVERSIONES

Functions:
- Saying how an event was
- Explaining why you couldn't do something
- Reporting what someone said

Grammar:
- Adjectives with **-ísimo/a**
- Absolute superlatives
- Superlatives: **mejor, peor**
- Verbs with prepositions
- Using **mientras** in the past
- Preterite of **decir**

Culture:
- El coquí
- **¿Cuáles son las fiestas más importantes de tu ciudad o país?**
- Holidays and festivals

Re-entry:
- Describing things
- Describing what you did
- The imperfect tense
- The preterite
- Months

CAPÍTULO 9: ¡DÍA DE MERCADO!

Functions:
- Asking for and giving directions
- Asking for help in a store
- Talking about how clothes look and fit
- Bargaining in a market

Grammar:
- Formal commands with **usted, ustedes**

Culture:
- Making purchases in a store
- Clothing and shoe sizes
- **¿Dónde compras tu comida?**
- Muralists

Re-entry:
- Comparisons
- Superlatives
- Direct and indirect objects
- Numbers
- **ser + de** + material
- Clothing material and pattern

CAPÍTULO 10: ¡CUÉNTAME!

Functions:
- Setting the scene for a story
- Continuing and ending a story
- Talking about the latest news
- Reacting to news

Grammar:
- The preterite versus the imperfect
- Preterite of **oír, creer, leer, caerse**
- The preterite and the imperfect to tell a story

Culture:
- **¿Te sabes un cuento?**
- An Ecuadorean legend
- **La Llorona**

Re-entry:
- Reflexive verbs
- Using **mientras**
- Imperfect of **hay**
- Preterite of **tener**
- Weather

CAPÍTULO 11: NUESTRO MEDIO AMBIENTE

Functions:
- Describing problems
- Talking about consequences
- Expressing agreement and disagreement
- Talking about obligations and solutions

Grammar:
- Negative words
- **Si** clauses in present tense
- **Nosotros** commands

Culture:
- The rain forest
- **¿Qué haces para proteger el medio ambiente?**
- Environmental protection agencies
- Packaging
- San Diego and Tijuana

Re-entry:
- Affirmative and negative words
- Travel-related terms

CAPÍTULO 12: VERANOS PASADOS, VERANOS POR VENIR

Functions:
- Exchanging the latest news
- Talking about where you went and what you did
- Telling when something happened
- Saying how you feel about people
- Describing places
- Saying when you're going to do something

Grammar:
- The subjunctive mood

Culture:
- Ecotourism
- **¿Cómo se celebran el fin de cursos?**
- Class trips
- **No hay servicio**

Re-entry:
- Chapter 12 is a global review of Chapters 1–11, *Level 2.*

Scope and Sequence: Spanish Level 3

CAPÍTULO 1: ¡QUÉ BIEN LO PASÉ ESTE VERANO!

Functions:
- Expressing interest, indifference, and displeasure
- Asking for information
- Describing yourself and others

Grammar:
- Stem-changing verbs in the present tense
- The present tense
- The preterite
- Formation of questions
- Adjectives
- **Saber** vs. **conocer**

Culture:
- Vacation activities of students from Costa Rica, Argentina, and Miami
- Seafood in Spain
- The sport **parapente**

Re-entry:
Chapters 1 and 2 are a global review of *¡Ven conmigo! Levels 1* and *2*

CAPÍTULO 2: POR UNA VIDA SANA

Functions:
- Asking for and giving advice
- Talking about taking care of yourself

Grammar:
- Informal commands
- Irregular informal commands
- Reflexive verbs
- The imperfect

Culture:
- Regional languages of Spain
- Work schedules in Spain
- Health habits of people in Spain and Latin America
- Socializing with friends in Spain

Re-entry:
Chapters 1 and 2 are a global review of *¡Ven conmigo! Levels 1* and *2*

CAPÍTULO 3: EL AYER Y EL MAÑANA

Functions:
- Talking about what has happened
- Supporting and expressing a point of view
- Using conversational fillers
- Talking about future events
- Talking about responsibilities

Grammar:
- The present perfect
- **Lo que**
- The future tense

Culture:
- Technology in the lives of Venezuelans today
- The role of oil in the Venezuelan economy
- The past and present of Caracas

Re-entry:
- electrical appliances
- **Todavía, ya, alguna vez**
- Comparisons of equality and inequality
- **Vamos a** + infinitive
- Supporting opinions

CAPÍTULO 4: ALREDEDOR DE LA MESA

Functions:
- Talking about how food tastes
- Talking about unintentional events
- Asking for help and requesting favors

Grammar:
- **Se** with unintentional events

Culture:
- The **sobremesa**
- Ways of getting assistance from service personnel
- Foods and holiday dishes of Venezuela
- Favorite foods of typical students from Miami, Quito, and Caracas
- The **causa picante**

Re-entry:
- Prepositions
- Making explanations
- Commands
- Double object pronouns
- Pronouns with commands
- The suffix **-ísimo**

CAPÍTULO 5: NUESTRAS LEYENDAS

Functions:
- Expressing qualified agreement and disagreement
- Reporting what others say and think
- Talking about hopes and wishes

Grammar:
- Impersonal **se**
- The subjunctive to express hopes and wishes
- Subjunctive of **ir, ser, dar**

Culture:
- La "leyenda negra"
- Aztec pictographs
- The legends "La llorona" and "La carreta sin bueyes"
- The legend of Quetzalcóatl
- The legend "El Quetzal"

Re-entry:
- Verbs followed by an infinitive

CAPÍTULO 6: EL ARTE Y LA MÚSICA

Functions:
- Introducing and changing a topic of conversation
- Expressing necessity
- Expressing an opinion
- Making suggestions and recommendations
- Turning down an invitation

Grammar:
- Gender of some words ending in **-a** and **-o**
- Irregular **yo** forms in the present subjunctive
- The use of **que** with the subjunctive
- **Ir, ser,** and **dar** in the subjunctive

Culture:
- The murals of Orozco
- The role of murals in Mexico
- How some Hispanic students express themselves through art
- Musical instruments
- Mexican pop music star Luis Miguel
- Life and works of Frida Kahlo

Re-entry:
- Expressing necessity with the subjunctive
- **Nosotros** commands
- Making invitations

CAPÍTULO 7: DIME CON QUIÉN ANDAS

Functions:
- Expressing happiness and unhappiness
- Comforting someone
- Making an apology
- Expressing gratitude

Grammar:
- Reflexive verbs for reciprocal actions
- The present perfect subjunctive
- The subjunctive with the unknown or nonexistent

Culture:
- The use of **vos**
- Cafés
- The popularity of movies
- The popularity of soccer

- How Spanish-speaking teenagers solve interpersonal problems

Re-entry:
- The use of the infinitive vs. the subjunctive
- Irregular subjunctive
- Past participle forms
- Affirmative and negative words

CAPÍTULO 8: LOS MEDIOS DE COMUNICACIÓN

Functions:
- Expressing doubt and disbelief
- Expressing certainty
- Talking about possibility and impossibility
- Expressing surprise

Grammar:
- the subjunctive after expressions of doubt and disbelief

Culture:
- The communications network in Argentina
- How commercials affect our attitudes and behavior
- Newsstands in Buenos Aires

Re-entry:
- The subjunctive after impersonal expressions

CAPÍTULO 9: LAS APARIENCIAS ENGAÑAN

Functions:
- Talking about your emotional reaction to something
- Expressing denial
- Expressing an assumption
- Making hypothetical statements

Grammar:
- The subjunctive after conjunctions of time
- The subjunctive with other conjunctions
- The subjunctive with expressions of denial
- The conditional

Culture:
- Hispanics in the United States
- Impressions Spanish-speaking people have of other cultures in the United States

Re-entry:
- The subjunctive

CAPÍTULO 10: TU APORTACIÓN AL MUNDO

Functions:
- Talking about accomplishments
- Talking about future plans
- Expressing cause and effect
- Expressing intention and purpose

Grammar:
- The subjunctive with certain expressions of time
- Verbs after prepositions
- The subjunctive with **para que**

Culture:
- Hispanics in New York City
- How Spanish-speaking students view themselves

Re-entry:
- The present perfect
- Reflexive verbs
- The conditional
- The subjunctive

CAPÍTULO 11: EL MUNDO EN QUE VIVIMOS

Functions:
- Pointing out problems and their consequences
- Talking about how you would solve a problem
- Talking about hypothetical situations

Grammar:
- Passive voice with **se**
- The past subjunctive

Culture:
- Environmental issues facing Central America
- Literacy in the Spanish-speaking world
- Political stability in Costa Rica

Re-entry:
- Impersonal **se**
- Talking about consequences
- The conditional

CAPÍTULO 12: MIS PLANES PARA EL FUTURO

Functions:
- Talking about former jobs and goals
- Talking about future career plans
- Giving advice and making recommendations about work

Grammar:
- Chapter 12 is a global review of Grammar in chapters 1–11.

Culture:
- Universities in Costa Rica
- Employment in Costa Rica

Re-entry:
- Preterite and imperfect
- Future tense
- The subjunctive
- The conditional
- The past subjunctive

Capítulo preliminar, pp. T68–11
Chapter Overview

The following material introduced in the **Capítulo preliminar** is presented again for testing in the chapters cited.

Acentos Chapter 1, page 23
Colores Chapter 6, page 158; Chapter 9, page 242
Números Chapter 1, page 27

RESOURCES FOR CAPÍTULO PRELIMINAR

Chapter Teaching Resources, Book 1
Teaching Transparencies—Maps
Textbook Audiocassette 1A/Audio CD 1
Practice and Activity Book, pp. 1–2
Video Guide
Video Program
Expanded Video Program
Videodisc Guide
Videodisc Program

Capítulo preliminar, pp. T68–11

Textbook Listening Activities Scripts

For scripts, see *Pupil's Edition,* page 5.

Nombres comunes, p. 5

2 Nombres en español

Marta
Claudia
Margarita
Andrés
Miguel
Luisa
Isabel
Cristóbal
Gregorio
Antonio

El alfabeto, pp. 6-7

A **a** de águila
B **be** de bandera
C **ce** de ciclismo
CH **che** de chaleco
D **de** de dinero
E **e** de ensalada
F **efe** de fruta
G **ge** de geografía
H **hache** de helicóptero
I **i** de iguana
J **jota** de jabón
K **ka** de karate
L **ele** de lámpara
LL **elle** de llanta
M **eme** de máscara
N **ene** de naranja
Ñ **eñe** de castañuelas
O **o** de oso
P **pe** de piñata
Q **cu** de quetzal
R **ere** de toro
erre de burro
S **ese** de salvavidas
T **te** de teléfono
U **u** de uvas
V **ve** de violín
W **doble ve** de Wálter
X **equis** de México
Y **y griega** de yate
Z **zeta** de zapatos

6 Por teléfono, p. 7

1. Pe, a, u, ele, a; Paula
2. I, ge, ene, a, ce, i, o; Ignacio
3. Jota, o, ere, ge, e; Jorge
4. Eme, a, ere, te, a; Marta
5. A, de, ere, i, a, ene, a; Adriana
6. Che, a, ere, o; Charo

Frases útiles para escuchar, p. 8

Abran el libro (en la página 20), por favor.
Levántense, por favor.
Siéntense, por favor.
Levanten la mano.
Bajen la mano.
Escuchen con atención.
Repitan después de mí.
Saquen una hoja de papel.
Silencio, por favor.
Miren la pizarra.

8 Simón dice, p. 8

1. Simón dice, "levántense, por favor".
2. Simón dice, "siéntense".
3. Simón dice, "saquen una hoja de papel".
4. Simón dice, "levanten la mano".
5. Bajen la mano.
6. Simón dice, "bajen la mano".
7. Miren la pizarra.
8. Simón dice, "repitan después de mí: ¡Gracias"!

Frases útiles para decir, p. 8

Buenos días.
Buenas tardes.
¿Cómo se dice... en español?
¿Cómo se escribe?
Más despacio, por favor.
¿Puedo ir por mi libro?
No entiendo.
No sé.
¿Puede repetir, por favor?
Perdón.
Tengo una pregunta.

13 Números de teléfono, p. 10

1. Me llamo Nicolás Guillén y mi número de teléfono es el 4-7-3-0-0-1-6.
2. Me llamo Juana Gómez Berea. Mi número de telefóno es el 3-9-1-2-3-4-6.
3. Soy Miguel Campos Romero. Mi número de teléfono es el 7-4-5-0-8-1-2.
4. Soy Cristina García. Mi número de teléfono es el 5-1-0-5-7-2-4.

Capítulo preliminar, pp. T68–11
Projects

In this activity students will consider their reasons for studying Spanish (motivation) and set personal objectives and goals. Students will share their ideas with the class through creative poster or brochure presentations that also serve to decorate the classroom and provide motivation through the semester. You may wish to have students make a brochure to include in their individual portfolios. (See pages T42–T43.) This project should be completed in English, unless you have fluent native speakers, who should complete it in Spanish. This may be assigned either as an individual or small-group assignment.

MATERIALS

✂ **Students may need:**

- Poster board
- Scissors
- Tape
- Travel brochures
- Construction paper
- Glue
- Magazines

OUTLINE

Students should address the following areas in their presentations:

- **Motivation** Why are you learning Spanish? For personal, academic, or professional reasons? AP credit at universities?
- **Objectives** What would you like to achieve in Spanish this semester? (Be realistic.)
- **Long-Term Application** What would you like to achieve in Spanish over the course of your life?

SUGGESTED SEQUENCE

1. Discuss the importance of being clear about personal objectives and goals for language learning. Mention that their perceptions are likely to change throughout the learning process. You may want to share with students your own learning experience. Explain what inspired you to study another language and why you began learning Spanish. Recount how your motivation, objectives, and goals unfolded over the years.
2. Describe the project and assign dates for oral presentations. Write project questions on the board, or distribute a project assignment sheet. Be sure to set a firm time limit for presentations.
3. Go over project questions and elicit a few sample answers from the class. If no one has any ideas at first, you might suggest a few of these examples.
   a. Motivation—need credit to graduate, need foreign language for college or future career; have Spanish-speaking relatives
   b. Objectives—carry on simple conversations in Spanish; write letters to a Spanish-speaking pen pal; get a good grade in this class
   c. Long-Term Application—test out of foreign language requirement in college; speak fluently enough to order meals at restaurants where they speak Spanish; talk to Spanish-speaking co-workers; travel in Spanish-speaking countries
4. Emphasize that students should be honest about their motivation, objectives, and goals. Give students some time in class to brainstorm and begin organizing their thoughts.
5. Students create their posters based on their personal motivations, objectives, and goals. You may want to suggest that they include information on culture, food, work opportunities, and so forth. Encourage students to be as expressive as they wish, using words, photos, and drawings. This can be done as classwork or homework, as an individual or a small-group assignment. Students present their posters or brochures to the class, explaining their motivation, objectives, and goals. Students may then select some of the goals presented as class goals.

GRADING THE PROJECT

The purpose of this project is to encourage students to think about why they are learning Spanish and what outcomes they expect. Because of the personal nature of the project, the subjective content should not be graded. Instead, holistic grading should focus on completion, presentation, and effort.

Suggested point distribution (total = 100 points)

Completion of assignment	30
Poster/Brochure	40
Effort	10
Presentation	20

Capítulo preliminar, pp. T68–11
Games

Teacher Note

Simulations and playful learning activities can be effective teaching tools, lowering students' anxieties and aiding language acquisition. For games to be most beneficial to your students, the atmosphere needs to be fun and playful—the class should look forward to doing the activity. Games can improve group interaction and motivation, and they can be cooperative rather than competitive. Here are some suggestions to help you incorporate games in your lesson plan.

- Games should be played in Spanish as much as possible. Ground rules may be explained in English, as necessary.
- Keep games simple so that a minimum of class time is spent explaining the rules.
- Involve students as scorekeepers or referees, to help with classroom management.
- Choose games that practice comprehension or production in meaningful contexts.
- Identify your teaching objective. Is the game for recognition only? for student production? for recycling previously presented material? to practice a particular skill? to develop higher-order thinking skills?
- Always set a time limit. If you stick to announced time limits, students will help each other stay on task.
- When you find a game that both you and your students respond to well, recycle it in new contexts throughout the year. This will give students a sense of security and continuity and reduce the set-up time.

ALPHABET

Recognition Write randomly chosen letters on the board or on a transparency. Ask students recognition questions, such as **¿Es una ere?** Students respond with either a thumbs up or thumbs down, or by holding up a **sí** or **no** card. Board races are appropriate at this level of recognition as well.

Production Students write a word at the board or on paper that you or a student dictates letter by letter. Try including names of famous people, students' first or last names, your school mascot, or local sports stars.

COLORS

Pair Work Each pair of students brings or is given magazine clippings showing colors taught in the **Capítulo preliminar.** Each student points out in Spanish the colors to his or her partner.

Tactile Learners Give each student small slips of paper, one of each color. Have them arrange the papers left to right or top to bottom on their desks in the order you name the colors. For a challenge: **Pongan el rojo a la izquierda del azul. Pongan el amarillo encima del blanco...**

NUMBERS

Recognition Have students listen as you say various combinations of numbers, then ask comprehension questions, **"Uno-tres-cinco-siete,** even or odd? **nueve-ocho-siete-seis,** forward or backward?" At this initial stage of recognition, student responses in English are acceptable. For a challenge, have students respond with **pares** *(even)*, **nones** *(odd)*, **progresivo** *(forward)*, or **regresivo** *(backward)*.

Challenge Have students solve simple arithmetic problems using numerals as you read the problem to them in Spanish. They will need to know **más** (+), **menos** (-), **por** (x), **dividido por** (÷), and **es/son** (=).

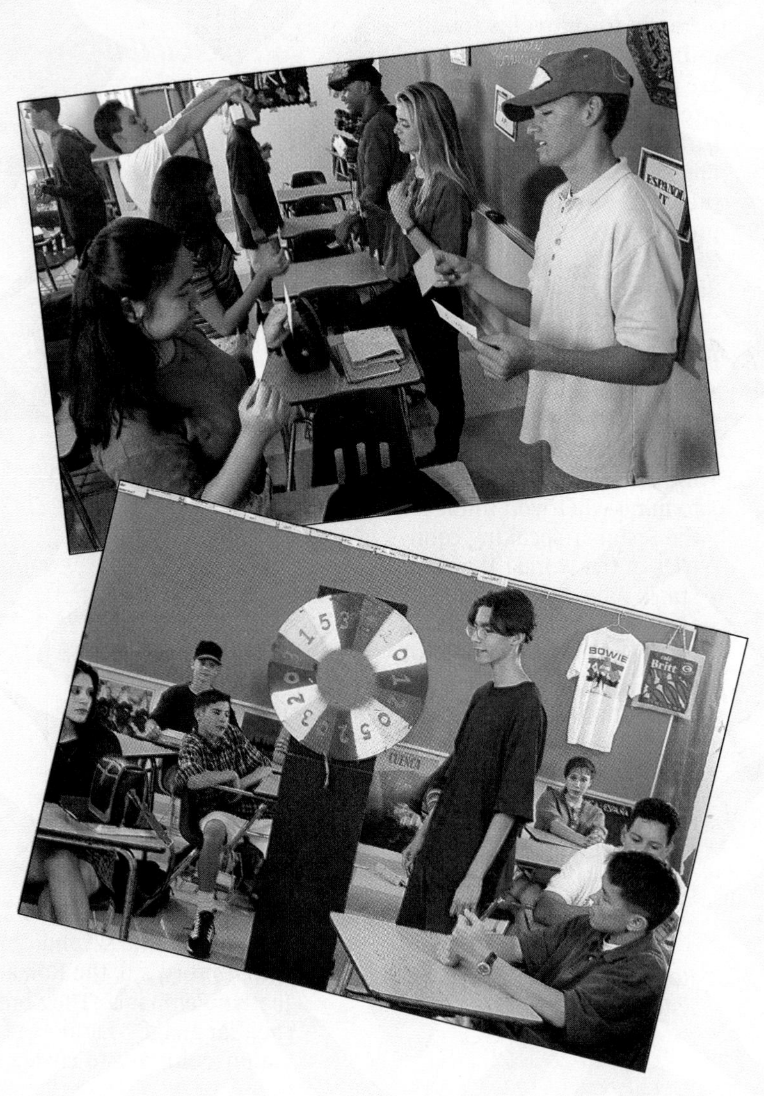

VIDEO PROGRAM OR EXPANDED VIDEO PROGRAM, Videocassette 1

OR VIDEODISC PROGRAM, *Videodisc 1A*

The video for the Preliminary Chapter will introduce your students to some of the people they will view in the rest of *¡Ven conmigo!* Some are the actors in **fotonovelas** found in **De antemano,** and others are people interviewed on the street for the **Panorama cultural** and authentic Video Clips. You may wish to play the video as a preview to the program and for your students to have an introduction to the Spanish language.

Motivating Activities

- Before students open their books, ask them to brainstorm answers to the following questions. What comes to mind when you think of the Spanish-speaking countries of the world? Which states have Spanish names? (Colorado, Florida, Nevada) Can you think of cities with Spanish names? (San Francisco, San Antonio, Boca Raton)
- Ask students to name any movies or TV shows in which Spanish is spoken, and any musicians who sing in Spanish. Ask if they know of singers or actors who have a Hispanic heritage. (Linda Ronstadt, Rosie Pérez, Emilio Estevez)

CAPÍTULO PRELIMINAR

¡Adelante!

Puerto Rico

los Estados Unidos

Ecuador

México

Argentina

Países hispanohablantes
Áreas hispanohablantes de los Estados Unidos
0 200 400 kilómetros
0 200 400 millas

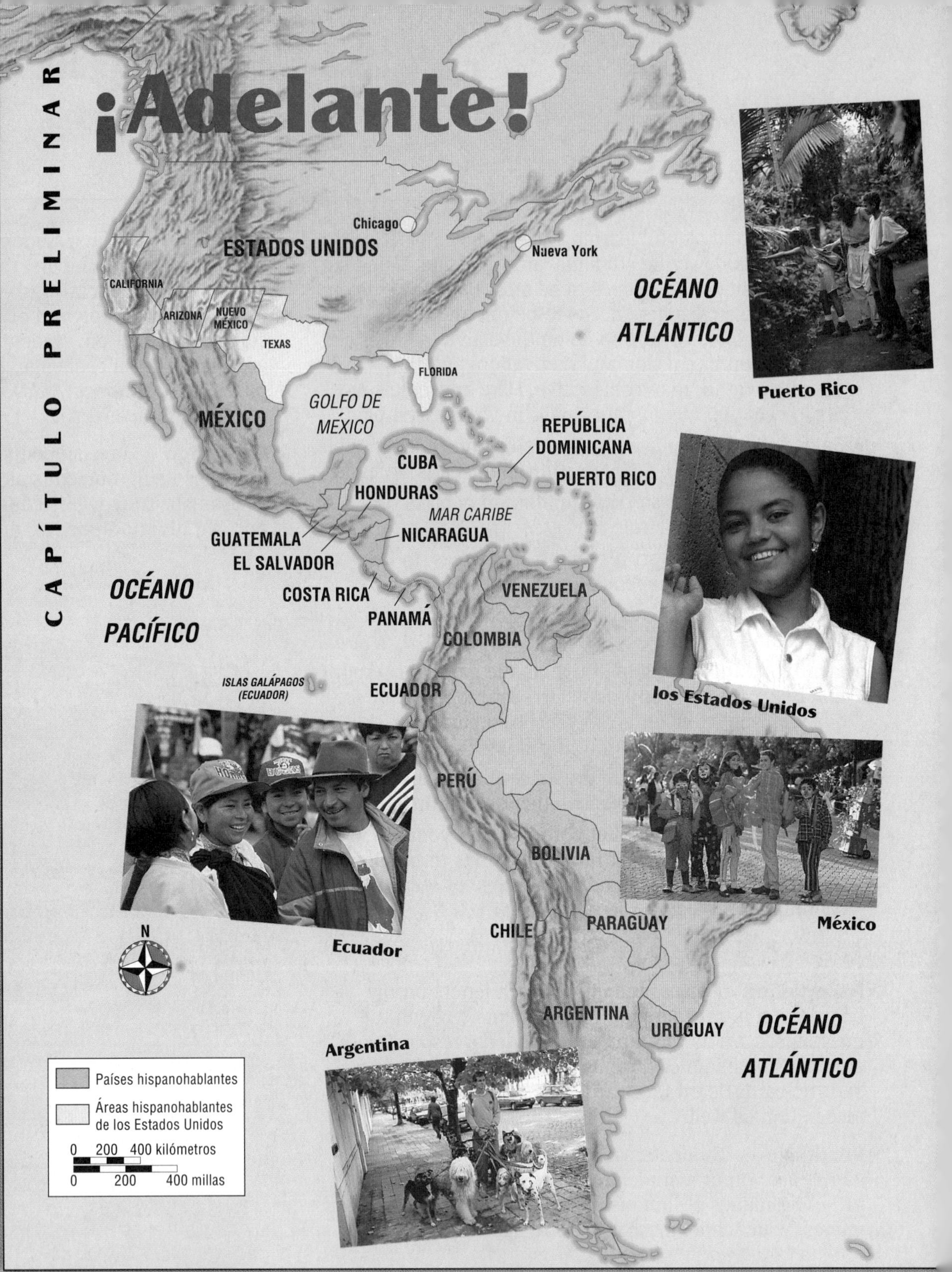

Culture Note

From the second century B.C. to the fifth century A.D. the Romans occupied the Iberian Peninsula. They brought not only their language—Latin—but also their civilization, culture, and customs.

Teacher Note

The **Capítulo preliminar** is a preparation for the study of Spanish. Students need not be expected to master the material—it will be presented again in subsequent chapters.

¡Bienvenido al mundo hispanohablante!

Spanish, one of the five official languages of the United Nations, is spoken by over 300 million people in the world today. Originally a dialect of Latin, Spanish was first recognized as a language in its own right about 700 years ago. Spanish is spoken in Spain (where it originated), in 19 Latin American countries, and in parts of Africa and the Philippines. It is also spoken in the United States, where about one out of ten residents is expected to be a Spanish speaker by the year 2000. Can you find the countries where these Spanish speakers live?

Photo Flash!

Photos on this page are of people that your students will view in the videos. Some are actors who play characters in the **fotonovelas,** and others are people interviewed on the street in numerous Spanish-speaking countries.

History Link

The Spanish began colonizing the Philippines in 1565 and ruled until 1898, when they lost control to the United States in the Spanish-American War. They named the islands after King Philip II (**Felipe II**). The Spanish legacy is still felt through religion. The Philippines has more Christians, most of whom are Roman Catholics, than any other Asian nation. Philippine food, a mixture of American, Chinese, Spanish, and indigenous Filipino cooking, is representative of the many cultures that have been a part of the nation. Although the two official languages of the Philippines are English and Pilipino, a small number of Filipinos still speak Spanish.

History Link

Guinea Ecuatorial Equatorial Guinea is a country on the West Coast of Africa. The territory that the country now occupies was ceded to Spain by Portugal in 1778. Although spoken only by a small minority, Spanish is the official language of Equatorial Guinea.

Pidgin English is spoken, and each ethnic group also speaks its own language. Hausa, a Hamito-Semitic language, has become a lingua franca that traverses ethnic and political boundaries. Another language spoken is Bantu.

Motivating Activities

- Have students bring in help wanted ads from national and local newspapers. Use the ads to point out job opportunities for bilingual people.
- Ask students if they have lived or traveled in a Spanish-speaking country. If they have, they may want to share their experiences.

Native Speakers

Ask students if they or any of their friends or family are Spanish speakers. Ask them to share how extensively they use Spanish. (All the time? in certain situations more than others? with certain people? for certain expressions only? Do they read Spanish-language newspapers, listen to Spanish-language radio stations, or watch Spanish-language TV?)

El español—¿Por qué?

There are many reasons for learning to speak Spanish. Which of these reasons is most important to you?

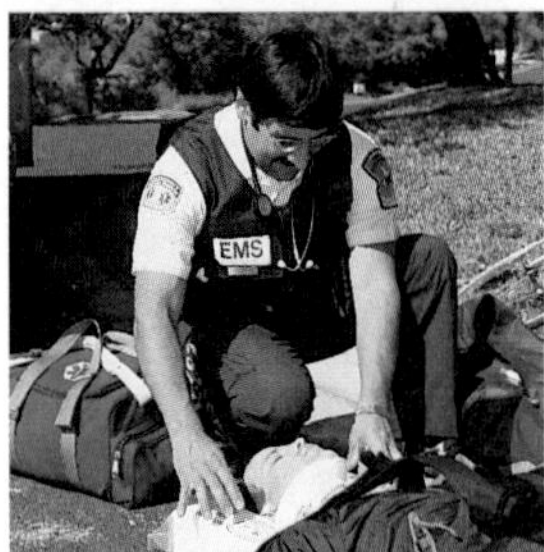

- Bilingual employees are increasingly in demand in business, social work, health care, education, journalism, and many other fields. Learning Spanish may help you find a more interesting, better-paying job.

- Each language has its own personality. To really get to know someone, you have to speak that person's language. Chances are good that someday you'll travel to a Spanish-speaking country. Whatever your reason for going, whether it be vacation, study, or business, you'll get a lot more out of your stay if you can speak the language.

- You're living in one of the major Spanish-speaking countries right now—the United States! Learning Spanish can open up a whole new world of information, entertainment, and adventure. Spanish-language movies, books, videos, magazines, TV shows, and music are all around you.
- If you plan to go to college, you'll find that many university programs require some foreign-language study. Taking a language now can improve your chances of admission and give you a head start on meeting your degree requirements.
- One of the best reasons for studying Spanish is for satisfaction. Studying another language is a challenge to your mind, and you get a great feeling of accomplishment the first time you have a conversation in Spanish.

History Link

In 1848 the Mexican Congress signed **el Tratado de Guadalupe Hidalgo,** ending the Mexican-American War. With this treaty Mexico ceded to the United States more than one-third of its total territory—the present-day states of Texas, California, Arizona, New Mexico, Nevada, and the Utah territory that included the present-day state of Utah and part of Colorado.

Social Studies Link

Ask students how the North American Free Trade Agreement (NAFTA) (**el Tratado de Libre Comercio de América del Norte,** or TLC) affects opportunities for trade between the United States and Mexico. What implications might this have for bilingual employment opportunities?

¿Sabías...? *Did you know...?*

Spanish language and culture are important parts of our national history. As you begin your study of Spanish, you should be aware that...

- the Spanish were among the first European explorers in what is today the U.S.
- the first European settlement in the United States was founded by the Spanish in 1565 at St. Augustine, Florida.
- parts of the U.S. once belonged to Mexico.
- many common words, such as *rodeo* and *patio,* came into English from Spanish.
- Spanish is the second most frequently spoken language in the U.S.
- many of the United States' most important trading partners in this hemisphere are Spanish-speaking nations.

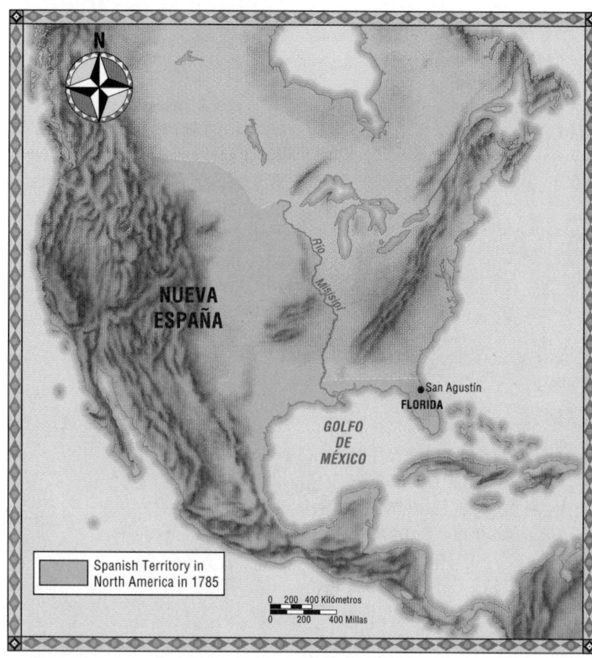

1 Herencia hispana *Hispanic heritage*

Working in small groups, choose and answer one of the following questions. Share your findings with the class. See answers below.

1. Using your knowledge of geography, list several major U.S. cities with Spanish names. Also list states with names based on Spanish words.
2. Using the map on page xxvii, name the major Spanish-speaking areas of the United States. What countries do many Spanish-speaking immigrants come from?
3. Under the headings *foods* and *cowboy lore,* list common English words you think may have been borrowed from Spanish.
4. Using the maps on pages xxi–xxvii, name 20 Spanish-speaking countries (one is a special part of the U.S.). Choose one country and list some things you know about it.
5. Name as many Spanish-language TV programs, radio stations, magazines, movies, and newspapers as you can.

Background Information

St. Augustine, Florida, was founded in 1565 by the Spaniard Pedro Menéndez de Áviles. It is considered the first permanent European settlement in what is today the United States. St. Augustine is on the northeastern coast of Florida.

Social Studies Link

Have students research the Spanish explorers who traveled through North America. Among the most famous was Alvar Núñez Cabeza de Vaca. After being shipwrecked, Cabeza de Vaca spent eight years in the Gulf region. His subsequent stories of the legendary El Dorado and the Seven Golden Cities of Cíbola inspired others to explore North America. Among these early explorers were Juan Ponce de León, who explored Florida searching for the mythical fountain of youth; Hernando (or Fernando) de Soto, who explored the southern Gulf Coast area and the Mississippi River; and Francisco Vázquez de Coronado, who explored the American Southwest. As an extension, have students research the indigenous peoples of North or South America or the Spanish **conquistadores.** You may want to show the film *Cabeza de Vaca.*

Teaching Suggestion

1 Students should be able to answer a few of the questions based on what they have learned in other classes. You may wish to make this an overnight assignment.

Answers

1 *Possible answers:* 1. Los Angeles, San Diego, San Antonio, Albuquerque, Santa Fe, Las Vegas; Colorado, New Mexico, Texas, Arizona, California, Montana, Florida, Nevada 2. Los Angeles, New York, Miami, Chicago, San Antonio, and the Southwest; Mexico, Puerto Rico, Cuba, and the countries of Central America 3. Foods: taco, enchilada, burrito, salsa, chocolate; Cowboy lore: lasso, lariat, ranch, chaps, chaparral, rodeo 4. *See maps pages xxi–xxvii for countries.* 5. *Answers will vary according to locale.*

Language Note

The word **chocolate** came into Spanish from Nahuatl, an indigenous language spoken in Central and Western Mexico. **Xocolātl** *(show-ko-lat-ul)* is the Nahuatl word for chocolate, meaning *bitter water.* The Aztec nobility drank it without sugar. Today, there are over one million native Nahuatl speakers in Mexico.

Thinking Critically

Analyzing Point out that Spanish speakers in the United States and much of Latin America come from diverse backgrounds. Spanish speakers' ancestors came from all parts of the world, including Africa, the Americas, Asia, Europe, and the Middle East.

Teaching Suggestion

Ask students to describe briefly other famous Spanish speakers or people of Hispanic heritage and have classmates guess whom they are describing. (Gloria Estefan, César Chávez, Kiki de la Garza, Edward James Olmos, Rosie Pérez, Emilo Estevez, Martin Sheen (a.k.a. Ramón Estevez), Charlie Sheen, Tish Hinojosa, Antonia Novello)

¿Los conoces? *Do you know them?*

Spanish speakers from all over the world have made valuable contributions in science, sports, politics, and the arts. These personality sketches may remind you of other famous Spanish speakers you know something about, like Gloria Estefan, Paul Rodríguez, or Arantxa Sánchez Vicario.

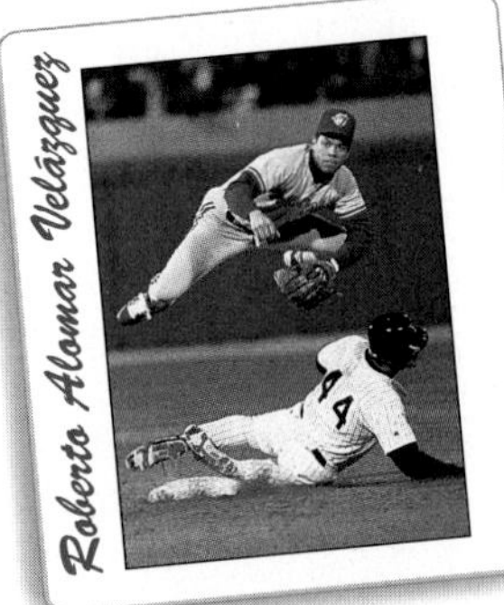

◀ **Roberto Alomar Velázquez** (b. 1968) is one of the world's finest second basemen. Born in Ponce, Puerto Rico to a family of baseball greats, Alomar has been chosen All-Star consecutively in recent years and has won several Golden Glove awards.

▲ **Miguel de Cervantes y Saavedra** (1547–1616) was the author of *Don Quijote de la Mancha*. His personal experiences of poverty, imprisonment, and warfare enabled him to paint a sharply realistic, yet sympathetic picture of Spanish life at the turn of the 17th century.

La Reina Isabel (Isabel I of Spain: 1451–1504) helped form the modern Spanish nation-state by marrying Fernando, King of Aragon. We know her best for financing Columbus's voyage to the New World. ▶

◀ **Frida Kahlo** (1907–1954), a Mexican artist born in Coyoacán, is best known for her powerful self-portraits. Like her husband, the famous muralist Diego Rivera, Frida Kahlo reflected the history and political life of her country in her work.

▲ **Simón Bolívar** (1783–1830), born in Caracas, Venezuela, led a brilliant campaign against Spanish colonialism that eventually resulted in independence for most of South America. He died in poverty and disgrace but is still honored as **el Libertador**, *The Liberator*.

Rigoberta Menchú (b. 1959), a Guatemalan Quiché woman, won the 1992 Nobel Peace Prize for condemning human rights violations against the indigenous people of Central America. ▶

Nombres comunes *Common names*

Here are some common names from Spanish-speaking countries. Choose a name for yourself from the list if you wish.

Me llamo **Ana Luisa.**

Me llamo **Javier.**

- Adela
- Alicia (Licha)
- Ana, Anita
- Ángela, Angélica
- Beatriz
- Carmen
- Catalina (Cata)
- Claudia
- Cristina (Tina)
- Daniela
- Dolores (Lola)
- Elena (Nena)
- Graciela (Chela)
- Inés
- Isabel (Isa)
- Juana
- Luisa
- Margarita
- María
- Marisol (Mari)
- Marta
- Mercedes (Merche)
- Natalia
- Paloma
- Pilar
- Rosario (Charo)
- Sara
- Susana
- Teresa
- Verónica (Vero)

- Alberto
- Alejandro (Alejo)
- Andrés
- Antonio (Toño)
- Carlos
- Cristóbal
- Diego
- Eduardo (Lalo)
- Francisco (Paco)
- Gregorio
- Guillermo
- Ignacio (Nacho)
- Jaime
- Jesús (Chuy)
- Jorge
- José (Pepe)
- Juan
- Julio
- Lorenzo
- Luis
- Manuel
- Mario
- Miguel
- Pablo
- Pedro
- Rafael (Rafa)
- Ricardo
- Roberto (Beto)
- Santiago
- Tomás

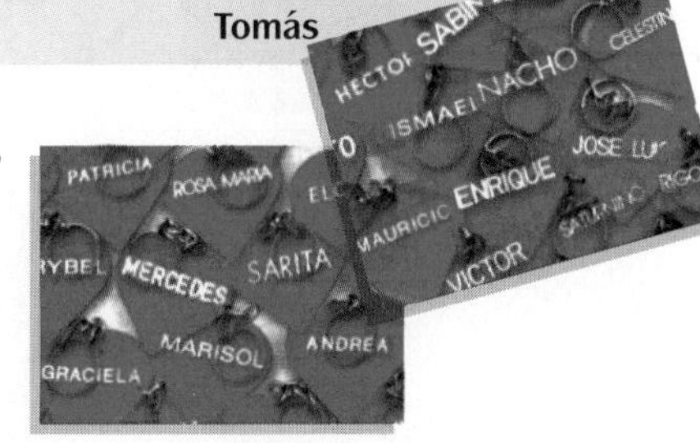

2 Nombres en español *Names in Spanish*

Listen to a series of names in Spanish and repeat them aloud after the speaker. Try to guess the English equivalent of each one. Does your name have an equivalent in Spanish? For answers, see script, page T65.

3 Mis amigos *My friends*

Find and write Spanish names that match the names of at least six of your family members, friends, or classmates. Check to see that you've used accents in the correct places. Answers will vary, see names above.

4 Me llamo... *My name is . . .*

Form a name chain in your row. The first person turns to a partner and asks his or her name. That person answers with a chosen name in Spanish, and then asks the next person's name. Keep going to the end of the row.

MODELO — ¿Cómo te llamas?
— Me llamo Carlos. ¿Cómo te llamas?

Los acentos

You may have noticed the accent mark (´) and the tilde (˜) on words in the name chart. They are used to help you pronounce the words correctly. You'll learn about these and other special marks, including the upside down question mark and exclamation point, in Chapter 1.

Motivating Activity

Ask students if they can think of any Spanish names that are not on the list. Have a volunteer write them on the board or on an overhead transparency.

Teaching Suggestions

- Play *Audiocassette 1A* or *Audio CD 1.* Have students listen without responding. Then replay the tape and have students repeat the names for practice.
- You may want to assign Spanish names for students to use in class. They can select a Spanish equivalent of their English name or assume a completely new Spanish name.
- Emphasize that Spanish and English do not sound the same. Encourage students to listen carefully to the tape and to your pronunciation of their names. Students should try to mimic correct pronunciation as closely as possible. For multi-syllabic names, you may wish to have the students do "backward buildup" so that their stress remains natural. (Wilfredo: -do, -fredo, Wilfredo)
- Emphasize the importance of practice. Language is a skill learned gradually, like a sport or playing an instrument.

Teaching Suggestion

3 Additional Practice

Have students find and list ten different Hispanic last names from the phone book.

Culture Note

It is very popular in the Dominican Republic to give children Russian names. (Vladimir, Katirina, Ivan, Tavia) It is also popular in the Dominican Republic to give children names of countries and cities. (América, Venecia, Roma, Australia)

Language Note

An **apodo** is an affectionate nickname, such as **el gallo** or **la rubia,** which is frequently given to fellow students in high school. In Chapter 1, the **fotonovela** story line is based on two pen pals who don't realize they are acquaintances from school, since they had known each other only by their shortened names.

Motivating Activity

To build confidence, help students identify the Spanish cognates and borrowed words such as **ciclismo, ensalada,** or **violín.**

For videodisc application, see *Videodisc Guide.*

Teaching Suggestions

- Before students try to produce the sounds themselves, have them point to the corresponding letter and picture as they listen to *Audiocassette 1A* or *Audio CD 1.*
- Ask students if they can identify the Spanish vowel sounds. Point out that Spanish vowel sounds are different from English ones.

For Individual Needs

Auditory Learners
Students may like to chant rhymes or make up rap tunes to learn the correct sounds. (**A–E–I–O–U, Yo me llamo María. ¿Cómo te llamas tú?**) As their vocabulary increases, encourage students who respond well to this approach to revise their rhymes to include new words.

Kinesthetic Learners
Working in pairs, students take turns dictating a design to their partner with Spanish letters, starting in the center of the design. English prepositions will be used, but all letters must be spoken in Spanish. (S1: "Put **ge** in the middle." S2: Writes the letter *G.* S1: "**Efe** is over **ge.**" S2: Writes the letter *F* over the *G.*)

El alfabeto *The alphabet*

The Spanish alphabet isn't quite the same as the English one. What differences do you notice? Listen to the names of the letters and repeat after the speaker.

águila

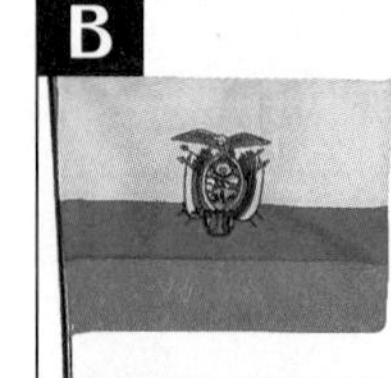

bandera

ciclismo

Although **ch** and **ll** have been officially dropped from the Spanish alphabet, dictionaries and glossaries published before 1994 will continue to show them as separate entries.

chaleco

dinero

ensalada

fruta

geografía

helicóptero

iguana

jabón

karate

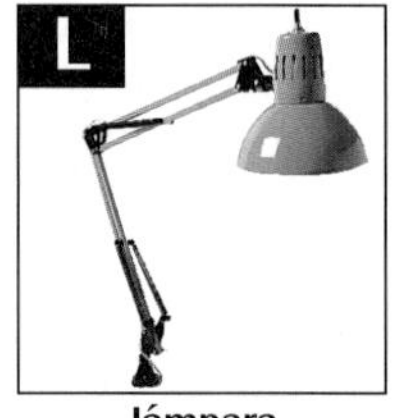

lámpara

llanta

5 Los cognados *Cognates*

Cognates are words that look the same in both Spanish and English. Although they're pronounced differently, they often have the same meaning—but not always! For example, **embarazada** means *pregnant,* not *embarrassed.* How many cognates do you see in this ad? What happens to the spelling of English *-tion* in Spanish? 23, **-ción** in Spanish

HOTEL TRYP MARÍA PITA

Situado en el límite de las Playas de Orzan y Riazor se encuentra muy próximo al centro histórico de la ciudad.

Sus 183 habitaciones están equipadas con teléfonos, radio, T.V. via satélite, caja fuerte y aire acondicionado.

Completan sus instalaciones: restaurante, cafetería, garaje, sauna, masaje y amplísimos salones apropiados para cualquier tipo de celebración.

Language Note

Point out that an **abecedario** is a Spanish primer used to teach the alphabet.

Community Link

Compile a class **abecedario** to be donated to a local children's center or library. Have students work in groups of three or four. Assign a portion of the alphabet to each group and have students cooperate to design and illustrate their letters. Students may use a Spanish dictionary.

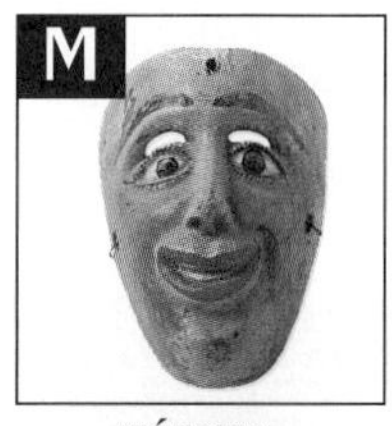

máscara

N
naranja

castañuelas

oso

P
piñata

quetzal

toro

burro

salvavidas

teléfono

uvas

violín

Walter

México

yate

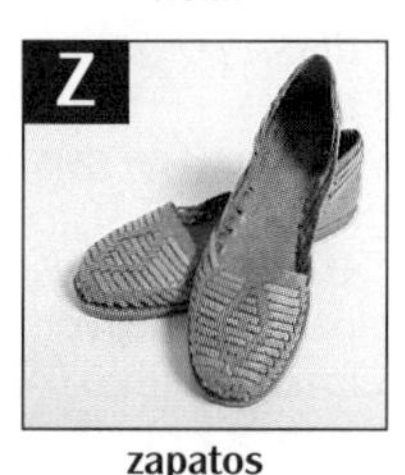

zapatos

6 Por teléfono *On the phone* Answers on p. T65.

Imagine that you work as a receptionist answering the telephone. Listen as several Spanish speakers spell their names for you. Write each name as you hear it spelled. Remember to use accents as needed.

7 ¿Cómo se escribe...? *How is . . . written?*

Work with a partner. Choose from the following items and spell each one aloud, letter by letter, in Spanish. Your partner will write the words as you spell them, then guess the number of the item you chose. Then switch roles. Answers will vary.

1. your first name
2. your last name
3. the name of your school
4. the name of your city or town
5. your best friend's first and last names
6. your favorite radio or TV station's call letters

Teaching Suggestions

- Dictate the spelling of words as students find them in the illustrations.
- Dictate a list of items for students to remember on a trip to the grocery store. **(jabón, fruta, naranja, uvas, dinero)**

For Individual Needs

6 Challenge Spell students' last names out loud and ask them to raise their hands when they recognize their own names.

Teaching Suggestion

7 Teach students **con mayúscula.** Point out that names are capitalized in Spanish just as they are in English. Teach **con acento** or **lleva acento** as well. **(eme con mayúscula, a, ere, i con acento, a: ...María)**

Language Notes

- Although the **Real Academia** has recently deleted the letters **ch** and **ll** from the alphabet, many dictionaries still have separate entries for these letters. The end-of-book vocabulary (pp. 348–361) follows the new rules, with **ch** and **ll** in sequence: "ce...ch...ci" and "li...ll...lo," with no separate entries for **ch** and **ll.**
- Although in the Americas **erre (rr)** is commonly recognized as a letter, the **Real Academia** does not officially recognize it.

Geography Link

Have students make up an alphabet book using the names of cities and countries in the maps on pages xxi–xxvii.

FRASES ÚTILES
CAPÍTULO PRELIMINAR

TPR Either play *Audiocassette 1A/Audio CD 1* or pronounce the commands for students yourself. Practice having students do the commands as you say them.

Games

MÍMICA Have students play charades. One student acts out a phrase without speaking and the other students guess what the phrase is in Spanish.

TIRITAS Divide the class into groups of three to five. Have the groups write each word in the phrases on a separate scrap of paper (i.e., one word per piece of paper). Have students scramble the scraps. With books closed, dictate the phrases while students arrange the scraps to form the Spanish phrases. The first group to get the correct answer gets a point. As students remove words from the pile, there are fewer scraps to look through.

8 Additional Practice
Play **Simón dice.** Have students take turns being Simón. Script is on p. T65.

Additional Vocabulary

Para escuchar If you use an overhead transparency instead of a chalkboard, you may wish to teach the phrase **Miren la transparencia**. Another command you may find helpful is **¡Libros al suelo!**

Para decir Additional phrases you may wish to teach your students are **¿Qué significa...?, No oigo, ¿Puedo ir al baño? ¿Puedo ir a la oficina?** and **¿Puedo ir a mi *locker*?**

Frases útiles *Useful phrases*

Para escuchar

Here are some phrases you'll probably hear regularly in Spanish class. Learn to recognize them and respond appropriately.

Abran el libro (en la página 20), por favor.	*Open your books (to page 20), please.*
Levántense, por favor.	*Please stand up.*
Siéntense, por favor.	*Please sit down.*
Levanten la mano.	*Raise your hands.*
Bajen la mano.	*Put your hands down.*
Escuchen con atención.	*Listen closely.*
Repitan después de mí.	*Repeat after me.*
Saquen una hoja de papel.	*Take out a sheet of paper.*
Silencio, por favor.	*Silence, please.*
Miren la pizarra.	*Look at the chalkboard.*

8 Simón dice *Simon says*

Listen to some commands and perform the action called for, such as raising your hand or opening your book. Respond only if the speaker says **Simón dice.** For answers, see script, page T65.

Para decir

Here are some phrases that you'll need to use often. Learn as many as you can and use them when they're appropriate.

Buenos días.	*Good morning.*
Buenas tardes.	*Good afternoon.*
¿Cómo se dice ... en español?	*How do you say . . . in Spanish?*
¿Cómo se escribe?	*How do you spell . . . ?* (lit., *How do you write . . . ?*)
Más despacio, por favor.	*Slower, please.*
¿Puedo ir por mi libro?	*Can (May) I go get my book?*
No entiendo.	*I don't understand.*
No sé.	*I don't know.*
¿Puede repetir, por favor?	*Can you repeat, please?*
Perdón.	*Excuse me.*
Tengo una pregunta.	*I have a question.*

9 Situaciones

What would you say in the following situations?
Choose your responses from **Frases útiles para decir.** See answers below.

1. You see your teacher at the store one afternoon.
2. You left your book in your locker.
3. You don't understand the directions.
4. Your teacher is talking too fast.
5. You don't know the answer.
6. You'd like to ask a question.
7. You need to hear something again.

Answers

9 1. Buenas tardes.
2. ¿Puedo ir por mi libro?
3. No entiendo.
4. Más despacio, por favor./ ¿Puede repetir, por favor?
5. No sé.
6. Tengo una pregunta.
7. ¿Puede repetir, por favor?

Answers

10 1. rojo, blanco, azul
2. blanco, negro
3. azul, gris
4. verde
5. anaranjado
6. gris, blanco, negro
7. marrón
8. amarillo
9. blanco
10. morado
11. negro
12. rojo

Colores y números *Colors and numbers*

10 Colores típicos

What colors come to mind when you think of the following items? Say them in Spanish.

1. the flag of the United States
2. a zebra
3. the sky
4. grass
5. a pumpkin
6. a cloudy day
7. coffee
8. a banana
9. snow
10. grape juice
11. a tire
12. a strawberry

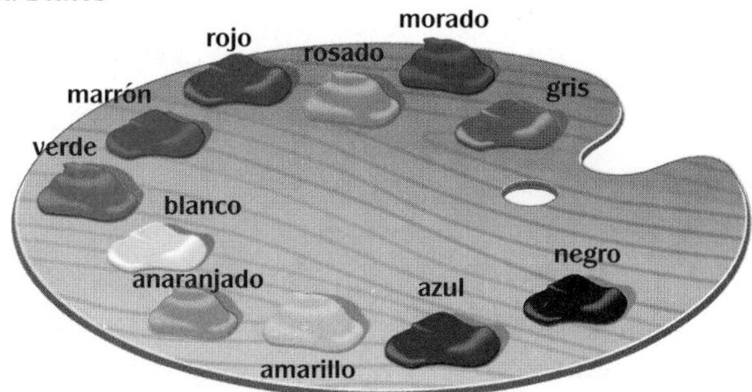

VOCABULARIO

cero

uno

dos

tres

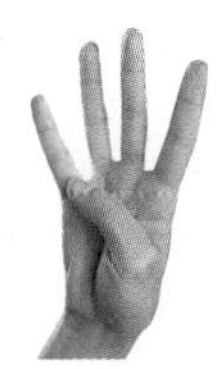

cuatro

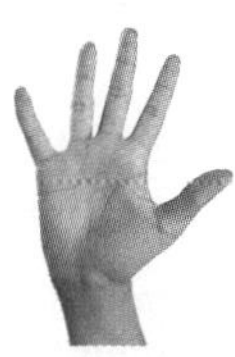

cinco

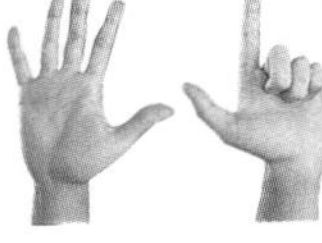

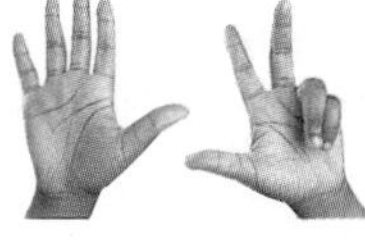

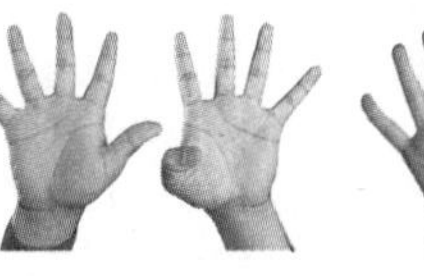

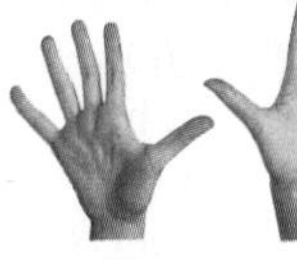

seis siete ocho nueve diez

11 ¿Cuántos dedos ves? *How many fingers do you see?*

Using the photos as a model, form a number with your hands and ask your partner to say the number. Switch roles after four or five tries.

12 Números cotidianos *Everyday numbers*

What numbers come to mind when you think of the following items? Make up your own item for question 8.

1. a pair of shoes 2
2. your fingers 5, 10
3. a tricycle 3
4. a pack of beverage cans 6
5. an octopus 8
6. a rectangle 4
7. a week 7
8. ¿? Answers will vary.

Multicultural Link

Europeans, Latin Americans, and North Africans write the numerals 1 and 7 a little differently than North Americans:

1 7

Additional Vocabulary

Violeta is another word for *purple*.

COLORES Y NÚMEROS
CAPÍTULO PRELIMINAR

Teaching Suggestions

- For personalization, point to various clothing items worn by students as you say the corresponding color.
- Ask students to name the colors of various classroom items. To evaluate listening comprehension, have students respond **cierto** or **falso** to your statements about colors in the room.
- Ask students what colors come to mind when they think of various holidays.
- Some of your students may be colorblind. (unable to distinguish among one or more of the colors red, green, and blue) With a colorblind student, you should stress color associations (fruits, plants, holidays) rather than color distinctions.

Game

CARRERAS Hang three sets of the nine colors (construction paper works well) vertically in three groups on chalkboard. Divide the class into three teams. You call out a color in Spanish and a representative from each team goes to the board and writes a word in English associated with that color next to it on their section of the board. The first student to write a correct answer earns a point for his or her team. Continue until all students have played, tally the points, and declare a winning team.

For Individual Needs

8 Challenge The following prepositions can be useful for TPR activities suggested in later chapters. You might put them on a transparency and teach for recognition: **en, en medio de, a la derecha de, a la izquierda de, debajo de, detrás de, delante de, al lado de.**

14 Group Work Have students write the numbers on scraps of paper. Collect the scraps and have students divide into groups of four or five. Shuffle and give each student four or five numbers. Students take turns dictating the number they receive, and the members of the group write the number as it is read. After verifying answers, the next student dictates, and so on.

Background Information

15 Items **a.** and **c.** are registration stickers that change yearly. Item **b.** is a license plate from the State of Mexico, and item **d.** is from Mexico, D.F. Cars keep the same plates for ten years. Registration stickers are placed on the inside of the windshield. Cars from Mexico City and surrounding areas must have a sticker to show that they have passed the six-month smog inspection, compared to once a year in many parts of the United States. Cars must also have a sticker (not shown in text, but on the *Videodisc*) for pollution control, called **la calcomanía** or **el engomado,** which says **Hoy No Circula.** This sticker designates the day of the week when the car may not be driven. This includes holidays. There are no restrictions between 10 P.M. and 6 A.M. on weekdays and any time on weekends. When the level of air pollution is too high, newspapers publish changes in the laws reducing the number of cars that can be used. Cars from out of town, including those with foreign license plates, are also subject to pollution control laws which restrict use according to the license plate number.

For videodisc application, see *Videodisc Guide.*

13 Números de teléfono

Listen as four Spanish speakers tell you their telephone numbers. Based on what you hear, match each speaker's name with the right number.

1. Nicolás
2. Juana
3. Miguel
4. Cristina

3 745-08-12 4 391-23-46
2 510-57-24 1 473-00-16

VOCABULARIO

once	11	dieciséis	16	veintiuno	21	veintiséis	26
doce	12	diecisiete	17	veintidós	22	veintisiete	27
trece	13	dieciocho	18	veintitrés	23	veintiocho	28
catorce	14	diecinueve	19	veinticuatro	24	veintinueve	29
quince	15	veinte	20	veinticinco	25	treinta	30

14 Datos importantes *Important facts*

Use numbers in Spanish to give the following information. Answers will vary.

1. your telephone number and area code
2. your zip code
3. the number of students in your row
4. your student I.D. number
5. the score of a recent game at your school or on TV

15 Placas y permisos en México

Your partner will read a number or name a color from these license stickers and plates. If you hear a number, name a color from the license plate that has that number, and vice versa. Switch roles after four or five tries. Answers will vary. See **modelo** for example.

MODELO —¿QZB 7829?
—Verde.
—¡Sí!

a. 

b. 

c. 996 FEP
DF 93 MEX

d. KZY 8762
DF MEX

Language Note

The numbers 16–19 and 21–29 can either be written as one word, **dieciséis,** or as three separate words, **diez y seis.** The form commonly listed in dictionaries is one word.

Culture Note

Increasingly, cities in Spanish-speaking countries use seven-digit telephone numbers. Often the first number is spoken alone, then the remaining numbers in pairs. (523-1628: **el cinco, veintitrés, dieciséis, veintiocho)**

Para mejor aprender el español

How best to learn Spanish

Listen

It's important to listen carefully in class. Take notes and ask questions if you don't understand, even if you think your question seems a little silly. Other people are probably wondering the same thing you are. You won't be able to understand everything you hear at first, but don't feel frustrated. You're actually absorbing a lot even when you don't realize it.

Speak

Practice speaking Spanish aloud every day. Talking with your teachers and classmates is an easy and fun way to learn. Don't be afraid to experiment. Your mistakes will help identify problems, and they'll show you important differences in the way English and Spanish "work" as languages.

Organize

Your memory is going to get a workout, so it's important to get organized. Throughout the textbook you'll see learning tips **(Sugerencias)** that can improve your study skills. For starters, here's a hint: see things with your mind. Associate each new word, sentence, or phrase with an exaggerated or unusual mental picture. For example, if you're learning the word **regla** *(ruler)*, visualize an enormous ruler on an enormous desk as you practice saying a sentence with the word.

Practice

Learning a foreign language is like learning to ride a bicycle or play an instrument. You can't spend one night cramming and then expect instantly to be able to ride or play the next morning. You didn't learn English that way either! Short, daily practice sessions are more effective than long, once-a-week sessions. Also, try to practice with a friend or a classmate. After all, language is about communication, and it takes two to communicate.

Expand

Increase your contact with Spanish outside of class in every way you can. You may be able to find someone living near you who speaks Spanish. It's easy to find Spanish-language programs on TV, on the radio, or at the video store. Many magazines and newspapers in Spanish are published or sold in the United States. Don't be afraid to read, watch, or listen. You won't understand every word, but that's okay. You can get a lot out of a story or an article by concentrating on the words you do recognize and doing a little intelligent guesswork.

Connect

Some English and Spanish words have common roots in Latin, and the two languages have influenced each other, so your knowledge of English can give you clues about the meaning of many Spanish words. Look for an English connection when you need to guess at unfamiliar words. You may also find that learning Spanish will help you in English class!

Have fun!

Above all, remember to have fun! The more you try, the more you'll learn. Besides, having fun will help you relax, and relaxed people learn better and faster. **¡Buena suerte!** *(Good luck!)*

Teaching Suggestion

You may wish to establish telephone partners to encourage students to use Spanish outside of class. This also will allow you to give assignments for oral practice (**tarea oral**) outside of class.

For Individual Needs

Tactile Learners Tell students that they should both envision and imagine themselves touching new vocabulary items as they hear, read, or say the Spanish word for the item. Explain that the more sensory associations they have for a word, the more likely they will be to remember the meaning of the word.

Challenge Give homework assignments that increase students' contact with Spanish outside class. Through creative assignments you can provide opportunities for them to experience the language in authentic situations. For example, many video stores carry movies in Spanish that students can watch for extra credit. They should report to the class what the movie was about and how much of the Spanish they understood.

LOCATION OPENER
CHAPTERS
1, 2

¡Ven conmigo a España! pp. 12–65

EXPANDED VIDEO PROGRAM, Videocassette 1

OR VIDEODISC PROGRAM, Videodisc 1A

Motivating Activity

Before students open their books, have them brainstorm about what they think Spain is like, what the people are like, and what the topography is like. Then have them compare their guesses to what they see in the photographs on pages 12–15.

Background Information

Toledo is the capital of the province of Toledo and is located 41 miles southwest of Madrid. The Tagus River (**el río Tajo**) flows in a deep ravine around the city, which is on a hill.

From 712 to 1085, Toledo was ruled by the Moors, an Islamic people from North Africa. During the Moorish period, Toledo was a thriving center of culture and learning, where Moslems, Jews, and Arabic-speaking Catholics (**mozárabes**) lived in relative peace and prosperity. The age of tolerance ended in the 14th century with a series of pogroms (riots against Jewish people). In 1492 Ferdinand and Isabella expelled everyone from Spain who would not become baptized as Catholic.

CAPÍTULOS 1 y 2

¡Ven conmigo a España!

The city of Toledo on the Tajo River

Language Note

The Ladino language, based on 15th-century Castilian Spanish mixed with many elements of Hebrew, is spoken by about 200,000 people, primarily living in communities in the Balkans, Israel, and Argentina. Like Yiddish, Ladino is written using the Hebrew alphabet. Ladino preserves many of the features that have been lost in modern Spanish. For example, **hijo** is *fijo,* **hablar** is *fablar,* and **ahora** is *agora.*

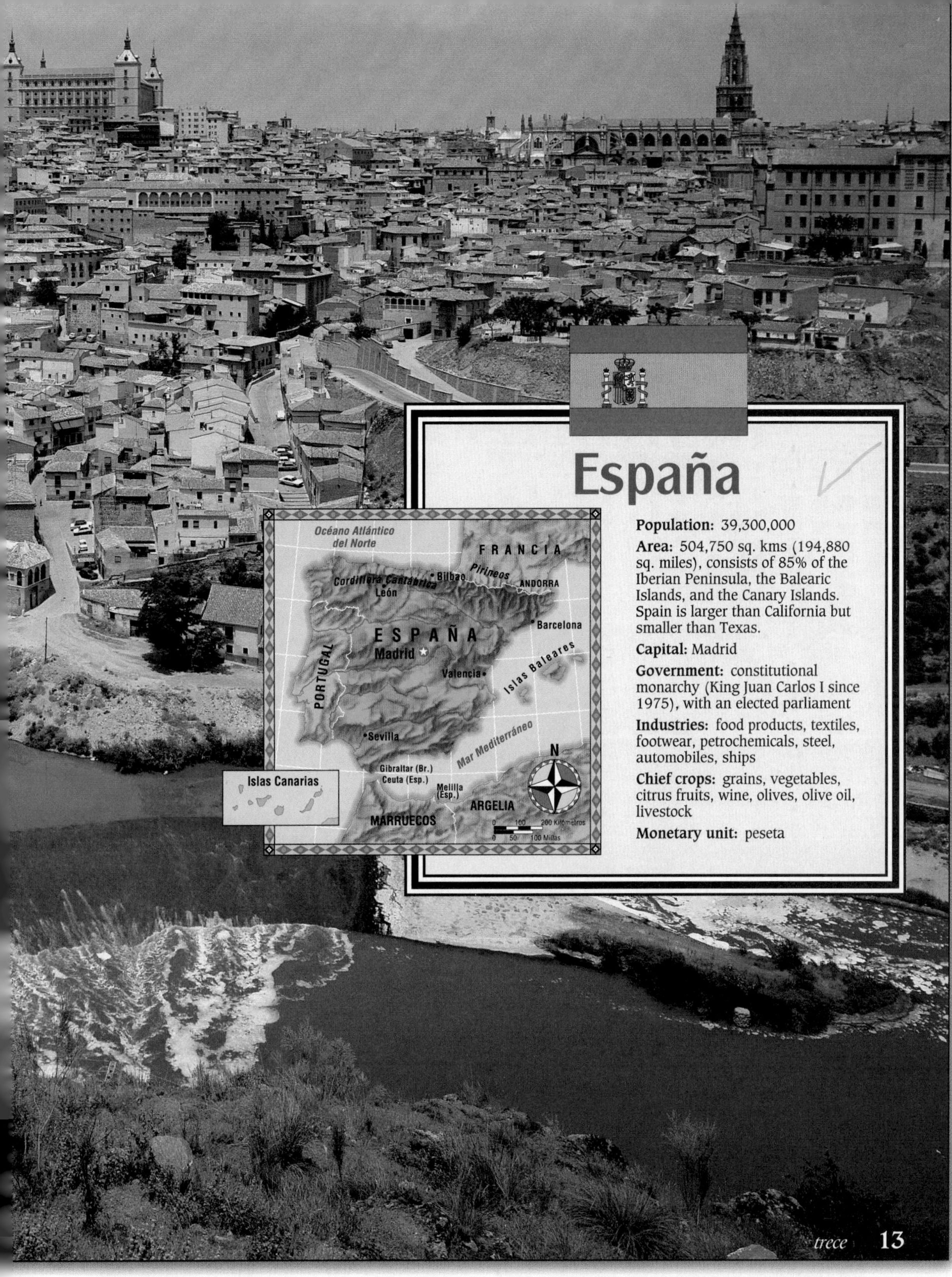

España

Population: 39,300,000

Area: 504,750 sq. kms (194,880 sq. miles), consists of 85% of the Iberian Peninsula, the Balearic Islands, and the Canary Islands. Spain is larger than California but smaller than Texas.

Capital: Madrid

Government: constitutional monarchy (King Juan Carlos I since 1975), with an elected parliament

Industries: food products, textiles, footwear, petrochemicals, steel, automobiles, ships

Chief crops: grains, vegetables, citrus fruits, wine, olives, olive oil, livestock

Monetary unit: peseta

trece 13

LOCATION OPENER
CHAPTERS 1, 2

Using the Almanac and Map

Terms in the Almanac

- **El gobierno:** The king serves as Spain's head of state. Although he does not have a direct role in running the government, he is an advisor. **El primer Ministro** heads the **Consejo de Ministros** (*Cabinet*) which carries out the day-to-day operations of the government. The **Cortes** (*Parliament*) makes the country's laws.
- **Las industrias: productos alimenticios** *food products;* **calzado** *footwear;* **petroquímicos** *petrochemicals;* **acero** *steel;* **automóviles** *automobiles;* **buques** *ships*
- **Cosechas principales: granos** *grains;* **vegetales** *vegetables;* **frutas cítricas** *citrus fruits;* **vino** *wine;* **aceitunas** *olives;* **aceite de oliva** *olive oil;* **ganado** *livestock*
- **Unidad monetaria: la peseta.** Five-peseta coins are commonly called **duros.**

Using the Map

- Have students identify the other country occupying the Iberian Peninsula. (Portugal)
- Have students identify Spain's neighbors to the north, west, and south. (France, Andorra, Portugal, Morocco)
- Have students locate Gibraltar. Ask students if they have heard of the Rock of Gibraltar, a large limestone mass that occupies most of Gibraltar's 2.3 square miles. You may want to point out that Gibraltar has been a British possession since 1713.
- Point out the short distance between Spain and Morocco. It is only about a two-hour ferry ride from the town of Algeciras to the coast of North Africa.

Thinking Critically

Comparing and Contrasting Have students compare the Canary Islands to the Balearic Islands. (The Canaries are made up of seven volcanic islands—Tenerife, Gran Canaria, La Palma, Gomera, Hierro, Fuerteventura, and Lanzarote—in the Atlantic west of Morocco. The inhabitants, called **canarios,** speak Spanish. The Balearics are made up of four islands—Mallorca, Menorca, Ibiza, and Formentera—located in the Mediterranean. The inhabitants speak Catalán.) You may want to have the students look up this information in the encyclopedia.

History Link

The Iberian Peninsula (**Península Ibérica**) takes its name from its first known inhabitants, **los ibéricos,** about whom little is known. It is believed that they came from North Africa, perhaps as long ago as 7,000 B.C.

LOCATION OPENER
CHAPTERS
1, 2

Using the Photo Essay

① ⑤ The Pyrenees (**los Pirineos**), stretching over 270 miles with a maximum width of about 100 miles, form the boundary between France and Spain. Spain is Europe's second most mountainous country, surpassed only by Switzerland. The tallest peak of the Pyrenees is the Aneto Peak (**Pico de Aneto**) in Aragon, at 11,169 feet. The Pyrenees have many international ski resorts.

② The hub of the oldest part of the city of Barcelona is formed by Las Ramblas, a spacious, tree-lined boulevard leading north to the commercial center, Plaza de Cataluña, and south to the Paseo Marítimo and the Puerto de Barcelona. Along Las Ramblas, you can buy birds, fish, turtles, and flowers, or you can sit and people-watch. If you enjoy Barcelona, you can drink from the Fuente de Canaletes and become a symbolic native of the city.

③ **Andalucía** is the region of Spain that most closely fits many people's image of Spain. It is the home of **flamenco** (a dance involving guitar music, finger-snapping, castanets, and heel-stomping), **gazpacho** (a spicy cold tomato soup), and the **corrida de toros** (bull fight). Much of Andalusian food, culture, and architecture is reminiscent of the ancient Moorish occupation.

ESPAÑA

What comes to mind when you think of Spain? Spain is a country of varied landscapes. In the north you'll find lush, green hills, along with ***los Pirineos*** *(the Pyrenees), a chain of rugged mountains separating Spain and France. Central Spain consists of a huge, dry plateau called the* ***Meseta,*** *home of the modern capital city of Madrid. Southern Spain has some of the most beautiful beaches in Europe. Spain's people are as diverse as its landscapes. They enjoy distinct customs and a strong sense of regional identity.*

① The swift rivers and rugged terrain in northern Spain are ideal for white water rafting adventures.

◀ ② The Plaza de Cataluña in Barcelona is situated at the end of the famous Ramblas boulevard, a short walk from the historical Barrio Gótico.

③ This young woman is wearing a traditional costume of Andalucía, a region in southern Spain where the music, architecture, and costume reflect almost 800 years of Moorish rule. ▶

④ Benidorm is a Mediterranean resort located on the Costa Blanca. The beautiful beaches make this one of Spain's most popular tourist destinations.

History Link

The Moors were a people from northwestern Africa who conquered Spain in the early 700s. They were Moslems, (**musulmanes**) followers of the religion of Islam. The Arabs brought their knowledge of mathematics, medicine, and other fields of study. They had also preserved many of the writings of the ancient Greek, Roman, and Middle Eastern civilizations. They ruled Spain for nearly 800 years.

Art Link

Many buildings in southern Spain feature Arabesque decoration, depicting curving patterns of fruits, flowers, and leaves or geometric shapes. Have students research buildings in Spain with Arabesque decoration. (Alhambra, Alcazaba, Alcázar) Ask students why Arabesque designs don't include people or animals. (Islamic religion forbids the portrayal of human or animal figures.)

(5) The Pyrenees Mountains form a natural border separating Spain from the rest of Europe. Abundant snowfall on the higher peaks makes them an excellent location for winter sports.

Chapters 1 and 2 will introduce you to some students who live in Madrid, the capital of Spain. Located in the geographical center of the country, Madrid is a large, modern city of over three million people. Both visitors and ***madrileños*** *(the residents of Madrid) love to explore the many cultural treasures, parks, and cafés of this busy city.*

(6) Once a year Andalusians in southern Spain celebrate the fine horses bred and trained here.

(7) This farmer uses traditional farming methods in the village of Navacepeda in the Gredos Mountains. Fresh air and pine woods make this a popular weekend spot for residents of nearby Madrid.

LOCATION OPENER
CHAPTERS 1, 2

Motivating Activity

Can students think of any regions of the United States that are similar to the Pyrenees? (the Colorado Rockies, the Adirondacks, the Appalachians)

(6) Álvaro Domecq and the Royal Andalusian School of Equestrian Art (**Escuela Real Andaluza de Arte Ecuestre**) have won many awards in Spain and in America for their talented horses. Every Thursday at noon the Jerez riding school puts on an equestrian ballet called **Cómo bailan los caballos andaluces,** which features horses that strut, goose-step, leap and dance. The rest of the working week, midday training sessions are open to the public. In May the whole city of Jerez de la Frontera celebrates these horses during the **Feria del Caballo.** Andalusian horses make up the stock of the Royal Lipizzaner Horses, which are trained at the Spanish Riding School of Vienna in Austria, and regularly tour the United States.

(7) Much of the land in Spain is used for farming, either as cropland or as pastureland. The country ranks among the world's leading producers of cork, lemons, olives, oranges, and grapes. Sheep are the chief livestock in Spain. Other important farm animals include beef and dairy cattle, chickens, goats, and pigs. About two-thirds of all Spanish farmers own their farms. Since about 1960, the government has introduced modern methods and equipment to Spanish farmers. Such advances have increased farm production, but there are still farmers who prefer to do their farming in the same style as their ancestors.

Multicultural Link

Have students interview someone from another culture to find out what types of annual celebrations take place in their area. (patron saint festivals, folk art celebrations, memorials for local heroes)

Language Note

Many words in the Spanish language that begin with **al-** are Arabic in origin. Words like **alcalde** *mayor* or *judge,* **almacén** *store,* **almohada** *pillow,* **alquilar** *to rent,* and **albóndiga** *meatball* are examples of words from Arabic.

Capítulo 1: ¡Mucho gusto!

Chapter Overview

	FUNCTIONS	GRAMMAR	CULTURE	RE-ENTRY
De antemano pp. 18–20	**¡Me llamo Francisco!**	*Practice and Activity Book*, p. 3	*Video Guide* OR *Videodisc Guide*	
Primer paso pp. 21–26	• Greeting people and saying goodbye, p. 21 • Introducing people and responding to an introduction, p. 22 • Asking how someone is and saying how you are, p. 24	• Punctuation marks, p. 23 • Pronouns **tú** and **yo**, p. 25	• **Nota cultural,** Greetings and goodbyes, p. 21 • **Nota cultural,** First names and Saint's Days, p. 23 • **Encuentro cultural, La distancia social**, p. 26	Accents (from **Capítulo preliminar**)
Segundo paso pp. 27–31	• Asking and saying how old someone is, p. 27 • Asking where someone is from and saying where you're from, p. 28	• **ser** (singular forms), p. 28 • Forming questions with question words, p. 30	**Panorama cultural**, **¿De dónde eres?**, p. 31	Numbers 0–30 (from **Capítulo preliminar**)
Tercer paso pp. 32–35	Talking about likes and dislikes, p. 32	Nouns and definite articles, p. 33		
Letra y sonido p. 35	Spanish vowels		**Dictado:** *Textbook Audiocassette 1A/Audio CD 1*	
Vamos a leer pp. 36–37	**Categorías**		**Reading Strategy:** Using cognates to determine meaning	
Review pp. 38–41	**Repaso,** pp. 38–39	**A ver si puedo...**, p. 40	**Vocabulario,** p. 41	
Assessment Options	**Quizzes** • *Chapter Teaching Resources, Book 1* **Primer paso,** Quiz 1-1, pp. 23–24 **Segundo paso,** Quiz 1-2, pp. 25–26 **Tercer paso,** Quiz 1-3, pp. 27–28 • *Assessment Items, Audiocassette 7A/Audio CD 1*		**Chapter Test** • *Chapter Teaching Resources, Book 1*, pp. 29–34 • *Assessment Guide*, Speaking Test, p. 28 • *Assessment Items, Audiocassette 7A/Audio CD 1* **Test Generator, Chapter 1**	

Video Program OR *Expanded Video Program, Videocassette 1,* OR *Videodisc Program, Videodisc 1A*	*Textbook Audiocassette 1A/Audio CD 1*

RESOURCES: Print	RESOURCES: Audiovisual
	Textbook Audiocassette 1A/Audio CD 1
Practice and Activity Book, pp. 4–6	
Chapter Teaching Resources, Book 1	
• Additional Listening Activities 1-1, 1-2, p. 11	*Additional Listening Activities, Audiocassette 10A/Audio CD 1*
• Student Response Forms, p. 20	
• Realia 1-1, pp. 15, 17	
• Situation Cards 1-1, pp. 18–19	
• Teaching Transparency Master 1-1, pp. 7, 10	*Teaching Transparency 1-1*
• Quiz 1-1, pp. 23–24	*Assessment Items, Audiocassette 7A/Audio CD 1*
Videodisc Guide	*Videodisc Program, Videodisc 1A*
	Textbook Audiocassette 1A/Audio CD 1
Practice and Activity Book, pp. 7–8	
Chapter Teaching Resources, Book 1	
• Communicative Activity 1-1, pp. 5–6	
• Additional Listening Activities 1-3, 1-4, p. 12	*Additional Listening Activities, Audiocassette 10A/Audio CD 1*
• Student Response Forms, p. 21	
• Realia 1-2, pp. 16, 17	
• Situation Cards 1-2, pp. 18–19	
• Teaching Transparency Master 1-2, pp. 8, 10	*Teaching Transparency 1-2*
• Quiz 1-2, pp. 25–26	*Assessment Items, Audiocassette 7A/Audio CD 1*
Video Guide	*Video Program* OR *Expanded Video Program, Videocassette 1*
Videodisc Guide	*Videodisc Program, Videodisc 1A*
	Textbook Audiocassette 1A/Audio CD 1
Practice and Activity Book, pp. 9–10	
Chapter Teaching Resources, Book 1	
• Communicative Activity 1-2, pp. 5–6	
• Additional Listening Activities 1-5, 1-6, p. 13	*Additional Listening Activities, Audiocassette 10A/Audio CD 1*
• Student Response Forms, p. 22	
• Realia 1-2, p. 16, 17	
• Situation Cards 1-3, pp. 18–19	
• Teaching Transparency Master 1-3, pp. 9, 10	*Teaching Transparency 1-3*
• Quiz 1-3, pp. 27–28	*Assessment Items, Audiocassette 7A/Audio CD 1*
Videodisc Guide	*Videodisc Program, Videodisc 1A*

Alternative Assessment

- Performance Assessment
  Primer paso, p. 25
  Segundo paso, p. 30
  Tercer paso, p. 35
- Portfolio Assessment
  Written: **Repaso,** Activity 7, *Pupil's Edition,* p. 39
  Assessment Guide, p. 14
  Oral: **Repaso,** Activity 8, *Pupil's Edition,* p. 39
  Assessment Guide, p. 14

Native Speaker Diagnostic Test
An informal diagnostic test to determine the skill level of native speakers is available in the *Native Speaker Activity Book,* pages 1–5

Capítulo 1: ¡Mucho gusto!
Textbook Listening Activities Scripts

For Student Response Forms, see *Chapter Teaching Resources, Book 1,* pp. 20–22.

Primer paso

Activity 6, p. 21

1. —Hasta luego, Miguel Ángel. Tengo que irme.
   —¡Chao, Alicia!
2. —Hola, Santiago.
   —¿Qué tal, Miguel Ángel?
3. —Buenos días, don Alonso.
   —Hola, Miguel Ángel.
4. —Adiós, Mariana.
   —Sí, hasta mañana, Miguel Ángel.
5. —Buenas tardes, doña Luisa. ¿Cómo está?
   —Buenas tardes. Estoy bien, gracias.
6. —Bueno, tengo clase.
   —¡Hasta luego, Polo!

Answers to Activity 6

1. leaving	3. arriving	5. leaving
2. arriving	4. leaving	6. leaving

Activity 9, p. 23

1. Mucho gusto.
2. Me llamo Abel. ¿Y tú? ¿Cómo te llamas?
3. Éste es mi amigo. Se llama Felipe.
4. Ésta es Evita, la estudiante del programa internacional.
5. Encantada.
6. Soy la señora Rivas.
7. Mucho gusto.

Possible answers to Activity 9

1. ¡Mucho gusto!	4. Mucho gusto.
2. Mucho gusto. Me llamo [*name*].	5. Igualmente.
	6. ¡Mucho gusto!
3. ¡Mucho gusto!; Encantado(a).	7. ¡Mucho gusto!; Igualmente.

Activity 13, p. 24

1. SARA ¿Cómo estás, Daniel?
   DANIEL Ay, muy mal.
2. SARA ¿Qué tal, Marta?
   MARTA Más o menos, Sara. ¿Y tú?
3. SARA Buenos días, Elena. ¿Cómo estás?
   ELENA Estoy muy bien, gracias, Sara.
4. SARA Hola, José Luis. ¿Qué tal?
   JOSÉ LUIS Pues, muy bien, Sara. ¿Y tú?
5. SARA Buenas tardes, Carlos. ¿Cómo estás?
   CARLOS ¡Excelente!
6. SARA ¿Qué tal, Juan?
   JUAN Pues, estoy muy mal, amiga, muy mal.

Answers to Activity 13

bien	regular	mal
Elena	Felipe	Daniel
José Luis	Marta	Juan
Carlos		

Segundo paso

Activity 18, p. 28

DANIEL Ésta es Marisa y tiene catorce años. Éste es José.
ARIANA ¿Cuántos años tiene?
DANIEL Tiene seis años.
ARIANA ¿Y éste? ¿Cómo se llama?
DANIEL Es David. Tiene once años.
ARIANA ¿Y ésta?
DANIEL Se llama Anita. Tiene veinticinco años.
ARIANA ¿Y éste?
DANIEL ¡Éste es Daniel! ¡Sí, soy yo! En esta foto tengo un año.

Answers to Activity 18

a. Marisa—14	c. David—11	e. Daniel—1
b. José—6	d. Anita—25	

Activity 21, p. 29

1. —¿Cómo se llama?
   —Se llama Gabriela y es de Buenos Aires, Argentina.
2. —¿Y ésta es Maricarmen?
   —Sí, es Maricarmen y es de Santiago de Chile.
3. —¿De dónde es David?
   —David es de Madrid, España.
4. —¿Cómo te llamas?
   —Mi nombre es Antonio y soy de Quito, Ecuador.
5. —¿Y tú? Eres Laura, ¿verdad?
   —Sí, Laura Alicia, encantada. Yo soy de San José, Costa Rica.
6. —¿De dónde es Pedro?
   —Pedro es de Santa Fe de Bogotá, Colombia.

Answers to Activity 21

1. Gabriela es de Argentina.
2. Maricarmen es de Chile.
3. David es de España.
4. Antonio es de Ecuador.
5. Laura es de Costa Rica.
6. Pedro es de Colombia.

Tercer paso

Activity 29, p. 32

CARLOS ¿Te gusta el voleibol?
ELENA Bueno, no. No me gusta mucho.
CARLOS ¿Te gusta la pizza?
ELENA No, no me gusta.
CARLOS Oye, ¿te gusta la música pop?
ELENA Pues, no me gusta.
CARLOS Bueno, entonces, ¿qué te gusta?
ELENA A ver... ¿te gusta la comida mexicana?
CARLOS Sí, me gusta.
ELENA ¡Estupendo! A mí también me gusta. ¿Te gusta el restaurante Taco Paco?
CARLOS Mmm..., no, no me gusta mucho.
ELENA Ah, bueno...

Answers to Activity 29

Likes	*Doesn't like*
la comida mexicana	el voleibol
	la pizza
	la música pop

Elena and Carlos should eat Mexican food together.

Activity 32, p. 33

AMIGO ¿Te gustan los deportes?
DIANA Sí, me gusta el béisbol. Y me gusta mucho el tenis. No me gusta mucho el golf.
AMIGO Bueno, y ¿qué comida te gusta?
DIANA Mmm, no me gusta la fruta. Me gusta la comida italiana. Y la ensalada. ¡Me gusta mucho la ensalada!
AMIGO Y a ti te gusta bastante la música, ¿verdad?
DIANA Sí, me gusta la música pero no me gusta el jazz. Me gusta más la música rock.

Answers to Activity 32

Likes	*Dislikes*
el béisbol	el golf
el tenis	la fruta
la ensalada	el jazz
la comida italiana	
la música rock	

Letra y sonido, p. 35

For the scripts for Parts A and C, see p. 35. The dialogue for Part B is below.

B. Dictado

— Buenos días, Marta. ¿Qué tal?
— Muy bien, Ana. ¿Cómo estás?
— Bien. Bueno, tengo que irme.
— Hasta luego.
— Chao.

Repaso

Activity 1, p. 38

MODELO Me llamo Mariana Castillo. Soy de España. Tengo quince años y me gusta mucho la música pop. No me gusta el tenis.

— Hola. Me llamo Liliana Rivera. Soy de Santiago de Chile y tengo dieciséis años. Me gusta mucho el tenis pero no me gusta hacer la tarea.

— Hola, ¿qué tal? Soy Pablo García. Soy de Monterrey, México y tengo quince años. Me gusta mucho el inglés. No me gusta la música clásica, pero la música rock, sí.

Capítulo 1: ¡Mucho gusto!
Projects

In this activity students will create picture collages of themselves with which to introduce themselves, state how old they are, and show some of their favorite things.

MATERIALS

✂ **Students may need**

- Poster board
- Glue
- Old magazines
- Scissors
- Tape
- Photos

SEQUENCE

1. Working individually, students start by making a list in English of what things they like and don't like. Students can refer to the dictionary on pp. 348–361 and the Additional Vocabulary on pp. 340–342 for Spanish equivalents.
2. Students plan how they can visually present who they are, especially their likes and dislikes.
3. Students find pictures in magazines or make their own drawings that illustrate their likes and dislikes, and then they start writing in Spanish. Students should mount their illustrations around the text on a large sheet of paper, using paper clips or small pieces of removable tape to hold the illustrations in place until they decide on the final layout.
4. Students write their text in Spanish and then ask another student to check it.
5. Students edit a partner's text.
6. Finally, students arrange their illustrations with the appropriate text.

GRADING THE PROJECT

For an oral grade, have students cover the Spanish text on their project and introduce themselves to their classmates in Spanish, stating their name, how old they are, and some of the things they like and dislike as they show their collages.

For a written grade, you might collect the projects and grade them, or you might have them all displayed around the classroom, giving you time to evaluate and grade each one.

Suggested point distribution (total = 100 points):

Completion of all steps	15
Self-Edit	15
Peer-Edit	15
Visual presentation	15
Accuracy of Spanish	40

NOTE

After—or instead of—grading these projects, you might suggest to students that they place them in their Portfolio (see pp. T52–T53). If the projects are for the Portfolio, tell them beforehand to save the notes they made in English, the first draft of the Spanish text, and also the final draft of the Spanish.

FAMILY LINK

Students might show their projects to a family member or a friend who is not taking Spanish. Ask students if they are able to make themselves understood by showing the pictures and the text to someone else.

Capítulo 1: ¡Mucho gusto!
Games

On this page you will find suggestions for games in which students practice some of the functions, structures, vocabulary, and cultural features studied in Chapter 1. When planning your lessons for this chapter, remember that games such as these not only make the students' classroom experience more enjoyable, they are also effective in motivating students to practice and review.

¿DÓNDE ESTÁ?

The objective of this game is to familiarize students with Spanish-speaking countries and their major cities. This may be played after the **Panorama cultural** on page 31.

Materials You will need a wall map of the world or a globe, folded slips of paper, and a container for the slips of paper.

Procedure On each slip of paper, write the name of a major city or county in which Spanish is spoken. Divide the class into two teams, Team A and Team B. Choose one student to be the scorekeeper. A member of Team A draws a name from the container and says to a member of Team B, **¿Dónde está** ______? A member of Team B must point to the country or city on the map; if he or she is successful, Team B receives a point. If he or she is unsuccessful, the turn goes to Team A. If successful, Team A receives the point. If neither is successful, then the teacher or another student supplies the correct information. Team B then draws a new slip of paper and the game continues. The team with the most points wins.

¿QUÉ TE GUSTA?

This word scramble is a quick vocabulary review. Play to review vocabulary presented in Chapter 1.

Procedure Students unscramble seven words from the chapter vocabulary list to find the answer to the question, **¿Qué te gusta?** Students place one letter in each blank to form the words. Students then arrange the circled letters to unscramble the answer to the question, **¿Qué te gusta?**

ME GUSTA LA

◯ _ _ _ _ ZAZPI
_ _ _ _ ◯ ARFTU
_ _ _ _ ◯ _ _ _ NSAEALAD
_ _ _ _ _ _ ◯ _ _ _ STIVNIÓLEE
_ _ _ _ ◯ ESLAC
_ _ ◯ _ _ _ ANAMÑA
_ ◯ _ _ _ _ DCIMOA

SOLUCIÓN: ME GUSTA EL _ _ _ _ _ _ _ _.

Answers
PIZZA, FRUTA, ENSALADA, TELEVISIÓN, CLASE, MAÑANA, COMIDA, ESPAÑOL

PONGA

This game, which is played exactly like Bingo, gives students the opportunity to practice numbers in Spanish while enjoying a familiar game. Use it to practice the numbers on page 27.

Materials Each student will need an index card or piece of cardboard and a permanent ink pen.

Procedure Students prepare their own PONGA card by drawing a card similar to a Bingo card on a sheet of paper. Cards should have five horizontal spaces and five vertical spaces. Students write a number between zero and 30 in each space on the card. Read a number between zero and 30 in Spanish and record it. Students cover or cross off numbers as they are called. When a player has marked off an entire row of numbers, he or she says PONGA. He or she then reads the numbers back to the teacher in Spanish. If the numbers are correct, that student is the winner. You may want to laminate the cards and reuse them with future classes. Students can use paper scraps to cover the numbers (if they have been written on before lamination), or write with a water-based marker.

P	O	N	G	A
12	9	30	27	0
20	15	4	2	7
1	23	18	25	18
17	13	5	16	3

Capítulo 1
¡Mucho gusto!
pp. 16–41

Using the Chapter Opener

Motivating Activity

Ask students the following: What do you say to someone you've just met? What would you write in a letter introducing yourself to a new pen pal? What differences would there be between meeting someone face to face and introducing yourself in a letter?

Photo Flash!

These photos were taken in Madrid.

(1) Pilar and Eva are from the province of **Ciudad Real,** in the region of **Castilla-La Mancha.** The girls have just finished dancing a **jota,** a traditional Castilian dance. The girls danced in a city park in Madrid to a chorus of traditional songs sung by other park visitors. Such impromptu performances are not unusual in Spain, where many people learn the traditional songs and dances of their region as children.

(2) This photo shows a young woman using a public telephone, or **cabina telefónica,** in a shopping district of Madrid.

(3) This photo shows Paco, the protagonist of the **fotonovela,** and the "imaginary girl." Paco has subscribed to a pen pal service and he has just received the first letter from Mercedes, his new pen pal. After reading her letter, Paco falls asleep and dreams of a meeting with Mercedes (as he imagines her to be). In the dream they are both wearing volleyball outfits and eating pizza at a local pizza parlor.

CAPÍTULO 1
¡Mucho gusto!

(1) Me llamo Pilar. Soy de Ciudad Real. Ésta es mi amiga Eva.

16 *dieciséis*

Culture Notes

- In Spain and Latin America sidewalk cafés are popular with people of all ages.
- Soccer is very popular in most Spanish-speaking countries, and teams from Spanish-speaking countries are usually among the finalists competing for soccer's world championship, the World Cup (**la Copa Mundial**).

Language Note

The Spanish word for a restaurant that specializes in pizza is **pizzería.**

The start of a new school year means seeing old friends but also meeting new ones. What's the first day of school like for you? What things do you look forward to?

In this chapter you will learn

- to say hello and goodbye; to introduce people and respond to an introduction; to ask how someone is and say how you are
- to ask and say how old someone is; to ask where someone is from and say where you're from
- to talk about likes and dislikes

And you will

- listen as people introduce themselves and tell their names, ages, and where they're from
- read a *fotonovela* and a letter from a pen pal
- write a short letter introducing yourself to a pen pal
- find out how Spanish speakers greet one another and introduce themselves

(2) **Hola, soy yo. Soy Ana. ¿Qué tal?**

(3) **¿Te gusta la pizza?**

CHAPTER OPENER
CHAPTER 1

Focusing on Outcomes

- Have students read the list of outcomes for this chapter, then have them match each of the first three outcomes to a photo. (Photo 1 represents introductions, photo 2 represents saying hello and asking how someone is, photo 3 represents talking about likes and dislikes.)
- Have students identify as many English expressions as possible to say hello and goodbye. When would they use each expression? What gesture (if any) do they use with these greetings? (a handshake, a kiss, a hug)

Thinking Critically

Observing Ask students if they can tell from the background where each photo might have been taken. (restaurant, park, city street) What in the photos provides clues to where they were taken?

For Individual Needs

Slower Pace Ask students: What do you think the people in the photo are eating? How and what would you order?

Challenge Have your students create an imaginary dialogue between the people in the photo. Name and describe them. What character traits do they have?

Multicultural Link

(2) Ask students to guess what the girl in this photo is saying and to whom she's speaking. Ask students why someone might need to make telephone calls from a telephone booth. Point out that although almost every household in the U.S. has a telephone, telephone service in Spain and Latin America is much more expensive and fewer people have telephones. In some countries, a family may be on a waiting list for two to six years before getting service.

VIDEO PROGRAM OR EXPANDED VIDEO PROGRAM, Videocassette 1

OR VIDEODISC PROGRAM, Videodisc 1A

Video Synopsis

Paco is looking out the window of his family's apartment, watching for Ramón, the mail carrier. Paco hopes Ramón is bringing a letter from his new pen pal. Paco sees Ramón coming and runs through his parents' grocery store, on the ground floor. Paco bumps into his mother, apologizes, and goes to get the letter. The mailman pretends not to have a letter for Paco because the letter is addressed to "Francisco," Paco's full name. Back in his room, Paco reads the letter and daydreams about his pen pal. Then Paco's friend Felipe stops by for a visit.

Motivating Activities

- Ask students if they have ever anxiously awaited a call or letter. How did they feel?
- Ask students if they have ever had a pen pal. Would they like to write to someone in a Spanish-speaking country?

Teaching Suggestion

Refer to page T56 for names and addresses of pen pal organizations. Have students begin corresponding with a pen pal at the beginning of the school year. Maintain the correspondence through assignments throughout the year.

DE ANTEMANO *Beforehand*

¡Me llamo Francisco! *My name is Francisco!*

Look at the characters in the **fotonovela,** or photo story. Where are they? What are their occupations? What do you think they're talking about? What do you suppose will happen in the story?

Paco

Felipe

Ramón

18

RESOURCES FOR DE ANTEMANO

Textbook Audiocassette 1A/Audio CD 1
Practice and Activity Book, p. 3
Video Guide
Video Program
Expanded Video Program, Videocassette 1
Videodisc Guide
Videodisc Program, Videodisc 1A

5

Madrid 3 de Septiembre

¡Hola Francisco!
Me llamo Mercedes Margarita Alvarez García y soy de Madrid. Tengo 15 años. Me gusta la pizza y me gusta mucho el voleibol. ¿Cuántos años tienes? ¿Qué te gusta a ti?

Mercedes

Sr. Francisco Xavier López Medina
C/Echegaray 21. 1.º D
28014 Madrid

6

¡Sí, señor! ¡Una carta de Mercedes! ¡Una chica fantástica!

¡Paco! ¡Paco! Está aquí tu amigo, Felipe.

7

Hola, Paco. ¿Qué tal?

Excelente. ¿Y tú?

8

Oye, ¿qué es eso?

Es una carta... de una chica.

9

¿Una chica? ¿Cómo se llama?

Felipe, es un secreto.

Paco, soy tu amigo. Por favor... cuéntame.

Bueno... mira...

19

Presentation

Ask students to guess what's happening. Who are the people pictured? What is their relationship?

Play the video or audio recording once. Discuss each picture; ask students what they understand. Model pronunciation and have students repeat after you. Read through the entire dialogue, having students guess the meaning from context.

Point out that **pizza** and **voleibol** are cognates (words that are similar in two languages, such as **voleibol** and *volleyball*). Tell students that looking and listening for cognates will help their comprehension. Play the video or audio recording a second time, then break the class into pairs for students to practice reading the dialogues and role-playing the parts of the different characters. As you circulate, check pronunciation.

Teaching Suggestion

(5) Ask students whether the handwriting in the letter looks unusual. Mention that handwriting styles differ from country to country. Ask them to name the letters that are hardest for them to recognize.

For Individual Needs

(5) **Challenge** Using the letter as a model, have students write a similar letter about themselves or an alter ego.

Language Note

Characters in the video episode for this chapter speak with a Spanish accent. Point out to students that they will have an opportunity through the Video Program to hear a variety of authentic accents from at least nine locations around the Spanish speaking world.

Video Integration

- ***Expanded Video Program,*** *Videocassette 1*
- ***Videodisc Program,*** *Videodisc 1A*

You may choose to continue with **¡Me llamo Francisco! (a continuación)** at this time or wait until later in the chapter. At this point in the story, Paco and Felipe go to meet Mercedes, Paco's pen pal. She arrives at the **pizzería** with her friend Juanita. Paco and Mercedes know each other from school as **Paco** and **Merche.** After some awkward moments, they realize that they are one another's pen pal under their full names—**Francisco** and **Mercedes.**

Teaching Suggestions

1 Allow approximately five minutes for pairs to prepare answers to the questions. Review with the entire class.

3 You may have asked students to write the expressions in Activity 3. In early stages of language acquisition, copying is a valid writing activity. Assure students that it is normal for the productive skills of speaking and writing to develop more slowly than the receptive skills of listening and reading. Allow time for students to develop their passive skills before asking them to speak and write. Not all students will develop their productive skills at the same pace.

5 After reading the **Nota cultural,** ask for volunteers to say what their last name would be if they used this naming convention. To create a comfortable and non-threatening atmosphere, it is especially important to ask only for volunteers to provide such personal examples.

1 ¿Comprendes? *Do you understand?*

How well do you understand what is happening in the **fotonovela**? Check by answering these questions. Don't be afraid to guess.

1. Who are the people in the **fotonovela**? Make a list of them. How are they related to Paco? Paco, his mother, his grandmother, his friend Felipe, and the mail carrier.
2. Why does Paco run out of the store? To see if the mail carrier has a letter for him.
3. What do you know about the family business? the family's home? They operate a fruit stand; the grandmother lives with them.
4. What do you think will happen next? Paco will tell Felipe about his new pen pal.

2 ¿Cierto o falso? *True or false?*

Based on the **fotonovela,** decide whether each statement is **cierto** *(true)* or **falso** *(false)*. If it's false, change one or two words to make it true.

1. La carta es de *(from)* Felipe. Falso, la carta es de Mercedes.
2. El nombre completo de Paco es Francisco Xavier López Medina. Cierto.
3. Felipe es el papá de *(of)* Paco. Falso, Felipe es el amigo de Paco.
4. Mercedes es de Toledo. Falso, Mercedes es de Madrid.
5. A Mercedes le gusta mucho el voleibol. Cierto.

NOTA CULTURAL

You might think Francisco Xavier López Medina is an unusually long name. Actually, Spaniards and Latin Americans commonly use both their first and middle names. They also generally use two last names: first the father's (in Paco's case, López) and then the mother's maiden name (for Paco, it's Medina). In the phone book, Paco's name would be listed under "L" as **López Medina.**

3 Cortesías *Courtesies* See answers below.

What Spanish phrases do the characters in the **fotonovela** use to say the following.

1. Hello.
2. Good morning!
3. I like volleyball.
4. My name is . . .
5. Thank you.
6. Goodbye.

4 ¡Soy yo! *It's me!*

Fill in the blanks in this passage with words or expressions from the **fotonovela.** See answers below.

PACO ¿Hay una __1__ para mí?
RAMÓN No, ésta no es. Esta carta es para __2__.
PACO ¡__3__ yo! ¡Soy __4__! ¡Yo __5__ Francisco! ¡Gracias! __6__ , ¿eh?
RAMÓN __7__, señor Francisco Xavier López Medina.

5 ¿Y tú?

What would your name be if you used both your father's and your mother's last names? Where would it be listed in the phone book? Answers will vary.

LOPEZ - 89

LOPEZ MATEOS, N. - Galileo, 21	248 9093
» **MATEOS, J.** - Alonso Cano, 33	730 1883
» **MATUTE, R.** - Giralda, 204	775 8964
» **MAYORAL, C.** - Palencia, 101	263 3276
» **MAYORAL, A.** - Luis Buñuel, 12	437 1806
» **MEDIAVILLA, P.** - Embajadores, 78	711 8419
LOPEZ MEDINA, A. - Av. S. Eloy, 301	472 4932
» **MEDINA, R.** - Amor Hermoso, 69	326 3771
» **MEDINA, F.** - Echegaray, 21	775 8964
» **MEDINA, T.** - Av. Valle, 35	464 7691
» **MEDRANO, A.** - Cerro Blanco, 14	558 2220
LOPEZ MEGIA, J. - Bolivia, 35	471 4936
» **MEIRA, L.** - Libertad, 45	792 2039

Answers

3
1. Hola.
2. Buenos días.
3. Me gusta mucho el voleibol.
4. Me llamo...
5. Gracias.
6. Hasta luego.

4
1. carta
2. el señor Francisco Xavier López Medina
3. Soy
4. yo
5. me llamo
6. Hasta luego
7. Adiós

PRIMER PASO

Saying hello and goodbye; introducing people and responding to an introduction; asking how someone is and saying how you are

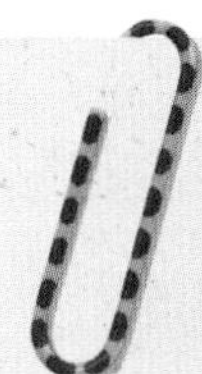

ASÍ SE DICE *Here's how you say it*

To greet someone, say:

¡Hola! *Hello!*

Buenos días, señor.
Good morning, sir.

Buenas tardes, señorita.
Good afternoon, miss.

Buenas noches, señora.
Good evening, ma'am.

To say goodbye to someone, say:

Adiós.	*Goodbye.*
Bueno, tengo clase.	*Well, I have class.*
Chao.	*'Bye.*
Hasta luego.	*See you later.*
Hasta mañana.	*See you tomorrow.*
Tengo que irme.	*I have to go.*

6 Escuchemos: Una recepción *Let's listen: A reception*

You're at an all-day open house celebration at Miguel Ángel's house. As you listen, decide whether the person is arriving or leaving. Answers on p.11C.

MODELO —¡Hola, Miguel Ángel!
—Buenos días, señora de López. *(Mrs. López is arriving.)*

1. Alicia
2. Santiago
3. don Alonso
4. Mariana
5. doña Luisa
6. David

NOTA CULTURAL

Spanish speakers often greet each other with a handshake or a kiss. In Spain, friends may greet each other with a light kiss on both cheeks. Latin Americans kiss on only one cheek. When men greet each other, they often shake hands, pat each other on the back, or hug. Young people often shake hands when they meet or say goodbye. Family members usually greet each other with a kiss.

Resources for PRIMER PASO

Textbook Audiocassette 1A/Audio CD 1
Practice and Activity Book, pp. 4–6
Native Speaker Activity Book, pp. 1–5
Videodisc Guide
Videodisc Program, Videodisc 1A

Chapter Teaching Resources, Book 1
- Additional Listening Activities 1-1, 1-2, p. 11
  Audiocassette 10A/Audio CD 1
- Student Response Forms, p. 20
- Realia 1-1, pp. 15, 17
- Situation Cards 1-1, pp. 18, 19
- Teaching Transparency Master 1-1, pp. 7, 10
  Teaching Transparency 1-1
- Quiz 1-1, pp. 23–24
  Audiocassette 7A/Audio CD 1

Jump Start!

Have students refer to the **fotonovela** on pages 18–19 and write all of the expressions they can find to greet someone and to say goodbye.

MOTIVATE

Ask pairs of student volunteers to demonstrate in front of the class how they greet people. Have them do this in several situations as if they were greeting close friends of the same or opposite sex, parents, grandparents, the school principal, a small child, a new student in school.

TEACH

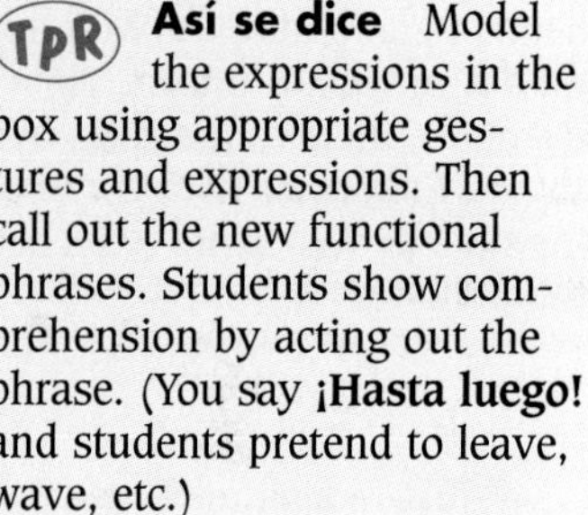

Presentation

TPR **Así se dice** Model the expressions in the box using appropriate gestures and expressions. Then call out the new functional phrases. Students show comprehension by acting out the phrase. (You say **¡Hasta luego!** and students pretend to leave, wave, etc.)

Teaching Suggestion

6 Use the Student Response Form for this activity, or have students number 1–6 on a separate sheet of paper.

Discuss the value of being a good listener both for language learning and as a general life skill. Play the recording, then verify answers with students. Play the recording again and have students repeat the Spanish. Encourage them to imitate the pronunciation they hear on the recording as closely as possible.

Teaching Suggestion

7 Ask students to work in pairs. Have them come up with as many **saludos** and **despedidas** as they can, referring to what they've learned so far.

Native Speakers

Ask native speakers to share a few other **saludos** and **despedidas** that they use.

Presentation

Así se dice Walk around the room greeting various students, using the suggested greetings. Encourage students to respond using the appropriate expression. Do a quick activity asking several students **¿Cómo te llamas?** As they respond, shake each student's hand and reply **¡Mucho gusto!** or **Encantado/a.** Then introduce them to the class by saying **Éste es** or **Ésta es.** Ask for student volunteers to model the phrases.

For videodisc application, see *Videodisc Guide.*

7 Saludos y despedidas *Hellos and goodbyes* Possible answers below.

How would you greet or say goodbye to the following people? How would they respond to your greetings? Choose your expressions from **Así se dice** on page 21.

a.

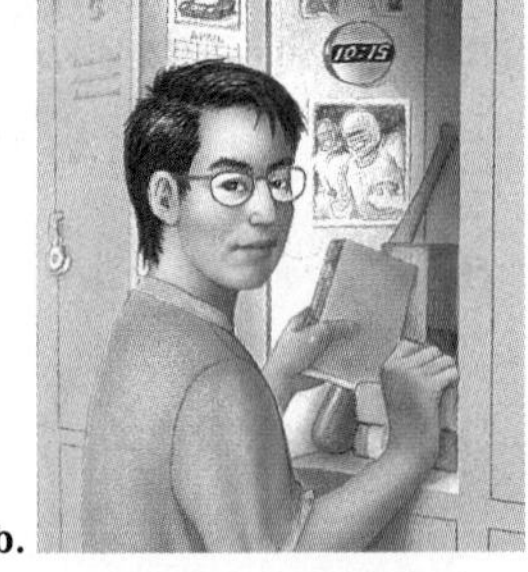

b.

c.

d.

e.

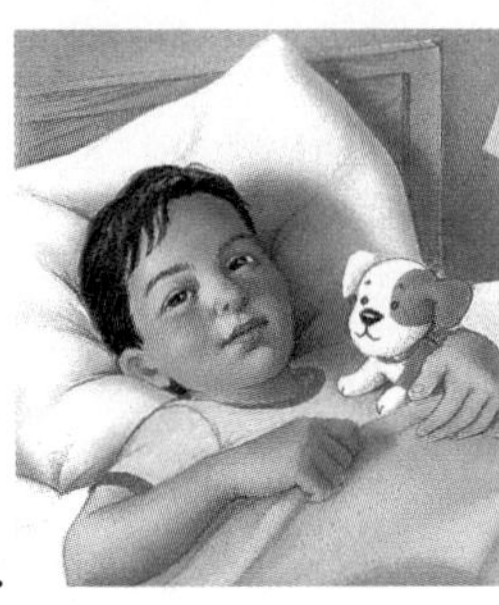
f.

8 Entre clases *Between classes* Sample answer below.

Work with a partner. Imagine you just ran into each other in the hall between classes. Greet each other briefly. Then tell your partner you have to go, and say goodbye. Switch roles and replay the conversation, this time using different expressions.

ASÍ SE DICE *Here's how you say it*

Introducing people and responding to an introduction

To introduce yourself, say:

Me llamo... *My name is . . .*

Soy... *I am . . .*

¿Y tú? ¿Cómo te llamas? *And you? What's your name?*

To introduce others, say:

Éste es mi amigo... *This is my (male) friend . . .*

Ésta es mi amiga... *This is my (female) friend . . .*

Se llama... *His/Her name is . . .*

To respond to an introduction, say:

¡Mucho gusto! *Nice to meet you!*

Encantado/a.* *Delighted to meet you.*

Igualmente. *Same here.*

*If you're male, use **Encantado.** If you're female, use **Encantada.** You'll learn more about masculine and feminine endings in Chapter 2.

Answers

7 *Possible answers:*

a. Buenos días, señorita; Buenos días.
b. ¡Hola!; ¡Hola!; Bueno, tengo clase.
c. Buenas tardes, señor; Buenas tardes.
d. Adiós; Hasta mañana.
e. Adiós, Chao; Hasta luego; Hasta mañana; Tengo que irme.
f. Buenas noches; Buenas noches; Hasta mañana.

8 *Sample answer:*

—Sí, tengo clase. ¡Adiós!; —Hasta luego.

9 Escuchemos: ¿Cómo respondes? *Let's listen: How do you respond?*

Look over the **Así se dice** section on page 22. Then, listen as some people at a party introduce themselves to you. Respond with one or two appropriate phrases.
Answers on p.11C.

10 Mini-situaciones

What would you say in the following situations? First find the expressions you need in **Así se dice**. Then, with a partner, act out each mini-situation. *Possible answers:* 1. ¡Mucho gusto!; Hola; Me llamo...

1. A friend introduces you to a new student.
2. You want to ask the person sitting next to you what his or her name is. ¿Cómo te llamas?
3. You've just been introduced to your new Spanish teacher. Mucho gusto.
4. You want to tell the new classmate who you are. Me llamo...; Soy...
5. Your new counselor has just said **"Mucho gusto."** ¡Mucho gusto!; Encantado/a.
6. You want to introduce your friend Ana to another classmate. Ésta es mi amiga, Ana.

Nota Gramatical

Have you noticed that Spanish uses upside-down punctuation marks to begin a question (¿) and an exclamation (¡)? An accent mark is sometimes needed over a vowel (**á, é, í, ó, ú**), usually to show which syllable is stressed. The mark on the **ñ** (as in **mañana**) is called the *tilde*. It indicates the sound *ny* as in *canyon*. How many of these new punctuation marks can you find in the **Así se dice** sections on pages 21 and 22? All of them.

11 Te presento a...

May I introduce you to . . .

A friend wants to introduce someone to you. Choose your responses from the expressions you've learned. Some blanks may have more than one possible answer.

TU AMIGO	Hola.
TÚ	__1__. ¡Hola!
TU AMIGO	Ésta es mi amiga, Patricia.
TÚ	__2__, Patricia. Mucho gusto
PATRICIA	Igualmente. Eh, perdón. ¿Cómo te __3__, por favor? llamas
TÚ	Me __4__ __5__. llamo [student's name]
TU AMIGO	Bueno, __6__ clase. Tengo que irme. tengo
TÚ	Hasta __7__. mañana/luego
PATRICIA	__8__. Chao

NOTA CULTURAL

Common first names among Spanish speakers are **José María** and **Juan Pablo** for males, **María José** and **Magdalena** for females. Many girls' names originally commemorated the Virgin Mary: **María del Pilar, María del Socorro, Ana María.** Roman Catholics often celebrate not only their birthdays, but also the feast day of the saint they are named after. For example, Susana might celebrate her **Día del Santo**, or *Saint's Day*, on August 11 in honor of St. Susan.

agosto

DOM	LUN	MAR	MIER	JUE	VIER	SAB
1 Sta. Esperanza	2 N.S. de los Ang.	3 Sta. Lydia	4 Sto. Domingo de G.	5 San Emigdio	6 San Justo	7 San Cayetano
8 San Emiliano	9 San Román	10 Sta. Paula	11 Sta. Susana	12 Sta. Clara	13 Sta. Aurora	14 Sta. Eusebia

Presentation

Nota gramatical Point out to students that the inverted question and exclamation marks used in Spanish signal the tone of a sentence before you start to read it. Explain that Spanish accent marks are part of the spelling of the words and that accent marks sometimes change the meaning of a word (**qué** = *what* vs. **que** = *that*).

Teacher Note

10 This pair-work activity should be done orally. Allow approximately three minutes for students to complete this activity.

For Individual Needs

10 Challenge Have students create their own dialogues and perform them for the class. They should change the setting. (school, home, outside, in a mall) After a pair has presented their dialogue, ask the class to paraphrase what was said.

Teaching Suggestion

11 For additional practice, students can go back to the **Así se dice** sections and copy words and phrases or make picture flash cards. As a follow-up, or to correct the activity, have groups of three read the completed dialogue to the class.

Game

PASSWORD® Use picture flash cards to play a game like Password®. Stand at the door and show an illustration to students as they pretend to leave class. They must each tell you the appropriate word or phrase in Spanish before they can leave. Change the picture after every student, shuffling the used cards to the back of your pile.

Presentation

Así se dice Model these expressions, and have students repeat after you, imitating your gestures. (**regular**—thumb up; **horrible**—thumb down; **más o menos**—hand rocking side to side with palm down; **estupendo** and **excelente**—emphatic gestures) Then have students pair off and practice asking and answering how they're doing, using the appropriate gestures while practicing the expressions.

For Individual Needs

Visual Learners

- Use gestures or sketch visual cues on index cards to represent each functional phrase. Have students call out the phrase as you perform the gesture or show the card.
- If students are developing their own word box, they should make cards representing these phrases. They can use the cards to verify comprehension and also for pair and small-group practice.

Cooperative Learning

13 Divide the class into groups of three. Assign one student to be the scribe and two to be performers. Each group should agree on the correct responses to the items in Activity 13. The group should make up a conversation, combining several of the verbal exchanges in an original dialogue. The students assigned to perform may use cue cards in presenting to the class. Each member of the group should be assigned the same grade based on the group's written responses and performance.

12 Nuevos amigos *New friends*

Role-play the following conversation with a classmate using expressions from **Así se dice** on page 22. If you'd like to use a Spanish name or nickname, choose one from the list on page 5. *Possible conversation:*

ESTUDIANTE 1 *Greet your classmate.* Hola; Buenos días; Buenas tardes.
ESTUDIANTE 2 *Respond and introduce yourself.* Buenos días, soy...; Hola, me llamo...
ESTUDIANTE 1 *Say "nice to meet you" and introduce yourself.* Mucho gusto, soy...; Encantado/a, me llamo...
ESTUDIANTE 2 *Respond to the introduction.* ¡Mucho gusto!; Igualmente.
ESTUDIANTE 1 *Say you have class now.* Bueno, tengo clase.
ESTUDIANTE 2 *Say that you also have class and say goodbye.* Tengo clase también, adiós.
ESTUDIANTE 1 *Say that you'll see your new friend tomorrow.* Hasta mañana.

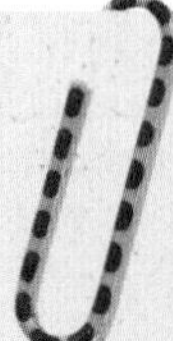

ASÍ SE DICE *Here's how you say it*

Asking how someone is and saying how you are

To find out how a friend is, ask:

¿Cómo estás? *How are you?*
¿Y tú? *And you?*
¿Qué tal? *How's it going?*

Your friend might say:

Estoy (bastante) bien, gracias. *I'm (pretty) well, thanks.*
Yo también. *Me too.*
Estupendo. *Great.*
Excelente. *Great.*
Regular. *Okay.*
Más o menos. *So-so.*
(Muy) mal. *(Very) bad.*
¡Horrible! *Horrible!*

13 Escuchemos: ¿Cómo estás?

As each friend tells Sara how he or she is, write the person's name under the appropriate heading. Answers on p.11C.

MODELO Buenas tardes, Felipe. ¿Qué tal?
Regular, gracias. ¿Y tú?

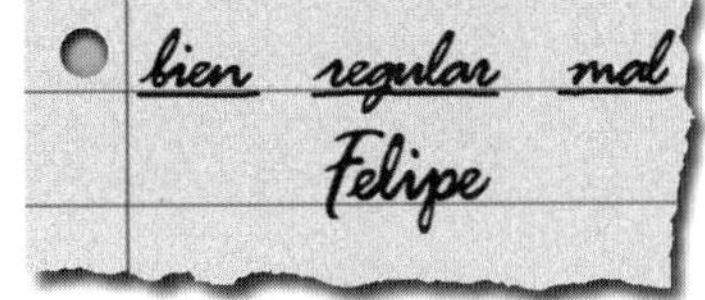

14 ¿Cómo contestas? *How do you answer?*

How would you answer the following? Select your responses from the expressions you've learned.

1. ¡Hola! ¿Qué tal? See possible answers below.
2. Ésta es mi amiga Charín.
3. ¿Cómo estás?
4. Soy Eduardo Robledo. ¿Y tú?
5. ¡Hasta luego!

In Spanish, there are many ways to ask a person how he or she is doing. Throughout Spain and Latin America you will hear **¿Qué pasa?** *(What's happening?)* and **¿Qué hay?/¿Qué tal?** *(What's up?)* In Mexico, you'll also hear **¿Qué hubo?** or **¿Qué onda?**

Answers

14 *Possible answers:*

1. Bien, gracias.
2. Mucho gusto, Charín.
3. Regular.
4. Me llamo *(name)*.
5. Adiós.

Gramática Subject pronouns tú and yo

1. Use the pronoun **yo** to refer to yourself. In Spanish, **yo** *(I)* is not capitalized, except at the beginning of a sentence. Use **tú** *(you)* when you're talking to another student, a friend, or to someone who is about your own age. Notice that **tú** has an accent.
2. In Chapter 4 you'll learn a different pronoun to use when speaking to someone older than you or when you want to be polite to a stranger. You'll also discover that subject pronouns like these aren't used as often in Spanish as in English.
3. How many expressions can you find in the preceding **Así se dice** sections where the pronoun **yo** is implied but not stated? [1]

15 ¿Tú o yo?

Which pronoun (**tú** or **yo**) is implied but not stated in each sentence?

1. ¿Cómo te llamas? tú
2. Me llamo Mercedes Margarita. yo
3. Soy Francisco. yo
4. ¿Cómo estás, Francisco? tú
5. Estoy bien, gracias. yo

16 Charla *Chitchat*

Mercedes is talking to a new classmate. Using words or phrases you've learned, write their conversation.

MERCEDES *greets her friend*
ELENA *responds and introduces her friend Pedro*
MERCEDES *says it is nice to meet Pedro*
PEDRO *responds and asks Mercedes how she is*
MERCEDES *responds and says she has class*
ELENA *says she also has to go now*
ALL *say goodbye*

Sample answer below.

17 Mini-drama

The two teens in the photo have just been introduced to each other by a friend. Together with two partners, role-play the three students. You may use the conversation you created in Activity 16. Be creative and change the dialogue as needed to suit your group.

[1] **Yo** is implied in: **(Yo) me llamo...**, **(Yo) estoy bien, mal...**, and in **(Yo) soy...**

Answers

16 *Sample answer:*

MERCEDES: ¡Hola Elena! ¿Qué tal?
ELENA: Muy bien, Mercedes. Éste es mi amigo Pedro.
MERCEDES: Mucho gusto, Pedro.
PEDRO: Igualmente. ¿Cómo estás?
MERCEDES: Muy bien, gracias, pero tengo clase.
ELENA: Sí, yo tengo que irme.
TODOS: ¡Adiós! ¡Hasta luego!

Presentation

Gramática Present subject pronouns with a Total Physical Response (TPR) activity. Give several sentences with either **tú** or **yo**. Students point to themselves whenever you say **yo**, and to another student as you say **tú**. Point out the accent mark on **tú**.

Teacher Suggestion

17 Allow time for students to prepare and practice the mini-drama. Circulate among the groups to check pronunciation and language.

For Individual Needs

17 Challenge Ask groups to perform their mini-drama for the rest of the class.

Close

To close this **Paso**, have students answer these questions: How do you say hello in Spanish? good morning? good afternoon? good evening?

Assess

Quiz 1-1, *Chapter Teaching Resources, Book 1,* pp. 23–24

Assessment Items, Audiocassette 7A/Audio CD 1

Performance Assessment

Hand pairs of students a three- to four-line situation written in English to practice one of the functional expressions learned in the **Primer paso.** *(One of you take the role of Mr. Villanueva, and the other the teenager, Gabriela. Greet each other as if it were three in the afternoon.)* Allow students one minute to prepare and then act out the situation in Spanish. You can do this with small groups while other students are working on a separate activity.

Presentation

Before students read this page, have two volunteers participate in a demonstration. Have them stand facing each other as they would if they were having a conversation. Measure the distance between them with a measuring tape. Then have the students move closer together until they begin to feel uncomfortable. Measure the distance again. Compare these distances with the interpersonal distance of Spanish-speakers from Spain and Latin America in photos throughout the book. Then have students read the **Encuentro.**

Thinking Critically

Comparing and Contrasting Encourage students to focus on cultural similarities as well as on differences. How does the information in the **Encuentro cultural** compare with what they observe in their own families, or in other countries they have visited or studied? Emphasize that cultural differences are natural and not necessarily good or bad.

ENCUENTRO CULTURAL

La distancia interpersonal

In a Spanish-speaking country, you may encounter differences in "interpersonal distance," or the distance people keep from each other when they are together. Answer these questions to see if you can keep the right distance in various settings.

Para discutir...

1. You're sitting on a crowded bus. When one more passenger gets on, you should . . .
   a. move over and make room for the newcomer, even if it means rubbing shoulders with the person next to you.
   b. keep your place and avoid touching your neighbor.

2. You're standing on the street corner talking to a close friend. Your friend will probably expect you to stand
   a. about an arm's length away.
   b. close enough to allow your friend to touch you without reaching.

Vamos a comprenderlo

1. (a) Buses are often crowded, and people expect to squeeze together. This may take some getting used to!
2. (b) Generally, Spanish speakers stand and sit closer to one another than most people in the United States do. Your Spanish-speaking friend might think you're a little bit unfriendly if you stand too far away.

Remember that there is seldom a single right answer in questions of etiquette. A good rule to follow in a new country is to watch what others do and let them take the lead in unfamiliar situations. As is said in Spanish, **Adónde fueras, haz lo que vieras.** *Wherever you go, do as you see. (When in Rome, do as the Romans do.)*

26

Multicultural Links

- Edwin Hall, an American anthropologist, has documented four distance zones in the United States: intimate (up to 18 inches apart), personal ($1\frac{1}{2}$ to 4 feet apart), social (4 to 12 feet apart), and public (12 to 25 feet apart).
- How people form lines can also indicate cultural differences. In Britain people usually form straight lines and stand quite far apart, whereas in Latin America they are much closer together and the line will probably meander more.
- Another cultural difference is how people walk together. For example, in the U.S., friends usually walk together side by side but do not touch; Arab and Latin American women often walk with their arms linked.

SEGUNDO PASO

Asking and saying how old someone is; asking where someone is from and saying where you are from

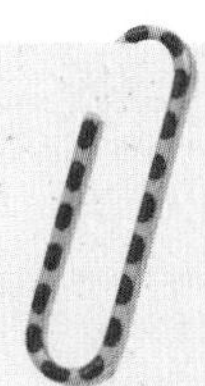

ASÍ SE DICE *Here's how you say it*

Asking and saying how old someone is

To ask how old someone is, say:

¿Cuántos años tienes?
How old are you?

¿Cuántos años tiene?
How old is (he/she)?

To answer, say:

Tengo ... años.
I'm . . . years old.

Tiene ... años.
(He/She) is . . . years old.

VOCABULARIO

Los números del 0 al 30

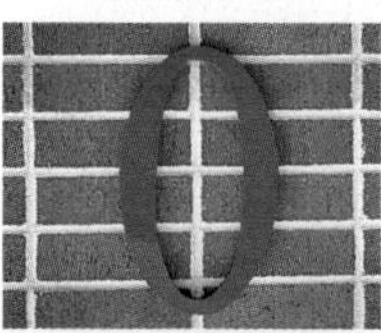
cero

uno

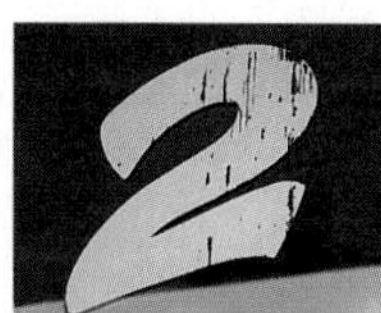
dos

tres

cuatro

cinco

seis

siete

ocho

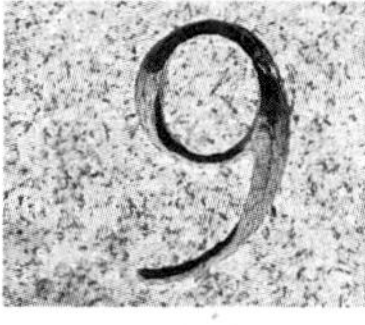
nueve

diez

11 once	12 doce	13 trece	14 catorce	15 quince
16 dieciséis	17 diecisiete	18 dieciocho	19 diecinueve	20 veinte
21 veintiuno	22 veintidós	23 veintitrés	24 veinticuatro	25 veinticinco
26 veintiséis	27 veintisiete	28 veintiocho	29 veintinueve	30 treinta

RESOURCES FOR SEGUNDO PASO

Textbook Audiocassette 1A/Audio CD 1
Practice and Activity Book, pp. 4–8
Native Speaker Activity Book, pp. 1–5
Video Guide
Video Program
Expanded Video Program, Videocassette 1
Videodisc Guide
Videodisc Program, Videodisc 1A

Chapter Teaching Resources, Book 1
- Communicative Activity 1-2, pp. 5–6
- Additional Listening Activities 1-3, 1-4, p. 12
  Audiocassette 10A/Audio CD 1
- Student Response Forms, p. 21
- Realia 1-2, pp. 16–17
- Situation Cards 1-2, pp. 18–19
- Teaching Transparency Master 1-2, pp. 8, 10
  Teaching Transparency 1-2
- Quiz 1-2, pp. 25–26
  Audiocassette 7A/Audio CD 1

Jump Start!

Have students write the answers to these questions: **¿Cómo te llamas? ¿Cómo estás?** Then have them write a short dialogue between two people who are meeting for the first time.

MOTIVATE

Take a quick poll of students' ages. Write the answers on the board. Discuss the meaning of age in our society and some of the rites of passage connected with age (getting a driver's license, voting, and registering for military service).

TEACH

Presentation

Así se dice Model the phrases and then, holding up fingers to represent ages, make a game of asking and having the students answer the questions. Introduce the statement **Tiene ... años** last.

Vocabulario Write numerals in sequence on the board. Point to the numerals in random order. Have students say or write each number as you point to it. Then have students number a piece of paper from one to 30. As you dictate a number have students write the numeral. Periodically check answers.

For videodisc application, see *Videodisc Guide.*

For Individual Needs

19 Challenge Teach students the phrase **Pienso en un número entre (uno y treinta)** and the words **más, menos, sí,** and **no.**

Building on Previous Skills

20 Before having the students break into pairs, briefly review expressions from **Así se dice,** pages 21 and 24.

Presentation

Así se dice Model sentences while saying **Me llamo...** and **Soy de...** Next use a puppet to present functional phrases. Ask the puppet **¿Cómo te llamas?** to which the puppet replies **Me llamo Adriana.** Then ask **¿De dónde eres, Adriana?** and the puppet may answer **Soy de Uruguay.** Point to Uruguay on a map as you introduce the puppet to them: **Clase, ésta es Adriana. Es de Uruguay.** Ask the class **¿De dónde es Adriana?** Students may want to use the puppet themselves, as it enables them to talk about some things in a less personal, revealing way.

Teaching Suggestion

Nota gramatical Teach these forms—**soy, eres, es**—as lexical items, without dwelling on the verb paradigm.

18 Escuchemos: Edades *Let's listen: Ages* Answers on p.11C

Daniel is showing Adriana pictures in the family album. Listen as he tells how old each relative is. Then match the correct picture to the age he gives.

a.

b.

c.

d.

e.

19 Número secreto *Secret number*

Try to guess the secret number your partner is thinking of (it must be between zero and 30). If you're wrong, your partner will point up or down to indicate a higher or lower number. Keep trying until you guess right. Then switch roles and play again.

20 Presentaciones *Introductions*

Introduce yourself to the three classmates sitting closest to you. Greet them and ask each one's name and age. Then introduce your three new friends to the class.
See answers below.

Nota Gramatical

The words **soy, eres,** and **es** are all forms of the verb **ser,** which is one way to say *to be* in Spanish. When talking about where someone is from, forms of **ser** are always used.

ASÍ SE DICE *Here's how you say it*

Asking where someone is from and saying where you're from

To find out where someone is from, ask:

¿De dónde eres?
Where are you from?

¿De dónde es...?
Where is . . . from?

To answer, say:

Soy de los Estados Unidos.
I'm from the United States.

Es de...
(She/He) is from . . .

Answers

20 *Possible conversation:*
—Hola, soy... Tengo ... años. ¿Cómo te llamas?; —Me llamo...; —¿Cuántos años tienes?; —Tengo ... años.
Possible introduction:
—Clase, éste/a es...Tiene ... años.; —Él/ella se llama... Tiene ... años.

Game

¿DE DÓNDE ERES? Holding a soft foam ball or beach ball, say **Soy de (Chile).** Tossing the ball to a student, ask **¿De dónde eres?** The student who catches answers **Soy de los Estados Unidos.** and then tosses the ball to another student, asking **¿De dónde eres?** Students can answer with the town they're from or with Spanish-speaking cities or countries. Have a map available for geographical reference.

Culture Note

Many high schools in Spain and Latin America have a photo I.D. card (**carné de identidad**) for their students. These cards double as library cards at the school library. National identification cards are issued to all citizens of Spain and most Latin American countries.

21 Escuchemos: ¿De dónde es?

You'll overhear students talking at a party. As you listen, write the name of the country each person is from. Then choose three of the students and write a sentence telling where each one is from.

1. Gabriela
2. Maricarmen
3. David
4. Antonio
5. Laura Alicia
6. Pedro

Un poco más...

Los países hispanohablantes

(la) Argentina
Bolivia
Colombia
Costa Rica
Cuba
Chile
el Ecuador
España
los Estados Unidos
Guatemala
Honduras
las Islas Canarias
México
Nicaragua
Panamá
(el) Paraguay
(el) Perú
Puerto Rico
(la) República Dominicana
El Salvador
(el) Uruguay
Venezuela

22 ¡Entrevista! *Interview*

Ask five classmates where they are from and note each person's name and place of origin. Then introduce one of them to the class: **Ésta es Shawna; es de Allentown.** Anyone else from Allentown raises his or her hand and says **yo también.**

Possible questions: ¿De dónde eres? ¿Cómo te llamas? *Possible answers:* Soy.../Me llamo.../Soy de....

23 Gente famosa *Famous people*

You and your partner will each list five famous women and five famous men. Include as many Spanish speakers as you can. Then take turns asking and answering where each famous person is from. See possible answers below.

MODELO —¿De dónde es Arantxa Sánchez Vicario?
—Es de España.

Arantxa Sánchez Vicario

24 Amigos hispanos *Hispanic friends*

Write at least one sentence about each of these people. Tell each person's name, age, and what country he or she is from. What is the last name of each student's father and mother? Then, find the two countries on the maps on pages xxii–xxiii and identify their capital cities. See possible answers below.

Instituto de Bachillerato
FELIPE GONZALEZ
SEVILLA, ESPAÑA
Apellidos: GARCIA JOVE
Nombre: JESUS MARIA
Nacido en: GRANADA
Día 21 de OCTUBRE de 19 81
Domicilio: Galera, 25 (7°-C)
Expediente n.° 123 Fecha 5-10-96 Curso 2° B.U.P.
El Director El Secretario

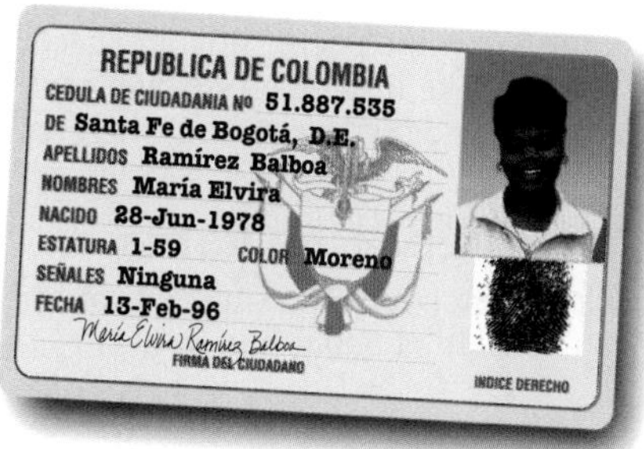

REPUBLICA DE COLOMBIA
CEDULA DE CIUDADANIA No 51.887.535
DE Santa Fe de Bogotá, D.E.
APELLIDOS Ramírez Balboa
NOMBRES María Elvira
NACIDO 28-Jun-1978
ESTATURA 1-59 COLOR Moreno
SEÑALES Ninguna
FECHA 13-Feb-96
FIRMA DEL CIUDADANO
INDICE DERECHO

Teaching Suggestion

22 Allow students to create imaginary names and origins for themselves.

Additional Practice

22 As homework, have students interview at least five people (school staff, faculty members, or other students). They are to draw a picture of the people they interviewed on a piece of paper and write captions. For example, **Ésta es (Sra. Carfora), es de (California)** or **Éste es (Nico), es de (El Salvador).**

Photo Flash!

The person pictured is professional tennis player Arantxa Sánchez Vicario. She is an outstanding professional tennis player from Spain.

Teaching Suggestion

23 You may wish to provide a list of famous men and women to choose from. Students could also use the library or media center to research names. As an alternative, students choose a hero or role model and explain their choice.

Answers

23 *Possible answers:*
Roberto Alomar—Puerto Rico; don Francisco—Chile; Julio Iglesias—España; Alberto Fujimori—Perú; Rigoberta Menchú—Guatemala; Gloria Estefan—Cuba

24 *Possible answers:*
Felipe González es de España. En 1994 tiene trece años. El apellido de su padre es González. El apellido de su madre es García. La capital de España es Madrid.
María es de Colombia. En 1994 tiene doce años. Su padre se llama Ramírez y su madre se llama Balboa. La capital de Colombia es Bogotá.

Presentation

Gramática Model pronunciation and the various usages of these question words at the beginning of questions. Toss a soft foam ball to students while asking a question. Whoever catches it answers your question, and then tosses it to another student while asking another question.

For videodisc application, see *Videodisc Guide*.

Teaching Suggestion

27 Tell your students that they are free to make up new identities for themselves. Students should refer to the map for ideas about origin.

Close

Have students give you several situations in which they might need to use the functional phrases from **Así se dice** on pages 27 and 28.

Assess

Quiz 1-2, *Chapter Teaching Resources Book 1,* pp. 25–26

Assessment Items, Audiocassette 7A/Audio CD 1

Performance Assessment

In small groups, have students create a situation (such as meeting a new exchange student or a famous person) in which they will introduce themselves and the chosen personality to each other and the class. Students need to introduce themselves by telling their name, their age, and where they are from (country or state). If time permits, set up a situation where students are entering a Spanish-speaking country and must pass through customs. The customs official asks for their names, ages, and countries of origin.

Gramática Forming questions with question words

1. So far, you've asked questions using several different words.
   ¿Cómo estás? *How are you?*
   ¿Cómo te llamas? *What's your name?*
   ¿Cuántos años tienes? *How old are you?*
   ¿De dónde eres? *Where are you from?*

   To ask questions like these, put the question word at the beginning of the sentence. These question words have accents.
2. Notice that **¿cómo?** can mean *how?* or *what?* depending on context. What does this tell you about translating?[1]

25 El comienzo de una amistad *The beginning of a friendship*

It's the first day of school for Ana, a new student at a **colegio** *(secondary school)* in Madrid. Fill in each blank with the correct word.

ANA Buenos días. ¿__1__ (Cómo/Cuántos) estás?
FEDERICO Bien, ¿y tú?
ANA Regular. Oye, soy Ana. Y tú, ¿__2__ (de dónde/cómo) te llamas?
FEDERICO Me llamo Federico. Tú no eres de aquí, ¿verdad? ¿__3__ (Cuántos/De dónde) eres?
ANA Soy de Andalucía. ¿__4__ (Cuántos/Cómo) años tienes?
FEDERICO Tengo quince años. ¿Y tú?
ANA Yo tengo quince también.

26 Una encuesta *A survey*

You're listening to Javier as he is being interviewed over the phone for a survey. Below are the answers Javier gave. For each answer, choose the question from the box. See answers below.

1. Bien, gracias.
2. De Madrid.
3. Catorce.
4. Javier Francisco González.

¿Cuántos años tienes?
¿Cómo te llamas?
¿Cómo estás?
¿De dónde eres?

27 Tres amigos *Three friends*

Get to know the people in your class! Form a group with three students you don't know well and take turns interviewing each other. Ask each other's names, how you're feeling today, how old you are, and where you're from. See possible conversation below.

28 Mi amigo/a se llama... *My friend's name is . . .*

Select one of your classmates from Activity 27 and write a brief paragraph telling what you've learned about him or her. *Possible answer:*
Mi amigo/a se llama... Tiene ... años y es de...

[1] There's not always a one-to-one match between words in different languages.

Answers

26 1. ¿Cómo estás?
2. ¿De dónde eres?
3. ¿Cuántos años tienes?
4. ¿Cómo te llamas?

27 *Possible conversation:*
—¡Hola! ¿Cómo estás?
—Muy bien, gracias. ¿Y tú?
—Bastante bien. Me llamo... ¿Cómo te llamas tú?
—Me llamo... Y tú, ¿cómo te llamas?
—Me llamo... Mucho gusto. Y tú, ¿cómo te llamas?
—Me llamo... Tengo ... años. ¿Cuántos años tienes tú?
—Tengo ... años. ¿Y tú?
—Tengo ... años, ¿y tú?
—Yo tengo ... años. ¿De dónde eres?
—Soy de... ¿Y tú?
—Soy de ... también.

¿De dónde eres?

Panorama cultural will introduce you to real Spanish speakers from around the globe, including Europe, Latin America, and the United States. In this chapter, we asked some people to tell us who they are and where they're from.

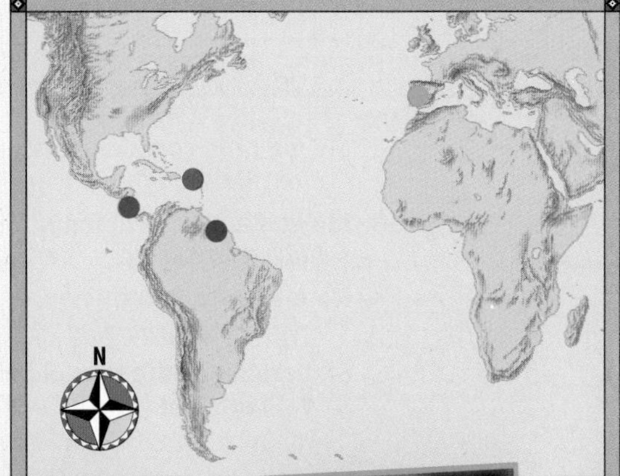

"Me llamo Mauricio. Vivo aquí también en San José, Costa Rica y tengo quince años."

"Mi nombre es Ivette Marcán. Yo soy de Ponce, Puerto Rico".

"Hola, buenas tardes. Me llamo Miguel Silva. Tengo dieciséis años y soy de Madrid".

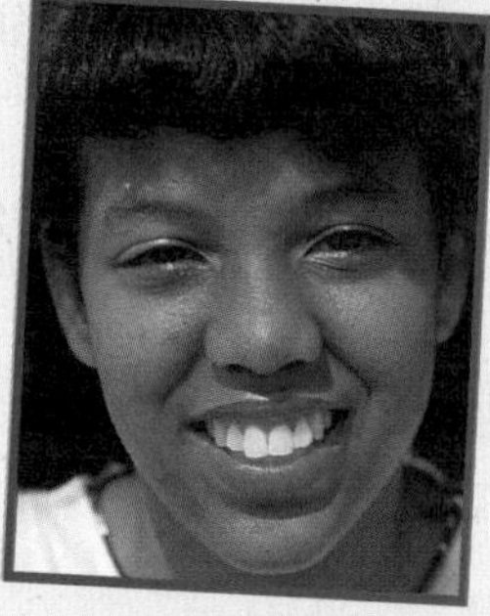

"Yo me llamo Sandra Terán y soy de Venezuela".

Para pensar y hablar... Things to think and talk about...

A. Can you find the places Mauricio, Ivette, Miguel, and Sandra are from on the maps in the front of your book? Using the legend on the maps, can you figure out how far apart all four countries are from each other?

B. What do you think these four countries are like? With a partner, describe each country in three or four sentences, using the maps in the front of the book and information you already know. Then, share your descriptions with another team.

VIDEO PROGRAM OR EXPANDED VIDEO PROGRAM, *Videocassette 1*

OR VIDEODISC PROGRAM, *Videodisc 1A*

Teacher Notes

- Each **Panorama cultural** section consists of authentic video interviews shot on location in different parts of the Spanish-speaking world. The videotape includes numerous interviews in addition to those featured in the Pupil's Edition. See *Video Guide* and *Videodisc Guide* for suggestions on different ways to use this versatile resource in the classsroom and for activities related to the **Panorama cultural.**
- Remind students that cultural material may be included in the Chapter Quizzes and Test.

Motivating Activity

Ask several students where they are from. Encourage a discussion of whether or not it is preferable to live in one place or to move frequently.

Presentation

First, view the video. Ask **¿De dónde es Miguel?** and **¿Cuántos años tiene él?** Repeat this process with the other interviewees. Play the video again, then have students ask each other **¿De dónde eres?** and answer **Soy de....** Play the video again and have students answer the **Preguntas.**

Preguntas

1. ¿Cómo se llama el chico de España? (Miguel)
2. ¿De dónde es Iva Marcán? (Ponce, Puerto Rico)
3. ¿Cuántos años tiene la persona de Costa Rica? (quince)
4. ¿De dónde es el chico que tiene dieciséis años? (Madrid)
5. ¿Cómo se llama la chica de Venezuela? (Sandra)

Geography Link

Have your students locate these countries and cities on the maps on pages xxi–xxvii.

Jump Start!

Have students answer the following questions in writing: **¿Cómo te llamas? ¿De dónde eres? ¿Cuántos años tienes?**

MOTIVATE

Write *Food, Sports,* and *School* as column heads across the top of a transparency. Ask students to name some things in English that they like and dislike in each category. Write their responses under the category heads. Leave room so that students can fill in the Spanish equivalents after presentation of the **Vocabulario.**

TEACH

Presentation

Así se dice Model pronunciation and sentence construction with **gustar.** Then using the transparency from MOTIVATE, point to a word and mime whether or not you like the item using **(No) me gusta...** and the Spanish equivalent.

Vocabulario Model pronunciation by teaching a word's last syllable first and then building "backwards." (**-ción, -tación, natación**) Then with one hand, hold up a visual of an item in the list. Use a puppet to ask silly comprehension questions. For example, while you are holding up a picture of a salad, the puppet asks **¿Qué es esto? ¿Una pizza?** You respond **No, no es una pizza, es una ensalada.**

TERCER PASO

Talking about likes and dislikes

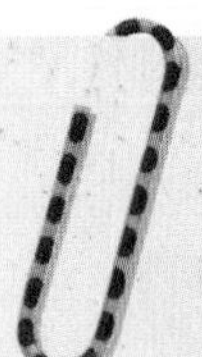

ASÍ SE DICE *Here's how you say it*

Talking about likes and dislikes

To find out what a friend likes, ask:	Your friend might answer:
¿Qué te gusta? *What do you like?*	**Me gusta la comida mexicana.** *I like Mexican food.* **Me gusta mucho el tenis.** *I like tennis a lot.* **No me gusta la natación.** *I don't like swimming.*
¿Te gusta el fútbol? *Do you like soccer?*	**Sí, pero me gusta más el béisbol.** *Yes, but I like baseball more.*

29 Escuchemos: Planes

Answers on p.11D.

Elena and Carlos are trying to make plans. As you listen to them talk, note which items Elena likes and doesn't like. Is there anything she and Carlos both like? What would you suggest they do together?

1. voleibol
2. pizza
3. la música pop
4. comida mexicana
5. el restaurante Taco Paco

VOCABULARIO

Los deportes *Sports*

el baloncesto
el béisbol
el fútbol
el fútbol norteamericano
la natación
el tenis
el voleibol

La comida *Food*

la cafetería
el chocolate
la comida mexicana (italiana, china...)
la ensalada
la fruta
la pizza

La música

el jazz
la música clásica
la música pop
la música rock
la música de...

Las clases

el español
la clase de inglés
la tarea *homework*

RESOURCES FOR TERCER PASO

Textbook Audiocassette 1A/Audio CD 1
Practice and Activity Book, pp. 9–10
Native Speaker Activity Book, pp. 1–5
Videodisc Guide
Videodisc Program, Videodisc 1A

Chapter Teaching Resources, Book 1
- Communicative Activity 1-2, pp. 5–6
- Additional Listening Activities 1-5, 1-6, p. 13
  Audiocassette 7A/Audio CD 1
- Student Response Forms, p. 22
- Realia 1-3, pp. 16–17
- Situation Cards 1-3, pp. 18–19
- Teaching Transparency Master 1-3, pp. 9, 10
  Teaching Transparency 1-3
- Quiz 1-3, pp. 27–28
  Audiocassette 7A/Audio CD 1

Gramática Nouns and definite articles

All the words in the vocabulary box on page 32 are nouns—words used to name people, places, and things. As you can see, all the nouns in the list have **el** or **la** *(the)* before them. Generally **el** is used before masculine nouns and **la** before feminine nouns. When learning new nouns, always learn the definite article that goes with the noun at the same time.

30 Gustos personales

For each category listed, write a sentence stating one thing in that category that you like and another that you don't like. Be sure to use the correct definite article (**el** or **la**) in your sentence.

MODELO deportes
Me gusta el tenis.
No me gusta el fútbol.

1. deportes
2. comida
3. música
4. clases

También se puede decir...

Just like English, Spanish has different words that express the same idea. It often depends on where you're from.

In Spain, the common word for basketball is **el baloncesto**. In many parts of the Spanish-speaking world, you'll also hear **el basquetbol**, or **el básquet**.

31 ¿Te gusta...? *Do you like . . .*

With a partner, take turns asking and answering whether you like the types of sports, music, food, and schoolwork listed in the **Vocabulario** on page 32. If your partner likes the same thing you do, you can say **¡A mí también!** *(Me too!)*

Possible conversation:
¿A ti te gusta el béisbol?
Sí, me gusta.
A mí también. *or* Pues, a mí no.
¿Te gusta la música de Pearl Jam?
No, no me gusta.

32 Escuchemos: Una fiesta

You're in charge of planning a party for Diana. Listen as a friend asks Diana what she likes and doesn't like. Take notes. Then, based on your list, decide one sport, one food, and one kind of music you would include in a party to please her.

Answers on p.11D.

33 ¡Juego de ingenio! *Guessing game!*

Work with a partner. First write three guesses about what your partner likes and doesn't like. Ask if your partner likes the items you listed. Take turns asking and answering, to see if you guessed right.

MODELO —¿Te gusta la natación?
—Sí, me gusta mucho la natación.
or No, no me gusta.

Although the best way to learn a new language is by spending time in a country where that language is spoken, you can still make the most out of your classroom opportunities to hear, speak, read, and write Spanish. From the moment you walk into the classroom, use as much Spanish as you can. Pay attention to everything your teacher says, even if you don't understand it all.

Presentation

Gramática Model a few of the vocabulary words from this chapter and ask students to tell which is the correct definite article. Then, have students identify the nouns and accompanying definite articles in the **fotonovela** on pages 18–19.

Teaching Suggestion

También se puede decir Students should keep a log of vocabulary variants. They can record the words in their notebooks, in their word boxes, or on a computer disk. You may want to have students do a bulletin board project with regional variants at some point.

Native Speakers

The **También se puede decir** features offer an excellent chance to confirm the validity of different dialects and vocabularies. Ask native speakers to share regional vocabulary differences they know with the class.

For Individual Needs

31 Challenge Have students poll five to ten people about their likes and dislikes. They should use sports, food, and school vocabulary. Have students report their findings to the class in an oral or written presentation. You might have them organize their collective results into graph or chart form.

For Individual Needs

Visual Learners Have students make review cards for new vocabulary. They can draw or paste pictures of sports, food, or school-related items on one side of each card and write the Spanish word on the back of the card.

For Videodisc application, see *Videodisc Guide.*

Teacher Note

You might explain to students that the **A lo nuestro** suggestions are to help make their Spanish sound more natural.

Teaching Suggestion

35 You may want to supply simple props for presentation of this activity. (balls, jam box, books)

34 La nueva estudiante *The new student*

Felipe is interviewing the new exchange student from Managua for the school newspaper. Take the role of the new student and write the words for his or her part. Possible answers:

FELIPE	Hola. Soy Felipe. ¿Cómo te llamas?
ESTUDIANTE	1. ______. Me llamo...
FELIPE	¿Cómo estás?
ESTUDIANTE	2. ¿______? Regular.
FELIPE	Bien. ¿De dónde eres?
ESTUDIANTE	3. ______. Soy de...
FELIPE	¿Y cuántos años tienes?
ESTUDIANTE	4. ______. Tengo ... años.
FELIPE	El béisbol es muy popular en Nicaragua. ¿Te gusta el béisbol?
ESTUDIANTE	5. ______. Sí, me gusta.
FELIPE	Personalmente, me gusta más el fútbol.
ESTUDIANTE	6. ¿______? ¿Te gusta el jazz?
FELIPE	No, no me gusta. Bueno, gracias y hasta luego.
ESTUDIANTE	7. ______. Chao.

35 ¡Mucho gusto!

See answers below.

Work with a partner and take turns playing the roles of two new friends, Pilar and Miguel. Use the drawing as a cue to answer questions about each other's names, ages, where you're from, and what kinds of things you like. Then switch roles.

A LO NUESTRO

There are many little words in Spanish that you can use to connect your ideas and to help you express yourself better. Some of these words are: **y** *(and)*, **también** *(too, also)*, and **más** *(more)*. Look back at the conversations in the **fotonovela** (pp. 18–19) and see how some of these words were used.

Answers

35 *Possible answers:*

—¿Cómo te llamas?
—Me llamo Pilar. ¿Y tú?
—Me llamo Miguel. ¿Cuántos años tienes?
—Tengo dieciséis años. ¿Cuántos años tienes tú?
—Yo tengo quince años. ¿Qué te gusta?
—Me gusta el fútbol, el voleibol, la música y las frutas. Y tú, Miguel, ¿qué te gusta?
—Me gusta el fútbol norteamericano, la comida italiana, la clase de inglés y el baloncesto.
—Pues, mucho gusto Miguel.
—Igualmente, Pilar.

36 ¡Entrevista! *Interview!* See answers below.

Now interview a classmate. Find out your partner's name, age, where he or she is from, and at least three things he or she likes and dislikes. Try to keep the conversation going as long as possible. Be prepared to reenact your interview for the class.

37 En mi cuaderno *In my journal*

Write a letter to a pen pal. Introduce yourself and give your age and where you're from. List three or four of your likes and dislikes. Then ask your pen pal some questions. Keep a copy of this letter in your journal.

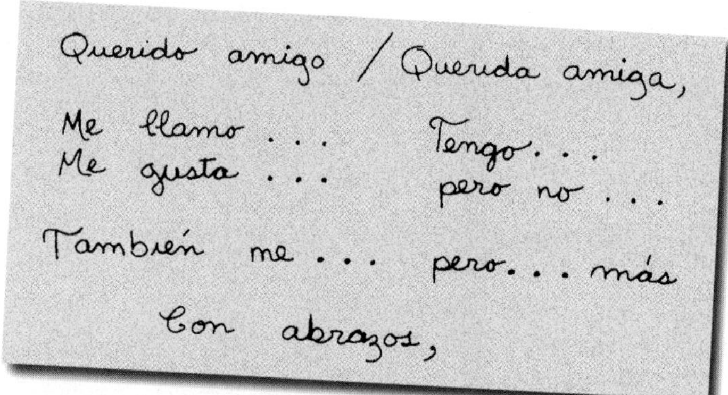

Querido amigo / Querida amiga,

Me llamo . . . Tengo. . .
Me gusta . . . pero no . . .
También me . . . pero. . . más

Con abrazos,

LETRA Y SONIDO

A. The Spanish vowels (**a, e, i, o, u**) are pronounced clearly and distinctly. Learn to pronounce them by mimicking the recording or your teacher.

1. **a:** as in *father,* but with the tongue closer to the front of the mouth
   Ana **cámara** **amiga** **tarea** **llama**
2. **e:** as in *they,* but without the *y* sound
   este **eres** **noche** **excelente** **café**
3. **i:** as in *machine,* but much shorter
   íntimo **isla** **legítimo** **Misisipí** **día**
4. **o:** as in *low,* but without the *w* sound
   hola **moto** **años** **dónde** **color**
5. **u:** as in *rule*
   fruta **uno** **fútbol** **único** **música**

B. **Dictado** Answers on p.11D.
Ana has just met several new friends in Madrid and is practicing the new phrases she has heard. Write what you hear.

C. **Trabalenguas**
¡A, e, i, o, u! Arbolito del Perú, ¿cómo te llamas tú?

Answers

36 *Possible questions:*
¡Mucho gusto! ¿Como te llamas? ¿De dónde eres? ¿Cuántos años tienes? ¿Te gusta el jazz?
Possible answers:
Me llamo...; Me llamo...; Soy de...; Tengo ... años.; No, no me gusta el jazz.

Portfolio

36 Oral You may want to suggest this activity as a potential oral portfolio item. For Portfolio suggestions, see *Assessment Guide,* pp. 2–13.

En mi cuaderno

37 For an additional journal entry suggestion for Chapter 1, see *Practice and Activity Book,* p. 145.

Additional Practice

Write the following **trabalenguas** *(tongue twisters)* on a transparency and have students repeat them after you. **Ana practica el alemán para viajar a Alemania. Elena entiende el español en vez del francés. Lili invita a Ignacio y Martín a ir a Ibiza. El lobo se comió todos los conos de chocolate. Al duque le gusta mucho el zumo de uva.**

Close

Conduct a short question-and-answer session in which students say what they like and dislike. They should use as much of the vocabulary from this **Paso** (sports, food, school) as possible. You might use the transparency from MOTIVATE on page 32 to show what students have learned.

Assess

Quiz 1-3, *Chapter Teaching Resources Book 1,* pp. 27–28

Assessment Items, Audiocassette 7A/Audio CD 1

Performance Assessment

In pairs, have students role-play the following situation. One is a famous sports figure, and the other a media interviewer. The interviewer asks the star questions related to his or her likes and dislikes (sports and food vocabulary). The star answers.

READING STRATEGY

Recognizing cognates. Tell students that the reading tips they learn in this section can be applied to anything they read.

PREREADING
Activity A

In each **Vamos a leer** section, the activities under **¡A comenzar!** focus on prereading skills.

Motivating Activity

Have students look through English-language magazines, looking only at the headlines. What information is in a headline?

Teacher Note

Be aware of your students' skill level in English. People seldom surpass their native-language abilities in a second language. If a student has difficulty reading in Spanish, he or she may lack English reading skills. Additionally, if you have students who have difficulty listening or spelling in Spanish, they may also be poor listeners or spellers in English. Talk to other teachers and to the students themselves to assess native language abilities or deficiencies.

READING
Activities B and C

Teaching Suggestion

B. Have students work with a partner on Activity B, then go over the answers as a class.

VAMOS A LEER

Categorías

Estrategia

Spanish shares many words with English. Words with similar meanings and spellings in both languages are called *cognates.** Recognizing cognates can help you understand more Spanish words.

¡A comenzar!

A. These headlines are from different Spanish-language magazines. How many Spanish/English cognates can you find in 20 seconds? 12 Compare your list with a classmate's and discuss the English meaning of each headline. Look up any you're not sure of in the glossary at the back of the book.

Al grano

B. Many cognates like the ones in the reading have similar endings in both languages: **personal, turismo** and **ecología.** How would you expect the Spanish versions of the following words to be spelled? Check your work against the dictionary and note any spelling changes. For example, what sometimes happens to the English spelling *ch* in Spanish? The English *ch* may become **c** or **qu** in Spanish.

sexism	racism	social
mechanism	sociology	zoology
chemistry	biology	legal
sexismo	racismo	social
mecanismo	sociología	zoología
química	biología	legal

*So-called false cognates can be misleading. For example, **librería** means *bookstore,* not *library.*

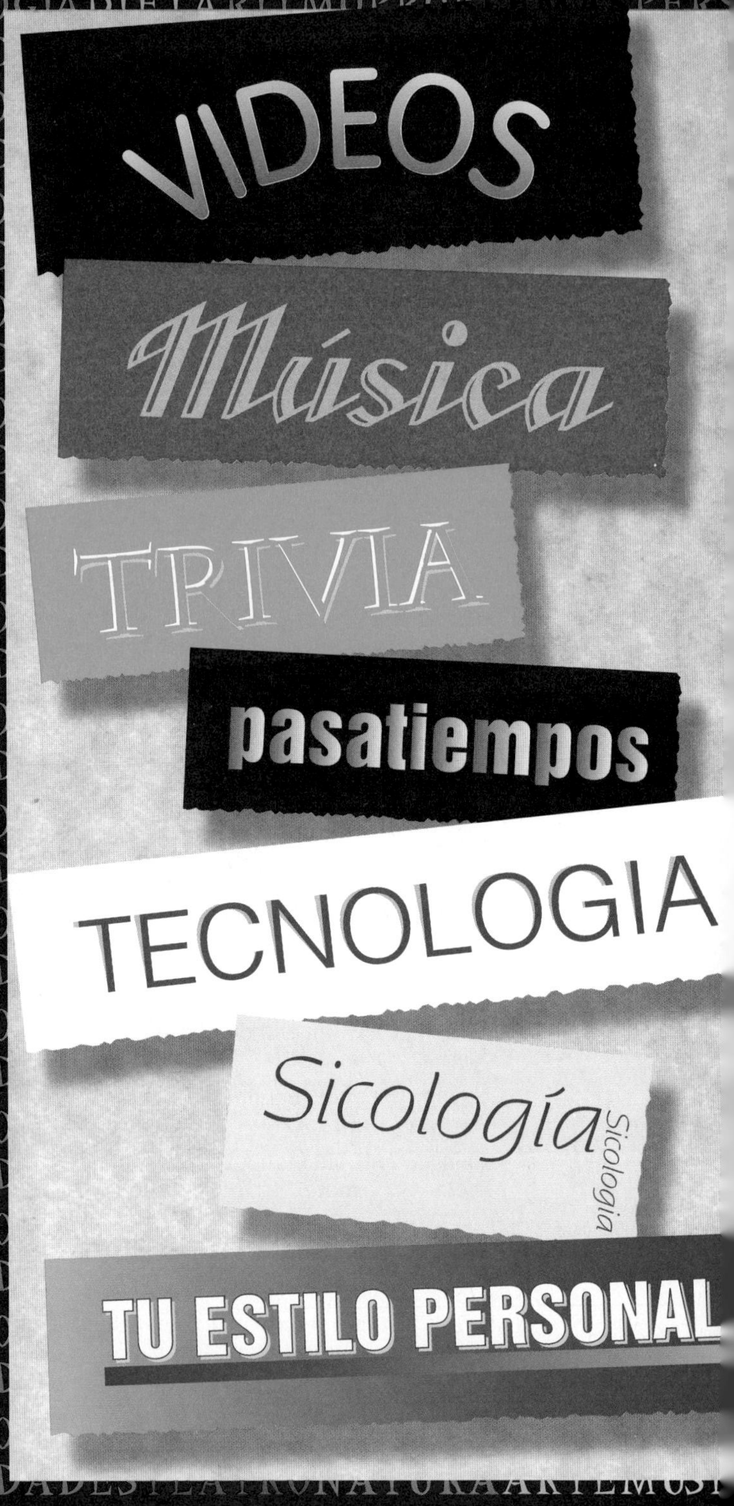

VIDEOS

Música

TRIVIA

pasatiempos

TECNOLOGIA

Sicología

Sicologia

TU ESTILO PERSONAL

C. The following are descriptions of articles from these magazines. In which section would you look to find each article? See answers below.

1. interesting tidbits about famous personalities
2. windsurfing in the Caribbean
3. the latest in compact disc players
4. what to say and do at a White House dinner
5. how to recognize the symptoms of depression
6. jokes and riddles
7. the latest styles in clothes and make-up
8. how to argue effectively
9. mural paintings in East Los Angeles
10. the new album by a Spanish rap group
11. suggestions about what to do on your next free Saturday

Cognados falsos

D. Some words look the same in both languages but don't mean the same thing. For example, **vaso** means *drinking glass,* not *vase.* List a similar English word for each Spanish word below. Then look up the Spanish words in a Spanish-English dictionary to see what they actually mean. How many are false cognates?

real **ropa** **sopa**
grupo **disgusto**

Four.
royal clothing soup group distaste

Cooperative Learning

C. Put students in groups of four. Ask them to choose a discussion leader, a scribe, a proofreader, and an announcer. Give students a specific amount of time in which to complete Activity C. Monitor the groups' work as you walk around. Help students as necessary. At the end of the activity, call on each group announcer to read the group's results. When group members have different assignments, remind them that they will receive a common group grade. This will keep each person on task and engaged in the total process.

POSTREADING
Activity D

Teaching Suggestion

After doing Activities A, B, and C, have students brainstorm as many English-Spanish cognates as they can in three minutes. Review their lists as a class. Clarify the meaning of any **cognados falsos** *(false cognates)* that may occur in the lists.

Native Speakers

Ask native speakers to bring in Spanish-language magazines or newspaper clippings. Have students look for cognates.

Teacher Note

For additional reading, see *Practice and Activity Book,* p. 11.

Answers

C 1. Trivia
2. Turismo
3. Tecnología
4. Etiqueta
5. Sicología
6. Humor
7. Tu estilo personal
8. Sicología
9. Arte
10. Música
11. Pasatiempos

The **Repaso** reviews and integrates all four skills and culture in preparation for the Chapter Test.

Teaching Suggestion

Before beginning the **Repaso**, have students turn to page 17 and review the learner outcomes. Ask them if they feel they have learned what was intended. Proceed through the **Repaso** activities. Encourage both group and individual work.

Additional Practice

1 Have students create a third card and fill it out for themselves. Then have students fill out a card for a partner, to practice asking in the **tú** form and reporting in the **él** or **ella** form.

REPASO

1 Imagine that you work for a pen pal service. Your job is to complete a set of cards with information left by the clients on the answering machine. One card has been done for you as an example. Create two other cards and fill them in as you listen to the messages.
Answers on p.11D.

NOMBRE: Mariana Castillo
ORIGEN: Es de España
EDAD: Tiene 15 años
LE GUSTA: la música rock
NO LE GUSTA: el tenis

2 Read the following letter that a client has sent to the pen pal service. Then decide which of the three candidates in Activity 1 would be a good pen pal for him according to their likes and dislikes. See answer below.

Hola. Busco un amigo por correspondencia. Me llamo José Luis Bazán. Tengo quince años y soy de Guatemala. Me gusta mucho el fútbol y el béisbol. También me gusta la música rock, pero no me gusta la música clásica.

3 Look at the picture of Paco and his friends in front of the pizzeria. Keeping in mind what you've learned about gestures and interpersonal distance, explain how the picture would differ if it took place in your hometown.
Possible answer: Paco and Mercedes would not kiss, and they would be standing farther apart.

4 Look at the people in the picture again. Write a brief conversation between Paco and Mercedes. Possible answer below.

Answers

2 Mariana would be a good match. Both like rock music.

4 *Possible answer:*
PACO: ¡Hola! ¿Cómo estás?
MERCHE: Bien. ¿Y tú?
PACO: Excelente. ¿Te gusta el voleibol?
MERCHE: Sí, me gusta mucho. ¿Te gusta la pizza?
PACO: Sí, me gusta la pizza también.

5 Working with a partner, role-play each of your dialogues from the previous activity. Add a phrase or two to end the conversation politely. Be prepared to present one of your dialogues to the class.

6 Think of one item you like and one you dislike in each of the categories in the box. Interview your group members to find who shares at least two of your likes and two of your dislikes.

comida	música
deportes	clases

See **Vocabulario**, page 32, for a list of vocabulary items students can use.

7 Write a short autobiographical paragraph. Be creative! Give yourself a new name, age, hometown, country, likes, and dislikes. Exchange papers with a partner and help each other correct mistakes. Possible answer below.

8 With your partner from Activity 7, take turns introducing each other to the class. Give as much information as you can. You and your partner should be prepared to answer questions about your likes and dislikes. See possible answer below.

9 The editor of your school newspaper has asked you to come up with a standard questionnaire for interviewing new students. Create an interview form using the questions you've learned, and try it out on a classmate. See possible questionnaire below.

10 Juan's full name is Juan Luis Fernández Jiménez. Where would you find his name in the telephone book? Answer: Under "Fernández."

11 **SITUACIÓN**

You've been asked to meet the new exchange student from Ecuador at the airport. Role-play the scene with a partner, using the information given. Be sure to exchange names, ages, where you're from, and several likes and dislikes in your conversation.

Possible conversation:

—Soy Pedro. ¿Cómo te llamas?
—Soy María Lorena de Malo.
—¿De dónde eres?
—Soy del Ecuador. Tú, ¿de dónde eres?
—Soy de California y tengo dieciséis años. ¿Cuántos años tienes?
—Tengo quince años. Me gusta mucho el tenis y el béisbol. ¿A ti qué te gusta?
—A mí me gusta el tenis también.

ECUADOR TENIS Y SQUASH CLUB

Esta tarjeta da al socio derecho de ingresar al Club a sus instalaciones.
La utilización de servicios.
En caso de pérdida notificar al Ecuador Tenis y Squash Club.

Nombre MARIA LORENA
DE MALO
Socio ESPECIAL Nº 12-911
Fecha Nac. 13-08-1979
María Lorena De Malo
Firma

Portfolio

7 Written Activity 7 may be used as a Portfolio entry. For Portfolio suggestions, see *Assessment Guide,* p. 14.

8 Oral Students might use Activity 8 as a Portfolio entry. For Portfolio suggestions, see *Assessment Guide,* p. 14.

Video Wrap-Up

- **Video Program**
- **Expanded Video Program, Videocassette 1**
- **Videodisc Program, Videodisc 1A**

At this time, you may want to use the video resources for additional review and enrichment. See *Video Guide* or *Videodisc Guide* for suggestions regarding the following:

- **¡Me llamo Francisco!** (Dramatic episode)
- **Panorama cultural** (Interviews)
- **Video Clips** (Authentic footage)

Answers

7 *Possible answer:*
Me llamo Pedro. Tengo 14 años. Soy de Cuba. Me gusta mucho la natación. No me gusta la tarea.

8 *Possible answer:* Clase, éste es mi amigo Pedro. Es de Cuba.

9 *Possible questionaire:* ¿Cómo te llamas? ¿De dónde eres? ¿Cuántos años tienes? ¿Qué te gusta? ¿Qué no te gusta?

This page is intended to help students prepare for the Chapter Test. It is designed for the students to work on their own initiative and consists of a brief checklist of the major points covered in the chapter. The students should be reminded that this is only a checklist and does not necessarily include everything that will appear on the Chapter Test.

Teacher Note

As this Chapter Test may be the first foreign language test your students will have taken, you may wish to give them some tips on test preparation. Point out that this is a skills test, not a knowledge test. Cramming will not help them because memorization is not what they will be tested on. Communicating is what language is about, so it is a good idea for students to study together. For example, they could re-read the **fotonovela** aloud, taking turns playing the characters' roles. Then they could identify vocabulary and phrases in the character's lines from the presentations in the chapter. You may also want to refer them back to page 11 for language study tips.

A VER SI PUEDO . . .

Can you say hello and goodbye? p. 21

1 How would you greet or say goodbye to these people? Possible answers below.
1. your best friend
2. the principal before classes
3. a classmate as the bell rings
4. your neighbor as he or she leaves your house one evening
5. a friend at the end of the school day

Can you introduce people and respond to an introduction? p. 22

2 What would you say in the following situations? Possible answers below.
1. You want to introduce yourself to an interesting new classmate at a party.
2. The new Spanish teacher asks your name.
3. You have just been introduced to Juan, the new exchange student from Spain.
4. Juan has just said, "Mucho gusto."

Can you ask how someone is and say how you are? p. 24

3 Juan has just joined your class and you want to get to know him. How would you . . .? Possible answers below.
1. ask him how he is doing
2. tell him how you're doing

Can you ask and say how old someone is? p. 27

4 How would you . . .? See answers below.
1. ask Juan how old he is
2. tell him how old you are
3. tell your friend how old Juan is

Can you ask and say where someone is from? p. 28

5 Can you . . .? Possible answers below.
1. tell Juan where you're from
2. ask him where he's from
3. tell your friend where Juan is from

Juan Luis Fernández Jiménez

Can you talk about likes and dislikes? p. 32

6 You'd like to ask Juan to do something with you on Saturday, but you don't know what he likes. Ask him if he likes these things, and tell him which ones you like. See possible answers below.
1. Chinese food
2. rock music
3. volleyball
4. baseball
5. Italian food
6. pop music
7. swimming
8. basketball
9. jazz

Answers

1 *Possible answers:*
1. ¡Hola!
2. Buenos días, señor(a).
3. Bueno, tengo clase.
4. Buenas noches; Adiós.
5. Hasta mañana.

2 *Possible answers:*
1. ¡Hola! ¿Cómo estás?
2. Me llamo…
3. Mucho gusto; Encantado/a.
4. Igualmente.

3 *Possible answers:*
1. ¿Qué tal?; ¿Cómo estás?
2. Bien; Regular.

4 *Possible answers:*
1. ¿Cuántos años tienes?
2. Tengo … años
3. Juan tiene … años.

5 *Possible answers:*
1. Soy de…
2. ¿De dónde eres?
3. Juan es de…

6
1. ¿Te gusta la comida china?
2. ¿Te gusta la música rock?
3. ¿Te gusta el voleibol?
4. ¿Te gusta el béisbol?
5. ¿Te gusta la comida italiana?
6. ¿Te gusta la música pop?
7. ¿Te gusta la natación?
8. ¿Te gusta el basquetbol?
9. ¿Te gusta el jazz? ...Me gusta...

VOCABULARIO

PRIMER PASO

Saying hello and goodbye

Adiós. *Goodbye.*
Buenas noches. *Good night.*
Buenas tardes. *Good afternoon.*
Bueno, tengo clase. *Well, I have class (now).*
Buenos días. *Good morning.*
Chao. *'Bye.*
Hasta luego. *See you later.*
Hasta mañana. *See you tomorrow.*
¡Hola! *Hello!*
señora *ma'am*
señorita *miss*
señor *sir*
Tengo que irme. *I have to go.*

Introducing people and responding to an introduction

¿Cómo te llamas? *What's your name?*
Encantado/a. *Delighted to meet you.*
Ésta es mi amiga. *This is my friend.* (to introduce a female)
Éste es mi amigo. *This is my friend.* (to introduce a male)
Igualmente. *Same here.*
Me llamo... *My name is . . .*
Mucho gusto. *Nice to meet you.*
Se llama... *His/Her name is . . .*
Soy... *I am . . .*
¿Y tú? *And you?* (familiar)

Asking how someone is and saying how you are

¿Cómo estás? *How are you?* (to ask a friend)
Estoy (bastante) bien, gracias. *I'm (pretty) well, thanks.*
Estupendo. *Great./Marvelous.*
Excelente. *Great./Excellent.*
Gracias. *Thanks.*
Horrible. *Horrible.*
Más o menos. *So-so.*
(Muy) mal. *(Very) bad.*
¿Qué tal? *How's it going?*
Regular. *Okay.*
tú *you* (informal)
yo *I*
Yo también. *Me too.*

SEGUNDO PASO

Asking and saying how old someone is

¿Cuántos años tienes? *How old are you?*
¿Cuántos años tiene? *How old is (she/he)?*
el número *number*
Tengo ... años. *I'm . . . years old.*
Tiene ... años. *She/He is . . . years old.*

Asking where someone is from and saying where you are from

¿De dónde eres? *Where are you from?*
¿De dónde es? *Where is she/he from?*
Es de... *He/She is from . . .*
Soy de... *I'm from . . .*
ser *to be*

Numbers 0–30

See p. 27.

TERCER PASO

Talking about likes and dislikes

el baloncesto *basketball*
el béisbol *baseball*
la cafetería *cafeteria*
la clase de inglés *English class*
la comida mexicana/italiana/china *Mexican/Italian/Chinese food*
el chocolate *chocolate*
el *the*
la ensalada *salad*
el español *Spanish*
el fútbol *soccer*
el fútbol norteamericano *football*
la fruta *fruit*
el jazz *jazz*
la *the*
más *more*
Me gusta... *I like . . .*
mucho *a lot*
la música clásica/pop/rock *classical/pop/rock music*
la música de... *music by . . .*
la natación *swimming*
no *no*
pero *but*
la pizza *pizza*
¿Qué te gusta? *What do you like?*
sí *yes*
la tarea *homework*
¿Te gusta...? *Do you like . . .?*
el tenis *tennis*
el voleibol *volleyball*

Game

¡A PESCAR! Each student makes a hand-held set of 31 playing cards, with the Spanish word and its corresponding numeral on one side. A pair of students shuffle their decks together and each draws five cards. Students play a variation of Go Fish—one student asks for a number in Spanish of a card that he or she has (**¿cinco?**), and if the partner has it in his or her hand, it must be handed to the caller. Upon collecting a matching pair of numbers, the player turns those two cards face down on the desk. The turn continues until the caller asks for something the partner does not have in his or her hand, at which point the partner says **¡A pescar!** The first student must draw one card from the deck. The turn then goes to the partner. The winner is the first to match all cards in his or her hand into pairs and therefore run out of cards.

For Individual Needs

Kinesthetic Learners Use actual objects as well as plastic replicas, drawings, and pictures to review the vocabulary. Put all items in a box. Have students take an item and use the name of the item in a Spanish phrase or sentence.

Chapter 1 Assessment

Chapter Test

- *Chapter Teaching Resources, Book 1*, pp. 29-34
- *Assessment Guide, Speaking Test*, p. 28
- *Assessment Items, Audiocassette 7A Audio CD 1*

Test Generator, Chapter 1

Alternative Assessment

Performance Assessment
Have students perform **Repaso** Activity 11, p. 39, as a cumulative performance assessment activity.

Portfolio Assessment

- **Written: Repaso** Activity 7, *Pupil's Edition*, p. 39
  Assessment Guide, p. 14
- **Oral: Repaso** Activity 8, *Pupil's Edition* p. 39
  Assessment Guide, p. 14

Capítulo 2: ¡Organízate!
Chapter Overview

De antemano pp. 44–46	**¡Mañana es el primer día de clases!**			*Video Guide* OR *Videodisc Guide*
	FUNCTIONS	**GRAMMAR**	**CULTURE**	**RE-ENTRY**
Primer paso pp. 47–51	Talking about what you want and need, p. 48	• Singular indefinite articles (**un** and **una**), p. 47 • Pluralization of nouns, p. 48 • Indefinite articles (**un** and **unos, una** and **unas**), p. 49 • Subject pronouns (**el** and **ella**), p. 50	• **Nota cultural**, The school day in Spain and Latin America, p. 50 • **Panorama cultural**, **¿Qué necesitas para el colegio?**, p. 51	Subject pronouns: **yo, tú**
Segundo paso pp. 52–55	Describing the contents of your room, p. 53	Agreement of **mucho** and **cuánto** with nouns, p. 54	**Nota cultural**, Apartments in Spain, p. 54	Talking about likes and dislikes
Tercer paso pp. 56–59	Talking about what you need and want to do, p. 56	Identifying infinitives, p. 57	Realia, Spanish currency, p. 58	• Numbers 0–30 • Forming questions with **cuántos**
Letra y sonido p. 59	**Pronunciación:** the letter **d** in Spanish		**Dictado:** *Textbook Audiocassette 1B/Audio CD 2*	
Vamos a Leer pp. 60–61	**Portadas**		**Reading Strategy**: Looking at pictures, titles, and subtitles first	
Review pp. 62–65	**Repaso**, pp. 62–63	**A ver si puedo...**, p. 64	**Vocabulario**, p. 65	
Assessment Options	**Paso Quizzes** • *Chapter Teaching Resources, Book 1* **Primer paso,** Quiz 2-1, pp. 81–82 **Segundo paso,** Quiz 2-2, pp. 83–84 **Tercer paso,** Quiz 2-3, pp. 85–86 • *Assessment Items, Audiocassette 7A/Audio CD 2*		**Chapter Test** • *Chapter Teaching Resources, Book 1*, pp. 87–92 • *Assessment Guide*, Speaking Test, p. 28 • *Assessment Items, Audiocassette 7A/Audio CD 2* **Test Generator, Chapter 2**	

RESOURCES: Print	RESOURCES: Audiovisual
Video Program OR *Expanded Video Program, Videocassette 1* OR *Videodisc Program, Videodisc 1B*	*Textbook Audiocassette 1B/Audio CD 2*
	Textbook Audiocassette 1B/Audio CD 2
Practice and Activity Book, pp. 14–16	
Native Speaker Activity Book, pp. 6–10	
Chapter Teaching Resources, Book 1	
• Additional Listening Activities 2-1, 2-2, p. 69	*Additional Listening Activities, Audiocassette 10A/Audio CD 2*
• Student Response Forms, p. 78	
• Realia 2-1, pp. 73, 75	
• Situation Cards 2-1, pp. 76–77	
• Teaching Transparency Master 2-1, pp. 65, 68	*Teaching Transparency 2-1*
• Quiz 2-1, pp. 81–82	*Assessment Items, Audiocassette 7A/Audio CD 2*
Videodisc Guide	*Videodisc Program, Videodisc 1B*
Video Guide	*Video Program* OR *Expanded Video Program, Videocassette 1*
	Textbook Audiocassette 1B/Audio CD 2
Practice and Activity Book, pp. 17–19	
Native Speaker Activity Book, pp. 6–10	
Chapter Teaching Resources, Book 1	
• Communicative Activity 2-1, pp. 63–64	
• Additional Listening Activities 2-3, 2-4, p. 70	*Additional Listening Activities, Audiocassette 10A/Audio CD 2*
• Student Response Forms, p. 79	
• Realia 2-2, pp. 74–75	
• Situation Cards 2-2, pp. 76–77	
• Teaching Transparency Master 2-2, pp. 66–68	*Teaching Transparency 2-2*
• Quiz 2-2, pp. 83–84	*Assessment Items, Audiocassette 7A/Audio CD 2*
Videodisc Guide	*Videodisc Program, Videodisc 1B*
	Textbook Audiocassette 1B/Audio CD 2
Practice and Activity Book, pp. 20–22	
Native Speaker Activity Book, pp. 6–10	
Chapter Teaching Resources, Book 1	
• Communicative Activity 2-2, pp. 63–64	
• Additional Listening Activities 2-5, 2-6, p. 71	*Additional Listening Activities, Audiocassette 10A/Audio CD 2*
• Student Response Forms, p. 80	
• Realia 2-2, pp. 74–75	
• Situation Cards 2-3, pp. 76–77	
• Teaching Transparency Master 2-3, pp. 67, 68	*Teaching Transparency 2-3*
• Quiz 2-3, pp. 85–86	*Assessment Items, Audiocassette 7A/Audio CD 2*
Videodisc Guide	*Video Program, Videodisc 1A*
Video Guide	*Video Program* OR *Expanded Video Program, Videocassette 1*
Videodisc Guide	*Videodisc Program, Videodisc 1B*

Alternative Assessment

- Performance Assessment
  Primer paso, p. 50
  Segundo paso, p. 55
  Tercer paso, p. 59
- Portfolio Assessment
  Written: **Repaso,** Activity 2, *Teacher's Edition*, p. 62
  Assessment Guide, p. 15
  Oral: **A ver si puedo...,** Activity 3, *Pupil's Edition*, p. 64
  Assessment Guide, p. 15

Capítulo 2: ¡Organízate!
Textbook Listening Activities Scripts

For Student Response Forms, see *Chapter Teaching Resources, Book 1,* pp. 78–80.

Primer paso

Activity 6, p. 47

ARTURO Para las clases, necesito unas gomas de borrar, cuadernos y libros, claro. Tú, ¿qué necesitas?

SUMIKO Necesito lápices y cuadernos, y una regla nueva.

Answers to Activity 6
gomas de borrar, cuadernos, libros, lápices, regla

Activity 8, p. 48

Necesito papel, una calculadora, lápices y una carpeta. Ya tengo una mochila, varios cuadernos, los libros y los bolígrafos.

Answers to Activity 8
Necesita: papel, calculadora, lápices, carpeta
Ya tiene: mochila, cuadernos, libros, bolígrafos

Segundo paso

Activity 16, p. 52

En mi cuarto, hay dos camas y dos escritorios. También hay dos sillas, una mesa y un televisor. En mi cuarto tengo también una radio, una lámpara y tres carteles. Claro que también hay una puerta y una ventana, un armario y ropa en el armario.

Answers to Activity 16
camas, escritorios, sillas, mesa, televisor, radio, lámpara, carteles, puerta, ventana, armario, ropa; *comparisons will vary*

Tercer paso

Activity 27, p. 57

Primero les digo lo que necesito hacer yo. Necesito organizar mi cuarto, poner la ropa en el armario y encontrar mi mochila. Necesito hacer muchas cosas. Mi hermano Tomás también necesita hacer muchas cosas. Él necesita ir al centro comercial para comprar una mochila nueva, pero primero necesita hacer la tarea.

Answers to Activity 27
1. both
2. Tomás
3. Tomás
4. Victoria
5. Victoria/both *(Students may point out that Tomás will need to find one in order to buy it.)*
6. Victoria
7. Tomás

Letra y sonido, p. 59

For the scripts for Parts A and C, see page 59. The script for Part B is below.

B. Dictado

Quiero ir de compras. Necesito varias cosas—diez lápices, una calculadora, dos cuadernos y un diccionario. No necesito bolígrafos—ya tengo cinco. Y carpetas, ya tengo cuarto. ¿Qué más? Ah, sí, ¡necesito el dinero!

Repaso

Activity 1, p. 62

Para las clases necesitas muchas cosas. Necesitas una mochila, cuatro cuadernos, cinco carpetas, diez bolígrafos, seis lápices y un diccionario.

Answers to Repaso Activity 1

a. 4 b. 1 c. 10 d. 5 e. 6 f. 1

Capítulo 2: ¡Organízate!
Projects

*In this activity students will use all four skills to create full-page magazine advertisements in Spanish, present their ads to the class, and read and listen to the presentations of other students. Advertising plays a very important role in Spanish-speaking countries, just as it does in the United States. Have students discuss how they use advertising to decide what to buy. Ask them what types of advertising they prefer. Then have students identify ways in which advertisers target certain consumer groups at certain times of the year. The theme of students' ads may be "Back to School" (**El regreso a clases**).*

MATERIALS

✂ **Students may need**

- Large sheets of white paper
- Old magazines
- A recent national newspaper
- Tape
- Scissors
- Markers
- Glue

SEQUENCE

Have students create advertisements individually or in groups. To create their ads they will need pictures of vocabulary items listed on page 65, which they can cut out of magazines. If some students are particularly artistic, they may choose to draw the items. Each item should have a price listed in **pesetas** that reflects the current exchange rate. Have students research the exchange rate in a recent national newspaper.

1. Talk to students about how they will be able to use the vocabulary they have learned for school supplies, clothing, and classroom items to create their ads. Ask them to make the ads appealing but accurate for the back-to-school theme.
2. Describe the project and assign a date for the rough draft, which is to be sketched on a separate sheet of paper. Assign a later date for final completion of the ad and a date for their oral presentations. Distribute a project assignment sheet and post it in the classroom, or write the assignment on the board.
3. Go over the project and answer any questions the students may have.
4. If they will be working in groups, give students time in class to brainstorm and organize their ideas.
5. Students complete their first draft for peer review and suggestions.
6. Students submit their rough draft for teacher review and suggestions.
7. Students complete the final draft, present their ads to the class, and submit their written ads to the teacher for evaluation.

FAMILY LINK

If students have worked individually on the project, they may also wish to present their ads to their families.

GRADING THE PROJECT

The purpose of this project is to encourage students to use their new vocabulary in both a written and an oral context. However, you may also consider students' ability to calculate the exchange rate when grading their ads.

Suggested point distribution (total = 100 points):

Newspaper Ad

Vocabulary use in ad	40
Creativity and appearance	20
Correct exchange rate	10

Oral Presentation

Comprehensibility	10
Vocabulary use	10
Delivery (poise and confidence)	10

NOTES

- You may wish to devote bulletin board space for finished products.
- The students may want to put their ads in their individual Portfolios.
- Oral presentations may be videotaped.

Capítulo 2: ¡Organízate!

Games

PARA LA CLASE

This game promotes cooperation and gives students an opportunity to practice the vocabulary in Chapter 2. It can be played with the **Vocabulario** *in each* **Paso** *or as a chapter review using the vocabulary on page 65.*

Procedure Students play the game with their books closed. Have one student in the class begin with **Para la clase necesito** ____. The student then adds any item from the **Vocabulario. (Para la clase necesito un cuaderno.)** The next student repeats what the first student said and adds an additional item **(Para la clase necesito un cuaderno y un libro.)** The third student repeats what the second student has said and adds an item.

The game continues with each student repeating what has been said before and adding an item. When a student cannot continue, another student or the teacher may help by pointing silently to the item in the classroom. You may consider rewarding winners.

Plurals Review The game may be played by asking each student to add two of the items. **(Para la clase necesito dos cuadernos.)** The next student repeats what the first student said and adds an additional two items. (**Para la clase necesito dos cuadernos y dos libros.**)

Numbers Review The game may be played by asking each student to increase the number of the next item by one. Student 1 says, **Para la clase necesito un cuaderno.** Student 2 says, **Para la clase necesito un cuaderno y dos libros.**

¿UN O UNA?

This game is played in pairs and practices gender agreement and indefinite articles.

Ask students to work in pairs, and to write words from the **Vocabulario** on small pieces of paper. On the back of each, they are to write **un** or **una.** Papers are placed in a stack with **un** and **una** face down. Students alternate turns, stating whether the noun requires **un** or **una** and turning the paper over to verify the answer. They continue until each has had a chance to match all nouns with articles.

SOBRE LA MESA

This game allows students to work in teams and to practice vocabulary from Chapter 2.

Procedure Before class, assemble as many items as possible from the **Vocabulario** on page 65. Place the items on a table or desk and cover them with a cloth. Divide students into teams.

Have all students gather around the table as you remove the cloth. Give students two minutes to study the items on the table. At the end of two minutes, replace the cloth and have them regroup into their teams. They are to make a list in Spanish of as many of the items as they can remember. You may wish to provide students a second look if they need to add to their lists. The team with the most correct list wins.

¿QUÉ FALTA?

This game practices vocabulary and improves memory.

Procedure Assemble vocabulary items on a table, as in SOBRE LA MESA. Have students gather around and study the items for two minutes. Disperse students or have them close their eyes while you or a student removes one or two items and hides them. Students must then say which items are missing. This can also be played as a team activity.

LA BÚSQUEDA

This game is a scavenger hunt to reinforce the vocabulary of Chapter 2, and to re-enter colors from the **Capítulo preliminar.** *It will work best in classrooms where the students have access to common supplies.*

Procedure Divide the class into small groups. Each group should make up a list of classroom items for another group. Tell them that lists should be as realistic as possible, but may include colors and numbers as modifiers as well. The items on the list are restricted to vocabulary from the chapter that is available in the classroom. (**una calculadora, dos lápices amarillos, una mochila roja, dos carpetas...**)

Then have groups exchange lists and allow time for a scavenger hunt for the items on their list. At the end of the time limit (five minutes, for example), have groups show their items while reading off the list. The group that has found the most items on its list is the winner.

Capítulo 2
¡Organízate!
pp. 42–65

Using the Chapter Opener

Motivating Activity

Returning to school in the fall can be very exciting. Ask students what they do to get ready to return to school and what they usually need to buy. What do they keep from year to year and what do they have to buy each year? Where do they go to buy their items? Who buys the things they need?

Presentation

Have students make a list in English of the items in the photo which they need for school. In pairs, have them compare their lists. Students keep the list and refer to it at the end of the chapter to see what they have learned.

Photo Flash!

(1) Point out to your students that the store in the photo is called a **papelería** because the store primarily sells paper. Tell students that they will learn the names of other stores and outlets which also end in **-ería** as they continue to study Spanish. **(cafetería, pizzería...)**

Building on Previous Skills

Remind students that they already know how to talk about likes and dislikes. How might the girl in the photo tell her friend that she likes her new notebook or ask him if he likes it? What might he answer?

CAPÍTULO 2
¡Organízate!

(1) **Necesito dos libros. ¿Qué necesitas tú?**

42 *cuarenta y dos*

Multicultural Link

If possible, have students interview exchange students or others from abroad regarding school schedules, necessities, and lifestyles in their countries. You might have students choose a country they are interested in and research these topics.

For Individual Needs

Auditory/Tactile Learners Ask students to point to the items in the photo as you read aloud: **fotos, mapas, diccionarios,** and **globos.** Point out that these are English cognates.

What do you usually do to get ready for school each year? Like Paco, you may need to take a look around your room, get things organized, and make a list of the school supplies you'll need.

In this chapter you will learn

- to talk about what you want and need
- to describe the contents of your room
- to talk about what you need and want to do

And you will

- listen to people talk about what they need, what they have in their rooms, and what they need to do
- read about some videos and books you might find interesting
- write a list of the things in someone's room
- find out how Spanish-speaking students prepare for the school year

(2) ¡Hombre! Necesitas organizar tus cosas.

Culture Note

In Spanish-speaking countries many items are sold in specialty shops like this **papelería.** There are not as many supermarkets or department stores that sell almost everything one might need as there are in the United States.

Focusing on Outcomes

Explain to students that in this chapter they will be learning the important language function of communicating to others what they need and want. Have them read the learner outcomes and match them to the photos. (Photo 1 talking about what you need; photo 2 talking about what you need to do; photo 3 describing the contents of your room.) Ask students to think of several items which they want at the beginning of a new school year and several additional items that they really need.

Photo Flash!

(2) This photo is taken from the video episode for Chapter Two. **Abuela** tells Paco that his room is a mess and that he needs to put his things away before he goes shopping. Paco can't tell what school supplies he needs until he straightens his room and finds out what he already has.

Additional Vocabulary

Students may ask about the following items seen in the photographs:

almohada *pillow*
manta, frazada *blanket*
colcha *quilt*
sobrecama *bedspread*
chal *shawl*
cortinas *curtains*
cuadro *picture*
marco *picture frame*
animal de peluche/un pelucho *stuffed animal*
alfombra *carpet*
moqueta *wall-to-wall carpeting* (Spain)
cómoda *dresser*
espejo *mirror*

VIDEO PROGRAM OR EXPANDED VIDEO PROGRAM, *Videocassette 1*

OR *VIDEODISC PROGRAM,* *Videodisc 1B*

SAMPLE

Video Synopsis

Paco is explaining to his grandmother that he needs to buy school supplies. His grandmother tells him to straighten his room first and gives him money to buy what he needs. While straightening his room Paco discovers that he doesn't really need everything he thought he did. When he tells his grandmother, she replies that he already has the money and to buy only what he needs. But now Paco can't find the money.

Motivating Activity

From the pictures in the text, have students predict what is going to happen in the **fotonovela.** Suggest that they formulate their predictions as answers to questions beginning *Who, How, Where, What, When,* and *Why.*

Presentation

Play the video or audio recording for students as they follow along in their books. Then read the **fotonovela** frame by frame, modeling the language and having students repeat after you. Encourage students to guess meaning from context and visual clues. Use Activity 1 on page 46 to check comprehension.

DE ANTEMANO

¡Mañana es el primer día de clases!

Look at the pictures in the **fotonovela.** Who are the characters? Where are they? Is there a problem? What clues tell you this?

Paco

Abuela

44

RESOURCES FOR DE ANTEMANO

Textbook Audiocassette 1B/Audio CD 2
Video Guide
Video Program
Expanded Video Program, Videocassette 1
Videodisc Guide
Videodisc Program, Videodisc 1B
Practice and Activity Book, p. 13

Teacher Note

For previewing, viewing, and postviewing activities, see *Video Guide.*

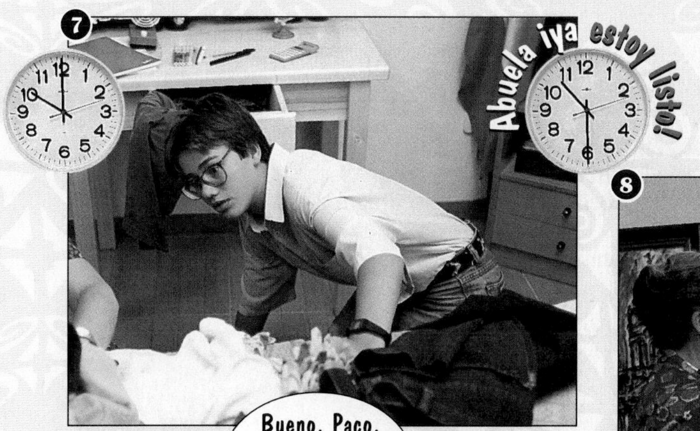

7

Abuela ¡ya estoy listo!

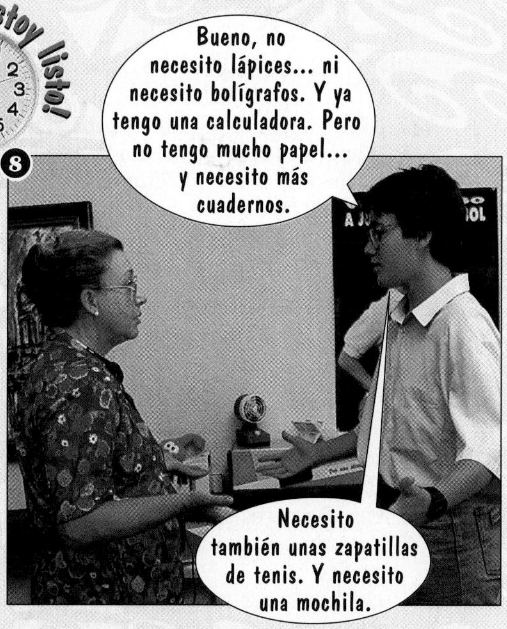

8

Bueno, no necesito lápices... ni necesito bolígrafos. Y ya tengo una calculadora. Pero no tengo mucho papel... y necesito más cuadernos.

Necesito también unas zapatillas de tenis. Y necesito una mochila.

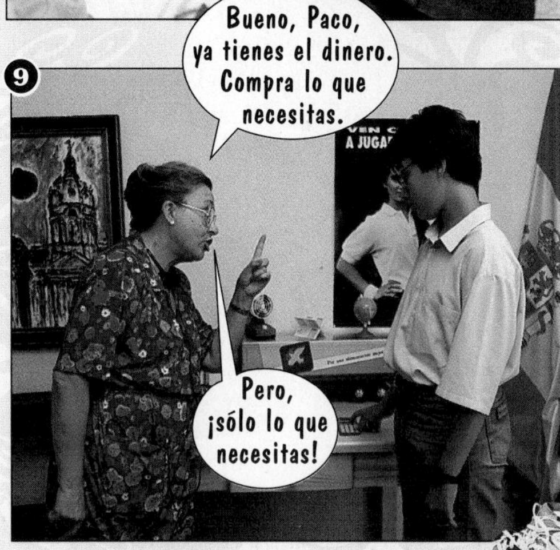

9

Bueno, Paco, ya tienes el dinero. Compra lo que necesitas.

Pero, ¡sólo lo que necesitas!

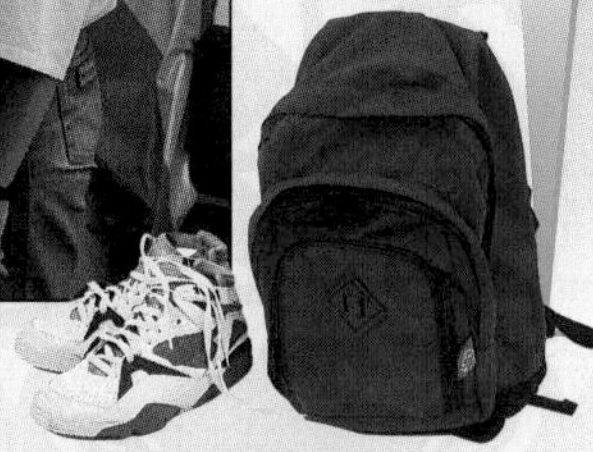

También se puede decir...

In many countries in Latin America, **la pluma** is used instead of **el bolígrafo.**

Other words for **el colegio** include **la escuela secundaria** and **el liceo.**

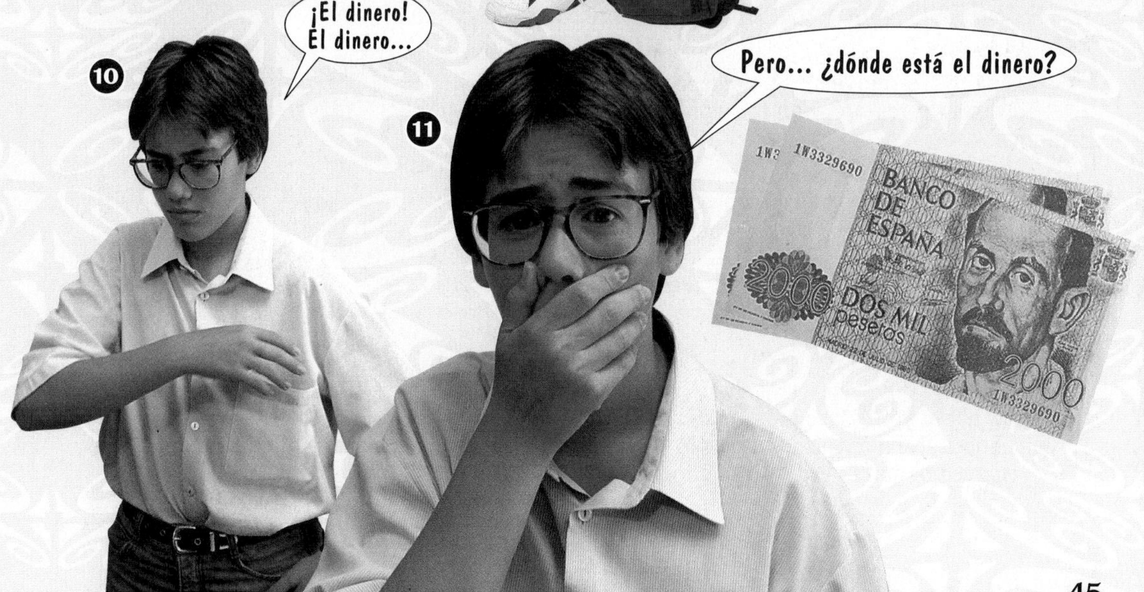

10

¡El dinero! El dinero...

11

Pero... ¿dónde está el dinero?

45

For Individual Needs

Kinesthetic Learners Pick up or point to the following items in the classroom: **mochila, cuaderno, lápiz, libro, papel, bolígrafo, calculadora, diccionario, zapatillas de tenis.** Then ask students to show you each article by picking it up or pointing it out. **(Muéstrame una calculadora.)** To review names and personalize the activity, ask **¿Quién tiene una calculadora?** Then have students ask other students the question.

Culture Note

In Spanish-speaking countries fewer teenagers have part-time jobs. Therefore, they need to ask their parents for spending money.

Thinking Critically

Predicting Ask students to think of different possible endings for the **fotonovela** episode.

Video Integration

- ***Expanded Video Program,*** *Videocassette 1*
- ***Videodisc Program,*** *Videodisc 1B*

You may choose to continue with **¡Mañana es el primer día de clases! (a continuación)** at this time or wait until later in the chapter. At this point in the story, Paco tears his room apart searching for the missing money. His grandmother comes in and is shocked at the mess. Paco calls Felipe and they go shopping together. First they visit a stationery store, next a shoe store, and finally a music store, where Paco buys a gift for his grandmother.

Cooperative Learning

1 Have students work in groups of three to answer the questions. One student asks the question and the second student answers. The third student indicates when to answer by saying **¡Contesta!** Students rotate these roles as they answer the questions.

Teaching Suggestions

1 Ask for volunteers to ask and answer questions. Have the class indicate whether or not answers are correct by thumbs up or thumbs down.

2 Write the words and phrases that make up these sentences on magnetic or felt board strips. Then ask students to manipulate the sentences to change what they say, changing negative sentences to positive ones and vice versa.

Additional Practice

Have partners make a shopping list for Paco. The list should include only the items he decides he needs after he has straightened his room. Ask students how much money Paco will have to spend on his school supplies. Ask pairs to compare their lists.

Language Notes

- The Spanish word **colegio** is generally used for elementary and secondary schools, both public and private. When referring to college, **universidad** is generally used.
- The word **goma** means both *eraser* and *rubber*. Use **borrador** for a chalkboard eraser.
- In some countries, **bulto** is used for *backpack* and **lapicero** means *pen.* **Carpeta** is also used for *notebook.*

1 ¿Comprendes?

Do you understand what is happening in the **fotonovela**? Check your understanding by answering these questions. Don't be afraid to guess! See answers below.

1. Where does the story take place?
2. At the beginning of the **fotonovela**, what does Paco say he needs?
3. What does Paco's grandmother tell him to do? Why?
4. At the end of the **fotonovela**, what does Paco end up needing for school? What else does he want?
5. How does the scene end? What problem does Paco have?

2 ¿Cierto o falso? See answers below.

Based on the ending of the **fotonovela**, are these statements true (**cierto**) or false (**falso**)? If a statement is false, change it to make it true.

1. Mañana es el primer día de clases.
2. Paco no necesita más cuadernos.
3. Paco no necesita más lápices ni bolígrafos.
4. La abuela organiza el cuarto de Paco.
5. Paco tiene unas zapatillas de tenis y necesita una calculadora.

3 ¿Cómo se dice...?

Find the words and phrases Paco uses . . . See answers below.

1. to say he needs something
2. to say he also needs something else
3. to say that he already has something
4. to say that he wants a backpack
5. to ask where the money is

4 ¿Listos? *Ready?*

Using the **fotonovela** as a guide, complete the following paragraph with the words from the box.

zapatillas cuadernos necesito clases dinero bolígrafos papel calculadora

Ay, ¡mañana es el primer día de __1__! Bueno, no __2__ lápices ni necesito __3__, y ya tengo una __4__. Pero no tengo mucho __5__ y necesito más __6__. Y también necesito unas __7__ de tenis. ¡Pero no tengo __8__!

1. clases 2. necesito 3. bolígrafos 4. calculadora 5. papel 6. cuadernos 7. zapatillas 8. dinero

5 ¿Y tú?

How about you? Have you run out of school supplies? Make a list of the supplies Paco mentions. Next to each, write **(No) necesito** or **(No) quiero** to say whether it is something you need or don't need, want or don't want. *Answers will vary. Example:* cuadernos. No necesito cuadernos.

Answers

1 1. At the house where Paco and his grandmother (**abuela**) live.
2. Una mochila, unos cuadernos, unos lápices, libros, papel, bolígrafos, una calculadora, un diccionario y unas zapatillas de tenis.
3. She tells him to clean up his room before he goes shopping, and to buy only the things he needs.
4. Paper, notebooks, tennis shoes, and a backpack.
5. Paco cannot find the money.

3 1. necesito
2. y necesito; necesito también
3. no necesito; ya tengo
4. quiero una mochila
5. ¿Dónde está el dinero?

PRIMER PASO

Talking about what you want and need

VOCABULARIO

También se puede decir...
In many countries in Latin America, **la pluma** is used instead of **el bolígrafo.** Other words for **el colegio** include **la escuela secundaria** and **el liceo.**

Nota Gramatical

Un and **una** mean *a* or *an.* Use **un** with masculine nouns: **un bolígrafo.** Use **una** with feminine nouns: **una regla.** Do you remember two ways to say *the* in Spanish?[1]

6 Escuchemos: Arturo y Sumiko

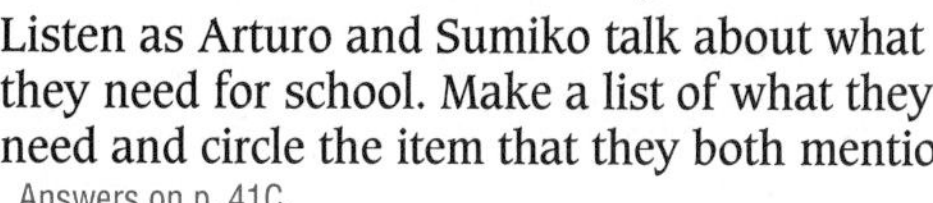

Listen as Arturo and Sumiko talk about what they need for school. Make a list of what they need and circle the item that they both mention.

Answers on p. 41C.

7 Cosas para el colegio

Things for school

Elena is telling her father what she has and what she needs for school. Complete each sentence with **un** or **una.**

Tengo __1__ (un) libro de matemáticas pero necesito __2__ (un) cuaderno. Tengo __3__ (un) bolígrafo, __4__ (una) goma de borrar y __5__ (una) carpeta. Necesito __6__ (un) diccionario, __7__ (una) calculadora, una regla y __8__ (un) lápiz. Y quiero __9__ (una) mochila nueva *(new)*.

[1] **El** and **la** are used to mean *the.*

RESOURCES FOR PRIMER PASO

Textbook Audiocassette 1B/Audio CD 2
Practice and Activity Book, pp. 14–16
Native Speaker Activity Book, pp. 6–10
Videodisc Guide
Videodisc Program, Videodisc 1B

Chapter Teaching Resources, Book 1
- Additional Listening Activities 2-1, 2-2, p. 69
  Audiocassette 10A/Audio CD 2
- Student Response Forms, p. 78
- Realia 2-1, pp. 73, 75
- Situation Cards 2-1, pp. 76–77
- Teaching Transparency Master 2-1, pp. 65, 68
  Teaching Transparency 2-1
- Quiz 2-1, pp. 81–82
  Audiocassette 7A/Audio CD 2

Jump Start!

To review punctuation and capitalization, write the following sentences on a transparency or the board. **(hola me llamo maria mercedes alvarez garcia y soy de madrid tengo 15 años y tu cuantos años tienes)** Have students rewrite the sentences using proper punctuation and capitalization.

MOTIVATE

Ask students what items on the vocabulary list are things they need for school. Ask if there is anything they still need to get.

TEACH

Presentation

Vocabulario As the class watches and listens, model the name of each item as you put it (or a picture of it) into a **mochila** on your desk. Then ask individual students to take certain items from the backpack using the question **¿Tienes...?** Divide the class into two teams and ask the first student on Team A: **¿Tienes...?** The student looks in the **mochila,** selects and names the item, and returns it to the **mochila.** If the student can't find the item, teammates can help out. A representative from Team B then identifies the next item you call out.

Nota Gramatical Explain that nouns in Spanish are divided into two groups: masculine and feminine. Review **el** and **la** using flashcards and draw a parallel between **un** and **una.** Note that using masculine and feminine articles becomes more natural with practice. Encourage students to guess when they are not sure of the appropriate article.

Presentation

Así se dice To model the phrases, take an item from a student's desk and ask "**¿Quieres (un libro)?**" Prompt the student to answer with "**Sí, quiero un libro.**" Then ask the class "**¿(Miguel) quiere un libro?**" Prompt the class to answer. Repeat the process with **necesitas.**

For videodisc application, see *Videodisc Guide.*

Teacher Note

8 You may wish to use the Student Response Form in the *Chapter Teaching Resources, Book 1*, page 78.

Additional Practice

8 You might set up a classroom store with play money and a list of school supplies for each student. Ask a few students to serve as clerks. The rest will be shoppers. Give shoppers a list of school supplies and ask them to check their own supplies against the items on the list. If they do not have something, they'll need to buy it at the classroom store.

Presentation

Gramática Ask students to make plural each of the vocabulary items on page 47. Then practice by holding up one or more of the items on the list and asking students **¿Cuántos hay?**

ASÍ SE DICE Talking about what you want and need

To find out what someone wants, ask:	To answer, say:
¿**Qué quieres?**	**Quiero** una mochila.
¿Paco **quiere** una mochila?	Sí, él **quiere** una mochila.
To find out what someone needs, ask:	
¿**Qué necesitas?**	**Necesito** un cuaderno.
¿**Necesitas** papel?	No, **ya tengo** papel. *No, I already have . . .*
¿Qué **necesita** Merche?	**¡Ella necesita muchas cosas!** *She needs a lot of things!*

8 Escuchemos: ¿Qué necesito?

Blanca is stocking up on school supplies before school starts. Listen as she makes up her shopping list. Ignoring the things she already has, write only the things she needs. Start your answer with **Necesito...** Answers on p. 41C.

9 ¿Qué necesitas para...? *What do you need for . . .?*

Using the drawing of the items in the bookstore and **Un poco más**, identify the Spanish words for the things you might need . . .

1. to write a report papel y bolígrafos
2. to carry loose papers una carpeta
3. to make a poster for art class un marcador
4. to add up your bill una calculadora
5. to do your geometry homework una regla
6. to take notes in class unos bolígrafos, papel
7. to carry your supplies una mochila
8. to look up unknown words un diccionario

Un poco más...

un lápiz de color	*colored pencil*
un marcador	*marker*
un pincel	*paintbrush*
(la) pintura	*paint*

Gramática Making nouns plural

1. So far, you've been talking about single things. To make a noun plural, add **-s** if it ends in a vowel: **diccionario → diccionarios.** If the noun ends in a consonant, add **-es: papel → papeles.**
2. If a noun ends in **-z**, change **-z** to **-c** and add **-es: lápiz → lápices.**
3. How would you make these nouns plural?
   a. cruz b. luz c. vez[1]

[1] The plurals are **cruces, luces, veces.**

Multicultural Link

Interview exchange students or others who have studied in Spanish-speaking countries. Inquire if students in those countries follow the same kind of schedule as students in your school. Do they stay in the same room all day? How does this affect what they bring to school? Do students wear uniforms? If there are no exchange students in your school, your students might ask these questions of pen pals. See page T56 for pen pal information.

10 ¡Necesito muchas cosas!

With a partner, play the roles of Paco and a friend. Each time Paco says he wants an item, his friend tells him he already has several. Use the numbers in parentheses.

MODELO (6) libro de béisbol. See answers below.
—Quiero un libro de béisbol.
—Pero Paco, ¡ya tienes seis libros de béisbol!

1. (3) calculadora
2. (11) lápiz
3. (9) cuaderno
4. (2) mochila
5. (15) bolígrafo
6. (5) carpeta
7. (20) goma de borrar
8. (4) regla

11 Una lista

Work in pairs. Find out if your partner needs or already has these school supplies. Then tell your partner which ones you need. Make a list for each partner. ¿Necesitas...? Yo necesito...

12 La lista de mi compañero/a *My partner's list*

Based on Activity 11, write a brief paragraph telling what school supplies your partner already has and what she or he needs. Use **Ya tiene..** and **Necesita...**
Possible answers: (Name) ya tiene...; *(Name)* necesita...

Gramática Indefinite articles (un, una, unos, unas)

1. You've already learned that **un** and **una** mean *a* or *an*. **Unos** and **unas** mean *some* or *a few*. This chart shows how the four forms of the indefinite article are used.

	SINGULAR	PLURAL
MASCULINE	**un bolígrafo**	**unos bolígrafos**
FEMININE	**una mochila**	**unas mochilas**

2. Use **unos** with a masculine plural noun. When referring to a group of people that includes both males and females, the masculine plural is used (**unos estudiantes**).
3. In a negative sentence, **un**, **una**, **unos**, and **unas** are often dropped.
   ¿Necesitas unos bolígrafos? No, no necesito bolígrafos.

For Individual Needs

10 Slower Pace Have students write the words for the numerals of how many items Paco has before joining their partner. Allow them to use the written responses as they role-play Paco and his friend.

Presentation

Gramática Model the usage of indefinite articles by walking around the room and picking up various items and then saying what you have. (**Tengo un bolígrafo. Tengo unos lápices.**) Then ask students questions to which they must respond appropriately, using indefinite articles. (**Paula, ¿necesitas un cuaderno? No, profesor, ya tengo unos cuadernos.**) You might have students ask each other questions as well.

Thinking Critically

Drawing Inferences Ask students why **el, la, los,** and **las** are called *definite articles* and why **un, una, unos,** and **unas** are called *indefinite articles.*

Answers

10 *Answers may vary. Possible answers:*

1. Quiero una calculadora. Pero Paco, ya tienes tres calculadoras.
2. Necesito unos lápices. Ya tienes once lápices.
3. Quiero unos cuadernos. Ya tienes nueve cuadernos.
4. Necesito una mochila. Ya tienes dos mochilas.
5. Necesito unos bolígrafos. Ya tienes quince bolígrafos.
6. Necesito una carpeta. Ya tienes cinco carpetas.
7. Necesito unas gomas de borrar. ¡Hombre! ya tienes veinte gomas de borrar.
8. Necesito una regla. Pero ya tienes cuatro reglas. ¡Qué desastre!

PRIMER PASO
CAPÍTULO 2

CLOSE

Fill a shopping basket with school items already presented. Put in two or three of some items. One by one, have students come up to the basket. Tell each person what he or she is to select using either, **Tienes, Necesitas,** or **Quieres** and an item or items in the basket. If you say **Miguel, necesitas cuadernos,** the student is to pick the item or items from the basket and say a sentence using the **yo** form of the verb you have used and the items selected. (**Necesito unos cuadernos**). Ask students to describe the items they find in the basket, using **un** or **unos,** and **una** or **unas.**

ASSESS

Quiz 2-1, *Chapter Teaching Resources, Book 1,* pp. 81–82

Assessment Items, Audiocassette 7A/Audio CD 2

Performance Assessment

Make a list of ten school supplies that students carry in their **mochilas.** Put these supplies in a **mochila.** Ask students to copy the list. Then pull an item out of a **mochila** and at the same time call out a number (**uno** for first item, **diez** for last). Ask students to write the number by the name of the item on their list.

13 Hablando con Felipe *Talking with Felipe*

It's the first day of school. Complete Paco and Felipe's phone conversation. Use the correct indefinite article (**un, una, unos** or **unas**) with the missing words.

PACO Felipe, ¿necesitas [un diccionario] ?

FELIPE Sí. También necesito [unos cuadernos] .

PACO Yo necesito [una calculadora] y [unas reglas] para la clase de matemáticas. Ah, y ¿quieres [una goma de borrar] ?

FELIPE Sí, y necesito [unos lápices] también.

14 ¿Qué necesitas?

What do you need for your classes? With a partner, take turns asking each other what school supplies you need for . . . See answers below.

1. la clase de español
2. la clase de arte
3. la clase de álgebra
4. la clase de historia

NOTA CULTURAL

In many high schools in Spain and Latin America, students stay in the same room for their classes all day and the teachers change classrooms. Because of this, it's rare to find a school that has lockers. Students carry their supplies to and from school each day in book bags or backpacks.

Nota Gramatical

In Chapter 1 you learned to use the subject pronoun **yo** when talking about yourself and **tú** when talking to another student or someone your own age. When you want to talk about someone else, use **él** to mean *he* and **ella** to mean *she.*

Paco y Merche quieren ir a la tienda. **Él** necesita una mochila y **ella** necesita muchas cosas.

15 Reportaje

Replace the name in the second sentence with **él** or **ella** as appropriate.

MODELO ¿Felipe? ¿Qué tiene Felipe? ¿Qué tiene él?

1. ¿Paco? Paco ya tiene papel. él
2. ¿Merche? Merche quiere una mochila. ella
3. ¿Leticia? No, Leticia no necesita un cuaderno. ella
4. ¿Juan Antonio? ¿Qué quiere Juan Antonio? él
5. ¿Noemí? Sí, Noemí necesita bolígrafos. ella

Answers

14 *Possible items:*

1. el libro de español, unos bolígrafos, un diccionario, papel, un cuaderno
2. unos marcadores, pintura, un pincel, una regla, papel
3. el libro de álgebra, unos lápices, una calculadora, una regla, papel, un cuaderno
4. el libro de inglés, unos bolígrafos, un diccionario, papel, un cuaderno

Game

DIBUJOS To review material from this **Paso,** divide the class into two teams and play this game. Ask the first player to go to the board. Show the student a vocabulary word. He or she draws a picture of the word and his or her team says the word in Spanish, including the correct definite article (**el** or **la**). The team has one minute to draw and guess the word before the opposing team may try. The successful team gets the point. The other team sends a student to the board next. Continue, this time with the indefinite articles.

¿Qué necesitas para el colegio?

In this chapter, we asked some people what they need to buy before the school year starts.

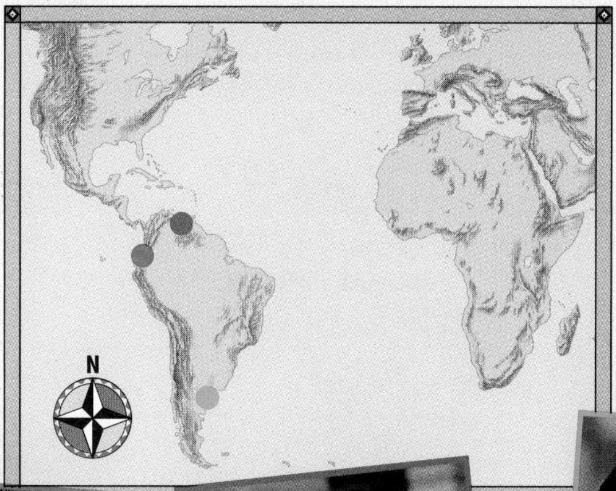

Paulina
Quito, Ecuador
"Tengo que comprar todos los cuadernos, los libros y mi uniforme".

Fabiola
Caracas, Venezuela
"Bueno, cuadernos, lápices, libros, borradores, calculadora".

Jimena
Buenos Aires, Argentina
"Tuve que comprar lápices, lapiceras, gomas, reglas, cartuchera, mochila, cuadernos y carpetas".

Para pensar y hablar...

A. What do you need to buy before the school year starts? In some countries of the Spanish-speaking world there's a basic list of school supplies. Do you find differences and similarities between the supplies you buy and the items mentioned by these Latin-American students?

B. Paulina mentions having to buy a uniform. How do you feel about wearing uniforms to school? What would be the advantages and disadvantages?

VIDEO PROGRAM OR EXPANDED VIDEO PROGRAM, Videocassette 1

OR VIDEODISC PROGRAM, Videodisc 1B

Teacher Notes

- See *Video Guide* and *Videodisc Guide* for activities related to the **Panorama cultural.**
- Remind students that cultural information on this page may be included in the Quizzes and Chapter Test.

Motivating Activity

Using the new vocabulary from Chapter 2, have the students make a list of the supplies that are necessary for school. Write their suggestions on the board or a transparency.

Presentation

Have students watch the video without looking at the written interview. Have the students recall the supplies that they heard. Check the items off the list from the Motivating Activity. Then have students read the interviews while listening to the tape a second time and check the answers that were given. Then play the video again and have students answer the **Preguntas.**

Preguntas

1. ¿Qué persona necesita un uniforme? (Paulina)
2. ¿El estudiante de qué país tiene que comprar una calculadora? (Venezuela)
3. En la Argentina, ¿necesitan los chicos comprar los libros? (No.)

Culture Notes

- You might point out that many schools in Spain and Latin America require their students to wear uniforms and that often, the students must purchase them.
- Schools in Latin American countries often do not provide as many materials as schools in the United States. It is common for students to have to purchase their books. They are not provided by the schools.

Language Note

In Argentina, **lapiceras** = *pens,* **cartuchera** = *zippered pencil case,* and **pluma estilográfica** = *cartridge pen.*

Jump Start!

Before class, display the following on a transparency or the board: a pen, an eraser, a backpack, a ruler, a notebook, and a book. Ask students to write in Spanish each item they have brought with them today.

Motivate

- Ask students to envision their ideal room; have several students describe their image. How do they envision their own rooms ten years from now?
- Ask students to jot down five things they consider essential for any student's room. Tally the number of times each item is listed, and put the most frequently listed items first when introducing this lesson.

Teach

Presentation

Vocabulario Have students pick out cognates in the **Vocabulario,** then model pronunciation of all items and have students repeat the new words. Ask them to turn to the Chapter Opener photo of the girl in her room and answer the question **¿Qué hay en su cuarto?**

Building on Previous Skills

Have students describe **El cuarto de Débora** using an indefinite article for each vocabulary item.

Answers

17 *Possible answers:*
HAY—sillas, ventanas, una puerta, un armario, un televisor, carteles, mesas, un reloj, escritorios, zapatillas de tenis;
NO HAY—cama, ropa, una radio, una lámpara, revistas

SEGUNDO PASO

Describing the contents of your room

VOCABULARIO

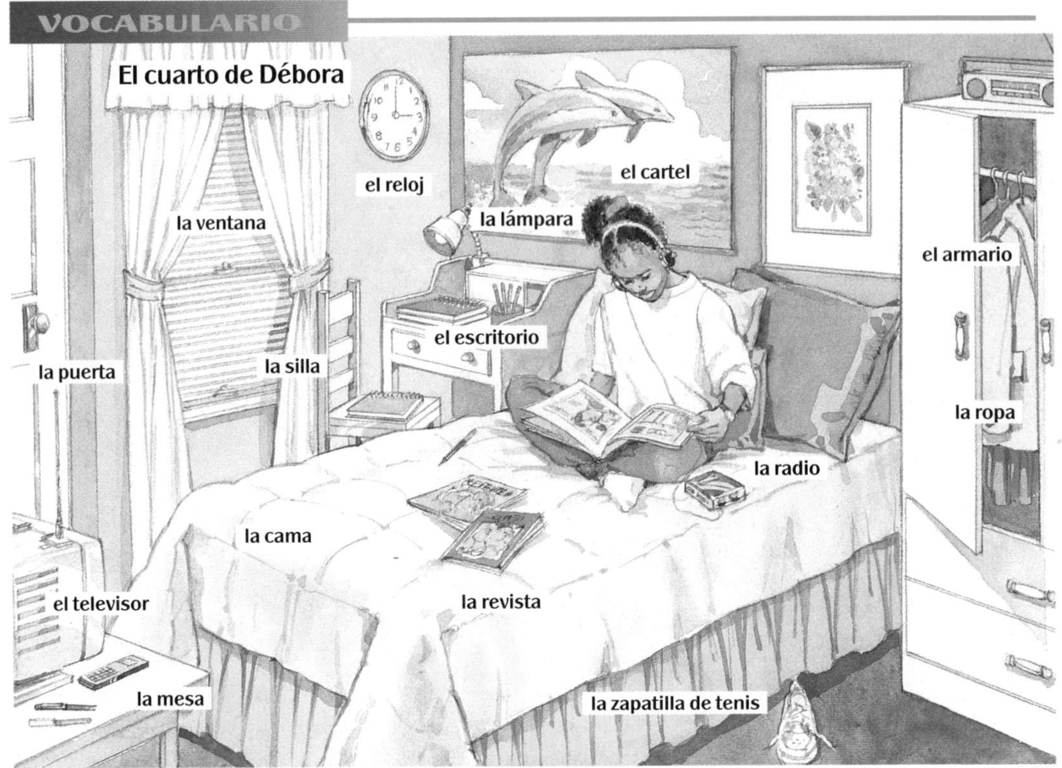

16 Escuchemos: ¿Qué hay?

Listen as Julio describes what's in his room. Write the items he mentions. How is the room he describes different from Débora's room in the picture?
Answers on p. 41C.

17 En la sala de clase *In the classroom*

Which of the things in Débora's room are also found in your classroom? Make two lists, one showing how many there are (**hay**) of each item, and another one showing what isn't there (**no hay**). See answers below.

También se puede decir...

In many Spanish-speaking countries, you will also hear **el pupitre** for **el escritorio** and **el afiche** or **el póster** for **el cartel.**

Un poco más...

el estéreo	*stereo*
la videocasetera	*VCR*
la computadora	*computer*
el teléfono	*telephone*

RESOURCES FOR SEGUNDO PASO

Textbook Audiocassette 1B/Audio CD 2
Practice and Activity Book, pp. 17–19
Native Speaker Activity Book, pp. 6–10
Video Guide
Video Program
Expanded Video Program, Videocassette 1
Videodisc Guide
Videodisc Program, Videodisc 1B

Chapter Teaching Resources, Book 1
- Communicative Activity 2-1, pp. 63–64
- Additional Listening Activities 2-3, 2-4, p. 70
  Audiocassette 10A/Audio CD 2
- Student Response Forms, p. 79
- Realia 2-2, pp. 74, 75
- Situation Cards 2-2, pp. 76–77
- Teaching Transparency Master 2-2, pp. 66, 68
  Teaching Transparency 2-2
- Quiz 2-2, pp. 83–84
  Audiocassette 7A/Audio CD 2

ASÍ SE DICE Describing the contents of your room

To find out what there is in someone's room, ask:

¿**Qué hay en tu cuarto?**

¿Qué hay **en el cuarto de Paco?**
. . . in Paco's room?

¿**Tienes un televisor?**
Do you have a TV set?

¿**Qué tiene** Merche **en su cuarto?**
. . . in her room?

To answer, say

Tengo una mesa y dos sillas **en mi cuarto.** *I have . . .*

Hay libros y cuadernos **en su cuarto.**
There are . . . in his room.

No, **no tengo** televisor.

Merche **tiene** unos carteles y una radio **en su cuarto.**

18 Describir el cuarto *Describing the room*

Look at the **Vocabulario** on page 52. How many of each item does Débora have in her room? Start your descriptions with **En el cuarto de Débora hay...** or **Débora tiene...**

un	1. bolígrafo	9. armario	un
una	2. ventana	10. zapatillas de tenis	una
tres	3. revista	11. silla	una
tres	4. cuaderno	12. radio	una
cuatro	5. lápiz	13. televisor	un
una	6. lámpara	14. reloj	un
una	7. cama	15. puerta	dos (o tres)
un	8. cartel		

Try making Spanish labels for things you use every day at school and at home (your school supplies, things in your room, etc.). This way, every time you look at an item you'll be reminded of how to say it in Spanish. And don't forget to include **el** and **la** to remind you which words are masculine and which ones are feminine.

19 Un cuarto perfecto

Look at the picture of this bedroom. Imagine that it is your room and write five sentences about it. Begin your description with **En mi cuarto hay...** Be as detailed as you can. See answers below.

20 ¿Qué hay en tu cuarto?

With a partner, take turns asking each other about what's in your rooms. Use both **¿Hay...?** and **¿Tienes...?** and refer to the drawing on page 52 for ideas. Use your imagination! See answers below.

Presentation

Así se dice Draw a picture of a room on a transparency and describe it. **(En el cuarto hay una cama, una silla...)** Then ask students personalized questions about their rooms. **(Pepe, ¿tienes una ventana en tu cuarto?)** Put students at ease by assuring them that their answers can refer to an imaginary or ideal room.

For videodisc application, see *Videodisc Guide.*

For Individual Needs

18 Visual Learners Label vocabulary items found in your classroom to help students remember the words.

18 Challenge Teach the prepositions **al lado de, encima de,** and **debajo de.** Ask students to tell you where an item is in relation to another. Use the picture of **el cuarto de Débora.**

20 Slower Pace Have students list the items they have before starting this activity.

Answers

19 *Sample answer:*
En mi cuarto hay una cama, una ventana y una lámpara blanca. Tengo unas carpetas, unos libros y unos cuadernos.

20 *Possible questions:*
¿Hay un reloj?
¿Tienes una silla?

Language Note

Las zapatillas de tenis is the common term for *tennis shoes* in Spain. In other countries one also hears **los zapatos de tenis** and **los tenis.**

SEGUNDO PASO
CAPÍTULO 2

Presentation

Gramática Point out to students that **cuánto/a** and **mucho/a** are sometimes used when referring to things we can't count or usually don't count. (**¿Cuánto papel hay en el escritorio? Hay mucho. ¿Cuánta leche hay en el vaso? Hay mucha.**) **Cuántos/as** and **muchos/as** are used when we could count the items to which we refer. (**¿Cuántos relojes hay en la escuela? Hay muchos. ¿Cuántas lámparas hay en la sala? Hay muchas.**)

Photo Flash!

Ask students to talk about the photograph, naming various items that they recognize and using the words **mucho** and **cuánto** as appropriate.

Additional Practice

21 Have partners ask and answer questions about classroom objects using **cuántos** and **muchos**. (**¿Cuántos diccionarios hay en la clase? Hay muchos diccionarios en la clase.**) Each student should ask a minimum of five questions.

Gramática Agreement of **mucho** and **cuánto** with nouns

1. Many nouns and adjectives have the following endings:

	SINGULAR	PLURAL
MASCULINE	**-o**	**-os**
FEMININE	**-a**	**-as**

Making the endings of adjectives and nouns match is called *agreement in gender* (masculine/feminine) *and number* (singular/plural).[1]

2. The forms of **¿cuánto?** are used to ask *how much?* or *how many?* Like other adjectives, **¿cuánto?** matches the noun it describes.

¿Cuánt**as** carpet**as** necesitas?
¿Cuánt**os** bolígraf**os**?
¿Cuánt**o** papel?
¿Cuánt**a** tarea tienes?

3. The forms of **mucho** mean *a lot, much,* or *many.* Like **cuánto**, **mucho** changes to match the noun it modifies.

No necesito much**as** carpet**as**, pero necesito much**os** bolígraf**os** y mucho papel.
Tengo mucha tarea.

21 ¿Cuántas cosas tengo? See answers below.

Patricia has just moved here, and her new friend David wants to know more about her. Fill in the blanks of their conversation using forms of **cuánto** and **mucho.**

DAVID ¿Te gusta el colegio? ¿__1__ clases tienes? ¿__2__ tarea hay?
PATRICIA Me gusta el colegio. Tengo siete clases y hay __3__ tarea.
DAVID ¿Te gusta tu cuarto? ¿Hay __4__ ventanas?
PATRICIA No hay __5__ ventanas. Sólo *(only)* hay una.
DAVID ¿__6__ carteles hay? ¿Y __7__ libros tienes?
PATRICIA Tengo __8__ carteles y __9__ libros. Pero David... no tengo __10__ amigos.
DAVID Ay, Patricia... ¡yo soy tu amigo!

NOTA CULTURAL

In Spain, most people live in **pisos** *(apartments)* in cities or towns. Bedrooms are often smaller, and sisters or brothers will sometimes have to share a room. Generally, the family shares a single TV set and a single phone. It's not common for teenagers to have a TV or a phone of their own in their bedroom.

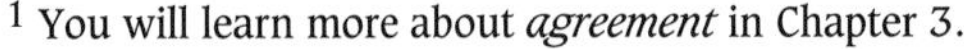

1 You will learn more about *agreement* in Chapter 3.

Answers

21
1. Cuántas
2. Cuánta
3. mucha
4. muchas
5. muchas
6. Cuántos
7. cuántos
8. muchos
8. muchos
10. muchos

22 Comparación de cuartos

Comparing rooms

Work with a partner. One of you is staying in the **Hotel Dineral,** and the other is staying in the **Hotel Pocovale.** Imagine that you're on the telephone to each other comparing your rooms. Tell your partner what's in your room, or tell about what's not there.

MODELO En mi cuarto hay dos camas. No tengo televisor pero hay una lámpara.

See answers below.

A lo nuestro

You have already learned to say if you like something using **(no) me gusta.** Here are some new phrases to express stronger reactions. If you like something a lot you can say, **¡Genial!, ¡Increíble!** or **¡Qué padre!** If you think something is just all right, you can say, **Está bien** or **No está mal.** If you think it's terrible, you can say, **¡Qué horrible!, ¡Qué pesado!** or **¡Pésimo!**

Hotel Pocovale

Hotel Dineral

23 Mi cuarto ideal

Survey three to five classmates to find out what's in each person's ideal room. Be prepared to tell the class what kind of room you would design for one member of your group.

MODELO —En el cuarto ideal de Ana, hay...

Un poco más...

un balcón	*balcony*
un estante	*bookcase*
una pecera	*fishbowl*
unas plantas	*plants*
unos videojuegos	*video games*
una alfombra	*rug*
unos discos compactos	*compact discs*
un tocador de discos compactos	*compact disc player*

24 En mi cuaderno

Answers will vary. Example: En mi cuarto ideal hay dos camas,...

Choose a picture of your ideal room from a magazine, or draw a room yourself. Imagine that it is your room, and write how many of each item you have.

Additional Practice

22 Have one partner ask the other questions about the room. **¿Cuántas ventanas hay en tu cuarto?** Partners should take turns asking questions.

En mi cuaderno

24 For an additional journal entry suggestion for Chapter 2, see *Practice and Activity Book,* p. 146

Close

To review the material introduced in this **Paso,** use Teaching Transparency 2-2. Have students identify new vocabulary as you point to it, asking **¿Qué es ésto?, ¿Qué hay en el cuarto?, ¿Tiene un televisor?,** and so on.

Assess

Quiz 2-2, *Chapter Teaching Resources, Book 1,* pp. 83–84

Assessment Items, Audiocassette 7A/Audio CD 2

Performance Assessment

Divide students into groups of three. Assign or let students choose these roles: librarian, scribe, proofreader. The librarian looks up words as needed, the scribe writes the description, and the proofreader checks for accuracy. Give each group a picture of a bedroom cut from a magazine. After discussing the things in the picture, each group writes a description of the room based on their discussion. All members of a group receive the same grade.

Answers

22 *Sample answer:*
Tengo un cuarto grande. Hay una cama y tres ventanas. También hay un armario y un televisor.

TERCER PASO

Talking about what you need and want to do

Jump Start!

Use *Teaching Transparency 2-2.* Give students five minutes to describe the room, listing as many items as they can.

MOTIVATE

Give students a task such as *wash a car, make a pizza, earn money,* or *make a sandwich.* Ask students what they would need to do to complete the task. Then call attention to some of the phrases that have been used to express need.

TEACH

Presentation

Así se dice Model the expressions in **Así se dice** for correct pronunciation and intonation. Have students repeat after you. Put a list of activities on the board in Spanish and have students tell you whether these are things that they want or need to do.

For videodisc application, see *Videodisc Guide.*

For Individual Needs

25 Challenge Ask students to complete the following sentences in as many original ways as possible.
1) **Necesito poner...**
2) **Necesito encontrar...**
3) **Necesito ir a...**
4) **Necesito conocer a...**
5) **Necesito comprar...**

ASÍ SE DICE **Talking about what you need and want to do**

To find out what someone needs to do, ask:

¿Qué necesitas hacer?

¿Y qué **necesita** hacer Paco?

To answer, say:

Necesito organizar mi cuarto.
... to organize my room.

Necesita ir a la librería.
... to go to the bookstore.

To find out what someone wants to do, ask:

¿Qué quieres hacer?

¿Y **qué quiere hacer** Merche?

No sé, pero no quiero hacer la tarea.
I don't know, but I don't want ...

Quiere ir a la pizzería.

25 ¿Qué necesita comprar?

Complete Paco and Abuela's conversation with the phrases in the box. First, read the sentences that come after the missing phrases so that the conversation makes sense.

ABUELA Oye, Paco. Manaña es el primer día de clases, ¿verdad? **1.** ¿ ______ ?
PACO Sí, es el primer día de clases. 2. Necesito ______.
ABUELA ¿Qué cosas necesitas hacer?
PACO 3. ______.
ABUELA Sí, es cierto. No tienes mucho papel.
PACO 4. Y también quiero comprar ______.
ABUELA Sí, también necesitas zapatillas de tenis. ¿Y cuadernos?
PACO 5. No, no ______.
ABUELA Bueno, no necesitas cuadernos.
PACO 6. ¡ ______ para la clase de álgebra.
ABUELA ¡Paco! 7. ¡ ______ ! Y tu cuarto es un desastre. **8.** ______ tu cuarto.

- 3 **necesito comprar papel**
- 4 **zapatillas de tenis**
- 7 **no necesitas una calculadora**
- 2 **hacer muchas cosas**
- 8 **necesitas organizar**
- 5 **necesito comprar cuadernos**
- 1 **qué necesitas hacer**
- 6 **pero necesito una calculadora**

26 Paco y su abuela

Now, with a partner, act out the roles of Paco and his grandmother, using the dialogue from the previous activity. Switch roles after you've done it once, and this time try to vary what the two characters have to say. Be creative! Answers modeled in Activity 25.

RESOURCES FOR TERCER PASO

Textbook Audiocassette 1B/Audio CD 2
Practice and Activity Book, pp. 20–22
Native Speaker Activity Book, pp. 6–10
Videodisc Guide
Videodisc Program, Videodisc 1B

Chapter Teaching Resources, Book 1
- Communicative Activity 2-2, pp 63–64
- Additional Listening Activities 2-5, 2-6, p. 71
  Audiocassette 10A/Audio CD 2
- Student Response Forms, p. 80
- Realia 4-2, pp. 74, 75
- Situation Cards 2-3, pp. 76–77
- Teaching Transparency Master 2-3, pp. 67, 68
  Teaching Transparency 2-3
- Quiz 2-3, pp. 85–86
  Audiocassette 7A/Audio CD 2

VOCABULARIO

Necesito....

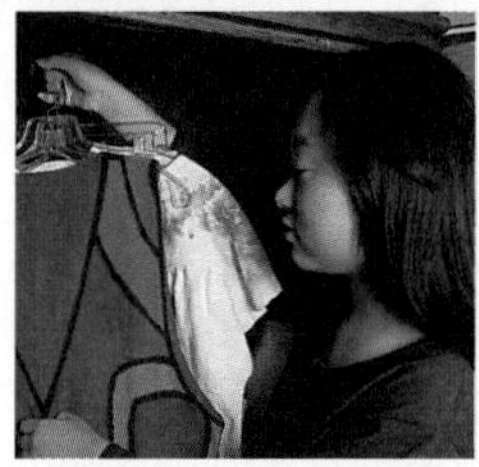
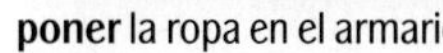

poner la ropa en el armario

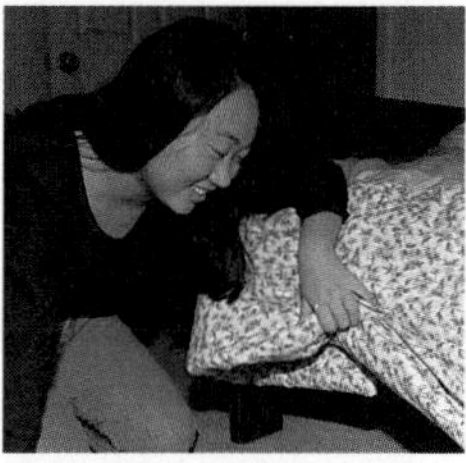

encontrar el dinero primero

Nota Gramatical

Comprar, **poner**, **conocer**, and **ir** are infinitives. The infinitive is the form of the verb found in the dictionary. There are three kinds of infinitive endings in Spanish: **-ar**, **-er**, and **-ir**.

Quiero...

ir al centro comercial

conocer a muchos nuevos amigos

comprar muchas cosas

27 Escuchemos: Victoria y Tomás

Listen as Victoria lists what she and Tomás need to do before Monday. Write the name of the person who needs to do each thing. What do both of them need to do? Answers on p. 41D.

1. hacer muchas cosas
2. ir al centro comercial
3. comprar una mochila
4. organizar el cuarto
5. encontrar la mochila
6. poner la ropa en el armario
7. hacer la tarea

28 Quehaceres *Chores*

Use verbs from the first column with phrases from the second to tell some things you plan to do this week. Start each sentence with **(No) Necesito...** or **(No) Quiero...** *Possible answers:*

No quiero organizar la sala de clase. Necesito poner los lápices en la mesa.

poner hacer comprar organizar ir encontrar	mi cuarto a clase los lápices en la mesa la sala de clase la tarea para mañana el dinero un diccionario de español mi libro de español en la mochila a la librería

29 Problemas

The following people need your help. Write what each person needs to do, wants to buy, or where each one needs to go, using as many new expressions as you can.

1. Juanita never knows what time it is.
2. Jorge's room is too dark.
3. María doesn't have enough clothes.
4. Isabel can't find tomorrow's homework in her cluttered room.
5. Rafael is trying to build his vocabulary.
6. Diego is totally out of pens, pencils, and paper.
7. Inés is new in town and is feeling lonely.

See possible answers below.

Answers

29 *Possible answers:*

1. Juanita necesita comprar un reloj.
2. Jorge necesita una ventana.
3. María necesita comprar ropa.
4. Ella necesita organizar el cuarto y hacer la tarea.
5. Rafael necesita un diccionario.
6. Diego necesita ir al centro comercial. Él necesita comprar muchas cosas.
7. Inés necesita conocer a nuevos amigos.

Presentation

Vocabulario Model the pronunciation of the phrases, having students repeat after you. Then ask the class **¿Necesitas poner la ropa en el armario en tu cuarto?** Have the class answer chorally first, then call on some individual students. Next practice **¿Quieres ir al centro comercial esta tarde?** and **¿Quieres comprar muchas cosas? ¿Necesitas muchas cosas o solamente quieres muchas cosas?** Then have students practice using the new phrases in pairs.

Teaching Suggestion

Ask students if they would like to make a pizza. If they would, write some of the ingredients on the chalkboard (**queso, champiñones, salsa,** and so on). Give students the phrase **Necesito poner... en la pizza.** Then ask **¿Qué necesitas hacer?** The student replies with an ingredient to be added. (**Necesito poner salsa en la pizza.**) Continue questioning students with each item until they know the pattern and the pizza is complete.

Additional Practice

The pizza activity above can be used in groups of two to four students, with one student asking questions and the others answering. The role of questioner alternates.

For Individual Needs

29 Auditory Learners

After writing the answers, have students orally check answers in pairs, asking each other what the various people need. (**¿Qué necesita hacer Juanita? Necesita comprar un reloj.**)

TERCER PASO
CAPÍTULO 2

Presentation

Vocabulario Count by 2's from 20 to 30, writing the numbers on the board as you say them. From 30 on, model the first number in each series (30, 40, 50, etc.) and have students continue until the next series is reached. Then play Ponga (see page 15F) to further practice the numbers. Students should prepare their Ponga card with numbers from 31 through 100.

Teaching Suggestion

32 Point out to students that **c/u** means **cada uno** and that they will have to calculate the answers.

Photo Flash!

Spanish currency comes in different-colored notes of 1000, 2000, 5000, and 10,000 **pesetas** (**pts.** and **ptas.** are both abbreviations for **pesetas**) and coins of 1, 5, 10, 25, 50, 100, 200, and 500 pts.

For Individual Needs

Slower Pace Introduce the word **mil** (one thousand), and have students use play money to practice shopping and counting in **pesetas.**

30 ¿Qué necesitas hacer?

Work in pairs. Tell your partner what each person in Activity 29 needs to do. Then find out if your partner wants or needs to do the same things. Switch roles after number four.

MODELO —Diego necesita ir a la librería. ¿Y tú? ¿Quieres ir a la librería?
—No, no quiero ir a la librería, pero necesito...

31 De vuelta al colegio *Back to school*

With a partner, take turns asking and telling each other how many of each item you need to buy and how much money you need.

MODELO —¿Cuántas carpetas necesitas comprar?
—Necesito comprar siete carpetas.
—Necesito ... dólares y ... centavos.

regla
cuaderno
mochila
libro

diccionario
lápiz
goma de borrar
bolígrafo

VOCABULARIO

¿Cuánto es en dólares?

31	treinta y uno	**40**	cuarenta	**101**	ciento uno
32	treinta y dos	**50**	cincuenta	**102**	ciento dos
33	treinta y tres	**60**	sesenta	**103**	ciento tres
34	treinta y cuatro	**70**	setenta		...
35	treinta y cinco	**80**	ochenta		...
36	treinta y seis	**90**	noventa		...
	...	**100**	cien	**199**	ciento noventa y nueve

Uno at the end of a number changes to **un** before a masculine noun and **una** before a feminine noun: **veintiún dólares** *(dollars)*, **veintiuna pesetas.**

32 ¿Cuánto dinero necesitas?

Play the roles of Paco and the bookstore clerk. Tell the clerk you need to buy these school supplies. Based on the prices given, the clerk tells you how much money you need.

MODELO —Necesito comprar dos lápices.
—Necesitas 70 pesetas.

See answers below.

1. cuatro gomas de borrar (a 15 ptas. cada una)
2. dos bolígrafos (a 90 ptas. cada uno)
3. un cuaderno (a 145 ptas. c/u)
4. tres lápices (a 35 pts. c/u)
5. dos reglas (a 99 ptas. c/u)

Culture Note

People in Spanish-speaking countries do not use personal checks for purchases as often as people in the United States. In Mexico many people pay their utility bills with personal checks, but in Spain bills are usually paid by direct withdrawal. Cash is universally accepted, and most stores also accept credit cards, especially in larger cities.

Answers

32 1. —Necesito comprar cuatro gomas de borrar.
—Necesitas 60 pesetas.
2. —Necesito dos bolis.
—Necesitas 180 pesetas.
3. —Necesito un cuaderno.
—Necesitas 145 pesetas.
4. —Necesito tres lápices.
—Necesitas 105 pesetas.
5. —Necesito dos reglas.
—Necesitas 198 pesetas.

33 ¿Cuántos años tiene?

In Chapter 1 you learned how to say how old someone is. Give the ages of the following people, using the person's name and **tiene ____ años.** If you don't know, you'll have to ask! If you can't ask, just guess. *Answers will vary. Example:* Mi padre tiene cincuenta años.

1. your parent or guardian
2. your teacher
3. the person sitting next to you
4. a TV star
5. the President
6. a grandparent or elderly person
7. your best friend
8. the person in your family nearest your age
9. your favorite movie star
10. a recording artist

34 Números de teléfono

Your partner will say a name and a telephone number. Write the number, then repeat it to your partner to verify that you copied correctly. Write three names and numbers, then switch roles and start over.

MODELO El teléfono de Mark es el cinco, cincuenta y cinco, ochenta y siete, treinta y seis.

35 En mi cuaderno

Most of us could use a little more organization in our lives. In your journal, write a paragraph about what you need to do this week. Include some things you need to do, where you need to go, and what you need to buy. Write how much money you need.

See sample entry below.

LETRA Y SONIDO

A. The letter *d* in Spanish represents two possible pronunciations.

1. At the very beginning of a phrase, or after an *l* or *n,* it sounds like the *d* in the English word *did* except with the tip of the tongue closer to the back of the teeth.
   dinero diez diccionario dar andar dónde el día falda
2. Anywhere else in the word or phrase (especially between vowels) its pronunciation is softened and is similar to the *th* in the English word *they.*
   qué día cerdo modo cada verdad estudiar calculadora

B. **Dictado**

Adriana is making a shopping list. Complete her list based on what she says.

Tengo... Necesito...

See page 41D for script.

C. **Trabalenguas**

Pronounce this tongue twister after your teacher or after the recording.

Cada dado da dos dedos,
dice el hado, y cada lado
de dos dados, o dos dedos,
da un dos en cada uno de los lados.

Native Speakers

To reinforce writing skills, have native speakers write the tongue twister in the **Letra y sonido** as you dictate it. After they have finished, ask them to look at the text to correct their work.

En mi cuaderno

35 For an additional journal entry suggestion for Chapter 2, see *Practice and Activity Book,* p. 146.

Close

To review material from this **Paso,** set up a **papelería** in the classroom with a variety of classroom objects "for sale" at various prices. Ask students to take the role of salesclerk and purchaser and to practice buying items in the store.

Assess

Quiz 2-3, *Chapter Teaching Resources, Book 1,* pp. 85–86

Assessment Items, Audiocassette 7A/Audio CD 2

Performance Assessment

Give each student a task to complete written on a sheet of paper (Clean up your room.) Students are to describe the steps that need to be accomplished to complete the task. This can be done on tape (video or audio) and presented to class, or it can be presented in written form.

Answers

35 *Sample answers:*
Necesito organizar mi cuarto.
También necesito hacer la tarea.
Necesito ir de compras.
Necesito comprar una calculadora.
Necesito 50 dólares.

Thinking Critically

Drawing Inferences Remind students that a store that sells paper **(papel)** is called a **papelería,** and that a store that sells books **(libros)** is called a **librería.** Have students guess what a store is called that sells shoes **(zapatos)**, flowers **(flores)**, and watches **(relojes)**. **(zapatería, florería, relojería)**

READING STRATEGY
Using pictures, titles, and subtitles first.

PREREADING
Activities A and B

Motivating Activity

Ask students to brainstorm the names of any books and movies from other countries that they might be familiar with.

READING
Activities C and D

Teaching Suggestion

C. Ask students to choose three of the items. What kinds of people would like these as gifts? (e.g., ***50 cosas que los niños pueden hacer para salvar la tierra;*** people who like nature, animals, oceans, recycling)

Thinking Critically

Drawing Inferences Ask students what they think they could learn from each of the items. Other than what the titles say, what information might be included? (*e.g.* ***Guía completa para el adiestramiento del perro:*** dog breeds, dog health, safety tips)

VAMOS A LEER

Portadas

A trip to the bookstore to buy school supplies is also a good opportunity to browse through some other interesting and fun items.

Estrategia
Look at pictures, titles, and subtitles before you begin to read. Also look for other words that "stand out" (bold or large print). By looking at these first, you can often tell what a passage is about without reading every word.

¡A comenzar!

A. Look at the pictures and titles on these two pages. Are these items . . .
1. advertisements? no
2. movie reviews? no
3. book covers and video tapes? yes
4. posters? no

B. By looking at just the pictures on the covers, can you tell which item is about . . . See answers below.
1. the environment?
2. kids on an island?
3. dogs?
4. marine life?

¿Te acuerdas?
Do you remember?
Remember the strategy you learned in Chapter 1. **Use cognates to figure out meaning.**

Mamíferos, aves, reptiles, anfibios y peces son los protagonistas de esta enciclopedia compuesta por tres tomos y magníficamente ilustrada. **ENCICLOPEDIA ILUSTRADA DE LOS ANIMALES** *Ed. Everest. 2.900 ptas. cada tomo.*

Educar para el futuro. 50 COSAS QUE LOS NIÑOS PUEDEN HACER PARA SALVAR LA TIERRA *The earth works group. Ed. Emecé. 1.110 ptas.*

LA ISLA DEL TERROR
Autor: Tony Koltz
Ilustró: Ron Wing

Buscando la utilidad GUÍA COMPLETA PARA EL ADIESTRAMIENTO DEL PERRO *V. Rossi. De Vecchi. 3.450 ptas.*

Answers
B 1. 50 cosas que los niños pueden hacer para salvar la tierra.
2. La isla del terror
3. Guía completa para el adiestramiento del perro
4. Mundo marino

LOS DINOSAURIOS. SU DESCUBRIMIENTO.
Transportados en la máquina del tiempo.
METROVIDEO.
2.495 ptas.

LAS NUEVAS AVENTURAS DE MOFLI
GATIVIDEO
Dibujos animados.
Doblada al español.
Duración: 90 minutos.

BILLIKEN PRESENTA: MUNDO MARINO
Video documental filmado en el oceanario de San Clemente del Tuyú.
ATLÁNTIDA

Al grano

For answers to C, D, and E, see below.

Now take a little more time and look at the words in bold print.

C. Which item would you buy as a gift for each of these people? Remember to rely only on pictures, titles, and subtitles!

For someone who . . .

1. is interested in dinosaurs
2. likes animals
3. wants to be a marine biologist
4. likes to watch cartoons on TV

D. Now read the information accompanying each picture and answer the questions.

1. Look at the *Enciclopedia ilustrada de los animales.* Is the book illustrated? Is it in color? Write the cognates that told you this.
2. Look at the *Guía completa para el adiestramiento del perro.* **Guía** means *guide.* What kind of a guide is this?
3. Look at *50 cosas que los niños pueden hacer para salvar la Tierra.* What's this book about? How do you know?
4. Look at *Las nuevas aventuras de Mofli.* This item isn't a book. What cognate on the cover tells you what it is?

E. Quieres comprar un video y un libro. Completa el párrafo *(paragraph)* para explicar *(to explain)* adónde necesitas ir, qué te gusta y cuánto dinero necesitas.

tienda *store*
interesante *interesting*
bueno *good*

Quiero comprar unos... Primero, necesito ir... donde está mi... favorita. De los videos que hay, me gusta... porque es... El libro que prefiero es... porque es... Necesito... dólares para comprar mis cosas.

Mathematics Link

The exchange rate of the dollar and the **peseta** varies. Check the current exchange rate in the newspaper and have students compute the cost of each book and video in dollars and cents. Do the prices seem reasonable?

POSTREADING
Activity E

E. All students may enjoy the challenge of doing the last activity in the **Vamos a leer** section in Spanish. It is also particularly suitable for native speakers of Spanish.

Teaching Suggestion

Ask students to think about their favorite book. What is the title? What do they like about the book? In their opinion, can you tell from the title everything the book is about?

Native Speakers

Ask native speakers to bring in their favorite book or video. See if non-native speakers can determine what it is about by reading the title. Then ask native speakers to describe its contents and why they like the book or video.

Teacher Note

For additional reading, see *Native Speaker Activity Book,* pp. 6–10 and *Practice and Activity Book,* p. 24.

Answers

C 1. Los dinosaurios, su descrubrimiento
2. Enciclopedia ilustrada de los animales
3. Las nuevas aventuras de Mofli

D 1. Yes, the book is illustrated and is in color. The cognates are **ilustrada, color.**
2. The guide is about dog training.
3. The book is about 50 things that children can do to save the Earth. The number 50, the picture of the planet Earth, and the English phrase *The Earth Works Group* provide the clues.
4. Video.

E *Answers will vary.*

The **Repaso** reviews and integrates all four skills and culture in preparation for the Chapter Test.

Portfolio

2 Written Suggest that students write a paragraph about a member of their family using vocabulary and functions learned in this chapter. A complete paragraph should include the following: what the person needs and wants to do, what he or she needs or wants to buy, and places he or she needs or wants to go. For Portfolio suggestions, see *Assessment Guide,* p. 15.

Additional Practice

4 Have students work in pairs or small groups to develop a conversation between an older and a younger sibling. The older sibling must buy his or her younger sibling what he or she needs for school. As the younger sibling says **Necesito tres bolígrafos** the older sibling is to question whether the younger child needs or wants the item by saying **¿Tienes bolígrafos?, ¿Qué hay en tu mochila?** or another appropriate question. The younger sibling should respond, and then the two siblings will decide to buy only what is needed. Encourage students to be creative.

For Individual Needs

4 Slower Pace Have students list the items before beginning this activity. If possible, have actual labeled items available.

REPASO

1 Imagine that you're an exchange student in Madrid. Your host brother Juan Carlos is helping you decide what you'll need for school. Based on what Juan Carlos says, how many of each item do you need? Script on p. 41D.

a. cuaderno 4
b. diccionario 1
c. bolígrafo 10
d. carpeta 5
e. lápiz 6
f. mochila 1

2 Look carefully at the photo of Paco and his grandmother. Imagine the conversation they are having. Create a dialogue between them with at least four lines for each character to say.
See sample answer below.

3 With a partner, role-play the dialogue you created for the photo in Activity 2. Your conversation should include listing what's in your room and talking about what you want and need. See sample dialogue below.

4 **Tienda Deco** is having a year-end sale. Working in a small group, look at the price list and decide which items you want to buy with the $199.00 you have. Be prepared to share your selections with the class.

MES DEL MUEBLE EN TIENDA DECO

Reloj Pared	$39.00
Mesa T.V.	$79.00
Lámpara Bima	$26.00
Silla Danesa	$50.00
Mesa Nido	$35.00
Armario 2 Puertas	$150.00

reloj pared
lámpara Bima

5 Your school will have some exchange students from Spain and Argentina this year. Based on what you've learned about schools in Spanish-speaking countries, name two things about your school that they would find familiar, and two things that might seem different.
Familiar: desks, books; Different: lockers, changing rooms

Answers

2, 3 *Possible dialogue:*

—Paco, necesitas organizar tu cuarto.
—Pero abuela, necesito ir de compras.
—¡Primero, a organizar tu cuarto!
—Bien, pero necesito muchas cosas. Necesito una mochila.
—Aquí tienes una mochila.
—Bien. Voy a organizar mi cuarto.

LOS DINOSAURIOS. SU DESCUBRIMIENTO.
Transportados en la máquina del tiempo.
METROVIDEO.
2.495 ptas.

LAS NUEVAS AVENTURAS DE MOFLI
GATIVIDEO
Dibujos animados.
Doblada al español.
Duración: 90 minutos.

BILLIKEN PRESENTA: MUNDO MARINO
Video documental filmado en el oceanario de San Clemente del Tuyú.
ATLÁNTIDA

Al grano

For answers to C, D, and E, see below.

Now take a little more time and look at the words in bold print.

C. Which item would you buy as a gift for each of these people? Remember to rely only on pictures, titles, and subtitles!

For someone who . . .

1. is interested in dinosaurs
2. likes animals
3. wants to be a marine biologist
4. likes to watch cartoons on TV

D. Now read the information accompanying each picture and answer the questions.

1. Look at the *Enciclopedia ilustrada de los animales.* Is the book illustrated? Is it in color? Write the cognates that told you this.
2. Look at the *Guía completa para el adiestramiento del perro.* **Guía** means *guide.* What kind of a guide is this?
3. Look at *50 cosas que los niños pueden hacer para salvar la Tierra.* What's this book about? How do you know?
4. Look at *Las nuevas aventuras de Mofli.* This item isn't a book. What cognate on the cover tells you what it is?

E. Quieres comprar un video y un libro. Completa el párrafo *(paragraph)* para explicar *(to explain)* adónde necesitas ir, qué te gusta y cuánto dinero necesitas.

tienda *store*
interesante *interesting*
bueno *good*

Quiero comprar unos... Primero, necesito ir... donde está mi... favorita. De los videos que hay, me gusta... porque es... El libro que prefiero es... porque es... Necesito... dólares para comprar mis cosas.

Mathematics Link

The exchange rate of the dollar and the **peseta** varies. Check the current exchange rate in the newspaper and have students compute the cost of each book and video in dollars and cents. Do the prices seem reasonable?

POSTREADING
Activity E

E. All students may enjoy the challenge of doing the last activity in the **Vamos a leer** section in Spanish. It is also particularly suitable for native speakers of Spanish.

Teaching Suggestion

Ask students to think about their favorite book. What is the title? What do they like about the book? In their opinion, can you tell from the title everything the book is about?

Native Speakers

Ask native speakers to bring in their favorite book or video. See if non-native speakers can determine what it is about by reading the title. Then ask native speakers to describe its contents and why they like the book or video.

Teacher Note

For additional reading, see *Native Speaker Activity Book,* pp. 6–10 and *Practice and Activity Book,* p. 24.

Answers

C 1. Los dinosaurios, su descrubrimiento
2. Enciclopedia ilustrada de los animales
3. Las nuevas aventuras de Mofli

D 1. Yes, the book is illustrated and is in color. The cognates are **ilustrada, color.**
2. The guide is about dog training.
3. The book is about 50 things that children can do to save the Earth. The number 50, the picture of the planet Earth, and the English phrase *The Earth Works Group* provide the clues.
4. Video.

E *Answers will vary.*

The **Repaso** reviews and integrates all four skills and culture in preparation for the Chapter Test.

Portfolio

2 Written Suggest that students write a paragraph about a member of their family using vocabulary and functions learned in this chapter. A complete paragraph should include the following: what the person needs and wants to do, what he or she needs or wants to buy, and places he or she needs or wants to go. For Portfolio suggestions, see *Assessment Guide,* p. 15.

Additional Practice

4 Have students work in pairs or small groups to develop a conversation between an older and a younger sibling. The older sibling must buy his or her younger sibling what he or she needs for school. As the younger sibling says **Necesito tres bolígrafos** the older sibling is to question whether the younger child needs or wants the item by saying **¿Tienes bolígrafos?, ¿Qué hay en tu mochila?** or another appropriate question. The younger sibling should respond, and then the two siblings will decide to buy only what is needed. Encourage students to be creative.

For Individual Needs

4 Slower Pace Have students list the items before beginning this activity. If possible, have actual labeled items available.

REPASO

1 Imagine that you're an exchange student in Madrid. Your host brother Juan Carlos is helping you decide what you'll need for school. Based on what Juan Carlos says, how many of each item do you need? Script on p. 41D.

a. cuaderno 4
b. diccionario 1
c. bolígrafo 10
d. carpeta 5
e. lápiz 6
f. mochila 1

2 Look carefully at the photo of Paco and his grandmother. Imagine the conversation they are having. Create a dialogue between them with at least four lines for each character to say. See sample answer below.

3 With a partner, role-play the dialogue you created for the photo in Activity 2. Your conversation should include listing what's in your room and talking about what you want and need. See sample dialogue below.

4 **Tienda Deco** is having a year-end sale. Working in a small group, look at the price list and decide which items you want to buy with the $199.00 you have. Be prepared to share your selections with the class.

MES DEL MUEBLE EN TIENDA DECO

Reloj Pared	$39.00
Mesa T.V.	$79.00
Lámpara Bima	$26.00
Silla Danesa	$50.00
Mesa Nido	$35.00
Armario 2 Puertas	$150.00

reloj pared

lámpara Bima

5 Your school will have some exchange students from Spain and Argentina this year. Based on what you've learned about schools in Spanish-speaking countries, name two things about your school that they would find familiar, and two things that might seem different.
Familiar: desks, books; Different: lockers, changing rooms

Answers

2, 3 *Possible dialogue:*

—Paco, necesitas organizar tu cuarto.
—Pero abuela, necesito ir de compras.
—¡Primero, a organizar tu cuarto!
—Bien, pero necesito muchas cosas. Necesito una mochila.
—Aquí tienes una mochila.
—Bien. Voy a organizar mi cuarto.

6 In pairs, take turns reading the items to each other. Then form sentences saying what each person wants or needs to do. Be creative!

MODELO Armando quiere jugar *(to play)* al tenis pero no tiene zapatillas.
Armando necesita ir al centro comercial para comprar zapatillas.

1. Joaquín dice *(says)*, "Me gusta la música de Juan Luis Guerra y tengo bastante *(plenty of)* dinero."
2. No tienes cuadernos ni gomas de borrar.
3. Tengo dinero en mi cuarto, sí, pero ¡el cuarto es un desastre!
4. Anabel no tiene muchos amigos.
5. Manuela dice, "Me gusta la revista *Tú.*"
6. Tengo muchos problemas en la clase de inglés.

Answers will vary. See example below.

7 With a partner, look at the pictures and match each of these descriptions to the person who said it. Then choose one of the two remaining pictures and describe it to your partner. See if she or he can guess which one you're describing.

1. Tengo veintiocho años. Me gusta la música clásica y tengo muchos discos compactos. ¿Quién soy?
2. Me gusta ir al centro comercial. Necesito zapatillas de tenis. Tengo quince años. ¿Quién soy?
3. Me gusta ir al centro comercial. Necesito zapatillas de tenis, pero necesito encontrar mi dinero primero. Tengo cincuenta años. ¿Quién soy?

3.

2.

1.

8 SITUACIÓN

Get together with two or three classmates. Imagine that you're students from different Spanish-speaking countries, with new names and ages. Introduce yourself to the group in Spanish. Keep your conversation going as long as you can by asking your partners questions about where they're from, things they have in their room, their likes and dislikes, and what they want to do.

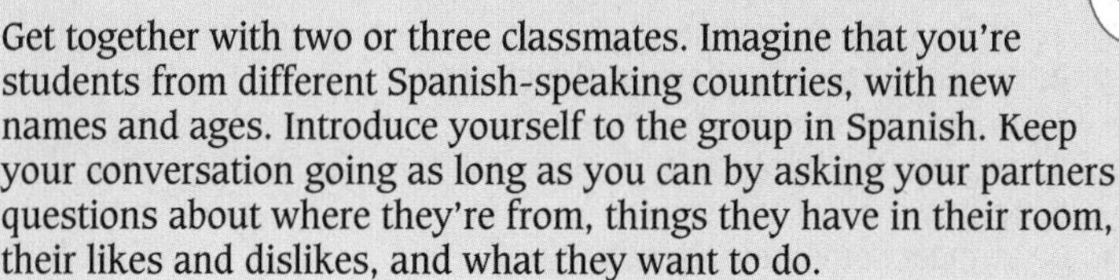

Answers

6 *Sample answer:*

1. Joaquín necesita ir a la tienda de música para comprar unos discos compactos de Juan Luis Guerra.

REPASO
CAPÍTULO 2

Additional Practice

Students work in pairs. One student says a sentence that poses a problem to the partner. (**No tengo dinero. Necesito un cuaderno.**) The partner should then offer a solution, using the phrases and vocabulary in the chapter. (**Necesitas ir al banco. Tienes que comprar un cuaderno.**)

Portfolio

8 Oral You may want to record the students' conversations from the **Situación** for their Portfolios. For Portfolio information, see *Assessment Guide,* pp. 2–13.

Video Wrap-Up

- ***Video Program***
- ***Expanded Video Program, Videocassette 1***
- ***Videodisc Program, Videodisc 4A***

At this time, you might want to use the video resources for additional review and enrichment. See *Video Guide* or *Videodisc Guide* for suggestions regarding the following:

- **¡Mañana es el primer día de clases!** (Dramatic episode)
- **Panorama cultural** (Interviews)
- **Video Clips** (Authentic footage)

This page is intended to help students prepare independently for the Chapter Test. It is a brief checklist of the major points covered in the chapter. The students should be reminded that this is only a checklist and does not necessarily include everything that will appear on the Chapter Test.

Portfolio

3 Oral Suggest that students record their dialogue from this activity as an oral Portfolio entry. For Portfolio suggestions, see *Assessment Guide,* p. 15.

A VER SI PUEDO . . .

Can you talk about what you want and need? p. 48

1 How would you ask these students if they need the items listed? How would the students answer? See answers below.

1. Juanita — some pens and paper
2. Paco — a calculator
3. Felipe — some notebooks
4. Mercedes — a backpack
5. Tú — ¿?

Can you describe the contents of your room? p. 53

2 How would you tell a friend how many, if any, of each item is in your room? How would you say you don't have a certain item but want one? Now write out the questions you would use to ask your friend if she or he has these items in his or her room. See answers below.

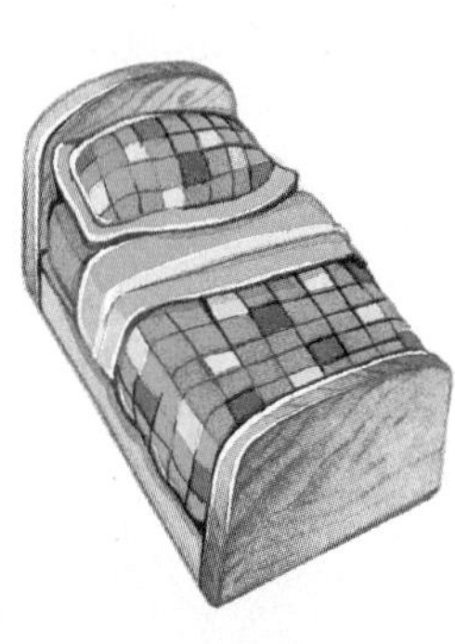

3 Tomorrow is the first day of class. Ask a friend how much or how many he or she needs of these things. How would your friend answer? See answers below.

1. paper
2. books
3. rulers
4. notebooks
5. folders
6. pencils

Can you talk about what you need and want to do? p. 56

4 Paco isn't very well prepared for the first day of class. How would you say he needs to do the following things? How would you say you want to do the same things? See answers below.

1. to organize his room
2. to put his tennis shoes in the closet
3. to find his money
4. to go to the bookstore
5. to buy a lot of things
6. to meet some new friends

Answers

1 *Possible answers:*

1. —Juanita, ¿tienes unos bolígrafos y papel?
   —Sí, tengo bolígrafos y papel.
2. —Paco, ¿tienes una calculadora?
   —No, no necesito una calculadora.
3. —Felipe, necesitas unos cuadernos?
   —Sí, necesito unos cuadernos.
4. —Mercedes, ¿necesitas una mochila?
   —No, no necesito una mochila.
5. —Mari, ¿necesitas un lápiz?
   —Sí, necesito un lápiz.

2 Hay _____ en mi cuarto. No tengo _____, pero quiero _____. ¿Tienes un armario en tu cuarto? _____ ¿una cama? ¿una radio? ¿un televisor?

3
1. ¿Cuánto papel necesitas?
2. ¿Cuántos libros necesitas?
3. ¿Cuántas reglas necesitas?
4. ¿Cuántos cuadernos necesitas?
5. ¿Cuántas carpetas necesitas?
6. ¿Cuántos lápices necesitas?

4
1. Necesita organizar su cuarto.
2. Necesita poner sus zapatillas de tenis en el armario.
3. Necesita encontrar su dinero.
4. Necesita ir a la librería.
5. Necesita comprar muchas cosas.
6. Necesita conocer a unos amigos nuevos.

VOCABULARIO

PRIMER PASO

Talking about what you want and need

el bolígrafo *ballpoint pen*
Bueno... *Well . . .*
la calculadora *calculator*
la carpeta *folder*
el colegio *high school*
el cuaderno *notebook*
el diccionario *dictionary*
él *he*
ella *she*
la goma de borrar *eraser*
el lápiz *pencil*
la librería *bookstore*
el libro *book*
la mochila *book bag, backpack*
necesita *she/he needs*
necesitar *to need*
necesitas *you need*
necesito *I need*
el papel *paper*
querer (ie) *to want*
quiere *he/she wants*
quieres *you want*
quiero *I want*
la regla *ruler*
un *a, an* (masc. sing.)
una *a, an* (fem. sing.)
unas *some, a few* (fem. pl.)
unos *some, a few* (masc. pl.)
ya *already*

SEGUNDO PASO

Describing the contents of your room

el armario *closet*
la cama *bed*
el cartel *poster*
¿cuánto/a? *how much?*
¿cuántos/as? *how many?*
el cuarto *room*
el escritorio *desk*
hay *there is, there are*
la lámpara *lamp*
la mesa *table*
mi *my*
mucho/a *a lot (of); a lot*
muchos/as *many, a lot of*
la puerta *door*
¿Qué hay en... *What's in . . .?*
la radio *radio*
el reloj *clock; watch*
la revista *magazine*
la ropa *clothing*
la silla *chair*
su *his; her*
el televisor *TV set*
tener (ie) *to have*
tengo *I have*
tiene *he/she has*
tienes *you have* (familiar)
tu *your* (fam.)
la ventana *window*
las zapatillas de tenis *tennis shoes* (Spain)

TERCER PASO

Talking about what you need and want to do

el centro comercial *shopping mall*
comprar *to buy*
conocer *to get to know* (someone)
la cosa *thing*
el dinero *money*
el dólar *dollar*
encontrar (ue) *to find*
hacer *to do, to make*
ir *to go*
No sé. *I don't know.*
nuevos amigos *new friends*
organizar *to organize*
la pizzería *pizzeria*
poner *to put*
primero *first*

For the numbers 31–199
See p. 58.

Game

¿Qué ves? This game re-enters the alphabet from the **Capítulo preliminar**. Any number of students may play, but it works well with small groups. One player tells the group that he or she sees something in the room (vocabulary restricted to this chapter). The others, each in turn, quickly try to guess what he or she sees. Whoever guesses correctly is the next student to describe. You will need to teach them **veo, ves,** and **cosa** as words to facilitate the game.

Player 1: Veo algo.
Player 2: ¿Es una persona o una cosa?
Player 1: Una cosa.
Player 3: ¿Con qué letra?
Player 1: Con la letra "c".
Player 4: ¿Es un cartel?
Player 1: Sí, por supuesto.

VOCABULARIO
CHAPTER 2

Teaching Suggestion

In the Chapter Opener the students made a list of items in the window of the **papelería**. Ask them to check the list to see which items they now know how to say in Spanish.

TPR Call out school items and have students hold them up as you say them. Start out by holding up a book saying **¡Libro!** Then move on to **¡Bolígrafo azul!...**

Chapter 2 Assessment

Chapter Test

- *Chapter Teaching Resources, Book 1,* pp. 87–92
- *Assessment Guide,* Speaking Test, p. 28
- *Assessment Items Audiocassette 7A Audio CD 2*

Test Generator, Chapter 2

Alternative Assessment

Performance Assessment

You might want to use the **Situación** (p. 63) as a cumulative performance assessment activity.

Portfolio Assessment

- **Written: Repaso,** *Teacher's Edition,* p. 62
  Assessment Guide, p. 15
- **Oral: A ver si puedo...,** Activity 3, *Pupil's Edition,* p. 64
  Assessment Guide, p. 15

LOCATION OPENER
CHAPTERS
3, 4

¡Ven conmigo a México! pp. 66–119

EXPANDED VIDEO PROGRAM, Videocassette 1

OR VIDEODISC PROGRAM, Videodisc 2A

Motivating Activity

Before students open their books, ask them what they know about Mexico today or what they think it might be like. Use *Map Transparency 5, México* to introduce students to the major regions and cities, and ask if any students have ever been to Mexico. What are the people like? What do they do for entertainment? Do they know anything about the indigenous people of Mexico? Then have them compare their guesses to what they see in the photographs on pages 66–69.

Background Information

Teotihuacán was already an ancient ruin when the Spaniards arrived. It is divided into quarters by two major intersecting avenues. The Avenue of the Dead (**la Calzada de los Muertos**) was the main north-to-south artery of the city.

The two great pyramids—the Pyramid of the Sun (**la pirámide del sol**) and the Pyramid of the Moon (**la pirámide de la luna**)—are the most prominent buildings in Teotihuacán. The Pyramid of the Sun stands 215 feet tall. The Pyramid of the Moon, 147 feet tall, is somewhat smaller.

CAPÍTULOS 3 y 4

¡Ven conmigo a México!

Ruinas de una civilización pre-azteca en Teotihuacán

Culture Note

Teotihuacán means *place of the gods* in Náhuatl. According to Nahua myth, the gods met here to create the sun and the moon. A huge pyre was built and the poor, brave god Nanauatzin threw himself without fear into the fire and became the sun. The richly attired Tecciztecatl, who had boasted of his bravery, hesitated before casting himself into the flames. He became the pale moon.

Multicultural Link

Ask students if they know how Egyptian pyramids are different from those in the Americas. (Americas: steps, flat tops, used as temples; Egypt: smooth sides, pointed tops, used as tombs and monuments)

México

Población: 92.000.000

Área: 1.949.706 km² (761.604 millas cuadradas); tres veces más grande que el estado de Texas

Capital: Ciudad de México (Distrito Federal), población 20.000.000

Gobierno: república federal

Industrias: acero, plata, químicos, electrodomésticos, textiles, caucho, petróleo, turismo

Cosechas principales: algodón, café, trigo, arroz, caña de azúcar, verduras, maíz, frutas

Unidad monetaria: el peso

Idiomas: español, más de cincuenta lenguas indígenas

LOCATION OPENER
CHAPTERS
3, 4

Using the Almanac and Map

Terms in the Almanac

- **La bandera:** The emblem in the center of the flag commemorates the legend of the founding of **Tenochtitlan,** the Aztec capital and the site of present-day Mexico City. (See **History Link** below.)
- **Capital:** Mexico City may be referred to simply as **México,** as **México, Distrito Federal,** or **México, D.F.**
- **República federal:** Mexico is comprised of 31 states and a federal district.
- **Industrias: acero** *steel;* **plata** *silver;* **químicos** *chemicals;* **electrodomésticos** *electrical household appliances;* **caucho** *rubber*
- **Cosechas principales: algodón** *cotton;* **café** *coffee;* **trigo** *wheat;* **arroz** *rice;* **caña de azúcar** *sugar cane*
- **Idiomas:** Spanish is the official language of Mexico, but many people speak indigenous languages, especially in the rural areas of Oaxaca, Chiapas, Michoacán, and the Yucatán. The main indigenous languages are **maya, mixteco, náhuatl, otomí, purépecha,** and **zapoteca.**

History Link

According to legend, the god Huitzilopochtli told the Aztecs to establish their capital, **Tenochtitlan,** where they saw an eagle perched on a cactus with a serpent in its mouth. They saw this on an island in the middle of Lake Texcoco, a large saline lake surrounded by volcanic peaks. Some parts of Tenochtitlán, now Mexico City, were built on artificial garden-islands known as **chinampas,** which also provided much of the city's food supply. The Spanish Conquerors were astounded at how developed Tenochtitlán was and took over the city for their own capital.

Using the Map

Refer students to the Map of Mexico on page xxvi to answer the following questions.

1. Have students point out countries that border Mexico. (United States, Guatemala, Belize)
2. Have students point out D.F. (Teotihuacán is about 30 miles from D.F.)
3. Have students locate Monterrey, an important industrial center.
4. Have students locate Guadalajara, an important agricultural and industrial center.
5. Have students locate Acapulco, Cozumel, and Cancún. Have they visited these popular places?

LOCATION OPENER
CHAPTERS
3, 4

Using the Photo Essay

① In Oaxaca you can find indigenous black pottery and Spanish-style green-glazed pottery. Also for sale in the **mercados** are weavings, textiles, filigree jewelry, ceramics, sculptures, baskets and colorful native dresses called **huipiles**. **Oaxaca** is a Zapotec word. The **x** is pronounced like the x in **México.**

② A **mariachi** band includes violins (**violines**), guitars (**guitarras**), harps (**harpas**), double basses (**contrabajos**), and **guitarrones,** a bass guitar adapted for this music. **Mariachi** ensembles are traditionally hired as serenaders, and the boyfriend frequently sings with the ensemble. Musicians also play in the city streets, weddings, parties, and in cafés. The **mariachi** style originated in Jalisco but has come to be regarded as a symbol of all Mexico. **Mariachi** is derived from the French word *mariage.*

③ **Popocatépetl,** often called "el Popo," is located 45 miles southeast of Mexico City. At 17,387 feet, it is second only to Mt. McKinley, the highest peak in North America. It has not erupted since 1802 but is still considered an active volcano. **Popocatépetl** means *smoking mountain* in Nahuatl.

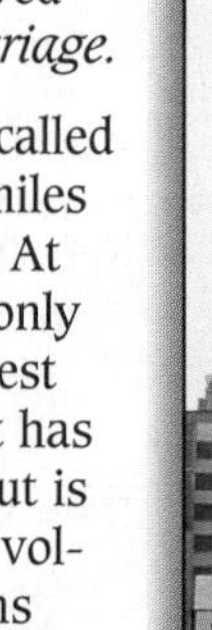

④ The Palace of Fine Arts (**El Palacio de Bellas Artes**), built between 1904 and 1934, is almost entirely of marble. Its great weight has caused it to sink about five to ten inches per year. It has been tied and lifted with cranes on several occasions. This major cultural center houses the National Theater, where concerts, dance programs, operas, and plays are performed, and art galleries featuring 19th and 20th century Mexican painting.

MÉXICO

Mexico, a rich and diverse nation with a wealth of resources, culture, and history, has been a cradle of advanced civilizations for more than two thousand years. Mexicans are of mixed indigenous and European descent. The country is a leading producer of petroleum, silver, corn, coffee, oranges, and cotton. Mexico City, the national capital, is the world's largest city.

① The markets of Oaxaca are a great place to find colorful pottery, weavings, jewelry, ceramics, and baskets.

② The Plaza Garibaldi is a popular place in Mexico City where many people come to enjoy mariachi music.

③ Popocatépetl, one of two volcanos near Mexico City, means "smoking mountain" in Nahuatl.

④ El Palacio de Bellas Artes, home of the Ballet Folklórico, is Mexico's most important theater.

68 sesenta y ocho

Geography Link

Ask students to suppose why numerous buildings in Mexico City are sinking. (When the Spaniards took over Tenochtitlán as their capital, flooding was a frequent problem and they undertook several drainage projects. As the lake drained, Mexico City expanded out onto the flat plains which had formerly been the muddy lake bed. The expanding city also required increasing amounts of drinking water, initially obtained from wells and springs in the south of the valley. The removal of water, however, has resulted in the compaction and shrinking of the ground underneath some parts of the city. Consequently, many of the buildings are sinking. The soft soils of the former lake bed are also very unstable during earthquakes. This is why destruction from earthquakes can be so dramatic in Mexico City as it was in 1985.)

(5) **Spectacular murals are found throughout Mexico, like this mosaic mural at the Universidad Nacional Autónoma de México.**

In Chapters 3 and 4 you will meet several students who live in Cuernavaca, a historic city of about 400,000 people that is the capital of the Mexican state of Morelos. Cuernavaca is a popular place where people from all over the world come to study Spanish. Young people from Mexico City come to Morelos for a fun-filled weekend of skiing on natural lakes, swimming in spring-fed pools, sailboat racing, and visiting historical sites like the **Palacio de Cortés** *or the ruins at Xochicalco.*

(6) **The Olmecs, Mexico's earliest recorded civilization, left behind huge carved stone heads, the earliest portraits of Native Americans.**

(7) **Chapultepec Park, the largest wooded area in Mexico City, is one of the best places for outdoor relaxation in the capital.**

(8) **The biggest rodeo rings in Mexico are in Mexico City and Guadalajara. These women are dressed in typical *charra* costume.**

sesenta y nueve 69

LOCATION OPENER
CHAPTERS 3, 4

(5) The mural at the library of the National Autonomous University of Mexico was created by Juan O'Gorman in 1950. It tells a symbolic history of Mexican culture.

(6) The statues probably came from San Lorenzo, one of the three major Olmec centers in the Tabasco region of the southern Gulf Coast. The heads were carved out of basalt, a volcanic rock, sometime between 1200 and 100 B.C. They are believed to represent rain spirits. Besides being highly skilled sculptors, the Olmecs were probably the Mesoamerican inventors of numbers, writing, and the calendar.

(7) Chapultepec Park (**el Parque de Chapultepec**) is a favorite spot for Mexicans, especially on a Sunday afternoon. It covers 40 square miles. Chapultepec has an amusement park, three lakes, and eight museums, including the famous Chapultepec Castle (**Castillo de Chapultepec**), which was the residence of the president until 1940. In Nahuatl, **Chapultepec** means *grasshopper hill.*

Thinking Critically

Comparing and Contrasting Ask students to compare Chapultepec Park to a park with which they are familiar.

(8) **Charreadas** are rodeo-like competitions popular in western Mexico. The male horsemen, called **charros,** wear dark blue suits made of doeskin or velvet with a short jacket known as a **bolero** and riding pants with gold or silver buttons down the sides. The **charras** wear a feminine version of the **charro** suit, and the **amazonas** wear long colorful dresses.

Art Link

Ask students if they know what a mural is. (a large picture painted on a wall or a ceiling) Can they describe a mosaic? (pictures or designs made by inlaying small bits of colored stone, glass, tile, etc., in mortar) Who are some famous Mexican muralists? (Diego Rivera, José Clemente Orozco, David Siqueiros)

Multicultural Link

The Olmecs are noted for their contribution to the development of the calendar. Ask students what other ancient cultures developed calendars. (Egyptian, Babylonian, Roman, Arabic, Chinese)

Capítulo 3: Nuevas clases, nuevos amigos
Chapter Overview

De antemano pp. 72–74		*Practice and Activity Book*, p. 25		*Video Guide* OR *Videodisc Guide*
	FUNCTIONS	**GRAMMAR**	**CULTURE**	**RE-ENTRY**
Primer paso pp. 75–79	• Talking about classes and sequencing events, p. 76 • Telling time, p. 77	• Plural definite articles, p. 75 • **ser** with time expressions, p. 78	• **Nota cultural,** Grade scales in different countries, p. 75 • **Panorama cultural, ¿Cómo es un día escolar típico?,** p. 79	• Present tense of **tener** • Numbers 0–199 • School supplies • Forming questions
Segundo paso pp. 80–83	• Telling at what time something happens, p. 80 • Talking about being late or in a hurry, p. 82	Possession with **de,** p. 81	• **Nota cultural,** Student course loads, p. 80 • **Encuentro cultural, Hora latina,** p. 83 • Mexican TV listing, p. 81	• Present tense of **tener** • Noun-adjective agreement • Forms of **necesitar, querer**
Tercer paso pp. 84–89	• Describing people and things, p. 84 • Talking about things you like and explaining why, p. 87	• Forms of **ser,** p. 84 • Adjective agreement, p. 85 • Tag questions, p. 88	Entertainment guide realia, p. 88	• Talking about likes and dislikes • Noun-adjective agreement • Question formation with **cómo**
Letra y sonido p. 89	Pronunciation: the letters **h, j, g**		**Dictado:** *Textbook Audiocassette 2A/Audio CD 3*	
Vamos a Leer pp. 90–91	**Calificaciones y horarios**		**Reading Strategy:** Using your background knowledge	
Review pp. 92–95	**Repaso,** pp. 92–93	**A ver si puedo...,** p. 94	**Vocabulario,** p. 95	

Assessment Options

Quizzes
- *Chapter Teaching Resources, Book 1*
  Primer paso, Quiz 3-1, pp. 139–140
  Segundo paso, Quiz 3-2, pp. 141–142
  Tercer paso, Quiz 3-3, pp. 143–144
- *Assessment Items, Audiocassette 7A/Audio CD 3*

Chapter Test
- *Chapter Teaching Resources, Book 1*, pp. 145–152
- *Assessment Guide,* Speaking Test, p. 29
- *Assessment Items, Audiocassette 7A/Audio CD 3*

Test Generator, Chapter 3

Video Program OR *Expanded Video Program, Videocassette 1* OR *Videodisc Program, Videodisc 2A*	*Textbook Audiocassette 2A/Audio CD 3*

RESOURCES: Print	RESOURCES: Audiovisual
	Textbook Audiocassette 2A/Audio CD 3
Practice and Activity Book, pp. 26–28	
Native Speaker Activity Book, pp. 11–15	
Chapter Teaching Resources, Book 1	
• Additional Listening Activities 3-1, 3-2, p. 127	*Additional Listening Activities, Audiocassette 9A/Audio CD 3*
• Student Response Forms, pp. 136–138	
• Realia 3-1, pp. 131, 133	
• Situation Cards 3-1, pp. 134–135	
• Teaching Transparency Master 3-1, pp. 123, 126	*Teaching Transparency 3-1*
• Quiz 3-1, pp. 139–140	*Assessment Items, Audiocassette 7A/Audio CD 3*
Videodisc Guide	*Videodisc Program, Videodisc 2A*
Video Guide	*Video Program* OR *Expanded Video Program, Videocassette 1*
	Textbook Audiocassette 2A/Audio CD 3
Practice and Activity Book, pp. 29–31	
Native Speaker Activity Book, pp. 11–15	
Chapter Teaching Resources, Book 1	
• Communicative Activity 3-1, pp. 119–120	
• Additional Listening Activities 3-2, 3-4, p. 128	*Additional Listening Activities, Audiocassette 9A/Audio CD 3*
• Student Response Forms, pp. 136–138	
• Realia 3-2, pp. 132, 133	
• Situation Cards 3-2, pp. 134–135	
• Teaching Transparency Master 3-2, pp. 124, 126	*Teaching Transparency 3-2*
• Quiz 3-2, pp. 141–142	*Assessment Items, Audiocassette 7A/Audio CD 3*
Videodisc Guide	*Videodisc Program, Videodisc 2A*
	Textbook Audiocassette 2A/Audio CD 3
Practice and Activity Book, pp. 32–36	
Native Speaker Activity Book, pp. 11–15	
Chapter Resources, Book 1	
• Communicative Activity 3-2, pp. 121–122	
• Additional Listening Activities 3-5, 3–6, p. 129	*Additional Listening Activities, Audiocassette 9A/Audio CD 3*
• Student Response Forms, pp. 136–138	
• Realia 3-2, pp. 132, 133	
• Situation Cards 3-3, pp. 134–135	
• Teaching Transparency Master 3-3, pp. 125, 126	*Teaching Transparency 3-3*
• Quiz 3-3, pp. 143–144	*Assessment Items, Audiocassette 7A/Audio CD 3*
Video Guide	*Videodisc Program, Videodisc 2A*
Video Guide	*Video Program* OR *Expanded Video Program, Videocassette 1*
Videodisc Guide	*Videodisc Program, Videodisc 2A*

Alternative Assessment

- Performance Assessment
  Primer paso, p. 78
  Segundo paso, p. 81
  Tercer paso, p. 89
- Portfolio Assessment
  Written: Activity 32, *Pupil's Edition,* p. 88
  Assessment Guide, p. 16
  Oral: Activity 29, *Pupil's Edition,* p. 87
  Assessment Guide, p. 16

Capítulo 3: Nuevas clases, nuevos amigos

Textbook Listening Activities Scripts

For Student Response Forms, see *Chapter Teaching Resources, Book 1,* pp. 136–138.

Primer paso

Activity 6, p. 75

— Hola, Lupita. ¿Qué tal?

— Hola, Álvaro. ¿Cómo estás?

— Bien, ¿y tú?

— Bueno, más o menos. Es el primer día de clase y ya tengo mucha tarea.

— ¿Qué clases tienes?

— Tengo ciencias, francés, arte, matemáticas, computación, educación física e historia con el profesor Maldonado. ¿Qué clases tienes tú?

— Yo tengo historia con la profesora Vázquez, ciencias sociales, computación y geografía.

— ¿A qué hora tienes clase de computación?

— A la una menos cinco.

— ¡Qué bien! Estamos en la misma clase, entonces.

— ¡Ay, no, llegamos tarde!

— ¡Vamos!

Answer to Activity 6

Lupita and Álvaro have the class of **computación** together.

Activity 10, p. 77

1. — Oye, Bernardo, ¿qué hora es?
   — Son las dos y media.
2. — Bernardo, dime, ¿qué hora es?
   — Son las tres y cuarto.
3. — No tengo reloj, Bernardo. ¿Qué hora es?
   — Son las seis.
4. — ¿Qué hora es, por favor?
   — Es la una y cuarto.
5. — Ahora, ¿qué hora es?
   — Son las diez. Vete a jugar.
6. — Bueno, Geraldo. ¡Despiértate!
   — ¿Qué hora es?
   — Son las ocho.
7. — Ya es tarde.
   — Pero, Bernardo, ¿qué hora es?
   — Son las ocho y media.
8. — Bernardo ¿Qué hora es?
   — Son las cuatro. ¡Vamos al parque!

Answers to Activity 10

1. h 2. f 3. g 4. a 5. c 6. e 7. b 8. d

Activity 13, p. 78

MODELO Son las doce y diez. Tengo la clase de computación.
12:10, computación

1. Ya son las nueve y cuarto. Tengo la clase de arte.
2. Ahora tengo ciencias sociales. Son las ocho y veinticinco.
3. Son las doce menos cuarto. Por fin tengo almuerzo.
4. ¡Ya es la una! Tengo clase de matemáticas.
5. Ya son las dos menos cinco. Tengo educación física.
6. Son las tres menos cuarto. Tengo la clase de francés.
7. ¿Son las diez y cinco? ¡Tengo geografía!

Answers to Activity 13

1. 9:15, arte
2. 8:25, ciencias sociales
3. 11:40, almuerzo
4. 1:00, matemáticas
5. 1:55, educación física
6. 2:45, francés
7. 10:05, geografía

Segundo paso

Activity 15, p. 80

1. Necesito ir a clase. ¿Qué hora es?
2. ¿A qué hora es el descanso?
3. Necesito organizar mi cuarto. ¿Ya son las tres?
4. ¿A qué hora es el almuerzo?
5. ¿A qué hora necesitas ir a la clase de inglés?
6. Quiero ir al centro comercial. ¿Qué hora es?

Answers to Activity 15

1. a 2. b 3. a 4. b 5. b 6. a

Tercer paso

Activity 29, p. 87

— Hola, Patricia, soy Gregorio. ¿Cómo estás?

— Muy bien. ¿Y tú?

— Bien. Oye, ¿qué haces esta tarde? Hay una fiesta a las ocho.

— ¡Ay, no, una fiesta no, por favor! No me gustan las fiestas. Pero me gustan los partidos de fútbol.

— Este, pues... No me gustan los partidos de fútbol. No son interesantes. Pero, a ver... me gustan los videojuegos. ¿A ti te gustan?

— Los videojuegos no me gustan. Bueno, Gregorio, ¿te gustan los partidos de tenis?

— Es que no me gustan los deportes. Pero me gustan los conciertos.

— ¡Ay, sí! Me encantan los conciertos. ¿Qué música te gusta? ¿Te gusta la música rock?

— Sí, me gusta la música rock. ¡Vamos a un concierto!

— ¡Fantástico! Oye, Gregorio, ¿tienes un coche?

— Pues, no...

Answers to Activity 29

1. cierto 2. falso 3. cierto 4. cierto

Letra y Sonido, p. 89

For the scripts for Parts A and C, see page 89. The script for Part B is below.

B. Dictado, p. 89

Necesito una goma de borrar y una regla en matemáticas. En geografía, necesito un bolígrafo y un cuaderno.

Repaso

Activity 1, p. 92

1. Son las tres de la mañana en la ciudad de Panamá.
2. En la ciudad de Los Ángeles son las doce del mediodía.
3. Aquí en Nueva York es la una y veinticinco de la tarde.
4. Son las tres y media de la tarde de un día fresco y nublado aquí en la bella ciudad de Miami.
5. Aquí en Caracas son las nueve menos cinco de la noche.

Answers to Repaso Activity 1

Answers will vary according to locale.

Capítulo 3: Nuevas clases, nuevos amigos
Projects

In this activity students will create a brochure of their school or town. This project may be done in class or as an outside assignment. Tell students to imagine that they are creating the brochures for a foreign exchange program. Exchange students in Spanish-speaking countries will decide where they want to attend classes, based on information they receive from U.S. schools.

MATERIALS

✂ **Students may need**

- Old magazines
- Old newspapers
- Construction paper
- Scissors
- Glue or tape
- Colored markers

SEQUENCE

1. Divide class into groups.
2. Set due dates for the brochure and oral presentation.
3. Students obtain pictures to illustrate the brochure. They may draw them, take photos, or cut pictures from magazines and newspapers. Groups decide which pictures to use.
4. Students should prepare a short written description in Spanish of each picture used. Each student is responsible for writing at least one description. Review **Vocabulario** (p. 95).
5. Groups make a preliminary two-page layout in which they indicate where pictures and descriptions will go.
6. Each group member proofreads the group's layout for accuracy. Option: Groups might critique each other's sections.
7. Groups glue or tape pictures on clean paper and write descriptions by the pictures.
8. Groups should also come up with a cover and a title for their brochures.
9. Each student reads the descriptions she or he has written to the class.

GRADING THE PROJECT

Suggested point distribution (total = 100 points):

Brochure content	40
Correct vocabulary and grammar	10
Originality	10
Appearance	10
Oral presentation	20
Individual participation	10

Teacher Note

If your class has a pen pal program, your students might send the brochure to their pen pal's school and ask for one in return.

Capítulo 3: Nuevas clases, nuevos amigos

LAS ESCALERAS

In this game, students can practice the vocabulary in this chapter or in preceding ones.

Preparation On the chalkboard draw two sets of stairs with eight to ten steps for students to write words on.

Procedure Divide the class into two teams. Ask one member from each team to go to the board and announce a word category. (school subjects, class schedules, time expressions, ways to describe a person) Students must write a word from that category on each step, beginning with the lowest. After they write their word, they are replaced by a teammate. The team filling all the spaces on the ladder correctly in the shortest time is the winner.

Categoría: Materias

______	______
______	______
______	______
______	historia
las ciencias	el francés
el arte	la geografía

PALABRAS REVUELTAS

This game is especially good for tactile learners. The objective is for students to be able to construct at least five Spanish words from scrambled letters.

Materials You will need 10 small squares of paper for each student.

Procedure Divide the class into two teams. Each person looks up a Spanish word from the **Vocabulario** on page 95. The students then write each letter that makes up that word on one of the pieces of paper. After everybody is finished, team members exchange their letters with a person on the other team. Students immediately try to arrange the letters in the correct order. Students who unscramble a word before their counterparts can win a point for their team.

CADENA

This game, which helps students review vocabulary, is good for auditory learners.

Procedure Have all students stand up. Begin by saying: **Este semestre tengo geografía**. The first student then says: **Este semestre tengo geografía y física.** The second student repeats what has already been said, adding a new school subject to the sentence. When someone gets the "chain" wrong, he or she sits down. This sequence continues until no one can add any more school subjects to the sentence. Then begin a new sentence, such as **Este año estudio arte.** The winners are the last three students to remain standing.

¿QUIÉN ES?

This game may be played after the ***Tercer paso.*** *It practices question formation and describing people.*

Procedure This may be played with the whole class, or by dividing the class into two groups and having the two groups play simultaneously. One player from the group is chosen to go first. He secretly selects another of the group as the **persona misteriosa.** Everyone in the group has a turn asking a question until the person's identity can be guessed. Questions should have yes or no answers.

QUESTIONER #1: ¿Es chico?
PLAYER: No, no es chico.
QUESTIONER #2: ¿Es rubia?
PLAYER: Sí, es rubia.
QUESTIONER #3: ¿Es alta?
PLAYER: No, no es alta.
QUESTIONER #4: ¿Le gustan los deportes?
PLAYER: Sí, le gustan los deportes.
QUESTIONER #5: ¿Es Julia?
PLAYER: Sí, ¡es Julia!

The student who guessed the person's identity now chooses a different person from the group, and the group continues to guess until that person's identity is revealed.

Capítulo 3 Nuevas clases, nuevos amigos

pp. 70–95

Using the Chapter Opener

Motivating Activities

- Ask students to make a list of what they might say to each other on the first day of a new school year. What might they ask new and old friends?
- Have students briefly discuss the classes they have this year and which they anticipate to be the best, worst, most useful, most fun, most interesting, etc.
- Ask students how they think they would feel about starting the year in a new school. Would they be excited about making new friends, or would they miss their old school?

1 ¿Te gustan las clases este semestre?

70 *setenta*

Culture Note

Students in Spain spend grades nine to 11 earning the **BUP** (**Bachillerato unificado polivalente**). Grade 12 is the **COU** (**Curso de orientación universitaria**), during which they prepare for university. Students in Mexico also spend grade 12 preparing for university. Mexican students must choose their subject area for university before they begin grade 12.

For Spanish-speaking students, a new school year means getting used to a new class schedule. It means finding out what new classes, teachers, and classmates are like. Best of all, the new school year means seeing old friends and meeting new ones. What is the beginning of the new school year like for you?

In this chapter you will learn

- to talk about class schedules and sequencing events; to tell time
- to tell at what time something happens; to talk about being late or in a hurry
- to describe people and things; to talk about things you like and explain why

And you will

- listen to conversations about classes and hear descriptions of people and their activities
- read class schedules and report cards from Spanish-speaking countries
- write a letter to someone in Cuernavaca
- find out about typical school schedules and grading systems in Spanish-speaking countries

(2) ¿A qué hora es la clase?

Focusing on Outcomes

Have students look at the chapter outcomes and match them with the three photos. (Photo 1 represents talking about things you like; photo 2 represents telling at what time something happens, telling time and talking about class schedules; and photo 3 represents describing people and things.) Point out to students that most of the people they meet and much of their time is spent in school, so it is important to be able to talk about these things.

Native Speakers

If any of your students have lived in or visited Mexico, ask them if they would be willing to share some of their knowledge. Ask them how Mexico is similar to the United States. How are the two countries different? What are Mexican schools like compared with those in the U.S.? Your advanced students may enjoy reading the interview on pp. 102–103 of *¡Ven conmigo! Holt Spanish Level 2.*

(3) Mis compañeros de clase son simpáticos.

Teacher Note

You may wish to assign your students the Additional Vocabulary on **asignaturas**, pp. 340–342.

VIDEO PROGRAM OR EXPANDED VIDEO PROGRAM, *Videocassette 2*

OR VIDEODISC PROGRAM, *Videodisc 2A*

Video Synopsis

Claudia is starting the year at a new school. She meets the school principal, who introduces her to her classmates in her first class. While waiting for their teacher to arrive, Claudia talks with her new acquaintances. The students are friendly, and one is particularly mischievous.

Motivating Activity

Divide students into small groups. From the pictures, have students predict what is going to happen in the **fotonovela.** Ask them to make their predictions by answering the questions *who? how old? where? what?* and *why*? This may be done in English or in Spanish, depending on your students' proficiency level.

Presentation

Have students follow along as you read the captions or play the audio recording. Next, have students repeat the dialogue after you. In their same groups from the Motivating Activity, encourage students to guess the meaning of the captions. Ask groups to revise their original predictions. Play the video and then have students describe what is happening in each frame of the **fotonovela.**

DE ANTEMANO

¡Bienvenida al colegio!

Look at the photos that accompany the story. Where and when do you think these scenes are taking place? What clues tell you this? What do you think will happen in the story?

María Inés, Fernando y Claudia

Director Altamirano

Profesor Romanca

1

DIRECTOR Bueno, ya son las ocho menos cinco. Aquí tienes el horario. Ahora tienes clase de ciencias sociales... y a las ocho y cincuenta tienes clase de francés. El descanso es a las nueve y cuarenta...

2

DIRECTOR Muchachos, buenos días. Ella es una compañera nueva. Se llama Claudia Obregón Sánchez. Es de la Ciudad de México.

3

MARÍA INÉS Me llamo María Inés.

FERNANDO Y yo soy Fernando. Encantado. Y ¡bienvenida a Cuernavaca!

MARÍA INÉS Eres de la Ciudad de México, ¡ay, qué padre! Hay muchas cosas interesantes allá, ¿no?

72

RESOURCES FOR DE ANTEMANO

Textbook Audiocassette 2A/Audio CD 3
Video Guide
Video Program
Expanded Video Program, Videocassette 1
Videodisc Guide
Videodisc Program, Videodisc 2A
Practice and Activity Book, p. 25

CLAUDIA Sí, la capital es muy divertida. Mira, me gusta ir al parque... visitar los museos... y también me gusta mucho jugar al basquetbol.

FERNANDO Miren, ya son las ocha. ¿Dónde está el profesor? Está atrasado.

CLAUDIA Fernando, ¿cómo es esta clase?

FERNANDO Ay, es horrible. El profesor es muy aburrido... ¡y no le gustan los exámenes fáciles!

MARÍA INÉS No te preocupes, Claudia, no es verdad. Esta clase es mi favorita. Es muy interesante, y el profesor, pues, es... así.

MARÍA INÉS Señor Rodríguez, una pregunta ¿Le gustan las ciencias sociales?

FERNANDO Sí, "profesora"... me gustan.

MARÍA INÉS ¿Y le gusta estudiar?

FERNANDO Sí, me gusta estudiar.

MARÍA INÉS Entonces, ¿por qué no le gusta estudiar las ciencias sociales?

73

Teaching Suggestions

- Point out that **bienvenida** in the title refers to Claudia, and that **bienvenido** changes in gender and number depending on who is being addressed.
- After students read the **fotonovela,** ask them if they have ever been in a similar situation (a new student in another country or simply in a new school). If so, how did they handle it? Were there differences in language or culture?

Video Integration

- ***Expanded Video Program,*** *Videocassette 1*
- ***Videodisc Program,*** *Videodisc 2A*

You may choose to continue with **¡Bienvenida al colegio! (a continuación)** at this time or wait until later in the chapter. When the story continues, María Inés receives an extra assignment from the teacher. The friends meet after school in the courtyard, and Claudia meets more of María Inés's and Fernando's friends.

Teaching Suggestion

1 Have students review questions with a partner. Then quickly ask for volunteers to answer questions. Ask the class to use thumbs up or thumbs down to indicate whether the answers are correct.

Additional Practice

2 Give the students these additional items:
Fernando es de la Ciudad de México.
La compañera nueva se llama María Inés.
La clase es de matemáticas.
María Inés es la profesora de la clase.
Put words and phrases that make up these sentences on sentence strips or a felt board, and have students move the words to make the true sentences false and the false ones true.

Additional Practice

5 Add these items to the activity:
Mis amigos son...
Mi familia es...
El fútbol americano es...
El video es...
El libro es...

1 ¿Comprendes? See answers below.

Check your understanding of the **fotonovela** by answering these questions. Remember that intelligent guessing is a useful way to increase your understanding in a foreign language.

1. What time is it when this story begins?
2. What do you think the principal is discussing with Claudia?
3. What's in the photographs that Claudia is showing Fernando and María Inés?
4. Can you compare María Inés and Fernando's opinions of this class?
5. Which of the students seems to be mischievous? Why?
6. How does the **fotonovela** end? How do you think María Inés feels?

2 Errores See answers below.

Based on the **fotonovela**, change these statements to make them true.

1. La primera clase de Claudia es la clase de francés.
2. Claudia es una profesora nueva en la clase.
3. Claudia es de España.
4. La capital de México es muy aburrida.
5. Para Fernando, la clase es fácil.

3 ¿Cómo se dice...? See answers below.

What phrases do these characters use in each situation?

Claudia
1. to say she also likes to do something
2. to ask Fernando what this class is like

the Principal
6. to say what time it is
7. to tell Claudia at what time she has French

María Inés
3. to tell Claudia not to worry
4. to say "it's not true"
5. to say the professor is "like this"

Fernando
8. to say he likes social sciences
9. to say what the teacher doesn't like

4 ¡Opiniones!

Using the **fotonovela** as a guide, fill in the blanks with words from the box.

Tengo la clase de __1__ a las ocho. No __2__ la clase. Es __3__ y los exámenes son __4__. Necesito más clases __5__. Mi clase de español es mi __6__ porque es __7__.

1 ciencias sociales
2 me gusta
interesantes 5
3 horrible
7 divertida
6 favorita
difíciles 4

5 ¿Y tú?

Complete the following sentences with your own ideas about what's fun, boring, or difficult.

1. La capital de mi estado es...
2. Mis clases son...
3. No me gusta mucho...
4. La clase de español es...
5. La música clásica es...
6. El tenis es...

Answers

1 1. 7:55
2. the school schedule
3. places in Mexico City
4. Fernando: doesn't like, horrible, professor boring, exams hard; Claudia: favorite class, interesting
5. María Inés; she mimics the teacher
6. The teacher discovers María Inés imitating him; embarrassed

2 *Possible answers:*
1. La primera clase de Claudia no es la clase de francés.
2. Claudia es (una/la) nueva estudiante en la clase.
3. Claudia es de la Ciudad de México.
4. La capital es muy divertida.
5. Para Fernando la clase no es fácil.

3 1. también me gusta
2. ¿cómo es esta clase?
3. No te preocupes, Claudia.
4. no es verdad
5. es... así
6. son las
7. a las ocho y cincuenta tienes clase de francés
8. me gustan
9. no le gustan

PRIMER PASO

Talking about class schedules and sequencing events; telling time

VOCABULARIO

¿Qué materias estudias? *What subjects are you studying?*

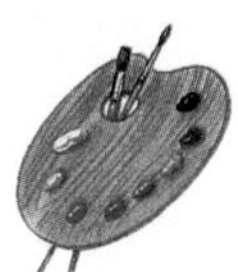

el arte

las ciencias

las ciencias sociales

la computación

el almuerzo

la educación física

el francés

la geografía

las matemáticas

el descanso

NOTA CULTURAL

How would you feel if you got a score of 18 on a test? In Peru, this would actually be a high grade, equivalent to a 90.

- Peruvian schools use a scale of 1 to 20, with 11 the lowest passing score.
- Mexican schools use a scale of 1 to 10; 6 is passing.

What would your grades be if you went to school in Peru? in Mexico?

También se puede decir...

In some Spanish-speaking countries **la computación** is called **la informática**. Another word for *subject* is **la asignatura**.

Nota Gramatical

With nouns referring to more than one thing, like **libros** or **clases,** use **los** or **las.** Both words mean *the.*

Tengo **los** libros

¿Tienes **las** gomas de borrar?

Also use **los** when referring to a group of people that includes both males and females.

Los profesores son de México.

6 Escuchemos: ¡Tenemos la misma clase!

Listen to Álvaro and Lupita discuss their new class schedules. What class do they have together? Answers on p. 69C.

Jump Start!

Write the following questions on the board and have students write their answers.

¿Qué necesitas para el colegio?
¿Cuántos cuadernos necesitas?
¿Cuántas carpetas necesitas?
¿Tienes una calculadora?
¿Tienes muchos bolígrafos?

MOTIVATE

Ask students what their favorite and least favorite courses are. As they mention different subjects, echo their responses in Spanish with **Entonces te gusta.../no te gusta...**

TEACH

Presentation

Vocabulario Have students scan the vocabulary for cognates and to establish recognition. Then ask **¿Quién tiene clase de arte?** Ask for a show of hands. Repeat for the other subjects. Continue by asking individuals if they like certain courses and eliciting answers to check pronunciation.

Nota gramatical Remind students that nouns in Spanish are divided into two groups, masculine and feminine. Review **el** and **la,** and introduce **los** and **las.** Ask students to call out the appropriate article for objects you hold up. Be sure to vary the number of objects you hold up.

RESOURCES FOR PRIMER PASO

Textbook Audiocassette 2A/Audio CD 3
Practice and Activity Book, pp. 26–28
Native Speaker Activity Book, pp. 11–15
Videodisc Guide
Videodisc Program, Videodisc 2A

Chapter Teaching Resources, Book 1
- Additional Listening Activities 3-1, 3-2, p. 127
  Audiocassette 9A/Audio CD 3
- Student Response Forms, pp. 136–138
- Realia 3-1, pp. 131, 133
- Situation Cards 3-1, pp. 134–135
- Teaching Transparency Master 3-1, pp. 123, 126
  Teaching Transparency 3-1
- Quiz 3-1, pp. 139–140
  Audiocassette 7A/Audio CD 3

For videodisc application, see *Videodisc Guide.*

Presentation

Así se dice Using a hand puppet, ask: **Lulú, ¿qué clases tienes este semestre?** Have the puppet "answer" you: **Bueno, tengo computación, ciencias sociales, inglés,** and so on. Continue to model the sentences in the function box in this manner, then have the class repeat them after you.

Additional Practice

Practice the time adverbs **primero, después, luego,** and **por fin** in a conversation with students. **(Carlos, ¿qué clase tienes primero? ¿Y qué tienes después? ¿Luego qué clase tienes?)** Then have students practice with a partner for three to four minutes.

Teaching Suggestion

7 Have students work in pairs to see if they have the same classes that are mentioned in the activity.

En mi cuaderno

8 Have students write a description of their class schedule in their journal. Ask them to use the time adjectives **primero, después, luego,** and **por fin** for sequencing the classes. For an additional journal entry suggestion for Chapter 3, see *Practice and Activity Book,* p. 147.

Math Link

8 Take a poll to find out what percentage of your class has other classes in common. Ask the class for a show of hands asking questions like **¿Quién tiene geografía?** Write the findings on the board. Have students create a bar graph labeled in Spanish using the results.

ASÍ SE DICE Talking about classes and sequencing events

To find out what classes a friend has, ask:

¿Qué clases tienes este semestre?
. . . this semester?

¿Qué clases tienes hoy?
. . . today?

¿Y mañana? *And tomorrow?*

Your friend might answer:

Bueno, **tengo** matemáticas, inglés, español y ciencias sociales.

Primero tengo geografía, **después** computación y **luego** francés.
First I have . . . afterwards . . . then . . .

¡Por fin tengo un día libre!
At last I have a free day!

7 ¿Qué clase tiene?

Read what Mrs. García's children tell her they need or want for school. Then, try to figure out what classes they are taking. Use **tiene clase de...** in your answers. See answers below.

BERTA Mamá, necesito una calculadora para mañana.
JAIME ¿Yo? Bueno, necesito un mapa de Europa y Asia.
PABLO Mamá, necesito ***Estudios de la Sociedad***.
CLARA Bueno, quiero un diccionario de inglés y español.
DIEGO ¡Ay! Hoy necesito zapatos de tenis para mi clase. Y Luis necesita un libro de computación.
SIMÓN Quiero comprar el libro ***Allez, viens***!

Un poco más...

el alemán *German*
el coro *choir*
la química *chemistry*

8 Primero tiene...

Complete this description of Claudia's weekly morning schedule, using the words provided in the box.

3, 4 **luego** 3, 4 **después** 5 **mañana**
2 **primero** 1 **hoy**

__1__ Claudia tiene siete clases. __2__ tiene la clase de ciencias sociales con el profesor Romanca. __3__ tiene francés y un descanso. __4__ tiene química, computación y un descanso. __5__ tiene física a las 10:00 y música a las 10:50.

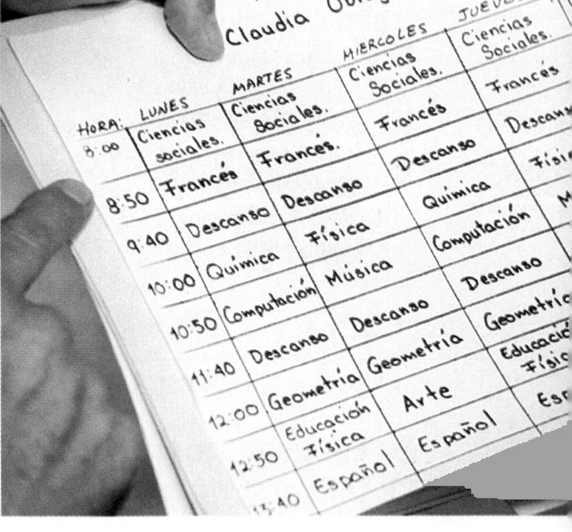

Culture Note

Students in Spain often receive comments instead of grades: **sobresaliente, bien, suficiente,** or **deficiente.** Students in many Spanish-speaking countries may be exempt from exams in a course if they have a good grade.

Answers

7 Berta: matemáticas;
Jaime: geografía;
Pablo: ciencias sociales;
Clara: inglés;
Diego: educación física;
Luis: computación;
Simón: francés

9 Pues, tengo...

Get together with a partner. Greet one another and ask how your partner is. Find out what classes you each have and in what order. Use the expressions you've learned for talking about your schedule.

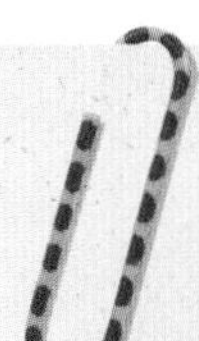

ASÍ SE DICE Telling time

To find out what time it is, ask:

¿Qué hora es?

¡Ay! **¿Ya son** las tres?

To answer, say:

Son las ocho. *It's 8 o'clock.*

Son las once y media. *It's 11:30.*

Es la una y cuarto. *It's 1:15. (It's a quarter after one).*

Sí, hombre, es tarde. ¡Vamos! *Yes, man, it's late. Let's go!*

10 Escuchemos: El reloj

Bernardo is babysitting today. You'll hear his brother at different times throughout the day ask him what time it is. Match each time mentioned with the correct clock below.

Answers on p. 69C.

a.

b.

c.

d.

e.

f.

g.

h.

11 Hora local

Generally, what time is it when . . . ?

1. the sun comes up
2. you wake up
3. you get out of bed
4. the school day begins
5. you eat lunch
6. you leave school
7. you eat dinner
8. you get in bed
9. you go to sleep

Presentation

Así se dice Use a large clock (or draw one on the board or a transparency) to model pronunciation and the use of the singular and plural forms of **ser** to express time. Have students in small groups construct paper-plate clocks, using pens or pencils for the hands. Students take turns calling out a time. The others move the hands on their clock to the right time. You might do this as a whole class activity as you check comprehension.

For Individual Needs

9 Slower Pace You might want to write times on the board and have students structure their conversation around them. (**10:30: ¿Qué clase tienes a las diez y media?**)

10 Slower Pace To prepare students for the listening task, ask them what time it is in each picture before playing the audio recording.

10 Challenge Bring in an old-fashioned round clock with accessible hands. Have a student come up and move the hands. He states the clock time. Class responds **cierto** or **falso.** Call on someone to correct. As a challenge, ask students to mentally advance time by various increments.

11 Kinesthetic Learners Have one or two volunteers pantomime several of the actions mentioned in this activity while the rest of the class guesses the associated time.

Language Note

Point out the difference between **cuatro** and **cuarto.** When telling time, in many countries **y quince** is used instead of **y cuarto.** A variation of **...menos quince** is **Faltan quince para...** . Due to digital watches, it is becoming more common to hear **Son las ocho y cuarenta y cinco.**

Presentation

Gramática Before beginning this section, prepare large flashcards. On each card write a time, such as 3:25. As you begin the presentation, point to the clock on the wall and tell the time: **Clase, son las diez y doce.** Then ask **Clase, ¿qué hora es?** Elicit a choral response and say with them **Son las diez y doce, profesor/a.** Next, show the cards one at a time and have the class chorally tell you the time in Spanish.

Close

TPR Ask a volunteer to come to the front of the class. Show the student a flashcard, but don't let the rest of the class see it. The student moves his or her body to visually represent the time. (3:00—Facing the class, the student may hold the right arm straight up and the left one perpendicular to the shoulder.) The rest of the class guesses the time in Spanish. Continue with other volunteers.

Assess

Quiz 3-1, *Chapter Teaching Resources, Book 1,* pp. 139–140

Assessment Items, Audiocassette 7A/Audio CD 3

Performance Assessment

In pairs, have students describe their schedules to each other as they would to a new friend. They should tell what classes they have at what time and indicate the order of their classes using **primero, después, luego,** and **por fin.** Have students present their dialogues to the class or record it on audio or videocassette.

Gramática Telling Time

1. To tell the hour (except for times around one o'clock), use **Son las...** plus the hour.
   Son las ocho. *It's 8 o'clock.*
2. For times after the hour, follow this pattern:
   Son las siete **y cuarto.** *It's a quarter after 7.*
   Son las ocho **y veinticinco.** *It's 8:25.*
   Son las once **y media.** *It's 11:30.*
3. For times before the hour, say:
   Es la una **menos veinte.** *It's 20 minutes to 1.*
   Son las doce **menos cuarto.** *It's a quarter to 12.*
   Son las ocho **menos diez.** *It's 10 minutes to 8.*
4. For times including 1:00, use **Es la una...**
   Es la una y veinte. *It's 1:20.*

12 ¿Qué hora es? See answers below.

With a partner, take turns asking and telling each other what time it is on each watch.

1. 
2. 

3. 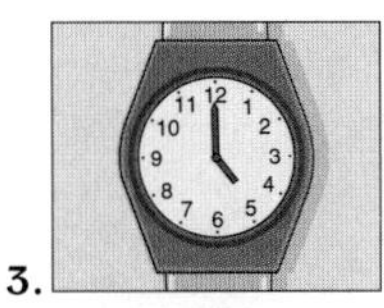
4. 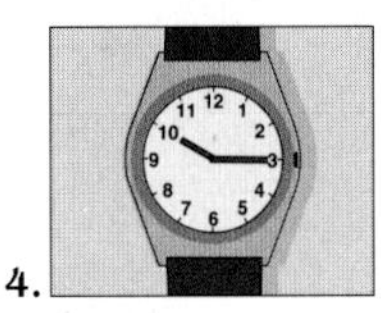
5. 

6. 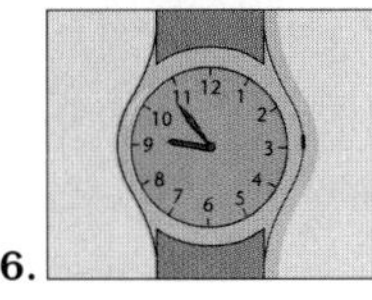

13 Escuchemos: ¿Qué clase tengo ahora?

Imagine that you're keeping your new friend Alberto company during a typical school day. Listen as he tells you about his schedule. First write the times of day he mentions. Then listen again and write the class he has at each time.

MODELO —Son las doce y diez. Tengo la clase de computación.
12:10—computación Answers on p. 69C.

14 Son las...

Take turns reading each item to your partner and asking what time it is. More than one time may be appropriate for some items. Create your own question for number 8.

1. Ya no tienes clases.
2. Necesitas hacer la tarea.
3. Necesitas ir al colegio.
4. Hay un descanso.
5. Tienes clase de español.
6. Es la hora del almuerzo.
7. Quieres ir a la pizzería con amigos.
8. ¿ ?

Answers

12
1. Son las tres y media.
2. Son las doce menos veinte.
3. Son las cinco.
4. Son las diez y cuarto.
5. Son las seis y cinco.
6. Son las nueve menos cinco.

¿Cómo es un día escolar típico?

In this chapter, we asked some students at what time they usually go to school, what they do after class and which classes they like.

PANORAMA CULTURAL

• Mario
Lagunilla de Heredia, Costa Rica

"Bueno... son varios horarios. En el horario de la mañana voy a las siete de la mañana, y en el horario de la tarde a las doce y media, más o menos."

• Lucía
Buenos Aires, Argentina

"Mi materia preferida es literatura y todas las que tengan que ver con lo humanístico."

• Natalie
Maracaibo, Venezuela

"Bueno... voy a la escuela de 7 de la mañana a 1:30 de la tarde; de ahí voy a mi casa, almuerzo; normalmente después me acuesto como hasta las 3 de la tarde y después me pongo a estudiar si tengo algo que estudiar."

Para pensar y hablar...

A. At what time do you usually go to school? How many hours are you in school? What do you do after school? In Costa Rica, Mario has classes almost all day with a lunch break. Why do you think he has such a schedule? What are the advantages and disadvantages of going to school for a longer period during the day?

B. In groups, ask your classmates what their favorite classes are and why. Discuss why some people like sciences and others humanities or social sciences.

Video Program or Expanded Video Program, Videocassette 2

or Videodisc Program, Videodisc 2A

Teacher Notes

- See *Video Guide* and *Videodisc Guide* for activities related to the **Panorama cultural.**
- Remind students that cultural information may be included in the Quizzes and the Chapter Test.

Motivating Activity

Ask students when their ideal class schedules would be, if they could choose all of their courses, and why.

Presentation

Stop the video after each interview and ask students to summarize what the person on the video said. When all three interviews have been viewed, have students answer the questions in the text. Play the video again, and have them answer the **Preguntas.**

Preguntas

1. **¿De dónde es Natalie? ¿Lucía? ¿Mario?** (Venezuela, Argentina, Costa Rica)
2. **¿Quién tiene dos horarios?** (Mario)
3. **¿A qué hora va Mario al colegio por la tarde?** (a las doce y media)
4. **¿Quiénes tienen clase a las siete de la mañana?** (Mario y Natalie)
5. **¿Qué le gusta a Lucía?** (la literatura)

Jump Start!

Write these questions on the board or on a transparency and have students write their answers.

¿Qué materias tienes este semestre?
¿Qué clases tienes hoy?
¿Qué clase tienes ahora?
¿Qué hora es?

MOTIVATE

Ask students when it is important to know what time something is. Are they ever late? When do they feel the need to hurry to get somewhere? In this **Paso** they will learn to talk about these things in Spanish.

TEACH

Presentation

Así se dice With your students, create a Spanish list of upcoming school-related activities. Make a calendar and enter the activities and the times they start. Ask students to practice questioning a partner about what time an event takes place.

—¿A qué hora es el partido de fútbol?
—A las siete.

Vocabulario Using the new vocabulary items, ask students when they have different classes during the day.

—Julia, ¿cuándo tienes la clase de educación física?
—Tengo educación física a las dos y media de la tarde.

SEGUNDO PASO

Telling at what time something happens; talking about being late or in a hurry

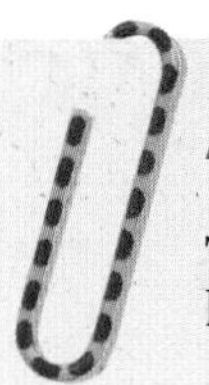

ASÍ SE DICE Telling at what time something happens

To find out at what time something happens, ask:

¿A qué hora es la clase?
At what time is . . .?

¿A qué hora es el almuerzo?

To answer, say:

(Es) a las tres de la tarde.

¡**Es ahora!** Son las doce **en punto.**
It's now! . . . on the dot.

VOCABULARIO

de la mañana *in the morning (A.M.)*
de la tarde *in the afternoon (P.M.)*
de la noche *in the evening (P.M.)*

15 Escuchemos: Horarios

Two new students are discussing their daily schedules. Listen to the questions, then choose the appropriate answer. Answers on p. 69C.

1. **a)** Es la una y veinte.
   b) Es a la una y veinte.
2. **a)** Son las doce y diez.
   b) A las doce y diez.
3. **a)** Sí, son las tres.
   b) Sí, es a las tres.
4. **a)** Son las once y media.
   b) A las once y media.
5. **a)** Son las tres y ocho.
   b) A las tres y ocho.
6. **a)** Son las seis de la tarde.
   b) Es a las seis de la tarde.

16 ¿A qué hora es la clase?

With a partner, take turns asking each other when these classes meet. Use the times listed given for each course.

1. matemáticas (10:35 A.M.)
2. computación (2:10 P.M.)
3. ciencias (11:40 A.M.)
4. inglés (9:40 A.M.)
5. educación física (3:40 P.M.)
6. francés (1:20 P.M.)
7. almuerzo (1:55 P.M.)

NOTA CULTURAL

Students in Spanish-speaking countries may take as many as nine different courses. They can take more courses because their schedules vary from day to day. Most of these are required courses.

RESOURCES FOR SEGUNDO PASO

Textbook Audiocassette 2A/Audio CD 3
Practice and Activity Book, pp. 29–31
Native Speaker Activity Book, pp. 11–15
Video Guide
Video Program
Expanded Video Program, Videocassette 1
Videodisc Guide
Videodisc Program, Videodisc 2A

Chapter Teaching Resources, Book 1
- Communicative Activity 3-1, pp. 119–120
- Additional Listening Activities 3-3, 3-4, p. 128
  Audiocassette 9A/Audio CD 3
- Student Response Forms, pp. 136–138
- Realia 3-2, pp. 132, 133
- Situation Cards 3-2, pp. 134–135
- Teaching Transparency Master 3-2, pp. 124, 126
  Teaching Transparency 3-2
- Quiz 3-2, pp. 141–142
  Audiocassette 7A/Audio CD 3

17 Los programas de televisión

Choose two programs from this television listing from Mexico City and tell your partner what time they begin. Your partner will guess which programs you chose. Then think of two television programs you like to watch at home. Tell your partner what time they begin and your partner will guess the programs.

JUEVES

7:00 NOCHE 5 **BEETLEJUICE.** Dibujos animados.
7 **ALF.** Comedia.
9 **ESPECIAL MUSICAL.** Variedades. "Timbiriche".
11 **HOY EN LA CULTURA** Entrevista especial a Octavio Paz. Premio Nobel de Literatura y Orgullo de México. Conducción: Sari Bermúdez.
7:30 2 **¡LLEVATELO!** Concursos para toda la familia, con Paco Stanley y Gabriela Ruffo.
5 **BATMAN.** Dibujos animados.
7 **SALVADO POR LA CAMPANA.** Aventuras.
11 **EL HOMBRE Y LA INDUSTRIA.** Reportajes. Juventud.
13 **SEÑORA.** Telenovela.
22 **POR AQUI PUEDEN PASAR. Animación infantil. Cuentos alrededor del mundo: Rumpelstkin.**
7:50 22 **ENCUADRE. Cartelera cinematográfica. Con Leonardo García Tsao y Nelson Carro.**
8:00 4 **LOS INTOCABLES.** Aventuras policíacas.
5 **INTRIGA TROPICAL.** Aventuras de un ex-agente antinarcóticos y su socia detective. Rob Stewart "Nick Slaughter", Carolyn Dunn "Sylvie Girard", Pedro Armendáriz "Lt. Carrillo".

18 Entrevista

Get together with two classmates. Imagine that you have just met. Exchange greetings with them and ask where they are from and how they're doing. Find out what classes they have today and at what times they meet. Then write their schedules, including classes and times. Be sure to use words like **primero, después,** and **luego** to help you sequence their schedules.

Nota Gramatical

In Spanish, to show that something belongs to someone, use **de**. This is the equivalent of *'s* (apostrophe *s*) in English.

los zapatos de David *David's shoes*

las clases de Eva *Eva's classes*

De combines with **el** to form the contraction **del.**

el perro del profesor *the teacher's dog*

la directora del colegio *the school's director*

SUGERENCIA

Sometimes students often don't know *how* to study a foreign language. Learning a language is like learning a new sport—you have to do a little bit every day. You also have to practice. Set aside time each day for Spanish. Study in a quiet place, where you can say words out loud. Review what you did in Spanish class that day, then go on to your homework. Keep at it and plan to study regularly with a classmate. All your hard work will pay off!

19 Una encuesta *A survey*

Work in a group of three. Each student completes the sentences below. Then exchange answers with your partners. Take turns reporting to the group.

MODELO —Mi actor favorito es Andy García.
—El actor favorito de Luis es Andy García.

1. Mi actor favorito es...
2. Mi actriz *(actress)* favorita...
3. Mi libro favorito es...
4. Mi deporte favorito es...
5. Mi clase favorita es...
6. Mi color favorito es...
7. Mi programa de televisión favorito es...
8. Mi grupo musical favorito es...
9. Mi comida favorita es...

SEGUNDO PASO
CAPÍTULO 3

For videodisc application, see *Videodisc Guide.*

TPR Ask students to demonstrate through gestures what they might be doing at the time you call out. (**Son las seis de la mañana.** Students might raise their arms and stretch, as though waking up.)

Group Work

17 This activity requires file cards and several TV guides. In groups of five, have students write the name and time of five of their favorite TV programs, one on each card. Give each group a TV schedule so that they may verify the program times. Then have groups exchange their file cards with other groups. On the back of each card, students write the hour of the program in Spanish. Students return the completed cards to the group. Have groups write up their ideal night of television in Spanish.

Presentation

Nota gramatical First, have the students read the grammar explanation. Then, walk around the class and pick up various objects. Ask for volunteers to answer questions such as **¿De quién es este libro?** Elicit answers such as **Es el libro de Beth.**

Family Link

Ask students to get together with someone at home and write out his or her daily schedule. Does the person do the same things at the same time every day, or does his or her schedule vary? Have students report their findings to the class, describing in Spanish a typical day in a family member's life.

Presentation

Así se dice Prepare a transparency with a list of names, events and times (**José, concierto—8:00 P.M.; Samuel, clase de inglés—1:15 P.M.**) Revealing one at a time, say a time later than the time on the transparency. **Son las ocho y media. ¡José, date prisa, estás atrasado!** After you have modeled various expressions in this way, show the entire list and call out a time to the class, to which they respond appropriately.
—Es la una y veinticinco.
—Samuel, estás atrasado, ¡córrele!

Close

To check comprehension of the material in this **Paso**, ask your students: **Clase, ¿a qué hora es la clase de español? ¿A qué hora es el almuerzo? Ay, clase, ¡estoy atrasado/a!** Use *Teaching Transparency 3-2* to further review the material from this **Paso.**

Assess

Quiz 3-2, *Chapter Teaching Resources, Book 1,* pp. 141–142

Assessment Items, Audiocassette 7A/Audio CD 3

Performance Assessment

Distribute copies of a TV schedule. Have students work in pairs to prepare a dialogue in which one asks the times of various programs, which the other provides. Students are to present their dialogues to the class or record them on an audio- or videocassette.

ASÍ SE DICE Talking about being late or in a hurry

To tell someone you are late, say:
Estoy atrasada. *(if you're female)*
Estoy atrasado. *(if you're male)*

To tell someone you are in a hurry, say:
Tengo prisa.

To say that someone else is late, say:
Está atrasada.
(if the person is female)
Está atrasado.
(if the person is male)

To tell a friend to hurry up, say:
¡Date prisa!

También se puede decir...
To tell a friend to hurry up, Mexicans also may say **¡Ándale!**, **¡Apúrate!**, or **¡Córrele!**

20 ¡Ya es tarde!

Everyone's running late today! Match the correct photo to the sentence below. Then, using phrases from **Así se dice** create captions for the remaining photos.

Ernesto, ¡date prisa porque la librería cierra *(closes)* a las siete!

a.

b.

c.

d.

21 ¿Quién está atrasado?

Of the people you know, who is always late and who is never late? Write sentences about five people you know, using **siempre** for always, and **nunca** for never.

MODELO Mi amigo Juan siempre está atrasado.

22 Lo siento, no tengo tiempo. *I'm sorry, I don't have time.*

Imagine that you and your partner have just run into each other. Write a dialogue in which one of you keeps on chatting while the other tries to end the conversation.

Teacher Note

Realia 3-1, in the *Chapter Teaching Resources, Book 1,* pp. 131, 133 is of a TV schedule. You may wish to copy this for your students to use in the Performance Assessment.

ENCUENTRO CULTURAL

Hora latina

Eric recently moved to Taxco, Mexico from Minnesota. Last weekend, he was invited to a party by his new friends Paloma and Consuelo. He arrived at 8:00 P.M., as Paloma and Consuelo had told him. When he got there, however, none of the other guests had arrived and the two girls weren't even ready. Eric felt really awkward.

Tomorrow, Eric has an interview with the principal at the school he'll be attending. His appointment is for 9:00 A.M. Eric isn't sure when to show up. Working with a partner, decide how to answer the questions under **Para discutir** below. Then check your answers in the **Vamos a comprenderlo** section to see if they are reasonable.

COLEGIO SAN ROQUE

Para discutir...

1. Should Eric show up for his interview at 9:00 on the dot?
2. What would have been a good time for Eric to arrive at Paloma and Consuelo's party?
3. What would you do if you arrived at a party before the hosts were ready?

Vamos a comprenderlo

In Mexico, as in other Spanish-speaking countries, people are expected to arrive a little late for a party—a half-hour to an hour later than they are told to come. This custom is called **hora latina** *(Latin time)*. But at school or on the job, people are expected to be on time. There's no set rule for what to do if you arrive too early to a social event. Eric could have made a polite excuse to leave and come back later, but it's likely that his hosts would have invited him in for a soft drink while he waited for the other guests.

ENCUENTRO CULTURAL
CAPÍTULO 3

Motivating Activity

Ask students to imagine they are friends with an exchange student from Mexico. They get along well and have many interests in common, but their friend is often very late for things. How would they deal with this? How important would it be to them? Would they consider it an individual failing or a cultural difference? Why?

For Individual Needs

Challenge Not all events in Spanish-speaking countries begin on time. Have students interview native speakers to discover when **hora latina** is appropriate. Suggest that they ask questions about concerts, dinners, hair appointments, or work. Compile their results to develop a profile of time customs in Spanish-speaking countries.

Thinking Critically

Synthesizing Have your students answer this question: How would you prepare a Mexican person for schedules in the United States?

Jump Start!

Write these questions on the board or a transparency and have students write their answers.

¿Qué hora es?
¿A qué hora tienes el almuerzo?
¿Te gusta el español?
¿Qué clase tienes después del español?
¿Te gusta?

MOTIVATE

Ask volunteers to ad-lib a conversation at the lost-and-found counter of a shopping mall. One student has lost a small child. The attendant at the counter must ask numerous questions to get an accurate description of the child. Have the class count the number of descriptors necessary to describe the child really well.

TEACH

Presentation

Así se dice, Vocabulario
Present the functional phrases and vocabulary by describing to the class several people in *Teaching Transparency 3-3*, in photos in the *Pupil's Edition,* or in magazine photos. Then play "20 Questions" using three pictures taped to the board. Say that you are thinking of one of the people, and have students ask yes-or-no questions until they can guess who you are thinking about. (**¿Es una persona cómica? ¿Tiene pelo moreno?**) You might have students play the game in small groups. You might refer to Communicative Activity 3-2 and *Teaching Transparency 3-3* for this presentation.

TERCER PASO

Describing people and things; talking about things you like and explaining why

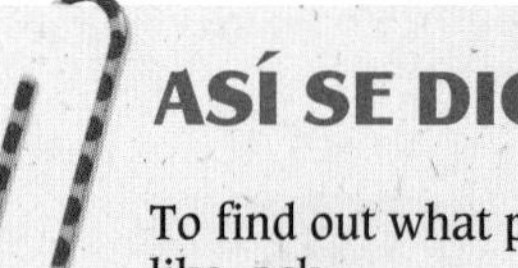

ASÍ SE DICE Describing people and things

To find out what people and things are like, ask:

¿Cómo es Fernando?
What's . . . like?

¿Cómo es la clase?

¿Cómo son los profesores?
. . . the teachers?

To tell what someone or something is like, say:

Él es alto. *He's tall.*

Es aburrida. *It's boring.*

No te preocupes. Ellos no son muy estrictos. *Don't worry. They aren't very strict.*

Nota Gramatical

You're familiar with the singular forms of **ser** *(to be)*. Here are all forms of the verb.

Soy alto.	Nosotros/as **somos** altos/as.
Eres baja.	Vosotros/as **sois** bajos/as.
Es cómico.	**Son** cómicos.
Es cómica.	**Son** cómicas.

VOCABULARIO

antipático/a *disagreeable*
bajo/a *short*
bonito/a *pretty*
bueno/a *good*
cómico/a *comical, funny*
difícil *difficult*
divertido/a *fun, amusing*
fácil *easy*
feo/a *ugly*
grande *big*
guapo/a *good-looking*
inteligente *intelligent*
interesante *interesting*
malo/a *bad*
moreno/a *brunette*
nuevo/a *new*
pequeño/a *small*
rubio/a *blond*
simpático/a *nice*

23 ¿Cómo son?

Match each drawing with the correct description.

a.

b.

c.

d.

c. **1.** Es nuevo pero es aburrido.
d. **2.** Son bajos y muy cómicos.
a. **3.** Son pequeños pero son muy malos.
b. **4.** Es alta y fea.

RESOURCES FOR TERCER PASO

Textbook Audiocassette 2A/Audio CD 3
Practice and Activity Book, pp. 32–34
Native Speaker Activity Book, pp. 11–15
Videodisc Guide
Videodisc Program, Videodisc 2A

Chapter Teaching Resources, Book 1
- Communicative Activity 3-2, pp. 121–122
- Additional Listening Activities 3-5, 3-6, p. 129
  Audiocassette 9A/Audio CD 3
- Student Response Forms, pp. 136–138
- Realia 3-2, pp. 132, 133
- Situation Cards 3-3, pp. 134–135
- Teaching Transparency Master 3-3, pp. 125, 126
  Teaching Transparency 3-3
- Quiz 3-3, pp. 143–144
  Audiocassette 7A/Audio CD 3

Gramática Adjective Agreement

Have you noticed that adjectives such as **divertido** change to match the nouns they modify?

	MASCULINE	FEMININE
SINGULAR	un libro **divertido**	una clase **divertida**
PLURAL	unos libros **divertidos**	unas clases **divertidas**

1. To describe one person or thing, use **es** + a singular adjective.
   El libro **es divertido.** La clase **es divertida.**
2. To describe more than one person or thing, use **son** + a plural adjective.
   Los libros **son buenos.** Las clases **son buenas.**
3. If you're describing a group of males and females, use a masculine plural adjective.
   Mis compañeros **son simpáticos.**
4. Adjectives ending in **-e** or a consonant such as **l**, **r**, or **n** have only two forms: singular and plural. To make these adjectives plural, add **-s** or **-es**.
   El libro es **interesante.** → Los libros son **interesantes.**
   La clase es **difícil.** → Las clases son **difíciles.**

24 La carta de Claudia

Claudia is writing to her cousin Marisa, telling her about her new school and her friends there. Complete her letter with the correct forms of the adjectives in the word box. Use each adjective only once.

bonito simpático inteligente
interesante
divertido difícil
guapo
cómico

Querida Marisa,
¡Hola! ¿Cómo estás? Bueno, aquí estoy en el Instituto Centro Unión. Me gusta mucho. Las clases son __1__ y __2__, pero no son __3__. Los profesores son muy __4__. Los estudiantes en este colegio son __5__. Mi amiga María Inés es __6__ y __7__. Fernando es el amigo de Sandra. Él es muy __8__. Bueno, ahora tengo clase. ¡Ya estoy atrasada!
¡Hasta luego!
Claudia

Presentation

Gramática Point out and model the four combinations of adjective agreement (feminine singular, masculine singular, feminine plural, and masculine plural) using **carpeta(s)** and **libro(s)**. Then, ask students questions about objects in the room and have them answer using adjectives.
(**—¿Qué son?**
—Son libros azules.)

For videodisc application, see *Videodisc Guide.*

Teaching Suggestion

Put magazine pictures in an envelope. Ask students to choose a picture of a person and describe him or her to a partner.

Teaching Suggestion

Place pictures of famous people in a bag. Have one student go to the front of the room. Select a picture from the bag and place it on the student's back. Other students take turns making up a descriptive sentence as a hint for who the famous person is. After each sentence, the student who is "it" must guess the name of the celebrity.

Additional Practice

24 Using Claudia's letter as a model, have students write a brief description of school, their friends, classes, and teachers.

Language Note

You might point out to students that **rubio/a** may also be used to describe someone who is fair-skinned. **Moreno/a** is often used to describe someone with dark coloring.

Teacher Notes

25 You may want to point out to your students that in number three, the adjective for *Texas* would agree with **el estado,** a masculine noun. As students will be describing other locations in future chapters, you may also wish to include **el país, la ciudad,** and **la provincia** in your explanation.

A lo nuestro **Oye** and **mira** are used as interjections and connectors in conversation. Students need practice hearing and using them to gain a sense of their use. Encourage students to use **mira** and **oye** in the hallways to greet each other. **(Oye Fulano, ¿cómo estás?)**

For Individual Needs

25 Slower Pace Have students brainstorm and list as many descriptors and adjectives from this chapter as they can before beginning this activity.

27 Tactile Learners Have students collect several objects from around the room (books, notebooks, pens, etc.) and pass them to each other as they describe them in Spanish. For added interest, have students close eyes and guess what is passed to them. You may wish to introduce *heavy* (**pesado**), *light* (**ligero**), *hard* (**duro**) and *soft* (**suave**). As a follow-up, have students label objects in the room.

25 ¡Al contrario!

Your friend is always talking, but everything he says is wrong. Change each statement to say the opposite of what your friend says.

MODELO Fernando es moreno.
—No, no es moreno. Es rubio.

1. Mis clases son fáciles.
2. La clase de español es aburrida.
3. Texas es pequeño.
4. Los profesores son antipáticos.
5. Alberto es alto.
6. Mis compañeros son malos.

26 Descripciones

Work with a partner and form as many sentences as you can describing the picture. Use the words from the **Vocabulario** on page 84.

A LO NUESTRO

What words do you use to get someone's attention? In Spanish, two common expressions are **¡Mira!** *(Look!)* and **¡Oye!** *(Listen!)*. When speaking to more than one person, use **miren** or **oigan.**

Oye, ¿cómo es la clase?
Hey, what's the class like?

Mira, es fácil, pero hay mucha tarea.
Look, it's easy, but there's a lot of homework.

Although **oye** and **oigan** mean *listen,* they are used like the English expression *"hey."*

27 Mis amigos son...

Working with a partner, describe the following things and people. Be prepared to share your opinions with the rest of the class.

MODELO —Oye, ¿cómo es tu cuarto?
—Mira, es pequeño, pero bonito.

1. el libro de...
2. los profesores de...
3. la cafetería
4. los centros comerciales
5. la clase de...
6. la tarea de...
7. tus amigos
8. la música de...

28 ¡Escribamos!

Write a short paragraph of six or seven sentences describing your classes, teachers, and friends at school this year.

Language Note

Dominicans and other native speakers from Caribbean countries use **bien** to replace **muy.**

Answers

25 *Possible answers:*

1. Tus clases no son fáciles. Son difíciles.
2. La clase de español no es aburrida. Es interesante.
3. Texas no es pequeño. Es grande.
4. Los profesores no son antipáticos. Son simpáticos.
5. Alberto no es alto. Es bajo.
6. Tus compañeros no son malos. Son buenos.

ASÍ SE DICE Talking about things you like and explaining why

To find out if a friend likes more than one thing, ask:

¿Te gustan las clases?

¿Cuál es tu clase favorita?
Which is . . . ?

¿A Claudia le gustan las ciencias?
Does Claudia like . . . ?

¿Por qué?
Why?

Your friend might answer:

Sí, **me gustan**. Son fáciles.

Mi clase **favorita** es inglés.

Sí. **Le gustan** mucho.

Porque son muy interesantes.
Because . . .

VOCABULARIO

el baile

el concierto

los deportes

el examen
(pl. los exámenes)

la fiesta

la novela

el partido de...

el videojuego

29 Escuchemos: Patricia y Gregorio

Patricia and Gregorio have just met at school. Listen to their conversation as they try to decide what to do. Based on their conversation, respond to these statements with **cierto** or **falso**. Answers on p. 69D.

1. A Patricia no le gustan las fiestas.
2. A Gregorio le gustan los partidos de fútbol porque son interesantes.
3. A Patricia no le gustan los conciertos.
4. A Gregorio le gusta la música rock.

Presentation

Así se dice On the board or a transparency, write the following to review the singular forms of **gustar.**
Me gusta el arte.
¿Te gusta el arte?
A Ana le gusta el arte.
Then ask students individual questions to elicit these forms.
— **¿Te gusta el arte, Ana?**
— **Sí, me gusta el arte.**
— **Juan, ¿a Ana le gusta el arte?**
— **Sí, a Ana le gusta el arte.**
Then move on to plural forms.

Vocabulario First, have students look at the drawings and read the captions. Then tell a story about yourself or someone else using the new vocabulary in sentences with **gustar.** (**A mí me gusta el baile folklórico. Y también me gusta ir a conciertos con mis amigos.**) After having modeled the pronunciation of the new vocabulary, practice with students as suggested in **Así se dice** above. Have students ask others in the class questions and have them report on what others have answered to elicit **le gusta.**

Portfolio

29 Oral Have students role-play the following situation: Two students are discussing their school schedule and activities. One student asks the other what classes the second is taking, and whether he or she likes the classes. The second replies, giving the reason for liking or disliking the classes. They should also ask about favorite and less favorite activities. For Portfolio suggestions, see *Assessment Guide,* p. 16.

Additional Practice

Así se dice Ask students to look at the examples you have written and those in **Así se dice.** To help them deduce the grammar rules, ask them what differences they see. What is the difference between **gusta** and **gustan?** After discussing the grammar rule, continue asking students questions in Spanish with plural nouns they already know.

For Individual Needs

30 Slower Pace If students are having trouble remembering vocabulary, put pictures of famous people on the board and number each one. Ask students if they can remember what adjectives were used to describe each person, and have them write a list of adjectives that go with each picture. It may be helpful for them to associate an image with adjectives. (a frog with **feo**) Then, have them check their adjective endings to be sure the form is correct.

Additional Practice

30 After students have completed the pairwork, create a graph of class **temperamentos** by having students report their partner's preferences to the categories in the activity.

Teaching Suggestion

32 Ask students to write to the Mexican Embassy or the Mexican Tourist Board (see p. T56.) to obtain information on Mexico. They might ask for information on specific cities such as Cuernavaca. Students may also supplement their knowledge with travel books on Mexico from bookstores or public libraries.

Portfolio

32 Written Point out to students that this activity would be an appropriate entry for their written portfolio. For Portfolio suggestions, see *Assessment Guide,* p. 16.

30 ¿Por qué te gusta?

Working with a partner, take turns asking whether or not you like the things in the list below. Explain why or why not, using the adjectives you've learned so far. Be prepared to report five of your partner's answers to the class. Answers will vary.

MODELO —Te gustan los bailes, ¿no?
—Sí, me gustan mucho.
—¿Por qué?
—Porque son divertidos.

1. la música pop
2. los exámenes
3. el basquetbol
4. las fiestas
5. el fútbol
6. los bailes
7. la música clásica
8. las novelas
9. la natación
10. los conciertos
11. el programa de...
12. los deportes
13. los videojuegos
14. el tenis
15. los videos de...

31 ¿A qué hora?

With a partner, take a look at this entertainment guide and try to figure out what to do. Take turns asking each other whether or not you like the events listed in the entertainment guide and what time they take place. When possible, try to use tag questions like those explained in the **Nota gramatical.**

MODELO —Te gustan los festivales de cine, ¿verdad?
—Sí, ¿a qué hora es el festival?
—A las doce de la tarde.

CALENDARIO DE EVENTOS

12h00:
FESTIVAL DE CINE FRANCES
LOCAL: AUDITORIO DEL MUSEO

15h00:
EXPOSICION DE ARTE
LOCAL: NUEVO MUSEO

17h00:
CONCIERTO DE PIANO
LOCAL: AUDITORIO DE MUSEO

18h30:
PRESENTACION DE DANZA
LOCAL: TEATRO CARLOS TAMARIZ

20h00:
FESTIVAL VIDEO-ROCK
LOCAL: AUDITORIO DE MUSEO

22h00:
GRAN BAILE: "LOS PRISIONEROS"
LOCAL: PARQUE DE SAN SEBASTIAN

Nota Gramatical

One way of asking a question is by adding **¿no?** or **¿verdad?** to the end of a sentence. These are called *tag questions.* The tag question can be translated several different ways, depending on the English context.

La clase es difícil, **¿no?** *isn't it?*

Te gustan los bailes, **¿verdad?** *don't you? right?*

32 De visita

Work in groups of three. Imagine that you are students at the Instituto Centro Unión in Cuernavaca. Prepare a list of questions you can use to interview a student from the U.S. Include questions about age, classes, friends, and teachers. Also, ask about likes and dislikes. Answers will vary.

33 Ahora, dime...

Choose a classmate to take the role of the visiting student in Activity 32. Interview your partner using the questions you've prepared. Then switch roles allowing your partner to ask you his or her list of questions.

34 Soy...

Form a group of five. On a sheet of paper, write a detailed description of yourself. In your description include your age, personality traits, physical characteristics, and things you like and dislike. Your classmates will try to guess who you are, so don't include your name!

35 En mi cuaderno

In your journal, write seven or eight sentences about what you need and want to do at different times tomorrow. Include such items as going to class, doing homework, and going shopping. Use expressions like **me gusta/n** to tell how you feel about the classes and places you mention, and explain why. Answers will vary.

MODELO Mañana necesito hacer la tarea de inglés a las cuatro y media. También quiero...

LETRA Y SONIDO

A. 1. **h**: The letter **h** in Spanish is always silent.
hora **ahora** **héroe** **Hugo** **hijo** **hospital**

2. **j**: The letter **j** in Spanish represents a sound that has no equivalent in English. It's pronounced like the *h* in the English word *house,* but much stronger and with the back of the tongue near the soft palate.
jugar **jefe** **ají** **joven** **pasaje** **caja** **juego**

3. **g**: The letter **g** before the vowels **e** and **i** has the same sound as the letter *j* in the examples above.
gente **general** **geografía** **gimnasio** **corregir** **agitar**

4. Before the vowels **a**, **o**, and **u** the letter **g** is pronounced like the *g* in the English word *go.*
ángulo **tengo** **gusto** **mango**
Between vowels this sound is much softer.
haga **agua** **agotar** **mucho gusto**

5. The **g** is pronounced "hard," like the *g* in *get,* when it's followed by **ue** or **ui**.
guerra **llegué** **guitarra** **guía**

B. **Dictado** Script on p. 69D.
Jimena describes for us what she needs in two of her classes. Write what Jimena is saying.

C. **Trabalenguas**
La gente de San José generalmente juega a las barajas con ganas de ganar.

En mi cuaderno

35 For an additional Chapter 3 journal entry suggestion, see *Practice and Activity Book,* page 147.

Close

To review the new material introduced in this **Paso**, hold up photos of famous people clipped from magazines. Ask students to describe the people. For example, while holding a photo of a famous athlete, ask: **Clase, ¿quién es? ¿Cómo es él/ella? ¿Es alto/a? ¿Es guapo/a? ¿moreno/a? ¿simpático/a? ¿Qué le gusta a él/ella? ¿Le gustan los deportes?** Repeat with various photos to review a variety of adjectives.

Additional Practice

Have students form groups of three. They are to create a dialogue using **ser** and singular and plural adjectives. One student makes an observation in the singular, which the other two students convert to the plural. (**—Yo soy simpática. —Ah, sí. Y nosotros somos simpáticos también.**) Then they present the dialogue to the class.

Assess

Quiz 3-3, *Chapter Teaching Resources, Book 1,* pp. 143–144

Assessment Items, Audiocassette 7A/Audio CD 3

Performance Assessment

Record TV advertisements on videocassette or clip some from a magazine. Have students choose an ad to critique. What do they like about the ad? (**Me gusta la música. Es divertida.**) What would they change? (**No me gusta el hombre. No es cómico.**) Have them design and describe their own ad. (**En mi aviso, hay un baile. El chico es simpático y la chica es bonita...**)

Motivating Activity

Discuss with students the basic reasons for having schedules and report cards. What information do they contain? What would schools be like without them?

READING STRATEGY

Using background knowledge.

PREREADING
Activities A and B

Teaching Suggestion

Discuss the 24-hour clock with the class prior to beginning the reading. To do this, use a clock with moveable arms and review telling time in Spanish.

—**¿Qué hora es, clase?** (11:00)
—**¿Son las once.**
—**¿Y ahora?** (12:00)
—**Son las doce.**

Then move the clock hands to 1:00 and ask:

—**¿Son las trece?**
—**No, es la una.**
—**Sí, es la una. Pero en un horario, son las trece.**

Check comprehension briefly in English, clarifying that 0:00 is midnight (**medianoche**).

Native Speakers

If you have students who have studied in other countries, ask them to write an essay comparing that country's system of schedules and grades to the system in your school.

VAMOS A LEER

Calificaciones y horarios

MATRÍCULA	ÓSCAR GONZÁLEZ LÓPEZ					(MÉXICO)
B0847842	SEPT.	OCT.	NOV.	ENE.	FEB.	MAR.
ESPAÑOL	7.7	9.8	9.5	9.5	9.2	8.4
MATEMÁTICAS	8.8	8.2	9.0	6.4	7.1	8.0
LENG.A.A/ESPAÑOLA	8.5	6.5	7.5	9.0	10.0	10.0
C. NATURALES	7.2	7.4	7.6	8.1	8.8	7.7
C. SOCIALES	9.0	7.7	9.6	10.0	9.7	9.4
EDUC. FÍSICA	10.0	7.5	10.0	9.5	9.6	9.5
EDUC. ARTÍSTICA	10.0	10.0	10.0	10.0	9.5	9.5
EDUC. TECNOLÓGICA	10.0	10.0	10.0	10.0	10.0	10.0

ALUMNA: JUANA ACOSTA RUIZ (ESPAÑA)

Segundo De B.U.P.	PRIMERA EVALUACIÓN			TERCERA EVALUACIÓN		
	Faltas de asistencia	conoci-mientos	Actitud	Faltas de asistencia	conoci-mientos	Actitud
L. y L. Españolas		7	C		7'5	C
Latín		8	B	1	5'5	C
Lengua Extranjera (____)		6'5	C		5	C
Geografía Humana		8	C		7	C
F. Polít. Soc. y Econ.						
Matemáticas		4'5	C		4'5	C
Física-Química		9	C		5'5	C
Religión		7	C		7	B
Educ. Física y Deport.					6	C
EATP. Ens. Ac. Tec-Prof.		4'5	C		5	C

Estrategia
As soon as you know the topic of a reading, spend a couple of minutes just thinking about the topic. What do you already know about it? The reading should then be easier to understand, and you'll be better able to guess unknown words and make sense of difficult passages.

¡A comenzar!

A. You'll probably be familiar with the topics of these items. Skim them briefly and then complete the following statement.

These items are . . .
a) TV schedules and sports scores
b) report cards and TV schedules
c) sports scores and class schedules
d) class schedules and report cards

B. Now, before you read them again more carefully, think about what you already know about these two topics. Would the following probably be found in a school schedule, in a report card, in both, or in neither?

1. letter grades report card
2. parents' names report card (or neither)
3. class names both
4. days of the week schedule
5. student's name both
6. textbook names neither
7. numerical grades report card
8. best friend's name neither
9. class times schedule

Now look at the schedules and report cards again. Find the topics.

Multicultural Link

Discuss with students ways of obtaining schedules and report cards from other countries. If students have pen pals, their correspondents might supply them. Or students may write to an education agency in Mexico (see p. T56.).

El horario de Gloria (México)

Hora	lunes	martes	miércoles	jueves	viernes
7:30-8:20	música	civismo	geografía	biología	historia
8:30-9:20	español	inglés	inglés	matemáticas	matemáticas
9:30-10:20	matemáticas	español	historia	educación física	civismo
10:30-11:20	historia	música	matemáticas	geografía	educación física
11:30-12:20	inglés	descanso	descanso	descanso	español
12:30-13:20	biología	matemáticas	español	español	biología
13:30-14:20					

El horario de María (España)

	lunes	martes	miércoles	jueves	viernes
9:20-10:10	historia	e. física	lit. gallega	latín	filosofía
10:10-11:00	latín	inglés	historia	l. gallega	matemáticas
11:00-11:50	inglés	filosofía	lit. española	l. española	latín
	descanso	descanso	descanso	descanso	descanso
12:10-13:00	matemáticas	inglés	diseño	diseño	inglés
13:00-13:50	e. física	latín	filosofía	filosofía	historia
13:50-14:40			matemáticas		lit. española
15:30-16:20	lit. española	religión			
16:20-17:10	religión	matemáticas			

Al grano

C. Comparaciones. Look at the last columns of the documents. See answers below.

1. The numerical grades are the achievement grades for the class. There are also letter grades. What do the letter grades on Juana's report card represent?
2. What is the highest grade each student got in science?
3. Who did better in physical education?
4. Who did better in Spanish?

D. ¿Qué horario prefieres? Read the class schedules carefully. Do you prefer Gloria's schedule, María's schedule, or your schedule? These questions may help you decide. See answers below.

1. Which classes do all three of you have?
2. How many days a week do you each have English?
3. What kinds of language classes do each of you take?
4. How many days a week do you each take physical education?

E. ¿Dónde te gustaría estudiar? Contesta las siguientes preguntas. See answers below.

1. ¿Cuántas clases tiene Gloria? ¿María? ¿Óscar? ¿Juana?
2. ¿Te gustan las clases de Gloria? ¿de María? ¿Por qué?
3. ¿A qué hora empiezan *(begin)* las clases de Gloria? ¿de María?

Answers

C 1. her attitude/behavior
2. Óscar: 8.8; Juana: 9
3. Óscar
4. Óscar
5. Óscar: ciencias naturales; Juana: matemáticas
6. Óscar: tecnología; Juana: geografía humana

D *Answers will vary.*
1. Gloria and María both have inglés, matemáticas, historia, and educación física
2. Gloria has English three times a week. María has it twice a week.
3. Gloria: inglés, español; María: inglés, latín
4. Gloria: twice; María: twice
5. Gloria: 3 descansos; María: 5 descansos

E 1. Óscar and Gloria are from Mexico. Juana and María are from Spain.
2. Gloria: 10; María: 10; Óscar: 8; Juana: 10
3. *Answers will vary.*
4. Gloria: 7:30; María: 9:20
5. *Answers will vary.*

Reading
Activities C and D

Have students work in groups of three. Ask them to scan the reading to find as many cognates as they can. Set a time limit of three minutes.

For Individual Needs

Slower Pace Before they work with all the schedules, have students work with just one until they understand its components.

Group Work

D. Have students review the schedules in groups of three. Each student takes a different schedule and presents its advantages to the group. Then students may vote as a class on which schedule is most appealing.

Postreading
Activity E

Have students choose either Spain or Mexico and make up their own "ideal" school schedule and report card as if they were a student in one of those countries.

Group Work

E. Have students work with a partner to answer these questions. Watch for students having difficulty. When finished, go over the answers as a class.

Teacher Note

For additional readings, see *Native Speaker Activity Book,* pp. 11–15 and *Practice and Activity Book,* p. 35.

The **Repaso** reviews and integrates all four skills and culture in preparation for the Chapter Test.

Teaching Suggestion

Review the learner outcomes on page 71 with students. Ask students if they feel they have learned all the outcomes listed. Tell them this review will highlight any area they need to concentrate on before the Chapter Test.

Cooperative Learning

4 Have students work in groups of three to answer these questions. All three should help create the answers. One student writes the answers, another checks for spelling, and the third presents the answers to the class. As a group, have them add one question that they create from one of the culture sections of the chapter.

Group Work

Divide the class into pairs. Tell them that they will create a conversation for a classroom competition. One of each pair plays a student who has recently arrived from Mexico to study at your school. He is unfamiliar with U.S. school schedules, classes, and what he should do at what time. The partner answers his questions. Partners are given fifteen to twenty minutes to plan the dialogues, which they then present to the class. At the end of the competition, the class votes on which pair has the most spontaneous, interesting, or humorous conversation. You may want to consider offering a prize, such as extra-credit points, to the winning pair.

REPASO

1 Look at the time zone map. Listen as times around Latin America and the U.S. are announced. For each time you hear, figure out what time it is where you are. Answers will vary.

2 These are the classes that Martín and Gabriela have on Monday. Answer the following questions in Spanish. See answers below.

1. ¿A qué hora tiene Gabriela la clase de español? ¿Y Martín?
2. ¿Qué clase tiene Gabriela primero? ¿Y Martín?
3. A las diez y media, ¿qué clase tiene Gabriela? ¿Y Martín?
4. Son las 8:40. ¿Qué clase tiene Gabriela? ¿Y Martín?

Hora	Martín	Gabriela
7:50 - 8:40	Francés	Ciencias sociales
8:40 - 9:30	Geografía	Computación
9:30 - 9:40	DESCANSO	DESCANSO
9:40 - 10:30	Arte	Inglés
10:30 - 11:20	Computación	Geografía
11:20 - 11:40	Inglés	Arte
11:40 - 12:30	ALMUERZO	ALMUERZO
12:30 - 13:20	Ciencias sociales	Español
13:20 - 13:30	DESCANSO	DESCANSO
13:30 - 14:20	Español	Educación física

3 Working with a partner, create two blank class schedules like the one in Activity 2. As you name your classes and the times they meet, your partner will fill in your schedule. Then switch roles. When you're through, discuss what your classes are like. Are they big? fun? interesting?

Answers

2 1. 12:30; 1:30
2. ciencias sociales; francés
3. geografía; computación
4. computación; geografía

4 Answer the following questions according to the culture sections of this chapter.

1. Would you be pleased if you got a 16 on your report card in Peru? How about a 9 in Mexico? maybe, yes
2. If you lived in Central America when might your school vacation be? November-February
3. Do students in Spanish-speaking countries have the same classes every day? How many classes can they take? no, nine
4. **Hora latina** means . . . Latin time, custom of arriving late at parties

5 How many sentences can you make using the words in the boxes?

A María Inés	(no) me	gusta	la clase de...	la música de...
A Claudia	(no) te	gustan	los deportes	la tarea
A Luis	(no) le		los exámenes	el videojuego
A Fernando			las fiestas	
A ti				
A mí				

Now challenge yourself and write why each person likes or doesn't like each thing. Use different adjectives to explain why.

MODELO A Luis no le gusta la clase de francés porque es aburrida.

6  Form a group of four. Imagine that one of you is showing this photo of your friends Claudia, María Inés, Fernando, and Luis. Role-play a dialogue in which your partners ask you what your friends in the photo are like, where each one is from, what they like or dislike, where they go to school, and what courses they take. Keep the conversation going as long as you can.

7  The City Council is holding a contest to find out which is the best school in town, and you want to write about your school. Write a short paragraph describing the classes, students, teachers, sports, and anything else that makes your school special.

8 SITUACIÓN

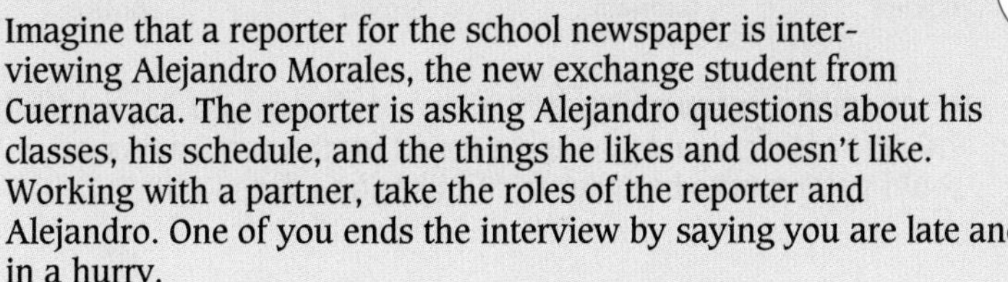

Imagine that a reporter for the school newspaper is interviewing Alejandro Morales, the new exchange student from Cuernavaca. The reporter is asking Alejandro questions about his classes, his schedule, and the things he likes and doesn't like. Working with a partner, take the roles of the reporter and Alejandro. One of you ends the interview by saying you are late and in a hurry.

Portfolio

7 Written Mention to your students that this essay would be an appropriate entry in their Portfolio.

8 Oral You may suggest that students include the **Situación** interview in their Portfolio. For Portfolio information, see *Assessment Guide,* pp. 2–13.

Reteaching

Ser, Adjective Agreement Prepare board with sentences made from different color coded cards. (verb = red, noun = blue, adjective = green) Have students replace existing cards with already prepared plural verb/noun/adjective cards. Use various examples, changing feminine to masculine and vice-versa. Build up sentence structure slowly.

Community Link

7 Have students write a proposal for their city council or the school board explaining why their school would benefit from having more exchange students. Have them expand on their essays about their school. Why is their school excellent for exchange students? What is good about their town for exchange students? Why is it important to have such programs?

Video Wrap-Up

- ***Video Program***
- ***Expanded Video Program, Videocassette 1***
- ***Videodisc Program, Videodisc 2A***

At this time, you might want to use the video resources for additional review and enrichment. See *Video Guide* or *Videodisc Guide* for suggestions regarding:

- **¡Bienvenida al colegio!** (Dramatic episode)
- **Panorama cultural** (Interviews)
- **Video Clips** (Authentic footage)

This page is intended to help students prepare independently for the Chapter Test. It is a brief checklist of the major points covered in the chapter. The students should be reminded that it is only a checklist and does not necessarily include everything that will appear on the Chapter Test.

A VER SI PUEDO . . .

Can you talk about classes and sequencing events? p. 76

1 How would you tell a classmate the sequence of your classes today? and tomorrow? Primero...luego...después... Mañana...

Can you tell time? p. 77

2 Write the time shown on each clock. See answers below.

a.

b.

c.

d.

Can you tell at what time something happens? p. 80

3 How would you ask each of these students what classes they have and at what time they meet? How would each student answer?

1. Sofía -physical education (8:13)
   -art (2:10)
2. César -French (11:40)
   -geography (2:25)
3. Simón -social sciences (9:07)
   -mathematics (3:15)
4. Adela -science (10:38)
   -computer science (12:54)

See answers below.

Can you talk about being late or in a hurry? p. 82

4 How would you . . .? See answers below.

1. say that you are in a hurry
2. say that you are late
3. say that a friend is late
4. tell a friend to hurry up

Can you describe people and things? p. 84

5 Imagine you're an exchange student in Cuernavaca. Describe the following people and things in your school in the U.S. to your new friends in Cuernavaca.

1. the teachers
2. Spanish class
3. the exams
4. physical education class
5. school friends
6. art class

6 Look at the photos. Write a sentence describing each person or thing.

Yolanda

Gabriela

Simón

Bruto

See sample answer below.

Can you talk about things you like and explain why? p. 87

7 How would you say which activities and classes you like or dislike, and why? How would you ask a friend for the same information? How would you report what your friend likes and doesn't like?

Answers

2 a. seis menos catorce
b. ocho y media
c. ocho menos diez
d. diez y diez

3 *Sample answer:*
— Sofía, ¿tienes clase de educación física? ¿y de arte?
— Sí, tengo educación física a las ocho y trece de la mañana y arte a las dos y diez de la tarde.

4 1. Tengo prisa.
2. Estoy atrasado/a.
3. Está atrasado/a.
4. ¡Date prisa!

6 *Sample answer:*
Yolanda es inteligente y estudia mucho.

VOCABULARIO

PRIMER PASO

Talking about classes and sequencing events

el almuerzo *lunch*
el arte *art*
las ciencias *science*
las ciencias sociales *social sciences*
la computación *computer science*
el descanso *recess, break*
después *after*
un día libre *a free day*
la educación física *physical education*
el francés *French*
la geografía *geography*
hoy *today*
las, los *the*
luego *then*
mañana *tomorrow*
las matemáticas *mathematics*
la materia *subject*
por fin *at last*
primero *first*
el semestre *semester*

Telling time

Es la una. *It's one o'clock.*
menos cuarto *quarter to (the hour)*
¿Qué hora es? *What time is it?*
Son las... *It's . . . o'clock*
tarde *late, afternoon*
y media *half past (the hour)*

SEGUNDO PASO

Telling at what time something happens

ahora *now*
¿A qué hora...? *At what time . . . ?*
de *of, from*
de la mañana *in the morning (A.M.)*
del *of the, from the*
de la noche *in the evening (P.M.)*
de la tarde *in the afternoon, (P.M.)*
en punto *on the dot*

Talking about being late or in a hurry

¡Date prisa! *Hurry up!*
Está atrasado/a. *He/ She is late.*
Estoy atrasado/a. *I'm late.*
Tengo prisa. *I'm in a hurry.*

TERCER PASO

Describing people and things

aburrido/a *boring*
alto/a *tall*
antipático/a *disagreeable*
bajo/a *short (to describe people)*
bonito/a *pretty*
bueno/a *good*
cómico/a *comical, funny*
¿Cómo es...? *What's . . . like?*
¿Cómo son...? *What are . . . like?*
el (la) compañero/a *friend, pal*
difícil *difficult*
divertido/a *fun, amusing*
ellas, ellos *they*
estricto/a *strict*
fácil *easy*
feo/a *ugly*
grande *big*
guapo/a *good-looking*
inteligente *intelligent*
interesante *interesting*
malo/a *bad*
moreno/a *brunette*
No te preocupes. *Don't worry.*
nuevo/a *new*
pequeño/a *small*
el (la) profesor, -a *teacher*
rubio/a *blond*
simpático/a *nice*
somos *we are*

Talking about things you like and explaining why

el baile *dance*
el concierto *concert*
cuál *which*
los deportes *sports*
el examen *exam (pl.* **los exámenes***)*
favorito/a *favorite*
la fiesta *party*
le gustan *he/ she likes*
me gustan *I like*
¿no? *isn't it?*
la novela *novel*
el partido de... *game of . . . (sport)*
¿Por qué? *Why?*
porque *because*
te gustan *you like*
¿verdad? *don't you?, right?*
el video(juego) *video (game)*

Game

ARREGLAR PALABRAS This game may be played at any time for vocabulary practice. Cut heavy paper or cardboard into one-inch squares. Leave a third of them blank and write the letters of the Spanish alphabet on the rest. (You may want to make extra squares with the most common letters: vowels, **s, t,** etc.) You will need enough pieces for each student to have 10 letters and five blanks. A blank serves as any letter the student chooses. Place the letters face down in one pile and the blanks in another pile. Each student picks 10 letters and five blanks. Using vocabulary they've learned so far, students arrange letters and blanks to form as many words as possible. The student with the most words wins. The student with the longest word is also a winner. This game may also be played in small teams.

Game

¿A QUÉ HORA ES...? Put a mock class schedule on a transparency or on the board. Divide the class into two teams. A member of Team A asks what time a class is. A member of Team B must answer in Spanish. Continue, alternating teams. Teams get one point for each correct response, and the winner is the team with the highest score.

CHAPTER 3 ASSESSMENT

CHAPTER TEST

- *Chapter Teaching Resources, Book 1,* pp. 145-152
- *Assessment Guide,* Speaking Test, p. 29
- *Assessment Items Audiocassette 7B Audio CD 3*

TEST GENERATOR, CHAPTER 3

ALTERNATIVE ASSESSMENT

Performance Assessment

You might want to use the **Situación** (p. 93) as a cumulative performance assessment activity.

Portfolio Assessment

- **Written:** Activity 32, *Pupil's Edition,* p. 88
  Assessment Guide, p. 16
- **Oral:** Activity 29, *Pupil's Edition,* p. 87
  Assessment Guide, p. 16

Capítulo 4: ¿Qué haces esta tarde?
Chapter Overview

De antemano pp. 98–100	*Practice and Activity Book*, p. 37		*Video Guide* OR *Videodisc Guide*	
	FUNCTIONS	**GRAMMAR**	**CULTURE**	**RE-ENTRY**
Primer paso pp. 101–105	• Talking about what you like to do, p. 101 • Discussing what you and others do during free time, p. 102	• Present tense of regular **-ar** verbs, p. 102 • **Con, conmigo, contigo,** p. 104 • The relative pronoun **que,** p. 105	• **Nota cultural,** Popular sports in Spanish-speaking countries, p. 103 • Greetings in Spanish-speaking countries, p. 105	Present tense of **tener**
Segundo paso pp. 106–110	Telling where people and things are, p. 106	• The verb **estar,** p. 106 • Subject pronouns, p. 109	• **Nota cultural, tú** and **usted** usage, p. 109 • **Panorama cultural: El paseo,** p. 110	• Subject pronouns **yo, tú, él, ella** • Describing with **ser**
Tercer paso pp. 111–113	Talking about where you and others go during free time, p. 111	• The verb **ir,** p. 111 • Days of the week, p. 112	• **Nota cultural,** Extracurricular activities in Spanish-speaking countries, p. 112	Telling time
Letra y sonido p. 113	Pronunciation: The letters **b** and **v**		**Dictado:** *Textbook Audiocassette 2B/Audio CD 4*	
Vamos a Leer pp. 114–115	**Anuncios personales**		**Reading Strategy:** Scanning for specific information	
Review pp. 116–119	**Repaso,** pp. 116–117	**A ver si puedo...,** p. 118	**Vocabulario,** p. 119	
Assessment Options	**Quizzes** • *Chapter Teaching Resources, Book 1* **Primer paso,** Quiz 4-1, pp. 197–198 **Segundo paso,** Quiz 4-2, pp. 199–200 **Tercer paso,** Quiz 4-3, pp. 201–202 • *Assessment Items, Audiocassette 7B/Audio CD 4*		**Chapter Test** • *Chapter Teaching Resources, Book 1*, pp. 203–210 • *Assessment Guide*, Speaking Test, p. 29 • *Assessment Items, Audiocassette 7B/Audio CD 4* **Test Generator, Chapter 4**	

Video Program or *Expanded Video Program, Videocassette 1* or *Videodisc Program, Videodisc 2B*	*Textbook Audiocassette 2B/Audio CD 4*

RESOURCES: Print	RESOURCES: Audiovisual
	Textbook Audiocassette 2B/Audio CD 4
Practice and Activity Book, pp. 38–40	
Native Speaker Activity Book, pp. 16–20	
Chapter Teaching Resources, Book 1	
• Additional Listening Activities 4-1, 4-2, p. 185	*Additional Listening Activities, Audiocassette 10B/Audio CD 4*
• Student Response Forms, pp. 194–196	
• Realia 4-1, pp. 189, 191	
• Situation Cards 4-1, pp. 192, 193	
• Teaching Transparency Master 4-1, pp. 181, 184	*Teaching Transparency 4-1*
• Quiz 4-1, pp. 197–198	*Assessment Items, Audiocassette 7B/Audio CD 4*
Videodisc Guide	*Videodisc Program, Videodisc 2B*
Video Guide	*Video Program* or *Expanded Video Program, Videocassette 1*
	Textbook Audiocassette 2B/Audio CD 4
Practice and Activity Book, pp. 41–43	
Native Speaker Activity Book, pp. 16–20	
Chapter Teaching Resources, Book 1	
• Communicative Activity 4-1, pp. 177–178	
• Additional Listening Activities 4-3, 4-4, p. 186	*Additional Listening Activities, Audiocassette 10B/Audio CD 4*
• Student Response Forms, p. 194–196	
• Realia 4-2, pp. 190, 191	
• Situation Cards 4-2, pp. 192, 193	
• Teaching Transparency Master 4-2, pp. 182, 184	*Teaching Transparency 4-2*
• Quiz 4-2, pp. 199–200	*Assessment Items, Audiocassette 7B/Audio CD 4*
Videodisc Guide	*Videodisc Program, Videodisc 2B*
	Textbook Audiocassette 2B/Audio CD 4
Practice and Activity Book, pp. 44–46	
Native Speaker Activity Book, pp. 16–20	
Chapter Resources, Book 1	
• Communicative Activity 4-2, pp. 179–180	
• Additional Listening Activities 4-5, 4-6, p. 187	*Additional Listening Activities, Audiocassette 10B/Audio CD 4*
• Student Response Forms, p. 194–196	
• Realia 4-2, p. 190, 191	
• Situation Cards 4-3, pp. 192, 193	
• Teaching Transparency Master 4-3, pp. 183, 184	*Teaching Transparency 4-3*
• Quiz 4-3, pp. 201–202	*Assessment Items, Audiocassette 7B/Audio CD 4*
Videodisc Guide	*Videodisc Program, Videodisc 1*
Videodisc Guide	*Video Program* or *Expanded Video Program, Videocassette 1*
Video Guide	*Videodisc Program, Videodisc 2B*

Alternative Assessment

- Performance Assessment
  Primer paso, p. 105
  Segundo paso, p. 109
  Tercer paso, p. 113
- Portfolio Assessment
  Written: **Repaso** Activity 7, *Pupil's Edition*, p. 117
  Assessment Guide, p. 17
  Oral: Activity 30, *Pupil's Edition*, p. 113
  Assessment Guide, p. 17

Capítulo 4: ¿Qué haces esta tarde?

Textbook Listening Activities Scripts

For Student Response Forms, see *Chapter Teaching Resources, Book 1,* pp. 194–196.

Primer paso

Activity 6, p. 101

1. Hola. Me llamo Tomás. Me gusta comprar muchas cosas. Por eso me gusta ir de compras.
2. ¿Qué tal? Me llamo Arturo. No me gustan las fiestas porque son muy aburridas.
3. Yo soy Bárbara. A mí me gusta hablar por teléfono... ¡día y noche!
4. Hola. Soy Patricia. No me gusta estudiar mucho, pero me gusta mirar la televisión.

Answers to Activity 6
1. c 2. b 3. a 4. d

Activity 8, p. 102

1. Hola, soy Carmen. Escucho música y miro la televisión en mi cuarto.
2. Me llamo Javier. Hablo por teléfono con Sofía, Manuel, Rebeca, Raúl...
3. Soy Armando. Ana y yo estudiamos en la biblioteca día y noche.
4. Me llamo Susana. Después de clases, practico el béisbol y el tenis.
5. Soy Pablo. En el tiempo libre, bailo y canto con mis amigos. Toco la guitarra también.

Answers to Activity 8
1. d 2. b 3. e 4. c 5. a

Segundo paso

Activity 18, p. 106

1. ¿El correo? Está en la Plaza de la Constitución.
2. Necesito encontrar mi mochila. No está en mi cuarto.
3. Hola. ¿Qué tal? Estoy atrasado. Todavía estoy en el trabajo.
4. ¡Estoy aquí, José! Mira, José, ¡estoy aquí!

Answers to Activity 18
1. c 2. d 3. b 4. a

Activity 21, p. 108

MODELO Paco es bajo y moreno. Le gusta jugar con su perro.

1. Marisa y Ana Luisa son guapas y morenas. Tienen catorce años.
2. El señor Contreras es bajo y le gusta comprar ropa.
3. Eva es muy inteligente y le gusta estudiar matemáticas.
4. Isabel tiene seis años y le gustan los videos cómicos.
5. Mario y José son antipáticos. Siempre necesitan hablar con el director del colegio.
6. Anabel nada muy bien. Tiene treinta y cinco años y es muy bonita.
7. Guillermo es alto y rubio. Juega mucho al basquetbol con sus amigos.

Answers to Activity 21
1. e 2. f 3. d 4. b 5. g 6. a 7. c

Tercer paso

Activity 26, p. 111

MODELO —Alicia, ¿adónde vas tú?
—Voy a la piscina.

1. —Y Pedro, ¿adónde va él?
—Él va a la casa de Graciela.
2. —David y Luisa, entonces. ¿Adónde van ellos?
—Ellos van al gimnasio.
3. —Y tú, Alicia, ¿adónde vas?
—Voy a la piscina. Trabajo allí hoy.
4. —Y Carlos, ¿va al cine?
—Sí, Carlos va al cine.
5. —Hola Carlos.
—Hola Filiberto. ¿Adónde vas?
—Voy al cine. ¡Contigo!

Answers to Activity 26

1. Pedro va a la casa de Graciela.
2. David y Luisa van al gimnasio.
3. Alicia va a la piscina.
4. Carlos va al cine.
5. Filiberto va al cine. *Carlos can give Filiberto a ride to the movies.*

Letra y sonido, p. 113

For the scripts for Parts A and C, see p. 113. The script for Part B is below.

B. Dictado, p. 113

veinte, bolígrafo, librería, basura, el tiempo libre, jueves

Repaso

Activity 1, p. 116

MODELO Hola, soy Carlos. El sábado vamos al parque para jugar al tenis. Vamos a las 10:00. ¿Quieres ir también?

1. Buenos días. Soy Carmen. Enrique y yo vamos a estudiar en la biblioteca hoy a las tres y media. ¿Quieres ir con nosotros?
2. Hola. Soy Gaby. ¿Cómo estás? Voy a la piscina mañana a las cuatro y media. ¿Quieres ir conmigo?
3. Buenos días. Soy Victoria. ¿Cómo estás? Sara y yo vamos al cine el domingo a las tres. A ti te gustan las películas, ¿no? Pues, ¡vamos!

Answers to Repaso Activity 1

Notes:

1. Carmen y Enrique van a la biblioteca hoy, a las 3:30
2. Gaby, va a la piscina mañana, a las 4:30
3. Victoria y Sara van al cine el domingo, a las 3:00

Capítulo 4: ¿Qué haces esta tarde?
Projects

COOPERATIVE LEARNING

This activity provides students the opportunity to tell visitors where things are in your town to help them get around. They will create a map and use it to present a guided tour in an oral performance.

INTRODUCTION

Talk to students about the importance of being able to use Spanish when traveling, meeting people, and helping others get around. Tell the class to imagine that a tourist group from Mexico will be coming to visit your town or city. Ask students if they have ever been on a guided tour. What was said on the tour? What would likely be part of a guided tour of your town? Then, explain that this chapter's project has two parts: the map and the guided tour.

MATERIALS

✂ **Students may need**

- Poster board
- Blank overhead transparencies
- Markers
- Rulers
- Pens/pencils
- Toy vehicle (optional)

SEQUENCE

1. Divide students into groups of four. Within each group assign the roles of script writer, script proofreader, tour guide, and tour demonstrator.
2. Groups will cooperatively draw a map of your town or the area around the school on poster board or an overhead transparency. The map will be used in the tour presentation and should include as many of the locations as possible from the **Vocabulario**, page 119.
3. Next, the students create a script for the guided tour. The script should include what is said as they arrive at a location and a short description of each site (what it is near or next to; what it looks like; what they like to do there). It is the role of the script writer to put the tour in writing.
4. The script proofreader peer-edits the written copy.
5. In front of the class, the tour guide narrates the trip their map represents. During the narration, the tour demonstrator indicates the sequence on the map by pointing or moving an object to each location as the tour guide mentions it.

GRADING THE PROJECT

Suggested point distribution (total = 100 points):

Map

Creativity and appearance 20

Legibility 10

Script

Appropriate vocabulary and detail 30

Spelling and grammar usage 10

Guided Tour

Coordination of script with demonstration . . . 10

Comprehensibility 20

Capítulo 4: ¿Qué haces esta tarde?

¿DÓNDE ESTÁ?

This game reviews the classroom vocabulary and provides the opportunity to work with the verb ***estar.***

Procedure One student writes the Spanish word for an object found in the classroom on a sheet of paper and gives it to you. The other students must ask questions of the first student to locate the object. (**¿Está debajo de la mesa?** or **¿Está cerca del escritorio?**) The student who guesses the object is the next to write a word and answer questions.

CEREBRO

This game, played like Concentration®, helps students learn and review vocabulary by using the skills of concentration and recall.

Preparation Have students make three pairs of cards.

1. On one card write a question from **Así se dice**, and on its mate write an appropriate response.
2. On one card write a verb from the chapter, and on its mate draw a stick figure that depicts the action.
3. Turn to page 104. On one card write a verb from the second box of Activity 10, and on its mate write an appropriate phrase from the third box. (Be certain that there is only one phrase from the third box that matches.)

Procedure Divide the class into pairs or small groups. Have students place the combined set of their cards in a pattern on the desk, blank side up. Players take turns turning over two cards each. If they match, the player removes them. If they don't match, the player replaces them in their original positions. Play continues until all the cards have been matched. The player with the most matches wins. For a challenge, have students make additional sets of cards.

FAMILY LINK

Teach a relative or friend five Spanish words. Have students take home their own set of CEREBRO cards. The assignment is to teach someone the three phrases by playing the game. Have students report orally how their **estudiante** is doing.

¿DÓNDE ESTOY?

Any number of students may play this game. For less experienced students you may want to list possible locations on the board. Choose one player to be "it." She picks a location (city, region, well-known landmark) and the other players question her and try to guess where she is.

— **¿Estás en la ciudad?**
— **Sí, estoy en la ciudad.**
— **¿Estás en una tienda?**
— **No, no estoy en una tienda.**
— **¿Hay cartas allí?**
— **Sí, hay cartas.**
— **¿Estás en el correo?**
— **Sí, estoy en el correo.**

The student who guesses correctly becomes "it" and the game proceeds. As a variation, you may wish to divide the class into teams.

¿Qué haces esta tarde?

pp. 96–119

Using the Chapter Opener

Motivating Activity

Ask students how they spent their leisure time during the past week. Have them discuss some of their favorite and least favorite free-time activities. You may wish to discuss whether or not last week was typical and why.

Photo Flash!

Many people in Spanish-speaking countries spend Sunday afternoons in the park, a favorite recreation spot. There are vendors in the park selling balloons, toys, soft drinks, ice cream, and other items that might attract passers-by.

Teacher Note

In presenting this chapter, you may want to refer your students to the **deportes y pasatiempos** section of the Additional Vocabulary, pp. 340–342.

CAPÍTULO 4

¿Qué haces esta tarde?

1 Siempre damos un paseo en el parque los domingos.

Multicultural Link

Discuss with students the tradition in Spain and Latin America of spending Sundays with the family. Ask students how they generally spend Sundays. (Do they sleep late, go to church, visit grandparents?) Ask them how their Hispanic friends usually spend their Sundays.

Spanish-speaking students enjoy a variety of activities after school. They like to get a bite to eat, have a fruit drink at a sidewalk café, or just listen to music. What do you do in your free time?

In this chapter you will learn

- to talk about what you like to do; to discuss what you and others do during free time
- to tell where people and things are
- to talk about where you and others go during free time

And you will

- listen to students talking about their plans for the weekend
- read about Spanish-speaking teenagers who are looking for pen pals
- write a short description of a typical week
- find out what teenagers in Spanish-speaking countries do in their free time

2 ¿El correo? Está en la Plaza de la Constitución.

3 ¿Adónde vamos?

Focusing on Outcomes

- Have students look at the photos and match them with the learner outcomes. (1. represents discussing what you and others do during free time, 2. represents telling where something is, and 3. represents talking about where you and others go during free time.)
- Ask students why they think it is important to be able to express in Spanish where people and things are. In what situations would this ability help them? Have they ever been in a situation in which they could not communicate with someone?

Photo Flash!

The photo of the teenagers packing the van is taken from the *Expanded Video Program.* They go to Taxco to visit relatives and to sightsee.

Culture Note

Point out that families in Spanish-speaking countries often do not have the luxury of owning more than one car. Therefore teenagers either walk, take the bus, or ride a moped to where they need to go.

VIDEO PROGRAM OR EXPANDED VIDEO PROGRAM, Videocassette 1

OR VIDEODISC PROGRAM, *Videodisc 1B*

Video Synopsis

Claudia and her friends decide to spend Saturday in Taxco. Knowing that María Inés enjoys Taxco, they try and find her, going to all the places she usually goes on Saturdays.

Motivating Activity

Ask students what they generally do with new friends. Ask them to discuss where they might take new friends who are visiting their city. What would they do? To whom might they introduce them?

Presentation

Have students read over the **fotonovela** silently. Have the students act out the pictures in pairs, then have them guess what might happen next.

Background Information

Taxco is a beautiful city in the state of Guerrero. The government has declared it to be a national monument. There are flowers and bougainvillea throughout the city. Its buildings are white with red tile roofs, and winding, cobblestone streets climb its steep hills. The church of Santa Prisca was ordered built in 1751 by José (Joseph) de la Borda, a Frenchman made wealthy by exploiting the local silver mines.

DE ANTEMANO

¿Dónde está María Inés?

You met Claudia and her new friends in Chapter 3. Look at the **fotonovela.** What do you think happens in this story? Where do you think Claudia and her new friends are going? Read the story and find out!

Rosa & Claudia

Luis

María Inés

1

Papi, él es mi amigo Luis. Después de clases, yo canto en el coro con Luis.

Sí, los miércoles y los viernes, ¿verdad?

No, papi, los martes y los jueves.

Ah... Entonces, Luis... ¿vas a Taxco con Claudia y Rosa?

Sí, señor... voy con ellas.

2

Hola, Luis. Claudia habla mucho de ti. Tú juegas al basquetbol muy bien, ¿no?

Pues... no sé.

Bueno, Luis, vamos a Taxco porque mi tío Ernesto tiene un regalo especial para mamá.

3

¡Tengo una muy buena idea! A María Inés le gusta mucho Taxco. ¿Llamo a María Inés?

Sí, cómo no. Buena idea.

4

Ah, pero los sábados por la mañana practica con su grupo de baile folklórico.

Pues, vamos allá. La escuela de baile donde tiene clase está en la Avenida Juárez.

98

RESOURCES FOR DE ANTEMANO

Textbook Audiocassette 2B/Audio CD 4
Video Guide
Video Program
Expanded Video Program, Videocassette 1
Videodisc Guide
Videodisc Program, Videodisc 2B
Practice and Activity Book, p. 37

5

Oye, María Inés... voy al centro. ¿Me acompañas?

Gracias, Juan, pero no. Necesito ir al correo. ¡Adiós!

6

¿Está aquí María Inés Hernández?

No, va ahora hacia el correo.

¿Dónde está?

En la Plaza de la Constitución.

7

Bueno, ¿qué hacemos? ¿Regresamos a casa?

Sí. Aquí no está.

Momento... por lo general, estudia en la biblioteca después de bailar. ¿Por qué no vamos allá?

8

María Inés no está en la escuela de baile, no está en el correo, y no está aquí en la biblioteca. ¿Qué hacemos?

Background Information

Folk dancing is a tradition carried on by many contemporary Mexicans. There are numerous regional dances performed by men, women, and children who wear traditional costumes at festivals and celebrations throughout the year. The **Ballet Folklórico de México** has contributed to the popularity of folk dancing. The dancers perform in the **Palacio de Bellas Artes** in Mexico City and in theaters throughout the world.

Photo Flash!

The dance student tells Luis and Claudia that María Inés has gone to the **correo.** Ask students if they have ever seen the phrase **correo áereo** on an envelope. Ask them to guess what it means. See if they can guess what building is on the Plaza de la Constitución. (the post office)

Teaching Suggestion

After students have listened to the audio recording or viewed the video, ask them to break into groups of three or four to practice introducing a friend to their parent(s). One or two of the students assume the role of parent(s) and the other student introduces his or her friend using the vocabulary from Chapter 1 and the example of Claudia introducing Luis.

Video Integration

- ***Expanded Video Program,*** ***Videocassette 1***
- ***Videodisc Program,*** ***Videodisc 2B***

You may choose to continue with **¿Dónde está María Inés? (a continuación)** at this time or wait until later in the chapter. At this point in the story, Claudia and Luis return home, where María Inés meets up with them. The three friends go to Taxco for the afternoon with Rosa, where they visit relatives and go sightseeing.

Language Note

The word **papi** is used often in Spanish and is similar in meaning to the English word *daddy*.

Native Speakers

You could assign native speakers the various roles in the **fotonovela** and ask them to act it out. This will also help those students who are auditory learners.

For Individual Needs

3 Challenge/Auditory Learners Have students close their books and listen as you read the sentences aloud. Read all of the sentences once, then read them again slowly, asking students to number the lettered sentences in order.

1 ¿Comprendes? ¡Contesta las preguntas!

Do you understand who the characters are and what they're doing in the **fotonovela**? Check your comprehension by answering these questions. Don't be afraid to guess!

1. Where does the story begin? Claudia's house
2. Where do Luis, Claudia, and Rosa plan to go? Taxco
3. Who are Luis and Claudia looking for? María Inés
4. Where do they look? gymnasium, post office, library
5. Do they find the person they're looking for? If not, why? No, they pass the store where she is without looking in.

2 ¿Cierto o falso?

Based on the end of the **fotonovela**, respond to these statements with **cierto** or **falso**. If a statement is false, change it to make it true. See answers below.

1. Luis y Claudia cantan en el coro los miércoles y los viernes.
2. Tío Ernesto tiene un regalo para la madre de Claudia y Rosa.
3. María Inés practica el béisbol los sábados por la mañana.
4. Claudia y Luis van al correo.
5. Por lo general, María Inés estudia en casa después de la clase de baile.

3 ¿Dónde está ella? *Where is she?*

In the **fotonovela**, Luis and Claudia go all over downtown Cuernavaca. Retrace their steps by putting the following events in order.

a. Claudia y Luis van a la clase de baile. 2
b. Ellos van al correo. 4
c. Luis va a la casa de Claudia. 1
d. Van a la biblioteca. 5
e. María Inés va al correo. 3

4 ¿Qué hacemos?

Complete these three conversations with words from the box. Use the **fotonovela** as a guide. One word will be used more than once.

5 correo
2 practica
vamos 3
1 sábados
6, 4 está
8 biblioteca
7 estudia

CLAUDIA Ah, pero los __1__ por la mañana María Inés __2__ con su grupo de baile folklórico.
LUIS Pues, __3__ allá. La escuela de baile donde tiene clase __4__ en la Avenida Juárez.

CLAUDIA Vamos al __5__. ¿Dónde está?
LUIS __6__ en la Plaza de la Constitución.

CLAUDIA Momento... por lo general __7__ en la __8__ después de bailar. ¿Vamos allá?
LUIS Sí, ¿por qué no?

5 ¿Y tú?

When was the last time you were at the places mentioned in the story? Make a list of each place, and write the day of the week when you were last there. Answers will vary.

Answers

2
1. Falso: Cantan en el coro los martes y los jueves.
2. Cierto
3. Falso: María Inés baila con un grupo de baile folklórico.
4. Cierto
5. Falso: María Inés estudia en la bibiloteca después de la clase de baile.

PRIMER PASO

Talking about what you like to do; discussing what you and others do during free time

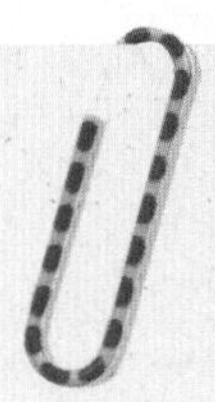

ASÍ SE DICE Talking about what you like to do

To find out what a friend likes to do, ask:	Your friend might respond:
¿Qué te gusta hacer?	**Me gusta pintar.** *I like to paint.*
¿A Manuel le gusta estudiar? *Does Manuel like to study?*	No, **no le gusta** estudiar. Pero le gusta **hablar por teléfono.** *. . . he doesn't like . . .* *. . . to talk on the phone.*
¿A quién le gusta bailar y cantar? *Who likes to dance and sing?*	**A mí me gusta** bailar y cantar. **Por eso me gustan** las fiestas. *I like . . .* *That's why I like . . .*

VOCABULARIO

cuidar a tu hermano/a	*to take care of your brother/sister*	**lavar el carro**	*to wash the car*
		lavar la ropa	*to wash the clothes*
dibujar	*to draw*	**mirar la televisión**	*to watch TV*
descansar en el parque	*to rest in the park*	**nadar en la piscina**	*to swim in the pool*
escuchar música	*to listen to music*	**sacar la basura**	*to take out the trash*

6 Escuchemos: Actividades

Listen to what the following people like to do. Match the name of each person with the appropriate picture.

1. Tomás
2. Arturo
3. Bárbara
4. Patricia

Answers on p. 95C.

7 ¿Qué te gusta hacer?

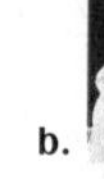

Look at the activities in **Así se dice** on this page or in the **Vocabulario.** List three activities you like to do and three that you don't like to do. Get together with a partner and compare lists. Be prepared to tell the class what your partner likes and doesn't like to do. Answers will vary.

a.

b.

c.

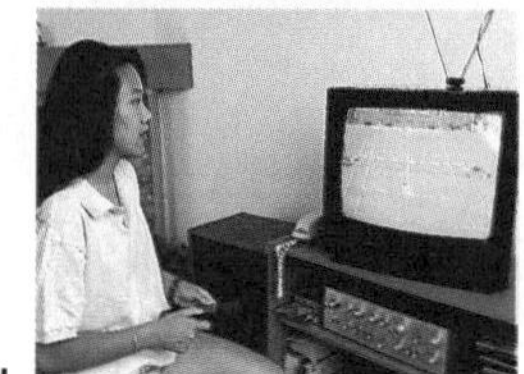

d.

Jump Start!

Write the following sentences on the board or a transparency and have students respond with one-sentence answers.

1. ¿Qué te gusta hacer a las ocho de la noche?
2. ¿A qué hora te gusta descansar?
3. ¿A qué hora es tu clase favorita?
4. ¿Qué deportes te gusta practicar?
5. Si (*if*) no te gustan los deportes, ¿qué te gusta hacer?

MOTIVATE

Ask students if they think teens in Spanish-speaking countries spend their free time the same way they do. Why or why not? What different chores or activities might kids around the world do?

TEACH

Presentation

Así se dice Ask **¿Qué te gusta hacer?**, respond with some of your own likes, then have students say their answer. Then repeat with **¿Qué no te gusta hacer?** Follow-up with some questions about the answers just given: **¿A ____ le gusta estudiar? ¿A quién le gusta ____?**

Vocabulario Put on *Teaching Transparency 4-1* to introduce and model the new vocabulary. Then, ask students to come up with other phrases using these new verbs and vocabulary they already know. **(sacar un cuaderno, lavar el perro)** To spiral in telling time and days of the week, ask questions such as the following. **¿Te gusta sacar la basura los lunes? ¿A qué hora necesitas lavar la ropa?**

RESOURCES FOR PRIMER PASO

Textbook Audiocassette 2B/Audio CD 4
Practice and Activity Book, pp. 38–40
Native Speaker Activity Book, pp. 16–20
Videodisc Guide
Videodisc Program, Videodisc 2B

Chapter Teaching Resources, Book 1
- Additional Listening Activities 4-1, 4-2, p. 185
  Audiocassette 10B/Audio CD 4
- Student Response Forms, pp. 194–196
- Realia 4-1, pp. 189, 191
- Situation Cards 4-1, pp. 192, 193
- Teaching Transparency Master 4-1, pp. 181, 184
  Teaching Transparency 4-1
- Quiz 4-1, pp. 197–198
  Audiocassette 7B/Audio CD 4

Presentation

Gramática Have students read through the forms of **hablar.** See if they can find differences in patterns between the Spanish and English conjugations. (English: needs pronoun and has two verb forms; Spanish: doesn't need pronoun, and has six verb forms.) Practice verb forms with the whole class first, then with individual students. **(¿Hablamos francés en esta clase? No, no hablamos francés, hablamos español. Lupe, ¿tú hablas francés? Juan y Gloria, ¿ustedes hablan francés?)**

Así se dice On the board, draw a day schedule, indicating hours in class and after class. Fill in the chart with verb phrases of what you do during the day. Then make statements about yourself referring to the chart as you speak. **(Después de clase me gusta tocar el piano. No me gusta sacar la basura.)**

For videodisc application, see *Videodisc Guide.*

Gramática Present tense of regular -ar verbs

1. In Spanish and English, verbs change depending on the *subject* (the person doing the action). This is called *conjugating the verb.*
2. In Spanish, there are three main groups of verbs; their infinitives (the unchanged form of a verb) end in **-ar**, **-er** or **-ir**. The first group you'll learn to conjugate is the **-ar** verbs: habl**ar** *(to speak)*, trabaj**ar** *(to work)*, estudi**ar** *(to study)*.
3. To conjugate **hablar** or any other regular **-ar** verb, take the part of the verb called the *stem* **(habl-)** and add these endings:

habl**o** *I speak*	habl**amos** *we speak*
habl**as** *you speak* (familiar)	**habl****áis** *you speak* (plural, Spain)
habl**a** { *you speak* (formal) / *she speaks* / *he speaks*	habl**an** { *you speak* (plural) / *they speak*

Look at the next section to see how these verb forms are used in context.

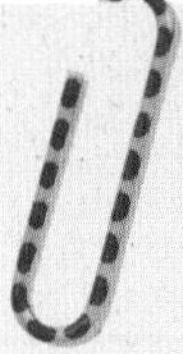

ASÍ SE DICE Discussing what you and others do during free time

To ask what a friend does after school, say:	Your friend might answer:
¿Qué haces después de clases? *What do you do after school?*	**¡Descanso!** *I rest!*
¿Tocas el piano? *Do you play the piano?*	No, pero **toco la guitarra.** *. . . I play the guitar.*
¿Baila María Inés **antes de regresar a casa?** *Does María Inés dance before returning home?*	Sí, ella **baila** con su grupo de baile.
¿Practican deportes Luis y Carmen **en el tiempo libre?** *Do Luis and Carmen practice sports during free time?*	No, ellos no **practican** deportes.

8 Escuchemos: El tiempo libre

Listen as each person tells you what he or she does during his or her free time. Match the person with the correct activity.

Answers on p. 95C.

1. Carmen	a. bailar y cantar
2. Javier	b. hablar con amigos
3. Armando y Ana	c. practicar deportes
4. Susana y yo	d. escuchar música
5. Pablo	e. estudiar

VOCABULARIO

pasar el rato con amigos

caminar con el perro

montar en bicicleta

trabajar en un restaurante

tomar un refresco/un helado

preparar la cena

También se puede decir...
In many Spanish-speaking countries, you'll also hear **andar en bicicleta** or **dar un paseo en bicicleta** in addition to **montar en bicicleta.**

NOTA CULTURAL

Soccer, cycling, tennis, and baseball are popular sports in Spanish-speaking countries. Fans in these countries have had a lot to cheer about! In 1993 and 1994, Sergi Bruguera of Spain won the French Open, one of the four grand slam events in professional tennis. In 1994, Conchita Martínez became the first Spanish woman to win the Wimbledon crown, tennis's premier tournament. In the United States, Spanish-speaking athletes have contributed greatly, especially to the sport of baseball.

9 Hacemos un poco de todo

Tell Mariana, your new classmate, what these people do in their free time. Write complete sentences using the information provided.
See answers below.

1. Yo/tocar/la guitarra en el tiempo libre
2. Mi hermana/trabajar/después de clases
3. Mi padre/caminar con el perro en el parque a las cinco
4. Beto y Shoji/hablar por teléfono después de clases
5. Maya y yo/nadar en la piscina antes de regresar a casa
6. Ellas/escuchar la radio antes de clases

Presentation

Vocabulario After looking at the pictures, ask students to raise their hands to answer the following questions about their own activities. (**¿A quién le gusta montar en bicicleta? ¿A quién no le gusta preparar la cena? ¿A quién le gusta caminar con el perro? ¿Quiénes de ustedes no toman el refresco ____ ? ¿Quiénes trabajan en un restaurante? ¿Cuántos de ustedes pasan el rato con amigos?**)

For Individual Needs

Auditory Learners Cut pictures from magazines or draw new vocabulary items. Then randomly number them, and, as you say the Spanish for a picture, students say the number in Spanish. Once they are familiar with the words the students can say the Spanish words for each picture as you cue them with the number.

Teaching Suggestion

9 You may want to have students do this activity orally.

Answers

9 1. Yo toco la guitarra en mi tiempo libre.
2. Mi hermana trabaja después de clases.
3. Mi padre camina con el perro en el parque a las cinco.
4. Beto y Shoji hablan por teléfono después de clases.
5. Maya y yo nadamos en la piscina antes de regresar a casa.
6. Ellas escuchan la radio antes de clases.

For Individual Needs

10 Kinesthetic Learners
Put these verbs and expressions on individual cards and give one to each student. Ask a student to stand and read his or her card aloud. Other students who have a card that combines with that card to make a meaningful phrase should also stand and say the full phrase. (A student with the card **Practicar** stands and says **Practico**, while showing the card to the class. Another student with the card **deportes** stands and says **Practico deportes.**)

Cooperative Learning

13 Have students do this activity in an interview format. One student asks a question, and the second answers. The third either writes the response or monitors his partners, helping when they get stuck. After a few questions, have students switch roles.

10 Combina las frases

Combine elements from the three boxes and write as many sentences as you can.
Answers will vary.

yo tú ella él	practicar nadar hablar trabajar montar caminar con el perro tomar escuchar tocar	en un restaurante el piano un refresco música deportes un helado en una fiesta en un baile en el parque por teléfono en la piscina en bicicleta

11 ¿Qué haces después de clases?

Work in pairs. Find out what your partner does in his or her free time with friends. Use the expressions **después de clases, antes de regresar a casa,** and **en el tiempo libre.** Take notes on your partner's responses and be prepared to report your findings to the class.
Answers will vary.

12 ¿Escuchas música también?

Using your notes from Activity 11, survey three other classmates and see if you can find at least two people who do the same activities as your partner.

Nota Gramatical

To talk about doing things with someone else, **con** is used with a pronoun like **él** or **ella.** The expressions *with me* and *with you* (familiar) have special forms.

¿Quién estudia **contigo?** *Who . . . with you?*

Mi amigo Miguel estudia **conmigo.** *. . . with me.*

13 Con mis amigos

Form a small group with two other classmates. Ask your partners what they do in their free time and with whom they do each activity. Switch roles after four questions. Use **siempre** *(always)* or **nunca** *(never)* before the verb when appropriate. Be prepared to share your findings with the class.

Culture Note

Explain to students that in Mexico and other Spanish-speaking countries, people often take a long lunch at midday. That means that schoolchildren often have at least an hour off for lunch. This gives families time to have their main meal together. In tropical areas with oppressive heat, this break may include a **siesta.**

14 ¡Conmigo!

Think about all the people you see every day. Tell who does the following activities with you.
Answers will vary.

MODELO participar en deportes
—¿Quién participa en deportes contigo?
—Mi papá participa en deportes conmigo.

1. tomar un refresco
2. practicar un deporte
3. dibujar
4. estudiar
5. mirar la televisión
6. escuchar música
7. caminar con el perro
8. montar en bicicleta
9. tomar un helado

15 ¿Con quién?

For each person or group listed, write two sentences telling what the person is like and what you or others do with that person. Answers will vary.

MODELO Carlos
Carlos es muy simpático. Lava la ropa y prepara la cena con su mamá.

1. yo
2. tu mejor amigo/a *(best friend)*
3. tus compañeros de clase
4. el profesor/la profesora de español
5. mamá
6. tu novio/a *(boyfriend/girlfriend)*
7. ¿?

a. trabajar
b. montar en bicicleta
c. estudiar
d. hablar por teléfono
e. preparar la cena
f. lavar la ropa
g. mirar la televisión

16 Preferencias

Take an informal survey involving two or three of your classmates. Be sure to use **que** in your answer. Answers will vary.

MODELO —¿Cuál es la clase que te gusta más?
—La clase que me gusta más es el español.

1. la música/te gusta escuchar
2. el estado/quieres visitar
3. el programa de televisión/te gusta mirar
4. una cosa/necesitas comprar
5. un deporte/te gusta practicar

Nota Gramatical

Que is a very common word in Spanish. It can refer to either people or things and can mean *that, which,* or *who.*

Tengo **una amiga que canta** bien.

La música que me gusta escuchar es rock en español.

17 Pienso en... *I'm thinking about*

Work with a partner and play this guessing game. Describe people using the pronoun **que.** Your partner has to guess who you're thinking of. Take turns guessing. Start with **Pienso en**.

MODELO —Pienso en una persona famosa que canta, toca la guitarra y es de Nueva Jersey.
—¿Es Bruce Springsteen?
—¡Sí, es él!

A lo nuestro

In Spanish there are many different ways to refer to your classmates and friends. To greet a friend in Peru, say **¡Hola, pata!** Throughout Latin America and Mexico, men call each other **compadre.** You'll hear friends call each other **mano/a** (short for **hermano/a**), or **compañeros/as** in Mexico and Central America. Other Mexican expressions for a friend are **chamaco/a, chavo/a,** or **cuate.**

Building on Previous Skills

15 Remind students to use times of day, days of the week, and places in their answers.

Teaching Suggestion

16 Have students report their findings to the class using the names of the students and the correct verb forms.

Close

Use *Teaching Transparency 4-1* to review activities and verb forms with the class.

Assess

Quiz 4-1, *Chapter Teaching Resources, Book 1,* pp. 197–198

Assessment Items, Audiocassette 7B/Audio CD 4

Performance Assessment

Have students describe their own preferences in free-time activities, and those of the ideal "roommate" in summer school (or camp). This could be done in writing or orally on audiocassette.

Jump Start!

On a transparency or the board, write a familiar Spanish word such as **LIBRO.** Ask students to use each letter in **LIBRO** to write a Spanish word. In this case, they should end up with five words (**Luego, estudIa, Bicicleta, maRtes, estO**).

MOTIVATE

Ask students when it is necessary to identify the location of something or someone (when you're meeting someone or giving directions), and what expressions are needed to indicate location.

TEACH

Presentation

Así se dice Ask students about where various people and objects are in the classroom. You may use all vocabulary learned so far. Individual students can point out the object and say **Está(n) aquí** or **Está(n) allá.**

Gramática To review time-of-day expressions while learning the verb **estar**, ask students questions. (**Los lunes a las cuatro de la tarde, ¿dónde estás normalmente?**)

SEGUNDO PASO

Telling where people and things are

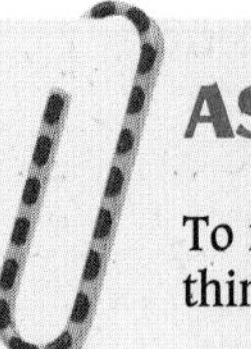

ASÍ SE DICE Telling where people and things are

To find out where someone or something is, ask:

¿Dónde estás?

¿No está en la escuela de baile? *Isn't she . . .?*

Your friend might answer:

Estoy en el centro. Necesito encontrar a María Inés. *I'm downtown.*

No, no está aquí. *No, she's not here.*

Está en el trabajo. *She's at work.*

18 Escuchemos: ¿Dónde está?

Listen to these people talking about where things are. Match each statement you hear with the correct picture. One statement will not have a matching picture. Answers on p. 95C.

a.

b.

c.

d.

Nota Gramatical

The verb **estar** *(to be)* is used to talk about location. Here are the present tense forms of the verb.

Estoy en la librería.
Estás con tu familia.
Está en el centro.
Estamos en casa.
Estáis en la clase.
Están en el cuarto.

19 ¡Vamos a Taxco!

This is the first time Luis has been to Taxco, so María Inés is acting as his guide. Read her description of the city and fill in the blanks with the correct form of **estar.** See answers below.

Estamos en un lugar magnífico. Luis, es la primera vez que tú ___1___ en Taxco, ¿no? Bueno, allá ___2___ el parque, y allá ___3___ Los Arcos. El Museo ___4___ en la Plaza Borda. Muchos hoteles buenos ___5___ en la calle Hidalgo. El cine y una tienda ___6___ en la Plazuela de San Juan.

RESOURCES FOR SEGUNDO PASO

Textbook Audiocassette 2B/Audio CD 4
Practice and Activity Book, pp. 41–43
Native Speaker Activity Book, pp. 16–20
Video Guide
Video Program
Expanded Video Program, Videocassette 1
Videodisc Guide
Videodisc Program, Videodisc 2B

Chapter Teaching Resources, Book 1
- Communicative Activity 4-1, pp. 177–178
- Additional Listening Activities 4-3, 4-4, p. 186
  Audiocassette 10B/Audio CD 4
- Student Response Forms, pp. 194–196
- Realia 4-2, pp. 190, 191
- Situation Cards 4-2, pp. 192, 193
- Teaching Transparency Master 4-2, pp. 182, 184
  Teaching Transparency 4-2
- Quiz 4-2, pp. 199–200
  Audiocassette 7B/Audio CD 4

20 ¿Quiénes y qué?

Name some people or things that are in the following places right now. Give as many answers as you can think of for each item. Answers will vary.

1. en la clase de español
2. en tu cuarto
3. en el centro
4. en tu armario
5. en tu casa
6. en México

VOCABULARIO

al lado de	*next to; to one side of*
allá	*there*
aquí	*here*
lejos de	*far from*
encima de	*on top of*
debajo de	*under; beneath*
cerca de	*near*

También se puede decir...
In Mexico, people say **la alberca** instead of **la piscina**; in Argentina and Uruguay, you'll hear **la pileta**.

Answers
19 1. estás
2. está
3. están
4. está
5. están
6. están

Presentation

Vocabulario Use local places to present the new vocabulary. **El cine "Expo" está en la calle Guadalupe. El supermercado "Mack's" está en la avenida Lincoln. Clase, ¿qué otros supermercados hay?** Students respond with the names of other local markets. Check comprehension by saying some false statements and having the students correct them.—**El cine "Expo" está en la avenida Lincoln. —No, profesora, está en la calle Guadalupe.** Have students practice with a partner: one gives a new vocabulary word, and the other responds with a proper name. They should create their own false statements to check comprehension.

Additional Practice

Teach the class the words for floor, wall, and ceiling. **(suelo, pared, techo)** Then walk around the class asking students if statements you make are true **(cierto)** or false **(falso)**. Have students correct false statements.

1. La pizarra está en la pared.
2. El/la profesor(a) está detrás de (students name).
3. El techo está al lado del suelo.
4. El escritorio está encima de la pizarra.
5. La mesa está cerca de (student's name).
6. El borrador está lejos de la pizarra.
7. El reloj está debajo del suelo.
8. El pupitre está encima del techo.

For videodisc application, see *Videodisc Guide.*

 **Cooperative Learning**

22 In this activity, students will make verb phrase flash cards. Divide the class into groups of three. Each group will choose two verb phrases using verbs they have learned **(hablar español, ir al parque)**. Each of the three students is responsible for two pronouns and verb forms so that all six forms are covered by the group. Cards should have one verb phrase and the two pronouns on the front **(hablar español—yo/usted)**, and the two completed sentences on the back **(Yo hablo español./Usted habla español.)**. Every group will end up with two complete sets of cards. Students then turn in their sets of cards. Keep the cards in sets for later use.

 **For Individual Needs**

Kinesthetic Learners To practice pronoun use after Gramática on p. 109, point out that you are talking with two students. Using gestures, demonstrate each pronoun. After you have modeled this ask students to break into groups of three or four and demonstrate each pronoun as you say it.

21 Escuchemos: ¿Quiénes son y dónde están?

Listen as Luis Miguel describes his friends and family to you. Match each picture with the description you hear. Then go back and write a sentence saying where each person is.

MODELO Paco es bajo y moreno. Le gusta jugar con su perro. Paco está en el parque. Answers on p. 95C.

MODELO

a. 
b. 
c. 
d. 

e. 
f. 
g. 
h. 

22 ¿Dónde están?

You and some friends are visiting a Mexican friend, Bernardo. No one knows the city very well. With a partner, refer to the downtown scene on page 107 to explain where everyone needs to go. Use the prepositions **en, cerca de, al lado de,** and **lejos de** to explain your directions from Bernardo's house **(la casa)**. See answers below.

MODELO Juan Luis quiere comprar fruta y chocolate. Él necesita ir al supermercado. Está cerca de la casa y al lado del cine.

1. Reynaldo necesita comprar ropa.
2. Berta quiere caminar con el perro.
3. Alejandro necesita comprar estampillas *(stamps)*.
4. Paula y Sergio quieren nadar.
5. Álvaro quiere ver una película *(to see a film)*.
6. Bárbara quiere jugar al voleibol.

Do you sometimes feel that all the Spanish you hear is too fast? It's frustrating to feel lost, but are you really missing *everything?* Try not to let anxiety get in the way of listening carefully and picking out the words you do understand. When you listen to your teacher or an audio tape, or when you watch a video in Spanish, focus on the words you recognize. Then do some intelligent guesswork to fill in the gaps. Don't give up!

23 ¿Dónde están las cosas en tu cuarto?

Get together with two other classmates. Take turns describing where four things are in your own rooms. While one person describes, the other two draw what they hear on a sheet of paper. Then compare the drawings and make corrections: **No, el reloj no está allí. Está encima del escritorio.**

Answers

22
1. Reynaldo necesita ir a la tienda. Está lejos de la casa.
2. Berta necesita ir al parque. Está cerca de la casa.
3. Alejandro necesita ir al correo. Está cerca de la casa.
4. Paula y Sergio necesitan ir a la piscina. Está lejos de la casa.
5. Álvaro necesita ir al cine. Está lejos de la casa.
6. Bárbara necesita ir al parque. Está lejos de la casa.

24 En mi ciudad... *In my city*

With a partner, complete these sentences about places you know. Make the sentences negative if you wish. Answers will vary.

1. El supermercado está lejos de...
2. El cine está al lado de...
3. El centro comercial está cerca de...
4. El restaurante está al lado de...
5. Hay ... debajo de mi cama.
6. En mi armario, hay...
7. Mi ventana está...
8. Normalmente mis libros están...

Gramática Subject pronouns

Spanish speakers don't use subject pronouns as often as English speakers do. That's because the verb ending usually indicates the subject of the verb. But the pronoun may be used to clarify or to emphasize the subject.

yo	compr**o**	**nosotros, nosotras**	compr**amos**
tú	compr**as**	**vosotros, vosotras**	compr**áis**
usted / **él, ella**	compr**a**	**ustedes** / **ellos, ellas**	compr**an**

1. In general, **tú** is used to speak to people you are on a first-name basis with. Use **usted** with adults and people in authority.
2. In Spain, **vosotros** is the plural of **tú**, while **ustedes** is the plural of **usted.** In the Americas, **ustedes** is the plural of both **tú** and **usted.**
3. The masculine forms (**nosotros** and **vosotros**) are used to refer to groups of males or groups including both males and females. The feminine forms **nosotras** and **vosotras** refer to groups including only females.

25 Bien, ¿y...?

During the course of the day, these people greet Octavio and ask how he is. Write both their greetings and Octavio's responses. Include pronouns in your sentences. See sample answer below.

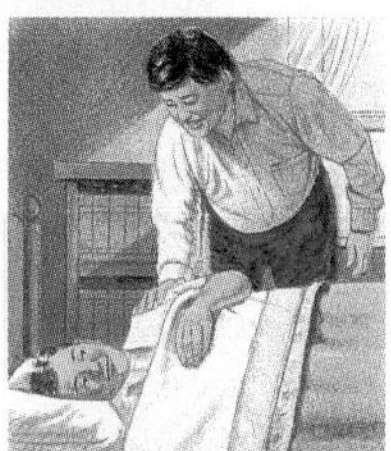
1.

2.

3.

4.

NOTA CULTURAL

The use of **tú** and **usted** varies from country to country. Children in some areas are likely to address a parent as **usted**, while children in other areas use **tú**. If you're in a Spanish-speaking area, listen to others and try to use **tú** and **usted** as they do. When in doubt, use **usted** and wait for the other person to invite you to be less formal.

Presentation

Gramática Point out that there are six different endings for regular -**ar** verbs, and that each ending corresponds to a subject pronoun (or group of pronouns). Because of this, the verb alone can often show who the subject is. Give students several sentences without subject pronouns and have them identify the subject. **Habla francés. (usted, él, ella)**

Close

Group Work

Divide class into the same groups of three who made the verb flash card sets earlier in this **Paso.** Give each group a set of cards that they did not make. Have them write sentences for the new cards. They "turn in" their sentences to the group who made the cards. This group reviews and corrects their classmates' work.

Assess

Quiz 4-2, *Chapter Teaching Resources, Book 1,* pp. 197–198.

Assessment Items, Audiocassette 7B/Audio CD 4

Performance Assessment

In groups, students develop and present a conversation in which they tell a new student where to find various persons and rooms in the school, and/or some of their favorite places around town.

Answers

25 *Answers will vary.*
1. El supermercado está lejos de la escuela.
2. El cine está al lado de las tiendas.

VIDEO PROGRAM OR EXPANDED VIDEO PROGRAM, Videocassette 1

OR VIDEODISC PROGRAM, Videodisc 2B

Teacher Notes

- See *Video Guide* and *Videodisc Guide* for activities related to the **Panorama cultural.**
- Remind students that cultural information may be included in the Chapter Quizzes and Test.
- **María Luisa** is a park in downtown Seville, with fountains, trees, walkways, and a conservatory.
- **Cartuja** is also known as **Isla de la Cartuja**, a neighborhood in Seville, and the site of the 1992 World Expo.

Motivating Activity

Ask students to discuss what they and their friends or relatives do to socialize. Where do they go to see and be seen by others?

Presentation

Watch the video and assign quotes for the students to read in unison using the video as a model. Then have students work with a partner, with one asking the questions and the other reading one of the quotes as an answer. Have students answer the questions in **Para pensar y hablar...** Then play the video again and have students answer the **Preguntas.**

PANORAMA CULTURAL

¿Te gusta pasear con tus amigos?

The **paseo** is a tradition in Spanish-speaking countries; people stroll around the **plaza** or along the streets of a town in the evening to socialize, and to see and be seen by others. In this chapter we asked some teens about the **paseo**.

Patricia
San Diego, California

"Me gusta ir con mis amigos a las tiendas, de compras... me gusta ir mucho... al parque, para ir a ver a los muchachos, y también a la playa".

Jimena
Buenos Aires, Argentina

"Vamos a pasear, vamos a muchísimos lugares... Me parece divertido estar todos juntos, es una manera de hacerse más amigos de todos".

David
Ciudad de México, México

"Sí, con mis amigos sí me gusta pasear... Podemos ir a la casa de uno o a la casa de otro".

Juan Pablo
Sevilla, España

"Sí, me gusta pasear. Vamos a la Cartuja, (al parque de) María Luisa, y hablamos de todo un poco... Que aquí en Sevilla es que es muy común, si no se sale de vacaciones, dar una vuelta ya que con el calor la casa es un infierno... y vamos, se pasa bien aquí con los amigos".

Para pensar y hablar...

A. Which interviewee has the best reason for going out on a **paseo**? Why?

B. Why do you think people enjoy the **paseo**? What activity do you participate in that serves the same purpose as the **paseo**?

Culture Note

Although the **paseo** is no longer a tradition in very large Latin American cities, urban families may still take strolls in their **barrio.** Urban neighborhoods in Latin American countries often have the feel of small towns, with family-owned shops and small cafés and restaurants. This is also true in urban **barrios** of the USA, such as in New York.

Preguntas

1. ¿Qué hacen David y sus amigos cuando pasean? (van a las casas de amigos.)
2. ¿De qué hablan Juan Pablo y sus amigos? (de la polución y de Sevilla)
3. ¿Por qué pasean los chicos? (Answers will vary.)

TERCER PASO

Talking about where you and others go during free time

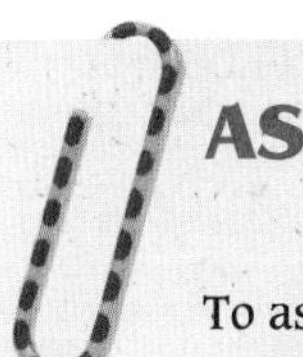

ASÍ SE DICE **Talking about where you and others go during free time**

To ask where someone is going, say:

¿Adónde vas?
Where are you going?

¿Adónde va María Inés?
Where is María Inés going?

Your friend might answer:

Voy a la biblioteca **para estudiar**.
I'm going . . . in order to study.

María Inés va al correo.

Nota Gramatical

Ir *(to go)* is an irregular verb since its conjugation doesn't follow any pattern. To ask where someone is going, use the question word **¿adónde?** *([to] where?)*.

Voy al cine.
¿Adónde **vas** ahora?
Va al gimnasio.
Vamos a la piscina.
Vais a casa.
Van al baile.

26 Escuchemos: ¿Adónde vas?

Listen as Filiberto asks his friend Alicia where everyone is going this afternoon after school. Write each person's name and where he or she is going. Then decide who can give Filiberto a ride to the movies. Answers on p. 95D.

27 ¿Adónde vamos?

Claudia and her friends are visiting Taxco and everyone is going to a different place. Fill in the blanks with the correct forms of the verb **ir**. See answers below.

ROSA Claudia __1__ a la casa de mi tío y yo __2__ con ella. Luis, ¿adónde __3__ tú?

LUIS Yo __4__ al parque. Oye, María Inés, ¿adónde __5__ tú? ¿A qué hora __6__ ustedes a la casa de su tío?

MARÍA INÉS Yo __7__ al centro.

CLAUDIA ¡Y nosotros __8__ a Cuernavaca a las nueve!

Jump Start!

On the board write two columns of phrases. Students will match the phrases correctly to form sentences. (Column one: **El libro está, Claudia y Luis están, Nosotros estamos Los lápices no están;** Column two: **en el gimnasio, encima del escritorio, en la escuela, debajo de la mesa)**

MOTIVATE

Ask students to make a list of the places where they will go this week. Have them share their list with a classmate. Where will they both go? Explain that they will learn how to express in Spanish that they are going to these places.

TEACH

Presentation

Así se dice, Nota gramatical Model the pronunciation of **Adónde.** Then point out the irregularities of **ir.** Walk around the room asking students questions. **(¿Adónde vas cuando nadas? ¿Adónde van tú y tus amigos cuando estudian?)** Then have students ask each other questions using the verb **ir. (Pedro, ¿vas al cine el sábado? No, el sábado voy a la piscina.)**

Answers

27 1. va
2. voy
3. vas
4. voy
5. vas
6. van
7. voy
8. vamos

RESOURCES FOR TERCER PASO

Textbook Audiocassette 2B/Audio CD 4
Practice and Activity Book, pp. 44–46
Native Speaker Activity Book, pp. 16–20
Videodisc Guide
Videodisc Program, Videodisc 2B

Chapter Teaching Resources, Book 1
- Communicative Activity 4-2, pp. 177–178
- Additional Listening Activities 4-5, 4-6, p. 187
  Audiocassette 10B/Audio CD 4
- Student Response Forms, pp. 194–196
- Realia 4-2, pp. 190, 191
- Situation Cards 4-3, pp. 192, 193
- Teaching Transparency Master 4-3, pp. 183, 184
  Teaching Transparency 4-3
- Quiz 4-3, pp. 201–202
  Audiocassette 7B/Audio CD 4

Building on Previous Skills

29 Have the pairs recycle question formation as well as previously-learned vocabulary in an oral variation. (**—¿Vas a la piscina?—Sí, voy a la piscina. —A qué hora vas? —Voy a las cuatro.**)

Presentation

Vocabulario Create on the chalk board one week from the current month's calendar, similar to that in the **Vocabulario.** Ask **¿Qué dia es?**, and give the answer. Then say **¿Y mañana? Mañana es ____. Y los otros dias de la semana son ____.** Have students repeat the names of the days after you, then check comprehension by asking what day of the week a certain date is. **¿Qué dia es el diez? el doce?** etc.

Nota gramatical Practice these new grammar rules by asking students what they're doing one day this week, and what they normally do on that day. (**Sara, ¿qué haces los domingos?** compared to **Sara, ¿qué haces el domingo?**)

For videodisc application, see *Videodisc Guide.*

For Individual Needs

Visual Learners Ask students to develop a Spanish calendar for the current month, putting in the days of the week and the dates in their proper places. Remind them that the days of the week are not capitalized. You might then have them fill in one week of the calendar with one sentence for each day, telling what they or someone they know normally does or is going to do on that day.

28 Cosas que hacer *Things to do*

You and a friend are trying to think of something to do this weekend. Look at the entertainment guide and say where you're going. Base your answers on the following. See answers below.

1. Te gusta jugar al tenis.
2. A tu compañero le gusta nadar.
3. Quieres hacer ejercicios aeróbicos (*to do aerobics*).
4. Quieres ver una película.

CINE

CINES LUMIERE. Pasaje Martín de los Heros o Princesa, 5. Tel. 542 11 72. Acceso directo desde el parking. Precio por sesión, 500 ptas. y otra película sin determinar. Confirmar cambios de horarios y película en taquilla.

GIMNASIOS

GIMNASIO GARCÍA. Andrés Bello, 21-23. Teléfono. 312 86 01. Karate (club campeón de España), clases de aeróbicos, gimnasia, jazz, voleibol, basquetbol y baile. Máquinas Polaris.

PISCINAS

MUNICIPALES ALUCHE (Latina). A. General Fanjul, 14 (metro Aluche, autobuses 17, 34 y 39). Tel. 706 28 68.

TENIS

CLUB DE TENIS LAS LOMAS. Avenida de Las Lomas. Tel. 633 04 63. Escuela de tenis. Todos los niveles. Todos los días de la semana.

29 Destinos

Using the vocabulary on page 107, write six sentences naming places where you, your friends, and your parents (**mis padres**) go in your free time. Answers will vary.

MODELO Voy al parque para montar en bicicleta.

VOCABULARIO

OCTUBRE

Monday — el fin de semana

lunes	martes	miércoles	jueves	viernes	sábado	domingo
	1	2	3	4	5	6
7	8	9	10	11	12	13

Nota Gramatical

1. Always use **el** before a day of the week except when stating what day it is. **Hoy es martes.**
2. To make **sábado** and **domingo** plural, add **-s.**
3. To say *on Monday, on Tuesday,* etc., use **el lunes, el martes.**
4. To say *on Mondays, on Tuesdays,* etc., use **los lunes, los martes.**
5. Days of the week are not capitalized in Spanish.

NOTA CULTURAL

In Spain and Latin America, there are fewer school-sponsored extracurricular activities for high school students than in the United States. Teenagers who play sports will often join independent teams since many schools don't have their own teams.

Culture Note

In many Spanish-speaking countries, calendars look slightly different than they do in English; **el lunes** (Monday), not **el domingo** (Sunday), is the first day of the week. Point out to your students that this makes more sense of the term "weekend," as Saturday and Sunday are visually together at the end of the week.

Answers

28 *Answers may vary.*
1. Voy al parque para jugar al tenis.
2. Mi compañero va al restaurante italiano.
3. Voy a la clase de ejercicios aeróbicos.
4. Voy al cine.

30 Si son las ocho, ¿dónde estás?

Compare schedules with a partner. Ask each other where you are at the following times during the week. Answers will vary.

MODELO —¿Dónde estás los lunes a las ocho de la mañana?
—Estoy en la clase de inglés.

1. los viernes a las cuatro de la tarde
2. los sábados a las diez y media de la mañana
3. los sábados por la noche
4. los martes a la una de la tarde
5. los jueves a las once de la mañana
6. los lunes por la noche
7. los domingos por la mañana
8. los miércoles por la tarde

31 ¡Una encuesta!

Take a survey of three classmates to find out where they go on the weekend. Write the name of each person and at least two places where he or she goes. Be prepared to present the class with the results of your survey.

32 En mi cuaderno Possible answers below.

Write a short description of a typical week in your life. Make a calendar for the week and include at least two activities for each day. Start some of your sentences with the phrases in the word box.

Después de clases, voy a...
En mi tiempo libre...
Los sábados estoy en...

LETRA Y SONIDO

A. The letters **b** and **v** in Spanish represent the same sound. That single sound has two possible variations.
   1. At the beginning of a phrase, or after an **m** or an **n**, these letters sound like the *b* in the English word *bean*.
      biblioteca basquetbol bailar invierno viernes
   2. Between vowels and after other consonants, their pronunciation is softened, with the lower lip slightly forward and not resting against the upper teeth.
      lobo lo bueno uva Cuba
   3. Note that the **b** and **v** in the following pairs of words and phrases have exactly the same pronunciation.
      tubo/tuvo a ver/haber
      los huevos/los suebos botar/votar

B. **Dictado** Answers on p. 95D.

Pablo hasn't learned to spell words that use **b** and **v** yet. As he says the words he's not sure of, write what you hear.

C. **Trabalenguas**

El lobo sabe bailar bien el vals bajo el árbol.

Answers

32 *Answers will vary.* Los lunes voy a la escuela. Después de clase toco el piano. Los martes voy a la clase de piano. En mi tempo libre estudio. Los sábados estoy en el centro comercial todo el día.

Game

Divide the class into groups of four. First, everyone should assume the identity of a famous person but not tell anyone who they are. The members of each group take turns guessing each other's identity and plans for the next two days. When everyone's identity and plans have been guessed, the groups share their findings with the class.

Portfolio

30 Oral You may wish to suggest this activity to your students as an appropriate oral Portfolio entry. For Portfolio suggestions, see *Assessment Guide,* p. 17.

Teaching Suggestion

31 If two people they interviewed go to the same place on the weekend, have students use the plural form.

En mi cuaderno

32 For an additional Chapter 4 journal entry suggestion, see *Practice and Activity Book,* page 148.

Close

Use *Teaching Transparency 4-3* to review material in this **Paso.**

Assess

Quiz 4-3, *Chapter Teaching Resources, Book 1,* pp. 201–202

Assessment Items, Audiocassette 7B/Audio CD 4

Performance Assessment

In pairs, have students role-play the following situation: You are going to spend the weekend with a close friend in a neighboring town. Call a relative and let him or her know your plans. Your relative asks where you and your friend are going and what times you expect to be at each location. You should plan at least four activities during the weekend.

Reading Strategies
Scanning for familiar words and specific information

Teaching Suggestion
Ask students to think of times, such as looking up a name in the phone directory, when they are scanning for information.

Prereading
Activities A and B

Motivating Activity
Ask students to think about what they like in a friend or pen pal. Do they like people with similar interests and hobbies, or do they prefer to spend time with people who are different from them?

Reading
Activities C and D

Teaching Suggestion
Have students scan the personal ads for obvious cognates **(música rock, teléfono)** and make a list of the ones they find. Then ask them to scan again for words or cognates that are not so easy (**turista, estudiar**). See if they can guess or derive their meanings.

VAMOS A LEER

Anuncios personales

Estrategia
Scanning for specific information means looking for one thing at a time, without concerning yourself with the rest of the information there. Some examples of scanning are looking up the spelling of a word in a dictionary or hunting through the TV listing to see what time a certain show comes on.

¡A comenzar!

The ads on these pages are for pen pals. They come from *Tú*, a magazine for Spanish-speaking teens. Before doing any scanning, let's gather more general information.

¿Te acuerdas?
Use your background knowledge before you read in depth.

A. If you were writing an ad for a pen pal, what kind of information would you include? Choose the ones you would want to include.
- your name
- your best friend's name
- your address
- the name of your school
- your age
- what you look like
- what your parents do
- your hobbies

B. Now look briefly at the ads. Of the eight possibilities listed above, which four are included in the ads?

LÍNEA DIRECTA

Nombre: Sandra Duque
Edad: 17 años
Dirección: P.O. Box #1752, Colón, República de Panamá, PANAMÁ.
Pasatiempos: Escuchar música, coleccionar unicornios, ver televisión, ir al cine, escribir cartas.

Nombre: Susana Tam
Edad: 13 años
Dirección: 4ta. Ave., N #41-07, La Flora, Cali, COLOMBIA.
Pasatiempos: Ir al cine, a fiestas, a bailar y hablar por teléfono. Pueden escribirme en inglés.

Nombre: Juan Dos Santos
Edad: 15 años
Dirección: 55 mts sur, Bomba Gasotica, Pérez Zeledón, COSTA RICA.
Pasatiempos: Oír música rock, hablar con los turistas y tener amigos.

Nombre: Juana Saldívar
Edad: 16 años
Dirección: P.O. Box 678, Hato Rey 00919, PUERTO RICO.
Pasatiempos: Conocer a chicos de otros países, oír música y pasear.

Nombre: Wilmer Ramírez
Edad: 16 años
Dirección: Urb. Las Batallas, Calle La Puerta #2, San Félix, Edo. Bolívar, VENEZUELA.
Pasatiempos: Leer, escuchar música e intercambiar correspondencia y estudiar.

Culture Note
Since European and Latin American countries are smaller geographically than the United States, it is often more common for people to travel to other countries and have friends in other countries. Ask students if they have been to another country or know someone abroad.

Al grano

Now that you have a general overview of the pen pal ads, you can *scan* for more details. See answers below.

C. Imagine that you're organizing a letter exchange for your Spanish class. Your classmates have listed their preferences regarding age and country where the pen pal lives. Which pen pal would be best for each classmate?

1. someone from Venezuela
2. someone who's 14 years old
3. a boy from Panama
4. a 16-year-old girl
5. someone from the United States
6. someone who lives in the city of Buenos Aires
7. a 17-year-old boy

D. Now it's time to choose a pen pal for yourself. You're hoping to develop a long-term friendship with someone who shares your own interests and hobbies. Whom will you choose if you . . .? See answers below.

1. like to dance
2. like to ride a bike
3. prefer to write letters in English
4. love listening to music

Whom *won't* you choose if you . . .?

5. don't like to study
6. don't like video games
7. don't like to swim

E. Escribe un anuncio *(ad)* personal en español. Usa vocabulario familiar. Después, lee el anuncio de un compañero o una compañera y trata de encontrarle un amigo o una amiga por correspondencia *(pen pal)*. Explícale a tu compañero o compañera por qué esta persona es su correspondiente ideal. Individual ads will vary.

Thinking Critically

Analyzing Ask students why they think they see so many cognates in Spanish. (English uses many words of French origin and both Spanish and French come from Latin; also, modern Spanish adopts many Anglicisms because of the universality of English in the fashion, travel, and business worlds.) Encourage students with this fact: Spanish may be easier to learn than they think!

Native Speakers

Activity E might be a good homework assignment for your native speakers or advanced learners.

Teacher Note

For additional readings, see *Practice and Activity Book*, p. 47 and *Native Speaker Activity Book,* pp. 16–20.

POSTREADING
Activity E

Teaching Suggestion

Have students copy their personal ad without putting their name or street address on it and turn it in. Randomly number the anonymous ads. Tape the ads around the room. Have students walk around and find the ad of someone they'd like to get to know. They should copy the number of the ad they like and that of their own ad and sit down. Then call out the numbers of the ads and ask whose they are. Students might be surprised at the people they've picked.

Answers

C 1. Wilmer Ramírez
2. Gerardo Vargas
3. Esteban Hernández
4. Juana Saldívar
5. Gerardo Vargas
6. Julia Ileana Oliveras
7. Pedro Manuel Yue

D *Answers may vary.*
1. Pedro, Gerardo, or Susana
2. Bessy
3. Julia or Susana
4. Pedro, Julia, Gerardo, Wilmer, Juana, Juan, or Sandra
5. Wilmer Ramírez
6. Esteban Hernández
7. Julia Oliveras

E *Answers will vary.*

The **Repaso** reviews and integrates all four skills and culture in preparation for the Chapter Test.

Teaching Suggestion

2 Have students write questions about the contents of the letter. With a partner, have them write five questions that María Elena's father could have asked her mother about the letter. Each pair might then role-play the conversation between the mother and father. They may wish to include the expression **María Elena dice** _____ or simply **Dice** _____.

For Individual Needs

3 Slower Pace Allow students to prepare by outlining the conversation or by writing some key words in Spanish before joining their partner.

REPASO

1 A friend has asked you to listen to some messages left on the answering machine. Take notes about who calls, what they want, and times or days they mention.
Answers on p. 95D.

Recado Telefónico
Nombre: Carlos
Asunto: 10:00, el sábado
jugar al tenis en el parque

2 Complete María Elena's letter to her family using forms of the verbs you've learned.
See answers below.

Queridos papás,

Aquí __1__ yo en St. Louis. Me __2__ mucho mi colegio. Es muy grande y está cerca de mi casa. Mis amigos son muy simpáticos. Nosotros __3__ al partido de fútbol los viernes, y yo __4__ con Gloria y Linda al centro comercial los sábados. Yo __5__ inglés, pero Miguel Ángel, un chico de Colombia, __6__ mejor *(better)*. Todos nosotros __7__ juntos en la biblioteca y hacemos la tarea. Mis amigos Ricardo y Andrés __8__ los sábados y domingos en el cine porque necesitan dinero, pero __9__ al fútbol todas las tardes a las cuatro. Yo __10__ a casa después de clases y __11__ con el perro. El perro __12__ "Spot". Es blanco y negro. Bueno, tengo que estudiar para un examen mañana. ¡Hasta luego!

Un abrazo para todos,
María Elena

3 Look at the photo of Claudia and her friends. With a partner, create a conversation in which the characters talk about what they do in their free time. Be sure to include times of day and days of the week. Answers will vary.

4 Now it's your turn to find María Inés! Use these notes to report her activities during the week. See answers below.

1. lunes (7:45) - ir al colegio
2. martes (5:00) - hablar por teléfono con Claudia
3. lunes (6:30) - practicar el basquetbol
4. jueves - estudiar con Luis por tres horas
5. viernes (después de clases) - tomar refrescos con amigos
6. sábado y domingo - montar en bicicleta en el parque

Answers

2 1. estoy 2. gusta 3. vamos 4. voy 5. hablo 6. habla 7. estudiamos 8. trabajan 9. practican 10. voy 11. camino 12. se llama

4
1. Los lunes a las ocho menos quince va al colegio.
2. Los martes a las cinco habla por teléfono con Claudia.
3. Los lunes a las seis y media practica el basquetbol.
4. Los jueves estudia con Luis por tres horas.
5. Los viernes después de clases toma refrescos con amigos.
6. Los sábados y domingos monta en bicicleta en el parque.

5 Look at the drawings of various places. Write sentences saying what you and others like to do there. Answers will vary.

6 Work with a classmate to talk about what you do during a typical week. Include days of the week, new verbs, and other expressions you've learned in this chapter, such as **conmigo, antes,** and **después de las clases.** Answers will vary.

7 Write a journal entry describing the daily activities you do and like to do, places you go, and when you go there. Write at least ten sentences, using at least eight different verbs. Use your imagination! Answers will vary.

8 En las siguientes oraciones, corrige *(correct)* las oraciones falsas. Basa tus respuestas *(answers)* en las **Notas culturales** y el **Panorama cultural** de este capítulo. See answers below.

1. El paseo ya no existe en Latinoamérica.
2. En los países hispanohablantes *(Spanish-speaking countries)* los colegios tienen muchas actividades después de clases.
3. Los estudiantes en los Estados Unidos trabajan mucho después de clases.
4. Un deporte muy popular en España es el tenis.
5. Por lo general, los jóvenes *(young)* usan el **tú** para hablar con su padre o su madre.

9 SITUACIÓN

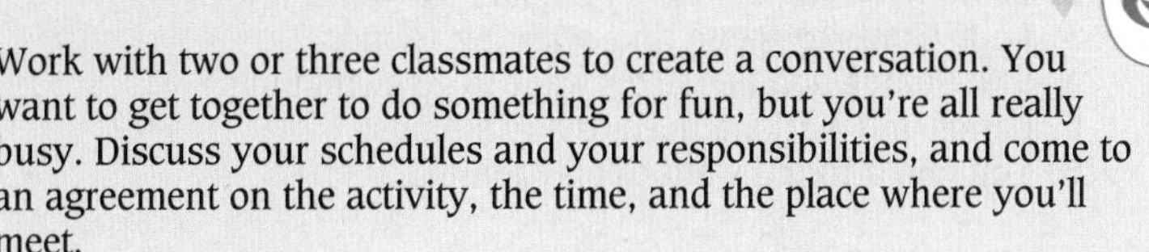

Work with two or three classmates to create a conversation. You want to get together to do something for fun, but you're all really busy. Discuss your schedules and your responsibilities, and come to an agreement on the activity, the time, and the place where you'll meet.

Answers

8 1. El paseo todavía existe en Latinoamérica.
2. En los países hispanohablantes los colegios no tienen muchas actividades después de clases.
3. Los estudiantes en los Estados Unidos no trabajan mucho después de clases.
4. Un deporte muy popular en la América Central es el fútbol.
5. Por lo general, los mexicanos usan el **tú** para hablar con su padre o su madre.

Portfolio

7 Written Your students may want to consider this activity as a potential Portfolio item. For Portfolio suggestion, see *Assessment Guide,* p. 17.

9 Oral You might consider this activity for students' oral Portfolio. For Portfolio information, see *Assessment Guide,* pp. 2–13.

Video Wrap-up

- ***Video Program***
- ***Expanded Video Program,*** *Videocassette 1*
- ***Videodisc Program,*** *Videodisc 2B*

At this time, you might want to use the video resources for additional review and enrichment. See *Video Guide* or *Videodisc Guide* for suggestions regarding the following:

- **¿Dónde está María Inés?** (Dramatic episode)
- **Panorama cultural** (Interviews)
- **Video Clips** (Authentic footage)

This page is intended to prepare students for the Chapter Test. It is a brief checklist of the major points covered in the chapter. The students should be reminded that it is a checklist only and does not necessarily reflect everything that will apprear on the Chapter Test.

Additional Practice

1 To review **gustar**, have students role play disagreement about where they shoiuld go on a day off.

A VER SI PUEDO . . .

Can you talk about what you like to do? p. 101

1 Write a sentence telling what these people like to do at the place given. See answers below.

MODELO Sr. López - la oficina
Le gusta trabajar.

1. Cecilia - la piscina
2. Gustavo - el centro comercial
3. Diego y Berta - la fiesta
4. Carlos y yo - el parque
5. Linda y Eva - la biblioteca
6. yo - el colegio

Can you discuss what you and others do during free time? p. 102

2 How would you tell someone that you . . .? Answers will vary.

1. play the guitar
2. wash the car
3. prepare dinner
4. paint and draw
5. watch television
6. swim in the pool

Can you tell where people and things are? p. 106

3 Write sentences in Spanish telling where the following people are. See answers below.

1. Rosa is reading books and must be very quiet.
2. Claudia is shopping for gifts for her parents.
3. Geraldo is walking the dogs.
4. Sofía is exercising and lifting weights.
5. You and your friends are watching a movie.
6. You're talking on the phone.

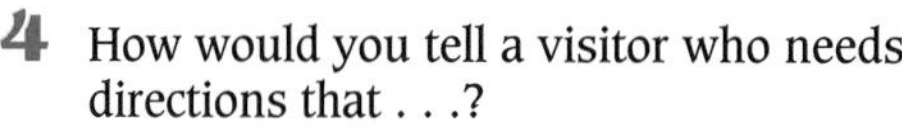

4 How would you tell a visitor who needs directions that . . .? See answers below.

1. the supermarket is next to the park
2. the bookstore is far from the store
3. the gym is near the library

Can you talk about where you and others go during free time? p. 111

5 Create a sentence telling where each person is going and why. See answers below.

MODELO Sr. Suárez is really thirsty.
Él va al restaurante para tomar un refresco.

1. Mariana wants to buy some books, notebooks, and pencils.
2. Pedro needs to talk to his English teacher.
3. Lupe wants to spend time with her friend.
4. Sra. Suárez and her sister want to go swimming.
5. Carlos and Adriana need to buy stamps.
6. You and a friend want to play tennis.

6 Think of a typical week in your life. Write a sentence telling at what time and on which day you're at the following places. Answers will vary.

1. el centro comercial
2. el cine
3. la casa de un amigo/una amiga
4. el parque

Answers

1 *Answers may vary.*
1. A Cecilia le gusta nadar en la piscina.
2. A Gustavo le gusta comprar ropa en el centro comercial.
3. A Diego y Berta les gusta bailar en la fiesta.
4. A Carlos y yo nos gusta jugar al tenis en el parque.
5. A Linda y Eva les gusta estudiar en la biblioteca.
6. Me gusta ir al colegio.

3 *Answers may vary.*
1. Rosa está en la biblioteca.
2. Claudia está en el centro comercial.
3. Geraldo está en el parque.
4. Sofía está en el gimnasio.
5. Nosotros estamos en el cine.
6. Estoy en casa.

4
1. El supermercado está al lado del parque.
2. La librería está lejos de la tienda.
3. La lámpara está encima de la mesa.

5
1. Mariana va a la librería para comprar libros, cuadernos y lápices.
2. Pedro va a la escuela para hablar con su profesor de inglés.
3. Lupe va a la casa para hablar con su amiga.
4. La señora Suárez y su hermana van a la piscina para nadar.
5. Carlos y Adriana van al correo para comprar estampillas.
6. Un amigo y yo vamos al parque para jugar al tenis.

VOCABULARIO

PRIMER PASO

Talking about what you like to do

¿A quién le gusta...? *Who likes . . . ?*
bailar *to dance*
cantar *to sing*
cuidar a tu hermano/a *to take care of your brother/sister*
descansar en el parque *to rest in the park*
dibujar *to draw*
escuchar música *to listen to music*
estudiar *to study*
hablar por teléfono *to talk on the phone*
lavar el carro *to wash the car*
lavar la ropa *to wash the clothes*
mirar la televisión *to watch TV*
nadar *to swim*
pintar *to paint*
la piscina *swimming pool*
por eso *that's why*
¿Qué te gusta hacer? *What do you like to do?*
sacar la basura *to take out the trash*

Discussing what you and others do during free time

antes de *before*
caminar con el perro *to walk the dog*
la cena *dinner*
conmigo *with me*
contigo *with you*
después de *after*
la guitarra *guitar*
el helado *ice cream*
montar en bicicleta *to ride a bike*
pasar el rato con amigos *to spend time with friends*
el piano *piano*
practicar *to practice*
preparar *to prepare*
que *that, which, who*
el refresco *soft drink*
regresar *to return*
restaurante *restaurant*
el tiempo libre *free time*
tocar *to play an instrument*
tomar *to drink, to take*
trabajar *to work*

SEGUNDO PASO

Telling where people and things are

al lado de *next to*
allá *there*
aquí *here*
la biblioteca *library*
la casa *house, home*
el centro *downtown*
cerca de *near*
el cine *movie theater*
el correo *post office*
debajo de *under, beneath*
¿dónde? *where?*
encima de *on top of*
estar *to be*
el gimnasio *gym*
lejos de *far from*
nosotros/nosotras *we*
el parque *park*
el supermercado *supermarket*
la tienda *store*
el trabajo *work, job*
usted *you (formal)*
ustedes *you (plural, formal)*
vosotros/vosotras *you (plural, informal)*

TERCER PASO

Talking about where you and others go during free time

¿adónde? *to where?*
al *to the*
el día *day*
el domingo *Sunday*
el fin de semana *weekend*
el jueves *Thursday*
el lunes *Monday*
el martes *Tuesday*
el miércoles *Wednesday*
para + infinitive *in order to*
la película *movie*
el sábado *Saturday*
la semana *week*
el viernes *Friday*

Game

Play MÍMICA to review verbs and prepositions. Write action verbs and prepositional phrases on cards. **(nadar, debajo de la mesa)** Divide the class into teams and give one card to each student. Taking turns, students act out their word or words while the other team guesses in Spanish. You may consider limiting the time that each team has to guess.

Game

CLAVE Divide class into two teams. On a dry erase board, chalkboard, or flipchart paper, write various Spanish phrases, verbs and nouns. Give a verbal clue describing one of the items listed. (**los días sábado y domingo**) A representative from each team points to the words described. (**el fin de semena**) The first to correctly identify it circles the item with that team's colored marker. The team with the most words circled at the end wins.

CHAPTER 4 ASSESSMENT

CHAPTER TEST

- *Chapter Teaching Resources, Book* 1, pp. 203–210
- *Assessment Guide,* Speaking Test, p. 29
- *Assessment Items Audiocassette 7B Audio CD 4* 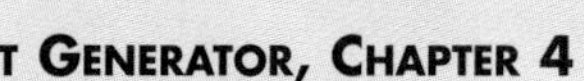

TEST GENERATOR, CHAPTER 4

ALTERNATIVE ASSESSMENT

Performance Assessment

You might want to use the **Situación** (p. 117) as a cumulative performance assessment activity.

Portfolio Assessment

- **Written: Repaso** Activity 7, *Pupil's Edition,* p. 117 *Assessment Guide,* p. 17
- **Oral:** Activity 30, *Pupil's Edition,* p. 113 *Assessment Guide,* p. 17

LOCATION OPENER
CHAPTERS
5, 6

¡Ven conmigo a la Florida! pp. 120–173

OR *VIDEODISC PROGRAM, Videodisc 3A*

SAMPLE

Motivating Activity

Ask your students what images, words or ideas make them think of Florida. What do they know about Florida's culture and people? Point out that Spanish is spoken widely in southern Florida, and that in these chapters they will learn how prevalent Latino culture is in this region of the United States.

Background Information

This photo features the Art Deco District of Miami Beach. Lovers of art deco lobbied to have the area recognized as a national treasure, and in 1979 it was placed on the *National Register of Historic Places,* becoming the youngest historic district in the nation.

CAPÍTULOS 5 y 6

¡Ven conmigo a la Florida!

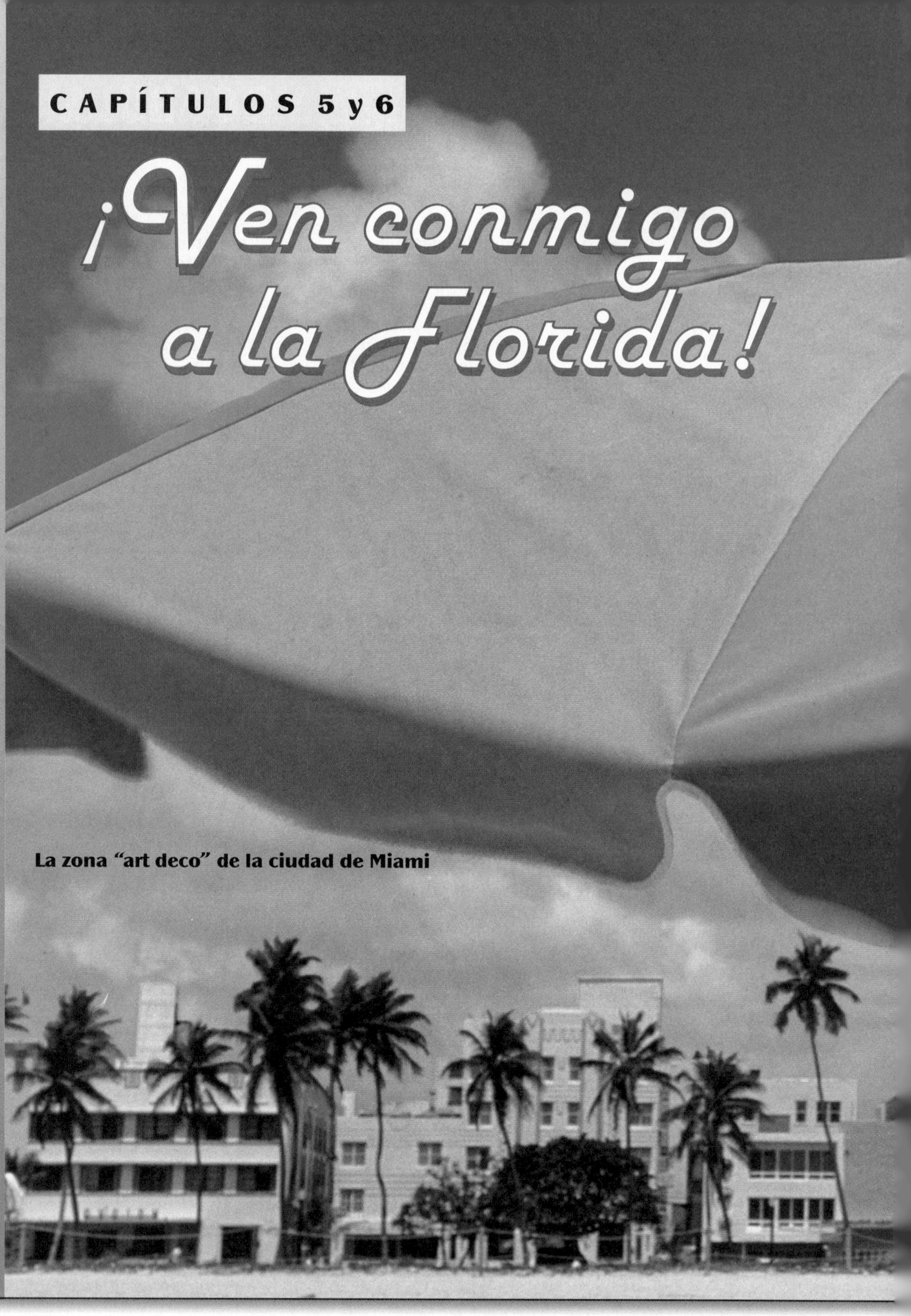

La zona "art deco" de la ciudad de Miami

Art Link

Ask students to research and define art deco. (Art deco was a decorative and architectural style of the period 1925–1940, characterized by geometric designs, bold colors, and the use of chrome, plastic, and other industrial materials. It was used mostly in architecture, furniture, jewelry, pottery, and textiles.) Why was art deco important for the industrial era? (Art deco artists aimed to lend elegance and sophistication to buildings and ordinary objects. Designers created objects that could be mass-produced rather than singular, original pieces like paintings and sculptures.) Can students name famous buildings that show the influence of art deco? (the Chrysler Building and Radio City Music Hall in New York City) You might have students research and report on Hispanic influence on architecture in the United States.

La Florida

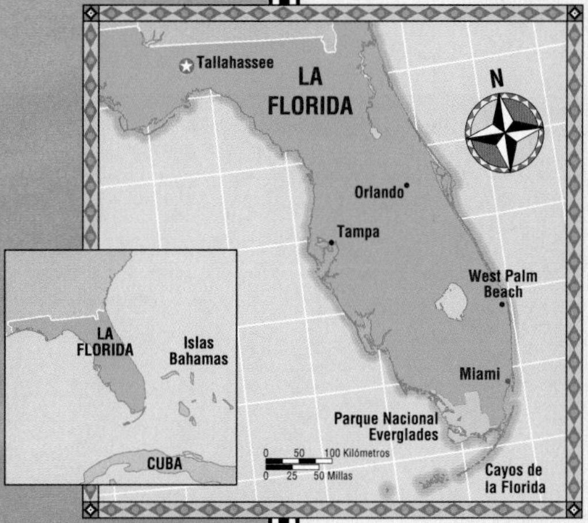

Población: Más de 13.500.000 habitantes

Área: 58.664 millas cuadradas

Capital: Tallahassee

Ciudad principal: Miami, 358.648 habitantes, de los cuales aproximadamente 224.000 son de origen hispano (Censo de 1990)

Clima: tropical y subtropical

Economía: manufactura, turismo, productos de frutas cítricas, caña de azúcar, pesca comercial, electrónica, comercio con Latinoamérica

Historia: Poblada por indígenas norteamericanos, entre ellos los Seminole, antes de la llegada del explorador español Ponce de León en 1513. Colonia francesa establecida en 1564. Colonia española establecida en 1565. España cedió el territorio a los Estados Unidos en 1819.

Using the Map

- Ask students to identify the two states that border Florida. (Alabama and Georgia)
- Have students measure the distance between Miami and Havana (approximately 200 miles). What significance might this short distance have? (The culture in Miami is very much like that of Cuba.)
- Tourism is crucial to Florida's economy. Ask students to locate some of the tourist spots on the map and to discuss their attractions.

LOCATION OPENER
CHAPTERS
5, 6

Using the Almanac and Map

Terms in the Almanac

- **La bandera:** The Florida state flag features crossed diagonal red bars on a white field. Its centerpiece is the state seal with a Native American woman strewing flowers, a sabal palm (the state tree), a steamboat, and the rising sun in the background.
- **Florida:** In the spring of 1513, Ponce de León became the first European to explore Florida, naming it **Pascua Florida,** meaning *Flowery Easter.* He discovered Florida while searching for the mythical Fountain of Youth.
- **Miami:** The name comes from a Native American word **Mayami,** which means *big water,* and perhaps referred to Lake Okeechobee.
- **Los Seminole:** The Seminole fled from the British in Georgia and Alabama and settled in south Florida in the 18th century. In 1829, the U.S. Government ordered them deported to the Oklahoma Indian Territory. The Seminole preferred to fight rather than leave their homes. Most were ultimately killed, forcibly resettled, or driven deep into the Everglades. A few descendants of those who escaped still live in the Everglades today.
- **Colonia española:** In 1565, the Spanish founded St. Augustine, the first permanent European settlement in what would become the United States.

LOCATION OPENER
CHAPTERS 5, 6

Using the Photo Essay

Thinking Critically

① **Comparing and Contrasting** Tell students that Florida is the site of the first undersea park in the continental U.S., the John Pennekamp Coral Reef State Park near Key Largo. Ask them why Florida is naturally more attractive to beach-goers and divers than other coastal states. (Florida is warm year-round and has more coastline than any other state except Alaska. Its beaches are exceptionally clean and beautiful.)

② At the turn of the century Miami began to boom, and the Everglades were in danger of being destroyed. In 1916, the Florida Federation of Women's Clubs purchased the first 4,000 acres of what would become Everglades National Park and set them aside for preservation. Southern Florida's metropolitan areas kept growing, but efforts continued to be made to protect the Everglades. In recent years, the commitment to save the Everglades has included expansion of the park and restoration of a more natural water flow to the wetlands.

Additional Vocabulary

You may want to present the following words with the Location Opener:

bucear *to scuba dive*
la sombrilla *parasol*
jugar al ajedrez *to play chess*
jugar al dominó *to play dominoes*
el arrecife de coral *coral reef*
el pantano *wetland*
la garza *heron*

Language Note

The English word *alligator* comes from the Spanish **el lagarto** (*lizard*).

LA FLORIDA

Florida has many attractions, such as the Kennedy Space Center, the wetlands of the Everglades, and hundreds of miles of fantastic beaches. The state also has a rich history, beginning with the Seminoles and other Native Americans. The Spanish came in the early 1500s, followed by other European settlers. A wide variety of ethnic heritages from other countries and other parts of the U.S. have greatly enriched the peninsula's population.

① **The warm waters of Biscayne Bay and the nearby Gulf Stream provide a fine setting for year-round water sports. Coral reef and keys (small islands) provide a magical world for scuba divers to explore.**

② **Home to alligators, manatees, and a riot of colorful aquatic birds, Everglades wetlands are one of the United States' great natural treasures.**

Culture Note

Southern Florida has a diverse population with an overall Hispanic flavor. Many of the state's Hispanic residents are of Cuban heritage and came to the United States to escape the communist policies of Fidel Castro after 1959. Cubans and Cuban Americans have often overcome difficult circumstances to excel in politics, business, sports, art and entertainment. (top corporate executives Roberto Goizueta, Rita DiMartino, and Remedios Díaz-Oliver; Chief of Protocol of the Organization of American States Ana Colomar O'Brien; Mayor of Miami Xavier Suárez; baseball player Tony Oliva; writer and premier ethnologist of Afro-Cuban folklore Lydia Cabrera; actor Andy García; salsa musician Celia Cruz and pop singer Gloria Estefan)

Chapters 5 and 6 will introduce you to Patricia, José Luis, and Raquel, some students who live in Miami. Spanish speakers make up about two-thirds of the city's population. The great majority of Spanish speakers here are Cuban in origin. You'll have a chance to find out a little about what ordinary life is like in this extraordinary North American city!

(3) Miami is internationally known for its lush beaches, romantic vistas, and exciting urban scene.

(4) Little Havana is the symbolic center of South Florida's thriving Cuban community, a place to enjoy a delicious meal or a game of chess or dominoes with good friends.

(5) The Venetian Municipal Pool, carved out of solid coral, attracts visitors from around the world.

LOCATION OPENER
CHAPTERS 5, 6

Background Information

The Florida East Coast Railroad was extended to Miami and completed in 1896. The railway boosted tourism and business in the region and enabled Miami to reach a population of 250,000 over the next fifty years. Miami is now an international financial center linking Latin America to the United States. It is also a major crossroads of international travel.

(3) South Florida's balmy climate (averaging 71°F to 81°F year-round) and cosmopolitan cities have long attracted vacationers and retirees.

(4) **El parque Máximo Gómez**, better known as Domino Park, is located on **la Calle Ocho,** in the heart of Miami's Little Havana (**la Pequeña Habana**). The park is popular with members of the Cuban community who come to play dominoes and chess. Ask students which article of the men's clothing would suggest that they might be Cuban to someone unfamiliar with the photo location. (their **guayabera** shirts)

(5) Built in 1924 by George Merrick, the Venetian pool is part of Coral Gables, the first fully planned community in the nation.

Culture Note

Thanks to its Cuban influence, southern Florida is virtually bilingual. Spanish is heard everywhere: in schools and shops, on the streets and over the airwaves. Spanish-language radio, television, and newspapers are popular and profitable. Florida's bilingualism is doubtless a strong attraction for Spanish-speaking tourists and business people from around the world.

History/Geography Link

- Florida and the states bordering Mexico bear the unmistakable stamp of Spanish influence. Ask students which states in the United States reveal a strong French heritage? (Louisiana, northern New England)
- Ask students if they can think of a Caribbean island that was colonized by both the French and the Spanish. (Hispaniola, divided between Haiti, a former French colony, and the Dominican Republic, a former Spanish colony) Have them locate it on the map on page xxv.

Capítulo 5: El ritmo de la vida
Chapter Overview

De antemano pp. 126–128	**¿Cómo es el ritmo de tu vida?**	*Practice and Activity Book*, p. 49	*Video Guide* OR *Videodisc Guide*	
	FUNCTIONS	**GRAMMAR**	**CULTURE**	**RE-ENTRY**
Primer paso pp. 129–131	Discussing how often you do things, p. 129	• Negation, p. 129 • **¿Quiénes?,** p. 130	**Tira cómica,** p. 131	**¿Quién?**
Segundo paso pp. 132–137	• Talking about what you and your friends like to do together, p. 132 • Talking about what you do during a typical week, p. 135	• Indirect object pronoun **les,** and **a ustedes, a ellos, a ellas,** p. 133 • **-er** and **-ir** verbs, p. 134	• **Nota cultural,** Getting together with friends, p. 134 • **Panorama cultural, ¿Cómo es una semana típica?,** p. 137	• **gustar** • Subject pronouns with **-er** and **-ir** verbs • Gender
Tercer paso pp. 138–141	• Giving today's date, p. 138 • Talking about the weather, p. 140	**Nota gramatical,** Giving the date, p. 138	**Nota cultural,** Seasons in South America, p. 139	Days of the week

Letra y sonido p. 141 — Stressing the correct syllable — **Dictado:** *Textbook Audiocassette 3A/Audio CD 5*

Vamos a leer pp. 142–143 — **Deportes en el agua** — **Reading Strategy:** Guessing meaning based on context

Review pp. 144–147 — **Repaso,** pp. 144–145 — **A ver si puedo...,** p. 146 — **Vocabulario,** p. 147

Assessment Options

Quizzes
- *Chapter Teaching Resources, Book 2*
  - **Primer paso,** Quiz 5-1, pp. 23–24
  - **Segundo paso,** Quiz 5-2, pp. 25–26
  - **Tercer paso,** Quiz 5-3, pp. 27–28
- *Assessment Items, Audiocassette 7B/Audio CD 5*

Chapter Test
- *Chapter Teaching Resources, Book 2*, pp. 29–36
- *Assessment Guide*, Speaking Test, p. 30
- *Assessment Items, Audiocassette 7B/Audio CD 5*

Test Generator, Chapter 5

RESOURCES: Print	RESOURCES: Audiovisual
Video Program OR *Expanded Video Program, Videocassette 2* OR *Videodisc Program, Videodisc 3A*	*Textbook Audiocassette 3A/Audio CD 5*
	Textbook Audiocassette 3A/Audio CD 5
Practice and Activity Book, pp. 50–52	
Native Speaker Activity Book, pp. 21–25	
Chapter Teaching Resources, Book 2	
• Additional Listening Activities 5-1, 5-2, p. 11	*Additional Listening Activities, Audiocassette 9B/Audio CD 5*
• Student Response Forms, pp. 20–22	
• Realia 5-1, pp. 15, 17	
• Situation Cards 5-1, pp. 18–19	
• Teaching Transparency Master 5-1, pp. 7, 10	*Teaching Transparency 5-1*
• Quiz 5-1, pp. 23–24	*Assessment Items, Audiocassette 7B/Audio CD 5*
Video Guide	*Video Program* OR *Expanded Video Program, Videocassette 2*
Videodisc Guide	*Videodisc Program, Videodisc 3A*
	Textbook Audiocassette 3A/Audio CD 5
Practice and Activity Book, pp. 53–55	
Native Speaker Activity Book, pp. 21–25	
Chapter Teaching Resources, Book 2	
• Communicative Activity 5-1, pp. 3–4	
• Additional Listening Activities 5-3, 5-4, p. 12	*Additional Listening Activities, Audiocassette 9B/Audio CD 5*
• Student Response Forms, pp. 20–22	
• Realia 5-1, pp. 15, 17	
• Situation Cards 5-2, pp. 18–19	
• Teaching Transparency Master 5-2, pp. 8, 10	*Teaching Transparency 5-2*
• Quiz 5-2, pp. 25–26	*Assessment Items, Audiocassette 7B/Audio CD 5*
Videodisc Guide	*Videodisc Program, Videodisc 3A*
	Textbook Audiocassette 3A/Audio CD 5
Practice and Activity Book, pp. 56–58	
Native Speaker Activity Book, pp. 21–25	
Chapter Teaching Resources, Book 2	
• Communicative Activity 5-2, pp. 5–6	
• Additional Listening Activities 5-5, 5-6, p. 13	*Additional Listening Activities, Audiocassette 9B/Audio CD 5*
• Student Response Forms, pp. 20–22	
• Realia 5-2, p. 16, 17	
• Situation Cards 5-3, pp. 18–19	
• Teaching Transparency Master 5-3, pp. 9, 10	*Teaching Transparency 5-3*
• Quiz 5-3, pp. 27–28	*Assessment Items, Audiocassette 7B/Audio CD 5*
Videodisc Guide	*Videodisc Program, Videodisc 3A*
Video Guide	*Video Program* OR *Expanded Video Program, Videocassette 2*
Videodisc Guide	*Videodisc Program, Videodisc 3A*

Alternative Assessment

- Performance Assessment
  - **Primer paso,** p. 131
  - **Segundo paso,** p. 137
  - **Tercer paso,** p. 141
- Portfolio Assessment
  - Written: **Repaso** Activity 4, *Pupil's Edition,* p. 145
    Assessment Guide, p. 18
  - Oral: Activity 30, *Pupil's Edition,* p. 141
    Assessment Guide, p. 18

Capítulo 5: El ritmo de la vida
Textbook Listening Activities Scripts

For Student Response Forms, see *Chapter Teaching Resources, Book 2,* pp. 20–22.

Primer paso

Activity 6, p. 129

— Hola, Teresa, ¿qué tal?

— Bien, Carlos, ¿y tú?

— ¡Fantástico! Oye, ¿cómo va todo en el trabajo?

— Bien...

— ¿Está todavía Alejandro?

— Sí... Alejandro está allí todos los días. Trabaja mucho.

— ¿Y los otros?

— Bueno... Maite trabaja los fines de semana. Ramón no está aquí mucho; trabaja sólo cuando tiene tiempo los jueves.

— ¿Y Flora? ¿Todavía trabaja con ustedes?

— Sí... Flora siempre trabaja los lunes, y a veces los jueves.

— ¿Y qué pasa con Juan Luis?

— Ay, no sé. Juan Luis nunca está aquí. Qué lástima, ¿verdad?

Answers to Activity 6

1. D, Juan Luis, nunca
2. B, Maite, los fines de semana
3. A, Alejandro, todos los días
4. E, Flora, siempre los lunes, a veces los jueves
5. C, Ramón, sólo cuando tiene tiempo los jueves

Segundo paso

Activity 13, p. 132

GLORIA Oye, Carlos, ¿qué les gusta a ti y a Eddie? ¿Les gusta practicar un deporte?

CARLOS Bueno, a mí me gusta esquiar, pero a Eddie no.

GLORIA ¿Les gusta bucear juntos?

CARLOS Pues sí, nos gusta bucear juntos. Especialmente los fines de semana.

GLORIA Eddie, ¿te gusta acampar con frecuencia?

EDDIE A mí me gusta mucho. Pero a Carlos no le gusta.

GLORIA Pero a ustedes les gusta pescar, ¿no?

CARLOS ¿Pescar? No, no pescamos nunca.

Answers to Activity 13

1. a 2. c 3. b 4. d

Activity 18, p. 136

Ese Fidel es inteligente y es un chico bueno. ¡Pero no le gusta hacer cosas difíciles! Por la mañana toma el autobús al colegio porque montar en bicicleta es muy difícil. A las doce sólo bebe jugo porque preparar un sándwich es muy difícil. Por la tarde, después de clases, sólo quiere descansar. No quiere ni asistir a clases ni practicar deportes. No, señor, ¡jugar al fútbol es muy difícil! Y no le gusta leer. Sólo lee las tiras cómicas, porque son fáciles. Y eso sí, a veces escribe a su amigo Pepe en Nueva York. Pero sólo tarjetas postales, ¡porque escribir cartas es muy difícil!

Answers to Activity 18

a. Incorrecto; Fidel no come un sándwich porque preparar un sándwich es difícil.
b. Incorrecto; Fidel no quiere jugar al fútbol porque es muy difícil.
c. Correcto

Tercer paso

Activity 23, p. 139

1. Hoy es el veinticinco de diciembre.
2. Hoy es el veintiséis de abril.
3. Hoy es el treinta y uno de octubre.
4. Hoy es el veintiséis de noviembre.
5. Hoy es el catorce de febrero.
6. Hoy es el cuatro de julio.

Answers to Activity 23
1. b 2. d 3. a 4. f 5. e 6. c

Letra y sonido, p. 141

For the scripts for Parts A, B, and D, see page 141. The script for Part C is below.

C. Dictado

Voy al almacén hoy porque necesito una cámara nueva. Pero, ¿dónde está mi suéter? ¿Y el cinturón para mi falda? Ah, aquí están. ¿Tú quieres ir conmigo?

Repaso

Activity 1, p. 144

1. Hoy en Nueva York, hace mal tiempo. No hace mucho frío, pero está lloviendo muchísimo.
2. En Chicago hace mucho viento otra vez. No va a nevar hoy, pero la temperatura va a llegar a los veinte grados.
3. En Miami va a ser un día maravilloso. Hace buen tiempo. Hace sol y la temperatura es de ochenta grados. Un buen día para la playa.
4. Hace frío en las montañas de Colorado. La temperatura es de treinta y dos grados. Un día perfecto para esquiar.

Answers to Repaso Activity 1
1. c 2. d 3. a 4. b

Capítulo 5: El ritmo de la vida
Projects

In this project students will create a brochure for a seasonal camp. This project is designed for individual or group work.

SITUATION

Tell students to imagine that they are the owners of a year-round camp. They have all the facilities to accommodate activities for every season. Have students prepare and present a brochure for their camp, telling about games, sports, lessons, and other activities to do there.

MATERIALS

✂ Students may need

- Poster board
- Glue
- Scissors
- Tape
- Markers
- Magazines

SEQUENCE

1. Decide whether to do this project as individual or group work, depending on your class size and time allotment.
2. Have students look for pictures to illustrate the activities that they would offer at their seasonal camp. If students cannot find pictures of certain items but would like to include them in their project, encourage them to draw.
3. Once they have selected several activities, students should make an outline of what they will include in their brochure.
4. Students must label each activity with its Spanish name and indicate the season when it is the most appropriate. **(Es posible acampar en el otoño.)**
5. Students in each group must check each other's features before putting the final descriptions in the brochure.
6. Each group presents its brochure. After brochures have been submitted, they will be displayed.
7. As a final step, have all students vote on where they would most like to spend their vacation.

GRADING THE PROJECT

If the outcome of the brochure is based on group cooperation and effort, one grade should be given to all members of the group.

Suggested point distribution (total = 100):

Content 25
Creativity 25
Grammar and Vocabulary 25
Oral Presentation 25

Capítulo 5: El ritmo de la vida

Games

PREGUNTAS

This game can be used to practice and reinforce the vocabulary presented in the **Así se dice** *sections of this chapter. You may also choose to include the functional phrases from the* **Así se dice** *sections of preceding chapters.*

Procedure Divide the students into two teams. Each team is to develop a list of the answers to the questions presented in the **Así se dice** sections. Then play begins with one student from each team facing off.

The Team 1 player reads the first answer from their list. The Team 2 player must ask a question that would be appropriate for the answer. If the Team 2 player is able to do so, Team 2 receives a point. Then the Team 2 player reads the first answer from his or her list and the Team 1 player must ask an appropriate question. If the Team 1 player is successful, Team 1 receives a point. The lists are then passed to the second player on each team and the play continues.

LA FECHA EN DIEZ PREGUNTAS

This game gives students the opportunity to practice asking questions and to use their critical thinking skills to determine the proper questions.

Procedure Write a date (day and month) on a piece of paper. Students take turns asking questions that can be answered by **sí** or **no** to determine the date. Students who can determine the date with ten questions or fewer are the winners.

You may wish to explain that the best way to win is to ask sharply focused questions. Questions should include the words **antes** or **después.** For example, **¿Es antes de junio? ¿Es después de marzo? ¿Es antes del 15?**

 **For Individual Needs**

Challenge You may wish to see if there are any students who can determine the date with only five questions.

TIC-TAC-TOE

Draw a Tic-Tac-Toe grid on the board. On pieces of paper, write new vocabulary words. Tape papers face down on each square. Dividing the class into teams, have students take turns picking a square and making a sentence with the word in the square.

If the student makes a complete sentence, his or her team marks an X or an O in that square. If not, the other team gets a chance to do so. If the second team fails to say a sentence, replace the word with a new one. The team that can connect three squares in a straight line wins. (You can make the game longer and more challenging by drawing a grid of four by four squares.)

VERDUGO

This game is the English "Hangman." It helps students review functions and vocabulary from this chapter or from preceding chapters.

Procedure Divide the class into two teams. Draw two scaffolds on the board or on a transparency. Name a category from this chapter (for example, talking about the weather, giving the date, or talking about what you and your friends like to do together) and make a blank for each letter of an expression in this category under each scaffold.

The first player of the first team suggests a letter. If the letter is found in the expression, write it in the appropriate blank. If the letter is not in the expression, begin the stick drawing of the hangman. If the first player's suggestion was correct, the next player on the team may suggest another letter. If the first player's suggestion was incorrect, the turn passes to the opposing team.

The rope and body are drawn in the following order: noose, head, torso, each arm, each leg, each hand, each foot, and hair. To break a tie score or to make the game last longer, additional features may be drawn. You might also use categories from preceding chapters to review vocabulary, functional expressions, or structures.

Capítulo 5
El ritmo de la vida
pp. 124–147

Using the Chapter Opener

Motivating Activity

Have students list what they typically do during an average week. Ask them to share: What do they have to do? What do they choose to do? How often?

Background Information

The southern part of Florida depends on rain for fresh water. It receives a drenching 40 to 65 inches a year, largely from May to October. You may wish to ask students how this compares with the amount typically received in the area where they live. (This is information they could get from a media weather forecaster.)

Photo Flash!

(1) This photo is of two of the video characters for Chapters 5 and 6, Armando and Raquel.

(1) **Armando y Raquel dibujan en el parque en el verano.**

124 *ciento veinticuatro*

Culture Note

Schools in Spanish-speaking countries are less likely than U.S. schools to have sports and extracurricular activities. Many teens in these countries participate in athletics through private sports clubs or city leagues.

In a typical week, Spanish-speaking teens go to school and spend time with friends and family. In many ways, they're probably a lot like you. For example, they worry about the weather when planning weekends or vacations!

In this chapter you will learn

- to discuss how often you do things
- to talk about what you and your friends like to do together; to talk about what you do during a typical week
- to give today's date; to talk about the weather

And you will

- listen to people talk about how they spend their time at different seasons of the year
- read a weather map in Spanish
- write a diary entry about your weekly routine
- find out about seasonal activities in Spanish-speaking countries

(2) **Todos los días hacemos ejercicio en el club deportivo.**

(3) **¡Está lloviendo a cántaros!**

Focusing on Outcomes

- Have students look at the chapter outcomes and match them with the three photos. Photo 1 represents discussing how often you do things; Photo 2 represents talking about what you and your friends like to do together; and Photo 3 represents talking about the weather.
- Ask students to talk about their plans for this week and how often they plan to do certain events.
- Ask students what they like to do together with their friends, and what a typical week is like.
- Bring in the weather map and the forecast from a local newspaper to provide students with some first-hand information about what the weather will be in their area. The students might then identify the expressions they will need to know to discuss the forecast in Spanish.
- Point out to students that they will learn how to talk about these things in Spanish in this chapter.

Additional Vocabulary

(3) You may want to teach your students **paraguas, guantes,** and **impermeable** to discuss this photo.

Language Note

A **cántaro** is a large, narrow-mouthed pitcher. Therefore the expression **Está lloviendo a cántaros** is the equivalent of the English expressions "rain is coming down in buckets," and "it's raining cats and dogs."

VIDEO PROGRAM OR EXPANDED VIDEO PROGRAM, *Videocassette 2*

OR VIDEODISC PROGRAM, *Videodisc 3A*

Video Synopsis

In this episode, students in Miami prepare a news broadcast program for their high school. There is a national weather forecast, interviews with students and a teacher about their free-time activities, and an interview with a new student. At the end of the episode, there is a problem with the camera and the broadcast is interrupted.

Motivating Activity

Have students imagine that a reporter has stopped them on the street to interview them about their free-time activities. Tell your students to make a list: What questions might he or she ask? What might you answer?

DE ANTEMANO

¿Cómo es el ritmo de tu vida?

Look at the pictures in the **fotonovela.** Can you tell what Patricia, José Luis, and Raquel are doing? Where are they? Does something go wrong? How can you tell?

Patricia

José Luis

Raquel

1

2

3

4

RAQUEL ¡Hola! Raquel Villanueva a sus órdenes. Todos estamos aquí, en el colegio, durante las horas de clase. ¿Pero qué hacemos cuando no estamos aquí? Ramón... ¿qué haces por la tarde?

RAMÓN Bueno... los martes y los jueves, trabajo en el restaurante de mis padres. Y cuando no trabajo, hago la tarea o paso el rato con mis amigos.

5

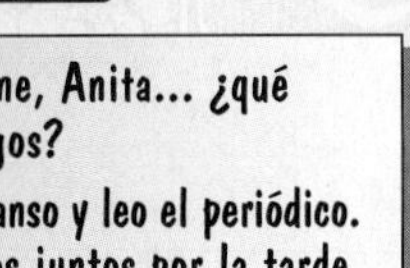

RAQUEL ¿Qué tal, Anita y Josué? Dime, Anita... ¿qué haces típicamente los domingos?

ANITA Eh... todos los domingos, descanso y leo el periódico. Y Josué y yo siempre corremos juntos por la tarde.

RAQUEL Ah, ¿sí? ¿Y corren mucho?

JOSUÉ Sí, mucho. Nos gusta correr. ¡Pero en el verano no, porque hace demasiado calor!

126

RESOURCES FOR DE ANTEMANO

Textbook Audiocassette 3A/Audio CD 5
Video Guide
Video Program
Expanded Video Program, Videocassette 2
Videodisc Guide
Videodisc Program, Videodisc 3A
Practice and Activity Book, p. 49

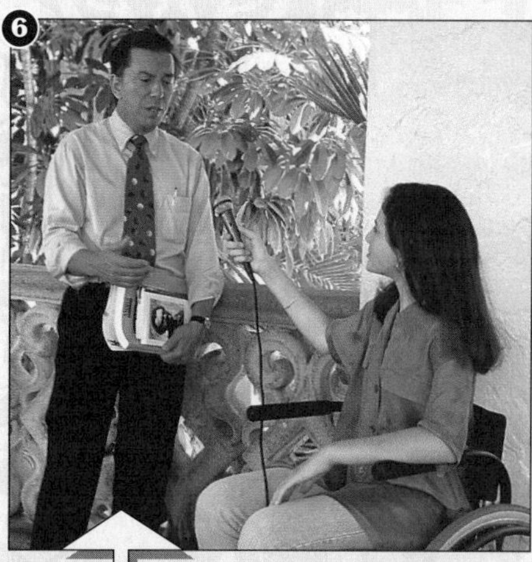

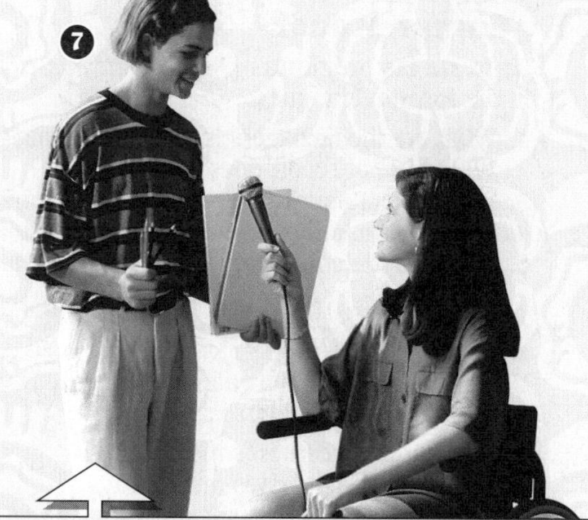

127

Presentation

Have students break into pairs and discuss in detail the visual clues in the photos that help them predict what is going on prior to reading the **foto-novela.** Then play the audio-recording or read aloud the different characters' parts, having students repeat each character's lines after you while reading along in the book. Then have the students practice with each other, taking turns reading the parts of different characters in the story. Finally, play the video. Have students see if their predictions based on the visual cues in the photos were accurate.

Thinking Critically

Comparing and Contrasting On a current weather map, ask students to locate Miami. Is the weather in Miami today the same as it is in the **fotonovela**? Students might then compare the weather in the other locations mentioned in the **fotonovela** with the current weather.

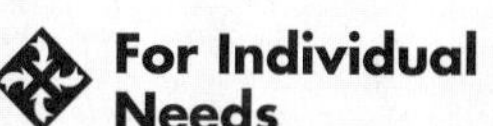

For Individual Needs

Challenge Ask students to locate newspaper and magazine articles about recent weather conditions around the world. They should read these and write a commentary on whether or not weather patterns are changing globally.

Video Integration

- ***Expanded Video Program,*** *Videocassette 2,*
- ***Videodisc Program,*** *Videodisc 3A*

SAMPLE

You may choose to continue with **¿Cómo es el ritmo de tu vida? (a continuación)** at this time, or wait until later in the chapter. When the story continues, the students resolve the camera problem that interrupted the show and clean up all the spilled papers as best they can. The next day the characters show Armando the Vizcaya Gardens.

Building on Previous Skills

Ask students to introduce the characters in the **fotonovela** using skills they have learned in Chapters 1 through 4. Have them give each character's name, age, country of origin, and likes or dislikes.

Teaching Suggestion

5 You may wish to have students compare their list with a partner's to see which activities they have in common and if their times for doing them are the same.

1 ¿Comprendes?

Contesta las preguntas *(Answer the questions)*. If you're not sure about what's happening in the **fotonovela,** guess!

1. What are the teenagers in the story doing? See answers below.
2. What kind of report does José Luis give? See answers below.
3. What does Raquel do in her special report? See answers below.
4. Who is Armando, and what does he have in common with Raquel? See answers below.
5. How will the crew deal with the accident at the end of the broadcast? See answers below.

2 ¿Cómo se dice?

Using the **fotonovela** as a guide, find the words and phrases you could use to See answers below.

1. say that the weather is nice
2. ask what a friend does on Sundays
3. say that you and a friend run a lot
4. say that you write letters
5. say that you paint and draw in your free time

3 Equivocaciones *Errors*

There are five errors in this paragraph describing Raquel and her friends. Find and correct the errors, then read the corrected paragraph aloud. See answers below.

Patricia y José Luis están en Nueva York, donde hace mucho sol. Anita trabaja en un restaurante los martes y los jueves. Josué y Anita corren todos los días. Raquel y Armando miran la televisión en su tiempo libre. ¿Y el profesor Williams? Él lee el periódico después de clases y prepara la cena con su esposa.

4 Cuando hace mal tiempo... *When the weather's bad . . .*

Read what Raquel says she and her friends do when the weather is bad. Then match the correct character's name with each activity.

Cuando hace frío, yo escucho música. Mi amiga Anita lee el periódico y el profesor Williams trabaja en casa. Cuando está lloviendo, Armando y yo dibujamos, Anita descansa y el profesor Williams y su señora escriben cartas.

1. Anita a, c
2. el profesor Williams b, e
3. Raquel d, f
4. Armando f
5. la señora del profesor b

a. leer el periódico
b. escribir cartas
c. descansar
d. escuchar música
e. trabajar en casa
f. dibujar

5 ¿Y tú?

Using the **fotonovela** for ideas, write several sentences about what you do during a typical week, and when. Answers will vary.

Answers

1 1. filming a TV show
2. weather report
3. interviews people about free-time activities
4. a new student; drawing and painting
5. *Answers will vary.*

2 1. Hace buen tiempo.
2. ¿Qué haces los domingos?
3. Corremos mucho.
4. Escribo cartas.
5. Pinto y dibujo en el tiempo libre.

3 1. Miami
2. Ramón
3. los domingos
4. pintan y dibujan
5. escucha música o escribe cartas

PRIMER PASO

Discussing how often you do things

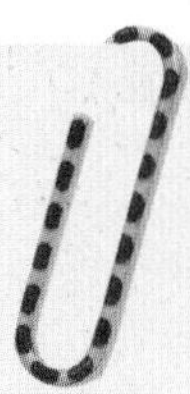

ASÍ SE DICE Discussing how often you do things

To find out how often a friend does things, ask:

¿Con qué frecuencia desayunas?
How often do you eat breakfast?

¿Siempre organizas tu cuarto?
(Do you) always . . .?

¿Y qué haces **durante la semana?**
. . . during the week?

¿Todavía tocas la guitarra?
(Do you) still . . .?

Your friend might respond:

Desayuno todos los dias.
I eat breakfast every day.

Nunca organizo mi cuarto.
(I) never . . .

A veces cuido a mi hermano.
Sometimes . . .

Muchas veces ayudo en casa.
Often I help at home.

Sí, pero **sólo cuando** no tengo tarea.
. . . only when . . .

6 Escuchemos: Viejos amigos *Old friends*

Listen as Teresa tells Carlos what some of his old friends are doing. Match the name of each friend with when he or she works with Teresa. Answers on p. 123C.

1. Juan Luis
2. Maite
3. Alejandro
4. Flora
5. Ramón

a. todos los días
b. los fines de semana
c. sólo cuando tiene tiempo los jueves
d. nunca
e. siempre los lunes, a veces los jueves

Gramática Negation

In Chapter 2 you learned to make sentences negative by putting **no** before the verb. To say *never* or *not ever,* put **nunca** before the verb.

Nunca tomo el autobús. *I never take the bus.*

In Spanish, you'll often use **no** and **nunca** or **no** and **nada** together in the same sentence. In that case, be sure to put **no** in front of the verb, and **nunca** or **nada** after the verb.

No tomo el autobús **nunca.** *I never take the bus.*
Los sábados **no** hago **nada.** *On Saturdays I don't do anything.*

Another negative word is **nadie**. It is always used with a singular verb form.

No toca la guitarra **nadie.** }
Nadie toca la guitarra. } *Nobody plays the guitar.*

RESOURCES FOR PRIMER PASO

Textbook Audiocassette 3A/Audio CD 5
Practice and Activity Book, pp. 50–52
Native Speaker Activity Book, pp. 21–25
Videodisc Guide
Videodisc Program, Videodisc 3A

Chapter Teaching Resources, Book 2
- Additional Listening Activities 5-1, 5-2, p. 11
  Audiocassette 9B/Audio CD 5
- Student Response Forms, pp. 20–22
- Realia 5-1, pp. 15, 17
- Situation Cards 5-1, pp. 18–19
- Teaching Transparency Master 5-1, pp. 7, 10
  Teaching Transparency 5-1
- Quiz 5-1, pp. 23–24
  Audiocassette 7B/Audio CD 5

Jump Start!

To review material from Chapter 4, ask students to write five things they are doing today. Ask them to write next to each of these activities how often they do them. (**Juego al baloncesto con mis amigos.** Always.)

MOTIVATE

Ask students how often they and their friends and family do things. Remind them that their answers may be fictional.

TEACH

Presentation

Así se dice Model the expressions by asking several questions and have students answer them. Then, have students ask and answer the questions in **Así se dice** with a partner.

Gramática Model the expressions by saying several sentences and then negating them. Then call on one student to say a sentence and ask another student to negate it.

For videodisc application, see Videodisc Guide.

Building on Previous Skills

Write on the board or a transparency: **Siempre, Muchas veces, A veces, Nunca.** Ask students to use the vocabulary from Chapter 4 for things they do and to write as many activities as they can under each heading.

Thinking Critically

7 Synthesizing Tell students to imagine they have found a list left by a parent or guardian asking the student to do three things immediately. Ask students to create such a note, using the activities from the word box.

Math Link

9 After groups have completed their **encuestas**, ask them to compile the results. Then ask each group to graph the results. Then display the graphs labeled in Spanish for the entire class.

For Individual Needs

10 Slower Pace Point out the clues in the text that signal the proper choice, as students may not associate the appropriate nouns with the blank. (In item 1, students may choose **¿Quiénes?** based on **muchas personas** rather than **¿Quién?** based on **chico**.) Review forms of **ser** with the interrogatives by pointing to individual students and have the class chorally respond **¿Quién es?** or **¿Quiénes son?** as appropriate.

Presentation

Nota gramatical Write five questions on the board. (**¿Quiénes estudian el arte? ¿Quién es cómico? ¿Quiénes son altos? ¿Quién es bajo? ¿Quiénes son divertidos?**) Elicit oral answers from several students, then have them write their answers to the questions on a sheet of paper. They can then compare their answers to a classmate's. You may want to point out that the change from **¿quién?** to **¿quiénes?** is not unusual. With the Spanish number system, everything reflects the change from singular to plural. (interrogatives, verbs, nouns, articles, adjectives)

7 Mi semana

What do you do during a typical week? Write six sentences using activities from the box. Be sure to explain how often you do each activity. Possible answers below.

practicar un deporte · desayunar · cuidar a tu hermano/a · caminar con el perro · trabajar · pintar · preparar la cena · estudiar en la biblioteca · tocar un instrumento · ir al colegio

8 Y tú, ¿qué haces?

a. Work in pairs. Using the word box in Activity 7, try to guess at least three activities you think your partner never does.
b. Then using your sentences from Activity 7, ask your partner how often he or she does the same things you do.

9 Una encuesta

Interview five classmates to find out how often they do the things mentioned in the first column. Your classmates will respond by using words from both columns.

MODELO —¿Con qué frecuencia lavas la ropa?
—Nunca lavo la ropa.

lavar la ropa	nunca
organizar tu cuarto	a veces
hablar por teléfono	sólo cuando tengo tiempo
ayudar en casa	los lunes, los martes, etc.
tomar el autobús	los fines de semana
sacar la basura	todos los días
mirar la televisión	

Nota Gramatical

You've already learned the question word **¿quién?** *(who?)*. **¿Quién?** is used to ask about one person. When asking about more than one person, use **¿quiénes?** *(who?)*. Compare the two sentences below.

¿Quién es el chico rubio?
Who is the blond boy?

¿Quiénes son las chicas altas?
Who are the tall girls?

10 ¿Quiénes son...? See answers below.

Fill in the blanks with **quién** or **quiénes** to complete David and Ana's conversation about guests at Ana's party.

DAVID Ana, hay muchas personas aquí, ¿no? ¿__1__ es el chico alto?
ANA Se llama Andrés.
DAVID ¿Y __2__ son las chicas al lado de Andrés?
ANA Se llaman Veronique y Marie Agnes. Son de París.
DAVID Ah, ¿sí? Yo tengo familia de Francia también.
ANA ¿__3__ es de Francia en tu familia?
DAVID Mi abuela. ¿Y __4__ son los chicos cerca de la puerta?
ANA Se llaman Mario, Roberto y Julia.

Answers

7 *Possible answers:* Practico el fútbol americano todos los días. Paseo al perro los sábados. Nunca preparo la cena. A veces estudio en la biblioteca.

10 1. Quién 2. quiénes 3. Quién 4. quiénes

11 ¿Quién hace eso? *Who does that?*

Who is doing what in the drawings? Get together with a partner and take turns asking and answering questions about the people and activities pictured. See answers below.

MODELO ¿Quiénes nadan en la Piscina Alberti?
Julia y Silvia nadan en la Piscina Alberti.

1. estar/gimnasio
2. mirar/televisión
3. ir/parque
4. cuidar/su hermano
5. pintar/la clase de arte
6. tomar/helado

Julia y Silvia

Rita

Li

Micki y Pablo

Roberto y Laura

Keesha

Ricardo y Daniel

Possible answers below.

12 ¿Tienes buena memoria?

Work in groups of four. On three slips of paper write the categories **siempre**, **a veces** and **nunca**. Under each category write two activities that you always, sometimes, and never do. Then one person in the group shuffles the papers. Each person draws three slips and asks **¿Quién...?** or **¿Quiénes...?** plus the activity to try and guess who wrote the activities on each slip.

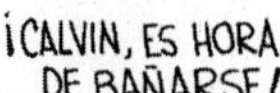

SUGERENCIA

At first, it's often hard to write in a foreign language. Remember that learning to write is like learning other skills in Spanish. Take it slowly, and go in small steps. Begin by writing short messages. For example, you can write brief reminders to yourself about what you need to do, or try writing out your weekly schedule in Spanish. Start now by making a list of activities you usually do during a particular day—for example, on Mondays.

Teaching Suggestion

Tira cómica First, ask your students to scan the comic for cognates and familiar words. What do they think is happening?

CLOSE

To review the functions and grammar of this **Paso**, do the following activity. On a small piece of paper, write an activity and an expression of frequency. Make enough of these to give one to each student. List some activities only once and other activities on several pieces of paper. If you use **mirar la televisión**, you might ask **¿Quién no mira la televisión nunca?** Students with this activity and **nunca** will raise their hands. Then have a student ask another question. **(¿Quién siempre hace ejercicios aeróbicos?)**

ASSESS

Quiz 5-1, *Chapter Teaching Resources, Book 2,* pp. 23–24

Assessment Items, Audiocassette 7B/Audio CD 5

Performance Assessment

Ask students to write a letter in Spanish to a friend who is spending the year in Mexico. Ask them to include information about what five of her friends are doing this year, the day of the week on which they do it, or how often they do it. You may wish to show the students the Spanish style of using numbers for the date. (25/1/96=January 25, 1996). The letter might begin with **Querido/a** ____ and end with **Un saludo de** ____.

Answers

11 1. ¿Quién está en el gimnasio? Keesha está en el gimnasio.
2. ¿Quiénes miran la televisión? Roberto y Laura miran la tele.
3. ¿Quiénes van al parque? Ricardo y Daniel van al parque.
4. ¿Quién cuida a su hermano? Rita cuida a su hermano.
5. ¿Quiénes pintan en la clase de arte? Micki y Pablo pintan en la clase de arte.
6. ¿Quiénes toman helado? Li toma helado.

12 *Possible questions and answers:*
(A veces preparo la cena.) —¿Quién prepara la cena a veces? ¿Tú, Roberto? —Sí a veces yo preparo la cena.
(Nunca organizo el cuarto.) —¿Quién no organiza el cuarto nunca? ¿Tú, Juana? —No, yo no. Yo siempre organizo el cuarto.

Jump Start!

Prior to class, write on the board or a transparency several phrases from Chapter 4 that students included in MOTIVATE, p. 129. Put blanks for some of the letters. Have students work independently to guess their meaning.

(m _ _ _ a _ _ n
_ i _ _ c _ _ t _ =
montar en bicicleta)

Thinking Critically

Analyzing Have an aphorism, cliché, or other well-known Spanish saying on the board when students arrive. (**En boca cerrada no entran moscas.** *Silence is golden.*) Ask if anyone can figure out what it means.

MOTIVATE

Tell students to imagine that they have just met a nice group of teenagers from Chile who speak no English. Have students jot down in English what types of questions they might want to ask the visitors. What might they want to be able to say to these people in Spanish?

TEACH

Presentation

Así se dice Ask students to raise their hand if their list from MOTIVATE includes the question *What do you like to do?* Have the class chorally repeat after you: **¿Qué les gusta hacer?** Model some more questions for the imaginary Chilean visitors, using those in the box as samples. Then model some answers to the questions.

SEGUNDO PASO

Talking about what you and your friends like to do together; talking about what you do during a typical week

ASÍ SE DICE Talking about what you and your friends like to do together

So far, you've been using **gusta** with the pronouns **me, te,** and **le** to talk about what just one person likes and dislikes.

To find out what a group of your friends likes to do, ask:

¿Qué **les gusta** hacer?
. . . do you like . . . ?

Y a Celia y Roberto, **¿les gusta esquiar juntos?**
. . . do they like to ski together?

¿Les gusta **acampar** y **pescar?**
. . . to camp . . . to fish?

Your friends might answer:

Nos gusta hacer ejercicio o correr por la playa. *We like to exercise or run on the beach.*

No sé, pero les gusta **bucear** juntos.
. . . to scuba dive . . .

Sí, **especialmente** durante **las vacaciones.**
. . . especially . . . vacation . . .

Answers on p. 123C.

13 Escuchemos: Mejores amigos

Gloria is writing an article about best friends for the school newspaper. Listen as she interviews Carlos and Eddie. Then, for each activity shown, choose the best answer.

1. Les gusta.
2. No les gusta.
3. Sólo le gusta a Carlos.
4. Sólo le gusta a Eddie.

a.

b.

c.

d.

RESOURCES FOR SEGUNDO PASO

Textbook Audiocassette 3A/Audio CD 5
Practice and Activity Book, pp. 53–55
Native Speaker Activity Book, pp. 21–55
Video Guide
Video Program
Expanded Video Program, Videocassette 2
Videodisc Guide
Videodisc Program, Videodisc 3A

Chapter Teaching Resources, Book 2
- Communicative Activity 5-1, pp. 3–4
- Additional Listening Activities 5-3, 5-4, p. 12
  Audiocassette 9B/Audio CD 5
- Student Response Forms, pp. 20–22
- Realia 5-2, pp. 15, 17
- Situation Cards 5-2, pp. 18–19
- Teaching Transparency Master 5-2, pp. 8, 10
  Teaching Transparency 5-2
- Quiz 5-2, pp. 25–26
  Audiocassette 7B/Audio CD 5

VOCABULARIO

asistir a una clase de ejercicios aeróbicos

comer un sándwich o una hamburguesa con papas fritas

beber agua o jugo

leer las tiras cómicas en el periódico

escribir tarjetas postales

recibir cartas

14 ¿Qué les gusta hacer?

Tell what you and your friends like to do at each of these times and places. For each answer, choose at least one item from the **Vocabulario** and at least one from vocabulary you already know. Answers will vary.

MODELO después de correr
Nos gusta descansar y beber jugo. A veces nos gusta nadar después de correr.

1. en casa los domingos
2. después de jugar a un deporte
3. los sábados (en el gimnasio, por ejemplo)
4. en la biblioteca
5. en la playa los fines de semana
6. durante las vacaciones

15 Preferencias

Work in pairs. Using the cues, ask a series of questions to find out which activities your partner likes to do and how often. Switch roles after three questions. Possible answers below.

MODELO correr: playa/parque
—¿Te gusta correr por la playa o en el parque?
—¿Y con qué frecuencia?

1. escribir: cartas/tarjetas postales
2. recibir: notas de amigos/cartas de amor *(love letters)*
3. comer: ensalada/un sándwich
4. leer: revistas/periódico
5. asistir: a clases/a un concierto de...
6. beber: jugo/agua

Nota Gramatical

Look at the examples in the **Así se dice** box on p.132. Notice that the same pronoun, **les,** can be used to mean both *to them* and *to you* (plural). The phrases **a ustedes** and **a ellos** or **a ellas** are sometimes added for clarification.

Look at the literal translations of these questions.

¿A ustedes les gusta nadar?
Is swimming pleasing to you?

¿A ellos les gusta preparar la cena juntos?
Is preparing dinner together pleasing to them?

What would the non-literal English translations be?[1]

1. *Do you like to swim? Do they like to fix dinner together?*

Answers
15 *Possible answers:*
1. —¿Te gusta escribir cartas o tarjetas postales?
—Me gusta escribir tarjetas postales.
—¿Y con qué frecuencia te gusta escribir?
—Me gusta escribir tarjetas todos los viernes.

Additional Vocabulary
los artes marciales *martial arts*
la alfarería *pottery*
el baile moderno *modern dance*
la autoescuela *driving school*
el ensayo *practice*

Presentation

Vocabulario Model pronunciation. Then ask students to work with a partner. Ask them to report to the class the activities they both like to do and the activities that neither likes to do. **(Nos gusta asistir a una clase de ejercicios aeróbicos.)** If one student likes to do the activity and the other does not, ask them to report that too. **(A mí me gusta hacer ejercicios aeróbicos, pero a Chitra no le gusta hacerlos.)**

Additional Practice

14 Have students break into different pairs and find three things that they both like to do. Then have pairs interview each other, practicing the plural forms, for about three minutes. Have several pairs report their findings to the class.

For Individual Needs

15 Kinesthetic Learners You may wish to divide the class into teams for this activity. Using a big clock or drawing one on the board, ask a student what he or she likes to do at this hour. The student is to pantomime the action, and the other students from the same team are to guess what is being pantomimed. The team will be given a point when they give a correct response. **(A las nueve le gusta hablar por teléfono.)**

Challenge Ask students to create a cartoon or **tira cómica** that incorporates vocabulary from this chapter.

Presentation

Gramática Practice the forms in the box with the whole class. Begin by asking a student **¿Qué comes?** The respondent answers **Como pizza.** Then turn to a second student and ask **¿Qué come él?** and that student reports **Come pizza.** To practice the plural forms ask two students: **Juan y Gloria, ¿qué comen ustedes?** Juan and Gloria together answer **Comemos pizza.** Ask another student **¿Qué comen ellos?** The student answers **Comen pizza.** Repeat the pattern with **escribir,** then move on to having the students ask and answer each other to use all of the forms. This exercise can be used quickly whenever a new verb is introduced.

Native Speakers

Ask any native speakers in your class to interview family members and report favorite public meeting places for the different generations. They can also report whether the information in the **Nota cultural** on car ownership holds true for their particular friends and family.

Gramática -er and -ir verbs

In Chapter 4 you learned to work with **-ar** verbs, such as **hablar.** Look at the conjugations of **comer** and **escribir** to see how **-er** and **-ir** verbs work. Which two endings aren't identical for both verbs?[1]

Como / Comes / Come } ensalada. Com**emos** / Com**éis** / Comen } ensalada.

Escribo / Escribes / Escribe } cartas. Escrib**imos** / Escrib**ís** / Escriben } cartas.

¿Se te ha olvidado? the subject pronouns Consulta la página 109

16 De vacaciones en Miami

Completa las oraciones sobre las vacaciones de Antonio y su familia. Usa la forma correcta del verbo entre paréntesis. See answers below.

1. Ana y yo (correr) por la playa por la mañana.
2. Luego descansamos y yo (leer) las tiras cómicas en inglés.
3. Los lunes y los miércoles mis padres (asistir) a una clase de ejercicios.
4. A Miguelito le gustan mucho las hamburguesas y las papas fritas. ¡Siempre (comer) mucho!
5. Mis padres no (comer) mucho. Están a dieta. *They are on a diet.*
6. Y tú, Diana, ¿por qué no me (escribir) una tarjeta postal?
7. Todos los días nosotros (recibir) cartas, pero ¡nada de ti! *Nothing from you!*

NOTA CULTURAL

Spending time with a group of friends is an important part of life for young adults in the Spanish-speaking world. Fewer young people own cars in Spain or Latin America than in the United States, so they often share rides with friends. Meeting friends in public is a big part of life for both young and old. Public gathering places like parks and cafés are common meeting places. The streets of a Spanish-speaking town are usually alive both day and night.

1. The **nosotros** forms are different: **com<u>emos</u>, escrib<u>imos</u>.** And the **vosotros** forms are different: **com<u>éis</u>, escrib<u>ís</u>.**

Culture Note

The beaches of Miami are famous for their size and beauty. On the weekends, it is common to see large families and groups of people at the beach together cooking out, listening to music and, of course, playing in the ocean.

Answers

16
1. corremos
2. leo
3. asisten
4. come
5. comen
6. escribe
7. recibimos

17 ¿Qué hacen?

What do the people in these pictures do during the week? See answers below.

MODELO Alejandra y sus amigos hacen la tarea juntos.

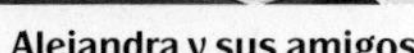
Alejandra y sus amigos

ustedes

la señora Pérez

tú

yo

nosotros

¿Te acuerdas?

Do you remember that masculine plural adjectives and nouns can refer to mixed groups of males and females as well as all-male groups? If you're talking about two males or a male and a female together, use **juntos.** If you're talking about two females, use **juntas.**

A LO NUESTRO

In Spanish, there are many ways to express how often you do things. Some of these expressions include: **una vez** *(once)*, **de vez en cuando** *(once in a while)*, **todo el tiempo** *(all the time)*, **cada día** *(each day)*, and **a menudo** *(often)*.

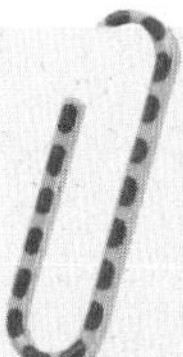

ASÍ SE DICE Talking about what you do during a typical week

To find out what your friends typically do during the week, ask:

¿Qué haces **típicamente** durante el día?

¿Qué hace Josué **por la mañana?** *. . . in the morning?*

¿Hacen ustedes ejercicio juntos?

¿Y qué hacen Raquel y Anita **por la noche?** *. . . at night?*

Some responses might be:

Asisto a clases, trabajo y paso el rato con amigos.

Corre **dos millas** por la playa. *. . . two miles . . .*

Sí, pero sólo **por la tarde.** *. . . in the afternoon.*

A veces van a un restaurante.

Additional Practice

17 Ask students to think about one activity shown here which they do during a typical week. Call on several students to say a few sentences about it. (**A mí me gusta correr en el gimnasio y en el parque. Corro todos los días a las cinco.**)

Presentation

Así se dice Tell the class a story about yourself, highlighting the vocabulary in **Así se dice: Típicamente, trabajo aquí en el colegio de siete a cuatro. Por la mañana enseño español, y por la tarde enseño geografía. Después de las cuatro, regreso a casa. Por la tarde a veces corro dos millas, o voy al gimnasio. Por la noche, típicamente preparo la cena para mi familia. A veces salimos a un restaurante, pero no con mucha frecuencia.** Then ask the students to respond to comprehension questions. (**—Clase, ¿qué hago típicamente por la mañana? —Usted enseña español. —¿Y qué hago por la tarde?**) Extend the pattern to several students, asking questions based on those in **Así se dice.** When it seems that comprehension is high, have students practice the pattern in pairs, including vocabulary from **A lo nuestro.**

Answers

17 Ustedes corren en la mañana.
La señora Pérez escribe tarjetas postales.
Comes hamburguesas con amigos en un restaurante.
Yo asisto a la clase de ejercicios aeróbicos.
Leemos las tiras cómicas en el periódico.

Teaching Suggestions

18 To focus students' listening, ask them to describe what Fidel is doing in each drawing before listening to the audiotape.

19 Remind students that **¿Tú?** questions and **Yo** answers should be included. Practice of these forms will help them prepare for Activity 20 as well.

20 To practice negation, consider varying Activity 20 so that students explain what they don't do on weekdays and weekends. **(En el colegio no miro la televisión, no escucho música. Los fines de semana no tengo clases...)**

Close

To review the functions and grammar of this **Paso,** have your students do the following activity. Ask students to form groups and give each group a list of several activities. Have students divide the activities into three categories—**por la mañana, por la tarde,** and **por la noche**—according to the time of day that they do each. Ask a spokesperson for each group to report to the class when the activities are done, using the correct form of the verb for each.

Assess

Quiz 5-2, *Chapter Teaching Resources, Book 2,* pp. 25–26

Assessment Items, Audiocassette 7B/Audio CD 5

Performance Assessment

Ask each student to make a daily planner for the coming weekend. Ask them to list the day of the week and use **por la mañana, por la tarde,** or **por la noche** with any activity they plan for that day.

18 Escuchemos: Un día típico en la vida de...

Answers on p. 123C.

Listen as Fidel's mother describes a typical day in his life, and decide which of these illustrations shows the real Fidel. Explain what is wrong with the incorrect illustrations.

a. 

b. 

c. 

19 ¿Quién lo hace?

Answers will vary.

Try to identify at least one person in your partner's family or circle of friends who does each of the activities listed. Also find out how often each person does the activity. Take notes, and try to find activities that your friends or family members have in common. If nobody does the activity, use **Nadie...** in your answer.

MODELO —Juana, ¿quién en tu familia lee revistas?
—Nadie, pero mi tío lee el periódico todos los días por la mañana.

leer: revistas, las tiras cómicas, el periódico, novelas
asistir a: una clase de ejercicios, bailes, conciertos
escribir: poemas, cartas, tarjetas postales
comer: ensaladas, fruta, hamburguesas
correr: en el parque, después de clases, cinco millas

20 ¿Cómo pasas tú los días? *How do you spend your days?*

Interview a partner to find out how she or he spends a typical weekday. Ask about morning, afternoon, and evening activities. Switch roles and answer your partner's questions about a typical weekend morning, afternoon, or evening.

MODELO —¿Qué haces los lunes por la mañana?
—Los lunes asisto al colegio y hablo con mis amigos.

21 Los sábados

Who do you usually spend Saturdays with? Write three paragraphs, one for the morning, one for the afternoon, and one for the evening. In each paragraph, tell who you're with, where you go, and what you typically do together. Use some of the expressions listed in the word box to make your paragraphs flow naturally.
See example below.

siempre **especialmente** **primero** **a veces** **vamos a** **nunca** **nos gusta** **por fin** **típicamente** **luego**

Answers

21 *Sample answer:*
Los sábados por la mañana siempre desayuno en casa. A veces miro la televisión. Luego corro con mi amiga Peggy. Por la tarde vamos juntas al centro comercial o al cine.

¿Cómo es una semana típica?

In this chapter, we asked some students what they usually do during the week and on weekends.

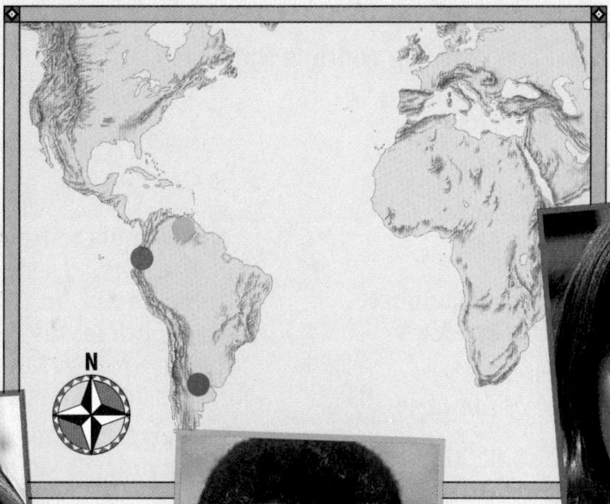

María Luisa
Quito, Ecuador

"Vengo al colegio y del colegio a la casa, y de ahí no hago nada más".

¿Y los fines de semana?
"Salgo a comer con mis amigas, me voy a casa de ellas o ellas vienen a mi casa".

Maikel
Caracas, Venezuela

"Ir al liceo, llegar a casa en la tarde, hacer mis tareas y descansar".

¿Y los fines de semana?
"Bueno, quedarme en mi casa o si no, salgo con mis padres".

Matías
Buenos Aires, Argentina

"Vengo al colegio a las ocho y cuarto; salgo doce y cuarto para irme a comer, vuelvo a la una y media y salgo de nuevo a las cuatro y cuarto, llego a mi casa, veo tele y como, y voy a dormir."

¿Y los fines de semana?
"Voy a andar en velero al club náutico, y después vuelvo tarde a eso de las ocho y vuelvo a mi casa directo a dormir".

Para pensar y hablar...

A. Read the interviews carefully. Whose weekday routine is most like yours? Whose weekend routine is similar to yours?

B. What you do says a lot about you. What do you think María Luisa, Matías, and Maikel are like?

VIDEO PROGRAM OR EXPANDED VIDEO PROGRAM, Videocassette 2

OR VIDEODISC PROGRAM, Videodisc 3A

Teacher Notes

- See *Video Guide* and *Videodisc Guide* for activities related to the **Panorama cultural.**
- Remind students that cultural information may be included in the Quizzes and Chapter Test.

Motivating Activity

Ask students how they imagine the daily routines of teenagers in Spain and Latin America. Do they think they are the same or different from their own? Why?

Presentation

Have students view the video. Stop the video after each interview and ask students to summarize in English what the person on the video said. When all interviews have been viewed, have students answer the questions in the text. Then show the video again and have students answer the **Preguntas.**

Language Note

As each of these interviewees is from South America, ask students to compare their accents to those they have heard from Spain and other Latin American countries. Note the aspiration of syllable-final **s** and **s** before a consonant.

Preguntas

1. ¿Cuál de los chicos no hace nada después del colegio? (María Luisa)
2. ¿Qué significa **liceo**? (high school)
3. ¿Quiénes salen con gente los fines de semana? (María Luisa, Maikel)
4. ¿Con quiénes salen? (sus amigas, sus padres)
5. ¿Qué quiere decir **andar en velero** y **a eso de**? (to go sailing; "around," in terms of time)

Native Speakers

If you have students from a Spanish-speaking country, ask if they are willing to share with the class how their daily routine is the same or different from the one they had in their country of origin. Students from other, non-Spanish-speaking cultures may also share how their daily routines were before they came to the United States.

Jump Start!

On the board or a transparency, write several simple addition and subtraction problems using numbers in written form from **uno** to **treinta y uno.** Have students solve the problems and write the answers in Spanish.

MOTIVATE

Ask students to each list five dates during the year that are important to them and to explain why.

TEACH

Presentation

Así se dice Write the date on the board, then say **Hoy es el... de...** Then ask the class to chorally answer the questions **¿Cuál es la fecha?** and **¿Qué fecha es hoy?** Then, ask volunteers to share some of their dates from MOTIVATE in Spanish. Write the date and why the student says it is important.

Vocabulario Use pictures from magazines or old calendars as flash cards for seasons, and tell the season and the months that comprise it. Have students read the **Nota cultural** on page 139. Then write four sentences on the board or a transparency. (**La estación de verano tiene los meses de...,** and so on for each season) Ask students to complete each statement for the northern hemisphere, then for the southern hemisphere. You might continue with questions such as **¿Qué te gusta hacer en el invierno? ¿Qué deportes practicas en el mes de mayo?**

TERCER PASO

Giving today's date; talking about the weather

ASÍ SE DICE Giving today's date

To find out today's date, ask:

¿Cuál es la fecha?
¿Qué fecha es hoy?

To give today's date, say:

Hoy **es el primero de diciembre.**
. . . is the first of December.

Es el quince de enero.
It's the fifteenth of January.

To tell on what date something happens, say:

El cuatro de este mes hay un examen.
On the fourth of this month . . .

Nota Gramatical

The formula for giving today's date is **el** + *number* + **de** + *month*: **el quince de junio.** The first day of the month is called **el primero.** Note that in Spanish you omit the "on" in expressions like *on the fifth.*

La fiesta es el cinco.
The party is on the fifth.

22 Fechas interesantes *Interesting dates* Answers will vary.

Working individually first, write a special date for each month of the year. You might include holidays and more personal dates like birthdays or upcoming special events. Then compare lists with your partner. For each date that you don't recognize, ask why that date is special to your partner. For holidays or other special occasions, see page 341.

VOCABULARIO

la primavera
- **marzo**
- **abril**
- **mayo**

el verano
- **junio**
- **julio**
- **agosto**

el invierno
- **diciembre**
- **enero**
- **febrero**

el otoño
- **septiembre**
- **octubre**
- **noviembre**

El otoño es una estación.
Hay cuatro estaciones en un año.

Octubre es un mes.
Hay doce meses en un año.

RESOURCES FOR TERCER PASO

Textbook Audiocassette 3A/Audio CD 5
Practice and Activity Book, pp. 56–58
Native Speaker Activity Book, pp. 21–25
Videodisc Guide
Videodisc Program, Videodisc 3A

Chapter Teaching Resources, Book 2
- Communicative Activity 5-2, pp. 5–6
- Additional Listening Activities 5-5, 5-6, p. 13
  Audiocassette 9B/Audio CD 5
- Student Response Forms, pp. 20–22
- Realia 5-2, pp. 16, 17
- Situation Cards 5-3, pp. 18–19
- Teaching Transparency Master 5-3, pp. 9, 10
  Teaching Transparency 5-3
- Quiz 5-3, pp. 27–28
  Audiocassette 7B/Audio CD 5

23 Escuchemos: Meses y estaciones

Listen and match the date you hear with the correct picture. Answers on p. 123D.

a.

b.

c.

d.

e.

f.

24 Actividades Possible answers below.

What do you usually do during different seasons of the year? Combine elements from all three columns to form answers. Then, create a sentence telling what you like to do in the places mentioned.

MODELO En el verano voy a la playa. Me gusta bucear, jugar al voleibol y descansar.

En el invierno	ir a...	el colegio
En la primavera	trabajar en...	el gimnasio
En el verano	hacer ejercicio...	el parque
En el otoño	comer...	la piscina
	beber...	la playa
	asistir a...	en casa
	leer...	el centro comercial
	escribir...	
	jugar al...	

NOTA CULTURAL

The seasons in the southern cone of South America occur at opposite times of year from seasons north of the equator. Summer begins in December, and winter begins in June. Much of South America is located on or near the Equator, where the weather is warm all year round. Here there are only two seasons, wet and dry. In the tropics, altitude plays a major role in climate. The Andes region is quite cold even though it's near the equator.

25 Y tú, ¿adónde vas?

Get together with a partner. Try to guess at least five sentences your partner wrote in Activity 24. Check how many of your guesses were right. What activities do you and your partner have in common?

26 ¿Cuál es la fecha?

Make a list of six dates, including at least one from each season. Then read them to your partner one at a time. Your partner will tell you what season it is, and at least one activity she or he associates with that time of year. Possible answers below.

MODELO —Es el treinta de abril.
—Es primavera, y juego al béisbol.

Additional Practice

Before class begins write three phrases on a transparency: **¿Quién cumple años el... de...? Yo, yo cumplo años el... de...,** and ____, **¿no cumples años el... de...?** This will be used later in the activity.

In Spanish, have students write their birthday on one side of a card, and their name on the other side. Collect the cards and have a volunteer shuffle and pass them out so that everyone has someone else's. Tell students that they cannot let anyone know whose card they receive.

Display the transparency and call on individual students to ask the first question using the date on their paper: **¿Quién cumple años el... de...?** The student recognizing his or her birthday will answer **Yo, yo cumplo años el... de...** If no one answers, then the student should ask using the student's name: **Juan, ¿no cumples años el cuatro de enero?** Juan should then answer in Spanish.

Continue until all students have participated. You may wish to save the cards for a quick review activity later in the chapter.

Teaching Suggestion

24 Have several students write sentences on the board or on a transparency to share with the class. You may wish to have the class peer-correct.

Answers

24 *Possible answers:*
En el invierno estoy mucho en casa. Me gusta leer novelas y mirar la televisión.

26 *Possible answers:*
—Es el catorce de agosto.
—Es el verano. Nadamos mucho en el verano.

Science Link

After reading the **Nota cultural,** ask students to explain why the seasons occur at opposite times of the year in the southern and northern hemispheres. (Due to tilt of the earth's axis, sunlight is more direct in the southern hemisphere in December than in June and more direct in the northern hemisphere in June than in December.)

Presentation

Así se dice, Vocabulario
Begin by having students follow along in their books as you talk about the weather map. **¿Qué tiempo hace hoy? En Portland está lloviendo. Llueve mucho. En Fargo, está nevando. Nieva bastante. En Chicago hace mucho viento. Y en San Antonio, hace sol. En Los Ángeles hace buen tiempo, pero en Milwaukee hace muy mal tiempo hoy.** After modeling the vocabulary, move into asking true/false comprehension questions. **(En Great Falls, hace mucho calor, ¿verdad?)** Finally, move into asking the students to answer your questions. **(Clase, ¿qué tiempo hace aquí hoy?)**

For videodisc application, see *Videodisc Guide.*

Additional Practice
Ask each student to bring in a weather map from a recent copy of a local newspaper. In pairs, students ask each other simple yes or no questions about actual current weather conditions. Answers should be truthful. Then ask them about the weather in various parts of the country. The symbols on the map will be helpful in practicing weather expressions.

Teaching Suggestion
Using a large calendar, you might keep an ongoing weather calendar for a period of time in the classroom. You can use this calendar to elicit conversation on both dates and weather expressions.

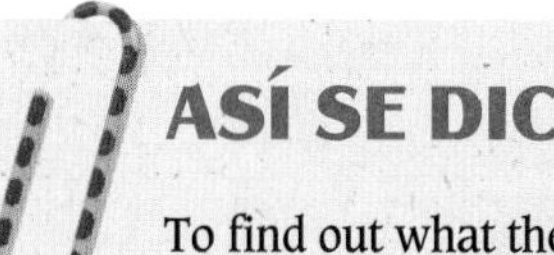

ASÍ SE DICE Talking about the weather

To find out what the weather is like, ask:

¿Qué tiempo hace?

To answer, say:

Hace buen tiempo.
Hace muy mal tiempo hoy.

VOCABULARIO

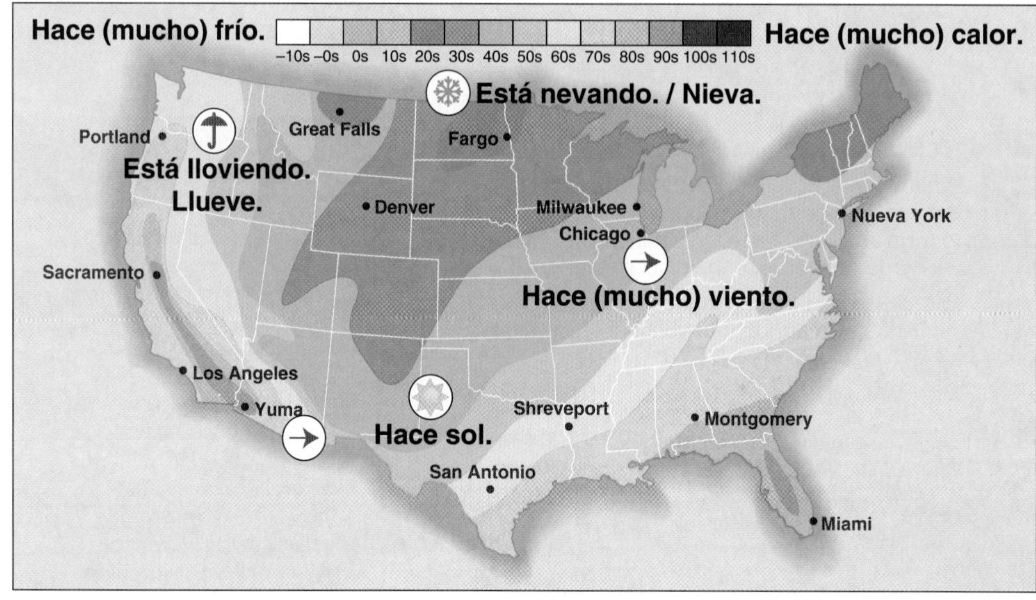

Está nublado. *It's cloudy.* **Hace fresco.** *It's cool.*

27 El pronóstico del tiempo *The weather report*

Look at the weather map and match the weather to the cities.

1. Miami a, c, d, h
2. Nueva York i
3. Portland c
4. Sacramento a, c, d, h
5. San Antonio a, c
6. Milwaukee e
7. Shreveport a, c
8. Chicago e

a. hace sol y hace buen tiempo
b. está lloviendo
c. hace buen tiempo
d. hace calor y hace sol
e. hace viento
f. hace mucho frío
g. hace frio y está nevando
h. hace calor
i. hace fresco

TPR Divide students into groups of three or four. Give each group a piece of paper with a month or a season on it. They are to develop a pantomime based on their month or season, and the class is to guess which one it is. Each student in the group should play a part in the pantomime.

28 El estudiante nuevo

Cristóbal is a new student from the Dominican Republic. Answer his questions about the weather in your town. Possible answers below.

MODELO —¿Qué tiempo hace en diciembre?
—Hace mucho frío y nieva.

1. julio
2. la primavera
3. octubre
4. marzo
5. el verano
6. febrero
7. agosto
8. el otoño

A LO NUESTRO

When it's really cold or hot, you can say **¡Hace un frío/calor tremendo!** If it's raining especially hard, you can say **Está lloviendo a cántaros** *(It's raining cats and dogs)*. If it's a beautiful day and you really can't complain, you can tell your friends **Hace un tiempo precioso.**

29 ¿Qué haces cuando...?

Find out what activities your partner does in the following kinds of weather. Use the -**ar**, -**er**, and -**ir** verbs you know. Be prepared to report your findings to the class. Possible answers below.

1. cuando hace frío
2. cuando llueve
3. cuando nieva
4. cuando hace mal tiempo
5. cuando hace sol
6. cuando hace calor

30 En mi cuaderno Answers will vary.

Write two paragraphs describing your favorite season and explaining why you like it. First, tell which months are in that season and describe the weather. Then, write about the activities that you and your friends like to do, and any special places where you go at that time.

LETRA Y SONIDO

A. One of the purposes of accent marks is to tell you which syllable to stress.

1. Words ending in a vowel, **n**, or **s** are stressed on the next to the last syllable.
   examen hablan discos toma quiero
2. Words ending in any consonant besides **n** or **s** are stressed on the last syllable.
   animal feliz Madrid hablar
3. Exceptions to rules 1 and 2 get an accent mark over the syllable to be stressed.
   semáforo lápices rápido lámpara música Víctor suéter
4. All question words have an accent mark.
   ¿qué? ¿cuándo? ¿quién? ¿cómo ¿cuánto? ¿dónde?

B. Some words have an accent mark to tell them apart from a similar word.

mi *my* **tu** *your* **si** *if*
mí *me* **tú** *you* **sí** *yes*

C. **Dictado** Answers on p. 123D.
Listen and read the phone conversation and rewrite the words that need accent marks.

Voy al almacen hoy porque necesito una camara nueva. Pero, ¿donde esta mi sueter? ¿Y el cinturon para mi falda? Ah, aqui estan. ¿Tu quieres ir conmigo?

D. **Trabalenguas**
Tin marín dedós pingüé, cúcara, mácara, títere fue

Portfolio

30 Oral You may wish to point this out to your students as an appropriate Portfolio entry to be audio- or videotaped. For Portfolio suggestions, see *Assessment Guide*, p. 18.

Close

Read statements like the following to your students and ask them to sketch a picture illustrating each.

- **Es el invierno, hace frío y nieva mucho.**
- **Está lloviendo y estoy en casa.**
- **Hace sol y mi amigo y yo nadamos.**
- **Es el otoño y hace viento.**
- **Hoy hace fresco y está nublado.**

Have students peer-check to verify comprehension.

Assess

Quiz 5-3, *Chapter Teaching Resources, Book 2*, pp. 27–28

Assessment items, Audiocassette 7B/Audio CD 5

Performance Assessment

Ask pairs of students to role-play the following conversation. One is a cousin from a Spanish-speaking country of South America who is coming to visit the cousin in the United States and, in order to know what to bring, needs to know what the weather will be like and what they will be doing. (They may choose any season.) One cousin asks various questions which the other student answers.

Answers

29 *Possible answers:*

1. —¿Qué haces cuando hace frío?
   —Cuando hace frío, me gusta leer en casa.
2. —¿Qué te gusta hacer cuando llueve?
   —Cuando llueve voy al cine.

Motivating Activity

Ask students to list the types of water activities they enjoy, and which they would like to try some day.

READING STRATEGY

Guessing meaning from context

PREREADING

Activity A

You may wish to ask students to look at the pictures and to guess what the reading will be about. You might then ask them what their favorite water sport is and if it is pictured here. Also, ask them which words they already know as a result of their knowledge of English.

Teacher Note

For additional readings, see *Native Speaker Activity Book,* pp. 21–25 and *Practice and Acitvity Book,* p. 59.

Native Speakers

Ask students to write an original paragraph describing their favorite sport.

VAMOS A LEER

Deportes en el agua

Estrategia

As you know, it's easy to understand pictures, cognates, and words you have already studied. Many other words can be understood, too, based on how they're used in the sentence or paragraph. When you come to an unknown word, try to guess its meaning based on context (the other words around it).

¡A comenzar!

A. Before you do any in-depth reading, first remember to get the general idea and to recall your background knowledge of the topic. It should be easy to tell what these readings are about because of the pictures.

¿Te acuerdas?

Look at pictures and titles first

What is the reading about?

a. a sporting goods store
b. racing
ⓒ water sports
d. the environment

Al grano

B. Imagine that your family will be vacationing in Miami this summer. Each of you wants to try out a different sport. Read the passages and decide which sport would be best for each member of your family. Then, find an appropriate activity for each family member on page 143. Be sure to tell what words or phrases support your choice.

El motoesquí es para los fanáticos de la velocidad. El piloto necesita moverse con el ritmo de las olas del océano. Es fácil usar estas máquinas y no es muy caro. Es posible alquilar una por $25 la hora.

¿Te gusta mirar deportes en la televisión? Las lanchas del offshore son un deporte similar a la Fórmula 1. Estas lanchas corren a aproximadamente 110 millas por hora. Pero no son baratas — ¡estas lanchas cuestan más de 200.000 dólares! Naturalmente, no hay muchas personas que participen en este deporte.

La natación es siempre el favorito de la estación. Es posible nadar en el océano o en una piscina. Hay muchas piscinas de tamaño olímpico que son muy grandes. Es bueno practicar aquí. La piscina está dividida en muchas calles, y todas las personas nadan en una calle diferente.

El windsurf es buen deporte para el verano. Si no tienes experiencia, es muy importante tomar lecciones de un instructor. También necesitas tener un buen sentido de equilibrio. Tu primera experiencia debe ser en el verano porque el viento es ideal. En la primavera, hace demasiado viento para las personas que no tienen experiencia en el deporte.

En el verano, hay muchos kayaks en el agua. Son barcos pequeños para una o dos personas. Las personas controlan el kayak con remos largos. Es normal operar un kayak en el río, no en el océano.

1. your father, who loves high speeds (What phrase in the text supports that decision?)
2. your mother, who likes the most popular of all water sports (What sentence says this sport is the most popular?)
3. your sister, who likes small, one- or two-person boats (What words in the text tell you this?)
4. your brother, who would rather watch sports than participate (What phrase says this is primarily a sport to watch?) See answers below.

C. Your parents are trying to read the descriptions of these sports, but they don't know Spanish as well as you do. They underlined the words they didn't know so that you could help them. Use your knowledge of context to help them guess the meanings of these words.

D. Choose one easy-to-recognize noun from each of the sports in the reading, but don't choose the name of the sport itself. Then tell your partner the noun you chose. Your partner will say which sport the noun is associated with. Switch roles after four nouns.

MODELO —Piscina.
—¡La natación!

E. Tus padres dicen que tienes todo el día libre para participar en tu deporte acuático favorito. ¿Cuál de estos cinco deportes prefieres? Busca dos o tres frases en la lectura *(reading)* que explican por qué prefieres este deporte.

READING
Activities B and C

Teaching Suggestion

B. There may be translations of the words other than those listed. Praise students for making logical guesses, even if it is not the exact word. For instance, **alquilar** could be translated as *use* or *get* in this context. After they've done one or two, check to see if they are guessing correctly. Talk them through the process in English if they are having difficulty. (1. "It's very important to take ____ from an expert.") Then ask the class to give you logical guesses.

Additional Practice

C. As a follow-up activity, put students in groups of two or three, give them a picture of a different sport than those listed here, and have them compose a brief caption.

POSTREADING
Activity D

Write the names of the sports in the photos on a transparency or on the board. Have students close their books. Then read a portion of the description of each photo from the text and ask students to identify the sport you are describing.

Teaching Suggestion

Ask each student to select the text from one of the photos and to record it on an audiocassette tape. Replay the tape and ask the student to assess how she or he sounds. You may wish to provide feedback to each student.

Answers

B 1. jet ski; "los fanáticos de la velocidad"
2. natación; "La natación es siempre el favorito de la estación".
3. kayaks; "barcos pequeños para una o dos personas"
4. offshore boating; "¿Te gusta mirar deportes en la televisión?" or "no hay muchas personas que participen"

C 1. a. lessons b. sense
2. a. size b. lanes
3. a. waves b. to rent
4. a. oars b. river
5. a. boats b. cost / they cost

D *Answers will vary.*
E *Answers will vary.*

The **Repaso** reviews and integrates all four skills and culture in preparation for the Chapter Test.

Teaching Suggestion

2 You might like to videotape the interview, asking one student to assume the role of Raquel. They can then reverse their roles.

Portfolio

4 Written You may wish to point out this activity as an appropriate entry for your students' Portfolio. For Portfolio suggestions, see *Assessment Guide,* p. 18.

Native Speakers

5 Ask students to share with the class details about the celebration of these holidays and others. You might try and determine if the festivities for each holiday vary from country to country.

REPASO

1 For each weather report you hear, determine which of the photos is being described. Answers on p. 123

a.

b.

c.

d.

2 Raquel needs to interview you in order to finish her segment on *Noticias Colegio Seminole*. Answer her questions.

1. Típicamente, ¿qué haces con tus amigos?
2. ¿Qué haces con tu familia durante la semana?
3. A tus amigos, ¿les gusta mirar la televisión? ¿Con qué frecuencia?
4. Cuando hace buen tiempo, ¿qué te gusta hacer?
5. ¿Qué haces con tus amigos cuando hace mal tiempo?

Answers will vary.

3 See if your partner knows who in your class likes to do the following activities and how often. Answers will vary.

1. escribir poemas
2. bailar
3. pescar
4. tocar el piano
5. dibujar
6. correr
7. comer ensaladas
8. organizar el cuarto
9. acampar
10. leer el periódico
11. asistir a conciertos
12. hacer ejercicio

4 Write a list of activities that you and your friends do during a typical week. Try to use several activities for each day. Possible answers below.

5 Write the following dates in correct Spanish form. See if you can locate a Spanish-language almanac or calendar to find out what special day each one represents. See answers below.

1. May 5 2. December 28 3. June 24 4. October 12 5. January 6

Answers

4 *Possible answers:*
Los lunes vamos a la biblioteca después de clase para estudiar. Después tomamos un refresco juntos. Los martes nos gusta ir a una clase de ejercicios aeróbicos. Los miércoles hablamos por teléfono.

5
1. el Cinco de Mayo; el día de independencia de México
2. el veintiocho de diciembre; el Día de los Inocentes *(April fools' day)*
3. el veinticuatro de junio; el Día de San Juan Bautista
4. el doce de octubre; el Día de la Raza (Columbus Day)
5. el seis de enero; el Día de los Reyes Magos

6 Pick four different cities from the weather map. Describe the weather there and list two different activities you might do in each place. Answers will vary.

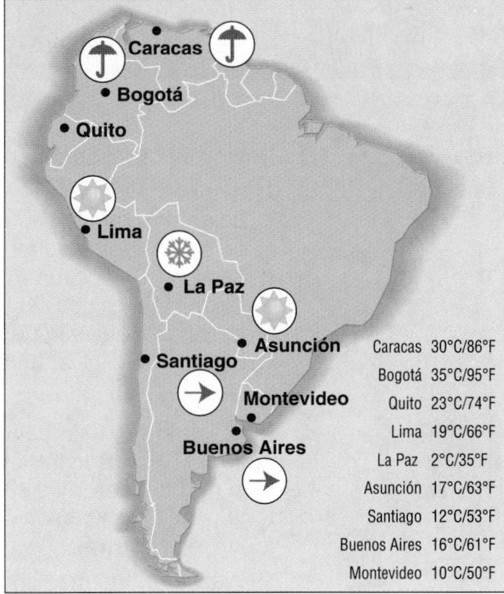

7 In groups of three, take turns interviewing and being interviewed. Ask your partners about each activity listed. In your answers, be sure to include when you do the activity and what the weather is like when you normally do it.

MODELO —¿Nadas mucho?
—Bueno, nado en el verano, cuando hace buen tiempo.

1. esquiar
2. bucear
3. leer novelas
4. acampar
5. cuidar a tu hermano
6. correr

8 Decide if the following statements would most likely be made by someone from the United States (**un estadounidense**) or someone from a Spanish-speaking country (**un hispano**). Some statements might be made by both! See answers below.

1. Bueno, durante la semana juego al fútbol con el equipo de mi colegio.
2. ¿En una semana típica? Pues, de lunes a sábado asisto a clases en mi colegio. Los domingos, mi familia y yo hacemos cosas juntos.
3. Trabajo todos los días después de clases en un restaurante.
4. A ver... por la tarde, mis amigos y yo paseamos por el centro. A veces tomamos algo en un café.
5. Generalmente, cuido a mis hermanitos después de clases, y los fines de semana mis amigos y yo vamos juntos al cine o a bailar.

9 SITUACIÓN

You are the host of your own late night talk show. With a partner, choose a famous person and role-play the interview. Be sure to ask what your guest does during certain times of the year, what he or she likes to do on vacation, where he or she likes to go, and why.

Answers

8 1. un estadounidense
2. un hispano
3. un estadounidense
4. un hispano/los dos
5. los dos

Additional Practice

6 Ask students to read or listen to the local weather forecast and to prepare their own brief **pronóstico del tiempo** for your city or town for the following day. It could be done as an audio or video recording or as a newspaper article. (You may wish to bring in a newspaper in case some students do not have access to a forecast.)

7 After students have done Activity 7, ask them whether or not one could normally expect to engage in a given activity, on a given date, in a given country. (**—¿Se puede nadar en Buenos Aires en julio?—No, porque hace frío.)**

Oral You might suggest that students include the **Situación** interview in their Portfolio. For Portfolio information, see *Assessment Guide*, pp. 2–13.

Video Wrap-up

- ***Video Program***
- ***Expanded Video Program, Videocassette 2***
- ***Videodisc Program, Videodisc 3A***

At this time, you might want to use the video resources for additional review and enrichment. See *Video Guide* or *Videodisc Guide* for suggestions regarding the following:

- **¿Cómo es el ritmo de tu vida?** (Dramatic episode)
- **Panorama cultural** (Interviews)
- **Video clips** (Authentic footage)

This page is intended to help students prepare for the Chapter Test. It is a brief checklist of the major points covered in the chapter. The students should be reminded that it is only a checklist and does not necessarily include everything that will appear on the Chapter Test. Remind students also that cultural information is included on the Chapter Test.

A VER SI PUEDO . . .

Can you discuss how often you do things? **p. 129**

1 How would José Luis say that . . .? See answers below.

1. he never swims
2. he always eats breakfast
3. he sometimes talks to Luisa
4. he always works on the weekends
5. he sometimes goes to the movies on Fridays
6. he never studies in the library
7. he always helps at home

Can you talk about what you and your friends like to do together? **p. 132**

2 How would you ask the following people or groups of people if they like to do each of the following activities? How would each person or group answer you? See answers below.

1. Franco/to organize his room
2. Cristina y Marta/to run in the park
3. Geraldo y Esteban/to scuba dive
4. Pablo/to read novels
5. Linda y Laura/to ski
6. Daniel/to exercise in the gym
7. Isabel/to write letters

Can you talk about what you do during a typical week? **p. 135**

3 How would you tell a classmate about five activities you typically do each week? Answers will vary.

Can you give today's date? **p. 138**

4 How would you tell a classmate the date of the following things? See answers below.

1. the Spanish test - March 5
2. the football game - Sept. 14
3. John's party - May 1
4. the school dance - July 29
5. the jazz concert - Jan. 18

Can you talk about the weather? **p. 140**

5 How would you describe the weather if it were . . .? See answers below.

1. rainy and cold
2. a nice, sunny day
3. cold and windy
4. snowy
5. hot and sunny
6. a cloudy day
7. cool
8. a terrible, rainy day

6 What would be a typical weather description in your hometown during the following times of the year? Answers will vary.

1. el otoño
2. el invierno
3. la primavera
4. el verano

Answers

1
1. Nunca nado.
2. Siempre desayuno. *or* Todos los días desayuno.
3. A veces hablo con Luisa.
4. Siempre trabajo los fines de semana.
5. A veces voy al cine los viernes.
6. Nunca estudio en la biblioteca.
7. Siempre ayudo en casa.

2
1. Franco, ¿te gusta organizar tu cuarto?
2. Cristina y Marta, ¿a ustedes les gusta correr en el parque? *or* ¿a vosotras os gusta correr en el parque?
3. Geraldo y Esteban, ¿a ustedes les gusta bucear?
4. Pablo, ¿te gusta leer novelas?
5. Linda y Laura, ¿les gusta esquiar?
6. Daniel, ¿te gusta hacer ejercicio en el gimnasio?
7. Isabel, ¿te gusta escribir cartas?

4
1. El examen de español es el cinco de marzo.
2. El partido de fútbol americano es el catorce de septiembre.
3. La fiesta de Juan es el primero de mayo.
4. El baile del colegio es el veinte y nueve de julio.
5. El concierto de jazz es el diez y ocho de enero.

5
1. Hace frío y está lloviendo.
2. Hace buen tiempo y hace sol.
3. Hace frío y mucho viento.
4. Nieva mucho hoy.
5. Hace calor y mucho sol.
6. Está nublado.
7. Hace fresco.
8. Hace mal tiempo y está lloviendo.

VOCABULARIO

PRIMER PASO

Discussing how often you do things

a veces *sometimes*
ayudar en casa *to help at home*
¿Con qué frecuencia? *How often?*
la chica *girl*
el chico *boy*
desayunar *to have breakfast*
durante *during*
muchas veces *often*
nada *nothing*
nadie *nobody*
nunca *never*
¿quiénes? *who? (plural)*
siempre *always*
sólo cuando *only when*
todavía *still, yet*
todos los días *every day*
tomar el autobús *to take the bus*

SEGUNDO PASO

Talking about what you and your friends like to do together

a ellos/ellas *to them*
a ustedes *to you (plural)*
acampar *to camp*
el agua *water (f.)*
asistir a *to attend*
beber *to drink*
bucear *to scuba dive*
la carta *letter*
una clase de ejercicios aeróbicos *aerobics class*
comer *to eat*
correr *to run*
escribir *to write*
especialmente *especially*
esquiar *to ski*
hacer ejercicio *to exercise*
la hamburguesa *hamburger*
el jugo *juice*
juntos/as *together*
les gusta *they/you (pl.) like*
leer *to read*
nos gusta *we like*
las papas fritas *french fries*
el periódico *newspaper*
pescar *to fish*
por la playa *along the beach*
recibir *to receive*
el sándwich *sandwich*
las tarjetas postales *postcards*
las tiras cómicas *comics*
las vacaciones *vacation*

Talking about what you do during a typical week

la milla *mile*
por la mañana *in the morning*
por la noche *at night (in the evening)*
por la tarde *in the afternoon*
típicamente *typically*

TERCER PASO

Giving today's date

abril *April*
agosto *August*
el año *year*
¿Cuál es la fecha? *What is today's date?*
diciembre *December*
enero *January*
las estaciones *seasons*
febrero *February*
el invierno *winter*
julio *July*
junio *June*
marzo *March*
mayo *May*
el mes *month*
noviembre *November*
octubre *October*
el otoño *fall*
la primavera *spring*
el primero *the first (of the month)*
¿Qué fecha es hoy? *What's today's date?*
septiembre *September*
el verano *summer*

Talking about the weather

Está lloviendo. *It's raining.*
Está nevando. *It's snowing.*
Está nublado. *It's cloudy.*
Hace buen tiempo. *The weather is nice.*
Hace calor. *It's hot.*
Hace fresco. *It's cool.*
Hace (mucho) frío. *It's (very) cold.*
Hace mal tiempo. *The weather is bad.*
Hace sol. *It's sunny.*
Hace (mucho) viento. *It's (very) windy.*
Llueve. *It's raining.*
Nieva. *It's snowing.*
¿Qué tiempo hace? *What's the weather like?*

Game

PONGA Ask students to prepare a card as in a game of Bingo, but not to write anything in the spaces. You will need to designate the number of spaces across and down. Then ask the student to fill in the spaces at random with words or expressions in Spanish from the vocabulary list. You may then proceed to give the word or expression in English, and if students have the word on their card, they can place a mark on the space. The first student to mark a straight or a diagonal line of spaces is the winner. A variation is to ask students to prepare a card and then exchange the card with another student before play begins.

Teaching Suggestion

To quickly review vocabulary, you may want to play TIC-TAC-TOE and VERDUGO. (See page 123F.)

CHAPTER 5 ASSESSMENT

CHAPTER TEST

- *Chapter Teaching Resources, Book 2,* pp. 29–36, 43, 44
- *Assessment Guide, Speaking Test,* p. 30
- *Assessment Items, Audiocassette 7B Audio CD 5*

TEST GENERATOR, CHAPTER 5

ALTERNATIVE ASSESSMENT

Performance Assessment

You might want to use the **Situación** (p. 93) as a cumulative performance assessment activity.

Portfolio Assessment

- **Written:** Repaso Activity 4, *Pupil's Edition,* p. 145
  Assessment Guide, p. 18
- **Oral:** Activity 30, *Pupil's Edition,* p. 141
  Assessment Guide, p. 18

Capítulo 6: Entre familia
Chapter Overview

De antemano pp. 150–152 | **¿Cómo es tu familia?** | *Practice and Activity Book*, p. 61 | *Video Guide* OR *Videodisc Guide*

	FUNCTIONS	GRAMMAR	CULTURE	RE-ENTRY
Primer paso pp. 153–157	Describing a family, p. 153	Possessive adjectives, p. 154	• **El compadrazgo,** p. 155 • **Encuentro cultural,** privacy in Hispanic culture, p. 157	• **Hay** • Possessive adjectives • Demonstrative adjectives • Use of **de**
Segundo paso pp. 158–163	• Describing people, p. 158 • Discussing things a family does together, p. 160	• **Hacer** and **salir** as irregular verbs, p. 160 • The personal **a,** p. 161	**Panorama cultural, La familia,** p. 163	• Colors • Descriptions of people • Pastimes/hobbies • **¿Con qué frecuencia?** • Adjective agreement
Tercer paso pp. 164–167	Discussing problems and giving advice, p. 164	• The verb **deber,** p. 164 • The verb **poner,** p. 165	**A lo nuestro,** diminutives, p. 167	Forming questions with **¿cómo?** and **¿cuántos?**

Letra y sonido p. 167 — The Spanish **r** — **Dictado:** *Textbook Audiocassette 3B/Audio CD 6*

Vamos a leer pp. 168–169 — **Cinco cosas curiosas para hacer en la Pequeña Habana** — **Reading Strategy:** Understanding organization by looking at pictures

Review pp. 170–173 — **Repaso,** pp. 170–171 — **A ver si puedo...,** p. 172 — **Vocabulario,** p. 173

Assessment Options

Quizzes
- *Chapter Teaching Resources, Book 2*
  - **Primer paso,** Quiz 6-1, pp. 81–82
  - **Segundo paso,** Quiz 6-2, pp. 83–84
  - **Tercer paso,** Quiz 6-3, pp. 85–86
- *Assessment Items, Audiocassette 7B/Audio CD 6*

Chapter Test
- *Chapter Teaching Resources, Book 2*, pp. 87–92
- *Assessment Guide*, Speaking Test, p. 30
- *Assessment Items, Audiocassette 7B/Audio CD 6*

Test Generator, Chapter 6

Video Program or *Expanded Video Program, Videocassette 2* or *Videodisc Program, Videodisc 3B*	*Textbook Audiocassette 3B/Audio CD 6*

RESOURCES: Print	RESOURCES: Audiovisual
	Textbook Audiocassette 3B/Audio CD 6
Practice and Activity Book, pp. 62–64	
Native Speaker Activity Book, pp. 26–30	
Chapter Teaching Resources, Book 2	
• Additional Listening Activities 6-1, 6-2, p. 69	*Additional Listening Activities, Audiocassette 9B/Audio CD 6*
• Student Response Forms, pp. 78–80	
• Realia 6-1, pp. 73, 74	
• Situation Cards 6-1, pp. 76–77	
• Teaching Transparency Master 6-1, pp. 65, 68	*Teaching Transparency 6-1*
• Quiz 6-1, pp. 81–82	*Assessment Items, Audiocassette 7B/Audio CD 6*
Video Guide	*Video Program* or *Expanded Video Program, Videocassette 2*
Videodisc Guide	*Videodisc Program, Videodisc 3B*
	Textbook Audiocassette 3B/Audio CD 6
Practice and Activity Book, pp. 65–67	
Native Speaker Activity Book, pp. 26–30	
Chapter Teaching Resources, Book 2	
• Communicative Activity 6-1, pp. 61–62	
• Additional Listening Activities 6-3, 6-4, p. 70	*Additional Listening Activities, Audiocassette 9B/Audio CD 6*
• Student Response Forms, pp. 78–80	
• Realia 6-1, pp. 73, 74	
• Situation Cards 6-2, pp. 76–77	
• Teaching Transparency Master 6-2, pp. 66, 68	*Teaching Transparency 6-2*
• Quiz 6-2, pp. 83–84	*Assessment Items, Audiocassette 7B*
Videodisc Guide	*Videodisc Program, Videodisc 3B*
	Textbook Audiocassette 3B/Audio CD 6
Practice and Activity Book, pp. 68–70	
Native Speaker Activity Book, pp. 26–30	
Chapter Teaching Resources, Book 2	
• Communicative Activity 6-2, pp. 63–64	
• Additional Listening Activities 6-5, 6-6, p. 71	*Additional Listening Activities, Audiocassette 9B/Audio CD 6*
• Student Response Forms, pp. 78–80	
• Realia 6-2, pp. 73, 74	
• Situation Cards 6-3, pp. 76–77	
• Teaching Transparency Master 6-3, pp. 67, 68	*Teaching Transparency 6-3*
• Quiz 6-3, pp. 85–86	*Assessment Items, Audiocassette 7B/Audio CD 6*
Videodisc Guide	*Videodisc Program, Videodisc 3B*

Alternative Assessment

- Performance Assessment
  Primer paso, p. 157
  Segundo paso, p. 163
  Tercer paso, p. 167
- Portfolio Assessment
  Written: **Repaso,** Activity 7, *Pupil's Edition,* p. 171
  Assessment Guide, p. 19
  Oral: Activity 22, *Pupil's Edition,* p. 161
  Assessment Guide, p. 19

Mid-term Exam
Assessment Guide, pp. 35–48
Assessment Items, Audiocassette 7B Audio CD 6

Capítulo 6: Entre familia
Textbook Listening Activities Scripts

For Student Response Forms, see *Practice and Activity Book,* pp. 78–80.

Primer paso

Activity 6, p. 153

1. Es una familia bastante grande. Hay nueve personas en total.
2. La familia es muy simpática. Tiene un perro muy travieso.
3. Los abuelos son de España. ¡Imagínate!
4. Es una familia muy unida. El padrastro es muy cariñoso con los hijos.
5. Los muchachos se ven muy guapos. El gato también.

Answers to Activity 6

1. b 2. d 3. ninguna foto 4. c 5. a

Segundo paso

Activity 15, p. 158

1. Alma tiene veintidós años y tiene el pelo blanco.
2. Guillermo es pelirrojo. Tiene los ojos negros.
3. Olivia tiene el pelo rubio y tiene ojos azules.
4. Adolfo tiene ochenta y cinco años. Tiene el pelo negro.
5. Liliana tiene los ojos blancos y el pelo verde.
6. Anselmo tiene pelo rubio y ojos de color café.

Answers to Activity 15

1. improbable
2. improbable
3. probable
4. improbable
5. improbable
6. probable

Activity 16, p. 159

1. Es pelirrojo, tiene ojos azules y es muy alto.
2. Es muy simpática y guapa. Tiene pelo negro y ojos de color café.
3. Es baja, tiene pelo rubio y ojos verdes. Es alto, tiene pelo moreno y tiene ojos verdes, también.
4. Es una persona muy especial. Tiene ojos negros y pelo negro. Es muy cariñosa conmigo. Tiene cincuenta años, pero se ve joven.
5. Son muy cómicos cuando están juntos. Uno de ellos es delgado y el otro es un poco gordo. Son muy traviesos.

Answers to Activity 16

1. David
2. Rebeca
3. Gabriel y Conchita
4. Maki
5. Simón y Quique

Activity 21, p. 160

1. Durante el verano mi familia y yo hacemos un viaje. Casi siempre visitamos a nuestros primos. Ellos viven en Colorado.
2. Salgo con frecuencia con mis amigos. A veces vamos a la playa.
3. Soy muy atlética. Hago ejercicio por la manaña con mis amigos. A veces los sábados corro con ellos en el parque.
4. Mi familia y yo salimos a comer juntos todos los viernes. Nos gusta hablar sobre nuestras actividades, las clases y el trabajo.

Answers to Activity 21

1. b 2. d 3. c 4. a

Tercer paso

Activity 28, p. 164

Mi tía es divorciada y vive con nosotros. Ella dice que mi mamá trabaja demasiado. Mi mamá sale de la casa a las siete de la mañana y regresa a las nueve de la noche. Debe descansar más, ¿verdad? Mi hermana es muy inteligente. Estudia ciencias y siempre está en la biblioteca con sus libros. Debe salir con amigos a veces. ¿Y yo? Pues, soy bastante perezosa. Toco la guitarra pero toco muy mal. Claro, debo practicar más.

Answers to Activity 28

1. c
2. a
3. b
4. su tía

Letra y sonido, p. 167

For the scripts for Parts A and C, see p. 167. The script for Part B is below.

B. Dictado

Rafael Ramírez es rubio y tiene ojos verdes. Él corre muy rápido en sus zapatos rojos de rayas.

Repaso

Activity 1, p. 170

Roberto, ésta es mi familia. Ésta es mi madre. Ella es inteligente y muy cariñosa. Lee muchas novelas. Y éste es mi padre. Él es muy alto, ¿verdad? También es muy cómico. Es artista y trabaja en un museo. Debe trabajar menos. Ésta es mi hermana. Ella es muy lista, pero debe estudiar más. Trabaja mucho en el jardín. Éste es mi tío Miguel. Es joven, tiene veinte años. A él le gusta tocar la guitarra día y noche. Éste es nuestro perro. Es muy travieso. También es un poco gordo porque come demasiado. Y finalmente éste soy yo. Yo soy muy simpático, porque siempre limpio mi cuarto.

Answers to Repaso Activity 1

1. el perro
2. el padre
3. la madre
4. Marcos
5. el tío Miguel
6. la hermana

Capítulo 6: Entre familia
Projects

In this activity, each student will create a family tree. Students may choose to diagram their own family, a fictional family, or a famous one. You may have them either write an essay or give an oral presentation to the class explaining the relationships on the tree.

MATERIALS

Students may need
- Posterboard
- Markers
- Photos

SEQUENCE

1. Explain the assignment to students. To familiarize students with the concept of diagramming relationships, draw a simple family tree on the board or a transparency. Or you might use the family tree on *Teaching Transparency 6-1.*
2. Have students sketch a rough draft of their tree. They should begin with one set of grandparents and add all of their children. Then they should add the marriages and children of the second generation, and so on.
3. Once they finish drawing the descendants of one set of grandparents, they should do the same for the other.
4. Upon finishing a rough draft of the entire family, they should outline the tree on a large piece of paper or posterboard. They should then transfer the information from the rough draft onto the final draft.
5. Students may embellish their trees with drawings or photos.
6. They should then either write a description in Spanish or present their tree to the class to explain the relationships on their tree.

Teaching Suggestion

Because some students might feel uncomfortable discussing their family background, offer all students the option of creating the family tree of an imaginary family or TV family. Suggest they use magazine photos or drawings to illustrate it. Or they might create a poster of important people in their life. For any of these, they should turn in a written description or make an oral presentation to the class.

GRADING THE PROJECT

You might grade this project on completeness, presentation and appearance, correct use and spelling of vocabulary, and either oral or written presentation.

Suggested Point Distribution (total = 100 points):

Completeness	30 points
Presentation/appearance	30 points
Use/spelling of vocabulary	20 points
Oral or written presentation	20 points

Capítulo 6: Entre familia

Games

¿ERES MI HIJO?

This game can be used to reinforce the acquisition of new vocabulary related to the family and descriptive adjectives. It can be played any time after the **Primer paso.**

Preparation For this game you will need to prepare a large family tree, the more complex the better. In addition to names, include details such as *deceased* (**muerto/a**), *divorced* (**divorciado/a**), and *adopted* (**adoptado/a**). Display the tree on the board. Or you might use the family tree on *Teaching Transparency 6-1.*

Procedure Divide the class into two teams. One player from each team chooses a person on the tree that he or she will be. The Team A player announces aloud the person he or she is going to be. The Team B player tells only you who he or she will be.

The Team A player asks the Team B player five questions to find out his or her identity—but never directly uses any names on the tree. (**¿Eres viejo o joven? ¿Tienes hijos? ¿Cuántos hermanos tienes? ¿Eres mi madre? ¿Eres la tía de mi padre?**)

If the Team A player can guess the Team B player's identity in five questions, Team A gets one point. If not, Team B gets one point. During the next round, the teams reverse roles: a Team A player has a secret identity and a Team B player asks the questions.

¿QUIÉN ES?

This game continues to review family terms and incorporates possessive adjectives into the play. It can be played to review material from the **Segundo paso.**

Preparation On the board, display the family tree you made for ¿ERES MI HIJO? You might also write descriptions of some of the persons on the tree.

Procedure Divide the class into teams and call one player from each team to the board. Describe a person on the tree using a string of relationships, never mentioning the name of the person. Start out with simple sentences and gradually make your sentences more complicated. (**Este hombre es viejo... Es el padre del tío de Jaime.**)

The player who identifies the person first gets one point and both players return to their seats. Then call up two more players and describe another person.

UNA PALABRA MÁS

The object of this game is for students to build logically on words and ideas to make complete sentences. The sentences can become odd or funny, but they should be grammatically correct.

Procedure Divide the class into two or more teams. Write one word on the board to begin a sentence (**Mi**). Have a student from another team come up and write a word to continue the sentence (**hermano**). The next team's player should write another word (**tiene**).

Play continues until the sentence is quite long and complicated. Students may add words either before or after previous ones to embellish the sentence. For example, a later student could write **inteligente** between **hermano** and **tiene.** Each time a student adds a word correctly, his or her team gets a point.

¡NO HAY SUJETO!

The object of this game is for students to identify the grammatical subject of a sentence by the context of the other words. It may be used at any time to review the vocabulary of the **Paso** *you are working on.*

Preparation Cut up small slips of paper, one for each student in your class. Write a Spanish sentence on each slip, omitting the subject in each and using the vocabulary of the **Paso** you are working on. For the **Primer paso,** you might write sentences such as **Mi ____ es el hijo de mis abuelos.** Place all the slips in a hat.

Procedure Divide the class into two teams. Have a player from Team A draw a slip, read it aloud, and supply the missing subject. For the example above, the Team A player could say **Mi padre es el hijo de mis abuelos.**

Follow the same procedure with Team B. Have teams alternate turns until each student has had a chance to make a complete sentence. Teams score one point for each sentence they make with a correct subject. The winner is the team with the highest score.

Capítulo 6 Entre familia

pp. 148–173

Using the Chapter Opener

Motivating Activity

Ask students to discuss what they do with their families. (weddings, birthdays, baseball games, etc.) Do members of their families advise each other? Who gives whom advice? Do they mostly solve dilemmas alone or do they seek help from friends and family?

Language Note

① **Jesús** is often used as a first name in Spanish. Some common nicknames for **Jesús** in Spanish-speaking countries are **Chucho** and **Chuy.**

Building on Previous Skills

① Use this photo to review numbers and **tener** and **llamarse,** asking several students to tell the class how many cousins they have and what their names are. (**Tengo tres primos. Se llaman Susan, Bill y Joe.**)

Photo Flash!

① This photo was taken in Mexico City. The three boys are students at the **preparatoria Centro Unión.**

① **Éstos son mis primos, Ramiro y Jesús.**

148 *ciento cuarenta y ocho*

Culture Note

Many Spanish speakers in Miami identify themselves as Cuban Americans, **cubanos,** or Cubans. Others, however, use the broader terms *Hispanic* and *Latino.* These are more general terms used to describe people who speak Spanish as their first language or whose ancestors did.

Many teenagers in the Spanish-speaking world live in large, close-knit families. Child care, parties, music, and meals are some of the many activities shared by all. How would you describe your family?

In this chapter you will learn

- to describe a family
- to describe people; to discuss things a family does together
- to discuss problems and give advice

And you will

- listen to some descriptions of different Spanish-speaking families
- read about some things to do in Miami
- write a description of a family and fill out a questionnaire
- find out what Spanish-speaking teenagers and their families do together

② **Tiene pelo negro y ojos de color café.**

③ **Cuando tienes problemas, debes hablar conmigo.**

Culture Note

• A family with three generations or more is usually termed an *extended family.* In Spanish-speaking countries, **la familia** often includes aunts, uncles, cousins, grandparents, and godparents. The U.S. extended family often includes members who are not biological relatives: stepparents, stepsiblings, step-grandchildren, and so on. In the United States, three generations do not live together as commonly as in Spanish-speaking countries.

• It is very common to see men, particularly older men, wearing berets in some Spanish-speaking countries. It is as much a Spanish tradition as a French one. The beret was originally worn by men in the Basque country in northern Spain and southern France.

Focusing on Outcomes

Refer students to the photos and have them match the outcomes with the photos. (Photo 1 represents describing your family, photo 2 represents describing people, and photo 3 represents discussing problems and giving advice.) Then have students look at these photos and describe the people. Ask some students to describe their family members. Then encourage a discussion about how families have changed and note the many different kinds of families today.

Teaching Suggestion

② Ask students if they can guess what color **ojos de color café** are. They can indicate some students in the class who have them using the correct form of the verb **tener**. (**María tiene ojos de color café.**)

Teacher Note

You may want to use the video to support the objectives. The self-check activities in **A ver si puedo...** on page 172 will help students assess their achievement of the learner outcomes.

Thinking Critically

Comparing and Contrasting
Have students write a short essay telling what it would be like to change places with a parent or sibling. Ask them to be honest and fair in their evaluation.

Photo Flash!

② This young woman is a high school student in Miami. She is the actress playing the role of Anita in the video.

③ This family is from Ciudad Real, although the photo was taken in Madrid. The grandfather is wearing a **boina**, the woolen beret typical of Northern Spain. His grandson and wife are sitting by him on the bench.

VIDEO PROGRAM OR EXPANDED VIDEO PROGRAM, Videocassette 2

OR VIDEODISC PROGRAM *Videodisc 3B*

Video Synopsis

Armando is visiting at Raquel's house and she is describing her family to him. As they look at a photo album, he asks her questions about her family members and she tells him about them and their interests. At the end of the scene, she is describing her dog when they are interrupted by a loud crash.

Motivating Activity

Ask students if they keep a photo album of their friends and families. As an assignment (extra-credit or regular), have them bring in their photo albums and, as they learn the vocabulary, write captions for photos telling who people are, describing them, and telling what they like to do.

Teaching Suggestion

You may want to have students read the comprehension questions in Activity 1, page 152, before viewing the video.

DE ANTEMANO

¿Cómo es tu familia?

Look at the pictures below. What is going on? Who is Raquel talking about with Armando? Does something surprising happen at the end? What could have happened?

Raquel

Armando

Pepe

Éstos son mis padres. Ellos son de Cuba. Les gusta mucho trabajar en el jardín. Mi mamá es muy buena cocinera. Alguna vez debes probar la barbacoa que ella prepara. ¡Es fenomenal!

Éstos son mis hermanos mayores. Y ella es mi hermana menor.

RESOURCES FOR DE ANTEMANO

Textbook Audiocassette 3B/Audio CD 6
Practice and Activity Book, p. 61
Video Guide
- *Video Program*
- *Expanded Video Program, Videocassette 2*

Videodisc Guide
- *Videodisc Program, Videodisc 3B*

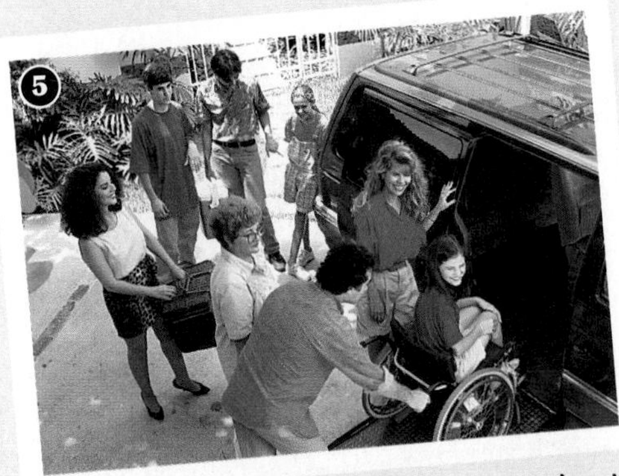

Nosotros hacemos muchas cosas juntos, especialmente los domingos. Primero, vamos a la iglesia. Después, comemos juntos y salimos a alguna parte. En esta foto, salimos al parque.

Aquí estamos en el parque. A mis hermanos les gusta mucho jugar al fútbol americano... y a mí también. Juego con ellos un poco todos los fines de semana.

Comemos de todo: arroz con frijoles negros, maduros, tostones, pollo asado... Ummm, el pollo asado de mi tía Gloria es fenomenal.

Aquí hay una foto de nuestro perro Pepe y de mí.

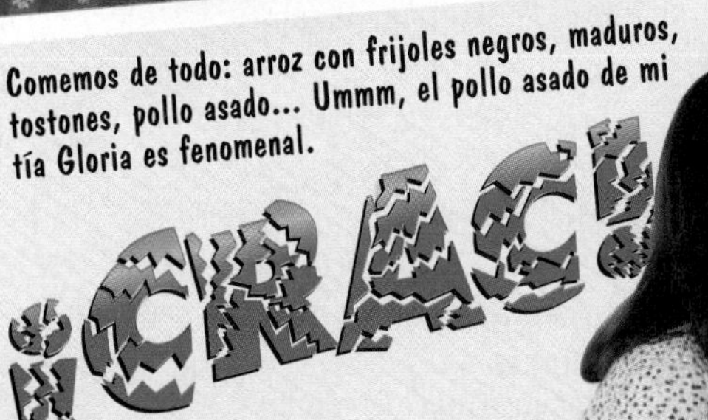

Presentation

Have students look at the **fotonovela.** What do they think is going on in the story? What visual cues help them to make intelligent guesses? Next, play the video. Have students work with a partner to see if they agree about what is happening. Discuss the plot with the whole class, then have them repeat the lines after you or the audio recording. If time permits, ask volunteers to read the lines aloud.

Teaching Suggestion

The reading for this **fotonovela** is relatively easy and students will probably be able to answer the questions without difficulty. Point out how much they are able to understand after having studied Spanish for only a short time.

Additional Practice

After you have presented the **fotonovela,** have students review the learner outcomes listed on page 149. Ask them to identify the phrases in the **fotonovela** that correspond to describing family, and describing people. Discussing problems and giving advice are functions modeled in the continuation of the **fotonovela** on the *Expanded Video Program* and *Videodisc Program.*

Video Integration

- ***Expanded Video Program,*** *Videocassette 2*
- ***Videodisc Program,*** *Videodisc 3B*

You may choose to continue with **¿Cómo es tu familia? (a continuación)** now, or wait until later in the chapter. When the story continues, Raquel discovers that her dog, Pepe, has created a mess. She scolds him, and he disappears. She becomes worried, and friends and family scour the neighborhood helping her look for the dog.

Teaching Suggestion

2 Have students identify the scene that proves or disproves each statement.

For Individual Needs

Visual Learners After the students have read the text and answered the questions, have them close their books and draw a picture of Raquel's family, identifying the members. Then have them open their books and check to see if they have included everyone. Have them add those they have omitted.

Additional Practice

5 Have groups of students who don't usually work together talk about their ideal families. How many share similar opinions? How many envision very different families?

Language Note

Ask students to compare the Spanish word **esposo/a** with the English word *spouse.* (Spanish cognates often have an **e** before **sp** or **st.**) You may also hear **mujer** for **esposa,** as well as **vieja** (*old lady*), a term that is used affectionately in Spanish.

Additional Practice

Have students clip pictures of families from magazines. Ask them to describe the members of the family, identifying them using the expressions Raquel used.

1 ¡Contesta las preguntas!

See answers below.

These questions will help you check your understanding of the **fotonovela.** Don't be afraid to guess if you're not sure of the answer.

1. ¿Dónde están Raquel y Armando?
2. ¿De qué hablan Raquel y Armando?
3. ¿Cómo es la familia de Raquel?
4. ¿Qué hacen juntos Raquel y su familia?
5. ¿Quién es Pepe y cómo es él?

2 ¿Son ciertas o falsas las oraciones?

Based on the story, respond to these statements with **cierto** or **falso**. If a statement is false, correct it. See answers below.

1. Armando y Raquel son hermanos.
2. Una tía de Raquel vive en casa con ella.
3. Raquel y sus hermanos tocan el piano.
4. Toda la familia hace algo los sábados.
5. Pepe es un primo de Raquel.

3 ¿Cómo se dice?

See answers below.

Look through the **fotonovela** and find the words and phrases you would use . . .

1. to ask what someone's family is like
2. to point out your parents in a photo
3. to ask a friend how many people live in his or her house
4. to say that you and a family member go out together on Sundays
5. to say that a friend should try your mom's barbecue

4 Un fin de semana con la familia

d, b, a, c

Con base en la fotonovela, pon las oraciones en orden lógico.

a. Los domingos siempre salimos juntos. A veces vamos al parque.

b. Los sábados mi mamá a veces prepara barbacoa. ¡La barbacoa de mi mamá es fenomenal!

c. Nuestro perro Pepe es muy travieso y por eso no va con nosotros al parque.

d. Los fines de semana hacemos muchas cosas juntos.

5 Y tú, ¿qué piensas? *What do you think?*

Answers will vary.

Completa las oraciones con tus opiniones personales.

1. La familia ideal es...
   a. grande **b.** pequeña **c.** ni *(neither)* grande ni *(nor)* pequeña
2. Las personas en una familia ideal hacen cosas juntas...
   a. a veces **b.** muchas veces **c.** todos los fines de semana
3. La familia ideal es...
   a. unida **b.** independiente **c.** independiente y unida también

Answers

1 1. Raquel and Armando are in the kitchen of Raquel's house.
2. They are talking about her family.
3. Raquel's family is fairly large.
4. Raquel and her family go to church and on picnics, play football, work in the garden, play music and sing.
5. Pepe is Raquel's dog. The dog possibly jumped and knocked something over.

2 1. Falso; Son amigos.
2. Cierto
3. Falso; Tocan la guitarra y la flauta.
4. Falso; los domingos.
5. Falso; Es el perro de Raquel.

3 1. ¿Cómo es tu familia?
2. Estos son mis padres.
3. ¿Cuántas personas viven en tu casa?
4. Salimos a alguna parte juntos los domingos.
5. Debes probar la barbacoa que prepara mi mamá.

4 d., b., a., c.

PRIMER PASO

Describing a family

VOCABULARIO

a. Ésta es la **familia** de Miguel: su **madre**, su **media hermana** *(half sister)* y su **gato**.

b. La familia Pérez es grande. Están aquí **el padre** y su **esposa** *(wife)*, los dos **hijos** y una **hija**, la **abuela** y el **tío** *(uncle)* de los chicos. La **tía** Catalina y el **abuelo** *(grandfather)* no están en la foto.

c. En mi casa hay cuatro personas: mi **medio hermano**, mi madre y yo, y el **esposo** *(husband)* de mamá, Rolando. Es mi **padrastro** *(stepfather)*.

los hermanos	*brothers and sisters*
los hijos	*children*
los abuelos	*grandparents*
la madrastra	*stepmother*
el hermanastro	*stepbrother*
la hermanastra	*stepsister*

d. Soy María. Están aquí mis padres (mi padre y mi madre) y mi **perro** Chuleta.

6 Escuchemos: ¿Quién es quién?

Answers on p. 147C.

Imagine that you're on the phone with the photographer who took the family portraits above. As she describes members of each family, find the picture that matches. If no picture matches, answer **ninguna foto**.

Jump Start!

On the board or on a transparency, write the expressions **Nos gusta... juntos** and **No nos gusta... juntos.** Students write five sentences listing what their families like or do not like to do together.

MOTIVATE

Have students talk about their family, the people with whom they live, or the family members from a popular movie or TV show. List as many words as possible that show family relationships. (mother, father, cousin, aunt, uncle)

TEACH

Presentation

Vocabulario Have students read along in their books as you read aloud the captions for each photo, modeling the new vocabulary. Next have students write a list of the words needed to describe their own family. With a partner, students then compare lists, describing their own family to each other. (**En mi familia hay ... personas. Tengo...**) You may wish to have students describe **la familia ideal** instead. Or you can use the family tree on *Teaching Transparency 6-1* to introduce basic family vocabulary.

Teaching Suggestion

With costumes and props, small groups can create a short skit (of five minutes or less) about a family. Ask them to write the script. For a topic they might use one of the following: going to the movies, visiting the grandparents, a day at the beach, the family vacation.

RESOURCES FOR PRIMER PASO

Textbook Audiocassette 3B/Audio CD 6
Practice and Activity Book, pp. 62–64
Native Speaker Activity Book, pp. 26–30
Video Guide
- *Video Program*
- *Expanded Video Program, Videocassette 2*

Videodisc Guide
- *Videodisc Program, Videodisc 3B*

Chapter Teaching Resources, Book 2
- Additional Listening Activities 6-1, 6-2, p. 69
  Audiocassette 9B/Audio CD 6
- Student Response Forms, pp. 78–80
- Realia 6-1, pp. 73, 74
- Situation Cards 6-1, pp. 76–77
- Teaching Transparency Master 6-1, pp. 65, 68
  Teaching Transparency 6-1
- Quiz 6-1, pp. 81–82
  Audiocassette 7B/Audio CD 6

Presentation

Así se dice Model pronunciation and intonation. Walk around the room and ask several students the questions from **Así se dice.** Assure students that they may give fictitious answers, perhaps describing their **familia ideal.** They might then work in pairs and ask these questions of their partners.

For videodisc application, see *Videodisc Guide.*

Presentation

Nota gramatical First review the singular of possessive adjectives. (—**¿De quién es esta mochila verde? ¿Es mi mochila? —No, profesora. Es la mochila de Raúl. —Raúl, ¿es tu mochila?**) Then model plural examples: **¿De quién es este colegio? ¿Es el colegio de los** (name of rival school's team)? **¡No, no es su colegio! Es nuestro colegio.**)

For Individual Needs

8 Slower Pace Have students refer to the pictures on page 153 and develop questions based on the people shown. You might have them work in pairs and alternate asking and answering questions about the pictures.

ASÍ SE DICE Describing a family

To find out about a friend's family, ask:

¿Cuántas personas hay en tu familia?

¿Cómo es tu familia?

Your friend might answer:

Hay cinco personas **en mi familia.**
Somos cinco.
También **tenemos** un perro.
. . . we have . . .

Nuestra familia es muy grande.
Tenemos muchos **primos**.
. . . cousins.

Somos muy **unidos**.
We're . . . close-knit.

Nota Gramatical

You've been using **mi(s)**, **tu(s)**, and **su(s)**, which are *possessive adjectives.* Here are some others:

nuestro/a(s)	our
vuestro/a(s)	your (when "you" is plural)
su(s)	your (when "you" is plural)
su(s)	their

1. Note that **nuestro** and **vuestro** have a feminine form:
   Nuestra familia es pequeña.
2. Like **mi**, **tu**, and **su**, these forms add an **-s** when they modify a plural noun: **sus primos, nuestros gatos.**

See sample answers below.

8 Una reunión familiar

Your friend doesn't know your family well. Answer her questions using the correct possessive adjectives.

MODELO —¿Quién es ella? ¿Es su tía?
—Sí, es nuestra tía. Se llama Melinda.

1. ¿El chico alto es el primo de ustedes?
2. ¿Es ella la madre de su papá?
3. ¿Los señores son tus tíos?
4. ¿Quiénes son ellas? ¿Son primas de ustedes?
5. Es el novio de su hermana, ¿no?

7 Retrato de familia

Family portrait

Work in pairs. Take the role of one of the people in the family pictures in the **Vocabulario**. Introduce yourself and the other members of your family to your partner.

¿Te acuerdas?

To point out two or more people at a time, use **éstos** and **éstas**.

Additional Vocabulary

Teach your students the word **parientes** and explain that it means *relatives.* Ask students to recall that the Spanish words for *parents* are **padres** and **papás.**

Photo Flash!

Ask students to describe the woman and her dog in the photo. After they have thought of several adjectives to describe them, have them combine two or more adjectives into one sentence.

9 ¿Quién en tu familia es...?

Work in pairs. Ask your partner, **¿Quién en tu familia es...?** using adjectives like those in the box.

guapo moreno bonito alto bajo simpático cómico inteligente rubio

10 Una entrevista

See sample answer below.

Work with a partner. Create six to eight questions about someone's family and take turns interviewing each other. Then, using forms of **nuestro** as needed, work together to write a paragraph telling two or three things you have in common.

NOTA CULTURAL

El compadrazgo is the relationship between parents and godparents of a child. When a man and a woman serve as **padrino** and **madrina** *(godfather* and *godmother)* at a baby's baptism, it's understood that they'll have a special life-long relationship with their godchild, giving love, advice, and even help with education or careers.

11 La familia Manrique

Answers will vary.

In groups of four, look at the drawing of the Manrique family and create a story. Each person in your group should describe a different family member. Include ages, likes and dislikes, pastimes, appearance, and personality. Be prepared to share your story with the class.

The Flying Manrique Family

For Individual Needs

Visual Learners Use the pictures on page 153 or bring in magazine photos. With the photos visible to everyone in the class, ask several students **¿Quién es alto? ¿Quién es cómico?** Students should answer appropriately according to the pictures displayed.

Teaching Suggestions

10 Have students write their paragraphs separately, then consult with a partner on a final version to be turned in.

11 Remind students that the word **nadie** is used alone before the verb to express *no one.* (**Nadie va a la fiesta.**) When **nadie** comes after the verb, the word **no** must be placed before the verb to negate the thought. (**No hay nadie.**)

Native Speakers

Have students create a puppet family. Using the puppets, they can develop a show in Spanish for younger children. It should have enough action to be interesting to children. Tell your students to focus on the repetition of terms, which will enable the children to learn some of the Spanish they are hearing. Your students could perform the show at a local library or other community center.

Answers

10 *Sample answer:*
Nuestras familias tienen mucho en común...

Culture Note

Many Spanish-speaking families select close friends to be godparents for their children. However, close relatives are also frequently chosen. The godfather (**el padrino** or **el compadre**) is often an uncle or brother, while the godmother (**la madrina** or **la comadre**) may be an aunt or sister. Godparents are traditional among Spanish-speaking families in the United States as well as in Spanish-speaking countries.

CLOSE

Refer students to the pictures on page 153. Ask questions using the expressions from this **Paso.** Students should use new vocabulary in their answers. (**¿Cuántas personas hay en la familia Pérez? Hay nueve personas...**) You might ask students to come up with their own questions to ask classmates.

ASSESS

Quiz 6-1, *Chapter Teaching Resources, Book 2,* pp. 81–82

Assessment Items, Audiocassette 7B/Audio CD 6

Performance Assessment

Ask students to develop a dialogue with a partner for presentation to the class. They are to pretend to be new acquaintances and ask each other about their families. They should demonstrate a real interest in each other's family with their questions. Answers should include descriptions of the family members. Remind students that their answers may be about an imaginary family. For additional Performance Assessment ideas, see Situation Cards 6-1.

Cooperative Learning

Have students work in groups of four to create a questionnaire. Each group member prepares two questions about a different family in the photos. (**¿Cuántos hermanos tiene Miguel? ¿Hay una hija en la familia Pérez?**) One person proofreads the questions and another puts them together as a questionnaire. Groups exchange questionnaires and answer their classmates' questions. Each questionnaire is then returned to the group that created it. The two remaining group members in each group check the answers to see if they are correct.

12 Cuestionario sobre la familia

Based on what you see in the questionnaire below, how would you describe this family? The verb **vivir** means *to live.*

1. Ésta es una familia...
2. En la familia, hay...
3. Viven en... con...
4. Probablemente tienen...
5. Les gusta...
6. Cuando tienen problemas...

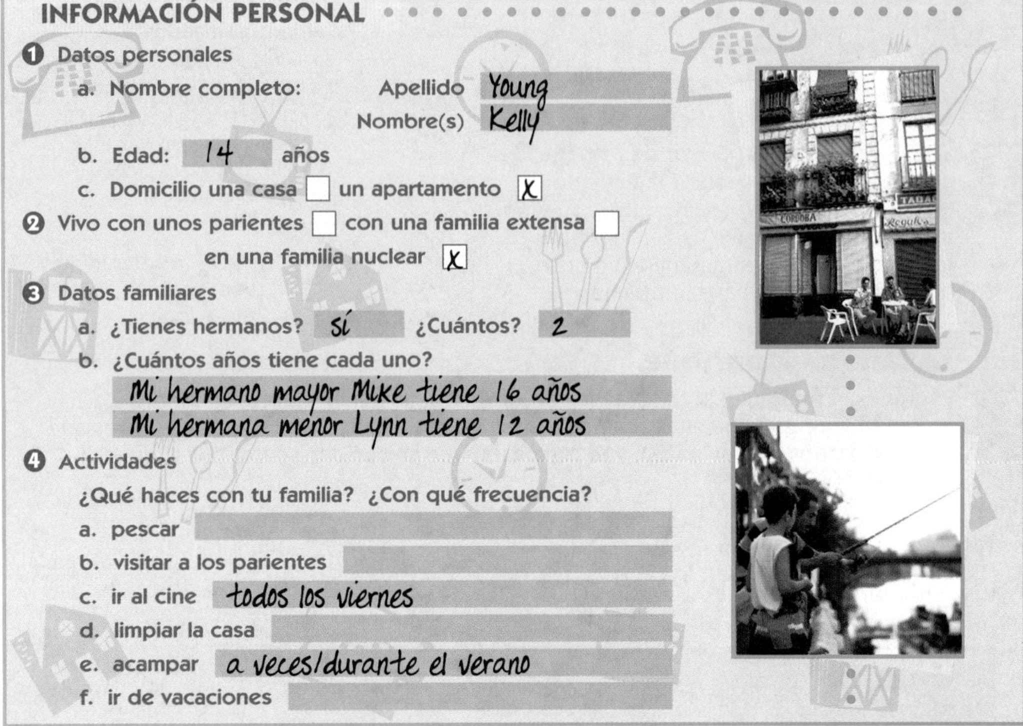

INFORMACIÓN PERSONAL

1. Datos personales
   a. Nombre completo: Apellido *Young* Nombre(s) *Kelly*
   b. Edad: *14* años
   c. Domicilio una casa ☐ un apartamento ☒
2. Vivo con unos parientes ☐ con una familia extensa ☐ en una familia nuclear ☒
3. Datos familiares
   a. ¿Tienes hermanos? *sí* ¿Cuántos? *2*
   b. ¿Cuántos años tiene cada uno?
      Mi hermano mayor Mike tiene 16 años
      Mi hermana menor Lynn tiene 12 años
4. Actividades
   ¿Qué haces con tu familia? ¿Con qué frecuencia?
   a. pescar
   b. visitar a los parientes
   c. ir al cine *todos los viernes*
   d. limpiar la casa
   e. acampar *a veces/durante el verano*
   f. ir de vacaciones

13 Mi familia imaginaria

Create your own questionnaire to find out about another family. Include questions about how people look, what they are like, what their house is like, and whether or not they have any pets.

14 ¿Cómo es tu familia?

First create an imaginary family or think of a TV family you and your partner are familiar with. Using the questionnaire you created in Activity 13, interview your partner about his or her "family," filling in the blanks as you go. Then switch roles. What characteristics do the families have in common?

Un poco más...

el animal doméstico	*pet*
el caballo	*horse*
el conejo	*rabbit*
la culebra	*snake*
el pájaro	*bird*
el pez de colores	*goldfish*
el ratón	*mouse*
la tortuga	*turtle*

Family Link

Have students create a questionnaire about what their family likes to do together. They are to have a member of their family answer it. Tell students that, if they prefer, they can make up answers about an imaginary family. Have students write a short report of their findings in Spanish.

¿Estás bien, hija?

Alison's spending her summer with Mrs. Saralegui and her children Marcela and Cristián in Concepción, Chile. After a busy day, Alison goes to her room to read and relax. Read the dialogues and try to answer the questions that follow.

MARCELA Oye, Alison, ¿no quieres tomar un té con nosotros? Estamos en la sala.
ALISON No, gracias, Marcela. Quiero leer esta novela.

Diez minutos después...

SRA. CECILIA ¿Te sientes mal, hijita? ¿Te hace falta[1] tu familia?
ALISON No. Estoy leyendo, nada más.

Quince minutos después...

CRISTIÁN Alison, ¿qué haces aquí solita? ¿Estás bien?
ALISON Sí, estoy bien. Sólo quiero leer ahora, gracias.

Para discutir...

A. Why do you think everyone assumes that Alison is upset or sick?
B. What do you do when you want to be alone?
C. In small groups, discuss what you think Alison is learning about privacy in Hispanic culture.

Vamos a comprenderlo

The concept of privacy is different in Spanish-speaking countries. People spend less time alone and more time among friends and family. Even though Alison just wants a few moments alone, the Saralegui family is worried that something must be wrong. Checking on her is their way of expressing concern.

1 **¿Te hace falta...?** Do you miss . . .?

Motivating Activity

Encourage a discussion among your students on the topic of privacy. How important is privacy to you? Why is it or isn't it important? When do you feel most strongly the need to be alone?

Presentation

Have students read the interactions between Alison and her host family members. Check comprehension with questions that students may answer with **cierto** or **falso.** (**Alison lee el periódico. Marcela le invita a tomar un té. Sra. Cecilia piensa que Alison se siente mal. Cristián quiere leer una novela también.**) Then have students answer the **Para discutir...** questions. As a class, discuss the content of the **Vamos a comprenderlo** paragraph.

Thinking Critically

Comparing and Contrasting Have students interview several people from three different age groups: teenagers, people their parents' age, and people their grandparents' age. Ask them to prepare several questions to ask each group. (Would you rather live alone or with others? Would you rather go to a movie alone or with others?) Do students' findings indicate that different age groups have different privacy needs? Can they determine what the reasons are for some of the differences? Have students turn in their findings in writing or make a brief presentation to the class.

Answers

12 *Possible answers:*
1. ...pequeña.
2. ...tres hijos.
3. ...un apartamento...
4. ...un gato.
5. ...ir al cine.
6. *Answers will vary.*

Multicultural Link

If library resources are available, have students research the differences in how privacy is regarded in two countries (e.g., Japan and Australia, or England and China). Ask them to include some of the reasons for differences in outlook (e.g., differences in population density, geography, history, or technology).

Jump Start!

Tell students there will be a family reunion with these people present: **madre, padre, hermanos, abuelos, tíos, madrastra.** Have them write four sentences, each one describing a different attendee with at least two adjectives.

MOTIVATE

Ask students if they can think of occasions on which it is important to be able to describe someone's appearance. (to point out people in a crowd, to describe a new classmate)

TEACH

Presentation

Así se dice Point out the use of the definite articles **el, la, los,** and **las** for parts of the body. Model pronunciation and ask students to identify others in the class who have each of the eye and hair colors. (**¿Quién tiene los ojos azules? ¿Quién tiene el pelo negro?**)

Vocabulario Model pronunciation and have students repeat the captions after you. Then have students describe themselves to a partner. Remind them to make the adjective endings agree with the nouns.

For Individual Needs

15 Challenge Ask students to make the improbable statements into probable ones.

Culture Note

Explain to students that **gordo** and **gorda** (or **gordito** and **gordita**) are often used as terms of affection.

SEGUNDO PASO

Describing people; discussing things a family does together

ASÍ SE DICE Describing people

To ask for a description of someone, say:

¿**Cómo es** tu abuelo?

¿**De qué color son los ojos de él?**

¿**De qué color es el pelo?**

Some responses might be:

Él es alto y cariñoso.

Los ojos de él son verdes.
He has green eyes.

Tiene canas.
He has gray hair.

Answers on p. 147 C.

15 Escuchemos: ¿Ciencia ficción?

Listen to the following descriptions of some fictional characters and use **probable** or **improbable** to tell what you think of their appearances.

También se puede decir...
Other words for *brown* are **marrón, castaño,** and **pardo.**

VOCABULARIO

La profesora Fajardo es muy lista. Es pelirroja, delgada y tiene los ojos azules.

Los hijos de Julio son traviesos. Pepe es mayor y Pedro es menor. Julio y sus hijos tienen pelo negro y los ojos de color café.

Los abuelos son muy cariñosos. La abuela es atractiva y un poco gorda. El abuelo es viejo. Tiene canas pero se ve joven.

RESOURCES FOR SEGUNDO PASO

Textbook Audiocassette 3B/Audio CD 6
Practice and Activity Book, pp. 65–67
Native Speaker Activity Book, pp. 26–30
Videodisc Guide
Videodisc Program, Videodisc 3B

Chapter Teaching Resources, Book 2
- Communicative Activity 6-1, pp. 61–62
- Additional Listening Activities 6-3, 6-4, p. 70
  Audiocassette 9B/Audio CD 6
- Student Response Forms, pp. 78–80
- Realia 6-1, pp. 73–74
- Situation Cards 6-2, pp. 76–77
- Teaching Transparency Master 6-2, pp. 66, 68
  Teaching Transparency 6-2
- Quiz 6-2, pp. 83–84
  Audiocassette 7B/Audio CD 6

16 Escuchemos: ¿Cómo son tus amigos?

Answers on p. 147C.

Listen as Rogelio describes some people and his cat to his Aunt Maki. Identify each character by name. Does Maki know one of them especially well?

Rebeca

Simón y Quique

Gabriel y Conchita

David

Maki

17 Los amigos de Rogelio

Answers will vary.

Write a description of each character in Activity 16, including hair and eye color, and how old each one probably is. Use some of the new words in the **Vocabulario** on page 158.

18 Una entrevista...

Work with a partner and interview each other about three of your relatives or characters in a TV series. Include at least one adult and at least one teenager. Describe each person as fully as possible and tell where he or she lives, works, and some things that person does. Be prepared to tell the class about one of the people you learned about.

Un poco más...

egoísta	*selfish*
leal	*loyal*
perezoso	*lazy*
trabajador	*hard-working*

What do you think these words mean?

agresivo	**generoso**
atlético	**independiente**
artístico	**responsable**
creativo	**romántico**
desorganizado	**tímido**

19 Adivina... ¿quién es?

Work in groups of three. Each pick a famous person and describe him or her in two to five sentences to the group. Your partners must guess who the person is you're describing.

20 Así soy yo.

See sample answer below.

Imagine that you're going to spend the next school year in Spain. Write a description of yourself for the agency that places students with host families. What do you look like? What things do you especially like or dislike? Make your description as detailed as you can. Be prepared to share your description with the class.

Answers

20 *Sample answer:*
Soy morena y baja. Tengo pelo y ojos de color café. Tengo 15 años y soy delgada. Soy tímida. También soy inteligente, trabajadora y responsable. Me gusta leer y viajar.

Teaching Suggestion

Students work in small groups to create a short skit based on the following situation: A hit-and-run driver has just left the scene of an accident. Fortunately, several witnesses got a good look at the driver. A police officer has just arrived and is taking their descriptions.

TPR To review colors and body parts, each student will need a group of items in various colors to move (small pieces of colored paper or crayons). Have students respond to simple commands in Spanish, such as: **Pongan el azul en el pelo.** Move into more complicated directions, such as **Si tienes el pelo castaño, pon el color verde en la silla,** or **Si tienes los ojos azules, pon el color negro en el suelo.** You may wish to have students peer-correct.

For Individual Needs

16 Slower Pace Have students orally describe the people in the illustrations before listening to the recording.

19 Visual Learners Display photos of several well-known personalities cut from magazines. Have a student describe one of the people in the photos. The other students guess which person is being described.

For videodisc application, see *Videodisc Guide.*

20 Auditory Learners Read several of the students' descriptions of themselves aloud and see if the class can guess who is being described. You may want to ask students in advance for permission to read their description to the class.

For Individual Needs

Kinesthetic Learners Work in groups of four or five. Using the **Vocabulario** and the words from **Un poco más,** ask each group to select at least five of the adjectives and think how they might mime them for the class. Ask each student to mime one of their words and ask the rest of the class to guess what the word is.

Presentation

Así se dice Ask several students, one by one, **¿Qué hacen Uds. los fines de semana?** Tell them you are referring to their family or friends and that they should answer in the first person plural, using the expressions in **Así se dice.** Then ask students to practice the questions and answers with a partner. Ask them to reverse roles so they can practice both the questions and the answers. Walk around the room and check comprehension and pronunciation.

Nota gramatical Explain the forms of **hacer** and **salir** in Spanish as follows: "Los verbos **hacer** y **salir** son regulares en el tiempo presente excepto en la forma **yo.** En esta forma la terminación es **-go.**"

Photo Flash!

Ask students to describe the people in the photo. To review you might also ask **¿Dónde están? ¿Qué tiempo hace? ¿Qué compran?**

For Individual Needs

21 Visual Learners Have students work in pairs. One partner describes one of the people in the photos. The other student guesses which person he or she is describing. Students should take turns describing and guessing.

ASÍ SE DICE Discussing things a family does together

To find out what a family does together, ask:

¿Qué hacen ustedes los fines de semana?
What do you do . . . ?

¿Hacen ustedes **algo** durante el verano?
. . . something . . .

Some responses might be:

Salimos juntos y **visitamos a** nuestros abuelos. **Casi siempre cenamos** con ellos los domingos.
We go out . . . we visit . . .
Almost always we eat dinner . . .

Sí. Siempre **hacemos un viaje.**
. . . we take a trip.

Caracas, Venezuela

Nota Gramatical

Hacer *(to do, make)* and **salir** *(to go out)* are regular verbs in the present tense except in the **yo** form, which has an irregular **-go** ending.

hago	hacemos	**salgo**	salimos
haces	hacéis	sales	salís
hace	hacen	sale	salen

21 Escuchemos: Con la familia

Answers on p. 147C.

Listen as four friends discuss what they do with their families and friends. Match the description you hear with the correct photo.

a. b. c. d.

Additional Practice

Assign students to bring in a picture of a family. (photo, clipped from a magazine, or hand-drawn) Have students describe the family to a partner, without showing her or him the picture. The partner is to draw the family described, asking questions to find out as many details as possible. They should find out each person's appearance, personality, age, and so forth. When the drawing is done, students compare their pictures and then reverse roles.

22 ¿Qué haces cuando sales?

Escribe un párrafo sobre lo que haces cuando sales. Utiliza las siguientes preguntas como guía.

1. ¿Sales los fines de semana?
2. ¿Qué te gusta hacer cuando sales?
3. ¿Con quién o con quiénes sales?
4. ¿Qué haces cuando sales con tus amigos?
5. ¿Qué te gusta hacer cuando sales con tu familia?
6. Si no sales mucho, ¿qué haces?

Nota Gramatical

When a person receives the action of a verb, a "personal **a**" is used before the direct object. If the direct object is a place or thing, no "**a**" is used.

Visito **a** mis tíos en Guatemala todos los veranos. Cuando estoy con ellos, siempre visitamos las ruinas mayas.

23 Visitas

See answers below.

Completa las siguientes oraciones con la **a personal**. Algunas oraciones no necesitan nada.

1. Visitamos ____ nuestros primos tres veces por mes.
2. Mario va a visitar ____ el Museo de Antropología con su hermana.
3. Llamo ____ mis abuelos todos los domingos.
4. Voy a visitar ____ mis amigos en Colorado este verano.
5. Paula quiere conocer ____ unos nuevos amigos este año.
6. Miro ____ la televisión por la noche con mi familia.

24 ¿Con qué frecuencia?

Use some of the following questions to interview a partner about his or her family, or about an imaginary family. Switch roles after four or five questions and be prepared to report your findings to the class.

1. ¿Dónde vives? ¿Quiénes viven contigo?
2. ¿Sales con tu familia los fines de semana? ¿Adónde van y qué hacen?
3. ¿Con quién vas a un centro comercial? ¿Cómo se llama el centro?
4. ¿Con qué frecuencia visitas a (tus abuelos, tus primos...)?
5. ¿A tu familia le gusta acampar, bucear o hacer esquí acuático?

¡Nos gusta bucear!

Sugerencia

Make your Spanish real by connecting what you learn in class to people or events in your life. For example, as you're learning how to describe families, imagine talking to someone you know about his or her family. That person might be a new friend or even a co-worker at your job. What kinds of questions would you want to ask? If you were living with a family in Venezuela, what do you think they'd like to know about your family in the United States?

For Individual Needs

22 Slower Pace In pairs, one student asks the other one or two of the questions. The second student answers them. Then have them switch roles before proceeding to more items.

Presentation

Nota gramatical Model the use of the personal **a** by using various people and objects in sentences. (**Veo la pizarra. También veo a Patricia.**) Then ask several students **¿Qué ves?** and point to an object or a person in the classroom. The student will answer by saying **Veo** ____ or **Veo a** ____.

Additional Practice

24 Teach the words for street (**la calle**), avenue (**la avenida**), and boulevard (**el paseo**) so that students will be able to give their addresses when asked **¿Dónde vives?** Teach them to say the street name first and then the number. (**Vivo en la calle Real número 254.**)

Portfolio

24 Oral Your students may wish to audiotape this interview for their Portfolio. For Portfolio suggestions, see *Assessment Guide,* p. 19.

Answers

23
1. a
2. nada
3. a
4. a
5. a
6. nada

Culture Note

The **a personal** is sometimes used with animals if they're treated as pets. (**Veo a mi perra Loli en las flores.**)

Additional Practice

25 Have students plan a trip to a city where they have friends or relatives. Ask them to indicate people and places they'd like to visit.

For Individual Needs

25 Challenge Have students tell what activities they will do at the places they visit and who will be with them.

Thinking Critically

26 Drawing Inferences Ask students to explain why they believe the expressions **la chica sándwich** and **el chico sándwich** are used.

CLOSE

Use *Teaching Transparency 6-2* to review descriptive adjectives and terms presented in the **Paso**. Ask students questions and elicit appropriate answers with these terms.

ASSESS

Quiz 6-2, *Chapter Teaching Resources, Book 2,* pp. 83–84

Assessment Items, Audiocassette 7B/Audio CD 6

Performance Assessment

Ask each student to develop a set of interview questions to find out about someone's family and what they like to do. You might set up your classroom like a TV talk show. Ask students to serve as host or hostess to interview someone in the class using their list of questions. Students should be sure to use questions and expressions from **Así se dice** on pages 158 and 160. For additional Performance Assessment ideas, see Situation Cards 6-2.

25 Una excursión

Answers will vary.

You and your family are planning a trip to Miami. Combine phrases from each box to make a list of people and places you want to visit. Use the personal **a** as needed.

MODELO Yo quiero visitar a un primo en Hialeah.

yo mis padres mi hermano/a todos nosotros mis abuelos	la piscina de Venecia mis tíos en Coral Gables los museos históricos nuestros primos una amiga de la familia

26 La chica sándwich

Together with a partner, read the descriptions of **la hermana mayor, la chica sándwich,** and **la hermana menor**. Imagine that you're one of the three pictured and describe yourself to your partner. See if your partner can guess if you're the oldest, the youngest, or the middle child in the family.

TRES HERMANAS, TRES PERSONALIDADES

Retrato de "La mayor": Madura, responsable. Nadie tiene que decirle que estudie; saca muy buenas notas. Siempre está presentable. Se puede abrir su closet sin miedo de ser sepultada en vida.

Retrato de "la chica sándwich": Es el polo opuesto de sus hermanas, pero ¿es ésta su verdadera personalidad o nada contra la corriente? Más conocida como "La chica camaleón".

Retrato de "baby de la familia": Es simpática, alegre, el alma de la fiesta. ¿Responsabilidad? Y eso... ¿con qué se come? De todas formas, todos la adoran. Pero ¡qué insoportable!

27 Un conflicto

See sample answer below.

Write a dialogue with six to nine sentences between a parent and a teenage son or daughter. The parent wants to do more things with the teenager as a family. The teenager feels that they already do too many things together. For example, will the teenager go with his or her parent to visit relatives this weekend, or go to the mall with friends? Follow these steps:

a. The parent asks to do something with the teenager.
b. The teenager objects, and tells what he or she really wants to do.
c. The parent says they never do things together.
d. The teenager says it's not true, and points out something they often do together.
e. Now create an ending! What do they end up doing?

Answers

27 *Sample answers:*

1. ¿Por qué no hacemos algo juntos este fin de semana?
2. Ay, no, papá. Pienso ir a la playa con mis amigos el sábado.
3. Pero hija, nunca pasamos tiempo juntos.
4. No es verdad, papi. Visitamos a nuestros primos casi todos los meses.

5–9. *Answers will vary.*

¿Cuántas personas hay en tu familia?

In this chapter, we asked some people about their families and what they do to help around the house.

Pablo
Quito, Ecuador
"En mi familia hay cinco personas. Mi mamá, mi papá y mis dos hermanas. Yo lavo los platos, limpio la cocina,... arreglo mi cuarto y limpio mi baño".

Arantxa
Madrid, España
"Somos cinco... Tengo dos hermanos menores... Cuando se van mis padres, me quedo con ellos en casa... Tengo que ayudar en casa... Ayudo a mi madre a recoger la casa".

Brenda
San Antonio, Texas
"Yo vivo en una familia de cinco... mi mamá es... muy protectiva... mi hermana es muy rebelde... mi hermano es como niño chiquito... y mi papá es... muy bueno... Mi hermano no hace muchas cosas; la que hace más soy yo, porque mi mamá va al trabajo todos los días y viene cansada. Soy yo, como soy la más grande de los niños, yo los cuido, hago los trastes *(dishes)*, trapeo *(mop)*".

Para pensar y hablar...

A. What responsibilities do you have? Are they similar to those mentioned above?

B. Many Hispanic families are large and close-knit. Family members spend a lot of time together and depend on each other for support. What advantages could this type of family offer?

Preguntas

1. ¿Quiénes tienen que cuidar a sus hermanos menores? (Arantxa y Brenda)
2. ¿Cuántos chicos limpian sus cuartos? (uno)
3. ¿Quién hace la mayoría del trabajo en la casa de Brenda? (Brenda)
4. ¿Qué hace Pablo que tú también hace en casa? (*Answers will vary.*)
5. ¿Qué chico tiene una familia como tu familia? ¿Por qué? (*Answers will vary.*)

Culture Note

Day-care centers are not as popular in South America as they are in the United States. South Americans usually don't feel comfortable leaving their children with a stranger—they'd much prefer to leave them with a relative or a servant. This is often possible, because grandparents often live close by and can baby-sit for working parents.

Video Program or Expanded Video Program, Videocassette 2

or Videodisc Program, *Videodisc 3B*

Teacher Notes

- See *Video Guide* and *Videodisc Guide* for activities related to the **Panorama cultural.**
- Remind students that the information in the **Panorama cultural** may be included in the Quizzes and Chapter Test.

Motivating Activity

Ask students what sorts of things they enjoy doing with their families. Would they like to spend more or less time with their families? Why? Would they like to spend more time with their grandparents if they could? Why or why not?

Presentation

Have students look at the map and photos and then read the captions. Next show the video. You might turn the **Para pensar y hablar** section into a written assignment one page in length. Have students compare and contrast their families' degree of interdependence. Ask them how much they identify with the people in the interviews. You may prefer to have them discuss the ideal family or a typical family if the issues seem too personal for your students.

Jump Start!

On the board or a transparency write the following scrambled expressions: 1. **ecahr nu jeavi** 2. **tarivis a ols obeausl** and 3. **rlias raap reocm.** Ask students to unscramble them to find three things they might do with their families. (1. **hacer un viaje** 2. **visitar a los abuelos** 3. **salir para comer**)

Motivate

Ask students to think of examples of advice they might give to their family and friends. Ask them to share some of those things they already know how to say in Spanish.

Presentation

Así se dice Read the problem and question from column one and have a student reply with the advice in column two. Repeat this two or three times. Then ask students to practice the new expressions in pairs, using a new problem and new advice.

Nota gramatical Explain **deber** in Spanish as follows: "El verbo **deber** es un verbo regular que termina en **-er.**" **Se usa con el infinitivo: Debemos hablar español en clase.** Have students list five things they should do that day. They should work in pairs and compare lists. Ask one student **¿Qué debes hacer hoy?** He or she should reply **Debo** ____. Then ask **¿Qué deben hacer Uds.?** to the other partner. He or she should answer with **Nosotros debemos** ____.

TERCER PASO

Discussing problems and giving advice

ASÍ SE DICE Discussing problems and giving advice

To discuss a problem, say:

Tengo un problema. El profesor **dice que** hablo **demasiado** en clase, pero **no es cierto.**
. . . says that . . . too much . . .

¿Qué debo hacer?
What should I do?

Your friend might answer:

Debes hablar **menos** en clase y escuchar más.
You should . . . less . . .

Nota Gramatical

The verb **deber** *(should, ought to)* is a regular **-er** verb.

debo	debemos
debes	debéis
debe	deben

Answers on p. 147D.

28 Escuchemos: Los problemas de Mónica

Listen as Mónica describes her family. Then match the pictures below to the correct description you hear. One of the people she describes isn't pictured. Who is it?

1. Mónica 2. su mamá 3. su hermana menor 4. su tía

a.

b.

c.

29 ¿Qué deben hacer?

Sample answers below.

With a partner, look at the pictures above of Mónica's family. First state the problem or situation and say what Mónica, her mother, and her younger sister should do. Then create an original solution for each problem. Be prepared to present your ideas to the class.

MODELO —La madre de Mónica trabaja demasiado. Debe trabajar menos y descansar un poco más.

Resources for TERCER PASO

Textbook Audiocassette 3B/Audio CD 6
Practice and Activity Book, pp. 68–70
Native Speaker Activity Book, pp. 26–30
Videodisc Guide
Videodisc Program, Videodisc 3B

Chapter Teaching Resources, Book 2
- Communicative Activity 6-2, pp. 63–64
- Additional Listening Activities 6-5, 6-6, p. 71
  Audiocassette 9B/Audio CD 6
- Student Response Forms, pp. 78–80
- Realia 6-2, pp. 73, 74
- Situation Cards 6-3, pp. 76–77
- Teaching Transparency Master 6-3, pp. 67, 68
  Teaching Transparency 6-3
- Quiz 6-3, pp. 85–86
  Audiocassette 7B/Audio CD 6

VOCABULARIO

¿Qué debes hacer en casa?

cortar el césped

trabajar en el jardín

hacer la cama

limpiar la cocina

pasar la aspiradora en la sala

poner la mesa

cuidar al gato

planchar

30 Los quehaceres domésticos

Household chores See answers below.

Ramón's mother is calling to see how he and his brother and sister are coming with the housecleaning. Complete their conversation with the appropriate forms of verbs from the box. Not all of the verbs will be used.

MAMÁ Hola, mi hijo. Todavía estoy en el trabajo y tus tíos __1__ con nosotros a las ocho. Ustedes __2__ limpiar todo.

RAMÓN Bueno, mamá, no te preocupes. Paco __3__ la aspiradora en la sala, Laura y José __4__ los platos y yo __5__ la mesa.

MAMÁ ¡Perfecto! Y yo les __6__ algo delicioso.

Nota Gramatical

On page 160, you learned the verbs **hacer** and **salir**. The verb **poner** *(to put, to place)* is similar in that it has **-go** in the **yo** form.

Pongo la mesa todos los días. Mi hermanita nunca la **pone**.

cenar pasar lavar sacar
deber preparar poner

Presentation

Vocabulario Model the vocabulary by telling the class which member of your family does or doesn't need to do each of the chores listed. Then ask students what they have to do at home. (**¿Quién debe cortar el césped?**)

Nota gramatical Write the paradigms of **hacer** and **salir** vertically on the board. Add the forms of **poner** as you use them in sentences. (**En mi casa, nunca pongo la mesa. ¿Pones la mesa en tu casa?**) Model pronunciation and then elicit sentences with forms of **poner** from students.

For videodisc application, see *Videodisc Guide.*

Additional Practice

30 Ask several students **¿Cómo ayudas en casa con los quehaceres?** Students answer **Debo...** After you have modeled the question for students, have students ask each other.

Group Work

Divide students into groups of three. Have them role-play a situation in which one student is a parent telling the children what should be done at home. The children agree to do it and tell the parent when they'll do it. Encourage students to use the time expressions they have already learned in their answers.

Answers

30 1. cenan
2. deben
3. pasa
4. lavan
5. pongo
6. preparo

Language Note

Point out to your students that in addition to the meanings *should* and *ought to,* **deber** also means *to owe.*

Additional Practice

32 Have students assign chores to people in their house, according to what members of their family like to do. (**Mi hermano debe lavar los platos porque come mucho.**)

For Individual Needs

34 Challenge Have students, working in groups come up with five chores they think are common. Then have groups survey other groups to determine which chore is the most common among them.

Additional Practice

35 (page 167) Tell students you are **el sabio** or **la sabia** (*the wise one*). Offer to help them with any problem they wish to tell you, as long as it's not real. Provide them with a suitable answer. After you have modeled this several times, have a student take your place as **el sabio** or **la sabia.**

31 ¿Qué pasa aquí? See answers below.

Look at these drawings and tell what these people should or should not be doing. Be prepared to share your pieces of advice with the class.

Pablo

Diana y Lola

Federico

Miguelito

Frida

32 ¡Todo bajo control! See answers below.

Assign everyone below a chore from the **Vocabulario** list on page 165. Try to assign each person the chore he or she likes. Some people may have more than one job.

1. A ti y a tu hermana menor les gustan los animales.
2. A tus abuelitos les gustan las plantas.
3. A tu primo le gusta pasar un rato con tus hermanos.
4. A tu hermano mayor le gusta preparar la cena.
5. A mí me gusta la ropa limpia *(clean)*.
6. A ti te gusta estar afuera *(outside)* y te gustan las máquinas *(machines)*.

33 Querida Amalia See answers below.

Complete this letter to Amalia by filling in the blanks with the correct forms of the words from the word box.

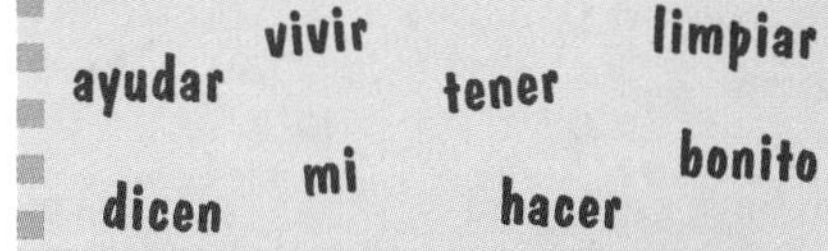

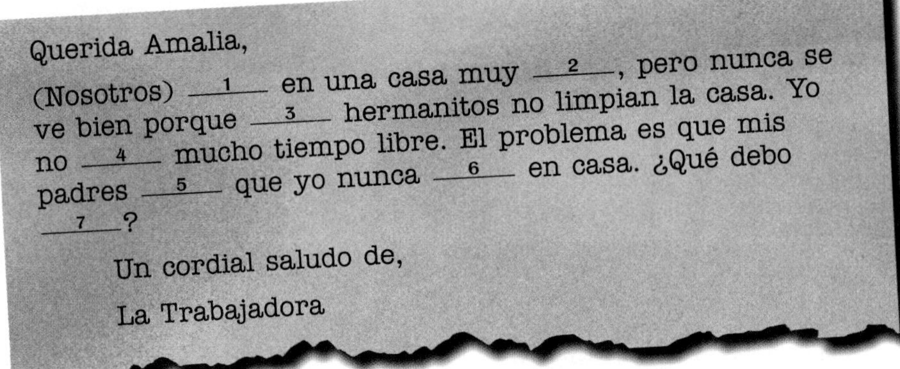

Querida Amalia,

(Nosotros) __1__ en una casa muy __2__, pero nunca se ve bien porque __3__ hermanitos no limpian la casa. Yo no __4__ mucho tiempo libre. El problema es que mis padres __5__ que yo nunca __6__ en casa. ¿Qué debo __7__?

Un cordial saludo de,

La Trabajadora

34 ¡Una encuesta!

Take a survey of five classmates. Ask them what chores they do around the house. Using **dice que**..., write five sentences reporting what your classmates say. Be prepared to share your survey with the class.

Answers

31 *Answers may vary.*

a. Pablo debe poner la mesa, no la cama.
b. Diana y Lola deben trabajar en el jardín, no en la sala.
c. Federico no debe pasar la aspiradora en el jardín sino en la casa.
d. Miguelito debe sacar la basura, no poner la basura en el ropero.
e. Frida debe darle de comer a un animal, no a la planta.

32 *Answers may vary.*

1. Mi hermana menor y yo cuidamos al perro.
2. Mis abuelos trabajan en el jardín.
3. Mi primo cuida a mis hermanitos.
4. Mi hermano mayor limpia la cocina y prepara la cena.
5. Yo limpio la ropa.
6. Tú cortas el césped.

35 Los consejos *Advice* See sample answer below.

With a partner, take the role of Amalia and answer the letter from **La Trabajadora** in Activity 33. Use **Debes...** and **Necesitas...** with the verbs you know. Be prepared to present your solutions to the class.

36 Problemas y más problemas

In small groups, get together and write a letter to an advice columnist. Your letter could be about housework, schoolwork, jobs, or friends. For additional vocabulary, see page 341. Exchange letters with another group and answer their letter.

A LO NUESTRO

Spanish-speakers often use special words when they are talking to someone they like a lot. These are called diminutives. For example, you could call your friend Juan, **Juanito,** or your friend Rosa, **Rosita**. You could call your grandmother **abuelita** and your father **papi**. Some other words adults often use to refer to people they care about are **mi cielo** or **mi vida** *(darling* or *dear)*. **Mi hijo/a** doesn't necessarily refer to an actual son or daughter, but to a young person the speaker is very fond of.

37 En mi cuaderno

Write a description of two friends or family members from a TV series. Include their ages, where they live, and what they're like. Next, describe any problems they may have, such as household chores they don't like doing, or problems they have at work or school. Finally, give them some advice about what to do. Write at least ten sentences in your journal.

LETRA Y SONIDO

A. The **r** in Spanish does not sound like the *r* in English. English does have a sound that is similar, however. It's the sound made by quickly touching the tip of the tongue to the ridge behind the upper teeth, as in bu*tt*er, ba*tt*er, la*dd*er.

1. The **r** is pronounced this way between vowels.
   cariñoso **cara** **moreno** **favorito** **pero**
2. At the beginning of a word or after an **n** or **l**, the single **r** has a trilled or rolled sound.
   rojo **rubio** **enrojecer** **Enrique** **alrededor**
3. The double **r** in Spanish always has a trilled or rolled sound.
   pelirrojo **perro** **carro** **correo**

B. **Dictado** Script on p. 147D.
Listen to a TV ad that features a famous athlete, Rafael Ramírez. Write what you hear.

C. **Trabalenguas**
La rata roe la ropa del Rey de Roma.

En mi cuaderno

37 For an additional journal entry suggestion for Chapter 6, see *Practice and Activity Book,* p. 150.

For Individual Needs

Auditory Learners Ask students to record the words in the **Letra y sonido.** This is to practice using **r** and **rr.** They should also record themselves reading the **trabalenguas.** Ask pairs to listen to each other's recording and check each other's pronunciation.

Close

To review material from this **Paso,** write common problems on slips of paper. (**Tengo mucho tarea..., No me gusta la comida en la cafetería.**) Place the slips in a bag, a **bolsa de problemas.** Have each student draw a slip of paper and write some helpful advice to solve the problem.

Assess

Quiz 6-3, *Chapter Teaching Resources, Book 2,* pp. 85–86

Assessment items, Audiocassette 7B/Audio CD 6

Performance Assessment

Ask students to create a note from a parent that lists at least five things a child should do around the house on a Saturday. For additional Performance Assessment ideas, see Situation Cards 6-3.

Answers

34
1. vivimos
2. bonita
3. mis
4. tengo
5. dicen
6. ayudo
7. hacer

35 *Sample answer:*
Querida Trabajadora,
Necesitas hablar con tu mamá sobre el problema. Ella puede hablar con tus hermanitos. Ellos pueden limpiar sus cuartos y poner sus juguetes en su lugar. Tú debes limpiar tu cuarto y ayudar en la cocina.
Buena suerte,
Amalia

READING STRATEGY
Using pictures, titles, and subtitles to determine the organization of a passage

Motivating Activity
Have students skim the reading spread to find words they already know. (**parque, restaurante, chino, baile, frutas...**)

PREREADING
Activity A

Building on Previous Skills
After students have skimmed for the answers to **¡A comenzar!** you might review vocabulary by asking **¿Te gusta la comida china? ¿Te gustan los restaurantes chinos? ¿Te gusta probar comida nueva? ¿Les gusta bailar? ¿Dónde bailan Uds.?**

Native Speakers
Ask native speakers to discuss traditional customs that their family or friends practice. Ask them if they know how these traditions began.

VAMOS A LEER

Cinco cosas curiosas para hacer en la Pequeña Habana

Estrategia
Before beginning to read, use the pictures, title, and subtitles to get a feeling for how the passage is organized. Knowing how the passage is organized will help you figure out what it's about. It can also help you hunt quickly through the passage to find a specific piece of information.

¡A comenzar!

A. This reading is from the **Guía oficial de la Pequeña Habana**, a guide for tourists in Miami. Skim it for one minute to find out which of these items are among the five suggestions.
- (•) buying fruit
- (•) watching a cultural dance
- walking tours
- (•) playing dominoes
- (•) going to clubs
- visiting museums
- (•) eating Chinese-Cuban food

Al grano

B. You have already studied two important ways to guess the meanings of words: using cognates and using context. Now you can combine these two skills to read more effectively.

Cognates. See if the unknown word looks like any English word. Does the English meaning you know make sense in context?

Jugar dominó en el Parque del Dominó

Éste es un espectáculo que no tiene igual en todo los Estados Unidos. Los hombres se reúnen alrededor de las mesas de dominó y ajedrez para jugar. Colgado del techo los vigila un aviso que dice: "No se permiten escándalos". Aquí los hombres (no hay mujeres) juegan sin hablar casi. No se permite hablar ni de política. Sólo se interrumpe el juego para ir al cafetín de al lado y comprarse un guarapo o un fuerte café cubano.

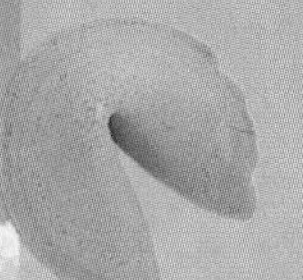

Ir a un restaurante chino-cubano y probar sus platos

Durante el siglo diecinueve muchos chinos llegaron a Cuba como esclavos y añadieron un sabor oriental a la cultura cubana. Sus descendientes mantuvieron las tradiciones culinarias chinas, y aquí en la Pequeña Habana se mantienen vivas en numerosos restaurantes.

Language Note
The expression **No se permiten escándalos** means that no loud noise or commotion is allowed.

Culture Note
Flamenco is an essential part of many Spanish-speaking cultures. It originated in 18th-century Spain in the southern region of Andalucía. At one time its sad songs of oppression and romance were looked down upon. Today, however, flamenco is very popular thoughout the Spanish-speaking world.

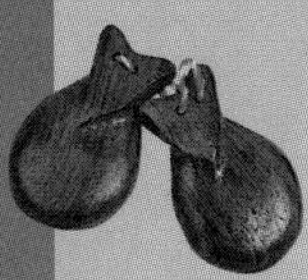

Ver un baile flamenco

Además de un baile, el flamenco es una expresión artística de pasión y rebeldía. Es un homenaje a la forma y movimientos del cuerpo humano. Tradicional en España, el flamenco es un espectáculo que se presenta diariamente en fabulosos restaurantes de la Pequeña Habana, como el Málaga.

Cabarets y discotecas

En un barrio donde predomina el español se encuentran los mejores clubes nocturnos de salsa, ritmo tropical y baladas. En lugares como "La Tranquera" se presentan artistas latinos de renombre.

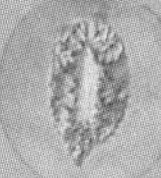

Comprar diferentes variedades de frutas

Abundan mangos, papayas, mamey, coco, plátanos, bananas, naranjas, toronjas en diferentes tiendas y paradores.

Context. Look at all the words before and after the word you want to guess. Understanding the rest of the sentence will help you guess what the unknown word means.

C. Your family needs help reading the guide. Listed here are the words they're having trouble with. For each person the first two words are cognates. The third word you can guess through context. After you guess the meaning of a word, go back and make sure your guess makes sense in the rest of the sentence.

1. Your brother might like to try a game of dominoes. Help him with these words:
   igual, **política**

   cafetín (**a.** caffeine **b.** game **(c.)** café)
2. Your mother is reading about the Chinese-Cuban restaurants, and these words are giving her trouble:
   culinarias, **numerosos**

   probar (**a.** break **b.** prepare **(c.)** taste)
3. Your sister is deciding between watching a **flamenco** dance and going dancing.
   pasión, **movimientos**

   barrio (**a.** bar **b.** language **(c.)** neighborhood)
4. You have decided to buy some fruit. Decide what these words mean:
   variedades, **coco**

   paradores (**(a.)** roadside stands **b.** walls **c.** parades)

D. En español, escribe una lista de cinco cosas interesantes que puedes *(you can)* hacer en el lugar donde tú vives. Después, discute tus ideas con un compañero o una compañera.

Community Link

Ask students what fruits are grown in their area and which are imported from other parts of the country. (**¿Qué frutas son de aquí y qué frutas son de otras partes del país?**) Ask them to interview a local grocer to find out what fruits are imported, and from which areas.

READING
Activities B and C

Have students do Activity B as individual work. If needed, this may be assigned as homework. Emphasize the importance of testing a word in context, even if the word is a cognate. For example, many students may want to guess that **política** means *political,* but an adjective does not fit in the context of the sentence. Also, some students may guess that **coco** is *cacao,* which is not a fruit and wouldn't make sense in context. Other words you may want your students to guess: **espectáculo, escándalos, siglo, esclavos, sabor, rebeldía, homenaje, diariamente, baladas.**

POSTREADING
Activity D

If your students have difficulty with the instructions to Activity C, go over the directions with them. The task itself may be challenging to some students, so you may choose to assign pairs so that one of each pair is able to help the other, if needed.

Group Work

As a longer project, have students construct a bulletin board about interesting things to do in your community. First, as a class, decide on five locations to highlight. Then assign students to groups and a location to each group. Each group prepares the Spanish description of a location and brings in photographs. You might display the bulletin board in the hall for other students and faculty to see.

Teacher Note

For additional readings, see *Native Speaker Activity Book,* pp. 26–30, and *Practice and Activity Book,* p. 71.

The **Repaso** reviews and integrates all four skills and culture in preparation for the Chapter Test.

Teaching Suggestions

2 Have students clip comic strips from the newspaper and cover the speech bubbles. Exchanging comics, students can then use Spanish to describe a problem and tell what should be done.

4 Remind students that they may discuss imaginary families or situations. Encourage them to be creative and talk about situations they've learned about.

Portfolio

5 Oral You might have students work in groups to create a dialogue for their one-act comedy. They might then perform their work for the class and record it for their oral Portfolio. For Portfolio information, see *Assessment Guide,* pp. 2–13.

REPASO

1 First read the statements below about Marcos and his family. Then listen as Marcos describes his family in detail. Decide which family member matches each numbered item below.

1. Debe comer menos.
2. Trabaja demasiado.
3. Lee muchas novelas.
4. Tiene un cuarto muy organizado.
5. Le gusta tocar la guitarra.
6. No estudia mucho.

Answers on p. 147D.

2 With a partner, look at the four pictures of these kids and their pets. For each, create what each person says. Use adjectives to describe the problem and use **deber** to tell what should be done.
See possible answers below.

Sebastián

Carlota

Nacho y Duquesa

Cervantes

3 Create a dialogue in which Raquel and Armando talk about what they do with their families on the weekend. Then get together with a partner and role-play your dialogues.

4 Using **deber** + infinitive, list the household chores these people should do. See sample answer below.

1. yo
2. mi hermano menor
3. mi padre
4. mi hermana mayor
5. mi abuela
6. mi madre

5 Your drama class is going to write a one-act comedy about a large family. Your task is to describe the cast of characters. Tell how many there are, where they live, their names, ages, and what each one looks like.

MODELO La abuela se llama Rosa. Ella es muy simpática. Tiene canas y tiene los ojos de color café. A ella le gusta...

Answers

2 *Possible answers:*
a. Sebastián no debe comer mucho.
b. La chica debe comprar una casa más grande para la Carlota.
c. Nacho y Duquesa deben jugar en el jardín, no en la casa.
d. Cervantes no debe leer el libro.

4 *Sample answers:*
1. Yo debo cortar el césped.
2. Mi hermano menor debe limpiar su cuarto.
3. Mi padre debe sacar la basura.
4. Mi hermana mayor debe cuidar al gato.
5. Mi abuela debe poner la mesa.
6. Mi madre debe pasar la aspiradora.

6 Imagine that you're going to study in Mexico next year and you've just received a letter from your host sister Carolina. Complete her letter by filling in the correct form of the verbs in the box. See answers below.

hacer	limpiar	cortar	vivir
visitar a		caminar	
ayudar	pasar	salir	sacar

¡Hola!

Me llamo Carolina. Mi familia y yo __1__ en Cuernavaca. Mi casa es grande. Por eso los sábados todos __2__ en casa. Primero todos nosotros hacemos las camas. Luego mi padre __3__ el césped. Mi mamá __4__ la aspiradora. Mi hermano __5__ la basura, y yo __6__ mi cuarto. Mi cuarto es muy desorganizado. Pero no sólo trabajamos. Por ejemplo, todos los sábados nosotros __7__ mis abuelos. Después, nosotros __8__ en el parque. Los sábados por la noche yo __9__ con amigos. Y en verano, siempre __10__ un viaje.

Recuerdos,
Carolina

7 Laura, Carolina's cousin, is coming to spend the year with you and your family. Write a letter to her and tell her about your family and one or two of your friends. Include a description of the people you mention, as well as what you do with your family. Ask Laura some questions about her family, too. Answers will vary.

8 Responde a las siguientes oraciones con **cierto** o **falso**. Corrige las oraciones falsas. Basa tus respuestas en las **Notas culturales**, el **Panorama cultural** y el **Encuentro cultural** de este capítulo. See answers below.

1. El compadrazgo ya no existe en Latinoamérica.
2. El concepto de la privacidad es diferente en la cultura hispana.
3. La familia nuclear es el ideal de muchos hispanohablantes.
4. La relación que existe entre una persona y sus padrinos termina *(ends)* cuando el niño tiene veintiún años.
5. En las familias hispanohablantes es menos común *(common)* pasar el tiempo solo.

9 SITUACIÓN

a. You've just arrived at your host family's house in Bolivia. Your host introduces the family to you, and then asks about your family. With a partner, role-play the situation. Be sure to include all your family members, a description of each one, and what you and your family like to do together.

b. You're going to have a party at your house on Saturday night. Five of your friends volunteer to help you get the house ready for the party. Tell each of them what he or she should do.

Answers

6
1. vivimos
2. ayudamos
3. corta
4. pasa
5. saca
6. limpio
7. visitamos a
8. caminamos
9. salgo
10. hacemos

8
1. Falso; El compadrazgo existe en Latinoamérica.
2. Cierto
3. Cierto
4. Falso; La relación que existe entre una persona y sus padrinos nunca termina.
5. Cierto

Portfolio

7 Written Your students may wish to enclose their letter to Laura as an addition to their Portfolio. For Portfolio suggestions, see *Assessment Guide,* p. 19.

Video Wrap-Up

- *VIDEO PROGRAM*
- *EXPANDED VIDEO PROGRAM, Videocassette 2*
- *VIDEODISC PROGRAM, Videodisc 3B*

At this time, you might want to use the video resources for additional review and enrichment. See *Video Guide* or *Videodisc Guide* for suggestions regarding the following:

- **¿Cómo es tu familia?** (Dramatic episode)
- **Panorama cultural** (Interviews)
- **Video clips** (Authentic footage)

This page is intended to help students prepare for the Chapter Test. It is designed for the students to work on their own initiative and consists of a brief checklist of the major points covered in the chapter. The students should be reminded that it is only a checklist and does not necessarily include everything that will appear on the Chapter Test.

A VER SI PUEDO . . .

Can you describe a family? p. 154

1 Can you tell Ramiro, a new student at your school, . . .? Answers will vary.
1. how many people there are in your family
2. how many brothers and sisters you have
3. what the names of your family members are
4. what they like to do in their free time

2 Can you complete each sentence with the correct family member?
1. La mamá de mi papá es mi ______. abuela
2. El hermano de mi mamá es mi ______. tío
3. La hija de mi tía es mi ______. prima
4. La hija de mis padres es mi ______. hermana
5. El hijo de mi padrastro es mi ______. hermanastro

Can you describe what people look like? p. 158

3 Describe these members of Florencia's family. See answers below.

mi abuelo

mi mamá

mi hermano, Toño

mi hermano, Óscar

Can you discuss things a family does together? p. 160

4 Write one or two sentences about each member of your family or an imaginary family. Include age, physical description, job, where they live, and what you do with them. See sample answer below.

Can you discuss problems and give advice? p. 164

5 Paula and her family need help solving these problems. What should each person do? See answers below.
1. Her sister is disorganized and can't find any of her things.
2. Paula's brother works all the time and he's very tired.
3. It's six o'clock in the evening and everyone's hungry.
4. Paula's sister is in trouble at school because she talks too much in class.

Answers

3 a. Su abuelo tiene canas. Es viejo y delgado y es muy cariñoso.
b. Su mamá tiene pelo negro y lleva anteojos.
c. Toño tiene pelo negro y ojos de color café. Es cómico.
d. Óscar es moreno. Tiene pelo castaño y es travieso.

4 *Sample answer:*
Mi hermano tiene veinte años. Es alto y delgado con pelo rubio. Trabaja en una oficina. Como nosotros vivimos cerca de un parque, los fines de semana jugamos juntos allí.

5 *Answers may vary.*
1. Debe limpiar su cuarto.
2. No debe trabajar todo el tiempo.
3. Deben preparar la cena.
4. Debe estudiar más y hablar menos en clase.

VOCABULARIO

PRIMER PASO

Describing a family

la abuela *grandmother*
el abuelo *grandfather*
los abuelos *grandparents*
la esposa *wife, spouse*
el esposo *husband, spouse*
éstas *these (feminine)*
éstos *these (masculine and feminine)*
la familia *family*
el gato *cat*
la hermana *sister*
la hermanastra *stepsister*
el hermanastro *stepbrother*
el hermano *brother*
los hermanos *brothers, brothers and sisters*
la hija *daughter*
el hijo *son*
los hijos *children*
la madrastra *stepmother*
la madre/mamá *mother/mom*
media hermana *half-sister*
medio hermano *half-brother*
mi/mis *my*
nuestro/a *our*
el padrastro *stepfather*
el padre/papá *father/dad*
los padres *parents*
la prima *female cousin*
el primo *male cousin*
su/sus *his, her, their, your (formal)*
la tía *aunt*
el tío *uncle*
tu/tus *your (familiar)*
unido/a *close-knit*
vivir *to live*
vuestro/a *your (pl. Spain)*

SEGUNDO PASO

Describing people

azul *blue*
cariñoso/a *affectionate*
de color café *brown*
¿De qué color es/son . . .? *What color is/are . . .?*
delgado/a *thin*
listo/a *clever, smart*
mayor *older*
menor *younger*
negro/a *black*
los ojos *eyes*
pelirrojo/a *redheaded*
el pelo *hair*
se ve joven *he/she looks young*
Tiene canas. *He/She has gray hair.*
travieso/a *mischievous*
un poco gordo/a *a little overweight*
verde *green*
viejo/a *old*

Discussing things a family does together

algo *something*
casi siempre *almost always*
cenar *to eat dinner*
hacer un viaje *take a trip*
salir *to go out, to leave*
visitar *to visit*

TERCER PASO

Discussing problems and giving advice

cortar el césped *to cut the grass*
cuidar al gato *to take care of the cat*
deber *should, ought to*
demasiado *too much*
dice que *he/she says that*
hacer la cama *to make the bed*
limpiar la cocina *to clean the kitchen*
menos *less*
No es cierto. *It isn't true.*
pasar la aspiradora *to vacuum*
planchar *to iron*
poner la mesa *to set the table*
un problema *a problem*
la sala *living room*
trabajar en el jardín *to work in the garden*

Teaching Suggestions

- To review the vocabulary in the **Primer paso,** you might wish to use the family tree on *Teaching Transparency 6-1* and ask students to identify the relationships.
- To review the vocabulary from each **Paso,** use pictures from magazines. Give groups one or two pictures each to describe. After they finish, groups can exchange pictures and describe the new ones. This can be repeated until they have described all the pictures.

Game

Béisbol is a board game for groups to review vocabulary or usage. For each group (1) prepare questions or cues like flashcards, (2) draw a baseball diamond on a sheet of paper, (3) bring a single die. To play, groups form two teams. The first player up draws a card. If the player answers correctly, he or she gets to roll the die. One is a single hit, two a double, three a triple, four a homerun, five a strikeout, and six a double play or (if this isn't possible) an out. Score is kept as in baseball.

Chapter 6 Assessment

Chapter Test

- *Chapter Teaching Resources, Book 2*, pp. 87-92
- *Assessment Guide, Speaking Test,* p. 30
- *Assessment Items, Audiocassette 7B Audio CD 6*

Test Generator, Chapter 6

Alternative Assessment

Performance Assessment

You might want to use the **Situación** (p. 171) as a cumulative performance assessment activity.

Portfolio Assessment

- **Written: Repaso** Activity 7, *Pupil's Edition,* p. 171
  Assessment Guide, p. 19
- **Oral:** Activity 22, *Pupil's Edition,* p. 161
  Assessment Guide, p. 19

Mid-term Exam

- *Assessment Guide,* pp. 35–48
- *Assessment Items, Audiocassette 7B/Audio CD 6*

LOCATION OPENER
CHAPTERS
7, 8

¡Ven conmigo a Ecuador! pp. 174–227

EXPANDED VIDEO PROGRAM, *Videocassette 3*

OR *VIDEODISC PROGRAM, Videodisc 4A*

Motivating Activity

Ask students what they think it would be like to live on the equator. Do they imagine a physical border dividing the northern and southern hemispheres? Ask if any students have ever been to a country in the southern hemisphere and give them the opportunity to tell the class what it was like.

Background Information

Quito is the capital and second largest city of the Republic of Ecuador. Set in the Quito Basin at the foot of the volcano Pichincha, at an altitude of 9,350 feet, Quito is the second highest major city in Latin America. It is also the oldest capital city in South America.

History Link

Quito was the ancient seat of the kingdom of Quitu, named after the people who lived here before the Spanish arrived in 1534. Between the 11th century and 1487, it was united with the Inca Empire. Quito remained the focal point of national affairs—political, social, and economic—from the 16th century until the early 20th century when economic dominance shifted to Guayaquil.

CAPÍTULOS 7 y 8

¡Ven conmigo a Ecuador!

Quito, la hermosa capital de Ecuador

Culture Note

Ecuador is divided into three regions with distinct cultures. The Coastal Lowland (**la Costa**) is made up primarily of descendants of African slaves brought over in previous centuries. The Andes Highland (**la Sierra**) is populated by many indigenous groups including Otavalos, Salasacas, and descendants of the Puruhá. The Eastern Lowland (**el Oriente**), which covers almost half the country, is composed primarily of indigenous Jívaro.

Language Notes

- The name **Ecuador** comes from the Spanish word for *equator.*
- Idigenous people make up nearly one-third of Ecuador's population. There are ten different native ethnic groups, each with its own language or dialect. Spanish is widely spoken by all Ecuadoreans, and Quechua is spoken by many indegenous people.

Ecuador

Islas Galápagos
el ecuador global
COLOMBIA
Otavalo
el ecuador global
Quito
Océano Pacífico
E C U A D O R
Guayaquil
Cuenca
La Cordillera de los Andes
PERÚ
N
0 50 Kilómetros
0 25 Millas

Población: 10.933.000

Área: 109.483 millas cuadradas (283.561 km^2), tamaño del estado de Colorado

Ubicación: En el noroeste de Sudamérica, con Colombia al norte, el Perú al sur y al este, y el océano Pacífico al oeste

Capital: Quito, con una población de 1.500.000

Gobierno: república federal

Industrias: comestibles, productos de madera, tejidos

Cosechas principales: plátanos, café, arroz, azúcar, maíz

Minerales: aceite, cobre, hierro, plomo, plata, azufre

Unidad monetaria: el sucre

Idiomas: español (lengua oficial), quechua, quichua

ciento setenta y cinco 175

LOCATION OPENER

CHAPTERS 7, 8

Using the Almanac and Map

Terms in the Almanac

- **Gobierno:** Ecuador has been an independent republic since 1822. The people elect a president to one four-year term, and the president appoints a 16-member cabinet. A 72-member Chamber of Representatives is the country's lawmaking body.
- **Industrias: comestibles** *food products,* **productos de madera** *wood products,* **tejidos** *fabrics*
- **Minerales: petróleo** *oil,* **cobre** *copper,* **hierro** *iron,* **plomo** *lead,* **plata** *silver,* **azufre** *sulphur*
- The **sucre** is Ecuador's currency, named after Antonio José de Sucre, who liberated Quito from Spain in the Battle of Pichincha.
- **Quechua:** The language of the former Inca empire. It is now widely spoken throughout the Andes highlands from southern Colombia to Chile.

Using the Map

- Ask students to identify the two countries that border Ecuador. (Peru and Colombia)
- Ask students to point out the equator. Do they know what general characteristics equatorial countries have? (Most equatorial lowlands have heavy rains and average temperatures over 68°F.)
- Have students locate the Andes (**la Cordillera de los Andes**). You may want to point out that they are the world's longest mountain chain. They stretch over 4,500 miles from Cape Horn at the tip of South America to Panama. Only the Himalayas of northern India and Tibet have higher peaks than the Andes.

Geography Link

Placed precisely at 0° latitude, the monument known as **La Mitad del Mundo** (*Middle of the World*) is located 15 miles north of Quito. It was at this location that an 18th century French expedition made the first scientific measurements of the equator, a 24,000-mile-long imaginary line encircling the globe and dividing the northern and southern hemispheres. A four-inch-wide strip of white pebbles marks the ground where the equator crosses the monument site. Many tourists have their photographs taken with one leg in each hemisphere. Have students use the map on pp. xxii–xxiii to point out other countries located on the equator. (Colombia, Brazil, Gabon, Congo, Zaire, Uganda, Kenya, Somalia, Indonesia)

LOCATION OPENER
CHAPTERS
7, 8

Motivating Activity

Ask students if they have ever seen a 500-lb. tortoise, a 4-ft. iguana, or a blue-footed booby bird. Have students describe the strangest animal that they have ever seen or that they have ever heard about.

Using the Photo Essay

① Many Ecuadoreans consider Cuenca to be the country's most beautiful city. Its colonial architecture stands aside new construction that usually has a neocolonial style to complement the old. There are no skyscrapers to obscure the view of the surrounding mountains. Instead, the three domes of the Catedral Nueva dominate the skyline. Construction on the Catedral Nueva began in 1880.

② The Galapagos archipelago (**el Archipiélago de Colón**) is located in the Pacific Ocean some 570 miles west of the coast of Ecuador. It consists of 13 major islands, six small islands and 42 islets that are barely more than large rocks. All are of volcanic origin and total more than 30,000 square miles in area. In 1959, the Galapagos were declared a national park, and human settlement was restricted to areas that had already been developed. A Marine Resources Reserve was created in 1986 covering 19,300 square miles. Both the park and reserve are designed to protect the islands and to encourage scientific research. The islands are home to 58 bird species, various types of iguanas and lizards, several species of giant tortoises, sea lions, dolphins, penguins, and many other forms of wildlife.

ECUADOR

*Ecuador is one of three Andean republics in which almost half the population is indigenous, the other two being Peru and Bolivia. The Andean mountain chain divides Ecuador into three very different geological regions—the coastal plain or **Costa**, the mountains or **Sierra**, and the eastern Amazonian jungle or **Oriente**. Ecuador's fourth geological region, the famous Galápagos archipelago, lies 570 miles off the coast in the Pacific Ocean.*

① **Ecuador's colonial architecture is famous worldwide, and some newer structures reflect the desire for architectural unity. Construction of the neo-Gothic *Catedral Nueva* in Cuenca began in 1880 and was halted in 1967. The blue cupolas of the cathedral overlook Cuenca's main square.**

② **The volcanic Galápagos Islands were declared a National Park in 1959. The islands are home to an extraordinary range of birds (58 resident species) and some very uncommon animals, such as the black marine iguana and the giant tortoise.**

176 *ciento setenta y seis*

Language Note

The word **galápago** means *giant tortoise* and refers primarily to the species *Geochelone elephantopus* found on the island.

Biology Link

Group your students with students from a biology class to research an animal that is found on the Galapagos Islands. Have them pretend they are working to protect this animal. Have them make a persuasive poster that encourages the animal's protection.

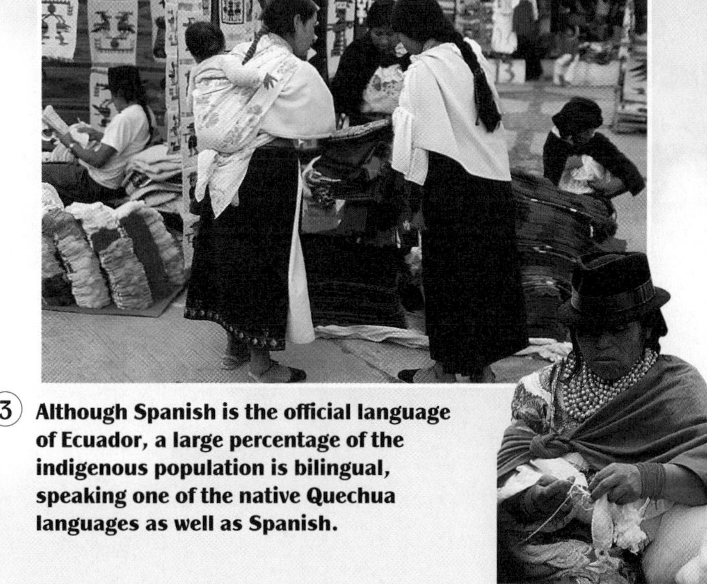

(3) **Although Spanish is the official language of Ecuador, a large percentage of the indigenous population is bilingual, speaking one of the native Quechua languages as well as Spanish.**

In Chapters 7 and 8, you'll meet Pablo, Diego, and Cristina, three friends living in Quito, Ecuador. The name "Ecuador" comes from the equator, which crosses the country. Ecuador is rich in natural resources and is proud of its culture. Quito, its capital, is a beautiful city steeped in thousands of years of cultural tradition, from long before the Incas to the present.

(4) **The fertile volcanic soil of the Ecuadorean *Sierra* has been farmed for centuries. Agricultural products native to the Andes include the potato and protein-rich quinoa.**

(5) **Traditional Andean music reflects Ecuador's rich cultural heritage: pre-Hispanic instruments such as the flute-like *quena* and drums blend harmoniously with the stringed instruments brought by the Spaniards.**

LOCATION OPENER

CHAPTERS 7, 8

(3) There are many native ethnic groups in Ecuador, each of which considers itself a distinct nationality with its own language and culture. The most numerous **indígenas** are the Quechuas who live mainly in the mountains of the Sierra. Among most groups are many **mestizos** (mix of European and indigenous races) and **sambos** (mix of african and indigenous races).

Culture Note

Women of Otavalo wear skirt wraps called **anakus** and shoulder wraps called **fachalinas** that are made of handspun wool or cotton. The clothing of Otavalo closely resembles that of the Incas.

(4) The Andes are formed by three parallel chains, or **cordilleras:** the eastern, central, and western ranges that divide the country into the costal region, the mountain region (the Sierra), and the east. Andean families live in a rugged environment. The land is rarely flat, so the Andean farmer must use creativity and horticultural knowledge handed down by his ancestors to terrace and cultivate the steep mountain slopes.

(5) Traditional instruments of the highlands included the following: flutes (**flautas**), panpipes (**rondadores**), conch shells (**conchas**), and various percussion instruments (**instrumentos de percusión**).

Flute-like instruments used today include the **quena,** a notched bamboo recorder, and a smaller flute called a **pingullu,** which has three or four holes. Probably the most characteristic Andean instrument is the **charango,** a five-string guitar that is about two feet long. Its body is sometimes made of wood, but is more often made from an armadillo shell.

Music Link

If possible, play a recording of Andean music. You may want to use the recording provided on *Audiocassette 11.* Have students guess what instruments they hear. You may want to present the musical instrument vocabulary before playing the recording.

Additional Vocabulary

arpa criolla *Andean harp*
bandolín *mandolin*
campana *bell*
bombo *drum*
maraca *gourd rattle*

Capítulo 7: ¿Qué te gustaría hacer?

Chapter Overview

De antemano pp. 180–182	**¿Qué hacemos?**	*Practice and Activity Book*, p. 73	*Video Guide* OR *Videodisc Guide*	
	FUNCTIONS	**GRAMMAR**	**CULTURE**	**RE-ENTRY**
Primer paso pp. 183–187	• Talking on the telephone, p. 183 • Extending and accepting invitations, p. 184	**e** to **ie** stem-changing verbs, p. 185	• Common telephone expressions, p. 183 • **Agenda,** p. 187	• Invitations: **gustar** • Days of the week
Segundo paso pp. 188–192	• Making plans, p. 188 • Talking about getting ready, p. 190	• **Pensar** + infinitive and **ir** + **a** + infinitive, p. 188 • Reflexive verbs, p. 190	• **Nota cultural,** Getting around without a car, p. 189 • **Panorama cultural, ¿Qué haces para conocer a una persona?,** p. 192	• Future expressions: **hoy, mañana,** etc. • Expressions of frequency: **todos los días, a veces,** etc.
Tercer paso pp. 193–195	Turning down an invitation and making an excuse, p. 193	Expressions with **tener,** p. 194	• **Tira cómica,** p. 193 • Party invitation, p. 195	The verb **tener**

Letra y sonido p. 195 — Pronouncing the letters **y** and **l** and **ll** — **Dictado:** *Textbook Audiocassette 4A/Audio CD 7*

Vamos a leer pp. 196–197 — **Caleidoscopio** — **Reading Strategy:** Previewing a text

Review pp. 198–201 — **Repaso,** pp. 198–199 — **A ver si puedo...,** p. 200 — **Vocabulario,** p. 201

Assessment Options

Quizzes
- *Chapter Teaching Resources, Book 2*
  Primer paso, Quiz 7-1, pp. 139–140
  Segundo paso, Quiz 7-2, pp. 141–142
  Tercer paso, Quiz 7-3, pp. 143–144
- *Assessment Items, Audiocassette 8A/Audio CD 7*

Chapter Test
- *Chapter Teaching Resources, Book 2*, pp. 145–150
- *Assessment Guide*, Speaking Test, p. 31
- *Assessment Items, Audiocassette 8A/Audio CD 7*

Test Generator, Chapter 7

RESOURCES: Print	RESOURCES: Audiovisual
Video Program OR *Expanded Video Program, Videocassette 3* OR *Videodisc Program, Videodisc 4A*	*Textbook Audiocassette 4A/Audio CD 7*
	Textbook Audiocassette 4A/Audio CD 7
Practice and Activity Book, pp. 74–76	
Native Speaker Activity Book, pp. 31–36	
Chapter Teaching Resources, Book 2	
• Additional Listening Activities 7-1, 7-2, p. 127	*Additional Listening Activities, Audiocassette 10A/Audio CD 7*
• Student Response Forms, pp.136–138	
• Realia 7-1, pp. 131, 132	
• Situation Cards 7-1, pp. 134, 135	
• Teaching Transparency Master 7-1, pp. 123, 126	*Teaching Transparency 7-1*
• Quiz 7-1, pp. 139–140	*Assessment Items, Audiocassette 8A/Audio CD 7*
Videodisc Guide	*Videodisc Program, Videodisc 4A*
	Textbook Audiocassette 4A/Audio CD 7
Practice and Activity Book, pp. 77–79	
Native Speaker Activity Book, pp. 31–36	
Chapter Teaching Resources, Book 2	
• Communicative Activity 7-1, pp. 119, 120	
• Additional Listening Activities 7-3, 7-4, p. 128	*Additional Listening Activities, Audiocassette 10A/Audio CD 7*
• Student Response Forms, pp.136–138	
• Realia 7-1, pp. 131, 132	
• Situation Cards 7-2, pp. 134, 135	
• Teaching Transparency Master 7-2, pp. 124, 126	*Teaching Transparency 7-2*
• Quiz 7-2, pp. 141–142	*Assessment Items, Audiocassette 8A/Audio CD 7*
Video Guide	*Video Program* OR *Expanded Video Program, Videocassette 3*
Videodisc Guide	*Videodisc Program, Videodisc 4A*
	Textbook Audiocassette 4A/Audio CD 7
Practice and Activity Book, pp. 80–82	
Native Speaker Activity Book, pp. 31–36	
Chapter Teaching Resources, Book 2	
• Communicative Activity 7-2, pp. 121, 122	
• Additional Listening Activities 7-5, 7-6, p. 129	*Additional Listening Activities, Audiocassette 10A/Audio CD 7*
• Student Response Forms, pp.136–138	
• Realia 7-2, p. 131, 132	
• Situation Cards 7-3, pp. 134, 135	
• Teaching Transparency Master 7-3, pp. 125, 126	*Teaching Transparency 7-3*
• Quiz 7-3, pp. 143–144	*Assessment Items, Audiocassette 8A/Audio CD 7*
Videodisc Guide	*Videodisc Program, Videodisc 4A*
Video Guide	*Video Program* OR *Expanded Video Program, Videocassette 3*
Videodisc Guide	*Videodisc Program, Videodisc 4A*

Alternative Assessment

- Performance Assessment
  Primer paso, p. 187
  Segundo paso, p. 191
  Tercer paso, p. 195
- Portfolio Assessment
  Written: **Repaso** Activity 4, *Pupil's Edition*, p. 198
  Assessment Guide, p. 20
  Oral: **Repaso** Activity 1, *Pupil's Edition*, p. 198
  Assessment Guide, p. 20

Capítulo 7: ¿Qué te gustaría hacer?

Textbook Listening Activities Scripts

For Student Response Forms, see *Chapter Teaching Resources, Book 2,* pp. 136–138.

Primer paso

Activity 6, p. 183

1. — Aló.
   — Buenas tardes, señorita. ¿Está Miguel, por favor?
   — Sí, un momento. ¿De parte, por favor?
   — De parte de Roberto.
2. — Bueno, Silvia. Ya es tarde y necesito estudiar para el examen.
   — Está bien. Hasta mañana, ¿eh?
   — Sí, hasta mañana Silvia. Chao.
3. — Bueno, Casa García a sus órdenes.
   — Buenos días. ¿Está el señor Alejandro García, por favor?
   — Lo siento mucho, pero el señor no está. ¿Quién habla?
   — Soy Pedro Castillo.
4. — Aló. Colegio La Salle.
   — Buenos días, señorita. ¿Está el señor Medina, por favor?
   — Un momento, por favor. ¿Quién habla?
   — Soy la doctora Isabel Martínez.
   — Gracias.
   — Lo siento pero la línea está ocupada.
5. — Bueno.
   — Buenas noches, señora. ¿Está María en casa?
   — ¿Eres tú, Alicia?
   — Sí, señora. ¿Cómo está usted?
   — Bien, gracias, pero María no está en casa.
   — Bueno, señora, llamo más tarde.
   — Adiós.

Answers to Activity 6

1. greeting someone
2. saying goodbye
3. unable to reach the person
4. unable to reach the person
5. greeting someone and unable to reach the person

Activity 9, p. 184

1. ¿Quieres jugar al tenis esta tarde?
2. ¿Quieres ir a cenar esta noche?
3. ¿Te gustaría ir al centro conmigo?
4. ¿Te gustaría estudiar con nosotras?
5. ¿Prefieres ir a la piscina el sábado?
6. ¿Prefieres la comida mexicana o la comida china?
7. ¿Te gustaría ir al cine conmigo esta tarde?

Answers to Activity 9

1. sí 2. no 3. sí 4. sí 5. no 6. sí 7. sí

Activity 12, p. 186

MÓNICA Oye, Carlos, ¿quieres hacer algo?

CARLOS Claro que sí, Mónica.

MÓNICA ¿Qué prefieres hacer — ir al circo o ir al parque de atracciones?

CARLOS Eh... no sé. Quiero ver la exhibición en el museo de antropología. ¿Quieres ir conmigo?

MÓNICA Ay, Carlos, no me gustan los museos. Tengo otra idea. Hace buen tiempo hoy, ¿verdad? ¿Te gustaría ir al lago o al campo?

CARLOS Prefiero ir al lago porque me gusta nadar.

MÓNICA A mí también. Entonces, vamos a las diez y media, ¿no?

Answer to Activity 12

Deciden ir al lago.

Segundo paso

Activity 19, p. 190

1. MAMÁ Manuel, aquí viene el autobús.
   MANUEL ¡Ay, no! Mamá, todavía necesito lavarme los dientes.
   MAMÁ Pues, ¡apúrate, hijo!
2. MAMÁ Gabi, ya son las ocho. Vas con tu novio a la fiesta de cumpleaños de Miguel a las ocho y media, ¿no? ¿Estás lista?
   GABI No, mamá. Estoy un poco atrasada. Necesito maquillarme.
3. MAMÁ Armando, ¿estás listo para ir al circo con tus primos?
   ARMANDO Sí...
   MAMÁ Pero hijo, tu pelo es un desastre.
   ARMANDO Ah, tienes razón, Mamá. Necesito peinarme.
4. MAMÁ ¿Estás listo, querido? Tenemos que estar en el teatro en media hora.
   PAPÁ Lo siento, mi amor. Todavía necesito afeitarme.
   MAMÁ Está bien, pero apúrate, por favor.
5. MAMÁ Berta, hoy es la boda de tu amiga Verónica, ¿verdad?
   BERTA Sí, mamá. A las tres. Hombre, son las dos y todavía necesito ducharme.

Answers to Activity 19

1. d 2. e 3. a 4. c 5. b

Tercer paso

Activity 23, p. 193

1. — Hola, Miguel. ¿Te gustaría ir con nosotros al partido de fútbol esta noche?
   — Lo siento, pero tengo que estudiar.
2. — Hola, Gabriela. Este fin de semana vamos al lago. ¿Te gustaría ir con nosotros?
   — ¡Qué lástima! Ya tengo planes para este fin de semana.
3. — Oye, Roberto, ¿te gustaría cenar con nosotros esta noche?
   —¿Esta noche? Ay, tengo una cita esta noche.
4. — Mariana, ¿te gustaría tomar un refresco esta tarde?
   — Estoy un poco cansada. Tal vez otro día, ¿eh?

Answers to Activity 23
1. c 2. b 3. a 4. d

Letra y sonido, p. 195

For the scripts for Parts A and C, see page 195. The script for Part B is below.

B. Dictado, p. 195

¡Qué lástima! Lupita y Yolanda quieren ir al lago el lunes, pero ya tengo planes con Lorena. Yo no voy allí con ellas.

Repaso

Activity 3, p. 198

1. ¿Te gustaría ir al cine esta noche?
2. ¿Quieres ir al museo el sábado?
3. ¿Te gustaría mirar la televisión?
4. ¿Quieres cenar en mi casa esta noche?
5. ¿Quieres ir a la librería para comprar unos cuadernos?
6. ¿Te gustaría ir al partido de fútbol el domingo?

Possible answers to Repaso Activity 3
1. No, gracias. Tengo una cita.
2. Sí, cómo no. Me gusta mucho la exposición de arte en el museo.
3. No, gracias. Tal vez otro día.
4. Lo siento pero no puedo cenar en tu casa esta noche. Tengo un examen mañana y necesito estudiar.
5. Sí. Vamos a la librería. Necesito comprar unos libros.
6. ¡Qué lástima! Ya tengo planes de ir a la casa de mis abuelos con la familia.

Capítulo 7: ¿Qué te gustaría hacer?
Projects

This project has two parts—an entertainment guide for the community and a TV entertainment show. After developing an entertainment guide, students will work together to create a television show based on this written work. Groups create a show entitled, "La semana divertida en (their city)." On the show they will talk about the entertainment events of the week (movies, plays, concerts, etc.), critique the events, and give their recommendations to the TV audience. Students might ask the entertainment critic of a local newspaper or television station how they can best describe or critique an event.

MATERIALS

✂ **Students will need**

- Paper
- Markers
- Word processor or typewriter, if available
- Magazines
- Entertainment section of local newspaper
- Videotaping equipment if available

SUGGESTIONS—ENTERTAINMENT GUIDE

1. Students may work alone or in small groups to create their guides. The guides should include at least six events and a short description of each. If students work in small groups, each person should create two or three events and descriptions. Each student should proofread the group's work and make sure that any one type of event does not appear too many times.
2. Explain the project to students by showing them an example of an entertainment guide from a newspaper. In their guide, they should include categories such as concerts, plays, movies, restaurants, museum and art gallery exhibits, events for children, and sporting events. They may wish to use the **Caleidoscopio** section as a guide (see pages 196–197).
3. Give students time in class to brainstorm and to check the local newspaper for material. Students may make events up; encourage them to be creative.
4. Students should include not only the events in their guide, but also a brief description of what each is about. They should use as much Spanish as possible.
5. Set a due date for the entertainment guide.
6. Ask students to exchange a rough draft of their guide with another group for peer review.
7. In the final draft of the guide, students may wish to include photos clipped from magazines that illustrate the event they describe in the guide. The guide might be formatted like a folded brochure, a small poster, or pages in a magazine.

SUGGESTIONS—TV SHOW

1. Allow time in class for groups to prepare their TV broadcast.
2. Groups should decide which events to talk about. Each person in the group should have a role (movie or theater critic, sports events reporter, restaurant critic, concert reviewer). Explain to students that the point of the show is to inform people about entertainment events in their city that week and to describe and critique the events as objectively as possible. Explain to students that good critics and reviewers do not express pure opinion in their critiques, but rather convey reasons for their judgments and thorough summaries of the events.
3. Encourage students to be creative in dramatizing their guides. They should embellish what they have written and try not to read their guides verbatim. Tell them that part of their grade will be determined by how much original Spanish they use and the ease with which they speak. This should be an exercise in using natural Spanish.
4. Set a date for groups to present the TV programs.
5. Push desks together to simulate a studio. Students might use toy microphones or set a up a creative backdrop that displays the name of the show.
6. If you choose to record or videotape the presentations, plan time at a later date for students to listen to or view them.

GRADING THE PROJECT

Suggested point distribution (total = 100 points):

Entertainment Guide

Vocabulary use	20
Appearance	10
Creativity	10
Grammar and clarity	10

TV Show

Vocabulary use	20
Creativity	20
Comprehensibility and natural speech	10

FAMILY LINK

Have students ask friends or family to go to one of the events in the guide if possible. They should then tell the student if his or her description or critique of the event was accurate. Students might later tell the class what their friend or family member said.

Capítulo 7: ¿Qué te gustaría hacer?

Games

LA LLAMADA

This game gives students an opportunity to practice telephone numbers, some telephone vocabulary, and the location of cities in Spain and Latin America.

Preparation Make two sets of cards, an A set and a B set. On each card write a different six-digit telephone number. (Use numbers; don't spell them out.) Make a list of phone numbers in A and those in B. You will also need a list of major cities in Spain and Latin America.

Procedure Divide the class into two teams and appoint a scorekeeper. Hand out the A cards to Team A and the B cards to Team B. When play begins, you will assume the role of the **operador/a.** Call out a telephone number from your list in Spanish. The student who has the card with the matching number says **Aló.** You will then say **Tengo una llamada de ______**, giving the name of a city on your list. The student is to say **Está bien, una llamada de ______**, repeating the name of the city and adding the country also. If the student answers **Aló** but does not give the country, his or her team receives only one point. Students receive one point for recognizing their phone number, and another point for giving the correct country.

LA PATATA CALIENTE

This game allows students to learn many vocabulary words at a time. It can be played with a large number of students or as few as six or eight.

Preparation Seat the participants in a large circle; the game works best if students can see each other. Choose a theme (foods, verbs, animals, family members, clothing) and assign one word to each player, including yourself. (For this example, the theme is verbs and you are **desayunar.**) You may want to make a list of the words if you have a large class. Go around the room and have each person say his or her word loudly and clearly. Make sure everyone knows his or her word and can pronounce it.

Procedure Start the game by saying a sentence with your word along with someone else's: **"Voy a desayunar y ducharme."** The person who is **ducharse** must make up a sentence quickly, using his or her verb first: **"Voy a ducharme y lavarme los dientes."** The person who is **lavarse los dientes** continues. Students may not choose previously used words. The game is meant to be fast-paced and funny. When a person fails to respond with his or her sentence, he or she should wear a funny hat until someone else makes a mistake. Depending on the theme, you'll want to change the repeated sentence. [*I'm wearing* (*clothing*), *I'm going to visit* (*family members*), *At the zoo I'm going to see* (*animals*).]

¿QUIÉN HABLA?

In this game, students apply the language they learn in this chapter by creating realistic telephone conversations.

Preparation Divide the class into pairs. If there is an odd number of students, have one trio. If desired, two to three telephones may be used as props. Consider asking the local phone company to donate a few unrepairable telephones to your classroom for use in role-plays, or asking a toy store to donate some play telephones.

Procedure Allow students a short period to plan mini-dialogues. They then present their conversations before the group. A trio could have a three-party conference call, an operator-assisted call, or call-waiting. Possible topics include dialing a wrong number, ordering take-out food delivery, or inviting someone to do something with you. Have students vote on the winning conversation.

ADIVINANZA

This game allows students to apply the expressions that they learned in this chapter and vocabulary. It can be played with a large number of students or as few as two.

Preparation Have available objects that one uses to get ready to go out. (a brush, a comb, a washcloth, a bar of soap, a towel, a razor, some clothing)

Procedure The first player leaves the room and the others select an object for him or her to guess. When the student returns, he or she asks the group a question about the use of the object with **¿cuándo? ¿por qué?** or **¿dónde?** For example, **¿Dónde lo uso?** Any member of the group may answer, for example, **En el baño.** The player who entered continues asking questions using the three question words until he or she guesses it. When the first player guesses the object, then someone else leaves the room, another object is chosen, and the second player questions the group in the same way as before.

¿Qué te gustaría hacer?

pp. 178-201

Using the Chapter Opener

Motivating Activity

The telephone is important to many teenagers regardless of the country in which they live. You might discuss with your students their use of the telephone. Whom do they call most often? What do they usually talk about? With whom do they have the longest conversations? the shortest? Are there rules at their house about the use of the telephone?

For Individual Needs

Challenge Ask your students personal questions in Spanish. **¿Con quién hablas más por teléfono? ¿Con quién hablas menos? ¿De qué hablan Uds.? ¿Con quién pasas la mayor parte del tiempo en el teléfono?**

Teaching Suggestion

Have students work in pairs and list five different situations in which they might turn down an invitation and make an excuse. Ask them to list as much as they can in Spanish.

CAPÍTULO 7

¿Qué te gustaría hacer?

1 Gracias, pero no puedo hoy. Ya tengo planes.

Multicultural Link

During certain times of the year in Spain, Mexico, Ecuador, and other Spanish-speaking countries, it is common to spend a weekend afternoon at a bullfight **(una corrida de toros)**. Families and friends go to the large bullrings **(plazas de toros)** to socialize, watch the bullfight and equestrian events, and eat many different foods. Have your students choose any country in the world and research in the library what people there do in their free time. Have them report their findings to the class.

Teenagers in Spanish-speaking countries do a variety of fun activities with friends after school and on the weekend. What do you invite your friends to do? Let's find out some of the ways Spanish-speaking teenagers invite each other to do things.

In this chapter you will learn

- to talk on the telephone; to extend and to accept invitations
- to make plans; to talk about getting ready
- to turn down an invitation and make an excuse

And you will

- listen to telephone conversations in Spanish
- read an entertainment guide from Ecuador
- write a note accepting or turning down an invitation
- find out about asking someone out in Spanish-speaking countries

(2) **Buenos días. ¿Está Pablo, por favor?**

(3) **Aaah... Necesito afeitarme y lavarme los dientes.**

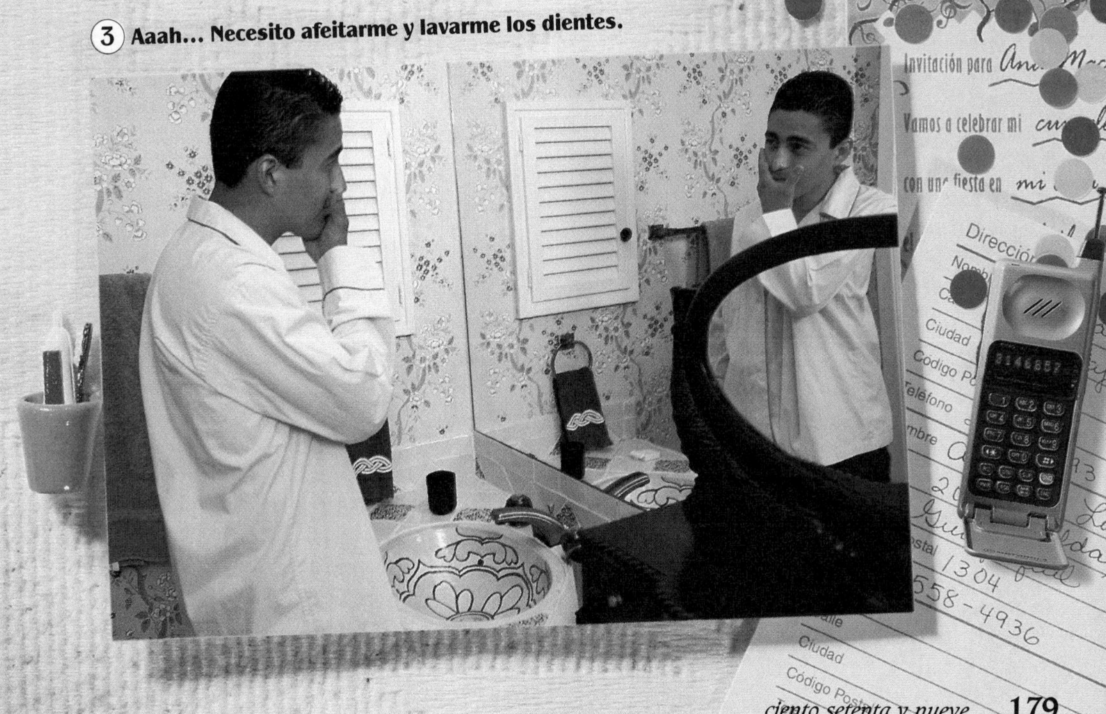

Focusing on Outcomes

Have students describe the people in these photos (see questions below) and match them with the learner outcomes. (Photo 1 represents talking on the telephone, photo 2, turning down an invitation and making an excuse, and photo 3, getting ready.) Ask students to make a list in Spanish of at least five things they do for fun with friends. Encourage them to use vocabulary from past chapters. They might mention things such as **ir a un partido de fútbol, salir, ir al cine, caminar, comer,** and **bailar.** Tell students that in this chapter they will learn how to invite people to do things, to accept or turn down an invitation, and to talk about what they do to get ready.

For Individual Needs

Challenge Based on the Multicultural Link on p. 178, conduct a class debate in English in the form of a talk show. Choose a panel of three or four students to be experts on the show's subject: Bull fight—right or wrong? The rest of the class will be the audience and should ask questions through you, the host, for the panel.

Preguntas

Have your students describe the people in these photos. Ask them the following questions. **¿Cómo es el chico en la foto número uno? ¿Con quién habla? ¿Qué dice? ¿Cómo es el chico en la foto número dos? ¿Es rubio? ¿Qué dice él? En la foto número tres, ¿cuántas personas hay? ¿Qué necesita hacer? ¿Dónde está?**

VIDEO PROGRAM OR EXPANDED VIDEO PROGRAM, *Videocassette 3*

OR *VIDEODISC PROGRAM,* ***Videodisc 4A***

Video Synopsis

Diego tells his friend Pablo that he is in a bad mood because Cristina is having a party on Saturday and he isn't invited. The two decide to go to a concert on Saturday, as Pablo doesn't have plans either. While they are at Pablo's house watching a video, Cristina calls to invite Pablo to the party. Pablo tells her that he is sorry but he has other plans for Saturday. While Diego is at Pablo's house, Cristina calls Diego's house and leaves a message with Diego's father about the party. The message gets buried under a stack of papers near the telephone. Will Diego find it?

Motivating Activity

Ask students what causes them to be in a bad mood. Do they ever feel left out of social activities? What do they do when they are feeling low? To put students at ease, remind them that they may make up answers to these questions.

DE ANTEMANO

¿Qué hacemos?

Look at the photos. What kind of mood is Diego in? How is Pablo trying to help Diego? Who is Cristina and how is she involved? Read the story and see what happens.

Pablo · Cristina · Diego · Sr. Andrade

1

¿Qué te pasa, Diego? ¿Por qué estás de mal humor?

Cristina va a hacer una fiesta el sábado. No me invitó.

2

¡Qué lástima! Oye, ¿tienes prisa ahora? ¿Tienes que hacer algo?

No, nada. ¿Por qué?

¿Quieres ver un video conmigo en mi casa?

¡Cómo no! Vamos.

3

Oye, Diego... tengo una idea. ¿Te gustaría hacer algo conmigo este sábado? No tengo planes.

Sí, ¿por qué no?

Bueno, ¿qué prefieres... salir o hacer algo en casa?

En realidad prefiero salir. Pero, ¿qué hacemos?

Hay un concierto de guitarra en el Coliseo Mayor. ¿Te gustaría ir?

Sí, ¡buena idea!

4

¿ Aló?

Hola, Pablo. Habla Cristina.

Ah... hola, Cristina.

Pablo, ¿quieres ir a una fiesta este sábado? Es para un estudiante de intercambio de los Estados Unidos.

180

RESOURCES FOR DE ANTEMANO

Textbook Audiocassette 4A/Audio CD 7
Video Guide
Video Program
Expanded Video Program, Videocassette 3
Videodisc Guide
Videodisc Program, Videodisc 4A
Practice and Activity Book, p. 73

Presentation

First, have students look at the photos and scan the captions. Remind them that scanning for familiar words and cognates will help them to understand new reading passages. Ask them frame-by-frame to guess what is happening in the story. Then play the video. As a follow-up, ask students if their predictions were accurate.

8 El señor Andrade deja el recado para Diego.

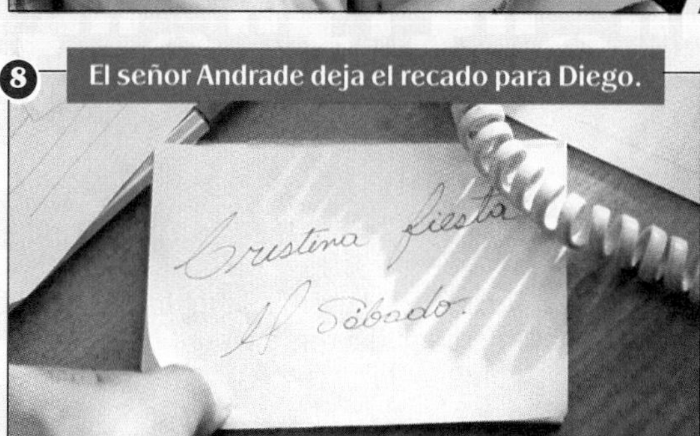

9 Pero...

181

Group Work

Divide students into groups of four. Assign each student the role of one of the persons in the **fotonovela.** Ask students to role-play the **fotonovela** with other members of their group, reading the various parts. You might have them change the ending and present their versions to the class.

For Individual Needs

Challenge Ask students to rewrite the end of the story. Encourage them to create original endings.

Language Notes

- **Los anteojos** and **las gafas** are two other common words for eyeglasses.
- **Chao,** an informal and popular way to say *good-bye,* comes from the Italian word *ciao.*
- Point out to students that the characters on the audio recording and videotape of Chapters 7 and 8 speak with typical Ecuadorean accent and inflection. Ask students if they find this regional accent easy to understand. Do they notice any particular differences?

Video Integration

- ***Expanded Video Program,*** *Videocassette 3*
- ***Videodisc Program,*** *Videodisc 4A*

You may continue with **¿Qué hacemos? (a continuación)** at this time or wait until later in the chapter. At this point in the story, Diego and Pablo discover that they were both invited to Cristina's party and revise their plans to attend. When they show up, Cristina isn't ready and it turns out that the guest of honor won't arrive for another week. The party had been postponed and Cristina's mother forgot to call Diego and Pablo. The three friends end up going out and spending the afternoon together.

DE ANTEMANO

CAPÍTULO 7

For Individual Needs

1 Slower Pace Have students work in small groups to discuss the comprehension questions. They should see how many different ideas and opinions they have about what happens in the **fotonovela.**

1 Challenge Ask students to close their books while you ask these questions in Spanish. **¿De qué hablan Diego y Pablo? ¿Cómo se siente Pablo? ¿Por qué? ¿Qué sugerencia le hace Pablo? ¿Por qué Cristina llama a Pablo? ¿Cómo reacciona? ¿Qué pasa cuando Cristina llama a la casa de Diego? ¿Va a haber un problema?** Encourage students to take risks and use as much Spanish as possible in answering. You might consider having students write their answers in Spanish first and then say them aloud.

Teaching Suggestion

3 Once students have identified the Spanish expressions, have them practice using them with a partner. If students have difficulty finding them, play the segment of the videocassette or videodisc where these expressions are used.

Additional Practice

After students have completed the exercises in **De antemano,** ask them to close their books. The class retells the story in Spanish, with each student adding one sentence to the story.

Teaching Suggestion

Have students exchange telephone numbers with a partner. After school one student calls the other and they converse completely in Spanish. The following day they should write or present a description of their **tarea oral.**

1 ¿Comprendes?

What's happening in the **fotonovela**? Answer the questions. If you don't know the answer, guess!

1. What are Diego and Pablo talking about? See answers below.
2. How does Diego feel? Why does he feel that way?
3. What suggestion does Pablo make?
4. Why does Cristina call Pablo? What is his reaction?
5. What happens when Cristina calls Diego's house? Will there be a problem?

2 ¿Cierto o falso?

Corrige *(Correct)* las oraciones que son falsas. See answers below.

1. Diego está de mal humor.
2. Pablo y Diego deciden ir a un concierto el sábado.
3. Cristina invita a Pablo, pero no a Diego.
4. Pablo no acepta la invitación de Cristina.
5. Diego recibe el recado de Cristina.

3 ¿Cómo se dice?

See answers below.

Find the words and phrases that . . .

1. Diego uses to say what he prefers to do
2. Pablo uses to ask if Diego has to do something
3. Cristina uses to invite Pablo to her party
4. Pablo uses to turn down Cristina's invitation
5. Mr. Andrade uses to ask who's calling

4 ¡Qué lío! *What a mess!*

Completa el párrafo de Diego con palabras de la lista. Usa la fotonovela como guía.

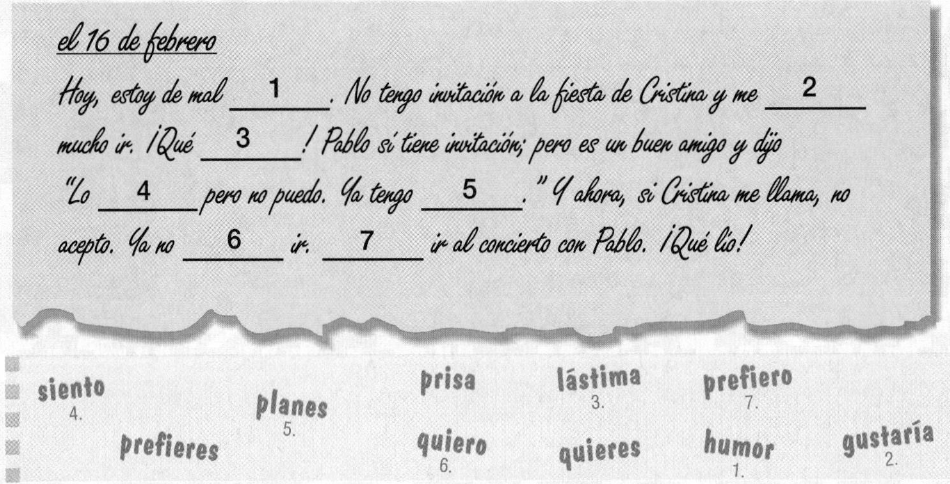

el 16 de febrero

Hoy, estoy de mal ___1___. *No tengo invitación a la fiesta de Cristina y me* ___2___ *mucho ir. ¡Qué* ___3___*! Pablo sí tiene invitación; pero es un buen amigo y dijo "Lo* ___4___ *pero no puedo. Ya tengo* ___5___*." Y ahora, si Cristina me llama, no acepto. Ya no* ___6___ *ir.* ___7___ *ir al concierto con Pablo. ¡Qué lío!*

siento 4. | planes 5. | prisa | lástima 3. | prefiero 7. | prefieres | quiero 6. | quieres | humor 1. | gustaría 2.

5 ¿Y tú?

Get together with a partner and discuss the following questions. Has something like Diego's problem ever happened to you? What did you do? If something like this ever did happen to you, what would you do? What do you think Diego is going to do? Answers will vary.

Answers

1 1. They're talking about Cristina's party.
2. Diego is in a bad mood because Cristina has not invited him to her party on Saturday.
3. He suggests they do something on Saturday.
4. Cristina calls Pablo to invite him to her party. Pablo says he can't go because he has plans.
5. Diego is not home, so Cristina leaves a message for Diego inviting him to the party. The message may get lost in other papers. Another problem is that now Diego has plans with Pablo.

2 1. Cierto
2. Cierto
3. Falso; Cristina invita a los dos muchachos.
4. Cierto
5. Falso; Pablo no recibe el recado de Cristina.

3 1. Prefiero salir.
2. ¿Tienes que hacer algo?
3. ¿Quieres venir a una fiesta este sábado?
4. Lo siento, pero no puedo. Ya tengo planes.
5. ¿De parte de quién?

PRIMER PASO

Talking on the telephone; extending and accepting invitations

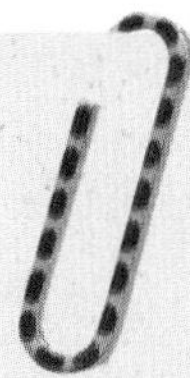

ASÍ SE DICE Talking on the telephone

If you called a friend who wasn't home, your conversation might go like this:

SEÑORA **Aló.**
Hello.
PABLO Buenos días, señora. ¿Está Cristina, por favor?
SEÑORA ¿Quién habla?
PABLO Soy yo, Pablo.
SEÑORA Ah, Pablo. ¿Cómo estás hoy?
PABLO Muy bien, ¿y usted?
SEÑORA Muy bien. Pero Cristina no está.
PABLO Bueno, **llamo más tarde.**
. . . I'll call later.
SEÑORA Adiós, Pablo.

If you needed to leave a message for someone, your conversation might go like this:

SECRETARIA **Diga.**
Hello.
DIEGO ¿Está la señorita Álvarez, por favor?
SECRETARIA **¿De parte de quién?**
Who's calling?
DIEGO De parte de Diego Vásquez.
SECRETARIA **Un momento...** lo siento pero **la línea está ocupada.**
One moment . . . the line is busy.
DIEGO Gracias. **¿Puedo dejar un recado?**
May I leave a message?
SECRETARIA **Está bien.**
All right.

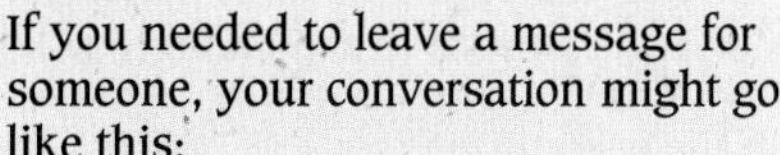

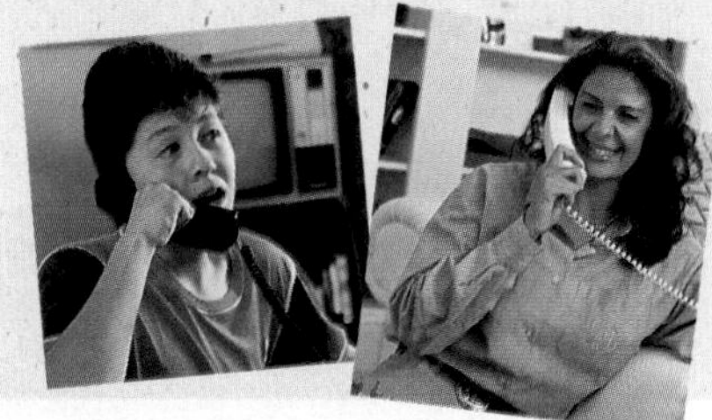

6 Escuchemos: Por teléfono

Listen to the following telephone calls. Decide if the caller is greeting someone, saying goodbye, or unable to reach the person. Answers on page 177C.

También se puede decir...
A common telephone greeting in Mexico is **Bueno.** In some other countries you will hear **Hola, Dígame,** or **Pronto.**

Jump Start!

Write the following telephone numbers on the board or a transparency: 15-41-21, 78.52.18, 53-69-10, 28.36.17, and 42-22-30. Have students write them as they would be spoken in Spanish. Remind them that phone numbers in Spanish-speaking countries are read two digits at a time. (15-41-21 = **quince, cuarenta y uno, veintiuno**) You might also point out that seven-digit numbers are increasingly common everywhere. In this case, the first digit is spoken alone, then the other six in pairs. (555–1234 = **cinco, cinquenta y cinco, doce, treinta y cuatro**)

Motivate

Ask students if they usually leave a message on the answering machine if a friend isn't home when they call. How do they feel about answering machines? Do they like or dislike leaving messages?

Teach

Presentation

Así se dice Have another teacher role-play the conversations with you, or use a puppet as a prop to play the role of a conversation partner. If possible, use phones as props. Have students practice the conversations with a partner, then reverse roles. After the class has practiced, walk around the room and take the role of one of the participants. Pick a student to take the other role. Repeat with different students.

Resources for PRIMER PASO

Textbook Audiocassette 4A/Audio CD 7
Practice and Activity Book, pp. 74–76
Native Speaker Activity Book, pp. 31–36
Videodisc Guide
Videodisc Program, Videodisc 4A

Chapter Teaching Resources, Book 2
- Additional Listening Activities 7-1, 7-2, p. 127
  Audiocassette 10A/Audio CD 7
- Student Response Forms, pp. 136–138
- Realia 7-1, pp. 131, 132
- Situation Cards 7-1, pp. 134, 135
- Teaching Transparency Master 7-1, pp. 123, 126
  Teaching Transparency 7-1
- Quiz 7-1, pp. 139–140
  Audiocassette 8A/Audio CD 7

Cooperative Learning

Divide the class into groups of three. One member of the group asks the others **¿Cuántos minutos pasas al teléfono?** and **¿Cuántas llamadas haces?** The second member adds up the totals of the three group members for each question. The third member reports the totals to the class. Ask the class **¿Qué grupo pasa más tiempo hablando por teléfono? ¿y menos tiempo? ¿Qué grupo hace el mayor número de llamadas? ¿y el menor número?**

Building on Previous Skills

On a transparency or on the board, write several names with phone numbers by them. **(Miguel—42.58.74, Sara—27.64.31)** Ask students the number for each name. **(¿Cuál es el número de teléfono de Miguel?)** Students should answer by saying the numbers in pairs.

Presentation

Así se dice Ask for two volunteers to come to the front of the class and help you role-play the dialogues. With one student at your side, ask the other student to read the role of "your friend" in the book. Invite the student while using hand gestures to be sure the class understands that it is an invitation coming from you and the person at your side. Then have students break into groups of three and practice the dialogues. Ask students to take turns inviting each other to other events such as **un partido de fútbol, una fiesta, un concierto, un baile,** or **una cena italiana.**

7 Situaciones

Possible answers below.

Choose four of the following situations. Write a telephone conversation for each situation you choose. Include greetings and farewells, and leave messages as needed.

1. You call your friend Marta, but she isn't at home. Her mother answers.
2. You call school to talk with Mrs. Castillo in the attendance office. The secretary in the office tells you that her line is busy.
3. You call Dr. Quintana, but the doctor is out.
4. You call your friend Benito and talk about school.
5. You call your mother or father at work. She/He is in a meeting and can't come to the phone.
6. You call your friend Pablo to ask him to play soccer.

8 Hablamos por teléfono

Work with a partner to role-play the conversations you chose in Activity 7. The "caller" should work from the written conversation, but the "answerer" should role-play without the script. Then change roles. See note below.

ASÍ SE DICE Extending and accepting invitations

To invite a friend to do something, say:	Your friend might answer:
¿Te gustaría ir al cine con nosotros? **Nos gustan** las películas de aventura y hay una a las nueve. *Would you like . . . ? We like . . .*	Sí, **me gustaría** ir con ustedes. *Yes, I would like . . .*
¿Quieres ir a comer el sábado? **Te invito**.. . . *It's my treat.*	**¡Claro que sí!** Gracias. *Of course!*

9 Escuchemos: Planes

Listen to the following questions. Do these sentences answer the questions you hear? If the sentence fits as a response, write **sí.** If it doesn't, write **no.**

1. Sí, me gusta mucho el tenis. sí
2. No me gustan los deportes. no
3. ¡Claro que sí! sí
4. ¡Cómo no! La clase es muy difícil. sí
5. Sí, me gustaría ir al partido de fútbol. no
6. Prefiero comida china. sí
7. No, no me gustan las películas. sí

Language Note

Point out that just as in English, Spanish has many different ways to express an idea. Ask the students if they can think of a functional equivalent for **te gustaría** and **me gustaría (quieres, quiero).** Tell students that as they continue their study of Spanish, they will learn many different ways of expressing themselves.

Answers

7 Possible answers:

1. —Aló. —Buenos días, señora. —¿Está Marta en casa? —No, Marta no está en casa. —Bueno, señora, llamo más tarde. —Está bien. —Adiós. —Adiós.
3. —¿Está el doctor Quintana? —No, el doctor no está. ¿Es muy importante? —No, estoy bien. Llamo más tarde.

8 *Answers will vary.* Students should include phrases like **te gustaría, qué lástima, prefieres,** and **tengo planes.**

Gramática e → ie stem-changing verbs

1. In **e → ie** stem-changing verbs, the letter **e** in the stem changes to **ie** in all forms except the **nosotros** and **vosotros** forms.
   You've been working with an **e → ie** verb: **querer**.
   quiero quieres quiere queremos queréis quieren
   Some other verbs that follow the same pattern are **preferir** *(to prefer)* and **empezar** *(to begin)*.
2. Another **e → ie** stem-changing verb is **venir** *(to come)*. It follows the same pattern as **tener**. Do you remember two other verbs with an irregular **-go** in the **yo** form?[1]
   tengo tienes tiene tenemos tenéis tienen
   vengo vienes viene venimos venís vienen

10 ¿Qué prefieres hacer?

Possible answers below.

¿Cuántas oraciones puedes *(can you)* escribir? Usa las frases en las tres columnas.

Yo Tú Mi amiga Mi amigo y yo Mis amigos	venir preferir tener querer	ir al cine o al concierto un examen mañana a la fiesta de Miguel ir al baile el sábado contigo a nuestra casa para cenar ¿?

11 Una fiesta

¿Qué pasa cuando Marta habla por teléfono con Luisa, la hermana de Paco? Usa las palabras de la lista para completar esta conversación.

See answers below.

empezar fiesta querer preferir
venir estar sábado hay

Paco – Fiesta
sábado 8:30
casa de Marta

LUISA ¿Aló?
MARTA Luisa, ¿qué tal? Habla Marta. Oye, ¿ __1__ Paco?
LUISA Ay, no está. ¿__2__ dejar un recado, o __3__ llamar más tarde?
MARTA Pues, un recado. __4__ una __5__ en mi casa el __6__. __7__ a las ocho y media.
LUISA Perfecto. Dime, ¿quiénes van?
MARTA Uy, van a __8__ muchos amigos.

1. **Hacer** and **salir** have irregular **yo** forms: **hago, salgo.**

Answers

10 *Possible answers:*
Prefiero ir al concierto.
Mi amiga tiene un examen mañana.

11 1. está 2. Quieres 3. prefieres 4. Hay 5. fiesta 6. sábado 7. Empieza 8. venir

Presentation

Gramática Have students silently read the grammar explanation. Then have them close their books and ask the following: What kind of verbs are we studying now? What are some examples of this kind of verb? (List the verbs that they mention on a transparency or the board.) How is this class of verbs different from those we've studied before? Does this change affect **-ar**, **-er**, and **-ir** verbs? Have them reopen their books and check if all of the information in the explanation has been mentioned.

Additional Practice

Gramática Put the subject pronouns up on the board or a transparency and ask them to secretly choose one. Write a few familiar phrases on the board **(querer un refresco, tener una bicicleta, venir al colegio)**. Then call out one of the phrases **(querer un refresco)**. Walk around the room and point to a student. He or she then gives a sentence that corresponds to the subject pronoun chosen. (A student who had chosen **yo** would say **¡Quiero un refresco!**)

Additional Practice

10 Have students build upon the sentences they write by adding time phrases or other information they have learned. **(Quiero asistir a la fiesta de Miguel el sábado a las siete.)**

Presentation

Vocabulario Have students look at the drawings and read the new vocabulary words. Then ask them a series of questions that they answer with **cierto** or **falso** by referring to nearby or well-known locations. ***Sea World* es un acuario, ¿no? (cierto) La ciudad de Nueva York está en el campo, ¿verdad? (falso)** Then, ask students **¿Qué lugares están cerca de la escuela? ¿de su casa? ¿Cuáles están lejos? ¿Te gusta asistir a las fiestas de sorpresa? ¿Por qué?**

For videodisc application, see *Videodisc Guide.*

Group Work

Have students converse in pairs or groups of three using the new vocabulary to say which places they like to visit with their families, which they prefer to go to with friends, and which places they do not like. Have a member from each group report to the class some of their findings.

VOCABULARIO

Lugares *Places*

el acuario

el campo

el circo

la ciudad

el lago

el museo de antropología

el parque de atracciones

el teatro

el zoológico

Eventos *Events*

la fiesta de cumpleaños
de aniversario
de graduación
de sorpresa

la boda

12 Escuchemos: Un sábado

Answers on page 177C.

It's Saturday morning and Mónica and Carlos are trying to figure out where to spend the day. Based on their conversation, where do they decide to go?

TPR Tape pictures of several places mentioned in **Vocabulario** around the classroom. Give students commands to practice the new vocabulary. (**Juan, ¡ve al campo! Clase, ¡miren los peces en el acuario!**)

Additional Vocabulary

el museo aeronaútico *aeronautical museum*
el museo de arte moderno *museum of modern art*
la exposición de dinosaurios *dinosaur exhibit*
el tanque de los tiburones *shark tank*
el espectáculo de los delfines *dolphin show*

13 Invitación

Answers will vary.

Work with a partner. Look at the new vocabulary on page 186 and make a list of three places where you both want to go. Then take turns inviting each other and accepting each other's invitations.

14 ¡Conversación!

Possible answers below.

Work with a partner. Choose one of these situations and create a conversation.

1. a. *Call and greet the person who answers.*
   b. *Say who's calling and ask to speak to your friend.*
   c. *Your friend's not there, so leave a message.*
   d. *Say goodbye to each other.*
2. a. *Call and greet your friend who answers.*
   b. *Invite your friend to go someplace with you.*
   c. *Your friend accepts your invitation.*
   d. *Say goodbye to each other.*

Many language students feel nervous about speaking. You might be worried about making mistakes, or you might think you won't sound right. To sharpen your speaking skills, practice aloud at home in Spanish using situations and material you've covered in class. You could role-play two friends talking on the phone and inviting each other to do something. What would each person say? These practice conversations will help prepare you to speak confidently in class.

15 Un fin de semana en Quito

Look at Cristina's schedule for the weekend. There are a lot of fun and interesting things to do in Ecuador. Write your weekend schedule modeled after Cristina's schedule. Include the times for each day. Then, compare your schedule with a partner's. See note below.

AGENDA

19	jueves	11:00 el museo 9:00 la fiesta de cumpleaños de Pablo
20	viernes	9:00 el zoológico 7:30 el teatro
21	sábado	10:00 el acuario 3:00 el parque de atracciones
22	domingo	12:00 el circo 4:00 el lago con Diego

For Individual Needs

14 Slower Pace Have students write some of the expressions they will need during the situation they choose.

14 Kinesthetic Learners Ask pairs of students to act out the conversations using prop telephones.

15 Slower Pace Allow students time to prepare their schedules before getting together with partners. Then have partners peer-edit each other's work.

Close

To review material and verify completion of objectives, use *Teaching Transparency 7-1.* You might point to different scenes and have students orally describe them in Spanish, or have students invite each other to some of the locations pictured.

Assess

Quiz 7-1, *Chapter Teaching Resources, Book 2,* pp. 139–140

Assessment Items, Audiocassette 8A/Audio CD 7

Performance Assessment

Working in pairs, have students role-play Activity 14, part 2. They should incorporate at least three verbs and three new vocabulary words. Have students role-play the phone conversation for the rest of the class. You may choose to record this for an oral portfolio entry or grade it as students perform. You may wish to allow some students to write the dialogue instead of acting it out.

Answers

14 *Possible answer:*

1. —¿Bueno? —Buenos días, Sr. Montes. —Soy yo, Margarita. —¿Está Eugenio? —Eugenio no está en casa. ¿Quieres dejar un recado? —Sí, por favor. Hay una fiesta en mi casa el sábado y quiero invitar a Eugenio. —Está bien. Adiós, Margarita.
   —Adiós, Sr. Montes.

15 *Answers will vary.* Students should include days, times, and location vocabulary. **(el teatro, el lago, el zoológico...)**

Jump Start!

On a transparency or the board write the question **¿Cuál es la estación del...?** and the following dates: **28 de diciembre, 5 de abril, 15 de julio, 3 de octubre,** and **16 de junio.** Students who need to review the names of the seasons may turn to page 138.

MOTIVATE

Ask students to discuss what they plan to do today, this weekend, or next year. Ask them what they will have to do to get ready for these plans. How do they respond to unexpected changes in plans?

TEACH

Presentation

Así se dice Have students read the cartoon, then read the text aloud. Ask comprehension questions in Spanish before beginning the **Nota gramatical.**

Nota gramatical First, have students read the grammar explanation. Then, write the forms of **pensar** on the board or on a transparency in the traditional paradigm of singular forms on the left, plurals on the right. Point out that the "shoe" or "boot" forms (the first, second, third person singular and third person plural) all have the stem change, while the **nosotros** and **vosotros** forms do not. Tell them that this visual representation may help them to remember the forms, as this pattern applies to all stem-changing verbs. Pronounce the forms and have students repeat them after you.

SEGUNDO PASO

Making plans; talking about getting ready

ASÍ SE DICE Making plans

Nota Gramatical

1. **Pensar** *(to think)* is another **e → ie** stem-changing verb.

   p**ie**nso, p**ie**nsas, p**ie**nsa,
   pensamos, pensáis, p**ie**nsan

   When followed by an infinitive, **pensar** means *to plan,* or *to intend* to do something.

   ¿Piensas jugar al tenis?
   Do you plan to play tennis?

2. You already know the verb **ir.** This verb can also be used to talk about the future, using the formula **ir + a +** infinitive.

   ¿Cuándo **vas a practicar** el piano?
   . . . are you going to practice . . .

   Voy a practicar mañana.
   I'm going to practice . . .

16 ¿Por qué no vienes? See answers below.

There's a party tonight, but several people have other plans. Explain why they can't come by completing the passage with the correct forms of **pensar** or **ir.**

Pues, Manuel no puede ir porque __1__ salir con unos amigos. Julio y yo __2__ ir al museo. Lupe y Gabriel no van a ir porque __3__ visitar el nuevo parque de atracciones. ¡Ellos __4__ a pasar todo el día allí! Y Elisa __5__ ir al teatro para ver un drama de Shakespeare. Y tú, ¿qué __6__ a hacer?

RESOURCES FOR SEGUNDO PASO

Textbook Audiocassette 4A/Audio CD 7
Practice and Activity Book, pp. 77–79
Native Speaker Activity Book, pp. 31–36
Video Guide
Video Program
Expanded Video Program, Videocassette 3
Videodisc Guide
Videodisc Program, Videodisc 4A

Chapter Teaching Resources, Book 2
- Communicative Activity 7-1, pp. 119, 120
- Additional Listening Activities 7-3, 7-4, p. 128
  Audiocassette 10A/Audio CD 7
- Student Response Forms, pp. 136–138
- Realia 7-1, pp. 131, 132
- Situation Cards 7-2, pp. 134, 135
- Teaching Transparency Master 7-2, pp. 124, 126
  Teaching Transparency 7-2
- Quiz 7-2, pp. 141–142
  Audiocassette 8A/Audio CD 7

17 ¿Qué piensas hacer? Possible answers below.

¿Qué vas a hacer? Escribe una frase para cada situación.

1. Tienes un examen muy difícil mañana.
2. El próximo sábado hay una fiesta de cumpleaños para tu mejor amigo.
3. Quieres jugar al basquetbol pero no tienes zapatos.
4. Tus abuelos vienen a visitar y la casa está completamente desorganizada.
5. No hay comida en la casa.

18 Y ustedes, ¿qué piensan hacer?

With a partner take turns asking each other what you plan to do during the days or times listed. Include where you're going to go or what you're going to do. Then get together with another pair and report your findings to each other. Answers will vary.

MODELO —¿Qué piensas hacer hoy?
—Hoy voy a lavar el carro.

hoy
este fin de semana

el miércoles
el viernes por la mañana

el sábado por la noche
el próximo (*next*) verano

mañana
el próximo domingo

NOTA CULTURAL

If you and a friend were making plans in Spain or Latin America, you probably would have to plan to get around without a car. There are several reasons for this. Cars are more expensive, so not all families have one. In some countries, you must be 18 years or older to get a driver's license. Finally, public transportation is inexpensive and convenient in most cities. In major cities, most people use the subway, taxis, buses, or **motos** (*mopeds*). Sometimes they just walk!

Answers

16 1. piensa 2. pensamos 3. piensan 4. van 5. piensa 6. vas

17 *Possible answers:*
1. Pienso estudiar esta noche.
2. Voy a asistir a la fiesta.
3. Voy a comprar unos zapatos.
4. Pienso organizar mi cuarto.
5. Voy al supermercado.

Multicultural Link

As a homework assignment, have your students compare public transportation in other countries with the United States. Here is a fact that they may find interesting: While London's subway is called the 'Underground,' it is the 'Metro' in Madrid, Paris, and Mexico City. Have them present what they find out to the class.

For Individual Needs

18 Slower Pace If students have trouble recalling vocabulary, write some familiar activities on the board. **(esquiar, hacer ejercicios, leer, pescar, hacer un viaje, salir, visitar)**

Additional Practice

18 After students have completed this activity, ask them to tell a partner how they plan to get to each of the activities they are planning. They might say **Pienso caminar a...** or **Pienso ir en el carro de mi amigo a...**

For videodisc application, see *Videodisc Guide.*

Thinking Critically

Comparing and Contrasting Ask students to use what they already know about teens in Spanish-speaking countries to compare and contrast how the plans of Hispanic teens might be different from those of teenagers in the United States. Ask about part-time jobs, different sports, the use of an automobile, and so on.

Building on Previous Skills

Ask students to pick a destination in a Spanish-speaking country they have read about. Have them write a short paragraph in Spanish telling where they plan to go and at least three things that they would like to see there.

Presentation

Así se dice, Nota gramatical Bring in some props (a washcloth, razor, toothbrush, comb, and make-up). Tell a story in Spanish to the class of some plans that you and someone else have for the evening and need to get ready for. **Esta noche, pienso ir al cine con mi esposa. Pero no estoy listo. Primero, necesito...** (pantomime different grooming verbs as you say them in Spanish). **Mi esposa/o (amiga/o) también necesita ducharse, afeitarse...** (Use the props as you tell about the other person as well.) Then hand the props to different students in the class and call upon them individually to pantomime as you ask the class to respond in unison to your question, **¿Qué necesita hacer (Juan)?**. The class responds with you, **Necesita afeitarse.**

Additional Practice

20 Ask students to tell their partner how their routine changes on Saturday and Sunday. **(Los sábados no tengo que levantarme temprano...)**

ASÍ SE DICE Talking about getting ready

To ask if a friend is ready, say:

¿Estás listo/a?
Are you ready?

Your friend might answer:

No, **todavía necesito ducharme y afeitarme.**
. . . I still need to shower and to shave.

No, porque **necesito lavarme los dientes, peinarme** y **maquillarme.**
. . . I need to brush my teeth, comb my hair, and put on make-up.

19 Escuchemos: ¿Todos listos?

Listen to some members of the Garza family as they talk about getting ready at different times of the day. Based on what you hear, write the letter of the item each person would need to use in order to get ready. See answers below.

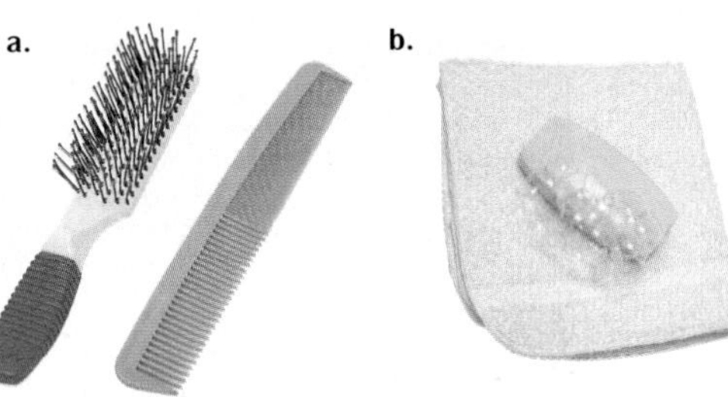

a. b.

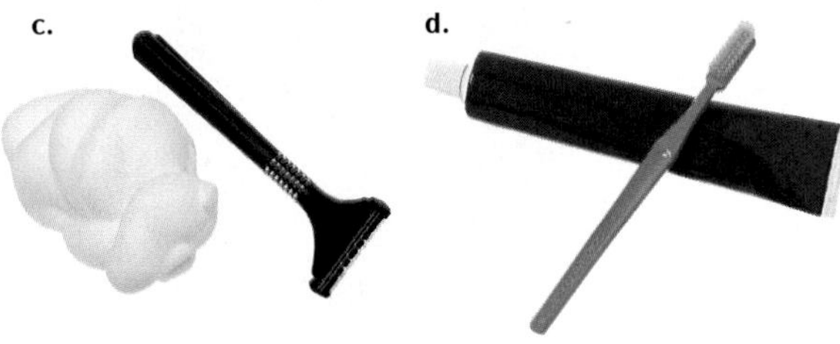

c. d.

e.

Nota Gramatical

A *reflexive verb* is a verb in which the action reflects back on the subject: *I bathe myself.* In Spanish, the infinitives of reflexive verbs have **se** attached to them **(afeitarse, ponerse)**. The **se** changes according to the subject of the verb:

(Yo) necesito **ducharme.**
(Tú) necesitas **afeitarte.**
Juanito necesita **peinarse.**

20 Mi rutina

See note below.

Work with a partner. Each of you write your daily routine, using **necesito** and the reflexive verbs you've just learned. Then ask each other questions about your daily routines. Include such phrases as **todos los días, ¿a qué hora?, a veces, nunca,** and days of the week.

Un poco más...

el cepillo *brush*
el cepillo de dientes *toothbrush*
el jabón *soap*
el maquillaje *make-up*
la navaja *razor*
la pasta de dientes *toothpaste*
el peine *comb*

Answers

19 a. peinarse
b. bañarse, lavarse, ducharse
c. afeitarse
d. lavarse los dientes, cepillarse los dientes
e. maquillarse

20 *Answers will vary.* Students should include **necesito, todos los días, ¿a qué hora?, a veces, nunca,** days of the week, and other vocabulary learned so far.

21 ¡Escribamos! Possible answers below.

Write a sentence telling what each person in the López family needs to do or is going to do. Make up a place where each person is going and the times when they go.

el señor López

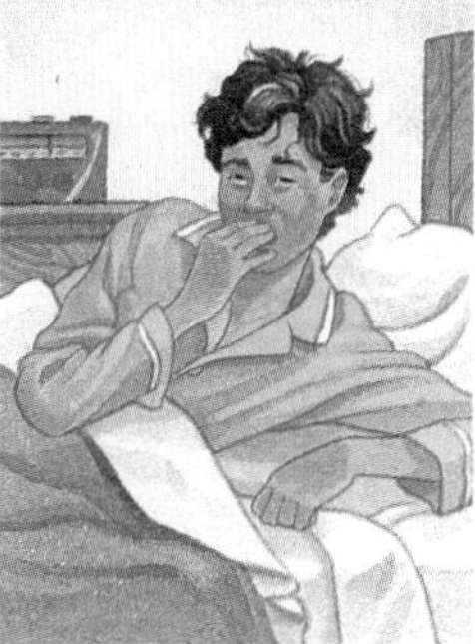

Ernesto

la señora López

Adela

22 ¿Estás listo/a?

Work in a group of three. Discuss what you are going to do in order to get ready for each of the activities listed in the box.

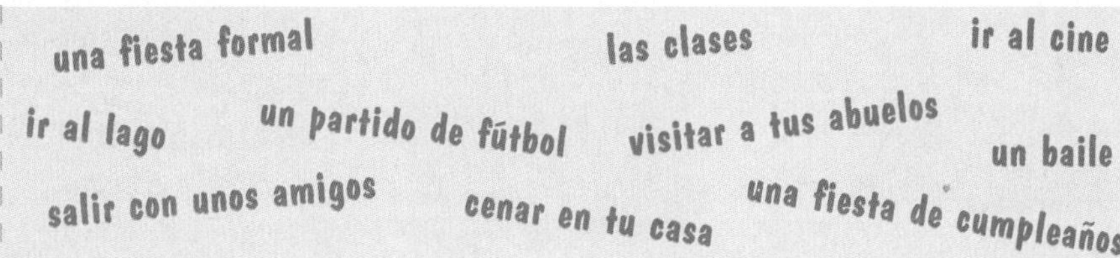

23 ¡Vamos a celebrar!

Tonight's the big party! Read the invitation with a partner and answer the following questions. Then tell each other whether or not you would like to go and why or why not. See answers below.

1. ¿Quién hace la fiesta?
2. ¿Dónde es?
3. ¿Dónde vive Ana?
4. ¿Cuál es la fecha de la fiesta?
5. ¿A qué hora empieza?
6. ¿Qué van a celebrar?
7. Son las cuatro de la tarde. ¿Qué vas a hacer antes de la fiesta? (ducharte, etc.)
8. ¿Qué piensas hacer en la fiesta?

Reteaching

Pensar + *infinitive* Write these sentences on the board or a transparency. **Yo pienso regresar a casa después de clases. Tú también piensas ir a tu casa, ¿no? Ana piensa desayunar en un café mañana. Mi amigo y yo pensamos cenar en un restaurante italiano este fin de semana. Mike y Diana piensan jugar al tenis.** Then have students write original sentences, exchange with a partner, and peer-correct.

Close

Ask students to close their books and write at least three things they will have to do to get ready for a party for which they have accepted an invitation. Check answers by asking several students **¿Estás listo/a?** and having them tell what they need to do.

Assess

Quiz 7-2, *Chapter Teaching Resources, Book 2,* pp. 141–142

Assessment Items, Audiocassette 8A/Audio CD 7

Performance Assessment

Ask students to work with a partner. Each pair is to create a party invitation that contains all the usual information: host, honoree, occasion, time, and place. Encourage them to embellish the invitation with activities planned, to indicate if it is a surprise party, and to give suggestions on what to bring. Have them decorate the invitations and post them on a class bulletin board.

Answers

21 *Possible answers:*

a. El señor López necesita afeitarse.
b. Ernesto va a peinarse ahora.
c. La señora López necesita lavarse los dientes.
d. Adela va a maquillarse.

23
1. Ana Macias Gómez va a dar la fiesta.
2. Es en su casa.
3. Ana vive en la calle Independencia, número 35.
4. La fecha de la fiesta es el 16 de abril.
5. La fiesta empieza a las seis menos cuarto.
6. Van a celebrar su cumpleaños.
7. *Answers will vary.*
8. *Answers will vary.*

PANORAMA CULTURAL

CAPÍTULO 7

VIDEO PROGRAM OR EXPANDED VIDEO PROGRAM, Videocassette 3

OR VIDEODISC PROGRAM, Videodisc 4A

Teacher Notes

- See *Video Guide* and *Videodisc Guide* for activities related to the **Panorama cultural.**
- Remind students that cultural information may be included in the Chapter Quizzes and Test.

Motivating Activity

Ask students what they do to get to know someone new. Do they invite them to participate with their friends or do they wait for the person to approach them first?

Presentation

Have students look at the map and photos. Then have them read the captions. Next, show the video or play the audio recording, and check comprehension by asking the **Preguntas.** Have students work in small groups to answer the activities in the **Para pensar y hablar...** section. Ask groups to present their list to the class.

PANORAMA CULTURAL

¿Qué haces para conocer a una persona?

How would you ask someone out in a Spanish-speaking country? Who would pay for the date? We asked these students to tell us about dating customs in their countries.

Rodrigo
Quito, Ecuador

"Me le acerco, le pregunto su nombre, me presento y le pido su número telefónico, o algo así. Los hombres pagamos la cita en Ecuador".

Jessica
San Miguel de Desamparados, Costa Rica

"Busco una persona amiga mía que me la presente. Él siempre paga la cita".

María Isabel
Sevilla, España

"Trato de que me lo presenten, y una vez que me lo presentan, pues trato de tener conversación con él. No nos dejan pagar. Me gusta que me inviten, pero yo también quiero; o sea, que me gusta invitar a mí también".

Para pensar y hablar...

A. In your opinion, which student has the best way of meeting someone new? Why? Who pays for dates according to these students? Why do you suppose that is, and how do you feel about it?

B. In small groups, talk about how you would meet someone you want to get to know. Compare what you would do to what these teens suggest, and write some similarities and differences between your ideas. Can you explain the differences? Be prepared to present your group's list to the class.

Thinking Critically

Comparing and Contrasting

Ask students to think about what the interviewees said about the males paying for the date. Do they think this is the case in the United States? Do they imagine that customs also vary in this country by region? Who pays for the date when they go out?

Preguntas

1. Cierto o falso: A María Isabel le gusta llamar al chico primero. (falso)
2. Cierto o falso: A María Isabel le gustaría pagar la cita de vez en cuando. (cierto)
3. Cierto o falso: Rodrigo espera que sus amigos le presenten a una chica. (falso)
4. ¿Qué le pide Rodrigo a las chicas? (su número telefónico)
5. Cierto o falso: A Jessica le gusta que sus amigas la presenten a un chico. (cierto)
6. Según las tres entrevistas, ¿quién paga la cita normalmente? (el chico)

Language Note

Ask students to compare the interviewees' accents. Which one(s) do they find easiest to understand? Why?

TERCER PASO

Turning down an invitation and making an excuse

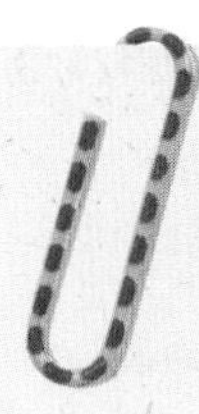

ASÍ SE DICE Turning down an invitation and making an excuse

To find out if your friend would like to do something with you, say:

¿Te gustaría ir al museo de arte conmigo hoy?

Your friend might say:

¡Qué lástima! Ya tengo planes. Tal vez otro día.
What a shame! I already have plans. Perhaps another day.

¿Hoy? **Lo siento,** pero no. Estoy **ocupado.** Tengo **una cita.**
I'm sorry . . . busy . . . a date (an appointment).

Lo siento hombre, pero **tengo prisa. Tengo que** trabajar.
. . . I'm in a hurry. I have to . . .

Me gustaría, pero no puedo. Estoy **cansado** y un poco **enfermo.**
I would like to, but I can't. . . . tired . . . sick.

También se puede decir...
Other words for **cansado** are **completamente muerto, agobiado, agotado, gastado,** and **rendido.**

24 Escuchemos: ¿Te gustaría...?

Listen as Margarita invites several friends to go with her to do some things. Match the name of the person with his or her excuse for not being able to go. Answers on p.177D.

1. Miguel
2. Mariana
3. Roberto
4. Gabriela

a. ¿Esta noche? Ay, tengo una cita esta noche.
b. ¡Qué lástima! Ya tengo planes para este fin de semana.
c. Lo siento, pero tengo que estudiar.
d. Estoy un poco cansada. Tal vez otro día, ¿eh?

Nota Gramatical

As you already know, **tener** means *to have.* But when used in certain phrases, it means *to be.* Do you remember **Tengo ... años** *(I'm . . . years old)* from Chapter 1? Here are some expressions with **tener** you can use for making excuses.

tener ganas de + infinitive
to feel like (doing something)

tener prisa
to be in a hurry

tener que + infinitive
to have to (do something)

tener sueño
to be sleepy

RESOURCES FOR TERCER PASO

Textbook Audiocassette 4A/Audio CD 7
Practice and Activity Book, pp. 80–82
Native Speaker Activity Book, pp. 31–36
Videodisc Guide
Videodisc Program, Videodisc 4A

Chapter Teaching Resources, Book 2
- Communicative Activity 7-2, pp. 121–122
- Additional Listening Activities 7-5, 7-6, p. 129
  Audiocassette 10A/Audio CD 7
- Student Response Forms, pp. 136–138
- Realia 7-2, pp. 131, 132
- Situation Cards 7-3, pp. 134, 135
- Teaching Transparency Master 7-3, pp. 125, 126
  Teaching Transparency 7-3
- Quiz 7-3, pp. 143–144
  Audiocassette 8A/Audio CD 7

Jump Start!

Write the following times on the board or a transparency. Ask students to write a sentence in Spanish for each, telling where they usually are or what they are usually doing at that time. **(a las 7:00 de la mañana, 1:30 de la tarde, 11:15 de la noche, 10:00 de la mañana, 4:30 de la tarde)**

MOTIVATE

Ask students to think of various excuses they have used in the past to turn down an invitation. You might list these on the board or on a transparency and ask the students to tell you which ones they find in **Así se dice.**

TEACH

Presentation

Así se dice Tell your students that someone you really don't want to go out with keeps inviting you to do things, but that you don't want to hurt his or her feelings. Then play the parts, using the new phrases from the box. **—Ramona, ¿te gustaría ir al museo de arte conmigo hoy? —¡Qué lástima, ____, ya tengo planes. Tal vez otro día.** Repeat the demonstration with other examples to model the other excuses. Then invite students to different events and have them respond with an excuse from the box.

Language Note

Explain to students that **cita** means *appointment* or *date,* while **fecha** is *calendar date.*

Portfolio

26 Oral or Written Have students choose three of the activities and invent outrageous excuses for not doing them. Ask them to be creative (**...voy a la luna, tengo que jugar con los Lakers de Los Ángeles...**). Have them enter these in their Portfolio as an oral or written entry. For Portfolio information, see *Assessment Guide,* pp. 2–13.

Additional Practice

26 Have students use the additional vocabulary on p. 186 and continue the activity.

Presentation

Nota gramatical On the board or a transparency write: **¿Qué tienes que hacer hoy? ¿Qué no tienes ganas de hacer? ¿A qué hora tienes prisa? ¿A qué hora tienes sueño?** Working in pairs, students ask each other these questions and write their partner's answer. Walk around and question students about their partner's answers. (**¿Qué tiene que hacer Jaime hoy?**) Jaime's partner responds. (**Jaime tiene que estudiar para un examen de inglés.**)

For Individual Needs

27 Challenge Ask students to form pairs and create a brief but complete dialogue for one of the three scenes illustrated and present it to the class.

25 Mucho que hacer

Read the following conversations containing invitations. Complete the sentences with words or phrases from the box. Some blanks will have more then one correct answer.

— Hola, Paco, ¿__1__ ir al cine esta noche?
— __2__ Roberto, pero __3__. Tengo __4__ con Marilú.

— Marta, ¿ __5__ ir a comer esta tarde?
— Sí, __6__. ¿A qué hora?

— Angélica, ¿__7__ el tenis o el voleibol?
— Pues yo prefiero el voleibol.
— ¿__8__ jugar el sábado?
— __9__. Yo __10__ trabajar el sábado. Pero __11__.

5 8 quieres
7 prefieres
1 te gustaría
Sí, muchísimas gracias
¡claro que sí!
¡qué lástima! 9
lo siento pero no puedo
2 me gustaría
11 tal vez otro día
4 una cita
tengo que 10
6 ¡cómo no!
ya tengo planes 3

26 ¡Qué problema!

Imagine that you've been invited to do the following activities, but you don't want to do any of them. Take turns inviting your partner and declining the invitations. Try to give a different excuse for each one. Answers will vary.

1. ir al museo de historia
2. estudiar para el examen de álgebra
3. ir al concierto de violín
4. comer en la casa del profesor
5. ir a un partido de fútbol
6. estudiar en la biblioteca

A LO NUESTRO

Ya is usually translated as *already,* but it can mean several different things. If someone wants to say *I'm on my way,* they'd use **Ya voy**. If someone asks if you're ready, you can answer **ya** *(just a minute)* or **todavía no** *(not yet)*. If you're being lectured and you're tired of listening, you might say **¡Ya, ya!** *(All right, already!)* or **¡Basta ya!** *(Enough!)*

27 Gracias, pero...

Sergio's too busy to spend time with his friends. Write what he's saying in each picture.

a. Tengo prisa.

b. No tengo ganas de jugar.

c. Tengo que estudiar ahora.

28 Pretextos *Excuses*

In groups of three, choose a picture from Activity 27 and create a conversation between Sergio and the other person in the picture. One of you should take notes. The other two should be prepared to present the conversation to the class.

29 En mi cuaderno

See note below.

You've just received an invitation from a friend to do something on Saturday night. Write a short reply in which you decline the invitation, give an excuse, and tell your friend what you plan to do instead. Use the **modelo** to help you get started.

MODELO

Querido Julio,
Gracias por la invitación, pero...

30 Un drama

Working with two classmates, choose one of the following situations to role-play. Be prepared to present the scene to the class.

a. You and your family are visiting your Aunt Emilia who has a very outdated video collection. Aunt Emilia tries to talk you into watching two of her favorites. Decline politely and give an excuse.

b. You and two friends are visiting your Uncle Celestino who always likes going to classical music concerts. Uncle Celestino would like you and your friends to go with him. Decline politely and give an excuse.

LETRA Y SONIDO

A. 1. The letters **ll** and **y** are usually pronounced alike. Their pronunciation in many Spanish-speaking countries is similar to the *y* in the English word *yes.*

yo	**yate**	**yema**	**yugo**	**yerno**
llamo	**lleva**	**llora**	**maquillaje**	**toalla**

2. The single **l** in Spanish is pronounced like the *l* in the English word *live.* Keep the tip of the tongue behind the upper teeth when pronouncing **l**.

zoológico	**lavarse**	**levantarse**	**¡Qué lástima!**
lo siento	**el lago**	**Aló**	**línea**

B. **Dictado** Answers on page 177D.

Lalo is trying to make plans with his friends. Write what he says.

C. **Trabalenguas**

La nublada neblina lava las lomas de un lugar lejano.

Answers

29 Answers should include **pero** + *excuse* and **pienso** + *infinitive.*

Teaching Suggestion

29 Remind students to use the feminine **Querida** when they write to a female.

En mi cuaderno

29 Have students decline the invitation, give an excuse, and tell their friend what they plan to do instead. For an additional journal entry suggestion for Chapter 7, see *Practice and Activity Book,* p. 82.

Close

To review expressions presented in this **Paso,** invite students to do several things they would likely prefer to avoid. Have them turn down your invitation and give a reasonable excuse. **¿Quieres estudiar conmigo este sábado? ¿Te gustaría lavar mi coche esta semana? ¿Quieres visitar a mi abuelita este viernes por la noche? ¿Te gustaría ir a la biblioteca conmigo el domingo por la mañana?**

Assess

Quiz 7-3, *Chapter Teaching Resources, Book 2,* pp. 141–142

Assessment Items, Audiocassette 8A/Audio CD 7

Performance Assessment

Group Work Divide the class into "families" of four or five. Ask each family to role-play a dialogue among family members. They should ask each other to do various things around the house. In response, each is to decline, refuse, or accept, what they are asked to do. Each family member should interact with at least two others. You might have groups present their conversations to the class. You could record the dialogues and enter them into student Portfolios if appropriate. For Portfolio information, see *Assessment Guide,* pp. 2–13.

READING STRATEGIES

Scanning for specific information Have students preview the readings. Then ask a few students to tell you briefly what they think the readings are about. Ask them how they figured this out. What clues did they get from prereading?

PREREADING
Activity A

Motivating Activity

Bring in a local entertainment guide. Have students identify the various parts of the guide (restaurants, nightclubs, theaters, movies, sports . . .) Ask students if they use entertainment guides. If not, how do they find out what is going on in their area?

READING
Activities B and C

Ask students to plan an extraordinary weekend for a friend who wants to experience as much as possible of Ecuadorean culture. Refer to the reading and have students write a letter to their friend telling him or her what they will be doing over the weekend, where they will go, and what time the events are.

Native Speakers

Ask native speakers to gather information on a Hispanic singer or theater actor. Have them research an individual to find out where the person is from, how they got started in their career, and what they do now. You might also ask students to find out whether that person is performing anywhere near them soon. Have them report what they find out to the class.

VAMOS A LEER

CALEIDOSCOPIO

Estrategia
An important strategy is to preview a reading passage by using titles, subtitles, and pictures to tell what it is about. Previewing a passage will give you a feel for its purpose, form, and content.

¡A comenzar!

If you were in Quito making plans with your friends, chances are you'd want to find out what there is to do. But before planning anything, you'll need to know what is going on in the city.

A. Based on what you see, what do you think the CALEIDOSCOPIO section is?
   1. a concert program
   2. a listing of restaurant reviews
   3. a general entertainment guide
   4. a movie magazine with film reviews

¿Te acuerdas?
Scan for specific information
You have already studied *scanning*, an important way to find information. When you scan, look only for specific pieces of information. Look for one thing at a time, and don't concern yourself with the rest of the information.

Al grano
See answers below.

B. Suppose you're in Quito with a group from your school. To find out what's going on, scan the **CALEIDOSCOPIO** section to answer these questions.

Diversiones

• Circo Rolan
Un nuevo concepto en circo
lunes a viernes: 17h30 y 19h30
sábados: 15h00 - 17h30 y 19h30
domingos: 15h00 - 17h30 y 19h30
Avenida Amazonas tras el CCNU.

• El Cafélibro
Peña cultural quiteña con anécdotas, música y poesía nacional. Participación espontánea de los asistentes.

• En el Museo de Arte Moderno de la Casa de la Cultura Ecuatoriana
Se abrirá un taller juvenil de dibujo para chicos entre los 13 y los 17 años que se llevará a cabo de miércoles a viernes de 10h00 a 12h00.

Teatro República presenta el gran espectáculo de teatro y marionetas ANGELONI ÚNICO, CÓMICO, MUSICAL sábado y domingo 11:00 - 14:30 - 16:30 horas s/6.000.

El mimo José Vacas presenta su nueva obra "Relatos para los que no quieren oír" en el Patio de Comedias, de jueves a domingo, a las 20h00.

Answers

B 1. In El Cafélibro you can hear national music and poetry. A drawing workshop for youths between 13 and 17 yrs. old
2. In El Patio de Comedias there is a mime performance. The marionetas ANGELONI are a puppet show with music and comedy.
3. In the Cafélibro you can listen to jazz. The concert in the Coliseo Rumiñahui with Miguel Bosé starts the latest at 8:00 P.M. Concerts in the U.S. usually begin around 8:00 P.M.
4. In the Normandie Cocina they serve French food. In the Restaurante La Choza they serve Ecuadorean food. There is a buffet in the Restaurante Rincón La Ronda.

Conciertos

Concierto de jazz con Larry Salgado y su grupo. Desde las 18h00 en el Cafélibro (Almagro y Pradera).

Banda sinfónica municipal Concierto de aniversario el jueves a las 19h30 en el Teatro Nacional.

¡El concierto del año! El viernes a las 20h00 en el Coliseo Rumiñahui el cantante español, Miguel Bosé.

Restaurantes

Restaurante LA CHOZA, El Palacio de la Cocina Ecuatoriana.- 12 de Octubre No. 1955 y Cordero.- Tfnos. 230-839 y 507-901 Quito.- Atención de lunes a viernes de 12 m. a 3.30 p.m.- y de 7 p.m. a 9.30 p.m. Sábados y domingos de 12 m. a 4 p.m.

Normandie Cocina francesa clásica. Lunes a viernes, almuerzo 12h30 a 14h30; y cena de 19h30 a 22h30. Sábados, sólo cena de 19h30 a 22h30 Leonidas Plaza 1048 entre Baquerizo y García (tras del teatro Fénix). Telfs: 233116, 507747 Quito

La Guarida del Coyote. Antojitos mexicanos. Bar restaurante mexicano. –Carrión 619 y Juan León Mera –Japón 542 y Naciones Unidas, Quito

Restaurante Rincón La Ronda. La mejor comida nacional e internacional, abierto los 365 días del año. Disfrute de nuestro tradicional buffet familiar todos los domingos. Belo Horizonte 400 y Almagro. Telfs: 540459, 545176 Quito

See answers to activities below.

1. Look at the ***Diversiones*** section. Where can you hear national music and poetry? What's going on at the Museum of Modern Art?
2. According to the ***Teatro*** section, where can you see a mime perform? Which event is a musical comedy?
3. Look at the ***Conciertos*** section. Where can you listen to jazz? Which concert begins the latest and when does it start? When do concerts in the U.S. usually begin?
4. Which restaurant in the ***Restaurantes*** section serves French food? What kind of food is served in ***Restaurante La choza***? Which restaurant has a buffet?

C. Imagine you're standing in line at a tourist information desk in Quito. What do you think the clerk would suggest from the listings for each person or group? Explain why it would be appropriate.

1. a family who likes animals, clowns, etc.
2. a young boy who enjoys puppet shows
3. a family who wants to try typical Ecuadorean food
4. a young woman who is interested in hearing local music
5. a woman who likes to draw and do artwork

D. Imagínate que estás en Quito con un grupo de turistas y ustedes tienen tres días libres. ¿Qué piensan hacer? Usa la guía para decidir qué lugares, restaurantes y atracciones piensan visitar. Invítale a un compañero o compañera a algunos lugares que quieres visitar. Si quieres ir, acepta la invitación. Si no quieres ir, dale una excusa y dile qué prefieres hacer. Al final, hagan una lista de seis actividades que quieren hacer juntos.

C 1. Circo Rolán. The circus usually has animals and clowns and is good family entertainment.
2. Teatro República. The marionette show is good for the young boy who likes puppet shows.
3. The Restaurante La Choza serves good Ecuadorean food.
4. El Cafélibro has national music.
5. El Museo de Arte Moderno. Depending on her age, she may be able to participate in the workshop.

D *Answers will vary.*

Language Note

Point out that many words in Spanish are derivatives of other words with similar meanings. For example, the word **asistente** comes from **asistir,** *to attend.* Knowing this, students may be able to deduce that **asistente** means *attendee.*

POSTREADING
Activity D

Teaching Suggestion

List some of the 24-hour times in the **CALEIDOSCOPIO** section on the board or a transparency. Ask students to give them in 12-hour times, referring to Chapter 3.

Thinking Critically

Drawing Inferences Ask students to compare and contrast the restaurant hours in Ecuador with those in the United States. What can they infer about when people eat in Ecuador? (They will learn more about this in Chapter 8.)

Portfolio

Oral Have students work with a partner to role-play a telephone conversation with a museum employee. They should ask for exhibit times and days, and what the exhibit is about. They could also ask for museum hours and whether there is a restaurant in the museum. Have them record the conversation and use it as a Portfolio entry. For Portfolio information, see *Assessment Guide,* pp. 2–13.

Teacher Note

For additional readings, see *Native Speaker Activity Book,* p. 35 and *Practice and Activity Book,* p. 83.

Culture Note

In Spain and many Latin American countries, the 24-hour clock is used for transportation timetables and entertainment listings. Ask students what time a movie starts if the 24-hour listing is 20h25. (8:25 P.M.)

The **Repaso** reviews and integrates all four skills and culture in preparation for the Chapter Test.

Portfolio

1 Oral This telephone conversation would be an appropriate entry for students to put in their Portfolio. For Portfolio suggestions, see *Assessment Guide,* p. 20.

For Individual Needs

2 Challenge Have students suggest alternatives to the invitations they decline. They may offer alternate times or activities.

Portfolio

4 Written You may wish to point this activity out to your students as a potential written Portfolio entry. For Portfolio suggestions, see *Assessment Guide,* p. 20.

REPASO

1 With a partner, prepare a telephone conversation that includes the following items:

a. Greet each other and ask for the person to whom you wish to speak.
b. Talk about what you both like to do and what you prefer.
c. One of you invites the other to join you in an activity.
d. The other accepts or politely declines the invitation.
e. If the invitation is accepted, give the details of time and place.
f. If the invitation is declined, suggest an alternate activity or time.
g. Say goodbye and make plans to see each other soon.

2 Work with a partner and take turns inviting each other to do the following activities. Accept four and decline four of the invitations.

1. visitar el museo
2. ir al parque de atracciones
3. bucear en el lago
4. jugar al voleibol en el parque
5. ir a una fiesta de sorpresa
6. escuchar música en un concierto
7. visitar el acuario o el zoológico
8. ir al teatro para ver un drama de Shakespeare

3 Listen to the following invitations and either accept or decline each one. Using the items in the word box, write your answers and be sure to use a different excuse for each situation. Try to combine some of the phrases in your answer.

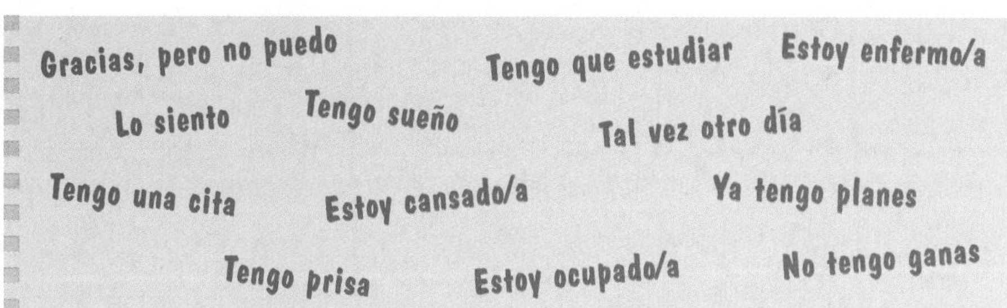

4 What are your plans for the weekend? Using the expressions you've learned in this chapter, choose five activities that might be part of your plans, and write a short paragraph about your weekend plans. Include what you have to do to get ready for each activity.

MODELO Este fin de semana... quiero ir a...
tengo que...
me gustaría...

Possible answers below.

5 Working in groups of three, take turns looking at the picture and inviting your partners to go to the places shown. Each person should either accept the invitation or decline it. If you decline an invitation, you should give an excuse or tell what you prefer to do.

6 Responde a las siguientes oraciones con **cierto** o **falso.** Corrige las oraciones falsas. Basa tus respuestas en la **Nota cultural** y el **Panorama cultural.**

1. En todos los países hispanohablantes, tienes que tener veintiún años para obtener una licencia de manejar.
2. Muchos jóvenes en los países en Latinoamérica tienen coches.
3. El transporte público es barato en España y en Latinoamérica.

7 **SITUACIÓN**

Imagine that your Great-Aunt Hortensia has two tickets to an accordion concert (**concierto de acordeón**) this Saturday and wants you to go with her. You already have plans to go out with your friends, but you don't want to hurt her feelings. With a classmate, take turns role-playing a conversation between you and your **tía abuela** Hortensia. Politely turn down her invitation and make an excuse, but remember to thank her for inviting you.

Answers

5 *Answers will vary.*

6 1. Falso; En algunos países hispanohablantes hay que tener 18 años para obtener una licencia de manejar.
2. Falso; Muchas personas en los países de Latinoamérica no tienen coches porque son muy caros.
3. Cierto

Additional Practice

5 Have students write a paragraph describing what people in this town do in their free time. Include as much detail as possible, such as what they like and dislike doing, show times, the cost of tickets, where people go on dates, and how the weather affects people's plans.

TEACH

To reduce students' fears of speaking Spanish, illustrate that there are many ways to say the same thing. Write an English word on the board and draw a sun around it. Draw several rays coming from the sun. At the ends of the rays, write Spanish synonyms for the English word. For example, if the word you write in the center is TRUE, the Spanish words could include **verdad, cierto, preciso, real, correcto, exactamente.** You might make this a contest among groups to see who can come up with the most synonyms.

Video Wrap-up

- ***Video Program***
- ***Expanded Video Program, Videocassette 3***
- ***Videodisc Program, Videodisc 4A***

At this time, you might want to use the video resources for additional review and enrichment. See *Video Guide* or *Videodisc Guide* for suggestions regarding:

- **¿Qué hacemos?** (Dramatic episode)
- **Panorama cultural** (Interviews)
- **Video clips** (Authentic footage)

This page is intended to prepare students for the Chapter Test. It is a brief checklist of the major points covered in the chapter. The students should be reminded that it is a checklist only and does not necessarily include everything that will appear on the Chapter Test.

A VER SI PUEDO . . .

Possible answers to activities below.

Can you talk on the telephone? p. 183

1 You're answering phones at the office at your school. What would you say in the following situation?

El teléfono suena.

TÚ ______

SR. GIBSON Buenas tardes. ¿Está la profesora Margarita Gibson, por favor?

TÚ ______

SR. GIBSON De parte de su esposo.

TÚ ______

SR. GIBSON ¿Puedo dejar un recado?

TÚ ______

Can you extend and accept invitations? p. 184

2 How would you invite the following people to do something with you? How might they accept your invitation?

1. tu mejor amigo/a
2. tu hermano/a
3. uno de tus padres
4. tu profesor/a
5. tu primo/a
6. tu novio/a

Can you make plans? p. 188

3 What do you plan to do this weekend? Give specific days, times, and places you plan to go, people you plan to see, and things you plan to do.

Can you talk about getting ready? p. 190

4 What do you usually need to do to get ready in these situations?

1. para ir al colegio
2. para salir con amigos
3. para ir a una fiesta formal
4. para ir a una boda
5. para hacer un viaje al campo
6. para ir al teatro

Can you turn down an invitation and make an excuse? p. 193

5 How would you turn down the following invitations?

1. your friend invites you to a surprise birthday party for his four-year-old brother
2. your parents invite you to go to the theater with them
3. your teacher invites you and your parents to go to the amusement park with him and his family

6 Regina is a new girl at school, and Samuel wants to get to know her better. Unfortunately, she has a different excuse for everything he asks her to do. What are some of her excuses?

1. Regina, ¿quieres ir al partido de béisbol del colegio el viernes después de clase?
2. ¿Quieres ir al zoológico el sábado?
3. Entonces, ¿te gustaría estudiar juntos el domingo por la tarde?

Answers

1 *Possible answer:*
—Aló, buenas tardes.
—¿De parte de quién?
—Lo siento, está ocupada.
—Sí, cómo no.

2 *Answers will vary.*

3 *Answers will vary.*

4 *Answers will vary.*

VOCABULARIO

PRIMER PASO

Talking on the telephone

Aló *Hello*
¿De parte de quién? *Who's calling?*
Diga *Hello*
Está bien. *All right.*
La línea está ocupada. *The line is busy.*
Llamo más tarde. *I'll call later.*
un momento *one moment*
¿Puedo dejar un recado? *May I leave a message?*

Extending and accepting invitations

el acuario *aquarium*
la boda *wedding*
el campo *country*
el circo *circus*
la ciudad *city*
¡Claro que sí! *Of course!*
empezar (ie) *to begin*
el evento *event*
una fiesta de aniversario *anniversary party*
de cumpleaños *birthday party*
de graduación *graduation party*
de sorpresa *surprise party*
el lago *lake*
el lugar *place*
Me gustaría... *I would like . . .*
el museo de antropología *anthropology museum*
Nos gustan... *We like . . .*
el parque de atracciones *amusement park*
preferir (ie) *to prefer*
el teatro *theater*
¿Te gustaría...? *Would you like . . .?*
Te invito *It's my treat*
venir (ie) *to come*
el zoológico *zoo*

SEGUNDO PASO

Making plans

¡Cómo no! *Of course!*
ir + a + infinitive *going to (do something)*
pensar (ie) + infinitive *to plan, to intend*

Talking about getting ready

afeitarse *to shave*
ducharse *to take a shower*
estar listo/a *to be ready*
lavarse los dientes *to brush your teeth*
maquillarse *to put on make-up*
peinarse *to comb your hair*

TERCER PASO

Turning down an invitation; making an excuse

cansado/a *tired*
una cita *a date, an appointment*
enfermo/a *sick*
Lo siento. No puedo. *I'm sorry. I can't.*
ocupado/a *busy*
¡Qué lástima! *What a shame!*
tal vez otro día *perhaps another day*
tener ganas de + infinitive *to feel like (doing something)*
tener que + infinitive *to have to (do something)*
tener sueño *to be sleepy*
Ya tengo planes. *I already have plans.*

TPR In two teams play MÍMICA. (See "Game," p. 119.) On slips of paper, write some of the sports, activities, and places of interest from this chapter. Alternating teams, players pantomime the word or words on their paper for the other team to guess.

VOCABULARIO
CAPÍTULO 7

For Individual Needs

Kinesthetic Learners Use a foam ball to review new vocabulary with students. Toss the ball to a student, calling out the English gloss for a new Spanish vocabulary word or phrase. If the student says the Spanish vocabulary correctly, then he or she can choose the next participant and toss the ball to that person. If he or she answers incorrectly, the ball must be handed back to the teacher, who chooses the next student.

Teacher Note

Remind students of the Additional Vocabulary feature starting on page 340.

CHAPTER 7 ASSESSMENT

CHAPTER TEST

- *Chapter Teaching Resources, Book 2,* pp. 145–150, 159, 160
- *Assessment Guide,* Speaking Test, p. 31
- *Assessment Items, Audiocassette* 8A *Audio CD 7*

TEST GENERATOR, CHAPTER 7

ALTERNATIVE ASSESSMENT

Performance Assessment
Have students perform **Repaso** Activity 7, p. 199, as a cumulative performance assessment activity.

Portfolio Assessment

- **Written: Repaso** Activity 4, *Pupil's Edition,* p. 198 *Assessment Guide,* p. 20
- **Oral: Repaso** Activity 1, *Pupil's Edition,* p. 198 *Assessment Guide,* p. 20

Capítulo 8: ¡A comer!
Chapter Overview

De antemano pp. 204–206 — **¿Qué vas a pedir?**, p. 204 — *Practice and Activity Book*, pp. 85–86 — *Video Guide* OR *Videodisc Guide*

	FUNCTIONS	GRAMMAR	CULTURE	RE-ENTRY
Primer paso pp. 207–211	Talking about meals and food, p. 207	• The verb **encantar** and indirect object pronouns, p. 208 • **o** to **ue** stem-changing verbs, p. 210	• **Nota cultural,** Breakfast in Spanish-speaking countries, p. 209 • **Nota cultural,** Lunch in Spanish-speaking countries, p. 210 • **Panorama cultural, ¿Cuál es un plato típico de tu país?,** p. 211	• Expressing likes and dislikes • **e** to **ie** stem-changing verbs • Times of day
Segundo paso pp. 212–215	Commenting on food, p. 212	• Use of **estar** to talk about how things taste, p. 212 • Expressions with **tener,** p. 213	• **Nota cultural,** Common Andean dishes, p. 214 • **Encuentro cultural, La comida de las Américas,** p. 215	• **estar** versus **ser** • Expressions with **tener**
Tercer paso pp. 216–221	• Making polite requests, p. 216 • Ordering dinner in a restaurant, p. 218 • Asking for and paying the bill in a restaurant, p. 218	**otro** and gender agreement, p. 216	• **Nota cultural,** Dinner in Spanish-speaking countries, p. 217 • **Nota cultural,** Latin American and Spanish **tortillas,** p. 220 • **Nota cultural,** Table manners in Spanish-speaking countries, p. 221	• Numbers from 200 to 100,000 • Question words **¿qué?** and **¿cuánto?**

Letra y sonido p. 221 — Pronouncing the letter **c** — **Dictado:** *Textbook Audiocassette 4B/Audio CD 8*

Vamos a Leer pp. 222–223 — **Batidos y sorbetes** — **Reading Strategy**: Recognizing text organization

Review pp. 224–227 — **Repaso,** pp. 224–225 — **A ver si puedo...,** p. 226 — **Vocabulario,** p. 227

Assessment Options

Quizzes
- *Chapter Teaching Resources, Book 2*
  Primer paso, Quiz 8-1, pp. 197–198
  Segundo paso, Quiz 8-2, pp. 199–200
  Tercer paso, Quiz 8-3, pp. 201–202
- *Assessment Items, Audiocassette 8A/Audio CD 8*

Chapter Test
- *Chapter Teaching Resources, Book 2*, pp. 203–208
- *Assessment Guide*, Speaking Test, p. 31
- *Assessment Items, Audiocassette 8A/Audio CD 8*

Test Generator, Chapter 8

RESOURCES: Print	RESOURCES: Audiovisual
Video Program OR *Expanded Video Program, Videocassette 3* OR *Videodisc Program, Videodisc 4B*	*Textbook Audiocassette 4B/Audio CD 8*
	Textbook Audiocassette 4B/Audio CD 8
Practice and Activity Book, pp. 86–88	
Native Speaker Activity Book, pp. 36–40	
Chapter Teaching Resources, Book 2	
• Additional Listening Activities 8-1, 8-2, p. 185	*Additional Listening Activities, Audiocassette 10A/Audio CD 8*
• Student Response Forms, pp. 194–196	
• Realia 8-1, pp. 189, 191	
• Situation Cards 8-1, pp. 192–193	
• Teaching Transparency Master 8-1, pp. 181, 184	*Teaching Transparency 8-1*
• Quiz 8-1, pp. 197–198	*Assessment Items, Audiocassette 8A/Audio CD 8*
Video Guide	*Video Program* OR *Expanded Video Program, Videocassette 3*
Videodisc Guide	*Videodisc Program, Videodisc 4B*
	Textbook Audiocassette 4B/Audio CD 8
Practice and Activity Book, pp. 89–91	
Native Speaker Activity Book, pp. 36–40	
Chapter Teaching Resources, Book 2	
• Communicative Activity 8-1, pp. 177–178	
• Additional Listening Activities 8-3, 8-4, p. 186	*Additional Listening Activities, Audiocassette 10A/Audio CD 8*
• Student Response Forms, pp. 194–196	
• Realia 8-1, pp. 190, 191	
• Situation Cards 8-2, pp. 192–193	
• Teaching Transparency Master 8-2, pp.182, 184	*Teaching Transparency 8-2*
• Quiz 8-2, pp. 199–200	*Assessment Items, Audiocassette 8A/Audio CD 8*
Videodisc Guide	*Videodisc Program, Videodisc 4B*
	Textbook Audiocassette 4B/Audio CD 8
Practice and Activity Book, pp. 92–94	
Native Speaker Activity Book, pp. 36–40	
Chapter Teaching Resources, Book 2	
• Communicative Activity 8-2, pp. 179–180	
• Additional Listening Activities 8-5, 8-6, p. 187	*Additional Listening Activities, Audiocassette 10A/Audio CD 8*
• Student Response Forms, pp. 194–196	
• Realia 8-2, pp. 190, 191	
• Situation Cards 8-3, pp. 192–193	
• Teaching Transparency Master 8-3, pp. 183, 184	*Teaching Transparency 8-3*
• Quiz 8-3, pp. 201–202	*Assessment Items, Audiocassette 8A/Audio CD 8*
Videodisc Guide	*Video Program, Videodisc 4B*
Video Guide	*Video Program* OR *Expanded Video Program, Videocassette 3*
Videodisc Guide	*Videodisc Program, Videodisc 4B*

Alternative Assessment

- Performance Assessment
  Primer paso, p. 210
  Segundo paso, p. 214
  Tercer paso, p. 221
- Portfolio Assessment
  Written: **Repaso,** Activity 6, *Pupil's Edition,* p. 224
  Assessment Guide p. 21
  Oral: **Repaso,** Activity 3, *Pupil's Edition,* p. 224
  Assessment Guide, p. 21

Capítulo 8: ¡A comer!
Textbook Listening Activities Scripts

For Student Response Forms, see *Practice and Activity Book,* pp. 194–196.

Primer paso

Activity 6, p. 208

MARCELA ¿Te gustan los huevos?
ROBERTO Sí, me encantan los huevos revueltos con tocino.
MARCELA A mí me encanta el pan dulce. ¿Y a ti?
ROBERTO No, no me gusta para nada.
MARCELA Bueno... a ver... ¿tomas café?
ROBERTO Uy, no me gusta el café para nada. Es horrible.
MARCELA Entonces, ¿qué prefieres tomar? ¿jugo de naranja o leche?
ROBERTO Prefiero tomar leche.
MARCELA A mí me gusta más el jugo de naranja. Me encantan las frutas.
ROBERTO A mí también. Especialmente los plátanos.

Answers to Activity 6

A Roberto le gustan los huevos revueltos con tocino, la leche y las frutas, especialmente los plátanos. A Marcela le gustan el pan dulce, el jugo de naranja y las frutas.

Activity 12, p. 210

ADELA Pablo, quiero saber cómo son las comidas en los Estados Unidos. En general, ¿a qué hora desayunas?
PABLO Bueno, en general desayunamos a las siete de la mañana.
ADELA ¿Y qué hay para el desayuno?
PABLO Hay de todo. Muchas veces hay huevos, pan tostado, jugo de fruta y café.
ADELA ¿Y a qué hora almuerzan Uds.?
PABLO Durante la semana, almorzamos a las doce.
ADELA ¿Y qué hay para el almuerzo?
PABLO A veces hay sopa, sándwiches y leche.

Answers to Activity 12

el desayuno: a las siete de la mañana; come huevos, pan tostado, jugo de fruta y café
el almuerzo: a las doce; toma sopa, sándwiches y leche

Segundo paso

Activity 16, p. 212

1. Este pescado está muy rico. ¡Me encanta!
2. Esta sopa no me gusta. Está fría.
3. ¿Qué tal la ensalada? ¡Está deliciosa!, ¿no?
4. Esta carne está muy picante. ¡Necesito agua!
5. La sopa está muy salada. ¡Qué horrible!
6. La ensalada de frutas no está muy buena hoy.

Answers to Activity 16

1. pescado: sí
2. sopa: no
3. ensalada: sí
4. carne: no
5. sopa: no
6. ensalada de frutas: no

Activity 21, p. 213

DIEGO ¿Tienes hambre, Isabel?
ISABEL No Diego, no tengo mucha hambre, pero tengo sed.
DIEGO ¿Por qué no tomas una limonada?
ISABEL Buena idea. Me encanta la limonada.
DIEGO Estela, ¿qué quieres almorzar? ¿Tienes hambre?
ESTELA Sí, sí, pero me gustaría desayunar. ¿Qué hay para el desayuno?
DIEGO Sólo hay jugo de manzana y pan tostado. Yo voy a comer la sopa de legumbres. ¡Me encanta la sopa aquí! Y Rafael, ¿qué vas a almorzar tú?
RAFAEL Nada. No tengo mucha hambre.

Answers to Activity 21

1. Estela
2. Isabel
3. Rafael e Isabel
4. Diego
5. jugo de manzana y pan tostado

Tercer paso

Activity 28, p. 217

1. —Voy a pedir una sopa de pollo, pescado, verduras y una ensalada, por favor.
   —Muy bien, señorita.
2. —¿Me trae fruta, café y pan tostado, por favor?
   —Sí, con mucho gusto.
3. —¿Nos trae café y un pastel, por favor?
   —Claro que sí, señora.
4. —No tengo mucha hambre. Voy a pedir una sopa de pollo, pan y un refresco, nada más.
   —Gracias, señor.
5. —Um, son las dos y media. Tengo mucha hambre. ¿Me trae la sopa de tomate, el bistec, papas fritas, zanahorias, una ensalada, pan y el postre, por favor? Y café más tarde. Gracias.
   —Muy bien, señor.
6. —¿Nos trae huevos revueltos con jamón, pan tostado, jugo de naranja y café, por favor?
   —Claro que sí.
7. —Voy a pedir una ensalada, arroz con pollo, postre y café.
   —Muy bien, señora.
8. —¿Tiene pasteles señor? ¿Me trae uno de chocolate? Y para mi amiga, uno de vainilla, por favor.
   —Gracias, señoritas.

Answers to Activity 28

1. lunch or dinner
2. breakfast
3. dessert
4. dinner or lunch
5. lunch
6. breakfast
7. dinner or lunch
8. dessert

Activity 32, p. 219

1. siete mil sucres
2. ocho mil quinientos sucres
3. cuatro mil sucres
4. cinco mil quinientos sucres
5. cuatro mil quinientos sucres
6. ocho mil setecientos cincuenta sucres

Answers to Activity 32

1. sancocho
2. ceviche de camarón
3. helado de naranjilla
4. ensalada mixta
5. canoa de frutas
6. pollo al ajillo

Letra y sonido, p. 221

For the scripts for Parts A and C, see p. 221. The script for Part B is below.

B. Dictado

Para este pastel de chocolate, necesito harina, azúcar y huevos. También quiero poner coco y dos cucharadas de cacao.

Repaso

Activity 1, p. 224

No me gusta para nada el pescado, pero el pollo sí, me gusta mucho. Los frijoles no me gustan porque son muy salados. Me encantan las legumbres, pero la carne no me gusta mucho. Para el desayuno los huevos revueltos con queso son muy ricos.

Answers to Repaso Activity 1

Ángel likes:	*Ángel doesn't like:*
el pollo	el pescado
las legumbres	los frijoles
los huevos revueltos con queso	la carne

Capítulo 8: ¡A comer!

Projects

In this project students plan a tasting party (**una fiesta internacional**) *of everyday dishes from Spanish-speaking countries. They write invitations, accept the invitations through acted-out phone calls, cook simple dishes, sample the dishes while conversing in Spanish with classmates at a fiesta, and write thank-you notes. The project will require one full class period and a portion of two or three others.*

MATERIALS

✂ **Students may need**

- Paper
- Markers
- Paper plates
- Paper glasses
- Plastic utensils
- Paper napkins

SEQUENCE

1. Students work in groups of four. Each group selects a recipe to prepare for the class. If students are unfamiliar with foods in Spanish-speaking countries, you might have them go to the school or public library and research international cookbooks for recipe ideas.
2. Set a date for the **fiesta.**
3. Students divide the responsibilities for the preparation and decide how they will accomplish everything. Dishes are to be prepared outside of class. Students only need to prepare enough for everyone to have a taste.
4. Tell students that their presentation of the prepared dish will be part of their grade.
5. Each student designs and writes an invitation in Spanish. Students exchange invitations with classmates from another group.
6. Pairs who have exchanged invitations act out calling each other to accept the invitation they have received. Their conversations might be recorded on audio- or videotape for grading purposes. Invitations are turned in.
7. At the **fiesta**, students sample the different items and use Spanish to converse and comment on the various dishes.
8. Students straighten up the classroom after they have finished the **fiesta.**
9. On the following day, students write and hand-deliver a thank-you note in Spanish to the person from whom they received their invitation. The thank-you notes become a part of the assessment.

GRADING THE PROJECT

Suggested point distribution (total = 100 points):

Written invitation	10
Telephone conversation	20
Selecting recipe and preparing food	10
Presentation of the dish	15
Using Spanish at **fiesta**	35
Thank-you note	10

Project Extension

In this project, individuals contribute recipes to a class cookbook.

MATERIALS

✂ **Students may need**

- Paper
- Markers
- Glue

SEQUENCE

1. Ask students to bring in a recipe for one of their favorite dishes.
2. Help students (and have students help each other) to translate their recipes into Spanish.
3. Students decorate their recipes with a drawing or a photo of the prepared dish.
4. Students explain their recipe to the class in Spanish. (If it is feasible, you might have them present the recipe and prepare it at the same time. This could be a "live," in-class presentation, or a videotaped presentation done in a kitchen, resembling a television cooking show.)
5. Collect the recipes and compile them into a ringed binder. You may want to make enough copies of the cookbook for each student to have his or her own.

GRADING THE PROJECT

Suggested point distribution (total = 100 points):

Translation of recipe	30
Design and creativity	30
Oral presentation	40

COMMUNITY LINK

If students know native Spanish speakers or people who have lived in Spanish-speaking countries, they might contact them to obtain recipes to prepare. You may want to invite native speakers to attend the **fiesta** and converse in Spanish with students.

Capítulo 8: ¡A comer!

Games

UN CRUCIGRAMA PARA TODOS

In this game, students use the chapter vocabulary to create a large crossword puzzle on the board. It may be played after the ***Primer paso.***

Procedure Write a vocabulary word on the board in large, separated, capital letters **(P L A T A N O).** Have a student come to the board and write a second word vertically through the first, using one of its letters.

```
  M
P L A T A N O
  N
  G
  O
```

Now ask another student to think of a word to write horizontally through the second word, and so on. This may also be played by two teams, creating puzzles on two different boards simultaneously. The team that adds the most words to their puzzle in a set time period wins.

This game can be made more or less difficult by limiting words to a narrow category (e.g. **frutas**), a broader category (e.g. **comida**), or opening it up to any Spanish words.

UNA COMIDA ENTERA

This game provides oral practice and a review of the vocabulary presented in this chapter. It may be played after ***Tercer paso.***

Procedure The teacher or a student leads the game. The leader begins the game by asking the first player **¿Qué le puedo traer?** The first player answers by requesting any item a customer might ask for at a restaurant, saying, for example, **Me puede traer un vaso.** The leader repeats the question to the next player who answers, adding an additional item to what the first player said. **(Me puede traer un vaso de jugo de naranja.)**

Play continues with each player adding an item to the list. Students may help each other remember the list by gesturing. You may want to play this game with two teams, alternating from one team to another. When a member of a team cannot continue the sequence, that team loses its turn.

MUCHOS NÚMEROS

This game helps students practice numbers from 1 to 100,000. It may be played after the ***Tercer paso.***

Procedure Divide the class into two teams. Write any number from 1 to 100,000 on the board. A player on Team A reads the number aloud in Spanish. If he or she gets it right, Team A gets a point. If he or she does not get it right, Team B gets a chance to read it correctly for a point.

Continue alternating teams until someone reads it correctly. Then change the number by adding, removing or changing one digit. (205 could become 105 or 215, for example, or 2056, or 20.) The next team starts this round by having a player read the new number.

DE VUELTA AL MUNDO

This is a fast vocabulary review game that is easy to set up and fun to play. It may be played after the ***Primer paso*** *and at the end of the chapter.*

Preparation You will need picture flash cards of vocabulary items. Before the game begins, tell students that after the game, they will have to write down as many vocabulary words as they can remember. You may want to have students clear their desks so they won't be tempted to write down the pool of words as the game proceeds. You may also want to ask for a volunteer to be the score keeper.

Procedure Divide the class into two teams. Representatives from each team stand side-by-side at a set location in the classroom. Hold up a flash card so that all students can see it. The first of the contestants to name the picture in Spanish wins a point for his team. If neither of the contestants can identify the picture, neither team wins a point on that round.

Teammates are not allowed to call out the correct answer to each other, as this behavior will reduce their team's score by one point. The round continues in this manner until each student has had a chance to play.

Play as many rounds as you like. When the game ends, have students write down as many of the vocabulary words used in the game as they can remember. You might give a prize to the student who recalls the most vocabulary.

Capítulo 8
¡A comer!
pp. 202–227

Using the Chapter Opener

Motivating Activity

Ask students to think about the cultural importance of food. What does it mean to them? Do they have fond memories associated with a particular food? (parent's cookie baking, special dishes used for special occasion) What do they usually eat at each meal? Do they eat with their families? What kind of restaurant do they prefer? Do their families cook any ethnic dishes?

Teacher Note

Throughout this chapter it would be helpful if the class could collect used magazines from which to clip pictures of food. You might also have them bring in non-perishable food items.

Photo Flash!

Ask students to name the fruits they recognize in the photo. They might mention **plátano** (*banana*), **piña** (*pineapple*), **fresa** (*strawberry*), and **coco** (*coconut*). Ecuador also has many fruits students may not have tried, such as **maracuyás** (*passion fruit*), **papayas, mangos, naranjillas** (*a fruit that tastes like a bitter orange*).

1 ¡Me encantan las frutas frescas!

202 *doscientos dos*

Multicultural Link

In this chapter students will learn about food in Ecuador and in other Spanish-speaking countries. Ask students what foods they identify with different areas of the world. Then ask students what they think people eat in Spain and Latin America. Have them make a list of their ideas. At the end of the chapter, you may have them revise their list and discuss what they have learned.

One thing that is always popular worldwide is good food! What do you enjoy eating at home? When you go out to eat, do you order your favorite foods? How much do you usually spend? In this chapter, you'll find out more about food and dining out in Spanish-speaking countries.

In this chapter you will learn

- to talk about meals and food
- to comment on food
- to make polite requests; to order dinner in a restaurant; to ask for and pay the bill in a restaurant

And you will

- listen to restaurant conversations
- read recipes on how to make batidos and sorbetes
- write a review of a restaurant
- find out the origin of different foods

2 ¡La sopa está muy rica!

3 Buenas tardes. ¿Qué le puedo traer?

Focusing on Outcomes

Have students match the learner outcomes to the photos on these pages. (1. represents talking about meals and food; 2. represents commenting on food; and 3. represents making polite requests and ordering dinner in a restaurant.) Point out that an important use of a language is talking about food. This includes being able to order and pay for meals and expressing their own preferences. By the end of the chapter, students will be able to participate in this important aspect of Spanish culture, whether in a Spanish-speaking country or a local Hispanic restaurant.

Photo Flash!

All of these photos were taken in Ecuador. The people in the first photo are shopping at an outdoor market, a popular place to shop in Ecuador and many other Spanish-speaking countries. The man in the second photo is eating **sancocho**, a typical Ecuadorean dish.

Language Notes

- In Spanish, fast-food restaurants are called **restaurantes de comida al paso.** Meals *to go* are **para llevar.**
- In addition to **sopa,** *soup* is also called **caldo** (or **locro,** if corn is used). Stews are called **guiso de pollo o carne,** or at times, **secos,** which means *dry.* Ask students why they think the word for stew is **seco.** (By comparison with soups, it is less liquid and "drier.")

Culture Note

Soups and stews are very popular dishes in Ecuador. **Caldo de pollo** (*chicken soup*) is among the most popular.

Video Program or Expanded Video Program, Videocassette 3

or Videodisc Program
Videodisc 4B

Video Synopsis

Raúl, Diego, and Cristina take Chen to a restaurant that serves typical Ecuadorean dishes. Diego orders **sancocho,** Christina orders **empanadas,** and Raúl orders **carne colorada.** They describe the food to Chen, who decides to order **sancocho.** After they have eaten and paid the bill, they leave the restaurant. They are driving along a mountain road when they suddenly have car trouble.

Motivating Activity

Ask students if they like trying new foods. If they were to visit a foreign country, would they like to try regional dishes? What foods from other countries are popular in their area? Which ethnic foods are their favorites?

Presentation

First, have students scan the **fotonovela.** Then, play the video. Have students repeat the dialogue lines after you, frame-by-frame. Periodically stop and ask comprehension questions. **(¿Quiénes van al restaurante? ¿Cómo se llama el hermano de Cristina? En el restaurante, ¿qué come Diego? ¿Cristina? ¿Raúl? ¿Chen?)** Play the video a second time, then have students practice the parts of the characters in groups of four.

DE ANTEMANO

¿Qué vas a pedir?

Cristina, her brother Raúl, and their friend Diego take Chen to the town of Otavalo, famous for its market. On the way, they get hungry, and stop to eat. Why won't they get to Otavalo on time?

Cristina

Diego

Chen

Raúl

1
En camino...

2
Tengo mucha hambre... Ya es la una y media,y generalmente almuerzo a las doce.
No te preocupes, vas a comer bien en el restaurante. Y para el almuerzo, hay platos especiales típicos de la región andina.

3
No sé... ¿qué van a pedir Uds.?
¿Qué vas a pedir?
Voy a pedir sancocho. El sancocho es delicioso aquí.
¿Sancocho?

4
Sí... mira, allí en esa mesa. Es una sopa de pollo, carne, plátanos, maíz y otras verduras.
Uf, no me gustan para nada las empanadas.
Sancocho está bien, pero a mí me encantan las empanadas. Empanadas, por favor.

5
¿Me puede traer carne colorada con papas, por favor?
Cómo no, señor. ¿Y para Ud., joven?
Emmmmmm... Sancocho, por favor.
Y para tomar, ¿nos trae cuatro aguas de Güitig?

Platos Del Día

Carne colorada	S/4.650
Sancocho	S/7.000
Yahuarlocro	S/8.000
Lomo al carbón	S/10.500
Empanadas de morocho	S/2.500
Llapingachos	S/7.500
Postres	
Helado de naranjilla	S/5.000
Tomatillos en almíbar	S/4.500

204

Resources for DE ANTEMANO

Textbook Audiocassette 4B/Audio CD 8
Video Guide
Video Program
Expanded Video Program, Videocassette 3
Videodisc Guide
Videodisc Program, Videodisc 4B
Practice and Activity Book, pp. 85–86

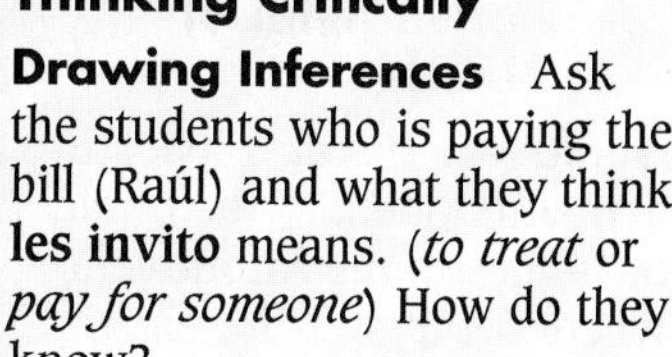

Thinking Critically

Drawing Inferences Ask the students who is paying the bill (Raúl) and what they think **les invito** means. (*to treat* or *pay for someone*) How do they know?

Language Notes

- **Carne colorada** is meat cooked with **achiote,** an orange spice that gives the cooked meat a reddish color and a special flavor. Achiote is made from the seeds of a shrub with decorative flowers that is grown in home gardens.
- **Empanadas** (also called **pasteles** or **hojaldías**) are small pies or turnovers, filled with seasoned meat or fish, but they can also be filled with vegetables or sweets. They are popular in almost all Spanish-speaking countries, although the preparation is time-consuming. Small **empanadas** are served as hors d'oeuvres. Like their European counterpart, pasties, meat **empanadas** are the typical food taken by miners into the mines for lunch or dinner breaks.

History Link

On January 12, 1551, the **cabildo** of Ciudad de los Reyes, today Lima, Peru, ordered that empanadas be made only by specialists, and applied other restrictions to assure their quality. During that period the bakers of Lima seem to have doubled as medical specialists, because on the same date they were forbidden from performing several first aid procedures. Beginning in 1552, bakers had to apply for a license to sell pies.

Video Integration

- ***Expanded Video Program,*** *Videocassette 3*
- ***Videodisc Program,*** *Videodisc 4B*

You may choose to continue with **¿Qué vas a pedir? (a continuación)** now or wait until later in the chapter. At this point in the story, the characters are helped with their car trouble by a passerby. They continue on their journey to Otavalo, a large and colorful market seen in the last frame of the **fotonovela.** They buy traditional sweaters and presents for Chen and his family, as well as some vegetables for Cristina and Raúl's mother. They return to Quito and recount their trip to the mother, showing her their purchases.

For Individual Needs

1 Slower Pace Have students first identify the frame or frames in the **fotonovela** where the answer for each question may be found. Then have them work in pairs comparing the frames they chose and checking the answers.

2 Challenge Have students work in small groups, ideally with a native speaker in each group. Ask them to discuss the phrases found in the **fotonovela** and try and come up with other ways to express them.

2 Visual/Auditory Learners Play the video again and have students raise their hands to pause the videotape or disc when they hear the phrase or see a visual clue to one of the answers. Then have them identify which question was being answered when they asked you to pause the recording.

Additional Practice

5 Ask students to respond with an original statement to each of the **cierto** and **falso** statements. Have them use the expressions they have learned so far. Instead of saying **falso** for the first statement, encourage them to express likes, dislikes and preferences. (**Generalmente no como muchas legumbres. No me gustan.**)

Teaching Suggestion

Have students work in groups of four to read and act out the restaurant scene. Ask one or two groups to perform it for the class.

1 ¿Comprendes? See answers below.

Answer these questions about the **fotonovela.** If you aren't sure, guess!

1. Where do Chen, Cristina, Diego, and Raúl go?
2. Is Chen familiar with the food of Ecuador?
3. What happens when Chen tastes the **ají**?
4. How does Chen like the food he orders?
5. What happens after the group leaves the restaurant?

2 ¿Cómo se dice? See answers below.

What phrases from the **fotonovela** can you use . . .?

1. to ask what someone will order
2. to explain what **sancocho** is
3. to say that you love **empanadas**
4. to ask a waiter to bring you **carne colorada**
5. to say that something is really good
6. to ask how much the bill is

3 ¿Quién lo diría? *Who would say it?* Answers may vary.

1. Me encanta la comida de Ecuador. Chen
2. ¿Empanadas? ¡Qué horrible! Diego
3. Y usted, ¿qué va a pedir? el camarero
4. No quiero sancocho. Y no quiero empanadillas. Raúl
5. ¿Empanadas? ¡Qué rico! Cristina

Los amigos y el camarero

4 ¡Qué lío!

Con base en la fotonovela, pon las oraciones en el orden correcto.

4 **a.** Para Chen, ¡el ají está muy picante!
6 **b.** Hay un problema con el carro.
2 **c.** Los amigos van a un restaurante que tiene comida típica de Ecuador.
5 **d.** A Chen le encanta el sancocho. ¡Está muy rico!
3 **e.** Diego quiere comer sancocho.
1 **f.** Chen tiene mucha hambre.

5 ¿Y tú?

Respond with **cierto** if a statement is true about you, or with **falso** if it is not.

1. Generalmente como muchas legumbres.
2. En casa no comemos comida picante.
3. Me encanta la sopa.
4. No me gustan para nada las empanadas.
5. Para tomar, prefiero el agua.
6. ¡Tengo hambre ahora!

Answers

1 1. to a restaurant
2. no
3. He thinks it is very spicy.
4. He likes it.
5. They have car trouble.

2 1. ¿Qué vas a pedir?
2. Es una sopa de pollo, carne, plátanos, maíz y otras verduras.
3. Me encantan las empanadas.
4. ¿Me puede traer carne colorada?
5. Está muy rico.
6. ¿Cuánto es?

PRIMER PASO

Talking about meals and food

ASÍ SE DICE Talking about meals and food

To ask your friend about meals and food, say:

¿Qué tomas para el desayuno?
What do you have for breakfast?

¿... para el almuerzo?
. . . for lunch?

Tengo sed. ¿Qué hay para tomar?
I'm thirsty. What's there to drink?

Your friend might answer:

A veces tomo un vaso de jugo y un poco de pan. **¡No me gusta** el cereal **para nada!**
I don't like . . . at all!

Por lo general tomo un sándwich, una manzana y un vaso de leche. *Generally I have a sandwich, an apple, and a glass of milk.*

Hay jugo, refrescos y agua. **¿Qué prefieres?**

VOCABULARIO

¡Me encanta el desayuno! *I love breakfast!*

el pan tostado
el tocino
los huevos

el desayuno fuerte

el desayuno ecuatoriano

el desayuno ligero

RESOURCES FOR PRIMER PASO

Textbook Audiocassette 4B/Audio CD 8
Practice and Activity Book, pp. 86–88
Native Speaker Activity Book, pp. 36–40
Video Guide
Video Program
Expanded Video Program, Videocassette 3
Videodisc Guide
Videodisc Program, Videodisc 4B

Chapter Teaching Resources, Book 2
- Additional Listening Activities 8-1, 8-2, p. 185
  Audiocassette 10A/Audio CD 8
- Student Response Forms, pp. 194–196
- Realia 8-1, pp. 189, 191
- Situation Cards 8-1, pp. 192–193
- Teaching Transparency Master 8-1, pp. 181, 184
  Teaching Transparency 8-1
- Quiz 8-1, pp. 197–198
  Audiocassette 8A/Audio CD 8

Jump Start!

On the board or a transparency write the following: **¿Cuál es la fecha?** and **¿Cuál es el pronóstico del tiempo para hoy?** Have students respond in writing.

MOTIVATE

Ask students to compare the breakfasts they eat on school days with those they eat on weekends. What are the similarities and differences?

TEACH

Presentation

Así se dice, Vocabulario
Model the phrases and vocabulary by describing what you and your family or friends have for breakfast and lunch. Then ask students the questions from **Así se dice** and have them answer referring to **Vocabulario.**

Additional Practice

Have students practice the expressions in **Así se dice** with a partner, alternating roles.

Teaching Suggestions

Have students make vocabulary flashcards. Ask them to label the back of the cards with the Spanish definitions. They can use magazine pictures, newspaper grocery ads, or their own drawings on the front. For additional food-related vocabulary, refer them to pages 209, 216, 217, and 340.

You might want to teach the word **blanquillos** for *eggs,* as some native speakers find **huevos** embarrassing.

Presentation

Gramática Model pronunciation by saying what you or others like to eat. Point out that the structure for **encantar** is the same as **gustar.** You may also wish to teach **disgustar** and **fascinar.** Ask each student to write in Spanish a list of ten breakfast foods. Then have them take turns asking a partner about the foods on their list. (**¿Te gusta(n)...? ¿Te encanta(n)? ...**) You might remind students that the use of tag questions like **¿verdad?** and **¿no?** are ways of making Spanish sound more natural.

Teaching Suggestion

7 After students have completed this activity, ask them to write what they and their families like for breakfast. Is there a difference in food between the weekdays and weekends? Do they eat at home or in restaurants? Are their favorite breakfast foods different from their parents'? their siblings'?

Native Speakers

7 Ask students to add a reason why they and their families like certain foods. (**Me encanta el jugo de naranja porque es dulce y muy rico.**) You might discuss what different kinds of foods people from different countries eat at each meal. For example, are foods that are normally eaten for breakfast in Ecuador or Mexico considered lunch items in the United States?

6 Escuchemos: El desayuno

Listen as Marcela and Roberto discuss what foods they like and dislike. Write what each person likes for breakfast.

Answers on p. 201C.

También se puede decir...

Food vocabulary often varies widely from region to region, even within a particular Spanish-speaking country. Other common words for **el plátano** are **la banana, el banano,** and **el guineo. El jugo** is usually called **el zumo** in Spain.

Gramática The verb **encantar** and indirect object pronouns

1. The verb **encantar** *(to really like; to love)* works just like the verb **gustar.**

   Me gusta la leche, pero **me encanta** el jugo de naranja.
   A Juan **le gusta** ser delgado, pero también ¡**le encanta** comer el pan!
   Nos encantan los plátanos.

2. The pronouns **me, te, le, nos, les** in front of the verbs above are called *indirect object pronouns,* which generally tell *to whom* or *for whom.* In this case they tell *to whom* something is pleasing.

   Te gusta la leche, ¿verdad? *Milk is pleasing to you, right?*

   You'll learn more about indirect object pronouns in Chapter 9.

3. Remember to use the definite article with **encantar** or **gustar** when you're saying that you like something in general.

   Me encanta **el** jugo de naranja.

7 ¿Qué te gusta desayunar? Answers will vary.

Forma cuatro oraciones con los siguientes elementos. Usa las formas correctas de **gustar** o **encantar** con **me, te, le, nos** o **les.** Tus oraciones pueden ser negativas.

A mí	gustar	tomar el desayuno juntos	el jugo de toronja
A nosotros	encantar	los huevos	el pan dulce
A mis padres		tomar un café por la mañana	tomar leche
A mi hermano/a			el cereal
A mi amigo/a			

8 ¿Qué hay para el desayuno? Answers will vary.

Prepara cuatro planes de comida. Escribe las comidas y las bebidas apropiadas en las siguientes categorías.

1. un típico desayuno ecuatoriano
2. tu desayuno típico
3. el desayuno ideal
4. un desayuno ligero
5. un desayuno vegetariano
6. un desayuno fuerte

Geography Link

Ecuador lies on the Earth's equator. Ask students what this means regarding Ecuador's climate and crops. (Ecuador has little change of climate throughout the year. For this reason, some fruits and vegetables are always in season and may be purchased all year long.) Have students working in pairs research what produce is grown all year round in Ecuador and what, if any, is seasonal. Have them report on what they find, using as much Spanish as possible.

9 Preferencias

Work with a partner. Read one of your meal plans from Activity 8 and see if your partner can guess what kind of meal it is. Switch roles until you've finished both of your lists.

VOCABULARIO

Para almorzar...

la sopa de legumbres	*vegetable soup*
el atún	*tuna*
la crema de maní y la jalea	*peanut butter and jelly*
el queso	*cheese*

También se puede decir...
Las legumbres are also called **los vegetales** or **las verduras**. Other words for **un sándwich** are **una torta** (Mexico) and **un bocadillo** (Spain). **El cacahuete** and **el cacahuate** are other words for **el maní**.

10 ¿Qué te gusta almorzar? Answers will vary.

Prepara una lista de comidas que puedes preparar con los siguientes ingredientes. Si necesitas más vocabulario, consulta la página 341.

1. queso
2. legumbres
3. pollo
4. atún
5. manzana
6. jamón

NOTA CULTURAL

Breakfast in Spanish-speaking countries is usually eaten around 7:00 or 8:00 A.M. People often eat **un panecillo** (a plain or sweet *roll*) and a piece of fresh fruit, such as **papaya** or **piña** *(pineapple)*. **Café con leche** (mostly warm milk with a little strong coffee), or **chocolate** (*hot chocolate*) are often served for breakfast.

11 Preguntas

Work with a partner. Pick three food items from the vocabulary or words you've learned before, but don't tell your partner what you've chosen. Using yes/no questions only, take turns trying to guess what your partner's choices are one by one.

MODELO	TU COMPAÑERO/A	TÚ
	—¿Es una fruta?	—Sí.
	—¿Es una piña?	—No.
	—¿Es una manzana?	—¡Sí!

Presentation

Vocabulario Model pronunciation of these words using a tag question format by asking students if they like the item illustrated. (**Te gusta la limonada, ¿verdad?**) Elicit responses from several students for each question. Then ask if students can find cognates. Are there any false cognates? (**sopa**) Then ask students **¿Qué hay para almorzar?** They should answer with a new vocabulary word.

Teaching Suggestion

Have students add pictures of the lunch items to their flashcard set.

For Individual Needs

10 Challenge Have students list some of the ingredients for several dishes as you call them out. (**ensalada de frutas, salsa de espagueti, un sándwich "club"**)

Building on Previous Skills

11 Remind students of adjectives they have learned in this and in previous chapters. Have them use these in their questions to their partners about the foods. (**¿Es grande?, ¿Es para el desayuno?, ¿De qué color es?**)

Additional Vocabulary

un sándwich de queso fundido *grilled cheese sandwich*
la sopa de tomate *tomato soup*
una ensalada de frutas *fruit salad*

Teacher Note

The additional food-related vocabulary on page 340 will allow students to personalize answers to any open-ended activities.

Presentation

Gramática Say "Yo almuerzo a las... Mis amigos Paco y Diana almuerzan a las..." Then ask students around the room **¿A qué hora almuerzas tú? ¿A qué hora almuerzan tú y tu familia? ¿A qué hora almorzamos nosotros en esta clase?** Students should respond using the appropriately conjugated verbs. Continue the practice with **desayunar** and **cenar.**

Close

Divide the class into groups of four or five. Each group develops a five-question survey **(encuesta)** of their classmates' eating habits. **(¿Tomas un vaso de jugo para el desayuno?)** All students should respond to every survey's questions. Students write their answers for each **encuesta** on a piece of paper and return it to the correct group.

Assess

Quiz 8-1, *Chapter Teaching Resources, Book 2,* pp. 197–198

Assessment Items, Audiocassette 8A/Audio CD 8

Performance Assessment

Have students make a shopping list of foods to buy for a week of breakfasts and lunches. They should then make a meal calendar for the week and describe to the class what they plan to eat at each meal.

Gramática o → ue stem-changing verbs

1. You've already learned about **e → ie** stem-changing verbs such as **querer.**
2. Another type of stem change is **o → ue. Almorzar** *(to eat lunch)* is an example; all forms have a stem-change except the **nosotros** and **vosotros** forms.

Almuerzo Almuerzas Almuerza	a la una.	¿Almorzamos ¿Almorzáis ¿Almuerzan	juntos?

3. Another **o → ue** stem-changing verb is **poder** *(can; to be able to)*.
   No puedo estudiar contigo esta noche porque tengo que trabajar.

12 Escuchemos: ¿Cómo es la comida aquí?

Listen as an Ecuadorean student asks about meals in the United States. Write the time her friend says he eats each meal in the U.S., and what he eats. Answers on p. 201C.

13 ¿A qué hora almuerzan Uds.?

Dos amigos almuerzan juntos por primera vez. Completa estas partes de su conversación con formas correctas de **almorzar** o **poder.** See answers below.

—¡Qué lástima! Simón no __1__ almorzar con nosotros hoy. En general, él y yo __2__ juntos aquí los miércoles.
—Y los fines de semana, ¿a qué hora __3__ Uds.?
—Nosotros siempre __4__ a las dos de la tarde. ¿ __5__ almorzar tú con Simón y conmigo este sábado a las dos?
—Este sábado yo no __6__ porque tengo que trabajar. Tal vez otro día, ¿no?
—Sí, ¡Cómo no!

Nota cultural

In many Spanish-speaking countries, the main meal—called simply **la comida**—is usually eaten around two o'clock. It is typically a heavier meal than lunch in the U.S. It consists of soup, meat, or fish with rice and vegetables, followed by dessert, and coffee. A typical Ecuadorean dish is **cazuela de marisco,** a casserole prepared in a clay pot with seafood and **maní.** For many people, it is traditional to have a rest, or **siesta,** after the **comida,** and then go back to work until late evening. What advantages can you see in eating the main meal early in the day?

14 Horarios diferentes

Write three sentences saying at what time each member of your household eats breakfast and lunch. Give your partner twenty seconds to look at each sentence. Then read the sentences aloud without saying the person's name, and see if your partner can remember who you're talking about. See answers below.

15 Y ustedes, ¿qué almuerzan?

Working in groups of four, take turns asking each other what time you have breakfast and lunch, and what you usually eat for each meal. Write what each person says. Then report on those who eat meals at the same time or have similiar foods for breakfast and lunch.

Culture Note

At some restaurants in Spanish-speaking countries, an inexpensive lunch menu consists only of two or three complete meals for which substitutions cannot be made. These **comidas corrientes** often include **una sopa, una ensalada, el primer plato, el segundo plato,** and **el postre.** These restaurants are popular, as cafeterias are rare and "fast food" places are economically accesible only to the upper class or upper-middle class.

Answers

13 1. puede 2. almorzamos 3. almuerzan 4. almorzamos 5. Puedes 6. puedo

14 *Sample answer:* Mi madre desayuna a las 7:30 y almuerza a las 2:00.

¿Cuál es un plato típico de tu país?

There are as many different "typical" dishes in the Spanish-speaking world as there are countries and regions. In this chapter we asked people to tell us about the dishes typical to their areas.

Diana
Miami, Florida
"Un plato típico... plátanos maduros con bistec empanizado... Tiene un bistec que está cocinado en pan, un poco de arroz y unos plátanos que están cocinados con azúcar".

Héctor
Valencia, Venezuela
"El pabellón. Es un plato que contiene arroz, caráota, carne mechada y tajada. Es el plato típico de Venezuela".

Juan Fernando
Quito, Ecuador
"El huevo frito con llapingachos y lechuga. Es uno de los platos más típicos que hay, que se inventó cuando vino la colonia española acá, ya que ellos no comían nada de lo preparado por los indígenas... Este plato lo comían los mineros en la época colonial. Llapingachos son tortillas de papa con queso".

Para pensar y hablar...

A. Do you think you would like the dishes that Diana, Héctor, and Juan Fernando describe? Which one would you most like to try? Which one least appeals to you? Why?

B. What characterizes a typical dish? List three things that could make a dish typical to a region. Then, using your list as a guide, answer the question **¿Cuál es un plato típico de tu país?**. What would you suggest visitors try if they were in your area?

Preguntas

1. ¿Qué es el plato típico de Miami, según Diana? (plátanos con bistec)
2. Según lo que dice Héctor, ¿qué plato es típico de Venezuela? (el pabellón)
3. Según Juan Fernando, ¿qué es un llapingacho? (tortilla de papa con queso)
4. ¿Qué se come con los llapingachos? (huevo frito y lechuga)
5. ¿Cuál es un plato típico de los Estados Unidos? (Answers will vary—apple pie, turkey, mashed potatoes)

Language Note

asado *grilled or roasted meat (usually beef)*
vacuno *pertaining to cattle*
pabellón *literally, pavillion; in Venezuela, a regional dish*
caráota *kidney bean, French bean*
carne mechada y tajada *beef prepared with bacon or ham and then sliced*
llapingacho *tortilla made with potato and cheese*

PANORAMA CULTURAL
CAPÍTULO 8

Video Program or Expanded Video Program, Videocassette 3

or Videodisc Program, Videodisc 4B

Teacher Notes

- See *Video Guide* or *Videodisc Guide* for activities related to the **Panorama cultural.**
- Remind students that cultural information may be included in the Quizzes and in the Chapter Test.

Motivating Activity

Ask students what is the most exotic food they have ever eaten and where they tried it. Did they like it? Have they had it since? Have they ever introduced a friend to a new food?

Presentation

Have students read the captions, then show the video. Discuss the questions in **Para pensar y hablar.** Play the video again and have students answer the **Preguntas.**

Thinking Critically

Comparing and Contrasting Héctor describes **el pabellón,** a Venezuelan dish of rice, kidney beans, and slices of meat. Ask students if they can think of a similar dish in the United States. Many Mexican and Tex-Mex restaurants serve **chili** and **fajitas** (strips of chicken or beef) with rice and beans.

Jump Start!

Ask students to look at the photos on p. 207 and decide what they would like to order for breakfast. Ask them to list each item they would like. Are their choices closest to a **desayuno fuerte, ligero,** or **ecuatoriano?**

MOTIVATE

Ask students to consider polite ways to comment on food. At a friend's or relative's, what do they do if they do not like something they are served? If they are served something disagreeable and are asked to comment on it, what should they say? to whom? Explain that in Latin America, etiquette requires that you eat it and simulate pleasure.

TEACH

Presentation

Así se dice Review the various descriptive uses of **estar.** (the weather, locations, people's moods and conditions) Then explain that **estar** is also used to describe food. Ask different students **En la cafetería aquí, ¿cómo están las verduras? ¿el pollo? ¿la fruta?** Use *Teaching Transparency 8-2* for more presentation ideas.

Teaching Suggestion

Ask students to add pictures of the vocabulary in **Así se dice** to their flashcard set.

SEGUNDO PASO

Commenting on food

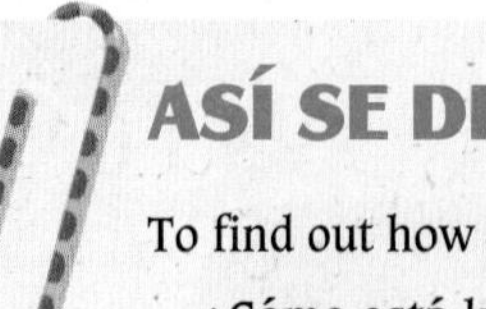

ASÍ SE DICE Commenting on food

To find out how something tastes, ask:

¿**Cómo está** la sopa?
How is . . . ?

¿Y cómo están los frijoles?
How do the beans taste?

¿Y cómo está el postre?
And how's the dessert?

Your friend might answer:

Está **deliciosa.** *. . . delicious.*
Está **fría** y **salada.**
. . . cold . . . salty.
¡Está **caliente**! *. . . hot.*

Están muy **picantes** pero están **ricos.**
. . . spicy . . . delicious.

¡Está muy dulce! *It's very sweet!*

16 Escuchemos: Comentarios

Listen as some customers comment on the food at El Rincón, a restaurant. Write the food item each person mentions. Then, if the person likes the food, write **sí**. If not, write **no**. Answers on p. 201C.

17 ¡La sopa no es mala palabra!

Look at the *Mafalda* comic strip and the soup advertisement. Then think of a sentence stating each of the following people's opinions about soup: Mafalda's, her mother's, and the chef's. What's your opinion? Answers will vary.

Nota Gramatical

The verb **estar** is often used to talk about how specific things taste, look, or feel. **Ser,** which also means *to be,* is used to tell what something is like, or to talk about the general nature of things. Look at the two sentences below. Which one is a general statement, and which is a comment about a particular dish?

Los camarones son ricos.
Shrimp are delicious.

Los camarones están ricos.
The shrimp are (taste) delicious.

RESOURCES FOR SEGUNDO PASO

Textbook Audiocassette 4B/Audio CD 8
Practice and Activity Book, pp. 89–91
Native Speaker Activity Book, pp. 36–40
Videodisc Guide
Video Program, Videodisc 4B

Chapter Teaching Resources, Book 2
- Communicative Activity 8-1, pp. 177–178
- Additional Listening Activities 8-3, 8-4, p. 186
  Audiocassette 10A/Audio CD 8
- Student Response Forms pp. 194–196
- Realia 8-2, pp. 190, 191
- Situation Cards 8-2, pp. 191–193
- Teaching Transparency Master 8-2, pp. 182, 184
  Teaching Transparency 8-2
- Quiz 8-2, pp. 199–200
  Audiocassette 8A/Audio CD 8

18 ¿Cómo está la comida?

Write a caption for each drawing. First ask how the food tastes. Then write what the person would say as a response. See answers below.

Cristóbal

Leticia

Mariano

Gloria

19 Comidas exóticas

Work in pairs. Ask your partner to name a food with an unusual combination of qualities, such as **una sopa fría.** If your partner can name a food that fits in the category (such as **gazpacho,** a cold soup served in Spain), your partner wins a point. If you stump your partner, you win a point.

comida	cualidades
sándwich	frío/a
sopa	picante
postre	dulce
ensalada	salado/a
¿?	caliente
	¿?

20 El menú del día

Imagine that you're planning daily menus at a local restaurant. You need to create different lunch specials for Monday through Friday lunch rushes. Be creative and come up with five tantalizing lunch specials. For additional food related vocabulary, see page 341.

Nota Gramatical

Do you remember the **tener** idioms in Chapter 7? Two other **tener** idioms are **tener hambre** *(to be hungry)* and **tener sed** *(to be thirsty)*. These are often used when talking about meals. Use the feminine form **mucha** with these expressions to mean *very*.

Tengo **mucha sed** pero no tengo **mucha hambre.**

21 Escuchemos: En el restaurante

Cuatro amigos están en un café popular. Escucha mientras hablan de lo que van a comer. Luego contesta estas preguntas. Answers on p. 201C.

1. ¿Quién quiere desayunar?
2. ¿Quién tiene sed?
3. ¿Quién no tiene hambre?
4. ¿Quién va a comer sopa?
5. ¿Qué hay para el desayuno?

Teaching Suggestion

Nota gramatical Present students with situations to respond to. For example, **Son las 10 y 12. Tengo hambre. Me gustaría ____. Tengo sed. Me gustaría ____.** Ask students to complete the sentences with a vocabulary word or words from this chapter.

Native Speakers

19 Ask native speakers or students who have lived in or traveled to a Spanish-speaking country to help other students compile lists of "unusual" foods.

For Individual Needs

19 Visual Learners Have students describe the foods illustrated in *Teaching Transparency 8-2,* based on each diner's reactions.

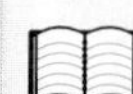

En mi cuaderno

20 For an additional Chapter 8 journal entry suggestion, see *Practice and Activity Book,* page 152.

Additional Practice

20 Give each student a paper plate. Have them draw (or paste magazine pictures of) a meal on their plate. Then ask the students to discuss with a partner their foods, using the vocabulary they have just learned. You might have students present their conversations to the class in pairs.

Answers

18 *Sample answer:*

— Cristóbal, ¿cómo está la comida?
— ¡Está terrible!

Culture Note

You might mention to students that Mafalda (page 212) is a popular comic strip, created by the Argentine cartoonist Quino. The children in the comic address social issues and make humorous, straightforward comments about the world.

CLOSE

Portfolio

Oral Have students review ways of commenting on food and discussing preferences. Then have students role-play a restaurant scene in groups of four or five. One student is the waitperson and the others are a group of friends who order lunch. They should incorporate the menus from Activity 20 as well as some of their conversations from Activity 24. They should discuss how the food tastes, what they would like to order, what don't you like, and what activities they will do after eating. For Portfolio information, see *Assessment Guide,* pp. 2–13.

Teaching Suggestion

You might use peer assessment of the above skits. Give each student a grading sheet with the following information:

People in Group _____
Use of appropriate vocabulary ___ points
Overall presentation ___ points
Creativity ___ points

Ask students to rate each group on a scale from 1 to 5 for each category (with 5 being the best score possible).

ASSESS

Quiz 8-2, *Chapter Teaching Resources, Book 2,* pp. 199-200
Assessment Items, Audiocassette 8A/Audio CD 8

Performance Assessment

Use the restaurant review from Activity 25 to evaluate students' performance. They should include a description of the establishment (diner, elegant restaurant, fast-food place) and what it serves (breakfast foods, lunch specials).

22 Mis preferencias Answers will vary.

Completa las siguientes oraciones con tus preferencias personales.

1. Cuando tengo hambre, prefiero comer...
2. Cuando tengo sed, prefiero tomar...
3. En el verano cuando hace mucho calor me gusta comer...
4. En el invierno cuando hace frío me gusta comer... y tomar...
5. No me gusta(n) para nada...

23 ¿Te gustaría almorzar conmigo?

Create a phone conversation in which you invite your partner to go out to lunch with you. Tell your partner what the menu is and what time you want to go. If your partner accepts, set a time. If your partner turns down the invitation, ask why he or she can't go and make sure he or she gives you a good excuse!

24 ¿Qué vamos a almorzar?

You and your partner from the previous activity are at a local restaurant for lunch. Get together with another pair and imagine that you have all run into each other there. Talk about the menu, whether or not you are really hungry and thirsty, and what you will order.

NOTA CULTURAL

Two common dishes in the Andes mountains are **sancocho** (a thick stew-like soup made of green plantains and corn) and **carne colorada,** (beef which has been prepared with **achiote,** or *annatto,* which gives it a characteristic red color). These dishes, like most Ecuadorean cuisine, are not spicy. **Ají,** a spicy condiment made of tomatoes, onions, and hot, red chili peppers is placed on most tables at mealtime for added flavor.

ají

sancocho

25 En mi cuaderno

What is your favorite restaurant? Write a brief review of one of your favorite places to eat. You could choose a fast-food place or an elegant restaurant. Comment on the service and the kind of food they serve. For more food-related vocabulary, turn to page 341.

Un poco más...

abierto	*open*
el ambiente	*atmosphere*
cerrado	*closed*
la especialidad	*specialty*
exquisito	*exquisite*
el plato del día	*daily special*

Multicultural Link

Point out that **achiote** is used to give food a reddish color and unique flavor. Ask students if they know what spice gives food a yellowish color (saffron), where it is from (the Mediterranean area, Asia Minor, and Iran) and what cuisines it is used in (Spanish, Oriental, Indian, North African). Saffron is the most expensive spice in the world and is considered a delicacy in the United States.

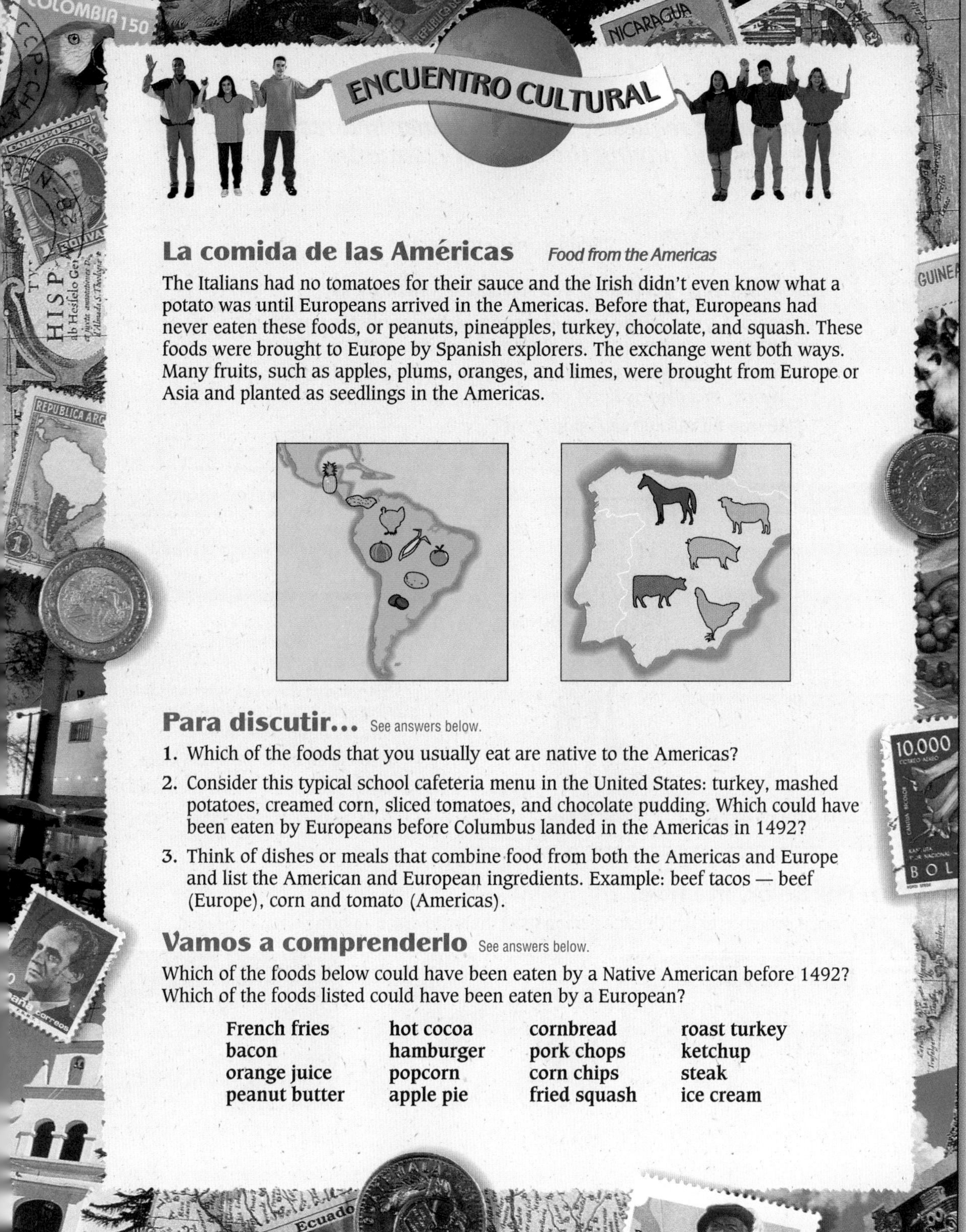

La comida de las Américas *Food from the Americas*

The Italians had no tomatoes for their sauce and the Irish didn't even know what a potato was until Europeans arrived in the Americas. Before that, Europeans had never eaten these foods, or peanuts, pineapples, turkey, chocolate, and squash. These foods were brought to Europe by Spanish explorers. The exchange went both ways. Many fruits, such as apples, plums, oranges, and limes, were brought from Europe or Asia and planted as seedlings in the Americas.

Para discutir... See answers below.

1. Which of the foods that you usually eat are native to the Americas?
2. Consider this typical school cafeteria menu in the United States: turkey, mashed potatoes, creamed corn, sliced tomatoes, and chocolate pudding. Which could have been eaten by Europeans before Columbus landed in the Americas in 1492?
3. Think of dishes or meals that combine food from both the Americas and Europe and list the American and European ingredients. Example: beef tacos — beef (Europe), corn and tomato (Americas).

Vamos a comprenderlo See answers below.

Which of the foods below could have been eaten by a Native American before 1492? Which of the foods listed could have been eaten by a European?

French fries	**hot cocoa**	**cornbread**	**roast turkey**
bacon	**hamburger**	**pork chops**	**ketchup**
orange juice	**popcorn**	**corn chips**	**steak**
peanut butter	**apple pie**	**fried squash**	**ice cream**

ENCUENTRO CULTURAL
CAPÍTULO 8

Presentation

Ask students to make a list of foods they eat frequently. Have them categorize each item under one of these headings: **De las Américas, De Europa,** or **Una combinación de las dos.** Have them compare their list with a partner's. Does their partner agree that each food is placed in the correct category?

Thinking Critically

Analyzing Ask students to consider how cuisines from around the world would be different if the early Spanish explorers and conquerors had not spread foods back and forth between Europe and the Americas. Potato, corn, pineapple, tomato and chocolate came from the Americas. (Perhaps there would be no famous Belgian chocolate, Italian tomato sauce or German potato salad.)

Multicultural Link

In the **Panorama cultural** interview on page 211, Juan Fernando describes an Ecuadorean dish eaten by the European colonists. The Pilgrims in Massachusetts were wary of the Native Americans' foods at first, but they soon came to cultivate and enjoy many of the same foods as their indigenous neighbors (corn, pumpkins). Ask students if they can think of any dishes that combine ingredients native to Europe and the Americas.

Answers
Encuentro cultural
1. corn, tortillas, chocolate, potatoes...
2. none
3. *Answers will vary.*

Vamos a comprenderlo
Native American: French fries, peanut butter, hot cocoa, popcorn, cornbread, corn chips, fried squash, roast turkey, ketchup;
European: bacon, orange juice, hamburger, apple pie, pork chops, steak, ice cream

Jump Start!

On the board or a transparency write **¿Qué hay en tu comida ideal?** Have students list five things and tell them the meal can be outrageous, and should include their favorite foods. When would they eat it? where? with whom?

MOTIVATE

Discuss the ideal meals from **Jump Start!** Have students say in Spanish what they love to eat. See how many unusual combinations students have come up with.

TEACH

Presentation

Así se dice Bring in the following items or pictures of them: a clean and a dirty napkin, a clean and a dirty plate, a clean and a dirty glass. Tell students what the items are using the expressions from **Así se dice.** Give items one by one to students and ask them to make appropriate requests from **Así se dice.** (When you give a student a dirty glass, he or she says **Este vaso está sucio. ¿Me trae otro, por favor?**)

Vocabulario Hold up real items and model the pronunciation of each as you arrange a table setting at the front of the room. Have a student come forward and "sit at the table." Ask the student to close his or her eyes while you remove one of the utensils from the setting. The student then opens his or her eyes, and asks you, the waitperson, to bring what is missing. Repeat this with several students, removing a different utensil each time.

TERCER PASO

Making polite requests; ordering dinner in a restaurant; asking for and paying the bill in a restaurant

ASÍ SE DICE **Making polite requests**

To ask the waitperson to bring you something, you might say:

Camarera, ¿nos puede traer el menú y unas servilletas por favor?
Waitress, can you bring us the menu and some napkins, please?

Camarero, este plato está sucio. ¿Me puede traer un plato limpio?
Waiter, this plate is dirty. Can you bring me a clean plate?

¿Me trae un vaso de agua **por favor?**

También se puede decir...

Another word that you'll commonly hear in Mexico for **el camarero** or **la camarera** is **el mesero** or **la mesera.** Another word for **el menú** is **la carta.**

VOCABULARIO

Nota Gramatical

Otro means *other* or *another*. It agrees in gender and number with the noun it modifies.

otro cuchillo	otra servilleta
otro**s** plato**s**	otra**s** cuchara**s**

26 Por favor, me trae... See answers below.

Write a sentence in which each person asks the waitperson to bring what is needed.

los chicos

Miyoko

Tanya

RESOURCES FOR TERCER PASO

Textbook Audiocassette 4B/Audio CD 8
Practice and Activity Book, pp. 92–94
Native Speaker Activity Book, pp. 36–40
Videodisc Guide
Videodisc Program, Videodisc 4B

Chapter Teaching Resources, Book 2
- Communicative Activity 8-2, pp. 179–180
- Additional Listening Activities 8-5, 8-6, p. 187
  Audiocassette 10A/Audio CD 8
- Student Response Forms, pp. 194–196
- Realia 8-2, pp. 190, 191
- Situation Cards 8-3, pp. 192–193
- Teaching Transparency Master 8-3, pp. 183, 184
  Teaching Transparency 8-3
- Quiz 8-3, pp. 201–202
  Audiocassette 8A/Audio CD 8

VOCABULARIO

La cena en el Café El Rancho

el batido de fresa	*strawberry milkshake*
la carne de res	*beef*
la cebolla	*onion*
los camarones	*shrimp*
el flan	*custard*
la galleta	*cookie*

NOTA CULTURAL

In Spanish-speaking countries, **la cena** is a light meal, usually eaten around 8:00 P.M., sometimes as late as 10:00 P.M. (or even later) in Spain. People generally eat a snack (**una merienda**) around 5:00 P.M. In Ecuador, **la merienda** usually consists of tea or coffee with bread, or perhaps a bowl of soup.

27 Y para comer...
See answers below.

Name the utensil or utensils you use to eat these foods.

1. el helado
2. las legumbres
3. la ensalada
4. el arroz
5. los huevos
6. la sopa

28 Escuchemos: Me trae...

Imagine you're eating at Restaurante El Molino, a busy restaurant in Quito. Listen to these orders and decide if each person is ordering breakfast, lunch, dinner, or dessert.

Answers on p. 201D.

Presentation

Vocabulario To model pronunciation, tell students you are very hungry and say which items on the menu you would like to eat. Then ask students, **¿Qué te gusta para cenar?** and **¿Qué hay para cenar?** Have them answer using the new vocabulary. Then have students practice ordering from the menu, with you playing the role of the **camarero/a.**

For videodisc application, see *Videodisc Guide.*

TPR Have a student set a table **(poner la mesa)** according to your instructions for when, where, and with whom they will be dining. Using **Pon** and **No pongas** and the prepositions of place, tell the student what utensils to put on the table and where to put them. After students have mastered the vocabulary, ask one of them to give instructions while another sets the table. You might also do this activity with all of the students while they sit at their own desks and use plastic utensils.

For Individual Needs

27 Kinesthetic Learners Have students hold up the utensil as they give the answers. Add several items from the menu to continue the activity.

Answers

26 1. Por favor, ¿nos puede traer servilletas?
2. Por favor, ¿me trae un tenedor?
3. ¿Me puede traer un cuchillo por favor?

27 1. la cuchara 2. el tenedor 3. el tenedor 4. el tenedor 5. el tenedor 6. la cuchara

Teaching Suggestion

If possible, plan a trip to a Spanish or Latin American restaurant. You might pre-arrange with the restaurant manager that employees speak only Spanish with the students (if the appropriate employees are available). Students should order their food in Spanish.

Presentation

Así se dice Use the menu on p. 217 as you model the expressions, asking several students **¿Tienes hambre? ¿Qué vas a pedir?** Then ask a student, **¿Qué le puedo traer?** The student responds with **Me puede traer...** Have the student turn to a classmate and ask the question as the **camarero/a.** The next student responds and then becomes the server, asking a pupil who will respond as a customer.

For Individual Needs

29 Auditory Learners Have students do this activity orally in pairs before writing the answers.

30 Visual Learners Have students refer to their flash-card set for help with this activity. Encourage them to compile their lists without looking at the Spanish definitions on the back of the cards.

Presentation

Así se dice Replay the restaurant scene from the **fotonovela.** Tell students to listen carefully to the phrases used by the server and the customers. Then have the class as a whole ask for the bill and about the tip, with you responding as the server. Then switch roles, so that they have practiced the entire dialogue.

ASÍ SE DICE Ordering dinner in a restaurant

To find out what a friend is going to order, ask:

¿Qué vas a pedir?
What are you going to order?

Your friend might say:

Voy a pedir los camarones.
I'm going to order. . .

The waitperson might ask:

¿Qué le puedo traer?
What can I bring you?

You might answer:

Yo **quisiera** el bistec.
I would like . . .

29 ¿Qué vas a pedir? See answers below.

You're in a restaurant and the waitperson wants to take your order. Read the waitperson's part of the dialogue and complete your part by ordering a meal. Use the foods you've learned so far. Don't forget to be polite!

EL CAMARERO	TÚ
Buenas tardes. ¿Qué le puedo traer?	Buenas tardes, pues, ___1___.
Excelente. La sopa del día es sopa de legumbres.	Muy bien, y ___2___.
¿Prefiere las zanahorias o el maíz?	Prefiero ___3___.
¿Quiere una ensalada?	Sí, ___4___.
¿Y para tomar? ¿Qué le puedo traer?	Me gustaría ___5___.
¿Algo más?	___6___.

30 ¿Qué van a pedir Uds.?

Imagine that your favorite restaurant is offering you a day of free meals. Make a list of what you want to eat for breakfast, lunch, and dinner. Write when you want to eat each meal. Then ask your partners when they want to eat each meal, and what they're going to order. Decide which person has tastes most like yours.

ASÍ SE DICE Asking for and paying the bill in a restaurant

To ask the waitperson for the bill, say:

¿Nos puede traer la cuenta?
La cuenta, por favor.

The waitperson might say:

¿Desean algo más?
Do you want anything else?

To ask about the amount of the bill and the tip, say:

¿Cuánto es?
¿Está incluida la propina?
Is the tip included?

The waitperson might say:

No, no está incluida. **Es aparte.**
. . . It's separate.

Culture Note

In Ecuador and other Spanish-speaking countries, servers in restaurants are generally male. Being a waiter is considered a profession. In many places, the bill is still hand-written.

Answers

29 *Possible answers:*
1. la sopa del día, por favor
2. una legumbre, por favor
3. el maíz
4. una ensalada,
5. tomar un refresco
6. No

VOCABULARIO

La cena en el Café El Rancho

el batido de fresa	*strawberry milkshake*
la carne de res	*beef*
la cebolla	*onion*
los camarones	*shrimp*
el flan	*custard*
la galleta	*cookie*

NOTA CULTURAL

In Spanish-speaking countries, **la cena** is a light meal, usually eaten around 8:00 P.M., sometimes as late as 10:00 P.M. (or even later) in Spain. People generally eat a snack (**una merienda**) around 5:00 P.M. In Ecuador, **la merienda** usually consists of tea or coffee with bread, or perhaps a bowl of soup.

27 Y para comer... See answers below.

Name the utensil or utensils you use to eat these foods.

1. el helado
2. las legumbres
3. la ensalada
4. el arroz
5. los huevos
6. la sopa

28 Escuchemos: Me trae...

Imagine you're eating at Restaurante El Molino, a busy restaurant in Quito. Listen to these orders and decide if each person is ordering breakfast, lunch, dinner, or dessert.

Answers on p. 201D.

Presentation

Vocabulario To model pronunciation, tell students you are very hungry and say which items on the menu you would like to eat. Then ask students, **¿Qué te gusta para cenar?** and **¿Qué hay para cenar?** Have them answer using the new vocabulary. Then have students practice ordering from the menu, with you playing the role of the **camarero/a.**

For videodisc application, see *Videodisc Guide.*

Have a student set a table **(poner la mesa)** according to your instructions for when, where, and with whom they will be dining. Using **Pon** and **No pongas** and the prepositions of place, tell the student what utensils to put on the table and where to put them. After students have mastered the vocabulary, ask one of them to give instructions while another sets the table. You might also do this activity with all of the students while they sit at their own desks and use plastic utensils.

For Individual Needs

27 Kinesthetic Learners Have students hold up the utensil as they give the answers. Add several items from the menu to continue the activity.

Answers

26 1. Por favor, ¿nos puede traer servilletas?
2. Por favor, ¿me trae un tenedor?
3. ¿Me puede traer un cuchillo por favor?

27 1. la cuchara
2. el tenedor
3. el tenedor
4. el tenedor
5. el tenedor
6. la cuchara

Teaching Suggestion

If possible, plan a trip to a Spanish or Latin American restaurant. You might pre-arrange with the restaurant manager that employees speak only Spanish with the students (if the appropriate employees are available). Students should order their food in Spanish.

ASÍ SE DICE — Ordering dinner in a restaurant

To find out what a friend is going to order, ask:

¿Qué vas a pedir?
What are you going to order?

Your friend might say:

Voy a pedir los camarones.
I'm going to order. . .

The waitperson might ask:

¿Qué le puedo traer?
What can I bring you?

You might answer:

Yo **quisiera** el bistec.
I would like . . .

29 ¿Qué vas a pedir? See answers below.

You're in a restaurant and the waitperson wants to take your order. Read the waitperson's part of the dialogue and complete your part by ordering a meal. Use the foods you've learned so far. Don't forget to be polite!

EL CAMARERO	TÚ
Buenas tardes. ¿Qué le puedo traer?	Buenas tardes, pues, ___1___.
Excelente. La sopa del día es sopa de legumbres.	Muy bien, y ___2___.
¿Prefiere las zanahorias o el maíz?	Prefiero ___3___.
¿Quiere una ensalada?	Sí, ___4___.
¿Y para tomar? ¿Qué le puedo traer?	Me gustaría ___5___.
¿Algo más?	___6___.

30 ¿Qué van a pedir Uds.?

Imagine that your favorite restaurant is offering you a day of free meals. Make a list of what you want to eat for breakfast, lunch, and dinner. Write when you want to eat each meal. Then ask your partners when they want to eat each meal, and what they're going to order. Decide which person has tastes most like yours.

ASÍ SE DICE — Asking for and paying the bill in a restaurant

To ask the waitperson for the bill, say:

¿Nos puede traer la cuenta?
La cuenta, por favor.

The waitperson might say:

¿Desean algo más?
Do you want anything else?

To ask about the amount of the bill and the tip, say:

¿Cuánto es?
¿Está incluida la propina?
Is the tip included?

The waitperson might say:

No, no está incluida. **Es aparte.**
. . . It's separate.

Presentation

Así se dice Use the menu on p. 217 as you model the expressions, asking several students **¿Tienes hambre? ¿Qué vas a pedir?** Then ask a student, **¿Qué le puedo traer?** The student responds with **Me puede traer...** Have the student turn to a classmate and ask the question as the **camarero/a.** The next student responds and then becomes the server, asking a pupil who will respond as a customer.

For Individual Needs

29 Auditory Learners Have students do this activity orally in pairs before writing the answers.

30 Visual Learners Have students refer to their flash-card set for help with this activity. Encourage them to compile their lists without looking at the Spanish definitions on the back of the cards.

Presentation

Así se dice Replay the restaurant scene from the **fotonovela.** Tell students to listen carefully to the phrases used by the server and the customers. Then have the class as a whole ask for the bill and about the tip, with you responding as the server. Then switch roles, so that they have practiced the entire dialogue.

Culture Note

In Ecuador and other Spanish-speaking countries, servers in restaurants are generally male. Being a waiter is considered a profession. In many places, the bill is still hand-written.

Answers

29 *Possible answers:*
1. la sopa del día, por favor
2. una legumbre, por favor
3. el maíz
4. una ensalada,
5. tomar un refresco
6. No

A LO NUESTRO

How do you get the attention of the waitperson in a crowded restaurant? Do you raise your hand? Do you call out loud? What is considered rude in one place may be perfectly acceptable somewhere else. In many Spanish-speaking countries it's considered rude to raise your voice in a crowded room. In Spain, for example, people make the sound *tch-tch* to get the waitperson's attention; in Costa Rica it's *pfft.* In Colombia people clap or raise their hands.

VOCABULARIO

Los números del 200 al 100.000

200 **doscientos/as**	700 **setecientos/as**	10.000 **diez mil**
300 **trescientos/as**	800 **ochocientos/as**	45.000 **cuarenta y cinco mil**
400 **cuatrocientos/as**	900 **novecientos/as**	80.000 **ochenta mil**
500 **quinientos/as**	1.000 **mil**	100.000 **cien mil**
600 **seiscientos/as**		

1. When numbers 200 to 900 modify a noun, they agree with the gender of the noun.
   seiscient**os** libr**os** seiscient**as** cas**as**
2. Notice that in Spanish you can use a period instead of a comma when writing large numbers (one thousand or greater).
   15.216 23.006 1.800 47.811 9.433

31 ¿Cómo se dicen? See answers below.

¿Cómo se dicen estos números en español?

1. 27.750
2. 3.609
3. 534
4. 94.800
5. 2.710
6. 615
7. 45.370
8. 8.112
9. 19.400
10. 100.000

32 Escuchemos: ¿Cuánto es? Answers on p. 201D.

Look at the menu and listen to the following prices. Match the price mentioned with the correct item on the menu.

Presentation

Vocabulario Make up large-number flashcards of the numbers in the box as well as some numbers in between. Begin by modeling the pronunciation. Have students read the explanation of gender agreement in the book. Then have students practice the masculine and feminine forms. For example, while holding up 800, say **ochocientos sucres, ochocientas pesetas,** then ask students **¿Cuántos sucres? ¿Cuántas pesetas?**

Additional Practice

Vocabulario Have students practice the new numbers, counting by hundreds. You say **cien.** Ask a student to continue with **doscientos.** Each subsequent student adds 100 until everyone has had a turn.

Math Link

Have students look up exchange rates for several currencies and convert prices of some common items they purchase (CDs, fast food items, clothing) from dollars into **pesos, pesetas, sucres,** etc.

Answers

31
1. veinte y siete mil setecientos cincuenta or veintisiete mil setecientos cincuenta
2. tres mil seiscientos nueve
3. quinientos treinta y cuatro
4. noventa y cuatro mil ochocientos
5. dos mil setecientos diez
6. seiscientos quince
7. ocho mil ciento doce
8. cuarenta y cinco mil trescientos setenta
9. diecinueve mil cuatrocientos
10. cien mil

Culture Note

In many Spanish-speaking countries, it is important for travelers to know how to express large numbers. Sometimes local currency units are hundreds or even thousands to the U.S. dollar.

Teaching Suggestion

33 Have students repeat this exercise, making sure they can leave a tip for their server. Now what can they order for dinner?

For Individual Needs

34 Auditory Learners Have students assume the role of waitperson as you place an order for a meal. Give the items you want and say the price as you order. (**Quisiera la sopa de legumbres a 185 pesetas, el pollo asado a 890 pesetas, y para tomar...**) See who gets the order correct and who gets the total of the bill correct.

TPR Use the recipes students collected for the Projects (page 201E) to reinforce food vocabulary. Assign each student an ingredient in one of the recipes. Students should provide a visual representation of their ingredient (find a magazine clipping of their ingredient and mount it on construction paper, or cut the shape out of poster board). Collect the images, review them with the class, shuffle them, and hand one out to each student. Then give commands to make the various recipes. For example, if the recipe is **paella**, you might say **Arroz, ¡levántate! Camarones, ven acá. Pollo, camina al lado de los camarones,** and so on.

33 Te invito

Role-play a restaurant scene with two classmates in which one of you is the waitperson and the other two are customers. One of you has 30,000 sucres and wants to treat the other to dinner. Using the menu from Activity 32, decide on a meal and comment on the food. Then, ask the waitperson for the bill and add it up.

34 La cuenta, por favor

Work with a partner. Use these receipts to role-play scenes in a restaurant. One will take the role of the customer and ask for the bill. The other will take the role of the waitperson and add up the receipt. Switch roles and repeat the scene with the second receipt.

ASADOR
—Castellano—
Secundino Mata Vázquez
D. N. I. 1.179.235

Lope de Vega, 27
Teléfono 429 76 13
28014 MADRID

№ 0000705

Cantidad	CONCEPTO	Pesetas
		360
1	Mixta	450
1	Judías verdes	1100
1	Salmón	300
1	Tortilla	700
2	Pan	150
1	Agua	160
1	Agua	300
1	Bombón glacé	100
1	Café	
	TOTAL	

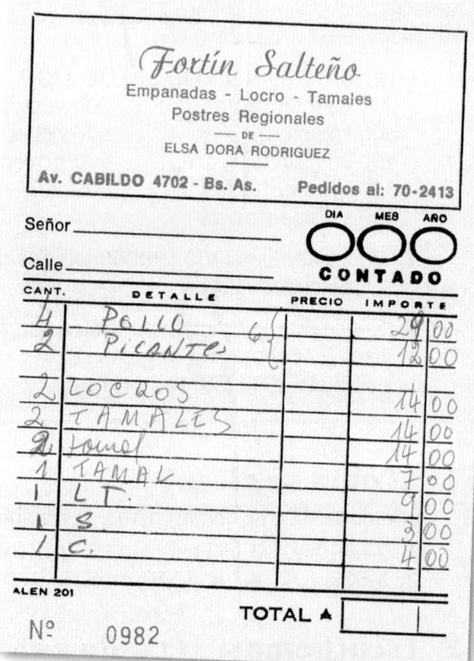

Fortín Salteño
Empanadas - Locro - Tamales
Postres Regionales
— DE —
ELSA DORA RODRIGUEZ
Av. CABILDO 4702 - Bs. As. Pedidos al: 70-2413

Señor
Calle
DIA MES AÑO
CONTADO

CANT.	DETALLE	PRECIO	IMPORTE
4	Pollo		29 00
2	Picante		12 00
2	Locros		14 00
2	Tamales		14 00
2	Humi		14 00
1	Tamal		7 00
1	L.T.		9 00
1	S.		3 00
1	C.		4 00

ALEN 201
TOTAL
Nº 0982

tortilla española

NOTA CULTURAL

In Spanish, as in English, a word can have more than one meaning. In Spain, a **tortilla** is a kind of omelet. The **tortilla española**, made of eggs, potatoes, onions, salt, and olive oil, is a popular dish for a light evening meal. In Mexico and Central America a **tortilla** is made from cornmeal or flour, pressed into a flat round shape and cooked on a griddle. These tortillas are the bread that goes with almost all meals. They are especially good when they're hot and fresh off the griddle.

Culture Note

Tortillas are a staple in Mexico and some Central American countries. Large supermarkets make and sell them fresh every day. These are made in huge quantities by machines called **tortillerías,** but many people still prefer to make them by hand. They are non-existent in most of South America, except in Mexican restaurants.

35 Vamos al restaurante

Using the food items you've learned so far, create a scene with two classmates. One of you take the role of the waitperson, the other two take the roles of the customers. Include in your conversation some small talk and requests for eating utensils and napkins. Also ask about dishes on the menu and ask for and pay the bill. Be prepared to present your scene to the class.

Learning a foreign language is like any other long-term project, such as getting into shape or taking up a new sport: it may take some time to see the results you want. Don't get discouraged, and remember that you *can* learn Spanish! Keep yourself motivated by setting short-term, realistic goals. A simple goal could be learning five additional words this week or reading an interesting-looking article in a Spanish-language magazine. Once you've learned more Spanish, you could make a goal of going to a store or restaurant in a Spanish-speaking part of town and doing some shopping or ordering a meal entirely in Spanish.

NOTA CULTURAL

In Spain and Latin America, people tend to use utensils more than people in the United States do when they eat. Spaniards usually cut chicken or fruit with a knife and a fork. When Spaniards and Latin Americans cut their food, they don't switch hands as some people in the United States do. The knife stays in the right hand and the fork in the left. When they're using only a fork in their right hand, Spanish speakers feel it's more polite to leave their left hand resting on the table.

LETRA Y SONIDO

A. The letter **c** before the vowels **e** and **i** is pronounced like **s**, as in **centro, cielo.** Before the vowels **a, o,** and **u** the letter **c** is pronounced like the **k** in the English word **kitchen.**

carne **rico** **cuchara** **cuchillo** **caliente** **picante** **camarero**

To spell the *k* sound of the word *kitchen* before the vowels **e** and **i**, use the letters **qu**

que **química** **saque** **quien** **quinientos** **queso**

Do you notice the pattern similar to the one you learned with the letters **g** and **j**?

B. Dictado Answers on p. 201D.

Anita needs help with a cake recipe. Write what she says.

C. Trabalenguas

¿Quién quiere pastel de chocolate?
¿Cuánto queso cabe en la caja?
¿Cómo quiere que Queta conduzca el carro?

Language Note

In **Castille** and most other parts of Spain, the letter **c**, when it precedes **e** or **i**, is pronounced like the English *th.* (**cinco** sounds like *think-o*) You may want to replay the video from **Capítulos 1** and **2** for students to listen for this accent by the Spanish actors.

For Individual Needs

35 Kinesthetic Learners

To heighten realism and facilitate role-play, provide two or three sets of props for students to use during this activity. Other groups may practice or work on written assignments while "waiting to be seated" at the "dining area."

Native Speakers

After you have covered the **Letra y sonido,** ask students to make up and write three additional **trabalenguas.** You might then distribute the **trabalenguas** to the class.

CLOSE

Use *Teaching Transparencies 8-1, 8-2,* and *8-3* to review vocabulary and target phrases. You might also hold up the number flashcards from the vocabulary presentation (page 219), asking **¿Cuánto es la cuenta (adición)?** To practice agreement, prompt student responses with **pesetas** for feminine forms and **pesos** or **sucres** for masculine forms.

ASSESS

Quiz 8-3, *Chapter Teaching Resources, Book 2,* pp. 201-202

Assessment Items, Audiocassette 8A/Audio CD 8

Performance Assessment

Use a modification of Activity 35 for performance assessment. Every time the customer asks for something, the server says they do not have it, and offers to bring the customer something else. The customer should ask for five different items, and the server should come up with five different alternatives. Students should present their conversation to the class.

READING STRATEGY

Recognizing text organization.

Prereading
Activity A

Teaching Suggestion

A. Have students paraphrase the title and subtitle of this essay in Spanish.

Teaching Suggestion

Group Work Working in pairs, ask students to make a list of all the cognates in one of the recipes. Ask if they are surprised at how many there are.

Thinking Critically

Drawing Inferences Ask students why they think these drinks are popular in many Spanish-speaking countries. (warm climates, fruit is plentiful and healthy, drinks are inexpensive)

Reading
Activities B and C

Teaching Suggestion

Al grano Have students read the passage and describe how it is organized. Once they recognize a rough outline, ask if they have any other ideas about how the author could have organized the essay. (recipes with orange first, recipes with other fruit second; discussion of tropical fruits first, recipes second)

Additional Practice

B. After students have finished adding the missing information to the outline, have them go back and reorganize a reading from a previous chapter.

C. Ask students to make up additional questions using more of the text.

VAMOS A LEER

Batidos y sorbetes

Estrategia

Many articles have a clear organization, showing that the author probably followed an outline. If you can find the organization of a text it will be easier to understand the main ideas, and you will know where to look for certain details. In this selection, the bold print and larger print will help you see some of the text's organization.

¡A comenzar!

Before you read the article, read the title and subtitle to find out what this article is about.

A. Which of the following best expresses the meaning of the title and subtitle?

1. Milkshakes and sorbets: Fruits, eggs, and milk make a healthy breakfast combination.
2. Milkshakes: Fruits and milk are very healthy when combined.
3. (circled) Milkshakes and sorbets: Fruits, ice, and milk can make a refreshing combination.

Al grano

B. The article "Batidos y sorbetes" is organized and easy to outline. Outlining is a great way to understand a reading, whether it be your social studies chapter or an article in Spanish like this one. On a piece of paper fill in the missing information.

por Bárbara Benavides

En junio, julio y agosto disfrutamos de unas combinaciones deliciosas, como los batidos y los sorbetes. Se puede combinar la leche, las frutas y un poco de hielo para producir una combinación refrescante.

Cuando hace mucho calor nos encantan siempre las bebidas frías. Una de las mejores maneras de disfrutar del verano es experimentar la increíble sensación de un buen refresco. Muchas veces tenemos ganas de tomar limonada o té helado o sólo agua fría. Pero a veces es más divertido preparar batidos y sorbetes.

Las frutas tropicales, como el plátano, la piña, la papaya y el mango, añaden un sabor exótico y son ideales para la creación de los batidos y los sorbetes. Existe una variedad enorme de frutas que se puede usar. También, tienen vitaminas y minerales importantes para la nutrición diaria.

LOS SORBETES

Sorbete de mango, pera y durazno (Sirve dos)

1 taza de pera
1 taza de mango
1 taza de durazno
2 vasos de jugo de naranja
1 taza de azúcar en polvo jugo de limón al gusto

Pele las frutas, quite las semillas y córtelas en pedacitos. Bata las frutas, el jugo de naranja y el azúcar en polvo en la licuadora. Ponga la mezcla en la sorbetera o siga las instrucciones de la receta anterior para hacer el sorbete en el congelador.

Sorbete de naranja (Sirve uno)

3 naranjas
1/2 limón
1/2 taza de azúcar en polvo

Exprima el limón y las naranjas. Agregue y disuelva bien el azúcar en polvo. Ponga los ingredientes en la sorbetera (máquina de hacer helado) y siga las instrucciones para hacer el helado-sorbete. Si no tiene sorbetera, ponga la mezcla en las bandejitas del congelador. Cuando se formen cubitos de hielo, pase todo a la licuadora y haga un puré. Coloque en un recipiente de plástico y vuelva a congelar en seguida.

Health Link

Ask students why fruits are considered one of the most healthful foods in our diet. (They supply carbohydrates, essential vitamins and minerals, and fiber.) Have students choose a specific fruit and research its nutritional value and then report their findings using as much Spanish as possible.

LOS BATIDOS

Los batidos se hacen con frutas combinadas con leche y hielo. Para darles una consistencia espesa, se necesita batir los ingredientes en una licuadora.

Batido de plátano con fresas

1/2 taza de plátanos
1/2 taza de fresas
1 vaso de leche
1/3 taza de hielo picado
azúcar al gusto

Mezcle en la licuadora y se sirve bien frío.

Batido de papaya (Sirve uno)

2 tazas de pulpa de papaya
1-1/2 taza de leche o agua
1/2 taza de azúcar
jugo de limón si se usa agua
hielo picado

Mezcle todos los ingredientes en la licuadora con leche o agua.

Batido de moras

1 vaso de leche
1 taza de moras (fresas, frambuesas, zarzamoras)
2 cucharadas de azúcar
hielo picado

Mezcle en la licuadora y se sirve bien frío.

Milkshakes and sorbets: fruits, ice and milk can make a healthy and refreshing combination

Title: ________ Batidos y sorbetes
Author: ________ Bárbara Benavides

I. Introduction
- **A. Frozen drinks are great in summer. (Paragraph 1)**
- **B. Tropical fruits are ideal for these drinks.**

II. ________ Los batidos
- **A.** ________ Batido de papaya
- **B. Batido de papaya**
- **C.** ________

III. Los sorbetes
- **A.** ________ Sorbete de melón
- **B.** ________ Sorbete de naranja

¿Te acuerdas?

Scan to find specific information. Make a list of what you're looking for and look for key words as you scan.

C. You'd like your school cafeteria to offer some of these delicious items. Your cafeteria director agrees, but has a few questions.

1. What kinds of fruits are recommended (according to the introduction)? tropical fruits
2. How many servings does the "Batido de papaya" make? 1
3. What fruit, other than an orange, is in the "Sorbete de naranja"? lemon

D. ¡Ahora te toca a ti! Inventa una receta nueva para un batido o un sorbete. Si usas palabras y frases de estas recetas, puedes hacer todo en español. Answers will vary.

POSTREADING
Activity D

For Individual Needs

D. Challenge Have students invent and write another kind of recipe. Have them use the various verbs and commands to invent a tropical fruit salad, a fruit-filled gelatin mold, or frozen fruit pops. Or, have students create an imaginary **batido** or **sorbete** using unlikely ingredients. Ask volunteers to read their recipes aloud and have the class vote on the ones they think would taste the best and the worst.

Family Link

Ask students to prepare one of the recipes for their family. Then have them report to the class what their family thinks of it.

Native Speakers

Have your students bring in a family recipe or find one in a Spanish-language cookbook. Have them write out the instructions, then write a paragraph explaining why they chose that recipe. Is it a personal favorite? representative of their culture?

Teacher Notes

- For additional readings, see *Native Speaker Activity Book,* pp. 36–40 and *Practice and Activity Book,* p. 96.
- You might find the following phrases helpful:
  un tercio de taza, la tercera parte de una taza a third of a cup
  media taza a half cup
  una taza y media a cup and a half

Multicultural Link

Some tropical fruits popular in Latin America are also popular in Africa. These include oranges, tangerines, bananas, pineapples, mangoes, papaws (**papayas**), soursop (**guanabana**), and sweetsop (also called sugar apple). Have students research what fruits are native to other parts of the world (Southeast Asia, East Africa, Australia). Ask them to report what they discover using as much Spanish as possible.

The **Repaso** reviews all four skills and culture in preparation for the Chapter Test.

Teaching Suggestion

1 Have students compare the foods that Ángel likes and dislikes with their own preferences. **(A Ángel le gusta el pollo, pero a mí no me gusta. A Ángel no le gusta el pescado y a mí no me gusta tampoco.)**

Portfolio

3 Oral Tell your students that a recording of their role-play would be an appropriate oral activity to include in their Portfolio. For Portfolio suggestions, see *Assessment Guide,* page 21.

Additional Practice

4 Have students alter these recipes to include ingredients that they especially like. What would they add or delete from the **ensalada**? How could they make a new kind of **empanada**?

Teaching Suggestion

5 Encourage students to include foods their families prepare for holidays and other special occasions. (religious holidays, birthdays, family reunions, Thanksgiving)

Portfolio

6 Written Your students may want to consider including their finished menus in their Portfolio. For Portfolio suggestions, see *Assessment Guide,* page 21.

REPASO

1 Listen as Ángel talks about some foods he likes and doesn't like. On a piece of paper make two columns, one for foods he likes, and the other for foods he doesn't like. Write the foods Ángel mentions in the correct columns. Answers on p. 201D.

2 Imagine that you're in a restaurant in Quito with Pablo. You're really hungry, but he's been snacking all day and just wants to have something light. Using the vocabulary you've learned, think of possible meals for both of you. Take notes and be prepared to present your choices to the class. See answers below.

3 Get together with a classmate and compare your choices from Activity 2. Now each one of you pick your favorite meal and take turns playing the roles of the customer and the waitperson. Order the food, comment on how it tastes, and then ask for and pay the bill.

4 Your school is having an international food festival and you've agreed to make **empanadas** and **ensalada.** Read the recipes and write a shopping list in Spanish, listing all the ingredients you'll need for the **empanadas** and the **ensalada.**

Ingredientes

ENSALADA MIXTA
Tiempo: 15 minutos
Raciones: 6-8
1a lechuga grande
4 tomates
1a taza de arroz cocido
100 g atún de lata
1/2 zanahoria rallada
1/2 cebolla

Se limpian las legumbres y se cortan en trozos. Se mezcla todo junto y se sirve con aceite, vinagre, sal y pimienta.

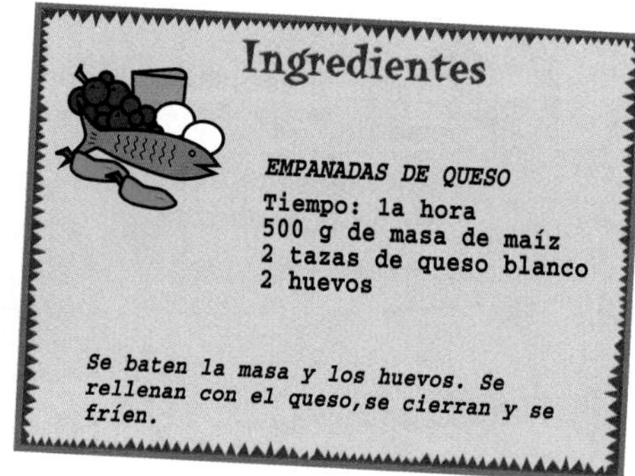

Ingredientes

EMPANADAS DE QUESO
Tiempo: 1a hora
500 g de masa de maíz
2 tazas de queso blanco
2 huevos

Se baten la masa y los huevos. Se rellenan con el queso, se cierran y se fríen.

5 In groups of three or four, plan—in Spanish—a menu for a holiday meal. Include a soup, beverage, main course with meat or fish, vegetables, salad, and a dessert. Remember to compromise! As items are suggested, say whether you like them a lot, a little, or not at all. Suggest alternatives using **Prefiero...** Choose a member of your group to write your holiday menu. Be prepared to share your menu with the class.

6 Imagine that you're going to open your own restaurant but you can't decide what kind. Create at least two menus, one for an elegant restaurant that is only open for dinner, and another for a 24-hour diner with inexpensive items.

Multicultural Link

8 Oranges have been cultivated in China since ancient times; they have been grown in Europe only since the thirteenth century. In southern China, people bring a small mandarin tree into their home for good luck during the Chinese New Year. Have students choose one country and research one custom from that country that includes food. Have them report what they find.

Answers

2 *Sample answers:*

Yo: arroz con pollo, una ensalada y un batido de chocolate;

PABLO: una ensalada de frutas y un refresco

7 Responde a las siguientes oraciones con **cierto** o **falso.** Corrige las oraciones falsas. Basa tus respuestas en las **Notas culturales**, el **Panorama cultural** y el **Encuentro cultural** de este capítulo.

1. En los países hispanohablantes, las personas desayunan entre las 10:00 y las 11:00 de la mañana. Falso, entre las 7:00 y las 8:00.
2. En los Estados Unidos, el almuerzo es generalmente más fuerte que en los países hispanohablantes. Falso, es más ligero.
3. La cazuela de marisco es un plato típico del Ecuador. Cierto
4. El sancocho es una sopa que se hace de plátanos, maíz y carne. Cierto
5. Un plato típico del Ecuador es es el pabellón. Falso, es típico de Venezuela.

8 Look at the picture of a woman at a juice stand in Mexico. Name as many kinds of fruit in the picture as you can.

9 With a partner, role-play ordering the following items. See answers below.

1. a glass of orange juice
2. a banana and strawberry shake
3. a glass of pineapple juice
4. a glass of grapefruit juice
5. a mango shake

10

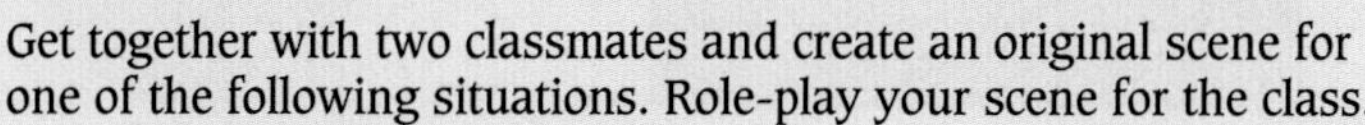

Get together with two classmates and create an original scene for one of the following situations. Role-play your scene for the class.

a. You and a classmate are eating breakfast at a restaurant. Another classmate is the waitperson. You're really hungry, but your friend isn't. Order two appropriate breakfasts and then talk about how the food tastes.

b. You and a friend have just finished eating lunch. The waitperson asks you if you want anything else and suggests a dessert. You politely decline and ask for the check. The waitperson tells you how much you owe. You pay the check and leave a tip.

c. You and your family are out for a nice dinner, but everything is going wrong! The waitperson forgets to give you the menu, the silverware is dirty, and when the food comes, it's cold and doesn't taste good. Point out the problems and politely request the things you need. Be creative, but mind your manners!

REPASO
CAPÍTULO 8

For Individual Needs

6 Slower Pace Have students create only one menu. You might let students choose the type of menu they make. As a class you could then compare and contrast the two types.

6 Challenge Ask students to write a paragraph or two comparing an elegant restaurant and an informal diner. What differences would there be other than in the menus?

9 Tactile/Kinesthetic Learners model food items or other vocabulary using playdough or plasticine clay. As students make the items, have them display them and ask the class what they are.

Video Wrap-Up

- ***Video Program***
- ***Expanded Video Program,*** *Videocassette 3*
- ***Videodisc Program,*** *Videodisc 4B*

At this time, you might want to use the video resources for additional review and enrichment. See *Video Guide* or *Videodisc Guide* for suggestions regarding the following:
- **¿Qué vas a pedir?** (Dramatic episode)
- **Panorama cultural** (Interviews)
- **Video Clips** (Authentic footage)

Answers

7 1. Falso; En los países hipanohablantes, las personas desayunan entre las 7:00 y las 8:00 de la mañana.
2. Falso; Generalmente, el almuerzo es más fuerte en los países hispanohablantes que en los Estados Unidos.
3. Cierto
4. Cierto
5. Falso; El pabellón es un plato típico de Venezuela.

8 naranjas, piñas, toronjas, fresas, papayas, mangoes, plátanos, naranjillas, cocos

9 *Sample answer:* 1. Me gustaría un vaso de jugo de naranja por favor.

This page is intended to prepare students for the Chapter Test. It is a brief checklist of the major points covered in the chapter. The students should be reminded that it is only a checklist, and does not necessarily include everything that will appear on the Chapter Test.

Teaching Suggestion

Have students make a list of foods that people in Spanish-speaking countries eat, according to what they have learned. Then have them compare their new list with the one they made at the beginning of **Capítulo 8.** Have their ideas changed? If so, how and why?

Teaching Suggestion

4, 5, 6 Have students practice Activities 4, 5, and 6 with a partner. Have them take turns role-playing each one and see if they can carry out short conversations without referring to their books.

A VER SI PUEDO . . .

Can you talk about meals and food? p. 207

1 How would you tell a classmate what your favorite breakfast foods are? How would you ask what he or she usually eats for breakfast? How would you tell a classmate what you eat for breakfast . . .?

1. on weekends
2. when you're very hungry
3. when you're in a big hurry
4. when someone takes you out for breakfast
5. on school days

See answers below.

2 How would you tell a classmate what you have for lunch and ask what he or she has for lunch? Sample answers: Para almorzar tomo... ¿Qué tomas tú para el almuerzo?

Can you comment on food? p. 212

3 Look at the pictures below. Can you write a sentence describing how you think each dish tastes? Answers will vary.

a.

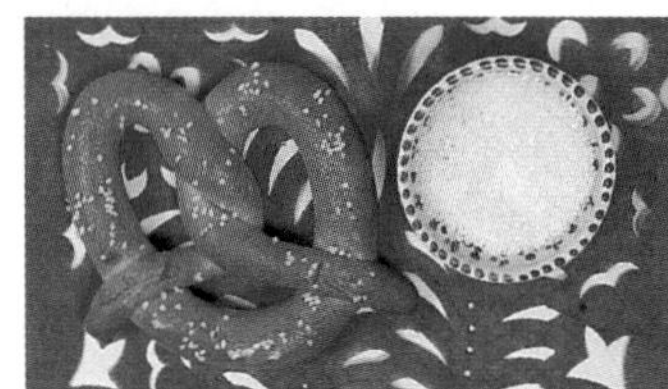
b.

c.

d.

Can you make polite requests? p. 216

4 You're eating with your family in a restaurant in Ecuador, and you're the only one who speaks Spanish. How would you ask the waitperson . . .? See answers below.

1. to bring spoons for everyone
2. to bring you a knife and a napkin
3. to bring the menu
4. to bring you a clean glass

Can you order dinner in a restaurant? p. 218

5 Imagine you and a friend are in El Rancho restaurant.

1. How would you ask your friend what he or she is going to order?
2. How would tell the waitperson that you want to order a salad?

See answers below.

Can you ask for and pay the bill in a restaurant? p. 218

6 How would you ask the waitperson how much the meal is? How would you ask him or her to bring you the bill? Sample answer: ¿Cuánto es la comida? Camarera, la cuenta por favor.

Answers

1 *Sample answers:*
Para el desayuno, mis comidas favoritas son los huevos revueltos y el jugo de naranja. Normalmente, ¿qué te gusta desayunar? Los fines de semana como cereal con leche y plátanos para el desayuno.

4 *Possible answers:*
1. Por favor, ¿nos puede traer unas cucharas?
2. ¿Me puede traer un cuchillo y una servilleta por favor?
3. ¿Nos puede traer los menús por favor?
4. Este vaso está sucio. ¿Me puede traer otro vaso limpio?

5 *Sample answers:*
1. ¿Qué vas a pedir?
2. Me gustaría una ensalada por favor.

VOCABULARIO

PRIMER PASO

Talking about meals and food

almorzar (ue) *to eat lunch*
el arroz *rice*
el atún *tuna*
café con leche *coffee with milk*
el cereal *cereal*
la crema de maní *peanut butter*
el desayuno *breakfast*
encantar *to really like, to love*
fuerte *strong, heavy*
los huevos *eggs*
el jamón *ham*
el jugo de naranja *orange juice*
la lechuga *lettuce*
las legumbres *vegetables*
ligero *light*
la limonada *lemonade*
el mango *mango*
la manzana *apple*
el pan dulce *sweet rolls*
el pan tostado *toast*
la papaya *papaya*
las papitas *potato chips*
para nada *at all*
el perro caliente *hot dog*
la piña *pineapple*
el plátano *banana*
poder (ue) *to be able; can*
el pollo *chicken*
el queso *cheese*
la sopa *soup*
el té frío *iced tea*
el tocino *bacon*
la toronja *grapefruit*
las uvas *grapes*
un vaso de leche *a glass of milk*

SEGUNDO PASO

Commenting on food

caliente *hot*
delicioso/a *delicious*
los frijoles *beans*
frío/a *cold*
picante *spicy*
el postre *dessert*
rico/a *rich, delicious*
salado/a *salty*
tener (mucha) hambre *to be (really) hungry*
tener (mucha) sed *to be (really) thirsty*

TERCER PASO

Making polite requests

la camarera *waitress*
el camarero *waiter*
la cuchara *spoon*
el cuchillo *knife*
limpio/a *clean*
el menú *menu*
¿Me puede traer...? *Can you bring me . . .?*
otro/a *other, another*
el plato *plate*
por favor *please*
la servilleta *napkin*
sucio/a *dirty*
el tazón *bowl*
el tenedor *fork*
traer *to bring*

Ordering dinner in a restaurant

el agua mineral *mineral water*
el batido *milkshake*
la bebida *beverage*
el bistec *steak*
los camarones *shrimp*
la carne *meat*
la carne de res *beef*
la cebolla *onion*
el flan *custard*
la fresa *strawberry*
la galleta *cookie*
el maíz *corn*
el pastel *cake*
pedir (i) *to order, to ask for*
el pescado *fish*
quisiera *I would like*
el tomate *tomato*
la zanahoria *carrot*

Asking for and paying the bill in a restaurant

¿Cuánto es? *How much is it?*
la cuenta *bill*
Es aparte. *It's separate.*
¿Está incluida? *Is it included?*
la propina *the tip*

Numbers 200–100,000

See p. 219.

Group Work

To review vocabulary, divide class into groups of four or five. Each student lists five situations in which they're hungry. Students practice each of the situations they've listed by taking turns telling each other that they're hungry and asking what they should eat. The other members of the group then suggest what to eat. (**—Son las siete de la mañana y tengo hambre. ¿Qué debo comer? —Debes comer el desayuno. —Sí, debes comer el cereal con plátano. —Y debes tomar jugo de naranja. —Yo creo que debes comer los huevos y tocino.**)

Game

TIRAR PALABRAS Bring in a foam ball. Call out a category based on the chapter vocabulary (**frutas, comida para el desayuno, comida en general, utensilios**). As you name the category, toss the ball to a student. The student is to say a related vocabulary word and toss the ball to another student, who is to give a different item from that category. When a student cannot come up with a word, he or she is out of the game. The winners are the last ones in. You decide when a category has been exhausted. At that time, change the category and have all students resume play.

CHAPTER 8 ASSESSMENT

CHAPTER TEST

- *Chapter Teaching Resources, Book 2,* pp. 203-208
- *Assessment Guide,* Speaking Test, p. 31
- *Assessment Items, Audiocassette 8A Audio CD 8*

TEST GENERATOR, CHAPTER 8

ALTERNATIVE ASSESSMENT

Performance Assessment

Have students describe the menus they made for **Repaso** Activity 7 to the class, trying to convince classmates to come to their restaurant. They should be evaluated according to their vocabulary and grammar usage and on their creativity and comprehensibility.

Portfolio Assessment

- **Written: Repaso,** Activity 6
  Pupil's Edition, p. 224
  Assessment Guide, p. 21
- **Oral: Repaso,** Activity 3
  Pupil's Edition, p. 224
  Assessment Guide, p. 21

LOCATION OPENER
CHAPTERS
9, 10

¡Ven conmigo a Texas! pp. 228–281

EXPANDED VIDEO PROGRAM, Videocassette 3

OR VIDEODISC PROGRAM, Videodisc 5A

Motivating Activity

Ask students to brainstorm about what they think Texas is like. Have them describe the topography of the state. Have them list any adjectives that come to mind.

Background Information

Texas is the second largest state in the United States. It is larger than Wisconsin, Michigan, Iowa, Indiana, and Illinois combined. Only Alaska is larger than Texas, but about 30 times as many people live in Texas as in Alaska. Six different flags have flown over Texas—those of Spain, France, Mexico, the Republic of Texas, the Confederacy, and the United States. The Republic of Texas lasted from 1836 to 1845. Because of the single star on its flag (adopted in 1839 by the Republic), Texas is often called the Lone Star State. Austin has been the state capital since 1845, when Texas joined the United States.

Language Note

The name *Texas* is thought to come from the Spanish pronunciation of the Caddo word for *friend* or *ally*.

CAPÍTULOS 9 y 10

¡Ven conmigo a Texas!

El centro de San Antonio, Texas

Social Studies Link

At least 30,000 indigenous people lived in what is today Texas when the first European settlers arrived. These indigenous groups, which varied widely in culture, technology, and language, included the Nacogdoches, Nasoni, Neche, Arkokisa, Attacapa, Darankawa, Comanche, Tonkawa, and the Coahuiltec. Divide the class into nine groups and assign each of them one of these indigenous groups to research. They should give a short oral presentation including information about where and how the group lived. The students might also look on a map of Texas for place names derived from the name of their group.

Texas

Población: 17.655.650, de los cuales 4.500.000 son hispanos

Área: 266.807 millas cuadradas. Sólo Alaska es más grande.

Capital: Austin

Ciudades principales: Houston, Dallas, San Antonio, El Paso, Austin, Fort Worth

Clima: desde ligeramente templado en el noroeste hasta subtropical en la costa del sur

Economía: productos químicos, comestibles, equipo de transporte, equipo eléctrico, productos petroleros, computadoras, petróleo, gas natural, ganado, algodón, leche, frutas

Historia: Poblado por indígenas norteamericanos, entre ellos los Caddo, antes de la llegada del explorador español Álvarez de Piñeda en 1519. Primeras misiones españolas establecidas en 1682. Colonia francesa establecida en 1685. Independencia de España en 1821. Independencia de México en 1836. La República de Texas se hizo un estado de los Estados Unidos en 1845.

LOCATION OPENER
CHAPTERS 9, 10

Using the Almanac and Map

Terms in the Almanac

- **Población:** Texas is the second most populous state after California. Houston, the largest city in Texas, is the fifth largest city in the United States.
- **Clima:** The climate of Texas varies greatly. Big Bend National Park in West Texas contains part of the Chihuahuan desert. It contrasts with the Sam Houston National Forest in East Texas with its pine trees, thickets, and bogs. There may be blizzards in the northern plains while winter temperatures in the Rio Grande Valley rarely dip below 60°F.
- **History:** Before the arrival of the Spanish explorer Alonso Álvarez de Piñeda in 1519, Texas was populated by the Caddos and other indigenous groups. The first Spanish missions were established in 1682. Texas gained independence from Spain in 1821 and from Mexico in 1836. The Republic of Texas became one of the United States in 1845.

Using the Map

- Have students name the U.S. states that border Texas. (Louisiana, Arkansas, Oklahoma, New Mexico)
- Have students name the Mexican states that border Texas by using the map on page xxvi. (Chihuahua, Coahuila, Nuevo León, Tamaulipas)
- Tell students to locate Houston, Dallas-Fort Worth, San Antonio, Austin, and El Paso. Ask students who have been to any of these cities to describe them to the class.

Thinking Critically

Comparing and Contrasting Divide the class into groups of four or five, and have them research NAFTA, the North American Free Trade Agreement (**TLC** or **el Tratado de Libre Comercio de América del Norte**). Have each group choose a pro or con position on the treaty and write a brief political TV or radio commercial promoting their point of view. Have groups present their commercials to the class

Culture Note

The Hispanic population of Texas is over four million, according to the 1990 Census. Hispanics now make up one-fourth of all Texans. By the year 2000, an estimated five million Hispanics will live in Texas.

LOCATION OPENER
CHAPTERS
9, 10

Motivating Activity
Have students brainstorm about the ways various ethnic groups influence life in the United States. (music, art, literature, cooking) Look at the photos on pages 228–231 and see if they confirm students' presuppositions.

Using the Photo Essay
① The Fiesta San Antonio tradition began in 1891 with a celebration on April 21, San Jacinto Day, in honor of the day on which Texas won its independence from Mexico. The Battle of Flowers Parade, which began around 1896, is an important part of the Fiesta tradition. The parade features historic commemorations, art shows, festivals, band concerts, sporting events, fireworks, and coronations.

② The San Antonio River winds through the heart of the city. Cobblestone walkways lead visitors to the river-level shops, restaurants, and an open-air amphitheater. The Riverwalk (**el Paseo del Río**) is the site of many of San Antonio's annual cultural events, such as art shows, Fiesta Noche del Río, and Fiesta San Antonio.

TEXAS

Texas was part of New Spain and Mexico for much longer than it has been part of the United States. Did you know that Texas was once an independent nation called the Republic of Texas? San Antonio is one of the world's most interesting cities. Its ties with Mexico make it an exciting place to be as the economies of Mexico and the U.S. become more interdependent.

② El Paseo del Río, the *River Walk*, attracts millions of visitors to its sidewalk cafes, restaurants, and shops. Visitors can take boat rides on the city's maze of canals.

① Fiesta San Antonio is a multicultural celebration held every April. This ten-day celebration includes parades, colorful dance shows, and band concerts.

③ Market Square is the scene of excitement and fun throughout the year. The festive atmosphere includes traditional Mexican music, food, and arts and crafts.

Music Link
The border region between Texas and Mexico has given rise to a unique culture, neither completely Texan nor Mexican, but a fusion of both. By the early 20th century, **música norteña,** or **conjunto** music, had grown deep roots along the border. The accordion, the heart of **conjunto** music, was introduced by German, Czech, and Polish settlers. In the last two decades **conjunto** music has spread throughout the United States and beyond. Have students research the music of a famous **conjunto** artist. (Narciso Martínez, Paulino Bernal, Ramón Ayala, José "Flaco" Jiménez) Ask them to give a short oral presentation about the artist, and if possible to play a recording of the music.

(4) The Tower of the Americas, built for the 1968 HemisFair, gives a bird's eye view of San Antonio. On a clear day you can see all the way to the Texas Hill Country.

In Chapters 9 and 10, you'll get to know Eva, Lisa, and Gabi, three friends who live in San Antonio, Texas, one of the ten largest cities in the United States. San Antonio is famous for its blend of cultures, with predominately Texan and Mexican flavors. As you'll see, people who live in Texas have lots of places to go and things to do.

(5) The Spanish missions formed the foundation for the city of San Antonio. The stately Mission Concepción looks as it did more than 200 years ago.

(6) Texas is home to many Mexican American people.

LOCATION OPENER
CHAPTERS 9, 10

(3) Market Square has been a shopping district since around 1840. It includes El Mercado, patterned after an authentic Mexican market, where San Antonians can shop for local art work, leather goods, and jewelry.

Culture Note

El Cinco de Mayo began as a commemoration of Mexico's liberation from France, but in Texas it has grown into a major celebration of Mexican American culture. The celebrations in San Antonio feature art exhibitions by Mexican artists as well as Tejano, **conjunto,** and **mariachi** music. Performances of **baile folklórico** include dances from throughout Mexico, especially the **jarabe tapatío,** often called the national dance of Mexico.

(4) The Tower of the Americas (**la Torre de las Américas**) stands 750 feet tall from its base to the tip of the antenna. Its observation decks offer a panoramic view of San Antonio and the surrounding area. The tower was originally built for HemisFair '68, a world's fair celebrating the city's 250th anniversary.

(5) San Antonio's missions were part of the chain of Franciscan missions established early in the 18th century serving as churches, schools, Native American pueblos, military barracks, fortifications, and granaries. Misión Concepción is the oldest unrestored mission in Texas. It was established in 1731.

(6) The Mexican Government sponsors the Mexican American Cultural Exchange Institute in San Antonio. It offers a program including art exhibits, lectures, workshops, movies, folk dancing, and concerts.

Literature Link

Texas has produced more contemporary Mexican American writers than any other state in the United States. Often Tejano writers are closely linked to the South Texas communities in which they spent their youth, and the subject of their work is linked to Tejano culture. One prominent Tejano writer is Tomás Rivera, from Crystal City, Texas. His work *...y no se lo tragó la tierra (. . . and the earth did not swallow him)* is the story of the struggles and triumphs a family of migrant farmworkers following crops through the Midwest and spending winters in Texas. It has been made into a film that won an award at the 1994 Santa Barbara International Film Festival.

Capítulo 9: ¡Vamos de compras!
Chapter Overview

De antemano pp. 234–236 | **¿Qué le compramos a Héctor?** | *Practice and Activity Book*, p. 97 | *Video Guide* OR *Videodisc Guide*

	FUNCTIONS	GRAMMAR	CULTURE	RE-ENTRY
Primer paso pp. 237–241	• Discussing gift suggestions, p. 237 • Asking for and giving directions downtown, p. 239	Indirect object pronouns: **le, les,** p. 238	• **Nota cultural,** specialty stores in Spain, p. 240 • **Panorama cultural, ¿Estás a la moda?,** p. 241	• **ir + a +** infinitive for planning • Describing family • Talking about locations • Talking about where things are
Segundo paso pp. 242–246	• Commenting on clothes, p. 242 • Making comparisons, p. 245	• **es/son + de +** material or pattern, p. 243 • Comparisons: **más... que, menos... que, tan... como,** p. 245	• Fine art: ***Tamalada,*** 1987, by Carmen Lomas Garza, p. 244 • Catalogue page with clothing, p. 246	• **ir + a +** infinitive for planning • Present tense of **ser** for description
Tercer paso pp. 247–249	• Expressing preferences, p. 247 • Asking about prices and paying for something, p. 248	Demonstrative adjectives: forms of **este, ese,** p. 247	Currency in some Spanish-speaking countries, p. 248	Numbers 0 to 100,000

Letra y sonido p. 249 | Pronouncing the letters **s, z,** and **c** | **Dictado:** *Textbook Audiocassette 5A/Audio CD 9*

Vamos a leer pp. 250–251 | **San Antonio** | **Reading Strategy:** Scanning for specific information

Review pp. 252–255 | **Repaso,** pp. 252–253 | **A ver si puedo...,** p. 254 | **Vocabulario,** p. 255

Assessment Options

Quizzes
- *Chapter Teaching Resources, Book 3*
  - **Primer paso,** Quiz 9-1, pp. 23–24
  - **Segundo paso,** Quiz 9-2, pp. 25–26
  - **Tercer paso,** Quiz 9-3, pp. 27–28
- *Assessment Items, Audiocassette 8A/Audio CD 9*

Chapter Test
- *Chapter Teaching Resources, Book 3*, pp. 29–36
- *Assessment Guide,* Speaking Test, p. 32
- *Assessment Items, Audiocassette 8A/Audio CD 9*

Test Generator, Chapter 9

Video Program OR *Expanded Video Program, Videocassette 3* OR *Videodisc Program, Videodisc 5A*	*Textbook Audiocassette 5A/Audio CD 9*

RESOURCES: Print	RESOURCES: Audiovisual
	Textbook Audiocassette 5A/Audio CD 9
Practice and Activity Book, pp. 98–100	
Native Speaker Activity Book, pp. 41–45	
Chapter Teaching Resources, Book 3	
• Additional Listening Activities 9-1, 9-2, p. 11	*Audiocassette 10A/Audio CD 9*
• Student Response Forms, pp. 20–22	
• Realia 9-1, pp. 15, 17	
• Situation Cards 9-1, pp. 18, 19	
• Teaching Transparency Master 9-1, pp. 7, 10	*Teaching Transparency 9-1*
• Quiz 9-1, pp. 23–24	*Assessment Items, Audiocassette 8A/Audio CD 9*
Video Guide	*Video Program* OR *Expanded Video Program, Videocassette 3*
Videodisc Guide	*Videodisc Program, Videodisc 5A*
	Textbook Audiocassette 5A/Audio CD 9
Practice and Activity Book, pp. 101–103	
Native Speaker Activity Book, pp. 41–45	
Chapter Teaching Resources, Book 3	
• Communicative Activity 9-1 pp. 3, 4	
• Additional Listening Activities 9-3, 9-4 p. 12	*Audiocassette 10A/Audio CD 9*
• Student Response Forms, pp. 20–22	
• Realia 9-1, pp. 15, 17	
• Situation Cards 9-2, pp. 18, 19	
• Teaching Transparency Master 9-2, pp. 8, 10	*Teaching Transparency 9-2*
• Quiz 9-2, pp. 25–26	*Assessment Items, Audiocassette 8A/Audio CD 9*
Videodisc Guide	*Videodisc Program, Videodisc 5A*
	Textbook Audiocassette 5A/Audio CD 9
Practice and Activity Book, pp. 104–106	
Native Speaker Activity Book, pp. 41–45	
Chapter Teaching Resources, Book 3	
• Communicative Activity 9-2, pp. 5–6	
• Additional Listening Activities 9-5, 9-6, p. 13	*Audiocassette 10A/Audio CD 9*
• Student Response Forms, pp. 20–22	
• Realia 9-2, pp. 16, 17	
• Situation Cards 9-3, pp. 18, 19	
• Teaching Transparency Master 9-3, pp. 9, 10	*Teaching Transparency 9-3*
• Quiz 9-3, pp. 27–28	*Assessment Items, Audiocassette 8A/Audio CD 9*
Videodisc Guide	*Videodisc Program, Videodisc 5A*
Video Guide	*Video Program* OR *Expanded Video Program, Videocassette 3*
Videodisc Guide	*Videodisc Program, Videodisc 5A*

Alternative Assessment

- Performance Assessment
  Primer paso, p. 240
  Segundo paso, p. 246
  Tercer paso, p. 249
- Portfolio Assessment
  Written: **Repaso,** Activity 7, *Pupil's Edition,* p. 253
  Assessment Guide, p. 22
  Oral: **Repaso,** Activity 5, *Pupil's Edition,* p. 253
  Assessment Guide, p. 22

Capítulo 9: ¡Vamos de compras!

Textbook Listening Activities Scripts

For Student Response Forms, see *Chapter Teaching Resources, Book 3,* pp. 20–22.

Primer paso

Activity 6, p. 237

a. A mi padre le encanta escuchar la música.

b. A mi madre le gusta mirar películas en casa.

c. A mi hermano Santiago le gustaría tocar un instrumento musical.

d. A mi hermana Eva le gusta practicar deportes.

e. A mi abuelo le encantan los animales.

f. A mi hermana Silvia le encanta decorar su cuarto con fotos grandes.

Answers to Activity 6

1. Los carteles son para su hermana Silvia.
2. El perro es para su abuelo.
3. Los zapatos de tenis son para su hermana Eva.
4. La radio es para su papá.
5. La guitarra es para su hermano Santiago.
6. Los videos son para su madre.

Activity 11, p. 240

1. Necesito comprar unas galletas y un pastel para el cumpleaños de mi hermanito.
2. Me gustaría comprar unos aretes para mi amiga.
3. Necesito comprar un juego de mesa para mi primo Luis.
4. Busco sandalias para la playa.
5. Busco una camisa elegante para llevar a la fiesta de Enrique este sábado.
6. Quiero comprar plantas para mi casa.
7. Voy a comprar pan dulce para la fiesta de mi papá.

Answers to Activity 11

1. d 2. c 3. e 4. a 5. g 6. f 7. b

Segundo paso

Activity 15, p. 243

CARLOS Necesito comprar unos bluejeans, una camiseta y unos zapatos de tenis.

ELENITA Quiero buscar un traje de baño porque hace mucho calor.

SERGIO Necesito unas camisetas, unos pantalones cortos y unos zapatos de tenis.

TERESA Necesito pantalones y una blusa de rayas. También necesito zapatos cafés.

LUIS Yo busco una camisa blanca, una corbata, calcetines y zapatos negros.

Answers to Activity 15

Possible answers:
Carlos—clases
Elenita—ir a la piscina
Sergio—jugar al tenis
Teresa—trabajar en la oficina/un baile
Luis—trabajar en la oficina/un baile

Activity 24, p. 246

1. La corbata de seda es más bonita que la corbata de lana.
2. ¡El perro es más gordo que el gato! ¡Necesita ponerse a dieta!
3. La falda negra es más corta que la falda amarilla.
4. Este vestido caro es más bonito que ese vestido barato.

Answers to Activity 24

Sample answer: El perro es más gordo que el gato.

Tercer paso

Activity 29, p. 248

1. — Perdón, señorita. ¿Cuánto cuesta esta blusa?
   — ¿La roja? El precio es $58.00.
   — ¡Qué cara!
2. — Bueno, me gustaría comprar esta camisa.
   — ¿La blanca?
   — Sí. ¿Cuánto cuesta?
   — Son ocho dólares con cincuenta y cinco centavos.
   — ¡Qué ganga!
3. — ¿Cuánto cuestan estas sandalias amarillas?
   — Son $27.00.
   — Creo que prefiero esas sandalias pardas.
   — Las pardas son más baratas. Sólo $18.00.
4. — Señorita, ¿cuánto es el pastel de chocolate?
   — Este es nuestro especial del día. Sólo cuesta $4.00.
   — ¡Qué barato!
5. — Perdón, señor. Necesito unos bluejeans.
   — Usted tiene suerte, señor. Aquí tenemos unos baratos.
   — ¿Sólo $17.00? ¡Qué baratos!
6. — Señorita, busco un vestido elegante para un baile.
   — Tenemos varios. Este azul, por ejemplo. O si prefiere otro color, lo tenemos también en rojo y en negro.
   — ¿Cuánto cuesta el vestido rojo?
   — Sólo $760.00.
   — ¡Ay, qué caro!
7. — Busco unos zapatos negros.
   — Aquí tenemos varios estilos. Éstos, por ejemplo, cuestan sólo $189.00.
   — ¡$189! ¡Qué caros! Gracias, pero no.

Answers to Activity 29

1. blusa roja: $58.00
2. camisa blanca: $8.55
3. sandalias amarillas: $27.00, sandalias pardas: $18.00
4. pastel de chocolate: $4.00
5. bluejeans: $17.00
6. vestido rojo: $760.00
7. zapatos negros: $189.00

Letra y sonido

For the scripts for Parts A and C, see p. 249. The script for Part B is below.

B. Dictado

Selena wants to go to the store for some gifts. Write everything she says.

Para la tía Silvia una blusa de seda.

Para César un suéter azul.

Para Simón unas sandalias.

Y para Celia unos zapatos.

Repaso

Activity 1, p. 252

SARA Ana, mañana es la fiesta de Lisa. ¿Ya tienes tu ropa?

ANA Sí, voy de King Kong. ¿De qué vas tú?

SARA Voy de payaso, pero todavía tengo que comprar mi ropa. ¿Me acompañas?

ANA Cómo no.

SARA Necesito una corbata bastante fea.

ANA Ay, sí. Compra una corbata de los años setenta.

SARA Ja, ja, ja. Oye, ¿qué te parece si vamos a una tienda ahora?

ANA Sí, perfecto. ¿Qué más necesitas?

SARA Bueno, una camisa de cuadros, unos zapatos grandes y unos pantalones grandes.

ANA ¿Sabes qué? Mi hermano tiene unos pantalones viejos que puedes usar.

SARA ¡Fantástico!

Answers to Repaso Activity 1

una corbata fea, unos pantalones grandes

Capítulo 9: ¡Vamos de compras!
Projects

Project 1

Students each research a famous Hispanic American and prepare a biographical report, in English. They also write a paragraph about the person in Spanish and present it to the class. The other students use Spanish as they try to guess who the famous person is.

MATERIALS

✂ Students may need
- Library resources
- Audiocassette recorder or camcorder

SEQUENCE

1. Students conduct library research to select a famous Hispanic American and obtain biographical information on the person. This might be a famous entertainer, sports figure, scientist, writer, poet, musician, politician, or human rights advocate.
2. Students write a biographical report in English using the writing process (outline, rough draft, peer-correction, final draft).
3. Students write a paragraph in Spanish from a first-person perspective (as if they were the famous person). They are not to mention the name of the person. Paragraphs are to end with **¿Quién soy yo?**
4. Students present their paragraphs to the class. The other students, asking questions in Spanish, try to guess the identity of the famous person.

GRADING THE PROJECT

Suggested point distribution (total = 100)

Biographical Report

Content 20
Organization. 10
Vocabulary and grammar 10

Paragraph in Spanish

Content 20
Vocabulary and grammar 20
Oral presentation 20

Project 2

Each student researches an item of traditional indigenous clothing. For a multicultural approach, you may want to allow them to choose the article of clothing from any indigenous group in the world, or any clothing that has become popular in a culture other than its own. You may want to have students compare styles, materials, dyes, embroidery, weaving techniques, and other aspects of clothing manufacture across cultures. They also create a poster displaying the styles and present it to the class.

MATERIALS

✂ Students may need
- Library resources
- Posterboard
- Glue or tape
- Scissors
- Markers or colored pencils
- Magazines

SEQUENCE

1. Students conduct library research to select a type of clothing and obtain information on it. Types of clothing might include **gauchos, huipiles, sarapes.**
2. Students prepare a presentation in Spanish on the clothes telling where they originated, what they are made of, and why they were worn. (climate, natural resources, aesthetic reasons, place of origin, marital status)
3. Students prepare posters representing the clothing they chose. They may use magazine pictures or draw the clothing themselves. Some students may be able to bring in authentic costumes or fabrics.
4. Students present their information to the class. When all of the presentations have been completed, display the posters around the room.

GRADING THE PROJECT

Suggested point distribution (total = 100)

Accuracy of information 40
Poster 20
Presentation to class 40

Capítulo 9: ¡Vamos de compras!
Games

¿QUÉ VEO?

This game is an excellent way to review both the vocabulary presented in the chapter and the vocabulary for classroom objects from Chapter 2.

Procedure One student writes the name of an object that is visible in the classroom on a small piece of paper and gives it to you. The student must tell the class either the color of the object or the material of which it is made (**Veo algo rojo** or **Veo algo de algodón**). The class then has one minute to guess what the item is. If a student guesses correctly, he or she writes the name of another object on a piece of paper and the game continues as before. If the class cannot guess the object in the allotted time, the student who wrote the word selects another student to continue the game by writing a new word on a piece of paper.

¿QUÉ ES ÉSTO?

In this activity, students identify objects by touch. It is good for tactile learners.

Preparation Place various objects representing vocabulary from this or past chapters into a large bag or pillowcase. For this chapter, items might include a CD case, a toy, a T-shirt, a plastic flower, a greeting card, a sock, and so on. Students may also choose to loan items to put in the bag for this game.

Procedure Hold the bag open as students one by one reach into the bag without looking and try to identify the objects in Spanish. Having the student wear a blindfold adds to the drama. (**Ah, ésta es una corbata, ¿no?**) The class can see what the object is but cannot tell. You may wish to break down the class into smaller groups and divide the objects among two to three bags.

LOS COGNADOS

This game will make students aware of the pervasive influence of Spanish on American English and will help students increase both their Spanish and English vocabularies.

Materials You will need index cards.

Preparation On one side of index cards write the following definitions (do not include the answers that are in parentheses). On the other side write the number of points the word is worth (10, 20, or 50) in large print.

10 points

Prairie wolf (coyote)
Rope used by cowboys (lariat or lasso)
Bothersome insect (mosquito)
Texas cattle farm (ranch)
Village square (plaza)
Reno is the capital (Nevada)
Helena is the capital (Montana)
Largest city in California (Los Angeles)
Denver is the capital (Colorado)
Tallahassee is the capital (Florida)
City featured in this chapter (San Antonio)
Corn (maize)

20 points

Wild horse (bronco)
Type of warfare (guerrilla)
Spotted horse or bean (pinto)
Cloak or rain garment (poncho)
Cowboy contest (rodeo)
Red fruit we think of as a vegetable (tomato)
Nice view (vista)
Deep valley (canyon)

50 points

Building material used in the southwest (adobe)
Tavern (cantina)
Group formed to rule (junta)
Very masculine (macho)
Mountain range (sierra)

Procedure Place the cards worth 10 points in one stack, those worth 20 in a second, and those worth 50 in a third. Divide students into two teams. The first player from Team A chooses a stack, draws the top card from it, and reads the definition aloud. If the Team A player can give the word that matches the definition within 10 seconds, his or her team receives the number of points on the card. If not, the first player on Team B gets a chance to answer. If the Team B player is successful, Team B receives half the points on the card. The second player on Team B then follows the same procedure the Team A player followed. When all cards in a stack have been used, the teams must draw from the remaining stacks—cards should not be reused. The game continues until all cards have been drawn. The team with the highest score is the winner. You may wish to set a time limit before you begin instead of playing until all the cards have been drawn.

Native Speakers

As a varient to Los cognados, suggest that native speakers make additional cards with words of their choosing.

Capítulo 9
¡Vamos de compras!
pp. 232–255

Using the Chapter Opener

Motivating Activity

Ask students to think about what they like to shop for and where they like to shop. Do they enjoy looking for clothes, sports equipment, or gifts for other people? Do they prefer shopping with a group of friends, one friend, or alone?

Photo Flash!

(1) This photo is taken in San Antonio, where the video program for this chapter was shot. The actors of the video episodes for Chapters 9 and 10 are natives of San Antonio.

Culture Note

San Antonio is a city with strong Spanish and Mexican influences on its history, culture, food, and shopping. There are an abundance of hand-crafted gifts from Mexico in the shops of El Mercado. Galleries and museums throughout the city are well known for their folk art and fine art inspired by the traditions of the Southwest.

CAPÍTULO 9

¡Vamos de compras!

(1) ¿Qué le compro a Héctor para su graduación?

232 *doscientos treinta y dos*

Culture Note

Ask students on what occasions they give or receive gifts (Christmas, Hanukkah, Valentine's Day, birthday). In Latin America and Spain children often receive gifts on both their birthday and their saint's day.

In Spain, gifts are customarily exchanged on **el Día de los Reyes Magos** (January 6) rather than on Christmas. This reflects the belief that the wise men arrived and presented their gifts on that date. Ask your students about the diversity of gift-giving customs in their community.

Do you enjoy shopping? Or does it bore you when someone takes you to the mall? Everyone shops once in a while, whether for gifts, music, clothes, food, or school supplies. Even if you're a reluctant buyer, shopping can still be an opportunity to get together with a group of friends and have some fun.

In this chapter you will learn

- to discuss gift suggestions; to ask for and give directions downtown
- to comment on clothes; to make comparisons
- to express preferences; to ask about prices and pay for something

And you will

- listen to people discuss clothes
- read store advertisements
- write a gift plan for family and friends
- find out what some teenagers in Spanish-speaking countries think about fashion

(2) ¿Cuál de estas camisetas prefieres?

(3) Oye, mira los vestidos. Son bonitos, ¿no?

CHAPTER OPENER
CHAPTER 9

Focusing on Outcomes

- Have your students read the learner outcomes and match them with the photos. (Photo 1 shows discussing gift suggestions, photo 2 shows expressing preferences and making comparisons, and photo 3 shows commenting on clothes)
- Ask students to think about the gifts they have bought in the past several months and the things they have bought for themselves. On what occasions are they expected to give a gift? In general do they give more gifts or receive more gifts? How much do they usually spend on a gift?
- Have students discuss alternatives to buying gifts. Do they make their own gifts? Do they enjoy giving or receiving personal gifts, such as washing the car, baking brownies, or cooking a meal for someone?

Teaching Suggestion

(3) Have students describe their favorite T-shirt to a partner. Ask them to explain why it is their favorite. Then, have several students describe the T-shirt to the class.

Thinking Critically

Synthesizing Teach your students the proverb **El que más tiene más quiere.** Ask them to work with a partner to translate it to English (*The more you have, the more you want*). Have each pair write a short paragraph telling whether or not they agree with the sentiment of the proverb, and why.

Language and History Note

Bluejeans are a worldwide fashion that originated in the United States. The first bluejeans were made in 1850 by Levi Strauss, a Bavarian Jewish immigrant living in San Francisco, California. Strauss made his overalls and pants from a durable cotton fabric he imported from France. The French name for this material was *serge de Nîmes.* In the United States the name was shortened to *denim.* In Spanish, denim is **mezclilla,** and in Mexico one hears **mezclillas** for bluejeans. You may want to present this information with the **Vocabulario** on page 242.

VIDEO PROGRAM OR EXPANDED VIDEO PROGRAM, Videocassette 3

OR VIDEODISC PROGRAM, Videodisc 5A

Video Synopsis

Eva, Lisa, and Gabi discuss what they might buy Héctor for a graduation gift. They begin shopping for his gift, also taking a few moments to look at some clothing for themselves. They continue looking for Héctor's gift but cannot decide what to get him. Finally they agree to separate for half an hour, and they will each buy Héctor a different gift—but they end up choosing the same poster as a gift.

Background Information

The girls in the video are shopping at El Mercado, a popular market in San Antonio. They are in the indoor shopping part of the market that was once the city's old Farmer's Market.

Motivating Activity

Ask students if they ever have problems deciding what gift to give someone. How do they solve this problem? Ask if they have any advice that could help others who have the same problem.

Teaching Suggestion

Before starting the video, have students look at the story frame by frame and guess what is happening. Next, play the video once without sound and have students revise their predictions. Then show the video again with the sound on.

DE ANTEMANO

¿Qué le compramos a Héctor?

Eva's brother, Héctor, is graduating from high school. Eva, Lisa and Gabi are downtown shopping for a graduation gift and doing some window shopping as well. Why do you think they'll be surprised when each girl sees what the others have bought?

Eva

Lisa

Gabi

LISA Bueno, ¿qué le van a comprar a Héctor para su graduación?

EVA No sé, tal vez unos discos compactos de Gloria Estefan.

GABI Me gustaría regalarle algo divertido.

LISA Gabi, ¡yo también quiero regalarle algo divertido!

EVA ¿Por qué no compran regalos divertidos las dos? Pero tenemos que encontrarlos hoy... ¡su fiesta de graduación es el viernes!

LISA ¿Quieren entrar en esta tienda de ropa? Para mirar, nada más. Y después, vamos a la papelería para comprarle a Héctor las tarjetas.

EVA ¿Cuál prefieren, la blusa roja o la blusa de rayas?

GABI Yo prefiero la roja. ¿Cuánto cuesta?

EVA Uy, cuarenta dólares. Es cara.

LISA ¿Qué te parecen estos pantalones cortos?

GABI Eh... de verdad, Lisa, no me gustan para nada los cuadros.

234

RESOURCES FOR DE ANTEMANO

Textbook Audiocassette 5A/Audio CD 9
Video Guide
Video Program
Expanded Video Program, Videocassette 3
Videodisc Guide
Videodisc Program, Videodisc 5A
Practice and Activity Book, p. 97

GABI ¿Qué tal esta falda?

EVA Es bonita.

LISA Y es de algodón...

EVA Y sólo cuesta 12 dólares. ¡Qué barata!

GABI Sí, ¡es una ganga!

LISA Bueno, ¿qué le compramos a Héctor?

EVA Uf... es difícil. No sé... le interesan los libros, ¿tal vez un libro? Hay una librería al lado de la zapatería.

GABI No, eso no, prefiero comprarle algo divertido.

LISA Vamos a ver quién le compra el regalo más divertido. ¿Por qué no vas a buscar algo, y yo voy también? Y nos vemos aquí en... ¿media hora?

EVA Y yo voy a buscar algo también. Muy bien, hasta luego... en media hora, aquí.

Primero Lisa...

...luego Gabi...

... y después Eva...

¿ pero qué hacen en la misma tienda?

235

Video Integration

- ***Expanded Video Program***, *Videocassette 3,*
- ***Videodisc Program***, *Videodisc 5A*

You may choose to continue with **¿Qué le compramos a Héctor? (a continuación)** at this time or wait until later in the chapter. At this point in the story, Eva, Lisa, and Gabi meet after shopping for Héctor's gifts. They window shop for jewelry and then listen to a mariachi band. Finally each unwraps what she has bought for Héctor and they discover that they all have identical gifts. Eva and Gabi decide to exchange theirs for another gift and they head off to the stores.

Presentation

Group Work First play the video or have students skim the **fotonovela.** Then have students work in pairs to make a list in Spanish of all of the things that Eva, Lisa, and Gabi consider buying for Héctor. Have them discuss with their partner which of the items they think Héctor would most like to have, and why. After completing their lists, each pair compares their list with another pair's list to make sure they haven't missed any items. Do they agree on which gift Héctor would most like to have?

Thinking Critically

Drawing Inferences Ask students to point out the various expressions in which **le** is used, and to infer what it means by the context of the expressions.

For Individual Needs

Challenge Ask the students to draw another frame for the **fotonovela** in which they include the conversation between Eva, Lisa, and Gabi when they meet each other after buying their gifts.

Native Speakers

As you present clothing, gift-giving, and shopping vocabulary in this chapter, you may want to have native speakers list the words for which they know an alternate form. Encourage them to share these regional variations with the class.

For Individual Needs

1 Slower Pace Before having students begin this activity, write on a transparency or the board the Spanish question words in one column and their English glosses in another. Have students match each English meaning with its Spanish counterpart and make up questions in Spanish using the question words. Then have them do the activity in the text.

Teaching Suggestions

4 After having answered the questions, have students look again at the **fotonovela** on pages 234–235 and justify their answers based on what each character says.

5 Ask students to complete the statements with one of their classmates in mind. Students then present their statement to a partner who tries to guess the subject of the statement.

1 ¿Comprendes? See answers below.

Contesta las preguntas. Acuérdate *(Remember)*... si no sabes, puedes adivinar.

1. ¿Para quién compran Eva, Lisa y Gabi los regalos?
2. ¿Por qué van a comprar los regalos?
3. ¿Adónde van primero? ¿Qué miran allí?
4. ¿Qué tipo de regalo quieren comprar Lisa y Gabi?
5. ¿Qué pasa cuando las chicas van solas a buscar sus regalos?

2 ¿Cierto o falso?

Corrige las oraciones falsas. See answers below.

1. Las chicas le compran regalos a Héctor.
2. Van a la zapatería para comprar tarjetas.
3. Gabi prefiere la blusa azul.
4. La falda es de algodón.
5. A Héctor no le interesan los libros.
6. Las chicas compran tres regalos diferentes.

3 ¿Cómo se dice? See answers below.

Imagine that you're a friend of Héctor's. Find the phrases you could use

1. to say you'd like to buy him something funny
2. to ask how much something costs
3. to say that something is made out of cotton
4. to ask "What should we buy him?"
5. to say he is interested in books

4 ¿Quién lo diría? *Who might say it?*

Identifica al personaje que podría decir *(could say)* lo siguiente.

Eva

Lisa

Gabi

1. A Héctor le interesan los deportes—el fútbol, el basquetbol... Eva
2. Me gustaría mirar la ropa en esta tienda. Lisa
3. Necesito unos nuevos pantalones cortos. Lisa
4. La falda no cuesta mucho—¡sólo veinte dólares! Eva
5. La librería está cerca de la zapatería. Eva

5 ¿Y tú? Answers will vary.

Completa las siguientes oraciones con referencia a un amigo o una amiga.

1. Su fiesta de cumpleaños es...
2. Me gustaría comprarle...
3. Le interesa(n)...
4. No le gusta(n) para nada...
5. Para comprarle un regalo, voy a...
6. Las cosas allí son más...

Answers

1
1. Héctor
2. para su graduación
3. a una tienda de ropa, blusas y pantalones cortos
4. algo divertido
5. compran el mismo cartel

2
1. cierto
2. falso; Van a una papelería para comprar las tarjetas.
3. falso; Gabi prefiere la blusa roja.
4. cierto
5. falso; A Héctor le interesan los libros.
6. falso; Las chicas compran el mismo regalo.

3
1. Me gustaría comprarle algo divertido.
2. ¿Cuánto cuesta?
3. Es de algodón.
4. ¿Qué le compramos a él?
5. Le interesan los libros.

PRIMER PASO

Discussing gift suggestions; asking for and giving directions downtown

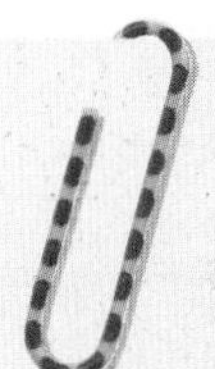

ASÍ SE DICE Discussing gift suggestions

To find out what gift a friend has in mind for someone, ask:

¿Qué piensas regalarle a tu hermano? *What are you planning on giving (as a gift) to . . .?*

¿Para quién es el regalo? *Who is the gift for?*

¿Qué tipo de regalo buscas? *What kind of gift are you looking for?*

Your friend might answer:

Le voy a dar unas camisetas. *I'm going to give him some T-shirts.*

El regalo **es para** mi novia.

Busco unos pantalones para mi primo. *I'm looking for some pants for my cousin.*

6 Escuchemos: Los regalos

Listen and take notes as Rodolfo tells you what his family members like. Then, answer the questions.

1. ¿Para quién son los carteles?
2. ¿Para quién es el perro?
3. ¿Para quién son los zapatos de tenis?
4. ¿Para quién es la radio?
5. ¿Para quién es la guitarra?
6. ¿Para quién son los videos?

Answers on p. 231C.

También se puede decir...

In some Spanish-speaking countries you will also hear **los pendientes** or **los aros** for *earrings*. Other words for *wallet* include **la billetera**, which is used more widely. **Cartera** is used to mean *purse* in many countries. In Costa Rica, **los confites** is used for *candy*, and in Argentina and Cuba you will hear *los caramelos*.

VOCABULARIO

un disco compacto

unos aretes y un collar

una cartera

unas corbatas

unos dulces

unas flores

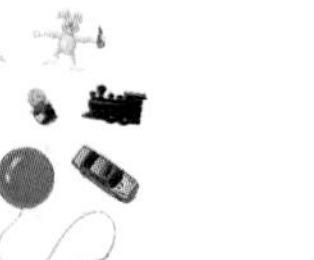

un juego de mesa

unos juguetes

una planta

una tarjeta

RESOURCES FOR PRIMER PASO

Textbook Audiocassette 5A/Audio CD 9
Practice and Activity Book, pp. 98–100
Native Speaker Activity Book, pp. 41–45
Videodisc Guide
Videodisc Program, Videodisc 5A

Chapter Teaching Resources, Book 3
- Additional Listening Activities 9-1, 9-2, p. 11
  Audiocassette 10A/Audio CD 9
- Student Response Forms, pp. 20–22
- Realia 9-1, pp. 15, 17
- Situation Cards 9-1, pp. 18, 19
- Teaching Transparency Master 9-1, pp. 7, 10
  Teaching Transparency 9-1
- Quiz 9-1, pp. 23–24
  Audiocassette 8A/Audio CD 9

Jump Start!

On the board or on a transparency write the following familiar poem, asking students to fill in the names of the months.
Treinta días tiene s ___,
a ___, j ___ y n ___.
F ___tiene veintiocho.
y los otros treinta y uno.
¿Qué son? Los m ___
del a ___.
Then have students list in Spanish the months of the year and the gift-giving dates they associate with those months.

MOTIVATE

In pairs, have students discuss what makes a gift good or bad. Have they ever received an inappropriate gift? What about a really great gift? What is the best gift they ever received? Ask volunteers to share some of the answers.

TEACH

Presentation

Ask students to look back at the **fotonovela** and have them find some of the expressions introduced in **Así se dice.** Point out to students that **¿Para quién es...?** is for one item and **¿Para quién son...?** is for more than one item. Then model pronunciation of the words in the **Vocabulario** and have students take the role of the friend to practice the expressions and the new vocabulary. You may want to have students work in pairs to practice the expressions and vocabulary.

For videodisc application, see *Videodisc Guide.*

PRIMER PASO
CAPÍTULO 9

Teaching Suggestion

7 Have students rewrite and personalize these statements. Point out the additional vocabulary on pages 340–341.

Presentation

Gramática Write the following sentences on the board or on a transparency: (**Le doy unos aretes a mamá. Mamá les regala los carteles a los niños. Los chicos quieren regalarles unas flores a las chicas.** Help students recognize the indirect objects in the sentences. Remind students that **le** and **les** can have several meanings and that **a** + pronoun or **a** + noun is often added for clarification.

For Individual Needs

8 **Slower Pace** Put this paragraph on a transparency and go through it as a whole-class activity, breaking it down into smaller parts as needed for comprehension.

Teaching Suggestion

9 Reinforce correct syntax by reminding students of correct word order in Spanish. For example, you may want to point out that the verbs **dar, regalar,** and **comprar** require that a preposition be placed before the stressed indirect object noun. (**dar ... a, regalar ... a,** and **comprar ... para**) When students are performing confidently, ask them to modify the activity by verifying each other's statements with a question in which they practice both positions of the indirect object pronoun. (Student 1: **Le quiero dar unas flores a mi amigo.** Student 2: **¿Quieres darle unas flores a tu amigo?**)

7 Regalos para todos

Using the gift items in the vocabulary list on page 237, write sentences telling what you'll buy these people. Base your choices on what they like. Possible answers below.

1. A tu hermano le gusta jugar en casa.
2. A tu hermana le encantan las joyas *(jewelry)*.
3. A tu mejor amiga/o le gusta escuchar música.
4. A tu padre le gusta vestirse bien *(dress well)*.
5. A tus abuelos les encanta su jardín.
6. A tu profesor/profesora le encanta el chocolate.

Gramática Indirect object pronouns

Indirect objects tell *to whom* or *for whom* something is intended.

1. Indirect object pronouns either precede a conjugated verb or may be attached to an infinitive.
   Le quiero regalar algo divertido a Héctor.
   Quiero regalar**le** algo divertido a Héctor.
   I want to give something fun to Hector (to him).
2. **Le** can mean *to him, to her* or *to you* (singular). **Les** can mean *to them* or *to you* (plural). To clarify **le** or **les**, you can add the phrase **a** + *pronoun* or **a** + *noun*.
   ¿Qué **le** compramos **a Héctor**?
   Les voy a regalar unos juguetes **a mis hermanos**.

8 Ir de compras

Completa el párrafo con **me**, **te**, **le**, **nos** o **les**.

¡Qué divertido ir de compras! A mi hermana Teresa __1__ voy a regalar un collar y a mi hermano __2__ doy una camiseta. A mamá y papá __3__ regalo un video de su película favorita. __4__ voy a regalar aretes a mi abuelita y a mi abuelito __5__ quiero regalar una corbata. ¿Qué crees que voy a regalar __6__ a ti? ¡Es una sorpresa! ¿Qué crees que Roberto __7__ va a regalar a mí? Mis papás __8__ van a regalar boletos para el concierto a mí y a mi hermano. ¿Qué te parece?

1. le; 2. le; 3. les; 4. Le; 5. le; 6. te; 7. me; 8. nos

9 Gustos y preferencias

Work in pairs. Decide which gifts each of you will give to the people listed in the last box. Be sure to include **le** or **les** in your sentences. Answers will vary.

MODELO Le voy a regalar un disco compacto a mi hermano para su graduación.

voy a	dar	unas flores	mi hermano
quiero	regalar	un cartel	mis padres
prefiero	comprar	una bicicleta	mi hermana
		un juego de mesa	mis amigos
		una planta	mi abuelo
		¿?	¿?

Answers

7 1. Le voy a comprar un juguete.
2. Le voy a comprar unos aretes o un collar.
3. Le voy a comprar un disco compacto.
4. Le voy a comprar una corbata.
5. Les voy a comprar una planta.
6. Le voy a comprar unos dulces de chocolate.

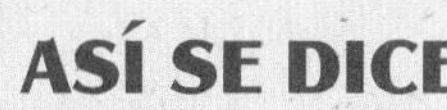

ASÍ SE DICE Asking for and giving directions downtown

To find out where a shop is located, ask:

Perdón, ¿dónde está el almacén? *Excuse me, where is the department store?*

¿Me puede decir dónde queda la joyería? *Can you tell me where the jewelry store is?*

Some responses might be:

Está a dos cuadras de aquí. *It's two blocks from here.*

Queda al lado de la zapatería. *It's next to the shoe store.*

10 En las tiendas

Working with a partner, look at the drawing of downtown Río Blanco and take turns asking and answering where each store is. Use **estar + lejos de, al lado de,** and **cerca de** in your sentences.

Sample answer below.

¿Te acuerdas?

You've already learned to say where someone or something is located using **estar** + *location.* If you've forgotten the prepositions of location, see page 106.

VOCABULARIO

Answers

10 *Sample answer:*
—¿Dónde está la dulcería?
—Está al lado de la juguetería.

Language Note

In Spain and Latin America **manzana** is often used instead of **cuadra** for *block.* Also, in direction-giving situations where English speakers would say "Walk four blocks," many Spanish speakers would say, **"Camine cuatro calles."**

Presentation

Así se dice Using a puppet to ask the questions, role-play the phrases in the box, altering them for local directions. For example, the puppet asks **Perdón, ¿dónde está el almacén ____?** and you respond with appropriate directions, using the phrases in the text. Then ask students to answer the puppet's questions.

For Individual Needs

Kinesthetic Learners
Arrange several of the students' desks to form a downtown area, placing a sign with the name of a store on each desk. One student then asks directions and a second student answers. The first student then walks to the desired location. You might change the signs around to provide additional practice.

Presentation

Vocabulario Put the name of each shop on an index card. Using props or pictures, set up eight stations in the classroom representing the shops, (e.g., bread for **panadería,** a flower for **florería,** etc.) Have a student select a card, show it to you and ask its location, (e.g. **¿Dónde está la panadería?**) The student brings the card to the appropriate station and responds **La panadería está aquí.** When the stations are all identified, ask location questions such as **¿Está la panadería al lado de la zapatería?**

Photo Flash!

Point out the use of **panadería** and **dulcería** in the photos. Ask students to try to guess the meanings of the signs based upon their current knowledge of Spanish. (**pan caliente** *hot bread,* **hornada de tarde** *batch of bread baked in afternoons,* **sucursal de Echegarayes** *branch of the Echegarayes company*)

Additional Practice

13 Ask students to work in groups of three or four to develop a dialogue in which they list a few items they want to buy, discuss the best places to shop for these items, and ask for directions to get to the store.

Close

Use *Overhead Transparency 9-1* to review the vocabulary and functions in this **Paso.** See suggestions for using the transparency, p. 10, *Chapter Teaching Resources, Book 3.*

Assess

Quiz 9-1, *Chapter Teaching Resources, Book 3,* pp. 23–24

Assessment Items, Audiocassette 8A/Audio CD 9

Performance Assessment

Ask students to write a note in Spanish to their parent or guardian saying that they are not going to be home after school because they have to buy a gift for a friend. They should include what they plan to give the friend and where they are going to buy the gift.

11 Escuchemos: De compras

Where is Eva going to shop? Listen as she talks about what she's going to buy. Match each item with the correct store. Answers on p. 231C.

1. pastel	a. Zapatería Monterrey
2. aretes	b. Panadería La Molina
3. juego de mesa	c. Joyería Central
4. sandalias	d. Pastelería Río Grande
5. camisa	e. Juguetería de San Antonio
6. plantas	f. Florería Martínez
7. pan dulce	g. Almacén Vargas

Nota cultural

When La Sra. Oviedo needs to buy groceries, she can go to a large supermarket or to some of the many specialty stores near her apartment. She usually prefers going to a specialty store. Like many Spanish housewives she shops almost every day, buying only what she needs for a day or two at a time. That way, the food in her kitchen is always fresh, she avoids traffic, and she has a chance to meet and chat with her acquaintances in the neighborhood.

12 ¿Dónde está? Answers will vary.

Imagine that you and your partner are in Río Blanco with this shopping list. Using the drawing on page 239, take turns deciding where you have to go to buy each item.

MODELO —Tengo que comprar un collar.
¿Sabes dónde está la joyería?
—Sí. Queda al lado de la zapatería.

collar
sandalias
flores
juguetes
zapatos de tenis
pan
galletas
corbata

13 Las tiendas

Get together with two or three classmates and write a list of four items you buy frequently, such as clothing, food, compact discs, and books. Then ask each other for the names of stores in your city or town where you can buy the different items you've listed. Include where the stores are located. Be sure to take notes and be ready to report to the class.

14 Amigos y familiares Answers will vary.

Describe the relationship, age, likes and dislikes and needs of these people to decide on a good gift for each.

1. your best friend
2. three family members
3. an elderly person you know

For Individual Needs

Challenge Teach students **doble a la derecha** (*turn right*), **doble a la izquierda** (*turn left*), and **siga derecho** (*continue straight ahead*). Students can then give more elaborate directions for a downtown area, using either a map of your town or the student desks (see **Kinesthetic Learners,** p. 239).

¿Estás a la moda?

Hispanic teens usually try to look as fashionable as they possibly can. Much of what is popular in the United States is also in style in Spain and Latin America. But what counts is quality, not quantity. Here are some comments from teenagers about what is usually **de moda** *(in style)* and what's definitely not.

Soledad
Madrid, España

"Yo cuando voy a una fiesta me pongo un vestido... y unos zapatos de tacón... Lo importante es uno mismo, y uno mismo nunca pasará de moda".

Gisela
Caracas, Venezuela

"Depende de la fiesta, pero una fiesta de mis amigos normalmente como estoy ahorita, ¿no? Un vestido, blue jeans... No es tan importante [estar a la moda], es más la ropa que me guste, más que la moda. No toda la moda me queda bien".

Pablo
San Vito, Costa Rica

"A como amerite, si es en el campo, vamos de esport, y si es algo ya normal nos ponemos traje... Claro que sí, [estar a la moda] es andar en la actualidad con todos, ¿verdad? No quedarse atrás".

Para pensar y hablar...

A. In small groups, discuss about what is fashionable. Make a list of the things your classmate is wearing and present it to the group.

B. With a classmate, suggest five reasons why people should or should not be **a la moda**.

VIDEO PROGRAM OR EXPANDED VIDEO PROGRAM, *Videocassette 3*

OR VIDEODISC PROGRAM, *Videodisc 5A*

Teacher Notes

- See *Video Guide* and *Videodisc Guide* for activities related to the **Panorama cultural.**
- Remind students that cultural information may be included on the Quizzes and Chapter Test.

Motivating Activity

Ask students to look at the clothing of teenagers in photos throughout this book and to compare it with the clothing they like to wear. Ask them to identify clothing styles that are popular both with them and the Spanish-speaking teenagers. Do they notice any differences?

Presentation

Have students listen to the audio recording or watch the video. Ask for volunteers to read one of the interviews aloud for pronunciation practice. Then have students answer the **Preguntas** below to check comprehension.

Language Note

zapatos de tacón *high heels*
uno mismo *oneself*
pasar de moda *to be out of fashion*
a como amerite *it depends* (***ameritar*** *to merit, to value)*
esport *casual, sporty*
andar en la actualidad *to be up to date*
quedarse atrás *to be behind the times*

Preguntas

1. ¿Quién es de España? ¿de Costa Rica? ¿de Venezuela? (Soledad, Pablo, Gisela)
2. ¿Qué dice Soledad que le gusta llevar a una fiesta? (un vestido y unos zapatos de tacón)
3. Según Gisela, ¿es importante llevar ropa elegante a las fiestas? (no)¿Por qué?
4. ¿A Pablo le importa estar a la moda? ¿por qué? (sí, porque le gusta andar en la actualidad)

Thinking Critically

Drawing Inferences Ask students to decide from the information in the interviews what each person would wear in the following situations: to school, to church, to the beach, to exercise, or camping.

Jump Start!

On the board or on a transparency write a list of several local stores. Have students identify what type of store each is. (Smith's Bakery—**panadería**) Use the types of stores included in the vocabulary on page 239.

Motivate

Ask students whether they prefer to wear new clothes or comfortable old clothes. When do they like to get all dressed up? When do they like to wear what is comfortable?

Teach

Presentation

Así se dice Model the expressions in the **Así se dice** box. Then call on several pairs of students to practice the first question and answer. After they practice with their books open, have them ask and answer the questions with books closed. Do the same for the second question. For additional practice, ask students to vary the dialogue by changing **fiesta** to **partido de fútbol, restaurante baile,** etc.

Vocabulario Fill a bag with the clothes listed. Name the objects as you hold them up. Then ask **sí/no** questions followed by either/or questions and finally short answer questions. Ask students to repeat the vocabulary after you and then to answer questions such as **¿De qué color es la blusa de la mujer? ¿Qué tipo de zapatos lleva la mujer? ¿Qué cosas son pardas?**

SEGUNDO PASO

Commenting on clothes; making comparisons

ASÍ SE DICE Commenting on clothes

To find out what someone is going to wear, ask:

¿Qué ropa vas a llevar a la fiesta?
What are you going to wear . . . ?

¿No tienes algo más formal?
Don't you have something more formal?

Your friend might say:

¡Lo de siempre! Una camiseta con bluejeans. *The usual!*

Sí, pero **prefiero llevar ropa cómoda.**
. . . I prefer comfortable clothes.

VOCABULARIO

¿Qué ropa vas a llevar tú?

Resources for SEGUNDO PASO

Textbook Audiocassette 5A/Audio CD 9
Practice and Activity Book, pp. 101–103
Native Speaker Activity Book, pp. 41–45
Video Guide
Video Program
Expanded Video Program, Videocassette 3
Videodisc Guide
Videodisc Program, Videodisc 5A

Chapter Teaching Resources, Book 3
- Communicative Activity 9-1, pp. 3, 4
- Additional Listening Activities 9-3, 9-4, p. 12
  Audiocassette 10A/Audio CD 9
- Student Response Forms, pp. 20–22
- Realia 9-1, pp. 15, 17
- Situation Cards 9-2, pp. 18, 19
- Teaching Transparency Master 9-2, pp. 8, 10
  Teaching Transparency 9-2
- Quiz 9-2, pp. 25–26
  Audiocassette 8A/Audio CD 9

15 Escuchemos: ¿Qué necesitas llevar? Answers on p. 231C.

Listen as various people talk about clothing they need for certain occasions. Choose an event for which the clothing would be appropriate.

Eventos: un baile, clases, jugar al tenis, ir a la piscina, trabajar en la oficina

16 Mis preferencias Possible answers below.

Completa las oraciones con tus preferencias personales.

1. Cuando hace calor, me gusta llevar...
2. En el invierno, cuando hace mucho frío, llevo...
3. Cuando voy al colegio, en general llevo...
4. Cuando salgo con mis amigos, llevo...
5. Cuando voy a una fiesta, me gusta llevar...
6. Me gusta jugar a los deportes. En general llevo...
7. Voy a ir a un picnic. Voy a llevar...
8. En la primavera, me encanta llevar...
9. Tan pronto como tenga el dinero *(As soon as I have the money)*, voy a comprar...

17 ¿Cómo es su ropa?

Work with a partner. Describe the clothing someone in your class is wearing. See if your partner can guess who you're describing.

18 El fin de semana

Working in pairs, tell your partner three or four places you'll be going this weekend. Then take turns suggesting what each of you should wear.

MODELO —Voy al cine y al centro comercial.
—Para ir al cine debes llevar bluejeans y una camiseta.

Nota Gramatical

In earlier lessons you've used **ser** to describe people and things and to tell where someone is from. The formula **es/son** + **de** + *material* or *pattern* is used to tell what something is made of.

El suéter es de lana.
¿Son de cuero tus botas?

VOCABULARIO

Answers

16 *Possible answers:*
1. los pantalones cortos y una camiseta
2. una chaqueta de lana y unas botas
3. unos bluejeans y una camiseta
4. los bluejeans y una camisa
5. un vestido y un suéter
6. los pantalones cortos y zapatillas de tenis
7. el traje de baño y unos pantalones cortos
8. las sandalias
9. una chaqueta de cuero

Language Note

Instead of **una camiseta,** some Spanish-speaking countries use **un jersey, una playera, un polo,** or **una remera.** Other words for **los bluejeans** include **los pantalones vaqueros, los mahones, los tejanos,** and **las mezclillas.** See Language and History Note, p. 233, for additional information on bluejeans.

Teaching Suggestion

Photo Ask students **¿Qué llevan los muchachos que juegan al baloncesto?** Then you might ask **¿Qué llevas tú cuando juegas al baloncesto?**

Teaching Suggestion

16 To start this activity, ask for a volunteer who will stand in front of the class to have his or her clothes described by the other students. Then say **¿Cómo es la ropa de ___?** Ask various students to add one sentence to the description. Repeat with several others for additional practice.

Presentation

Vocabulario Hold up photos of people wearing the new articles of clothing. Point out the items to the students and model the vocabulary, having students repeat. Then shuffle the photos and ask, **¿Qué lleva ___?** Have them include vocabulary from page 242. If time permits, you may want to include vocabulary from **Un poco más...** on page 244.

For Individual Needs

Tactile Learners Bring in pieces of cotton, wool, silk, leather, striped fabric, and plaid fabric. Let students see and feel them as you teach the vocabulary words. Ask students to group the fabric by season.

Reteaching

16 Colors Review the names of the colors using square pieces of construction paper. You may want to have students re-read the introduction to colors in the Preliminary Chapter, page 9.

Background Information

19 The artist Carmen Lomas Garza often paints about her own life as a young Mexican American growing up in the small South Texas town of Kingsville. She has largely concentrated on depicting the traditions of Mexican American culture. Drawing on her childhood memories, she captures the magic of daily life found in family and neighborhood activities such as gathering cactus during Lent, or making **tamales** during the Christmas season (as depicted in *Tamalada*).

For Individual Needs

19 Auditory/Visual Learners Describe orally several of the outfits or have students describe them. The rest of the class should listen and then point to the outfit being described as soon as they recognize it. Check comprehension by walking around the class to observe student reaction.

For videodisc application, see *Videodisc Guide.*

Reteaching

Clothing Cut pictures of clothing from a magazine or construction paper. Hang them with tape on a clothesline that you have drawn on the board. As you point to an article of clothing, ask the students **¿Qué es esto?** Then ask individual students to go to the board and point out the article of clothing you ask for. (**Enséñame una camisa.**)

19 ¿Qué llevan? Possible answers below.

Look at the picture and describe at least four different outfits. Include colors in your descriptions. What do you think they're doing?

Carmen Lomas Garza, ***Tamalada,*** 1987, Gouache on paper. 20" × 27".

20 ¡Qué ropa tan rara!

Look at these drawings of different people in different situations. What do you think is wrong in each drawing? Write a sentence telling what the people are wearing. Then write a sentence telling what you think they should be wearing instead. For additional clothing vocabulary, see page 342.

Possible answers below.

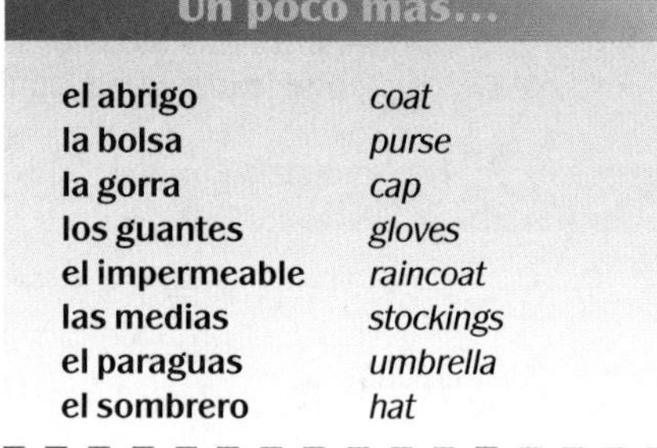

Un poco más...

el abrigo	*coat*
la bolsa	*purse*
la gorra	*cap*
los guantes	*gloves*
el impermeable	*raincoat*
las medias	*stockings*
el paraguas	*umbrella*
el sombrero	*hat*

1.

2.

3.

4.

Answers

19 *Possible answer:* El hombre lleva anteojos, un suéter, y una camisa. La niña lleva un vestido, unos calcetines, y unos zapatos.

20 *Possible answers:*
1. Lleva un traje de baño. Debe llevar una chaqueta, pantalones y botas.
2. Lleva una chaqueta formal con pantalones cortos. Debe llevar pantalones largos.
3. Lleva una camiseta. Debe llevar las botas.
4. Lleva pantalones largos. Debe llevar un traje de baño.

21 Una encuesta

Working in groups of three or four, take a survey of clothing preferences for the items listed. Make a chart of what each person prefers and report to the class. Compare your findings with other groups.

1. to wear to school
2. to wear on a date
3. for a class trip
4. the middle of the summer
5. to go to the park
6. to walk the dog
7. to go to a formal dance
8. to play tennis

22 Me gustaría comprar...

Possible answers below.

You've just won a $500 gift certificate for your favorite department store. Write six or eight sentences describing what you'd like to buy for your friends and family. Be sure to describe colors, patterns, and material. Use the words in the box.

tener · *necesitar* · *llevar* · *me gustaría* · *preferir* · *comprar* · *ir de compras*

23 ¿Y ustedes?

Now get together with two classmates. Create the "ultimate gift list" by combining your individual lists from Activity 22. Be ready to report the group's choices to the class.

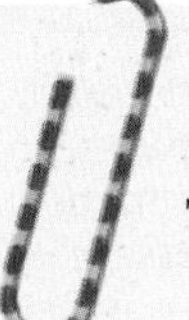

ASÍ SE DICE Making comparisons

To compare things, you might ask:

¿Cúal es más barato — el reloj o el disco compacto? *Which is cheaper . . . ?*

¿Son los carteles tan caros como el juguete? *Are the posters as expensive as the toy?*

Some responses might be:

El disco compacto **es menos caro.**

Sí. **Son del mismo precio.** *They're the same price.*

Gramática Making comparisons

1. To make comparisons with adjectives in Spanish, use the following formulas:
   - **más** + *adjective* + **que** — *more . . . than*
   - **menos** + *adjective* + **que** — *less . . . than*
   - **tan** + *adjective* + **como** — *as . . . as*
2. The adjective agrees in gender and number with the item it describes.
   La camisa blanca es **más bonita que** el vestido azul.
   Las sandalias son **menos caras que** los zapatos de tenis.
   El cinturón es **tan barato como** la corbata.

Teaching Suggestion

21 You may wish to provide each group with a transparency for their chart. Compile the data in the charts on one transparency and make generalizations about class preferences. Have a simple discussion about **la ropa favorita de los jóvenes. (Los jóvenes prefieren los bluejeans, zapatos de tenis, camisas de rayas o de cuadros. Para un baile las chicas prefieren vestidos elegantes, zapatos, y medias.)**

Presentation

Así se dice/Gramática Explain how to form comparisons. First write the formulas from the **Gramática** box on the board or on a transparency. Then demonstrate how the formulas relate to the sentences by giving example sentences for each. Next divide the class into trios. Give each trio an envelope that contains components of sentences written on slips of paper. (Be sure to prepare these ahead of time.) For example, on six slips of paper, write **Rosa/es/más/alta/que/Raúl.** It is better if the adjective only agrees with the subject. Have the trios arrange the words to form a sentence. For an extra challenge, put two or three sentences in the same envelope. For a slower pace, give English explanation of the sentences.

Additional Practice

Gramática Bring in pictures of famous people for a photo bank. Compare yourself to one of the people. Have students guess the person to whom you are comparing yourself.

22 *Possible answer:* Me gustaría comprar un vestido de seda. También necesito unos zapatos de cuero. Voy a comprar suéteres de lana para el invierno. También me voy a comprar un abrigo de piel y lana que cuesta $300.

Culture Note

The sizes used for clothes in Spain and Latin America are different from those used in the United States. For example, women's pants that are size 10 in the United States are size 42 in Europe and Latin America, and U.S. men's size 32 pants correspond to European size 81 pants.

For Individual Needs

23 Slower Pace Have students describe the items pictured to each other before listening to the audio recording.

Additional Practice

24 To provide additional practice with comparisons and to review the food vocabulary in Chapter 8, bring in food store ads from newspapers. Ask each pair of students to make at least five price comparisons. Then have two or three students share their comparisons with the rest of the class.

Close

Teaching Suggestion

Walk around the classroom and ask the class about the material in various students' clothing. **(¿De qué es el suéter de ____?)** After you have done this, ask students to work in pairs. They are to tell their partner what they are wearing, and describe its material and color. How are their clothing choices affected by the seasons?

Assess

Quiz 9-2, *Chapter Teaching Resources, Book 3,* pp. 25–26

Assessment Items, Audiocassette 8A/Audio CD 9

Performance Assessment

Use Activity 25 as a Performance Assessment, or have students write a letter to a friend describing their favorite outfit. They should include colors, fabrics, information about where they wear it, and a comparison of this outfit with others.

24 Escuchemos: ¿Cómo son? Answers on p. 231C.

Look at the drawings. Listen and match what you hear to the correct pair of items. When you're finished, write sentences to compare each pair of items using the adjectives you've learned.

25 Regalos y más regalos

You need to buy gifts for your family and friends. Look at the catalog page and decide what to buy for each person. Be sure to say what each person needs. Use comparisons in deciding upon which item to buy.

MODELO Mi hermana necesita ropa nueva. Quiero comprarle una blusa porque es más barata que un vestido. Los vestidos son caros.

Sometimes you don't know the exact word for something even in your native language. Remember that one way you can still get your message across is by describing what you can't remember. Use a phrase like **Es una cosa que...** and then tell what it does, how it's used, or where it is. As practice, look around your room or classroom and pick three things you don't know how to say in Spanish. How could you describe them so a Spanish speaker would understand? Test your skills on a classmate! Look at these four drawings. Can you describe these items to a friend?

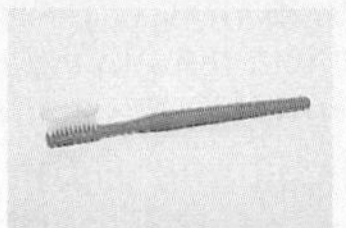

Math Link

Realia Ask students to determine how much money they can save per item if they purchase them on sale. Then have them calculate their total savings. On the board or on a transparency write the following:

Precios reducidos:	Originalmente	Ahora
Trajes de seda	$225.00	$189.95
Camisas de algodón	25.95	18.00
Zapatos de cuero	63.00	49.98

(Answers: $35.05, $7.95, $13.02; $56.02)

TERCER PASO

Expressing preferences; asking about prices and paying for something

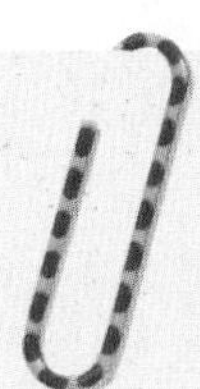

ASÍ SE DICE Expressing preferences

To find out which item a friend prefers, ask:	Your friend might say:
¿Cuál de estos trajes prefieres? *Which of these suits do you prefer?*	**Prefiero el azul.** *I prefer the blue one.*
¿Qué camisa te gusta más? ¿La verde o la amarilla? *Which shirt do you like more? The green one or the yellow one?*	La verde. **Además, te queda muy bien.** *Besides, it fits you very well.*

Nota Gramatical

Demonstrative adjectives point out people and things. Like other adjectives, they agree in gender and number with the noun they modify.

Masculine

este vestido *this . . .*	**estos** vestidos *these . . .*
ese vestido *that . . .*	**esos** vestidos *those . . .*

Feminine

esta falda	**estas** faldas
esa falda	**esas** faldas

26 Opiniones

Alicia and her sister Mónica are shopping for clothes. Write Alicia's comments on what they see. See answers below.

MODELO blusa/feo
—Oye, Mónica. Esta blusa es fea, ¿no?

1. camisa/caro
2. botas/feo
3. suéter/pequeño
4. zapatos/barato
5. falda/grande
6. cinturón/bonito
7. chaqueta/barato
8. vestido/caro

27 Opiniones diferentes

Now it's Mónica's turn! Work with a partner. Using your sentences from Activity 26, take turns giving Mónica's responses to Alicia's comments. See answers below.

MODELO —Oye, Mónica. Esta blusa es fea, ¿no?
—No, Alicia, esa blusa no es fea. Es bonita.

28 Preferencias

Work in groups of three. Look at the pictures on pages 242 and 244. What are your tastes in clothing? Tell which items you like and don't like.

Jump Start!

Have students write the answers to the following questions: **¿Qué ropa llevas hoy? ¿Siempre llevas un abrigo en el invierno? ¿Te gusta llevar ropa elegante? ¿Qué lleva el profesor/la profesora hoy?**

MOTIVATE

Ask students on what occasions they would discuss a purchase with family or friends before buying the item. What phrases do they use? Do they shop around for a good price? What stores do they go to?

TEACH

Presentation

Así se dice Bring in magazine pictures of people wearing various types of clothing to introduce expressing preferences from **Así se dice.** Ask the class questions about the appropriateness of types of clothing in certain situations as you hold up two pictures, then answer the questions. (**¿Cuál de estas camisas prefieres para un partido de fútbol? Yo prefiero la roja.**) Model contrasting items of different gender to present the **Nota gramatical.** (**¿Qué gusta más para ir a la iglesia, esta falda o este suéter?**) Then include students in the question and answer process.

RESOURCES FOR TERCER PASO

Textbook Audiocassette 5A/Audio CD 9
Practice and Activity Book, pp. 104–106
Native Speaker Activity Book, pp. 41–45
Videodisc Guide
Videodisc Program, Videodisc 5A

Chapter Teaching Resources, Book 3
- Communicative Activity 9-2, pp. 5–6
- Additional Listening Activities 9-5, 9-6, p. 13
  Audiocassette 10A/Audio CD 9
- Student Response Forms, pp. 20–22
- Realia 9-2, pp. 16, 17
- Situation Cards 9-3, pp. 18, 19
- Teaching Transparency Master 9-3, pp. 9, 10
  Teaching Transparency 9-3
- Quiz 9-3, pp. 27–28
  Audiocassette 8A/Audio CD 9

Answers

26
1. Esta camisa es cara, ¿no?
2. Estas botas son feas, ¿no?
3. Este suéter es pequeño, ¿no?
4. Estos zapatos son baratos, ¿no?
5. Esta falda es grande, ¿no?
6. Este cinturón es bonito, ¿no?
7. Esta chaqueta es barata, ¿no?
8. Este vestido es caro, ¿no?

27 *Answers will vary.*

Presentation

Así se dice/Vocabulario To introduce talking about prices, put price tags on the articles of clothing used for the Presentation on page 247. The tags should be large enough to be easily read by the whole class. Then ask questions one by one about their prices. Include the expressions from the **Vocabulario. (¿Cuánto cuesta esta corbata? Cuesta treinta dólares, ¡Es un robo!)** Then hold up objects and ask individual students to answer the question **¿Cuánto cuesta(n) ___?** Each student is to answer by giving a price and an appropriate expression from the **Vocabulario.**

Nota cultural Have students find out the current exchange rates for three of the countries listed and report back to the class.

Teaching Suggestions

29 Review colors (pp. 9, 158, 242) and numbers (pp. 9, 10, 27, 219) before having students listen to this activity.

Culture Note

Other currencies of Spanish-speaking countries are as follows:

Bolivia *el boliviano*
Chile *el peso*
Cuba *el peso*
El Salvador *el colón*
Filipinas *el peso*
Guinea Ecuatorial *el franco*
Honduras *la lempira*
Nicaragua *la córdoba*
Panamá *el balboa*
Paraguay *el guaraní*
Perú *el inti*
República Dominicana *el peso*
Uruguay *el peso*

ASÍ SE DICE Asking about prices and paying for something

To ask how much one item costs, say:

¿Cuánto cuesta esta chaqueta?
How much does . . . cost?

Some responses might be:

Cuesta 90 dólares.

To ask how much two or more items cost, say:

¿Cuánto cuestan...?
How much do . . . cost?

Cuestan 175 sucres.

VOCABULARIO

¡Es un robo!	*It's a rip-off!*
¡Qué barato!	*How cheap!*
¡Qué caro!	*How expensive!*
¡Qué ganga!	*What a bargain!*

29 Escuchemos: ¡Qué caro!

Listen to conversations between a clerk and some customers. Write the name, price, and color of the items mentioned.

Answers on p. 231D.

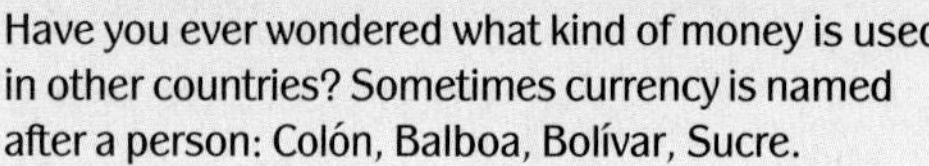

Have you ever wondered what kind of money is used in other countries? Sometimes currency is named after a person: Colón, Balboa, Bolívar, Sucre.

Argentina	*el peso*	**Guatemala**	*el quetzal*
Colombia	*el peso*	**México**	*el peso*
Costa Rica	*el colón*	**Puerto Rico**	*el dólar*
Ecuador	*el sucre*	**Venezuela**	*el bolívar*
España	*la peseta*		

30 En la tienda

Mateo and Pedro are shopping for gifts. In groups of four, decide what Pedro would say in the conversation. Then, two members of the group take turns role-playing the scene. The other pair in the group can prompt and critique. Use your imagination!

MATEO Necesito comprar algo para mi novia. ¿Te gusta esta combinación?
PEDRO Pues, ______
MATEO Bueno, entonces. Este vestido azul, ¿te gusta?
PEDRO Sí. ¿______?
MATEO El precio es $89. Es mucho, ¿no?
PEDRO ¡______!
MATEO Pues, mira ______
PEDRO ¿______?
MATEO ¡Ay, hombre! ¡Cuesta $700!
PEDRO ¡______!

For Individual Needs

30 Slower Pace Write the English equivalents of the missing phrases on the board. (*not much, how much is it, a whole lot, this one, how much, what a rip-off*)

31 De compras con los amigos

Work with a partner to prepare a scene like the one you wrote in Activity 30. One of you plays the clerk, the other the customer. The customer asks questions about material, price, and quality, and the clerk answers. Decide if the items are a bargain and if the colors match other clothing. Then make arrangements to pay. Be prepared to present your scene to the class.

A LO NUESTRO

If you want to tell a friend he or she looks good today, you can say **¡Qué bien te ves!** or **¡Qué guapo/a estás!** *(You look great!)*. To compliment someone on his or her outfit, say **Estás a la última** *(You're stylish)* or **Tu ropa hace juego** *(Your clothes go well together)*. To say something doesn't match, use **No hace juego**.

32 En el almacén *In the department store*

Role-play a scene with a partner in which one of you is the store clerk and the other a customer who needs to buy gifts. When the customer chooses a gift, compare his or her selection with another item and give reasons why he or she should or shouldn't buy the item chosen. Finally, have the customer pay for the gifts.

33 En mi cuaderno Possible answers below.

Write a dialogue for your journal in which you are a clerk who tries to talk a customer out of buying clothing that doesn't match. Convince the customer that the colors don't coordinate, that plaids and stripes really don't look good together, and that the outfit is out of fashion. Then, compare the clothing the customer chooses with clothing that actually does look good.

LETRA Y SONIDO

A. 1. **s:** The letter **s** in Spanish is pronounced like the *s* in the English word *pass*.
camiseta flores pastelería gris suéter seda

2. **z:** In Latin America, the letter **z** before the vowels **a, o,** and **u** is also pronounced like the *s* in the English word *pass.*
azul zapatos zanahoria zarzuela zapatería
However, in Spain, the letter **z** before the vowels **a, o,** and **u** is pronounced much like the *th* in the English word *think.*

3. **c:** In Latin America, the letter **c** before the vowels **e** and **i** is also pronounced like an *s.*
almacén dulces dulcería calcetines cinturón
In Spain, the letter **c** before the vowels **e** and **i** is also pronounced like the *th* in English.

B. **Dictado** Answers on p. 231D.
Selena wants to go to the store for some gifts. Write everything she says.

C. **Trabalenguas**
La señora Sánchez sazona la sopa con sal y sasafrás.
César y Cecilia cocinan cinco cebollas con cilantro a las once.

TERCER PASO
CAPÍTULO 9

Teaching Suggestion

A lo nuestro Tell students that **hacer juego, hacer buena combinación,** and **combinarse bien** are three ways to say that an outfit matches.

For videodisc application, see *Videodisc Guide.*

Native Speakers

Ask students to make a shopping list with at least ten items that contain the sounds covered in **Letra y sonido.** They are not to use any of the examples in **Letra y sonido.** Have students exchange lists to check spelling.

CLOSE

Use *Teaching Transparency 9-3* to review the material from this **Paso** with students. If time permits, use *Teaching Transparencies 9-1* and *9-2* for a comprehensive review.

ASSESS

Quiz 9-3, *Chapter Teaching Resources, Book 3,* pp. 27–28

Assessment Items, Audiocassette 8A/Audio CD 9

Performance Assessment

Pairs of students create a dialogue between a customer and the clerk in a clothing store. Have them include expressions of courtesy, express preferences, inquire about prices, and pay. The work may be performed or written. Encourage students to try out different selling styles. (hard sell, soft sell)

Answers

33 *Possible answer:*
Lo siento, señor, pero este traje no le va muy bien. La camisa no queda muy bien con la chaqueta anaranjada. Y creo que la corbata de cuadros amarillos no hace juego con los pantalones rojos. Sinceramente, este traje no está de moda. ¿Por qué no se pone el traje azul con la camisa blanca? Sí, esta ropa es mucho mejor.

Additional Practice

Ask students to create a catalog of clothing that they like. They should write a description of each item and give its price.

READING STRATEGY
Scanning for specific information

Teacher Note
After they have read **Estrategia,** ask students what additional strategies they have used in previous readings that might be helpful. They might mention using cognates, using background knowledge, or guessing words from context.

PREREADING
ACTIVITIES A AND B

Motivating Activity
Ask students what they know about San Antonio. Have they ever visited it, read about it, or seen anything about it on TV? Do they know anything about San Antonio's festivals? If so, ask them to share their knowledge with the class.

Building on Previous Skills
Listening In Spanish read aloud descriptions of the five activities in the reading as a listening comprehension activity. Students are to respond with the name of the corresponding activity.

Native Speakers
Have native speakers choose another city in the United States that has a strong latino influence. They should research the history of that community and write a report on it in Spanish. You may wish to have them present their reports orally to the class. Another option would be to have native speakers prepare a brochure on your town or community.

VAMOS A LEER

San Antonio

Estrategia
Scanning for specific information means looking for one thing at a time, without concerning yourself with the rest of the information. Some examples of scanning are looking up the spelling of a word in a dictionary or hunting through the TV listing to see what time a certain show comes on.

¡A comenzar!
Let's look at the pictures and subtitles in this brochure about San Antonio.

A. Using pictures only, determine which of these topics are addressed in the article.

1. sports
2. a zoo
3. eating
4. police protection
5. shopping
6. night clubs
7. holiday activities
8. a river near the city
9. an old Spanish building

B. Suppose you're in a hurry and don't have time to read every section. Look only at subtitles to determine where you could read about the following. Write the appropriate subtitle.

1. where the good shopping is
2. the river that runs through the city
3. churches
4. where to have dinner
5. what to do on holidays

See answers below.

SAN ANTONIO

ofrece generosas porciones de su vida cosmopolita, incluyendo finos restaurantes, vida nocturna, deportes profesionales y bellas artes.* Nuestros grupos étnicos *añaden su propio sabor.

Restaurantes.
Nuestra herencia multicultural hace posible que usted pueda escoger entre muchos restaurantes, desde parrilladas de estilo tejano y picantes platillos mexicanos hasta la cocina continental, oriental y "alta americana".

Compras.
¿Listo para ir de compras? Tome un taxi acuático al refrescante centro comercial al lado del Paseo del Río. Encuentre tesoros deslumbrantes en los centros comerciales de la ciudad. Disfrute de las artesanías de La Villita y El Mercado.

Answers
B 1. Compras
2. Río San Antonio
3. Las Misiones
4. Restaurantes
5. Festivales

¿Te acuerdas?

Use pictures, titles, and subtitles first.

- *It will make understanding easier.*
- *It will save you time.* Sometimes you're only interested in one small part of an article.

Al grano See answers below.

From the pictures and subtitles you got a general overview of this article about San Antonio. You know what areas are mentioned, and you should be able to locate important details very quickly.

C. Imagine that you work for the San Antonio Chamber of Commerce. Answer the tourists' questions, using the information in the brochure. You already know where to look for the answers, but you will have to read the descriptions thoroughly to find out the details.

1. Are there any Chinese or Japanese restaurants in town?
2. The river front shopping district is surrounded by water. How do I get there?
3. What's the name of the river front area that has stores, galleries, and cafés?
4. In which Mission does the Mariachi Mass take place?
5. In what month does the **Muestra Ganadera** festival occur?

D. Además de responder a las preguntas, otra de tus tareas en la Cámara de Comercio es la de hacer itinerarios de muestra para los turistas. Crea tu propio folleto en el que describas tres cosas que se pueden hacer en San Antonio en un día. Las tres actividades deben provenir de lo que has leído.

READING
ACTIVITY C

Additional Practice

C. Students might also develop a telephone conversation between an employee of the San Antonio Chamber of Commerce and a prospective visitor to the city.

Group Work

Have each student write one question about each section of the reading. Have them ask these aloud in small groups and see which group member can correctly answer first.

POSTREADING
ACTIVITY D

Teaching Suggestion

Have students do class presentations on some aspect of San Antonio. Information on historical places such as the Alamo is readily available and travel guides discussing restaurants and shopping can be obtained from many libraries. Or you could create a bulletin board about San Antonio, with students bringing in pictures or drawings with Spanish captions.

Teacher Note

For additional readings, see *Native Speaker Activity Book,* pp. 41–45 and *Practice and Activity Book,* p. 107.

Answers

C 1. yes
2. by water taxi
3. El Paseo del Río
4. Misión San José
5. February

Multicultural Link

Divide the class into two groups to research and write a report on the Battle of the Alamo and the events that led up to it. One group will write their report from the perspective of the Texans, and the other from the Mexican perspective. Follow a presentation of the reports with a discussion of how and why the two reports are different.

The **Repaso** reviews and integrates all four skills and culture in preparation for the Chapter Test.

Reteaching

Expressing preferences
Hold up two magazine or catalogue photos of clothing and tell the class which you prefer. Repeat with several pairs of pictures. Then show two pictures of the same item and ask **¿Cuál de estos/as ___ prefieres?** or **¿Qué ___ te gusta más?** Have students answer. Pass out catalogues or photos and have students continue this activity in small groups.

Teaching Suggestion

1, 2 You may wish to have students use these activities for oral practice.

For Individual Needs

3 Slower Pace Allow students to conduct this activity using notes.

REPASO

1 Listen as Sara and Ana talk about what Sara needs for the costume party (**fiesta de disfraces**). Choose the items she mentions. Not all will be used.

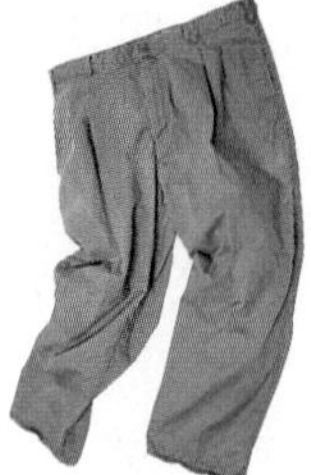

Answers on p. 231D.

2 Look at this photo. Choose a person who is wearing clothing you like. Describe the clothing in three or four sentences. If you cannot see certain items of clothing, such as shoes or socks, guess what colors they might be. Possible answers below.

Possible answers below.

3 What gifts do you suppose each of the following people plans to give their friends and family members? Write a sentence to say what you think each gift will be.

MODELO Mi hermano → a mí
Mi hermano me va a regalar un disco compacto.

1. mi mamá → a mi hermana
2. yo → a mi amigo
3. tú → a tu prima
4. mi amiga → a su hermano
5. mi abuela → a nosotras
6. mis tíos → a mí
7. yo → a mi primo
8. mi mejor amigo/amiga → a mí

Answers

2 *Possible answer:*
Me gusta la ropa que lleva esa persona en la foto. Lleva una falda negra con botas negras. Lleva una camisa gris con un suéter de varios colores.

3 *Possible answers:*
1. Mi mamá le va a regalar una bicicleta a mi hermana.
2. Yo le voy a regalar una camiseta a mi amigo.
3. Tú le vas a regalar aretes a tu prima.
4. Mi amiga le va a regalar un libro a su hermano.
5. Mi abuela nos va a regalar dinero.
6. Mis tíos me van a regalar pantalones.
7. Yo le voy a regalar un reloj a mi primo.
8. Mi mejor amigo/a me va a regalar un disco compacto.

4 *Possible answers:*
Toda la ropa del verano está rebajada. ¡Qué ganga! Las camisas y camisetas de algodón de todos los colores cuestan entre $5.00 y $15.00 dólares.

4 Write an advertisement for a newspaper, announcing a big sale on all types of clothing for the next season. Include different colors, materials, and prices. Make certain you stress that there are bargains at the store! Be creative! Possible answers below.

5 Working with a partner, discuss your tastes in clothing, where you prefer to shop, and which local stores have the best prices. Be sure to include colors, styles, and materials. Be prepared to present your conversation to the class.

6 Work in groups of three or four to take a survey of the information collected in Activity 5. Take notes and be prepared to present the information to the class. Make a list for a new student of the best places to shop. Compile the information from the entire class.

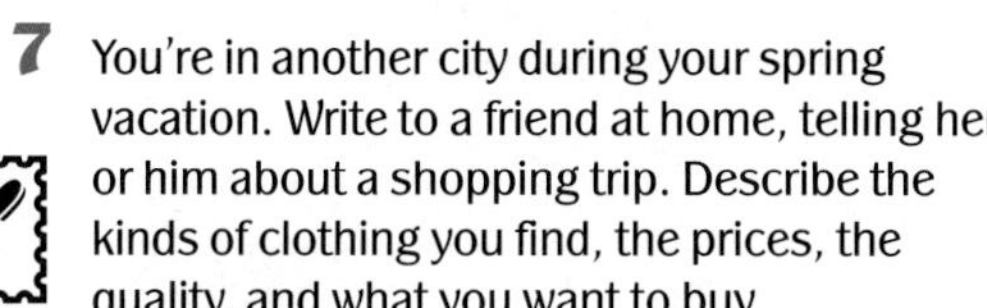
7 You're in another city during your spring vacation. Write to a friend at home, telling her or him about a shopping trip. Describe the kinds of clothing you find, the prices, the quality, and what you want to buy. Possible answers below.

8 Compare how teenagers in the United States feel about fashion compared with how teenagers in Spanish-speaking countries feel. Possible answers below.

9 How would you tell a friend that you are going to give these items to various relatives for their birthdays? See answers below.

a. mi papá

b. mi hermana

c. mi tía

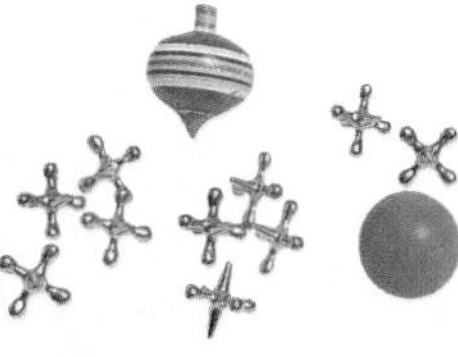
d. mis primos

10 SITUACIÓN

Create a store within your classroom. Gather materials to "sell," choose clerks, make signs and price tags, and set up a cashier's station. Then use the vocabulary and grammar from this chapter to "buy and sell" the merchandise.

Portfolio

5 Oral Suggest that students record their dialogue from this activity as an oral Portfolio entry. For Portfolio suggestions, see *Assessment Guide,* p. 22.

7 Written This activity may be used as a written Portfolio entry. For Portfolio suggestions see *Assessment Guide,* p. 22.

Teaching Suggestion

10 You may wish to have students use play money as they buy items so they can practice making change. Have students create a cashier's booth. Explain that in many stores in Spanish-speaking countries customers pay at the cashier's booth, where they are given a receipt stamped "paid." They then return to the check-out counter, where the clerk delivers the merchandise and gives them another receipt. Have students price the items using one of the currencies in **Nota cultural,** page 248.

Video Wrap-Up

- ***Video Program***
- ***Expanded Video Program, Videocassette 3***
- ***Videodisc Program, Videodisc 5A***

At this time, you might want to use the video resources for additional review and enrichment. See *Video Guide* or *Videodisc Guide* for suggestions regarding the following:
- **¿Qué le compramos a Héctor?** (Dramatic episode)
- **Panorama cultural** (Interviews)
- **Video Clips** (Authentic footage)

7 *Possible answers:*
Querida amiga: Estoy en Dallas para pasar las vacaciones de primavera. Aquí hay muchos centros comerciales y tiendas de ropa de buena calidad. Venden ropa muy barata en algunas tiendas. En una tienda cerca de la casa quiero comprar un vestido rojo de algodón y pantalones azules. Hasta luego. Tu amiga.

8 *Possible answers:*
Teenagers in all countries want to wear the most up-to-date styles. Bluejeans are popular in every country.

9 a. Le voy a dar una corbata a mi papá.
b. Le voy a regalar un reloj a mi hermana.
c. Le voy a dar una planta a mi tía.
d. Les voy a regalar unos juguetes a mis primos.

A VER SI PUEDO . . .

This page is intended to help students prepare for the Chapter Test. It is designed for the students to work on their own initiative and consists of a brief checklist of the major points covered in the chapter. The students should be reminded that it is a checklist only and not necessarily everything that will appear on the test. Remind students that cultural information is included in the Chapter Test.

Cooperative Learning

Divide the class into groups of three. Each group member is responsible for helping the other members practice two language functions from **Así se dice.** Then have students practice the functions with their group until everyone can do each one. At random select a student from each group and have her or him demonstrate one of the functions by responding to your cues. Give the entire group the grade which that student earned. Select a person from another group for a second function, and so forth.

Can you discuss gift suggestions? p. 237

1 You and a friend are shopping for a birthday gift for your Spanish teacher. How would you ask your friend about what you should get for your teacher? How might he or she make a suggestion? See answers below.

Can you ask for and give directions downtown? p. 239

2 You're at the spot marked X on this map. Can you ask someone where the bookstore and the bakery are? How would he or she answer? See answers below.

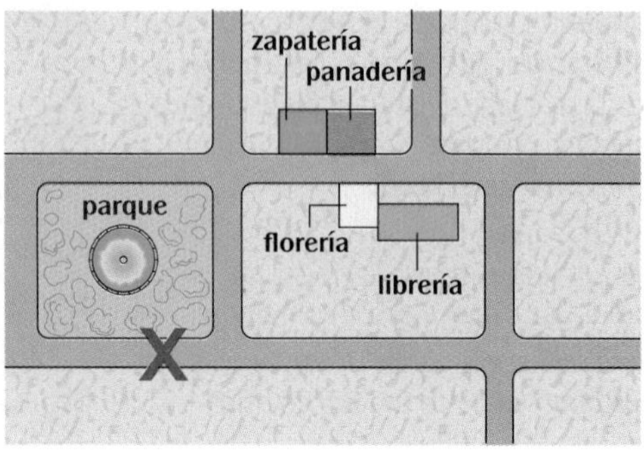

Can you comment on clothes? p. 242

3 How would you describe the clothes you're wearing right now? Describe the color, pattern, and material of each item. Possible answers below.

Can you make comparisons? p. 245

4 How would you compare the two items in each drawing? Possible answers below.

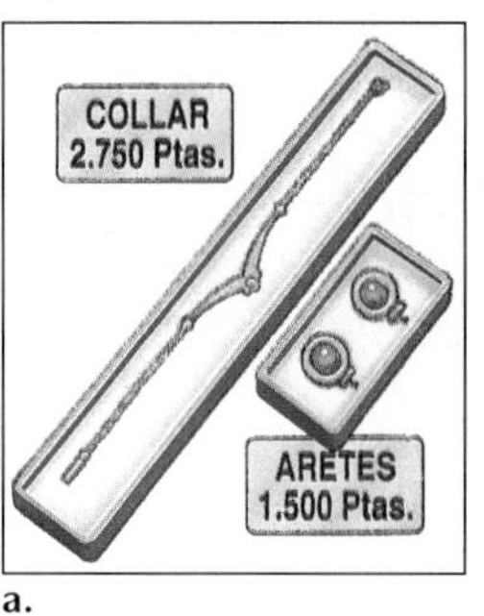

a.

b.

c.

Can you express preferences? p. 247

5 Look at the pictures in Activity 4. For each pair of items, tell which one you prefer and why. Answers will vary.

Can you ask about prices and pay for something? p. 248

6 You're in a shopping center in Mexico and the salesclerk doesn't speak English. How would you ask the prices of the following items? How might the clerk answer? See answers below.

a. a yellow cotton blouse
b. a silk tie
c. a box of candy
d. a greeting card

Answers

1 *Sample answer:*—¿Qué le regalamos a la profesora? —Vamos a comprarle chocolates porque (a ella) le encantan los dulces.

2 *Answers may vary.*
—¿Dónde está la librería?
—Está a dos cuadras de aquí.
—¿Me puede decir dónde queda la panadería?
—Queda al lado de la zapatería.

4 *Answers may vary.* a. Los aretes son más caros que el collar. b. La chaqueta de cuero es más formal que la chaqueta de cuadros. c. El florero de cristal es más bonito que el florero cerámico.

5 *Answers will vary.*

6 a. ¿Cuánto cuesta la blusa amarilla de algodón?
b. ¿Cuánto cuesta la corbata de seda?
c. ¿Cuánto cuestan estos dulces?
d. ¿Cuánto cuesta esta tarjeta?

VOCABULARIO

PRIMER PASO

Discussing gift suggestions

el arete *earring*
buscar *to look for*
la camiseta *T-shirt*
la cartera *wallet*
el collar *necklace*
cómodo *comfortable*
la corbata *tie*
dar *to give*
el disco compacto *compact disc*
los dulces *candy*
las flores *flowers*
formal *formal*
el juego de mesa *(board) game*
los juguetes *toys*
le *to/for her, him, you*
les *to/for them, you (pl.)*
me *to/for me*
nos *to/for us*
los pantalones *pants*
¿Para quién...? *For whom . . .?*
la planta *plant*
regalar *to give (as a gift)*
el regalo *gift*
la tarjeta *greeting card*
te *to/for you*

Asking for and giving directions downtown

el almacén *department store*
la cuadra *city block*
la dulcería *candy store*
la florería *flower shop*
la joyería *jewelry store*
la juguetería *toy store*
¿Me puede decir...? *Can you tell me . . .?*
la panadería *bakery*
la pastelería *pastry shop; sweet shop*
Perdón *Excuse me*
el precio *price*
quedar *to be (situated)*
la tienda de comestibles *grocery store*
la zapatería *shoe store*

SEGUNDO PASO

Commenting on clothes

de algodón *cotton*
amarillo *yellow*
anaranjado *orange*
blanco *white*
los bluejeans *bluejeans*
la blusa *blouse*
las botas *boots*
los calcetines *socks*
la camisa *shirt*
la chaqueta *jacket*
el cinturón *belt*
de cuadros *plaid*
de cuero *leather*
la falda *skirt*
gris *gray*
de lana *wool*
llevar *to wear*
morado *purple*
los pantalones cortos *shorts*
pardo *brown*
de rayas *striped*
rojo *red*
las sandalias *sandals*
de seda *silk*
el suéter *sweater*
el traje *suit*
el traje de baño *bathing suit*
el vestido *dress*

Making comparisons

barato *cheap*
caro *expensive*
más ... que *more . . . than*
menos ... que *less . . . than*
Son del mismo precio. *They're the same price.*
tan ... como *as . . . as*

TERCER PASO

Expressing preferences

además *besides*
esa, ese *that*
esas, esos *those*
esta, este *this*
estas, estos *these*
Te queda muy bien. *It fits you very well.*

Asking about prices and paying for something

¿Cuánto cuesta...? *How much does . . . cost?*
¿Cuánto cuestan...? *How much do . . . cost?*
¡Es un robo! *It's rip-off!*
¡Qué barato! *How cheap!*
¡Qué caro! *How expensive!*
¡Qué ganga! *What a bargain!*

Game

To review colors, articles of clothing, and the materials from which they are made, have students play the game ¿QUÉ VEO? The instructions are on page 231F.

Teaching Suggestion

Put the articles included in the vocabulary in a shopping bag and, as you take each one out, ask questions beginning with **¿Para quién son...?** or **¿Para quién es...?** (—**¿Para quién son los juguetes? —Los juguetes son para mi hermanita.**)

VOCABULARIO
CAPÍTULO 9

Game

REGALOS Give each student an index card on which a word for a gift is written or a picture of a gift is pasted or drawn. Be sure to give yourself a card also. Put the following questions on the board or on a transparency to practice the vocabulary and the indirect object pronouns: **¿Qué le vas a regalar a ___? ¿Qué me vas a regalar a mí? ¿Qué te voy a regalar a ti? ¿Qué les vas a regalar a ___ y a ___?** Students will answer with the item they have on their card. Practice placing the pronoun before the verb, then expand by attaching the pronoun to the infinitive.

CHAPTER 9 ASSESSMENT

CHAPTER TEST

- *Chapter Teaching Resources, Book 3,* pp. 29–36
- *Assessment Guide,* Speaking Test, p. 32
- *Assessment Items, Audiocassette 8A Audio CD 9*

TEST GENERATOR, CHAPTER 9

ALTERNATIVE ASSESSMENT

Performance Assessment

Have students perform **Repaso** Activity 5, p. 253, as a cumulative performance assessment activity.

Portfolio Assessment

- **Written: Repaso** Activity 7, *Pupil's Edition,* p. 253 *Assessment Guide,* p. 22
- **Oral: Repaso** Activity 5, *Pupil's Edition,* p. 253 *Assessment Guide,* p. 22

Capítulo 10: Celebraciones
Chapter Overview

De antemano pp. 258–260	**¡Felicidades Héctor!**	Practice and Activity Book, p. 109		*Video Guide* OR *Videodisc Guide*

	FUNCTIONS	GRAMMAR	CULTURE	RE-ENTRY
Primer paso pp. 261–265	• Talking about what you're doing right now, p. 262 • Asking for and giving an opinion, p. 264	Present progressive, p. 263	• **Nota cultural, Día de Santo,** p. 262 • **Panorama cultural, ¿Qué hacen ustedes para celebrar?** p. 265	• **Estar** • Dates, months, seasons • Extending, accepting, and turning down invitations
Segundo paso pp. 266–270	• Asking for help and responding to requests, p. 266 • Telling a friend what to do, p. 268	Informal commands, p. 268	• **Nota cultural, La quinceañera,** p. 260 • **Encuentro cultural, ¿Cómo se celebra una boda?** p. 270	• **Tú** versus **usted** • Household chores
Tercer paso pp. 271–275	Talking about past events, p. 271	• Preterite tense of regular **-ar** verbs, p. 271 • Direct object pronouns **lo** and **la,** p. 274	Realia: **Agenda,** p. 273	• Days of the week • **¿Quién? ¿Quiénes?** • Free-time activities • Places • Household chores

Letra y sonido p. 275	Listening for Spanish syllables	**Dictado:** *Textbook Audiocassette 5B/Audio CD 10*
Vamos a Leer pp. 276–277	**Festivales del mundo hispano**	**Reading Strategy**: Making comparisons while reading
Review pp. 278–281	**Repaso,** pp. 278–279 **A ver si puedo...,** p. 280 **Vocabulario,** p. 281	
Assessment Options	**Quizzes** • *Chapter Teaching Resources, Book 3* **Primer paso,** Quiz 10-1, pp. 81–82 **Segundo paso,** Quiz 10-2, pp. 83–84 **Tercer paso,** Quiz 10-3, pp. 85–86 • *Assessment Items, Audiocassette 8B/Audio CD 10*	**Chapter Test** • *Chapter Teaching Resources, Book 3,* pp. 87–92 • *Assessment Guide,* Speaking Test, p. 32 • *Assessment Items, Audiocassette 8B/Audio CD 10* **Test Generator, Chapter 10**

Video Program OR *Expanded Video Program, Videocassette 4* OR *Videodisc Program, Videodisc 5B*	*Textbook Audiocassette 5B/Audio CD 10*

RESOURCES: Print	RESOURCES: Audiovisual
	Textbook Audiocassette 5B/Audio CD 10
Practice and Activity Book, pp. 110–112	
Native Speaker Activity Book, pp. 46–50	
Chapter Teaching Resources, Book 3	
• Additional Listening Activities 10-1, 10-2, p. 69	*Additional Listening Activities, Audiocassette 10B/Audio CD 10*
• Student Response Forms, pp. 78–80	
• Realia 10-1, pp. 73, 75	
• Situation Cards 10-1, pp. 76–77	
• Teaching Transparency Master 10-1, pp. 65–68	*Teaching Transparency 10-1*
• Quiz 10-1, pp. 81–82	*Assessment Items, Audiocassette 8B/Audio CD 10*
Video Guide	*Video Program* OR *Expanded Video Program, Videocassette 4*
Videodisc Guide	*Videodisc Program, Videodisc 5B*
	Textbook Audiocassette 5B/Audio CD 10
Practice and Activity Book, pp. 113–115	
Native Speaker Activity Book, pp. 46–50	
Chapter Teaching Resources, Book 3	
• Communicative Activity 10-1, pp. 61–62	
• Additional Listening Activities 10-3, 10-4, p. 70	*Additional Listening Activities, Audiocassette 10B/Audio CD 10*
• Student Response Forms, pp. 78–80	
• Realia 10-1, pp. 73, 75	
• Situation Cards 10-2, pp. 76–77	
• Teaching Transparency Master 10-2, pp. 65–68	*Teaching Transparency 10-2*
• Quiz 10-2, pp. 83–84	*Assessment Items, Audiocassette 8B/Audio CD 10*
Videodisc Guide	*Videodisc Program, Videodisc 5B*
	Textbook Audiocassette 5B/Audio CD 10
Practice and Activity Book, pp. 116–118	
Native Speaker Activity Book, pp. 46–50	
Chapter Teaching Resources, Book 3	
• Communicative Activity 10-2, pp. 63–64	
• Additional Listening Activities 10-5, 10-6, p. 71	*Additional Listening Activities, Audiocassette 10B/Audio CD 10*
• Student Response Forms, pp. 78–80	
• Realia 10-2, pp. 74, 75	
• Situation Cards 10-3, pp. 76–77	
• Teaching Transparency Master 10-3, pp. 65–68	*Teaching Transparency 10-3*
• Quiz 10-3, pp. 85–86	*Assessment Items, Audiocassette 8B/Audio CD 10*
Videodisc Guide	*Videodisc Program, Videodisc 5B*
Video Guide	*Video Program* OR *Expanded Video Program, Videocassette 4*
Videodisc Guide	*Videodisc Program, Videodisc 5B*

Alternative Assessment

- Performance Assessment
  Primer paso, p. 264
  Segundo paso, p. 269
  Tercer paso, p. 275
- Portfolio Assessment
  Written: *Teacher's Edition,* p. 279
  Assessment Guide, p. 23
  Oral: **Repaso,** Activity 8, *Pupil's Edition,* p. 279
  Assessment Guide, p. 23

Capítulo 10: Celebraciones
Textbook Listening Activities Scripts

For Student response Forms, see *Chapter Teaching Resources, Book 3,* pp. 78–80.

Primer paso

Activity 7, p. 262

1. Me llamo Rolando. Vivo en Miami. Nosotros celebramos el Día de Acción de Gracias, pero como todas las familias, nuestra cena tiene cosas especiales de nuestra tradición cubana. Servimos pavo, pero también servimos arroz con frijoles negros.
2. Soy Marta. Vivo en San Antonio. Mi día favorito es el Día de los Enamorados que celebramos en febrero. Mando tarjetas a mis amigos y mi novio siempre me regala chocolates, flores o algo especial.
3. Soy Daniela. En mi familia nuestra fiesta favorita es la Navidad. Toda la familia va a la casa de mis abuelos. Vamos a misa a las doce de la noche y luego regresamos a casa para una cena fabulosa.
4. Yo me llamo Bernardo. Tengo seis años. Mi día favorito es mi cumpleaños. Este año mi mamá me va a llevar al zoológico. Luego vamos al cine y después voy a tener una fiesta.

Answers to Activity 7
1. d 2. a 3. c 4. b

Activity 9, p. 263

Esta tarde va a haber una fiesta estupenda en nuestra casa. Es el cumpleaños de mi abuelo y mi familia y yo vamos a hacer una fiesta para él. Pero hay muchas cosas que tenemos que hacer antes de la fiesta. Julia está limpiando la cocina. Mi tía Rosita está preparando una cena muy especial para mi abuelo. Mi hermana Sarita está en el patio. Ella está poniendo la mesa. Mis primos Teresa y Mauricio están lavando los platos. Roberto está decorando la sala. Y yo, ¿qué estoy haciendo yo? Bueno, yo estoy organizando mi cuarto. ¡Es un desastre!

Answers to Activity 9
1. Sarita, e
2. Guadalupe, d
3. Roberto, a
4. Rosita, b
5. Teresa y Mauricio, f
6. Julia, c

Segundo paso

Activity 18, p. 267

1. Roberto, ¿me puedes ayudar a decorar la sala?
2. Elenita, ¿me haces el favor de llamar a Gregorio? Toca muy bien la guitarra.
3. Oye, ¿quién me ayuda con las decoraciones?
4. Jaime, ¿me haces el favor de ir a la pastelería?
5. Laura, ¿quiénes van a traer la música para bailar?
6. Mamá, ¿me ayudas a preparar los sándwiches?
7. ¿Me traes una silla, por favor?

Answers to Activity 18
1. d 2. a 3. c 4. g 5. e 6. f 7. b

Activity 22, p. 268

1. —Buenos días. Habla Nicolás. ¿Qué necesitan para la fiesta?
   —Este... trae unos refrescos, por favor.
2. —Hola, soy Soledad. ¿Qué hago para la fiesta?
   —A ver... eh... ve al supermercado y compra helado, por favor.
3. —¿Qué tal? Habla Gustavo. ¿Qué puedo traer a la fiesta?
   —Trae unos discos compactos, por favor.
4. —Buenas tardes. Habla Verónica. ¿Ya está todo listo para la fiesta? ¿Puedo preparar algo especial?
   —A ver... prepara una ensalada de frutas, por favor.
5. —¿Qué tal? Habla Gloria. ¿Qué puedo hacer para la fiesta?
   —Bueno... Tú tienes una cámara, ¿verdad? Saca fotos de todos, por favor.
6. —Hola, soy Cristóbal. ¿Necesitan algo para la fiesta?
   —Sí, Cristóbal. Compra los globos, por favor.

Answers to Activity 22
1. a 2. b 3. d 4. c 5. f 6. e

Tercer paso

Activity 28, p. 272

Ay, ¡qué fiesta tan estupenda! Patricia preparó un postre muy rico para la fiesta anoche. Bárbara bailó con su novio Miguel. Ellos bailaron en la fiesta toda la noche. Raquel y Gloria jugaron a las cartas con Felipe y su hermano Guillermo. Y Francisco, ¡a él le encanta nadar! Nadó mucho en nuestra piscina. Pablo miró la televisión. ¡A él no le gustan las fiestas para nada! Yo hablé mucho con mis amigos. Un amigo mío, Shoji, cantó unas canciones en español y Kerry tocó la guitarra. Gracie y Kim jugaron a los videojuegos. Andrés y Valerie escucharon música.

Answers to Activity 28

1. a 2. c 3. b 4. d 5. g 6. e 7. h 8. f

Letra y sonido, p. 275

For the scripts for Parts A and C, see p. 275. The dialogue for Part B is below.

B. Dictado

Bueno, primero tengo que ayudar a lavar la ropa. Después, a las seis, voy a comprar unas zapatillas nuevas. Y luego, a las ocho, voy a una película con unos amigos.

Repaso

Activity 1, p. 278

Me llamo Mariana y vivo en San Antonio. En diciembre viajamos a Monterrey para celebrar las fiestas de Navidad con mis abuelos. ¡Qué viaje más fantástico! Mi abuela preparó unas decoraciones bonitas. Todos mis primos llegaron de Guadalajara y preparamos una cena maravillosa de pavo, enchiladas, bacalao y ensalada de Nochebuena. Cenamos a las ocho. Después bailamos, cantamos y hablamos toda la noche. La Navidad es mi día festivo favorito porque siempre la pasamos en México con mis abuelos.

Answers to Activity 1

1. Monterrey
2. para celebrar la Navidad con sus abuelos
3. diciembre
4. decoraciones bonitas
5. bailaron, cantaron y hablaron toda la noche
6. la pasan en México con sus abuelos

Capítulo 10: Celebraciones
Projects

In this project students will work in groups to create puppet shows about holiday celebrations. Each group will research the history, customs, and cultural significance of a different holiday. They will then produce a five- to ten-minute puppet show that tells a story about that celebration. Students will enjoy gathering information with others and will be able to use all four language skills as they write, practice, and present their shows to the class.

MATERIALS

✄ **Students may need**
- Small paper bags, socks, or other materials to make puppets
- Glue
- Marker
- A table large enough for students to sit under
- A sheet to cover the front and sides of the table
- Audio or video recording equipment if you choose to tape the shows

SEQUENCE

1. Explain the project to the students and set due dates for their research, a written script, and the show.
2. Divide the students into groups of four or five. If possible, you may want to have a native speaker in each group. Ask students to work together to decide on a holiday they'd like to learn more about. You might assist each group in selecting a celebration.
3. Allow the students time to do their research and to write their script. Remind the students to use the Spanish they know in writing their scripts. You might suggest they use a dictionary as needed.
4. Have students turn in a rough draft of their script. Review it and return it to them.
5. Make puppets one day in class. Have students bring in various materials they feel would be useful for making puppets (socks, yarn, string, buttons). You may wish to have them look up the Spanish for these materials in a dictionary, write them on the board, and speak in Spanish as much as possible.
6. Allow the students time to rehearse their shows either in class or as groups outside of class.
7. Groups hand in a written copy of their script. You might also ask students to write a short paragraph describing key information about the celebration they researched.
8. Students present their shows to the class.

GRADING THE PROJECT

Suggested point distribution (total = 100 points):

Cultural research	20
Accurate Spanish in script	25
Creativity in script	10
Accurate Spanish in show	25
Creativity in show	10
Individual contributions	10

You might ask students to assess their own contribution to the script and to the show. On a sheet of paper ask each student to rate his or her contribution on a scale of 1 to 5 (5 being the highest).

COMMUNITY LINKS

- You might invite a person from a Spanish-speaking country to speak to the class about holidays in his or her country. This will create interest in other cultures and will help students decide on a celebration that they might like to know more about. If possible, have the guest bring realia that is unique to his or her culture to share with the class.
- Encourage students to perform their puppet plays for younger children. They might do so in a school, hospital, library, foster-care center, or day-care center.

Capítulo 10: Celebraciones
Games

MI REGALO

This game provides practice with vocabulary, reading, and writing skills. Play this game after the ***Tercer paso*** *to review vocabulary.*

Preparation Give each student three index cards. On the front of each card, have them write four sentences describing a gift. Remind students to match the adjectives to the gift being described. **(Es roja. Es de algodón. No es muy grande ni muy pequeña. La llevo mucho.)** On the back of the card have them write the Spanish word for the gift. **(una camiseta)**

Procedure Divide the class into two teams. Ask the first player on Team 1 to read his or her clues to a Team 2 player. The Team 2 player has four opportunities to guess what the gift is. He or she should guess by saying **Creo que es** ___. The Team 1 player answers either **Sí, tienes razón** or **No, no tienes razón.** If the Team 2 player guesses correctly, Team 2 gets a point. If the Team 2 player is unable to name the gift in four guesses, the Team 1 player reveals the gift and Team 1 receives a point. Next it is Team 1's turn to guess. The team with the most points wins.

Es roja.
Es de algodón.
No es muy grande ni muy pequeña.
La llevo mucho.

una camiseta

UN AÑO DE CELEBRACIONES

This game provides practice with the preterite tense and the names of several holidays. It also tests students' knowledge of various holidays and festivals. Use it as a review at the end of the chapter.

Preparation On index cards, have students write verbs associated with activities or celebrations. **(acampar, ayudar, bailar, bucear, caminar, cenar, comprar, cortar, cuidar, decorar, descansar, inflar, mandar, escuchar, llevar, tomar)** These should be placed in a pile face down so that students may draw from a deck. On the board, write the 12 months of the year in order. Then ask students to name one holiday in each month. These may be holidays discussed in this chapter or other celebrations, such as someone's birthday or a special day at school.

Procedure 1 Divide the class into two teams. The object of the game is for each team to proceed through the year and "celebrate" each holiday. Teams celebrate a **día festivo** by having a player from the team use a preterite verb correctly in a sentence about the holiday. A Team 1 player starts in **enero.** The class has chosen to celebrate **el Día de los Reyes Magos**, for example. A Team 1 player takes a card **(caminar)**. He or she must construct a sentence using that verb in the preterite tense. The sentence must have something to do with the holiday. **(El Día de los Reyes Magos, los reyes caminaron por los pueblos.)**

If the student makes a logical sentence and uses the verb correctly, Team 1 advances and the play switches to Team 2. If he or she does not make a logical sentence, Team 1 does not advance and the play switches to Team 2. Whenever Team 1 has a turn again, the player will make a sentence with a new verb about the holiday in **febrero.** The first team to celebrate all 12 holidays wins.

The following variation of the game may be helpful if you have a large class or if you'd like to elicit longer, more creative sentences.

Procedure 2 Students play on several small teams. All teams simultaneously construct a sentence for the same holiday. Each team has a different verb, however. Set a time limit and some rules about looking up words in the book or in a dictionary. (Students may not look up verb conjugations!)

When time is up, have one representative from each team read the group's sentence. Groups whose sentences are correct advance to the next month to make a new sentence about that month's holiday. Groups whose sentences are not right must draw another verb and make a new sentence about the same holiday. The first team to celebrate all 12 holidays wins.

Celebraciones

pp. 256-281

Using the Chapter Opener

Motivating Activity

Ask students what holidays they celebrate. Which holiday is their favorite, and why? Do they celebrate with family, with friends, or both? What do they do? What do they eat?

Teaching Suggestion

Ask each student to make a list of the holidays for which their family decorates. Then suggest they compare their list to a partner's to see if they are similar. Have them discuss the kinds of decorations they use for each holiday. What significance do the decorations have for them?

Culture Note

You may want to point out to your students that since Roman Catholicism is the majority religion in Spanish-speaking countries, a nativity scene (**nacimiento, pesebre,** or **belén**) is much more common than a tree for commemorating Christmas. Ask students to choose one country and research one holiday and its customs. Have them report to the class what objects or practices symbolize that holiday.

1 ¿Bailaste mucho en la fiesta anoche

Multicultural Link

Ask students if they can think of any traditions from Spanish-speaking countries that have been adopted by people in the United States who are not Hispanic. (They might mention **piñatas, luminarias,** and **poinsetias,** all of which have come to the United States from Mexico.) Ask students to research a holiday in the United States that originated in Europe, Asia, or Africa. Have them report on what they find.

Building on Previous Skills

Ask students to think back to Chapter 8, **¡A comer!**, and recall what they learned about foods in Spanish-speaking countries. What are some typical dishes in various countries? (Several are mentioned in the Location Opener almanac boxes throughout *¡Ven Conmigo!*) Which are prepared for parties?

Teenagers in Spanish-speaking countries love to get together with friends and relatives to celebrate special occasions. Usually the whole family, both young and old, attend these celebrations. Do you enjoy getting ready for a party? What do you do to celebrate different holidays?

In this chapter you will learn

- to talk about what you're doing right now; to ask for and give an opinion
- to ask for help and respond to requests; to tell a friend what to do
- to talk about past events

And you will

- listen to Spanish speakers talk about how they celebrate holidays
- read about different celebrations
- write an agenda of your activities for the past week
- find out how holidays are celebrated in the Spanish-speaking world

2 Estamos celebrando el Cinco de Mayo.

3 ¿Me ayudas a preparar los tamales?

Culture Note

Tamales are a popular delicacy throughout Mexico, Central America, and parts of the United States. They are less common in South America. They are generally served on festive occasions. There are many types of **tamales,** some of them sweet. They are usually made of cornmeal dough spread on cornhusks, then stuffed with a variety of fillings and steamed. In the Yucatán and in Central America, **tamales** are made with plantain leaves, not cornhusks. In Honduras, **nacatamal** is a meat tamale and a **tamal** is without meat. In Venezuela, **tamales** are called **hallacas.**

Language Note

The Spanish word **tamal** (plural **tamales**) comes from the Nahuatl word **tamalli** and was a food staple of the Aztec empire.

Focusing on Outcomes

Ask students to look at the photos and say which photos correspond to which of the outcomes. (Photo 1 represents talking about past events, photo 2 represents talking about what you're doing right now, and photo 3 represents asking for help.) Explain that they will learn a new way to express an ongoing action. To get students to focus on the first outcome, ask them to tell you a few things they are doing right now and point out the difference between present tense and the present progressive. Do they know how to express any of these actions in Spanish?

Culture Note

El cinco de Mayo is a holiday celebrated by both Mexicans and Mexican Americans to commemorate the Mexican victory at the Battle of Puebla, 1862, between the army led by President Benito Juárez and the invading army sent from France by Napoleon III. Although the French forces later overwhelmed the Mexicans and installed a Habsburg (Maximilian) as emperor of Mexico, the Mexicans eventually defeated the invaders in 1867, when Maximilian was executed and Benito Jaúrez was restored as president. The Battle of Puebla is still considered the first and most symbolic Mexican victory of the war. While in power, Maximilian restored the **Castillo de Chapultepec** and created the **Paseo de la Reforma,** Mexico City's most elegant boulevard.

Native Speakers

Ask students from Spanish-speaking families whether they observe any holiday customs that originated in Hispanic countries. They might be interested in researching how a particular holiday is celebrated in their family's country of origin and telling the class about it.

VIDEO PROGRAM OR EXPANDED VIDEO PROGRAM, Videocassette 4

OR VIDEODISC PROGRAM, *Videodisc 5B*

Video Synopsis

The Villarreal family is busy making all the preparations for Héctor's graduation party. While making the tamales, Grandmother Dolores tells Lisa, Eva, Gabi, and Aníbal about holidays in Mexico and which is her favorite. Manuel Villarreal and his brother Tomás are talking in the backyard when Tomás holds up a package. Manuel realizes he has forgotten something very important.

Building on Previous Skills

Ask students to write a paragraph about a male and a female in the **fotonovela.** They should describe what each is wearing and what each looks like, including color of hair and eyes and height. You might ask students also to imagine what the two people are like—what they like to do and where they like to go.

Teaching Suggestions

- As a previewing or prereading task, have students read the questions in Activity 1, p. 260.
- To encourage students to focus on non-linguistic cues, play the video once without sound and ask them to hypothesize about what is happening in the story. Then play the video again with the sound on.

DE ANTEMANO

¡Felicidades Héctor!

Lots of things are going on at once in the Villarreal house. They're getting ready for a really big celebration! Look at the photos to see what they're doing. Has something been forgotten?

Abuelo, abuela, Eva, Héctor, Rebeca y Manuel Villarreal

Tío Tomás, Tía Marcela y Juan

Lisa y Gabi

1
¡Tomás! Mira... ¿qué te parece?
No sé... pregúntale a Juan.
Perfecto. Oye, Marcela. ¿Dónde están los globos?
¡Juan! ¿Tienes los globos?

2
¿Me ayudas a inflar los globos?
Aquí están.
¡Claro que sí, papá! ¿Qué tal si usamos de todos los colores? Hay de violeta, rojo, azul, verde...

3

4

5

258

RESOURCES FOR DE ANTEMANO

Textbook Audiocassette 5B/Audio CD 10
Video Guide
Video Program
Expanded Video Program, Videocassette 4
Videodisc Guide
Videodisc Program, Videodisc 5B
Practice and Activity Book, p. 109

Thinking Critically

Analyzing Tell students that a rite of passage is a ritual that is observed when a person changes status in life. Four major rites of passage are birth, initiation, marriage, and death. An initiation rite marks the transition from childhood to adult status. Do students think Héctor's graduation party can be considered a rite of passage? Why or why not?

6
Eva, ¿me pasas las hojas? Gracias.
Preparar tamales es mucho trabajo, ¿no?
Sí, hija, es verdad, pero es la comida favorita de Héctor. Generalmente, sólo preparamos muchos tamales en diciembre para la Navidad. Es una tradición de la cultura mexicana.

7
¿Hay tradiciones mexicanas para otros días festivos también?
Claro que sí, hay muchas. Durante las Pascuas, sobre todo en Semana Santa, hay desfiles... el Día de la Independencia, que es el 16 de septiembre, hay fuegos artificiales. Pero mi día festivo favorito es el Día de los Muertos. Me acuerdo de un año en particular...

8
¿Qué hiciste, abuela?
Pues, lo de siempre. Mi mamá preparó comida para llevar a las tumbas de la familia. Yo ayudé también. Ese año, yo compré la comida en la pequeña tienda cerca de la casa. Pero pasó algo especial...

9
Manuel... ¡Manuel! ¿Qué son éstos, hermano?
¿Mmmm? Ah... son las invitaciones.

10
¿Las invitaciones? ¡No mandé las invitaciones!

259

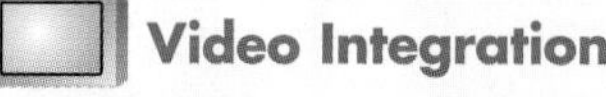

Video Integration

- ***Expanded Video Program,*** *Videocassette 4*
- ***Videodisc Program,*** *Videodisc 5B*

You may choose to continue with **¡Felicidades Héctor! (a continuación)** at this time or wait until later in the chapter. At this point in the story, Héctor's mother suggests calling the guests to make sure they know about the party. Eva goes to the bakery to pick up the cake and, upon returning home, discovers they have given her the wrong one. She returns to the bakery to exchange the cake, but en route she sees Héctor and must avoid being seen by him.

Motivating Activity

Ask students to list what they already know about holiday celebrations in Spanish-speaking countries. Transfer their answers to a master list on a poster or a large sheet of paper to hang in the room. At the end of the chapter, ask them what items they could add to their list.

Presentation

After students have watched the video, ask them what Héctor's family did to get ready for the party. What remains for them to do? Ask students to list what they think the Villarreal family will do to solve the problem. Use Activity 1, p. 260, to check comprehension.

Teaching Suggestion

Ask students to write a list in English of different expressions they use to give an opinion, to ask for help, or to respond to a request. Ask them to keep their list until they complete the **Segundo paso.** They will then check to see how many of the expressions they can say in Spanish.

Motivating Activity

Ask students to brainstorm about the things they might do to get ready for a party at their house. How many of these words do they already know in Spanish?

For Individual Needs

Kinesthetic Learners Assign the role of each of the persons in the video to a student in the class. Ask the students to act out the video, beginning with an introduction of themselves as they appear in the first three photos. Continue with the photos that follow, asking each student to read his or her lines.

DE ANTEMANO
CAPÍTULO 10

Teaching Suggestions

1 You might wish to have students work in pairs to answer the comprehension questions.

3 Have students identify the frame in the **fotonovela** where each expression is found.

Additional Practice

5 Have groups of students who don't usually work together talk about these **categorías.** Do any of the students have similar experiences? How many have very different opinions about holidays?

Language Note

Your students may be interested to know that the word **globo** is used in several different ways in Spanish. Depending on the context, it can mean *balloon, globe,* or *hot air balloon.*

Native Speakers

- If any native Spanish speakers in your class have been to a **quinceañera,** ask them to write a page reporting on it. Ask them to describe the music, the decorations, and anything else that made it a special occasion.
- If any native speakers have not been to a **quinceañera** but know someone who has had a **quinceañera,** they might interview the person to obtain a description of the party. Have them write a short report on their interview.
- If more than one native speaker has been to a **quinceañera,** ask them to prepare a joint report in which they relate similarities and differences between the **quinceañeras** they attended.
- Ask students who prepare a report also to make a presentation to the class.

1 ¿Comprendes?

¿Comprendes lo que pasa en la fotonovela? Contesta las preguntas. Si no estás seguro/a, adivina. See answers below.

1. ¿Quiénes son las personas en la fotonovela?
2. ¿Qué tipo de fiesta preparan? ¿Para quién es la fiesta?
3. ¿A quién llama Manuel? ¿Por qué?
4. ¿Qué hacen Eva, Lisa y Gabi? ¿Quién les ayuda?
5. ¿Qué descubre Manuel al final?
6. ¿Qué crees que Manuel debe hacer en esta situación?

2 Ordena las oraciones See answers below.

Con base en la fotonovela, pon estas oraciones en el orden correcto.

a. Manuel Villarreal llama a la pastelería.

b. Tía Marcela ayuda con las decoraciones.

c. Abuela Dolores explica unas tradiciones mexicanas.

d. Juan y su papá inflan los globos.

e. Tío Tomás pregunta sobre las invitaciones.

3 ¿Cómo dirías? See answers below.

If you were having a party, what words and phrases from the **fotonovela** might you use . . .?

1. to ask for help with the balloons
2. to say that you didn't send the invitations
3. to tell the bakery to put "Congratulations" on the cake
4. to ask someone what they think of the music
5. to say "I'm talking with the bakery"

4 Una fiesta bien organizada

Aquí tienes una lista de cosas necesarias para una fiesta de cumpleaños. Pregúntale a tu compañero/a quién va a hacer estos preparativos. See answers below.

comprar la comida	mandar las invitaciones
preparar la comida	comprar el pastel
inflar los globos	comprar un regalo

5 ¿Y tú? Answers will vary.

Nombra *(Name)* una cosa que corresponde a cada categoría.

1. un plato que sólo comes los días de fiesta
2. un/a pariente que sólo ves cuando hay una fiesta
3. un baile típico de tu cultura
4. la celebración más importante de tu vida
5. la fiesta que más le gusta a tu familia

NOTA CULTURAL

The fifteenth birthday for many Hispanic girls is a coming of age celebration with a party at home. This party is called a **quinceañera** and can range from a small, informal gathering to a celebration resembling a wedding. In most cases a local **conjunto** *(group of musicians)* plays. It is customary for the **padrino** or **madrina** to present the honoree with a special gift.

Answers

1 1. la familia Villarreal
2. una fiesta de graduación para Héctor
3. a la pastelería para pedir el pastel
4. preparan tamales; abuela Dolores
5. que no mandó las invitaciones
6. *Sample answer:* Debe llamar a los invitados.

2 1. Tía Marcela ayuda con las decoraciones.
2. Juan y su papá inflan los globos.
3. Manuel Villarreal llama a la pastelería.
4. Abuela Dolores explica unas tradiciones mexicanas.
5. Tío Tomás pregunta sobre las invitaciones.

3 1. ¿Me ayudas a inflar los globos?
2. No mandé las invitaciones.
3. Que pongan "Felicidades" en el pastel.
4. ¿Qué te parece la música?
5. Estoy hablando con la pastelería.

4 ¿Quién va a comprar la comida? ¿Quién va a preparar la comida? ¿Quién va a inflar los globos? ¿Quién va a mandar las invitaciones? ¿Quién va a comprar el pastel? ¿Quién va a comprar un regalo?

5 *Answers will vary.*

PRIMER PASO

Talking about what you're doing right now; asking for and giving an opinion

VOCABULARIO

Los días festivos

la Nochevieja y el Año Nuevo

la Nochebuena y la Navidad

las Pascuas

el Día de los Enamorados

el Día de Acción de Gracias

el Día de la Madre

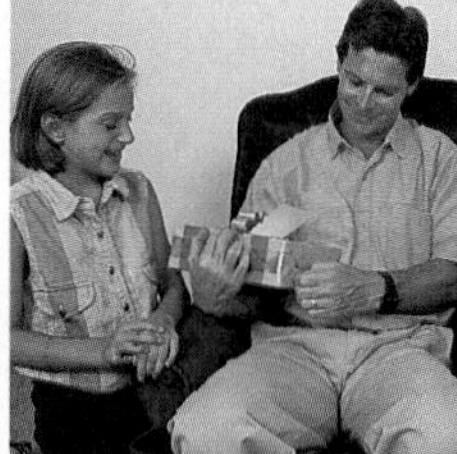
el Día del Padre

el Día de la Independencia

6 Los días de fiesta

Choose four holidays from the list above. List at least four things you associate with each holiday. For additional words and phrases you might want to use, see pages 341–343.

Answers will vary.

MODELO el Día de la Independencia en los Estados Unidos

Un picnic con la familia, el béisbol, el mes de julio, hace mucho calor...

A LO NUESTRO

Feliz *(happy)* turns up in many expressions used during holidays and celebrations. On your birthday, a friend will say **Feliz cumpleaños. Feliz Navidad** means *Merry Christmas*. What do you think **Feliz Año Nuevo** and **Feliz aniversario** mean? To congratulate someone, you say **Felicidades** or **Te felicito.**

RESOURCES FOR PRIMER PASO

Textbook Audiocassette 5B/Audio CD 10
Practice and Activity Book, pp. 110–112
Native Speaker Activity Book, pp. 46–50
Videodisc Guide
Videodisc Program, Videodisc 5B

Chapter Teaching Resources, Book 3
- Additional Listening Activities 10-1, 10-2, p. 69
  Audiocassette 10/Audio CD 10
- Student Response Forms, p. 78–80
- Realia 10-1, pp. 73, 75
- Situation Cards 10-1, pp. 76–77
- Teaching Transparency Master 10-1, pp. 65–68
  Teaching Transparency 10-1
- Quiz 10-1, pp. 81–82
  Audiocassette 8B/Audio CD 10

Jump Start!

On the board or a transparency write the following sentence: **¿Qué necesitas para preparar una comida especial festiva?** Give students three minutes to list as many items as they can.

MOTIVATE

Ask students to make a list of holidays they celebrate. Are they all included in the vocabulary list? Ask them to write the Spanish equivalent beside each item. If they celebrate a holiday that is not on the list, have them look it up in a dictionary and add it to their list.

TEACH

Presentation

Vocabulario Have students look at the photos as you describe them in Spanish. **(La Nochevieja es el 31 de diciembre. El primero de enero es el Año Nuevo. La Navidad es el 25 de diciembre. La Nochebuena es el 24 de diciembre.)** Continue in this manner describing each of the photos, pausing between each. Then ask several students when each holiday is this year. **(¿En qué mes es el Día de las Madres este año?)** Have a current calendar available to prompt answers.

For Individual Needs

Tactile Learners Show students how to make a simple calendar. Give students each a sheet of paper and ask them to fold it into 12 squares. They should label each square with a month of the year, then fill in the holidays from the **Vocabulario** in the correct squares.

Additional Practice

8 Give students several minutes to work alone and write a short description of a holiday without mentioning the name of the day. The description should be filled with clues about the holiday. Then have several students read their descriptions aloud. Other students guess what holiday is being described.

Presentation

Así se dice Model the dialogue between Lisa and her friend, using gestures to emphasize meaning. For example, while asking **Lisa, ¿qué estás haciendo?** look at a student as though he or she were Lisa. Pretend to hang decorations as you answer **Estoy colgando las decoraciones.** Explain that **-ando** is generally the equivalent of *-ing* in English. Walk around the classroom describing what you are doing, using gestures to reinforce meaning: **Estoy caminando. Ahora estoy hablando a la clase. Estoy pensando.** Then ask **¿Estás (Están) escuchando/hablando conmigo/pensando?** to elicit the appropriate response.

Language Note

The Spanish word *fiesta* comes from the Latin *festa* meaning *joyous* or *festive.* Some common words for *holiday* include **día festivo, día de fiesta, día feriado,** and **día holgado.**

Teaching Suggestion

Have students work in pairs or small groups to make holiday greeting cards. They will need paper, pictures from magazines, colored markers, and glue or tape. Allow them to use bilingual dictionaries.

7 Escuchemos: ¡De fiesta!

You'll hear four conversations, each about a different holiday. Match each conversation with the most appropriate greeting card.

a. 2

b. 4

Feliz Navidad

c. 3

d. 1

Answers on p. 255C.

NOTA CULTURAL

In small towns and cities throughout the Spanish-speaking world, there are special celebrations for all kinds of occasions. You've already learned that in Spanish-speaking countries many people celebrate not only their birthday, but also their **Día del Santo**. Many cities and countries have Saint's days which they often celebrate as holidays. Spain's patron saint, for example, is Santiago. July 25 is the Feast of Santiago and is an important holiday in Spain. Juan Carlos, the king of Spain, has his Saint's day on June 24, **el Día de San Juan**, making it a national holiday.

8 ¿Cuál es tu día festivo favorito?

Ask a classmate about his or her favorite holidays and what he or she does to celebrate. In the word box are some questions to get you started. Answers will vary.

¿Miras un partido en la televisión?
¿Con quién(es) pasas el día?
¿Adónde vas?
¿Cantas o bailas?
¿Comes algo en especial?

ASÍ SE DICE — Talking about what you're doing right now

To find out what someone is doing right now, ask:	He or she might say:
Lisa, **¿qué estás haciendo?** *. . . what are you doing?*	**Estoy colgando las decoraciones.** *I'm hanging the decorations.*
¿Y tu hermano?	Él **está limpiando** la sala. *He is cleaning . . .*
¿Todos **están decorando** la casa? *Are you all decorating . . .?*	Sí, **estamos decorando** la casa. *. . . we are decorating . . .*

Culture Note

June 24, the Roman Catholic feast day of Saint John the Baptist (**el Día de San Juan Bautista**), is a very important holiday in many Spanish-speaking countries. Many traditions surrounding it are inspired by the concept of baptism (**bautismo, bautizo**). For example, in Puerto Rico the residents of San Juan (**sanjuaneros**) walk backward into the ocean three times at midnight on June 23. In Mexico people celebrate with water activities, such as a swimming parties or playfully sprinkling each other with water. Other traditions are unrelated to water, such as in Bolivia, where neighbors gather around bonfires to stay warm and celebrate by dancing and singing all night long.

Gramática Present progressive

The *present progressive* is used to talk about what's happening right now. Use **estar** + the *present participle* of the verb.

- For **-ar** verbs, add **-ando** to the stem:
  Estoy bailando. No **están cantando.**
- For **-er** and **-ir** verbs, add **-iendo** to the stem:
  ¿Qué **están comiendo** Uds.? Enrique **está escribiendo** las invitaciones.
- If the stem ends in a vowel the **-iendo** changes to **-yendo**:
  ¿Estás leyendo el periódico?

9 Escuchemos: Un día especial

What are these people doing right now? Listen to Guadalupe's statements and match the person or persons with the correct picture. Answers on p. 255C.

1. Sarita e
2. Guadalupe d
3. Roberto a
4. Rosita b
5. Teresa y Mauricio f
6. Julia c

a.

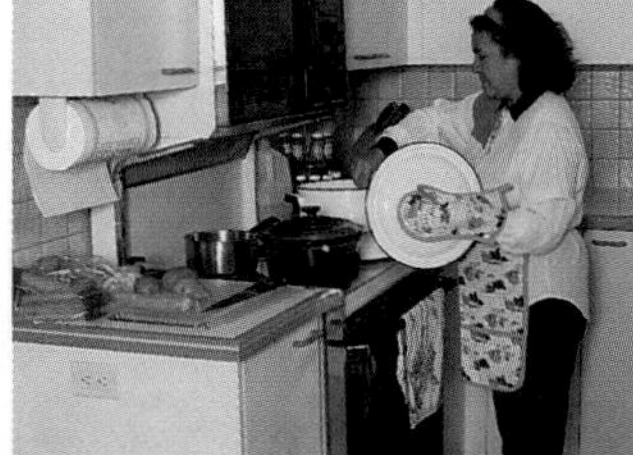
b.

c.

d.

e.

f.

10 ¿Qué están haciendo?

Pregúntale a tu compañero o compañera qué es lo que están haciendo tres de las personas en las fotos en la Actividad 9. Después, contesta las preguntas de tu compañero o compañera sobre las otras tres personas en las fotos.

11 ¡Escribamos!

Write a short paragraph about what each person is doing in Activity 9. Give a different reason why each person is doing what they're doing to get ready for the party.

MODELO A Julia le encanta limpiar todo. Por eso ella está limpiando la cocina.

Presentation

Gramática First, have students silently read the explanation. Then model pronunciation of several examples and go over the formation of the present progressive. Ask each student to write five sentences describing things he or she is or is not doing right now. (**Estoy pensando. No estoy nadando. Estoy aprendiendo español. No estoy comiendo.**) Then ask students to share their sentences with the class.

Reteaching

11 On index cards, write questions similar to those in **Así se dice** on page 262. (**¿Qué está haciendo la tía Rosita?**) Hand out the cards to students. Have each student answer their question, referring to the pictures in Activity 9. (**Está preparando la comida porque necesitan comida en la fiesta.**)

Building on Previous Skills

Have students work in pairs. One student makes a request of his or her partner and the partner makes an excuse because he or she is doing something else right at the moment. (**—¿Quieres ir al parque? —Lo siento, pero no puedo. Estoy estudiando.**) You might refer them to Chapters 7 and 8 for some of these expressions. Ask students to share their exchanges with the class.

Teaching Suggestion

This activity requires advance planning and scheduling. Divide the class into small groups and have each group choose a holiday to present to the class. Groups then research their holiday and write a short report on it, which they read to the class. Groups accompany their report with a physical representation of the holiday, such as food (just enough for each student to have a taste), costumes, props, photographs, or music.

Teaching Suggestion

12 Assign roles in each pair and allow students three to five minutes to prepare. One will determine the type of celebration and kinds of preparation going on, the other will come up with a list of questions to be asked.

Presentation

Así se dice Model the expressions in **Así se dice** for correct pronunciation and intonation. Then ask a student one of the questions and have him or her respond with an appropriate answer. Call on individual students to give their opinions on some original questions with their books closed. (**¿Crees que tenemos bastante tarea? ¿Qué te parece la clase de ciencias naturales? ¿Qué te parece si asistimos al colegio durante el verano?**)

Teaching Suggestion

14 This activity may be done as an individual assignment with answers discussed by the entire class.

Close

Write several holidays and their dates on the board or a transparency. Then tell the class to imagine today is that holiday. Have a student choose one of the dates you have written. (**¿Con quién pasas el día?**) The student should answer appropriately. (**Paso el Día de las Madres con mi madre y mi abuela.**) Vary the questions for each student.

12 Todos están ocupados

Work in pairs. Imagine that one of your friends calls while you and your family are in the middle of getting ready for a big celebration. Your friend wants to know what you're doing to prepare for it. Take turns asking and answering questions about what's going on and what each person is doing to help.

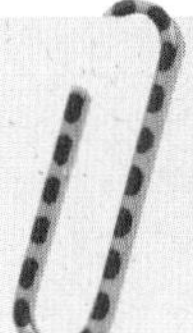

ASÍ SE DICE — Asking for and giving an opinion

To find out what a friend thinks about something, ask:

¿Crees que hay bastante comida para la fiesta?
Do you think that . . .?

¿Qué te parece si llamamos a Eva?
How do you feel about . . .?

Your friend might say:

Creo que sí.
Creo que no.

Me parece bien.
Perfecto.
Buena idea.

13 Y tú, ¿qué crees?

Pregúntale a tu compañero/a qué piensa de los días festivos. Pregúntale por qué a algunos le gustan y a otros no. Después, contesta las preguntas de tu compañero/a. Usa **Creo que es..., Me parece...** y **porque...** en las respuestas.

14 Compramos regalos

Answers will vary.

You and a classmate must decide on gifts for various relatives' birthdays. Read the statements and take turns giving your opinion on an appropriate gift item for each person.

1. A Carolina le gusta mucho el arte.
2. A Ricardo le encanta cocinar.
3. A Marcos le gustan todos los deportes.
4. A Patricia le encantan las joyas.
5. A Malena le gusta leer.
6. A Ángela le encanta sacar fotos.

15 ¡Vamos a la fiesta!

Work with two or three classmates to plan a celebration for a holiday of your choice. Plan who will attend, the food you would like to serve, and what kind of activities there will be. When your partners say what they want to do, give your opinion. Appoint a spokesperson to report your plans to the class. Use **Nos parece** to tell about an opinion you all have.

16 Una celebración diferente

Having a celebration doesn't necessarily mean having a party. Choose a holiday or event you would like to add to the calendar. Write two paragraphs in Spanish explaining why and how we should celebrate it.

Assess

Quiz 10-1, *Chapter Teaching Resources, Book 3,* pp. 81–82

Assessment Items, Audiocassette 8B/ Audio CD 10

Performance Assessment

Ask students to imagine that it is the morning of a holiday. Have them work in pairs to develop a phone conversation in which one person describes what everyone is doing to prepare for the celebration and the other asks questions. (**—¿Con quién pasas la Nochebuena? —Paso el día con mi familia. Mi padre está preparando una sopa porque siempre la comemos en la Nochebuena.**)

¿Qué hacen ustedes para celebrar?

Festivals are a very important part of life in Spanish-speaking countries. Often the whole community participates. Here is how some people celebrate.

Verónica
San Antonio, Texas

"El 16 de septiembre significa la independencia de México... En Laredo tenemos como un baile... o tenemos una fiesta... Si México no hubiera ganado su independencia de España, nunca estuviéramos nosotros aquí, los hispanos, aquí donde estamos hoy".

Familia Pardo
La Coruña, España

"La fiesta de la Virgen del Rosario es una fiesta (en que) tocan la música tradicional, hay bailes típicos gallegos, como la muñeira y luego canciones, música popular gallega. . ."

Angélica
Caracas, Venezuela

"El 5 de julio se celebra la batalla de Carabó. Eso se celebra en Los Próceres, que es un parque que queda cerca... Todos los militares salen a desfilar, sale la armada, la aviación, el ejército y la guardia. Eso fue por... la independencia de Carabó, del estado de Carabó".

Para pensar y hablar...

A. Are any of the holidays mentioned by the interviewees similar to holidays you're familiar with? Which ones? How are they similar? How are they different?

B. Choose your favorite holiday and write a description in Spanish of the way you usually celebrate it. Then find out how a classmate celebrates the same holiday. Are there any differences? If so, what might explain them?

Preguntas

1. ¿Quién menciona un evento festivo religioso? (la familia Pardo)
2. ¿Qué tipo de música escucha la familia Pardo durante la fiesta de la Virgen del Rosario? (música gallega, de origen celta)
3. ¿Cuál es la fecha de la celebración de la batalla de Carabobo? (el 5 de julio)
4. Según Veronica, ¿cómo se celebra la independencia de México en la ciudad de Laredo? (con un baile o una fiesta)

Teaching Suggestions

- You may want to have your students research the life of Simón Bolívar as an outside assignment.
- Point out that Veronica was interviewed in San Antonio, but her answer implies that her family is from Laredo, Texas.
- Ask your students to listen closely to the three distinct accents on the audio or video recording. What similarites and differences can they identify?

Video Program or Expanded Video Program, Videocassette 4

or Videodisc Program, Videodisc 5B

Teacher Notes

- See *Video Guide* and *Videodisc Guide* for activities related to the **Panorama cultural.**
- Remind students that cultural information may be included on the Quizzes and Chapter Test.

Motivating Activity

Have your students list the elements that make their favorite celebration or holiday special to them.

Presentation

Play the video and ask students to take notes on the key points that each interviewee makes. Then ask students to compare notes with a partner and to discuss what they have learned from the interviews. Then play the video again and have students answer the **Preguntas.**

History Link

On June 24, 1821, the forces of Simón Bolívar fought the final battle of independence against the Spanish army commanded by Field Marshal Miguel de la Torre. The Battle of Carabobo won the country its independence. The State of Carabobo is located in the north-center of Venezuela. Its capital is Valencia, an important industrial city.

Jump Start!

On the board or a transparency write **REGALO,** with space between each letter. Under the letter **R** write the word **Radio.** Tell students to imagine that a friend's birthday is coming up, and they need to think of five more ideas for gifts using the remaining letters.

Motivate

Ask students to think of three instances when they asked someone for help recently. How did they ask, and what were the verbal responses others gave? Ask them to name as many different ways to ask for and agree or refuse to help as they can.

Teach

Presentation

Así se dice Model pronunciation and question construction, pointing out the position of the indirect object pronoun **me.** Have students work in pairs to practice asking for help and responding to requests. Remind them to reverse roles so that each person practices both the requests and the responses. Finally, ask each person to make up at least three new requests and have the other person respond appropriately.

Vocabulario Replay the **fotonovela** to model pronunciation of new vocabulary. Then ask several students questions from **Así se dice** that include the new vocabulary. **(¿Me ayudas a inflar los globos?)** Students should respond with an expression from **Así se dice.** When students are comfortable with the new words, call on a student to ask a classmate a question using a vocabulary word.

SEGUNDO PASO

Asking for help and responding to requests; telling a friend what to do

ASÍ SE DICE Asking for help and responding to requests

To ask for help, say:

¿Me haces el favor de llamar a Gabi?
Can you do me the favor of . . .?

¿Me ayudas a decorar la sala?

¿Me traes una silla, por favor?

¿Me pasas el helado?

To agree to help, say:

Claro que sí.

Cómo no.

¡Con mucho gusto! *Sure!*

Un momentito. *Just a second.*

To politely refuse to help, say:

Lo siento, pero en este momento estoy ocupado.
I'm sorry, but right now . . .

Perdóname, pero no puedo.
Excuse me, but . . .

17 Las fiestas

Look at the drawings in the **Vocabulario.** How would each person ask you to help with what she or he is doing? Sample answer: ¿Me ayudas a inflar los globos?

VOCABULARIO

inflar los globos
llamar a los invitados

colgar las decoraciones
decorar la casa

mandar las invitaciones

recibir regalos
abrir los regalos

Resources for SEGUNDO PASO

Textbook Audiocassette 5B/Audio CD 10
Practice and Activity Book, pp. 113–115
Native Speaker Activity Book, pp. 46–50
Video Guide
Video Program
Expanded Video Program, Videocassette 4
Videodisc Guide
Videodisc Program, Videodisc 5B

Chapter Teaching Resources, Book 3
- Communicative Activity 10-2, pp. 61–62
- Additional Listening Activities 10-3, 10-4, p. 70
  Audiocassette 10B/Audio CD 10
- Student Response Forms, pp. 78–80
- Realia 10-2, pp. 73, 75
- Situation Cards 10-2, pp. 76–77
- Teaching Transparency Master 10-2, pp. 65–68
  Teaching Transparency 10-2
- Quiz 10-2, pp. 83–84
  Audiocassette 8B/Audio CD 10

18 Escuchemos: ¿Me ayudas?

Listen as various people help each other get ready for the upcoming party. Choose the correct response to each question you hear. Answers on p. 255C.

a. Sí, cómo no. Él canta y baila también. 2
b. Sí. ¿Necesitas algo más? 7
c. Todos te ayudamos, Hilda. 3
d. Sí. ¿Dónde pongo los globos? 1
e. Creo que todos van a traer música. 5
f. En este momento no puedo, pero más tarde, sí, te ayudo con los sándwiches. 6
g. Sí. ¿Dónde está? ¿En el centro? 4

19 ¿Necesitas ayuda? Answers will vary.

Look at the drawings of Fernando getting ready for his party tonight. He forgot to do a lot of things, and now he needs some help. Create miniconversations for each picture. Fernando asks for assistance and the other person agrees or refuses to help. Be creative!

a.

b.

c.

d.

20 ¿Me puedes ayudar?

Imagine you're getting ready for a party at your house next week. Make a list of six questions to ask others for help with the preparations. Be sure to include food, decorations, and invitations in your requests. Sample questions below.

21 ¡Claro que sí!

Now get together with a partner and ask for help with the preparations on your list from Activity 20. Your partner must either offer to help, politely refuse, or suggest someone else who can do the job. Take turns asking questions.

Additional Practice

18 Play the audio recording again and ask students to come up with original responses to the questions that the characters ask. You might ask students to come up with questions that are not on the page.

Teaching Suggestion

19 Have students work in pairs to create these conversations. Ask them to present them to the class and have the class guess which picture corresponds to their conversation.

For Individual Needs

21 Slower Pace Have students work in pairs to list the items they need to prepare for the party. Together, pairs create the questions asking for help with each item.

Multicultural Link

Ask students to find out about coming-of-age celebrations in another culture. Have them report their findings to the class. (For example, Jewish people celebrate coming of age for both boys and girls. The bar mitzvah and bat mitzvah celebrations take place when a child turns thirteen. In addition to a religious ceremony, a large party is often given for the child by his or her extended family and friends.)

Answers

20 *Sample questions:*

Anita, ¿puedes traer algo en especial para decorar la casa?
Pedro, ¿me ayudas a colgar las decoraciones por favor?
Philip, ¿me haces el favor de llamar a los invitados?

Game

Play a variation of **Simón dice** by combining it with **me haces el favor de...** If a request is not preceded by **Simón dice** then the students should answer with **Lo siento, no puedo. (Simón dice, ¿me haces el favor de abrir el libro?)** You may want to refer your students to page 8 of the Preliminary Chapter for ideas.

Presentation

Have several students mime various party preparations as you give them simple commands. (**Cuelga las decoraciones, por favor. Prepara la ensalada. Decora la sala,** etc.) Then have students give each other commands in pairs, with partners miming in response.

For Individual Needs

22 Challenge Play the audio recording again. After each short conversation, stop the tape and ask students to write a response to each request in which they say they cannot bring the item asked for. They should offer an alternative or an excuse. (**Buenos días. Habla Nicolás. ¿Qué necesitan para la fiesta? Este... trae unos refrescos, por favor. —Lo siento, no puedo traer refrescos. ¿Qué te parece si traigo unos discos compactos?**) Play the recording as many times as necessary.

24 Slower Pace Allow partners several minutes to write a list of **Cosas que hacer.** Have them list tasks using the infinitive of the verb, changing it to the command form during role-play.

Native Speakers

Have a native speaker teach the class his or her favorite hobby using the polite command forms. For example, a student could bring a tennis racquet and give the class a tennis lesson. (**María, ¿me haces el favor de usar la raqueta de esta manera?**) Students could then ask questions in Spanish.

ASÍ SE DICE Telling a friend what to do

To tell a friend what to do, say:

Prepara la ensalada y **limpia** la cocina, **¿quieres?**
Prepare . . . clean . . .

Por favor, **decora** la sala y **llama** a los invitados.
. . . decorate . . . call . . .

Your friend might say:

De acuerdo. *Agreed.*

Está bien.

Nota Gramatical

Informal commands are used with people you would address as **tú.** To state an informal command in Spanish, take the second person singular of the verb and drop the **-s.** For example:

cantas minus **s** = **canta** *(sing!)*

Several command forms are irregular and should be memorized because they don't follow a single pattern. A few of these are:

haz *do, make!* **pon** *put, place!*
ve *go!* **ven** *come!*
vete *go away!*

22 Escuchemos: Preparativos

Listen as several people call the Villarreal house asking what they can do to help with the preparations for Hector's graduation party. Match each person with the correct task. Answers on p. 255C.

1. Gustavo
2. Soledad
3. Cristóbal
4. Verónica
5. Nicolás
6. Gloria

a. trae unos discos
b. ve al supermercado
c. prepara la ensalada
d. compra los globos
e. saca las fotos
f. trae unos refrescos

23 ¡Qué divertido! See answers below.

Imagine that you're at Hector's graduation party and Mr. Villarreal wants everyone to have a good time. How would he tell each person to do the following things?

1. María/sacar unas fotos del grupo
2. Guillermo/comer más tamales
3. Mercedes/bailar con Héctor
4. Gabi/cantar canciones populares
5. Eva/tocar la guitarra para Gabi
6. Lisa/poner la música de tu grupo favorito
7. Héctor/abrir los regalos pronto
8. Rebeca/descansar un poco

24 Cosas que hacer See answers below.

You're having a party and your partner is helping you get ready. You've already done some of the preparations, but you still have some things left to do. Take turns telling each other to do the items left on the list. Don't forget to be polite!

comprar los refrescos
preparar la comida

decorar la sala
inflar los globos

limpiar la sala
llamar a nuestros amigos

poner la ropa en el armario
traer los discos compactos

Answers

23 1. María, saca unas fotos del grupo.
2. Guillermo, come más tamales.
3. Mercedes, baila con Héctor.
4. Gabi, canta canciones populares.
5. Eva, toca la guitarra para Gabi.
6. Lisa, pon la música de tu grupo favorito.
7. Héctor, abre los regalos pronto.
8. Rebeca, descansa un poco.

24 *Sample answers:* Compra los refrescos, por favor. Me haces el favor de preparar la comida?

25 Antes...

What a party! You and your friends had a great time last night, but now it's time to clean up the mess. Look at the picture and make a detailed list of all the things that need to be done to get the house back in order.

26 ...y después

Work with a partner. Using the lists you made in Activity 25, take turns telling your partner what he or she can do to help you get the house together. Don't forget—you also promised your parents that you would wash the clothes, walk the dog, and cut the grass!

When you learn new material, add what you're learning to what you already know, and think about how to use it in a conversation. For example, instead of just making a list of informal commands (like **haz**, **ven**, and **pon**), put them into a context by thinking of sentences that go with each one (like **¡Haz la tarea!**, **¡Ven conmigo!**, and **¡Pon la mesa!**). When you learn a new word, make up sentences about your own life for each of the new vocabulary items.

For Individual Needs

25 Slower Pace Use the illustration to review home-related vocabulary before students do Activity 25.

25 Challenge Have students write a paragraph describing the house and what must be done.

Group Work

26 Ask students to work in groups of four or five as they role-play the following conversation: After a party, the host or hostess asks friends one by one to help out by doing specific things to clean up the mess. Some friends respond affirmatively, others politely refuse and offer an excuse. **(—¿Me ayudas a lavar los platos? —Lo siento, pero tengo que caminar con el perro. —¿Me haces el favor de pasar la aspiradora? —Cómo no.)** Have group members take turns playing the host or hostess. You might have groups present their conversations to the class.

Close

TPR Ask individual students to comply with a command that involves moving around the room. **(ven acá, escribe en la pizarra, pon el cuaderno en este escritorio)** After you have given several commands, ask students to give an appropriate command to another student.

Assess

Quiz 10-2, *Chapter Teaching Resources, Book 3,* pp. 83–84zz

Assessment Items, Audiocassette 8B Audio CD 10

Performance Assessment

Tell students that a family is planning a big party for the grandparents' wedding anniversary. The person in charge of planning the party has errands to run and cannot direct preparations. Ask students to write a list telling each member of the family what he or she is to do to help prepare for the party. They may include any number of people in the family for this activity.

Motivating Activity

Ask students to think of a celebration they know of that proceeds in stages, with certain parts being more important than others. Some people's families might put greater emphasis on Christmas Eve than on December 25, for example, but both days commemorate Christmas.

Culture Note

Weddings in Mexico are similar to those in the United States in many ways. However, wedding receptions are generally more elaborate, lenghty celebrations. The reception for a noon wedding often lasts until two or three in the morning—and commonly goes until dawn. Good food and dance music (usually with mariachis) are considered a must.

Additional Vocabulary

madrina *maid of honor*
damas de boda *bridesmaids*
padrino *best man*
chambelanes *groomsmen*
pajes *flower girl and ring bearer*

ENCUENTRO CULTURAL

¿Cómo se celebra una boda?

GUADALUPE ¿Quieres ir conmigo esta tarde? Mi hermana Clara y su novio Simón se van a casar.

CHARLIE ¿Hoy?

GUADALUPE Sí, la ceremonia no dura mucho tiempo. Estoy segura de que tenemos suficiente tiempo para ir al museo.

CHARLIE Pero, tus padres están en Nueva York, ¿no? ¿No van a asistir a la boda?

GUADALUPE ¡Claro que sí! Regresan el jueves antes de la boda.

CHARLIE Pero... la boda es hoy, ¿verdad?

GUADALUPE Sí, pero es la ceremonia civil, nada más.

CHARLIE Entonces, ¿la boda es el domingo? ¡No entiendo!

Para discutir...

1. Why does Charlie seem so surprised that Guadalupe's sister is getting married today without her parents being present?
2. Why are Clara and Simón having two different wedding ceremonies?

Vamos a comprenderlo

In Latin American countries, many couples participate in two ceremonies. For most, the civil ceremony is just a formality, similiar to getting a marriage license. The religious ceremony is the important one for the family and the one after which all the festivities occur. Although the civil ceremony is fully legal and binding, family and friends often don't consider the couple married until after the ceremony in church.

Answers

27
1. Probablemente Pilar pasó la aspiradora, limpió la cocina y lavó los platos anoche.
2. Probablemente Luis compró la comida, la cocinó y la preparó anoche.
3. Probablemente Liliana no miró el partido ni escuchó la radio ni habló con sus amigos anoche.
4. Probablemente Federico no miró la televisión anoche pero estudió mucho y no habló por teléfono con amigos.
5. Probablemente Marta y Patricia caminaron mucho, trabajaron muy tarde y regresaron a casa tarde anoche.
6. Probablemente Bernardo viajó el año pasado a Santo Domingo donde nadó y esquió en el agua.

TERCER PASO

Talking about past events

ASÍ SE DICE — Talking about past events

To find out what a friend did, ask:

¿Qué hiciste anoche en la fiesta?
What did you do last night . . .?

¿Qué hizo Kathy **ayer?**
What did . . . do yesterday?

¿Lo pasaron bien la semana pasada? *Did you have a good time last week?*

Your friend might answer:

Bailé un poco y **hablé** con Lisa.
I danced . . . I talked . . .

Cantó unas canciones. *She sang . . .*

Sí, **lo pasamos bien.**

VOCABULARIO

anteayer	*day before yesterday*
el año pasado	*last year*
el sábado pasado	*last Saturday*
el verano pasado	*last summer*

Nota Gramatical

Use the preterite tense to talk about events completed sometime in the past. The preterite endings for **trabajar,** a regular **-ar** verb, are:

trabaj**é**	trabaj**amos**
trabaj**aste**	trabaj**asteis**
trabaj**ó**	trabaj**aron**

Notice the accent marks and how they affect pronunciation in the **yo** and the **él/ella/usted** forms.

27 Anoche See answers below.

Based on the cues, list what each person or persons did or didn't do and when.

MODELO — Raúl no tiene mucha hambre a la hora del desayuno. (tomar helado, cenar tarde)
—Probablemente **tomó helado** y **cenó tarde** anoche.

1. La casa de Pilar está muy limpia. (pasar la aspiradora, limpiar la cocina, lavar los platos)
2. La comida para la fiesta de Luis está lista. (comprar, cocinar, preparar)
3. Liliana no sabe los resultados del gran partido de fútbol. (mirar el partido, escuchar la radio, hablar con sus amigos)
4. Federico sabe todas las respuestas para el examen de hoy. (mirar la televisión, estudiar mucho, hablar por teléfono con amigos)
5. Marta y Patricia están muy cansadas hoy. (caminar mucho, trabajar muy tarde, regresar a casa tarde)
6. Bernardo está aburrido con sus vacaciones este verano. (viajar a Santo Domingo, nadar, esquiar en el agua)

RESOURCES FOR TERCER PASO

Textbook Audiocassette 5B/Audio CD 10
Practice and Activity Book, pp. 116–118
Native Speaker Activity Book, pp. 46–50
Videodisc Guide
Videodisc Program, Videodisc 5B

Chapter Teaching Resources, Book 3
- Communicative Activity 10-2, pp. 177–178
- Additional Listening Activities 10-5, 10-6, p. 187
  Audiocassette 10B/Audio CD 10
- Student Response Forms, pp. 78–80
- Realia 10-2, pp. 74, 75
- Situation Cards 10-3, pp. 76–77
- Teaching Transparency Master 10-3, pp. 65–68
  Teaching Transparency 10-3
- Quiz 10-3, pp. 85–86
  Audiocassette 8B/Audio CD 10

Jump Start!

Write the following on the board or a transparency: **Hay un gran baile este fin de semana. Todos se visten muy de moda. ¿Qué vas a llevar tú?** Students are to include as many details as possible.

MOTIVATE

Have each student write at least five things in Spanish that they are doing today. Then ask them to write **Ayer ____ también** next to those they also did yesterday. Have them keep their lists to see how many blanks they can fill in after they have completed this **Paso.**

TEACH

Presentation

After you model pronunciation of the target phrases in **Así se dice,** have students read the **Nota gramatical.** Explain the importance of accent marks in pronouncing verbs correctly. (**Baile** is a formal command, **bailé** is *I danced.*) Then have students work with a partner to practice the questions and answers in **Así se dice.**

Vocabulario Write the following expressions on the board or a transparency: **bailar el sábado pasado, trabajar en un restaurante el verano pasado mirar la televisión anteayer; estudiar mucho el año pasado.** Have students move around and ask their classmates questions, using the **tú** form of the preterite tense. The person asked responds affirmatively or negatively in the **yo** form. Ask them to find at least one person who did each of the activities.

Additional Practice

28 After doing this activity as a listening comprehension exercise, call on several students and ask questions about the characters on the audio recording. (**¿Qué hicieron Andrés y Valerie?**) Students should answer appropriately, according to the answers given in the listening activity. You might have students ask their classmates questions.

Cooperative Learning

29 When students understand verbs in the preterite fairly well, divide them into groups of three. On the board or a transparency write the following: **comprar un regalo, mirar la televisión, acampar el verano pasado, caminar mucho anoche, descansar después de la escuela,** and **llevar la camiseta roja.** Have one student ask another if he or she did one of these things. The second student will answer and a third student will report what the second said. (One: **¿Compraste un regalo?** Two: **Sí, le compré un regalo a José.** Three: **Le compró un regalo a José.**) Ask the students to switch roles to practice all of the expressions.

For Individual Needs

30 Visual Learners Have students bring in photos, magazine ads, or travel brochures. Have them use these to illustrate what they did on a recent vacation.

30 Challenge Have students choose a memorable vacation and write about it. Allow them to use a dictionary to look up additional vocabulary as necessary.

28 Escuchemos: La fiesta de Abby Answers on p. 255D.

Abby's party was great! Listen as she tells her parents about what some of her friends did at her party last night. Match the name(s) of the person(s) to the correct drawing.

a.

b.

c.

d.

e.

f.

g.

h.

1. Raquel y Gloria a
2. Kerry y Shoji c
3. Bárbara y Miguel b
4. Pablo d
5. Patricia g
6. Gracie y Kim e
7. Andrés y Valerie h
8. Francisco f

29 La semana pasada Possible answer below.

Work with a partner and take turns asking each other if you did the following things last week. Be sure to include where, on what day, and with whom you did each activity.

1. hablar por teléfono
2. nadar
3. escuchar música
4. caminar con el perro
5. tomar helado
6. estudiar
7. montar en bicicleta
8. mirar la televisión
9. desayunar
10. trabajar

30 ¿Qué hicieron todos? Possible answers below.

Imagine that you and your friends spent a great day outdoors. Write a paragraph about the fun things everyone did there by answering the following questions. Be creative!

1. ¿A qué hora llegaron?
2. ¿Quiénes montaron a caballo?
3. ¿Nadaron todos?
4. ¿Quién pescó?
5. ¿Quiénes jugaron al voleibol?
6. ¿Quién no hizo nada?

Additional Vocabulary

andar por la arena *to walk in the sand*
empinar el papalote *to fly a kite*
construir un castillo de arena *to build a sandcastle*
buscar caracoles del mar *to look for seashells*

Game

¿QUÉ DIBUJAS? Whisper to a student a vocabulary word or phrase. The student draws a simple representation of it on the board. This can be a drawing or a symbol and can be clarified through mime. The rest of the class must then guess the word or phrase.

31 ¿Qué pasó aquí?

With a partner, look at the two drawings. What did Gloria do to the room that makes it look so different? Take turns looking for and pointing out five differences each.

antes

después

32 Una semana ocupada

Look at Hector's agenda. With a partner, take turns asking each other and answering questions about his activities for the week.

MODELO —¿Qué hizo Héctor el lunes?
—El lunes Héctor tomó un examen a las nueve y media.

AGENDA

lunes:	tomar un examen	(9:30)
martes:	estudiar con Gabi	(4:00)
miércoles:	visitar a mis tíos	(7:30)
jueves:	cantar en el coro	(8:15)
viernes:	tomar un helado con Eva	(9:00)
sábado:	acampar con mis primos	(3:00)
domingo:	hablar con los abuelos	(2:00)

33 Mi semana

Now, create your agenda for a typical week, like Hector's agenda in Activity 32. Then, get together with a partner and ask each other questions about what you did day by day. Did you and your partner do any of the same things?

Additional Practice

31 Have students work with a partner to come up with five sentences about the picture labeled **después.** They should write sentences in the preterite tense explaining what was done to clean up the room. (**Alguien lavó los platos.**) You might have students share their sentences with the class. An alternative is to have students make up a story. (like *Goldilocks*—**el padre lavó los platos, la madre recogió...**)

For Individual Needs

31 Visual Learners After students have done this activity, ask them to look closely at both pictures and memorize as many details as they can. Then have them close their books and recall the pictures without looking at them. See how many differences between the pictures the class can remember.

32 Slower Pace Allow students to write what Héctor did on each day before doing this activity orally.

Teaching Suggestion

33 Ask several pairs of students to share some of their questions and answers about their agendas with the class.

Language Note

Point out the similarity of the words *camp* and **acampar.** Many English words for sports and activities are used in other languages. Sometimes the meaning of the word changes slightly. In Spain, for example, *jogging* is sometimes known as **el footing.** In Puerto Rico, it is called **joguear** (pronounced with an English *j*).

Reteaching

Preterite Make cards and fasten them on the board in vertical columns as follows : (1) subject pronouns and people's names, (2) verb stems of regular -**ar** verbs, (3) preterite endings of -**ar** verbs, (4) direct objects, adverbs, and prepositional phrases. Model an example sentence for each verb ending. Then have students make sentences using a card from each column. For further practice, students can also write the sentences.

Presentation

Nota gramatical First have students read the explanation. Then walk around the room asking students a variety of questions to which they will respond using a direct object pronoun (**un pronombre de complemento directo**). (**¿Estudias el español todos los días? ¿Miras la televisión con frecuencia? ¿Sacas la basura todas las semanas? ¿Tienes el libro de matemáticas contigo?**) Check for comprehension and pronunciation.

Additional Practice

34 As a follow-up to the pair work, ask students these questions in the past tense, and have them respond appropriately. This will provide them practice with the preterite tense and with direct object pronouns.

For Individual Needs

34 Slower Pace Have students write answers to numbers one to five to prepare for the oral activity.

34 Challenge If students do not do a particular activity during the week, have them respond to their partner appropriately, and include further information about who in their family actually does. (**No lo hago nunca. Mi madre hace las camas todas las mañanas.**)

34 ¿Qué haces durante la semana? Sample answers below.

Take turns asking each other if you do these activities during the week. Include when and how often you do each activity. Use the correct direct object pronoun.

MODELO —¿Cuándo lees el periódico?
—Lo leo todos los días.

1. hacer la cama
2. practicar la guitarra
3. preparar el almuerzo
4. mirar la televisión
5. escribir una carta
6. limpiar el cuarto
7. estudiar español, álgebra, ...
8. lavar la ropa o lavar el carro
9. hacer la tarea
10. poner la mesa

Nota Gramatical

Just as we use subject pronouns to avoid repetition of names, we can use direct object pronouns to refer to someone or something already mentioned. The singular forms of these pronouns are:

lo *him, it, you (formal)*
la *her, it, you (formal)*

The pronoun agrees in gender with the noun replaced and comes right before the verb.

Sarita compró **el regalo** ayer.
Sarita **lo** compró ayer.

Daniel, ¿lavaste **la ropa** anoche?
Sí, ya **la** lavé anoche.

35 ¿Todo listo? See answers below.

Mr. Villarreal wants to make sure that everything is ready for Hector's graduation party. How would the following people answer his questions? Be sure to use the correct direct object pronoun in your answers.

MODELO —Rebeca, ¿ya compraste el pastel? (No)
—No, no lo compré todavía.

1. Eva, ¿ya invitaste al profesor de Héctor? (No)
2. Gabi y Lisa, ¿ya limpiaron la casa? (Sí)
3. Lisa, ¿ya decoraste el patio? (No)
4. Abuela, ¿ya preparaste la comida? (No)
5. Tomás y Juan, ¿ya compraron el regalo? (Sí)
6. Marcela, ¿ya llamaste a Victoria? (Sí)
7. Aníbal, ¿ya ayudaste a tu papá? (Sí)
8. Juan, ¿ya alquilaste *(you rented)* el video? (No)
9. Gabi y Eva, ¿ya compraron el helado? (No)

36 ¿Y qué hizo...?

Find out at least one thing your partner and his or her friends or family members did at the following times:

1. el año pasado
2. el domingo pasado
3. anteayer
4. ayer por la mañana
5. ayer a las doce
6. hoy antes de llegar al colegio

Teaching Suggestion

Students often have difficulty with negative answers that begin **No, no...** Point out that the second **no** is required to make the verb negative. You might also point out that an affirmative answer can also be introduced by a **no** when the answer is unexpected: **¿Limpiaste la cocina? No, la limpió Abel.**

Answers

35
1. No, no lo invité todavía.
2. Sí, ya la limpiamos.
3. No, no lo decoré todavía.
4. No, no la preparé todavía.
5. Sí, ya lo compramos.
6. Sí, ya la llamé.
7. Sí, ya lo ayudé.
8. No, no lo alquilé todavía.
9. No, no lo compramos todavía.

37 Un sábado ocupado

Last Saturday was a busy day at the Ramírez house. With a partner, take turns telling each other who did the following things.

MODELO Susana (limpiar la cocina)
—Susana la limpió.

Yo	lavar la ropa
Tú	preparar la cena
Carlos y yo	lavar el carro
El señor Ramírez	cortar el césped
Tía Elena	pasar la aspiradora
Diana y Bernardo	limpiar la cocina
Susana	cuidar al hermano

38 En mi cuaderno

Create a journal entry telling what you did each day last week. Tell about the activities you participated in each day. Use the verbs you've worked with so far in the preterite. For the preterite forms of other verbs, see page 347.

LETRA Y SONIDO

A. You may sometimes feel that Spanish is spoken very fast. This is because Spanish divides the chain of speech into even syllables. It does not mark word boundaries. Here are some guidelines to help you.

1. Two vowels that come together are joined and are not separated even if they are part of different words.

   él va⊂a⊂hablar **entra⊂en la casa**
   lo⊂encuentro **hablo⊂inglés**

2. If a word ends in a consonant and the next one begins with a vowel, the preceding consonant begins the new syllable.

   Daniel⊂es⊂inteligente. **Quieren⊂nadar.**
   Tiene los⊂ojos⊂azules.

3. Identical vowels and consonants are reduced to a slightly longer single sound.

   ¿Tienes⊂soda? **Sus⊂hijos⊂son⊂nuestros⊂amigos.**

B. **Dictado** Script on p. 255D.
Listen as Ricardo tells you what he's going to do tonight. Write what you hear.

C. **Trabalenguas**
Abre, cierra, saca afuera.
No tires chicle en la acera.

Teaching Suggestion

Letra y Sonido Dictate the following two sentences for students. **Mi madre es profesora de español. Trabaja en una escuela secundaria.** Ask students to mark where they would link sounds together. Then have students practice pronouncing the sentences.

Teaching Suggestion

34 Ask students to tell a partner who at their house did each of the tasks listed in the activity the last time it was done. Ask them to use direct object pronouns. (**En mi casa yo la preparé.**) Remind them that it is acceptable to give imaginary "facts" about their families, or to talk about another family.

En mi cuaderno

38 For an additional Chapter 10 journal entry suggestion, see *Practice and Activity Book,* page 154.

CLOSE

Write the following questions on the board or a transparency: **¿Quién lavó la ropa? ¿Quién limpió la cocina la semana pasada? ¿Quién preparó la cena anoche? ¿Quién lavó el carro ayer? ¿Quién organizó el cuarto?** Call on students to answer one of the questions based on the information in Activity 36. Then ask more questions, having students answer with their books closed.

ASSESS

Quiz 10-3, *Chapter Teaching Resources, Book 3,* pp. 85–86

Assessment Items, Audiocassette 8B/Audio CD 10

Performance Assessment

Have students work in pairs to role-play a telephone conversation in which they talk about what they did this past weekend. Students should be prepared to present their dialogue to the class.

READING STRATEGY

Making comparisons while reading

PREREADING
Activity A

Motivating Activity

Have students take a few moments to look at the background objects and the pictures on these pages. Ask them to call out adjectives these pictures and objects bring to mind. Have a volunteer write these on the board. Then have the class break into groups of three or four to complete Activity A.

READING
Activities B and C

Teaching Suggestion

Ask students to use other reading strategies they have learned to help them to understand these passages. Ask them to point out cognates, skim for main ideas, and make an outline of each of the festivals described here.

Native Speakers

Ask native speakers to share with the class what their favorite aspects of various holidays are. Ask them which celebrations or activities are most important to them, and why. Then open the discussion up to the class and see if non-native speakers can make some comparisons with holidays that they celebrate. Ask students if they think there are common aspects to celebrations around the world that make holidays special to everyone. (time with family and friends, special foods, costumes) As a variation, have native speakers write a description of their favorite holiday.

VAMOS A LEER

Festivales del mundo hispano

Estrategia

Make comparisons while reading. When you read a passage that discusses the same thing from different perspectives, it's logical to make comparisons. When you consciously try to compare and contrast new ideas, they will be clearer in your mind. You can either make comparisons in your head as you read, or you can write them. You will remember the most if you write your comparisons while you are reading.

¡A comenzar!

These reading passages are about festivals around the world. You won't read about the same things for every place, but there will be enough in common to make comparisons with some local and national festivals in the United States.

¿Te acuerdas?

Use your background knowledge before you read in depth.

A. In groups of three or four students, complete these statements about festivals. Be sure to write your answers.

In your hometown . . .

1. people often visit during ______.
2. some favorite festival foods are ______.

San Antonio

Los eventos de Fiesta San Antonio, los cuales muestran la individualidad de San Antonio y sus influencias multiculturales, comienzan al principio del mes de abril. Esta celebración de 10 días de comida y diversión incluye desfiles, remembranzas históricas, coronaciones de la realeza, exhibiciones de arte, festivales, conciertos musicales, eventos deportivos, fuegos artificiales y mucho, mucho más. Hay pocos eventos de Fiesta en donde no puede ir toda la familia junta a divertirse.

España

España tiene más de 3,000 festivales cada año. Los más famosos son: las "Fallas de Valencia", la "Feria de Abril" en Sevilla, la "Fiesta de San Fermín" y la "Semana Santa" sevillana. En las Fallas, en marzo, se erigen "ninots"; el nombre "ninot" se refiere a las pequeñas figuras hechas a mano. Todas estas figuras son quemadas en la noche de San José, excepto la mejor, la cual se envía a un museo especial. La procesión de la Feria de Abril en Sevilla incluye hombres a caballo y mujeres en vestidos alegres. A lo largo de los bulevares se colocan puestos que sirven comida típica; hay bailes, música y diversión general.

Miami

La noche de carnaval ilumina el Tazón de la Naranja a principios de marzo con un desfile de estrellas de la música latina y del entretenimiento en el inicio del "Carnaval de Miami". Música salsa, disfraces coloridos y platillos cubanos dan sabor a la celebración de una semana que culmina con la fiesta de un día entero en la Calle Ocho, en el corazón de la Pequeña Habana. El propósito del festival es festejar la herencia hispana de Miami.

Multicultural Link

Major festivals like **la Feria de Sevilla, el Día de los Muertos** in Mexico, **Las Fallas de Valencia,** and **Fiesta** in San Antonio unite entire cities in the spirit of goodwill. Some cities or regions are very proud of their famous festivities. Ask students what other regional festivals they know about. (Mardi Gras in New Orleans and French-speaking countries; Chinese New Year in China and in cities with large Chinese populations; Carnival in Brazil; Oktoberfest in Germany)

Puerto Rico

El "Festival de las Máscaras" se celebra del 24 al 28 de diciembre en Hatillo, al noreste de la isla. El festival muestra las raíces primitivas de la música folklórica y los desfiles de los "vejigantes" con sus máscaras y disfraces coloridos.

México

En las tres últimas semanas de octubre, Guanajuato se convierte en la ciudad anfitriona del Festival Cervantino, una amalgama internacional de conciertos musicales, obras de teatro en auditorios o en las calles de la ciudad, exhibiciones de arte y espectáculos para niños. En la Plaza de San Roque se presentan compañías de ballet, obras de teatro y conciertos. Varios espectáculos callejeros que no están programados son: la pantomima, el mariachi, las estudiantinas, la música folklórica y la de rock.

Ecuador

En Quito del 28 de diciembre al 6 de enero, la fiesta de año nuevo, conocida como la fiesta de los "inocentes", hace que se llenen las calles de gente. Otro festival, el de la semana que termina el 5 de diciembre, celebra la fundación de la ciudad. Hay música y toros en las calles. El carnaval en Shrovetide se celebra, como en todos los países andinos, arrojando bolsas de plástico con agua a los paseantes (especialmente turistas), de modo que se necesita un impermeable y un paraguas en esa estación.

3. some special festival activities for adults or children include ______.
4. typical festival music is ______.

Al grano

B. Now read about festivals in six different places. Use the reading passages to answer the same six questions that you've just answered for San Antonio, Mexico, and Miami.

C. You've read about festivals in other places, and you've written information you can use to make comparisons. In Activity D you'll decide in which place you think the festivals are most appealing. But before making any decisions, answer the following questions:

1. What are four of Spain's most famous festivals?
2. What are three things that give the **Carnaval de Miami** its flavor?
3. In what city in Puerto Rico and during what time of year do they celebrate the **Festival de las Máscaras**?
4. What two things should you bring with you when you go to **El Carnaval** in Ecuador?
5. What are some things you may see at the **Festival Cervantino** in Mexico?
6. What are five things to do at the **Fiesta San Antonio**?

D. Imagina que tú puedes visitar uno de estos seis lugares. Escoge uno de los festivales y haz una lista de los eventos que te gustaría ver. Después, reúnete con dos compañeros de clase y decide a qué lugar quieren ir juntos. ¡Todos deben estar de acuerdo! Asegúrense de tomar sus decisiones según la lectura.

POSTREADING
Activity C

Teaching Suggestions

- Have students write three pairs of sentences, one pair for each of the three Spanish-speaking countries featured in **Vamos a leer.** The first sentence should be about a festival in Spain, Ecuador, or Mexico. The second sentence should be about a festival in the United States. The two sentences should show how the festivals are similar. **(Ecuador: Durante el carnaval en Shrovetide, la gente tira bolsas de plástico con agua. Los Estados Unidos: En los desfiles del Día de Acción de Gracias, la gente tira confeti serpentinas y dulces.)**
- Have students prepare an oral presentation highlighting the music, the dances, and the traditional costumes of a Spanish-speaking country or region within the country. A few suggestions: **La Zarzuela** of Spain, **El Flamenco** of Andalucía, **La Jota** of Aragón, **El Baile Folklórico (El Jarabe Tapatío)** of Mexico, **El Merengue** of the Dominican Republic, **el Tango** of Argentina.
- Native speakers and other students familiar with today's music scene might enjoy reporting on current music and dances. **(La rumba y el mambo son bailes tradicionales de Cuba. Hoy día los cubanos jóvenes que viven en Miami prefieren escuchar la música de Gloria Estefan del conjunto el Miami Sound Machine...)**

Teacher Note

For additional readings, see *Native Speaker Activity Book,* pp. 46–50 and *Practice and Activity Book,* p. 119.

History Link

Have students research why the Roman Catholic church has had such a great influence on Spain and Latin America. Who financed the early voyages to Latin America? (the Catholic monarchs) What was going on in Spain and in the rest of Europe at the time? (a struggle between Roman Catholic and Protestant religions) Have students present what they learn to the class.

Thinking Critically

Comparing and Contrasting Have students research the Mexican **Día de los Muertos** and write a short paper comparing attitudes toward death in Mexico and the United States. Or you might tell the class about this holiday and encourage a class discussion on this topic. You could mention Octavio Paz's statement: "The Mexican is familiar with death, jokes about it, caresses it, sleeps with it, celebrates it."

Repaso reviews all five skills and culture in preparation for the Chapter Test.

For Individual Needs

2 Challenge You might ask students to work in groups so they can pool their information to create a detailed description of the picture and what the people are doing. Challenge the groups to add as much information as possible. Ask the groups to share their descriptions with the class.

Teaching Suggestion

3 Ask students to come up with as many combinations of commands, requests, and responses as they can for these pictures based on what they've learned in the chapter. Encourage them to be imaginative.

Portfolio

Written Ask students to write a letter to a friend or relative who will be coming home to celebrate a special family holiday. They should tell what each person is doing now to prepare for the occasion and ask the person's opinion about a special gift for someone in the family. For Portfolio suggestions, see *Assessment Guide*, pp. 2–13.

REPASO

1 Listen to Mariana tell about her favorite holiday. Write the information requested for each question.

1. ¿Adónde viajaron Mariana y su familia?
2. ¿Por qué viajaron allí?
3. ¿En qué mes viajaron?
4. ¿Qué preparó la abuela?
5. Después de la cena, ¿qué hicieron todos?
6. ¿Por qué es la Navidad su fiesta favorita?

Answers on p. 255D.

2 Look at the picture of everyone at the Villarreal house getting ready for Hector's graduation party. Write a sentence telling what each person is doing right now.

3 Look at the pictures and create a conversation with a partner in which one person tells the other what to do to help, and the other responds to the request.

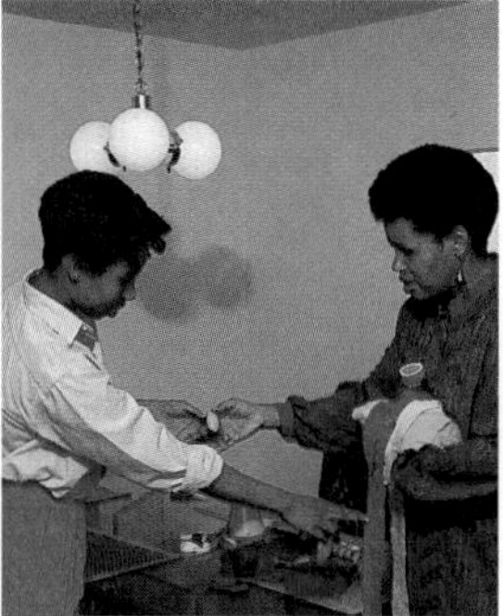
a.

b.

c.

4 You're in charge of planning a celebration. Choosing elements from each of the boxes, decide what kind of food and drink you want to have, what time the party will start, and how many guests you'll invite. Make a list of your decisions.

comida	bebidas	hora	invitados
hamburguesas	refrescos	7:30	15
ensalada	limonada	9:00	25
comida china	café	8:30	10
comida mexicana	agua	5:00	30
sándwiches	batidos	¿?	¿?
fruta	¿?		
pizza			
¿?			

Family Link

Ask the students to talk with an older relative or friend to find out how they celebrated holidays when they were younger. Tell them to be sure to ask where the person grew up. Have students share their findings with the class.

5 List six activities related to school, preparing for a party, or spending time with your family. Then get together with a partner and take turns asking each other what you think of each activity on the list. Do you and your partner share the same opinion of any of the activities? Be prepared to report your findings to the class.

6 Write a short paragraph about what you learned about celebrations in Spanish-speaking countries. In your paragraph, compare these celebrations to those in the United States. State three differences and three similarities in the way in which celebrations are observed.

7 Read the minutes from the last Spanish Club outting and answer the questions that follow.

Las noticias del Club de español **Semana no. 3**

El sábado todos lo pasamos bien. Todos llegaron al parque para el picnic del Club de español a las nueve de la mañana. Cada persona preparó algo para comer. Yo preparé un postre y la profesora preparó unos sándwiches muy ricos. Celebramos el cumpleaños de la profesora. Compramos un reloj para ella. En la fiesta, Alicia tocó la guitarra y Felipe y Sara cantaron canciones en español. Muchas personas bailaron también. Nadamos en el lago y jugamos al béisbol y al tenis. A las nueve de la noche llegamos a casa cansados, pero contentos.

Tomás Wilson, secretario

1. ¿Cuándo llegaron los estudiantes a la fiesta?
2. ¿Qué preparó la profesora para la fiesta?
3. ¿Qué le compraron a la profesora? ¿Por qué?
4. ¿Qué hizo Alicia? ¿y Felipe?
5. ¿A qué hora llegaron todos a casa? ¿y cómo?

8 **SITUACIÓN**

You're on a committee to plan the end-of-the-year dance. But there are some problems. Your class doesn't have enough money. Work with three or four classmates to discuss a solution to the problem. Give your opinion about food, activities, and a location that will fit your budget. You may also suggest ways to earn money for the project. Be prepared to present your conversation to the class.

Teaching Suggestion

7 Ask the groups of students to brainstorm about three other gift-giving occasions. Have them discuss what they would need to do or buy according to the party theme. You might have them share their ideas with the class. Encourage them to be creative.

Portfolio

Written Ask each student to create a greeting card to send to a friend or relative using expressions from Chapter 10 and helpful information from previous chapters. They should be clever and include drawings or magazine photos. Students may wish to include their greeting card in their written Portfolio. For Portfolio suggestions, see *Assessment Guide,* p. 23.

8 Oral You might have students include their conversations from **Situación** in their oral Portfolio. For Portfolio suggestions, see *Assessment Guide,* p. 23.

Video Wrap-Up

- ***Video Program***
- ***Expanded Video Program, Videocassette 4***
- ***Videodisc Program, Videodisc 5B***

At this time, you might want to use the video resources for additional review and enrichment. See *Video Guide* and *Videodisc Guide* for suggestions regarding:
- **¡Felicidades Héctor!** (Dramatic episode)
- **Panorama cultural** (Interviews)
- **Video clips** (Authentic footage)

Game

Treinta segundos Prior to class prepare a list of questions to ask what people are doing at that moment. (**¿Qué está haciendo el profesor de matemáticas? ¿Qué están haciendo tus amigos? ¿Qué estoy haciendo?**) Divide the class into two teams. Each team receives one point per logical answer given in 30 seconds. An answer might be **El profesor está hablando y está escribiendo en la pizarra.** As a variation, ask students what people did in the past, using **-ar** verbs. (**Qué compraste ayer? Compré un regalo para María.**)

A VER SI PUEDO...
CHAPTER 10

This page is intended to help students prepare independently for the Chapter Test. It is a brief checklist of the major points covered in the chapter. The students should be reminded that it is only a checklist and does not necessarily include everything that will appear on the Chapter Test.

Teaching Suggestions

2 Ask students the same questions using the preterite tense. (How would you say that Manuel bought the cake?) Have them answer appropriately.

3 Ask students to list possible answers to these questions.

4 Ask students to write response notes from two of the Spanish club members, one responding positively and one responding negatively.

Additional Practice

5 Have students say that they are doing the activities mentioned in this exercise. **(1. Estoy estudiando más. 2. Estoy haciendo mi tarea.)**

A VER SI PUEDO . . .

Can you talk about what you're doing right now? p. 262

1 How would you ask a classmate what her or his favorite holiday is, why it's a favorite, and how it's celebrated? See answers below.

2 How would you say that . . .?
1. Héctor is opening gifts
2. Manuel is buying the cake
3. Rebeca is calling the guests
4. Mario and Juan are decorating the living room
5. Abuela is preparing the tamales
6. We are all eating and drinking
7. Aníbal is talking on the phone
8. Eva and Lisa are blowing up balloons

See answers below.

Can you ask for and give an opinion? p. 264

3 How would you ask a guest what she or he thinks of . . .?
1. the party
2. the food
3. the music
4. the dessert

See answers below.

Can you ask for help and respond to requests? p. 266

4 The Spanish Club is planning an end-of-the-year party. Can you write notes to five club members asking for their help in completing the preparations?

Can you tell a friend what to do? p. 268

5 How would you tell a friend to do the following things?
1. study more
2. do your homework
3. organize your room
4. read your book
5. eat more vegetables
6. do exercises
7. attend class every day
8. help at home

See answers below.

Can you talk about past events? p. 271

6 Can you write a sentence for each drawing saying what these people did last night? Use your imagination and create a name for each person. Answers will vary.

a.

b.

c.

d.

e.

f.

Answers

1 *Sample answers:* ¿Cuál es tu día festivo favorito? ¿Por qué? ¿Cómo se celebra ese día?

2
1. Héctor está abriendo regalos.
2. Manuel está comprando el pastel.
3. Rebeca está llamando a los invitados.
4. Mario y Juan están decorando la sala.
5. La abuela está preparando los tamales.
6. Todos estamos comiendo y bebiendo.
7. Aníbal está hablando por teléfono.
8. Eva y Lisa están inflando los globos.

3 *Answers may vary.*
1. ¿Qué piensas de la fiesta?
2. ¿Qué piensas de la comida?
3. ¿Qué te parece la música?
4. ¿Te gusta el postre?

5
1. Estudia más.
2. Haz tu tarea.
3. Organiza tu cuarto.
4. Lee tu libro.
5. Come más vegetales.
6. Haz ejercicios.
7. Asiste a clase todos los días.
8. Ayuda en casa.

6 *Answers will vary.* Students should use chapter vocabulary.

VOCABULARIO

PRIMER PASO

Talking about what you're doing right now

el Año Nuevo *New Year's day*
colgar (ue) las decoraciones *to hang decorations*
decorar *to decorate*
el Día de Acción de Gracias *Thanksgiving*
el Día de los Enamorados *Valentine's Day*
el Día de la Independencia *Independence Day*
el Día de la Madre *Mother's Day*
el Día del Padre *Father's Day*
los días festivos *holidays*
la Navidad *Christmas*
la Nochebuena *Christmas Eve*
la Nochevieja *New Year's Eve*
las Pascuas *Easter*

Asking for and giving an opinion

Buena idea. *Good idea.*
creer *to believe, to think*
Creo que no. *I don't think so.*
Creo que sí. *I think so.*
Me parece bien. *It seems fine with me.*
Perfecto. *Perfect.*
¿Qué te parece si...? *How do you feel about . . .?*

SEGUNDO PASO

Asking for help and responding to requests

abrir los regalos *to open gifts*
¡Con mucho gusto! *Sure!*
inflar los globos *to blow up balloons*
llamar a los invitados *to call the guests*
mandar las invitaciones *to send invitations*
¿Me ayudas a...? *Can you help me . . .?*
¿Me haces el favor de...? *Can you do me the favor of . . .?*
¿Me pasas...? *Can you pass me . . .?*
¿Me traes...? *Can you (familiar) bring me . . .?*
Perdóname. *Excuse me.*
recibir regalos *to receive gifts*
Un momentito. *Just a second.*

Telling a friend what to do

De acuerdo. *Agreed.*
haz *do, make!*
pon *put, place!*
ve *go!*
ven *come!*
vete *go away!*

TERCER PASO

Talking about past events

anoche *last night*
anteayer *day before yesterday*
el año pasado *last year*
ayer *yesterday*
la, lo *it/her/him*
¿Qué hiciste? *What did you do?*
¿Qué hizo? *What did he/she/you do?*
el sábado pasado *last Saturday*
la semana pasada *last week*
el verano pasado *last summer*

Teaching Suggestion

Group Work Have students work in groups of three or four and write a letter in which they include as many vocabulary words as possible. Suggest that they underline vocabulary words each time they use them. You might set a time limit for this activity. When time is up, have one student from each group tell the class how many words they were able to include. Ask another student from each group to read the letter. You might like to have the class judge which letter was the most creative.

Chapter 10 Assessment

Chapter Test

- *Chapter Teaching Resources, Book 3,* pp. 87–92
- *Assessment Guide, Speaking Test,* p. 32
- *Assessment Items, Audiocassette 8B Audio CD 10*

Test Generator, Chapter 10

Alternative Assessment

Performance Assessment

You might have students present the **Situación** on page 279 as a cumulative performance assessment.

Portfolio Assessment

- **Written:** *Teacher's Edition,* p. 279
  Assessment Guide, p. 23
- **Oral: Repaso** Activity 8, *Pupil's Edition,* p. 279
  Assessment Guide, p. 23

Game

Palabras prohibidas Make cards with one vocabulary word on each card. Divide the class into two teams and set up a desk at the front of the classroom with two chairs facing each other. A student from each team plays in turn. One student is the reader (**lector/a**) and the other is the guesser (**adivinador/a**). Give the reader five cards and tell him or her not to look at them yet. Set a time limit of one minute (may be varied as needed). When you say **¡Empieza!** the reader looks at the first card. He or she gives the guesser verbal clues without saying the word on the card or a derivative of it. (If the word is **invitación,** the reader might say **fiesta, planear, tarjeta, hora,** or **persona que hace la fiesta,** but words like **invitado** and **invitar** are not allowed.) Neither student may use gestures. If the guesser gets the word right, the reader moves on to the next card. The team gets one point for each word the guesser gets in one minute.

LOCATION OPENER
CHAPTERS
11, 12

¡Ven conmigo a Puerto Rico!

pp. 282–335

EXPANDED VIDEO PROGRAM, *Videocassette 4*

OR VIDEODISC PROGRAM, *Videodisc 6A*

Motivating Activity

Ask students to name a territory in the Caribbean that belongs to the United States. (Puerto Rico, U.S. Virgin Islands) Ask students what they already know about Puerto Rico. Ask students who have been there to describe it, or have students tell what they think it may be like.

Background Information

Puerto Rico is the smallest of the Greater Antilles Islands. It is 100 miles long and 35 miles wide. The first known inhabitants of Puerto Rico were the Taíno, who greeted Columbus and the Spanish settlers in 1493. During the first three centuries of the Spanish colonial period, the settlers frequently battled their Dutch and English rivals in order to maintain control of the island. The seven-square-block area of Old San Juan was once completely enclosed by a wall and patroled day and night. At sundown, access to the city was restricted. One of the most famous fortresses of San Juan is **La Fortaleza**, also known as **Palacio de Santa Catalina.**

CAPÍTULOS 11 y 12

¡Ven conmigo a Puerto Rico!

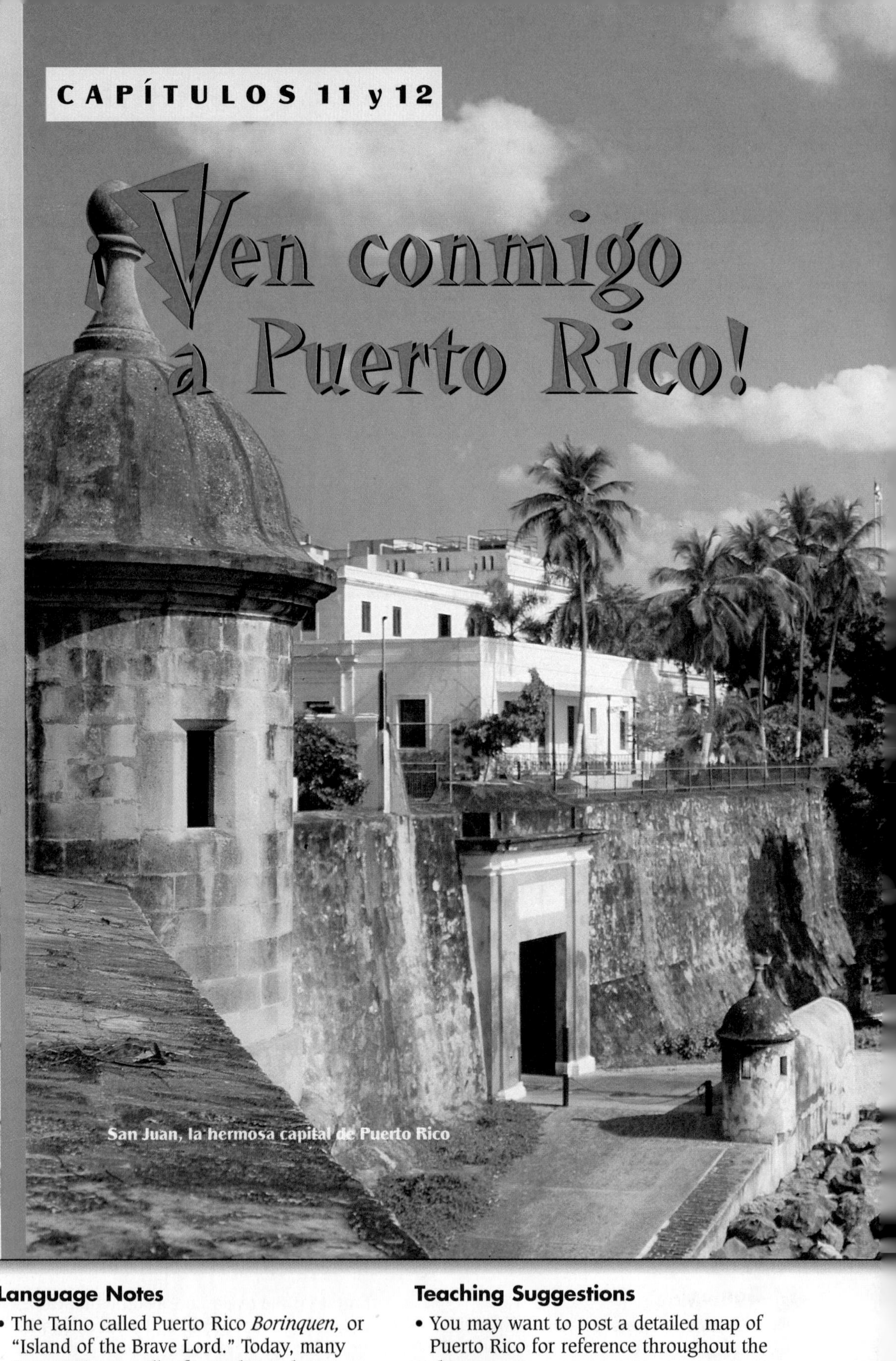

San Juan, la hermosa capital de Puerto Rico

Language Notes

- The Taíno called Puerto Rico *Borinquen,* or "Island of the Brave Lord." Today, many Puerto Ricans still refer to themselves as **boricuas.**
- Oranges are a popular fruit in the Caribbean. They originated in the part of Asia that now includes southwestern China. For this reason, oranges are usually called **chinas** in Puerto Rico.

Teaching Suggestions

- You may want to post a detailed map of Puerto Rico for reference throughout the chapter.
- You may want to put up photographs of famous Puerto Rican people including Rosie Perez, Rita Moreno, Jimmy Smits (actors), Chayanne (singer), Juan González, Iván Rodríguez (baseball players), and the late Raúl Julia (actor).

Puerto Rico

Población: 3.580.332 (el 99.9% habla español, pero la mayoría habla inglés también)

Área: 8.897 kilómetros cuadrados (3.435 millas cuadradas)

Ubicación: una isla entre el océano Atlántico al norte y el mar Caribe al sur

Capital: San Juan, con una población de 840.000

Gobierno: estado libre asociado

Industrias: la pesca, productos farmacéuticos, maquinarias y metales, turismo

Cosechas principales: azúcar, tabaco, café, piña, plátanos, coco

Minerales: arcilla, caliza, cobalto, cobre, hierro, níquel

Unidad monetaria: el dólar

Idiomas: español, inglés

LOCATION OPENER
CHAPTERS
11, 12

Using the Almanac and Map

Terms in the Almanac

- **Gobierno:** Since 1952 Puerto Rico has been a commonwealth of the U.S., or **estado libre asociado.** When living on the island, Puerto Ricans cannot vote in presidential elections and do not pay federal income tax. However, Puerto Ricans do have full U.S. citizenship. If they move to the U.S. mainland, they may vote, and they must also pay federal taxes.
- **Minerales: arcilla** *clay;* **caliza** *limestone;* **cobalto** *cobalt;* **cobre** *copper;* **hierro** *iron;* **níquel** *nickel*
- **Unidad monetaria:** Puerto Rico uses U.S. currency, but the names of units may be different. A *dollar* is sometimes called a **peso.** The *half-dollar* is called **medio peso,** a *quarter* is a **peseta,** a *nickel* is a **níquel** or **vellón,** and a *penny* is a **chavo** or **centavo.** As in English, a ten-cent coin is pronounced *dime.* People sometimes say **chavo** for money, and if you don't have any, you are **pelado** or **sin chavo.**
- **Idiomas:** On January 28, 1993, Governor Luis Muñoz Marín declared both Spanish and English the official languages of Puerto Rico.

Using the Map

- Direct students to point out the West Indies archipelago. (Greater Antilles, Lesser Antilles, Bahama Islands)
- Have students locate the islands that constitute the Greater Antilles archipelago. (Cuba; Jamaica; Hispaniola, which includes Haiti and the Dominican Republic)
- Ask students to identify the bodies of water that surround Puerto Rico. (Atlantic Ocean and Caribbean Sea) You may want to tell students that it only takes about six hours to drive around the island.

LOCATION OPENER
CHAPTERS
11, 12

Using the Photo Essay

① The City Hall (**la Alcaldía**) was built in stages from 1604 to 1789. It is one of the government buildings that surrounds the **Plaza de Armas,** so named for the drills carried out by the city's inhabitants in preparation for attack by pirates. Planned in the 16th century as San Juan's main square, the **Plaza de Armas** later became a social gathering place.

② Hotels and high rise condominiums along the shore of Isla Verde were built within the last 30 years. Today, Isla Verde is one of San Juan's top tourist centers, with miles of beaches, hotels, restaurants, and boutiques. Puerto Rico has 280 miles of shoreline dotted with popular resorts including Luquillo, Condado, Miramar, and Ocean Park.

Culture Note

La música salsa is derived from the **rumba,** a dance music of Afro-Cuban origin. The instruments normally used for **salsa** are the piano, trumpet, saxophone, and percussion instruments like the **güiro,** conga and bongo drums. Vocals are crucial to **salsa:** the lyrics often combine poetry and politics. **Salsa** was introduced in 1930s in the dance halls of New York City where it became wildly popular. Since then legendary **salseros** Willie Colón, Celia Cruz, Rubén Blades, and Tito Puente have made **salsa** a favorite musical style throughout the Spanish-speaking world and beyond.

PUERTO RICO

Discovered by Columbus on November 19, 1493, Puerto Rico is one of the most beautiful islands in the Caribbean. The island is mostly mountainous and has a tropical climate and many picturesque beaches. Puerto Rican cultural life is a mixture of Antillean, African, Spanish, and North American influences.

② Puerto Rico has magnificent beaches scattered along hundreds of miles of coastline. This makes the island an ideal location for water sports activities for islanders and visitors from around the world.

① Begun in 1602, the historic Alcaldía *(City Hall)* houses both the local government and small businesses. The adjacent Plaza de Armas served as the training field for Spanish soldiers defending the islands.

Language Note

Puerto Ricans speak differently depending on where they are from on the island. For example, the people from Mayagüez on the west coast pronounce the **r** similarly to the uvular [r], as in French, and people from Jayuya in the central Cordillera end words by pronouncing the final **e** as an **i** (**leche** would be pronounced *lechi*). You may want to refer to the Language Note on page 289 for more information on Puerto Rican accents.

③ The main shopping avenue in old San Juan is Calle de Cristo. The narrow cobblestone streets are busy day and night.

Chapters 11 and 12 will introduce you to Ben and his sister Carmen, two New Yorkers visiting relatives in Puerto Rico. They, along with their mother and grandfather, visit some of the fascinating and beautiful places on the island of Puerto Rico. How would you like to spend two weeks on an island?

④ Throughout Puerto Rico you'll find tantalizing foods, ranging from a wide variety of seafood to delicious, tropical fruits.

⑤ The Castle of El Morro, built by the Spanish between 1539 and 1584, is a six-level fortress, with walls 140 feet high and 20 feet thick. It was once the first line of defense for all of Spain's possessions in the Americas.

⑥ Almost every holiday is an occasion for a festival in Puerto Rico.

Culture Note

The Taíno cultivated corn (**maíz**), peanuts (**maní**), yams (**ñame**), taro (**yautía**), and cassava (**yuca**). Fruits such as guava (**guayaba**), pineapple (**piña**), and sea grapes (**uvas playeras**) grew wild. These foods are all still popular in Puerto Rico today. The Taíno also cultivated arrowroot (**arrurruz**), which they called *aru-aru,* meaning "meal of meals."

LOCATION OPENER
CHAPTERS 11, 12

③ Cristo Street in Old San Juan is the home of the **Centro Nacional de Artes Populares y Artesanías** of the Institute of Puerto Rican Culture. Nearby is the **Casa del Libro,** a collection of rare books, some pre-16th century. At the end of the street is the **Capilla de Cristo,** a chapel with a small silver altar.

Culture Note

During the 18th century, horse racing in the streets of San Juan was common. According to legend, in 1753 a horse racer named Baltasar Montáñez failed to make the turn at the south end of Calle Cristo and plunged over the cliff—but miraculously survived. Capilla de Cristo was built both to commemorate the miracle and to block off Calle Cristo.

④ Some typical Puerto Rican dishes include deep-fried **tostones,** made from sliced plantains or breadfruit (**pana**). Pork dishes include fried rinds (**chicharrón**), a tripe stew (**mondongo**), and **gandinga,** made from minced liver, heart, and kidney. Bananas are often fried to make a sweet dessert. Another popular food is **pastel,** which is not a dessert, but a **tamal** made with meat, olives, onions, and plantain flour.

⑤ **El Morro** (*headland* or *promontory*) is the oldest and most strategic in San Juan. Its six levels rise more than 140 feet and dominate the harbor entrance. It was originally named **San Felipe del Morro,** in honor of King Philip III of Spain. A deep moat surrounds its 18-foot-thick walls, and it is equipped with barracks, wells, supply rooms, dungeons, a chapel, and an armory.

Capítulo 11: Para vivir bien
Chapter Overview

De antemano pp. 288–290 — **Un recorrido por San Juan** — *Practice and Activity Book,* p. 121 — *Video Guide* OR *Videodisc Guide*

	FUNCTIONS	GRAMMAR	CULTURE	RE-ENTRY
Primer paso pp. 291–293	Making suggestions and expressing feelings, p. 291	Present tense of **sentirse,** p. 291	• Realia, **Drogas no y cuestionario,** p. 293 • Questionnaire about living well, p. 293	• **e** to **ie** stem-changing verbs • Food vocabulary • Expressions of frequency
Segundo paso pp. 294–299	Talking about moods and physical condition, p. 294	The verb **doler** with **me, te, le,** p. 296	• Magazine article on relieving stress, p. 297 • **Nota cultural,** Baseball in Spanish-speaking countries, p. 298 • **Panorama cultural, ¿Qué deporte practicas?,** p. 299	• Definite articles • **estar** + condition • **o** to **ue** stem-changing verbs
Tercer paso pp. 300–305	• Saying what you did, p. 300 • Talking about where you went and when, p. 302	• The verb **jugar** in the preterite, p. 300 • **ir** in the preterite, p. 302	• **Nota cultural,** American football versus soccer, **jai alai,** p. 301 • **Encuentro cultural, Remedios caseros,** p. 305	• Use of preterite tense to discuss past events • Sports

Letra y sonido p. 304 — **Pronunciación:** Strong versus weak vowels — **Dictado:** *Textbook Audiocassette 6A/Audio CD 11*

Vamos a leer pp. 306–307 — **Para estar en forma** — **Reading Strategy:** Using background knowledge

Review pp. 308–311 — **Repaso,** pp. 308–309 — **A ver si puedo...,** p. 310 — **Vocabulario,** p. 311

Assessment Options

Quizzes
- *Chapter Teaching Resources, Book 3*
  Primer paso, Quiz 11-1, pp. 139–140
  Segundo paso, Quiz 11-2, pp. 141–142
  Tercer paso, Quiz 11-3, pp. 143–144
- *Assessment Items, Audiocassette 8B/Audio CD 11*

Chapter Test
- *Chapter Teaching Resources, Book 3,* pp. 145–150
- *Assessment Guide,* Speaking Test, p. 33
- *Assessment Items, Audiocassette 8B/Audio CD 11*

Test Generator, Chapter 11

RESOURCES: Print	RESOURCES: Audiovisual
Video Program OR *Expanded Video Program, Videocassette 4* OR *Videodisc Program, Videodisc 6A*	*Textbook Audiocassette 6A/Audio CD 11*
	Textbook Audiocassette 6A/Audio CD 11
Practice and Activity Book, pp. 122–124	
Native Speaker Activity Book, pp. 51–55	
Chapter Teaching Resources, Book 3	
• Additional Listening Activities 11-1, 11-2, p. 127	*Audiocassette 10B/Audio CD 11*
• Student Response Forms, pp. 136–138	
• Realia 11-1, p. 131, 133	
• Situation Cards 11-1, pp. 134–135	
• Teaching Transparency Master 11-1, pp. 123, 126	*Teaching Transparency 11-1*
• Quiz 11-1, pp. 139–140	*Assessment Items, Audiocassette 8B/Audio CD 11*
Videodisc Guide	*Videodisc Program, Videodisc 6A*
	Textbook Audiocassette 6A/Audio CD 11
Practice and Activity Book, pp. 125–127	
Native Speaker Activity Book, pp. 51–55	
Chapter Teaching Resources, Book 3	
• Communicative Activity 11-1, pp. 119–120	
• Additional Listening Activities 11-3, 11-4, p. 128	*Audiocassette 10B/Audio CD 11*
• Student Response Forms, pp. 136–138	
• Realia 11-1, pp. 131, 133	
• Situation Cards 11-2, pp. 134–135	
• Teaching Transparency Master 11-2, pp. 124, 126	*Teaching Transparency 11-2*
• Quiz 11-2, pp. 141–142	*Assessment Items, Audiocassette 8B/Audio CD 11*
Video Guide	*Video Program* OR *Expanded Video Progarm, Videocassette 4*
Videodisc Guide	*Videodisc Program, Videodisc 6A*
	Textbook Audiocassette 6A/Audio CD 11
Practice and Activity Book, pp. 128–130	
Native Speaker Activity Book, pp. 51–55	
Chapter Teaching Resources, Book 3	
• Communicative Activity 11-2, pp. 121–122	
• Additional Listening Activities 11-5, 11-6, p. 129	*Audiocassette 10B/Audio CD 11*
• Student Response Forms, pp. 136–138	
• Realia 11-2, pp. 132, 133	
• Situation Cards 11-3, pp. 134–135	
• Teaching Transparency Master 11-3, pp. 125, 126	*Teaching Transparency 11-3*
• Quiz 11-3, pp. 143–144	*Assessment Items, Audiocassette 8B/Audio CD 11*
Videodisc Guide	*Videodisc Program, Videodisc 6A*

Alternative Assessment

- Performance Assessment
  Primer paso, p. 293
  Segundo paso, p. 298
  Tercer paso, p. 304
- Portfolio Assessment
  Written: Activity 31, *Pupil's Edition*, p. 302
  Assessment Guide, p. 24
  Oral: **Repaso** Activity 3, *Pupil's Edition*, p. 308
  Assessment Guide, p. 24

Capítulo 11: Para vivir bien
Textbook Listening Activities Scripts

For Student Response Forms, see *Chapter Teaching Resources, Book 3,* pp. 136–138.

Primer paso

Activity 6, p. 291

1. No sé qué me pasa. Siempre me siento muy cansada. ¿Qué hago?
2. Bueno, me gusta mucho mirar la televisión. No hago mucho ejercicio pero quiero empezar a hacerlo.
3. No me gusta para nada la leche. Prefiero tomar refrescos.
4. Yo trabajo día y noche. Siempre estoy aquí en la oficina.
5. Me encanta comer pizza, hamburguesas y papas fritas.
6. No me siento bien porque casi siempre estoy en casa. Debo salir más.

Answers to Activity 6
Sample answer:
1. Natalia

Segundo paso

Activity 13, p. 294

1. ¡Uy! ¡Me siento muy mal! Tengo una fiebre de 102 grados.
2. ¡Hombre! No sé qué hacer. Hoy tengo un examen muy difícil en la clase de álgebra.
3. Esta noche voy a cantar por primera vez en un concierto y no estoy preparado.
4. ¡Qué lástima! No puedo pasar las vacaciones con mi tía en Puerto Rico.
5. Ay, mi hermanita es terrible. Siempre quiere llevar mis camisas y mis suéteres.
6. Aquí estoy en el restaurante con mi novia. No tengo el dinero para pagar la cena. ¿Qué voy a hacer?
7. No me siento bien. No puedo asisitir a clases hoy.
8. Todo el mundo está enfermo. Yo también.

Answers to Activity 13
1. 6 2. 2, 5 3. 2, 5 4. 4 5. 3 6. 2, 5 7. 7 8. 1, 8

Activity 17, p. 296

1. Ay, no puedo correr más. Estoy muy cansado.
2. Profesora, lo siento pero no puedo escribir más.
3. ¡Ay! Tomé dos batidos y cuatro hamburguesas.
4. Levanto pesas todos los días.
5. Estoy resfriada y no puedo hablar.
6. Hago muchos ejercicios aeróbicos.
7. Me gusta leer novelas día y noche.

Answers to Activity 17
1. d 2. e 3. g 4. a 5. f 6. c 7. b

Tercer paso

Activity 33, p. 303

1. Ricardo y Miguel fueron al estadio a desayunar.
2. Angélica y Marta fueron a la cancha de tenis a bailar con Roberto y Sergio.
3. Gabriel fue a la piscina a nadar.
4. Yo fui a la pista de correr a hacer yoga.
5. María y Pablo fueron a la biblioteca a escuchar el concierto.
6. Mi hermano fue al gimnasio a levantar pesas.
7. Mis padres fueron al estadio a ver un partido de fútbol.
8. Mis hermanos y yo fuimos al cine a jugar al basquetbol con nuestros primos.

Answers to Activity 33
1. no; Fueron al estadio a ver un partido de béisbol.
2. no; Fueron a la cancha de tenis a jugar al tenis con Roberto y Sergio.
3. sí
4. no; Fui a la pista de correr a hacer ejercicio.
5. no; Fueron a la biblioteca a leer.
6. sí
7. sí
8. no; Fuimos al cine y vimos una película muy buena.

Letra y sonido, p. 304

For the scripts for Parts A and C, see p. 304. The script for Part B is below.

B. Dictado

Mi horario no es fácil. Estudio geometría, historia y física. Me gusta estudiar por la tarde y ver televisión por la noche.

Repaso

Activity 4, p. 309

RAFI Ay, Sara. Estoy muy triste. El lunes regresamos a casa y yo quiero quedarme en Puerto Rico.

SARA Yo, también Rafi. Pero estoy muy contenta porque pasamos unas vacaciones maravillosas con nuestra familia. Visitamos muchos lugares en Puerto Rico.

RAFI Me gustaría regresar a El Yunque. ¡Qué interesante! Y ¡qué hermoso! Las flores, los pájaros, todo.

SARA También me gustó mucho El Yunque. Pero a mí me gusta más pasar todo el día en la playa, como la semana pasada. Nadamos, llevamos comida, jugamos al voleibol y cantamos. Ay, qué bien lo pasé.

RAFI Me gustó mucho el museo y también me gustaron los cuentos del abuelo.

SARA Sí, éstas fueron unas vacaciones maravillosas.

Answers to Repaso Activity 4

1. Rafi está muy triste.
2. Sara está triste pero también contenta.
3. Rafi quiere regresar a El Yunque. Sara quiere pasar el día en la playa.
4. A Sara le gustaron el Yunque y la playa.
5. A Rafi le gustó el museo y también le gustaron los cuentos del abuelo.

Teacher Note

The following suggestion for native speakers is a poem by Cuban poet Nicolás Guillén. It is not recorded on the scripts and is included as an application of Caribbean culture and language.

Native Speakers

In the poem **Búcate plata** Cuban poet Nicolás Guillén illustrates some of the characteristics of Caribbean Spanish. Have native speakers read the poem aloud with a Caribbean accent, substituting an aspiration where each **s** is missing. You may want to do this after the Language Note on page 289.

Búcate plata,
búcate plata,
poqque no doy un paso má:
etoy a arró con galleta,
na má.
Yo bien sé cómo etá to,
pero biejo, hay que comé:
búcate plata,
búcate plata,
poqque me boy a corré.

Depué dirán que soy mala,
y no me quedrán tratá,
pero amó con hambre, biejo,
¡qué ba!
Con tanto sapato nuebo,
¡qué ba!
Con tanto reló, compadre,
¡qué ba!
Con tanto lujo, mi negro,
¡qué ba!

Capítulo 11: Para vivir bien
Projects

A. *In this activity students will translate a Spanish refrán (proverb) and make a poster to illustrate it.*

MATERIALS

✂ **Students may need**
- Poster board
- Pens and markers
- Magazines
- Scissors
- Glue
- Bilingual dictionary

REFRANES

(Give students only the Spanish proverbs, not the English equivalents.)

Más vale pájaro en mano que cien volando.
A bird in the hand is worth two in the bush.

Hijo no tenemos y nombre le ponemos.
Don't count your chickens before they are hatched.

El hábito no hace al monje.
Clothes don't make the man.

Querer es poder.
Where there's a will, there's a way.

Ojos que no ven, corazón que no se siente.
Out of sight, out of mind.

No todo lo que brilla es oro.
All that glitters is not gold.

Cara vemos, corazón no sabemos.
Appearances are deceiving.

Donde una puerta se cierra, otra se abre.
Every cloud has a silver lining.

En boca cerrada no entran moscas.
A closed mouth does not catch flies.

Dime con quién andas y te diré quién eres.
You are known by the company you keep.

SEQUENCE

1. Divide class into small groups.
2. Assign one of the **refranes** from the list to each group.
3. Students look up the words in a bilingual dictionary and write a literal translation.
4. Students try to think of an English proverb with the same meaning and add it to their literal translation.
5. Students make a poster in which they write and illustrate the **refrán.**
6. Students present their posters to the class in Spanish, explaining what the **refrán** means and why they illustrated it as they did. Group members participate equally in talking about the poster.

GRADING THE PROJECT

The same grade should be given to all members of each group.

Suggested point distribution (total = 100 points):

Literal translation (accuracy) 30
Equivalent English proverb 20
Poster (content, design) 20
Oral presentation (grammar, vocabulary) 30

FAMILY LINK

If students are not familiar with an English proverb that has the same meaning as their **refrán,** they might ask their parents or grandparents if they know one.

B. *In this activity students will plan, script, and film an exercise video in Spanish.*

MATERIALS

- Video recorder
- Videocassettes

SEQUENCE

1. Divide class into two or three groups. Explain that the students in each group will cooperatively create a whole-body exercise video. Have students do simple exercises so as to avoid injuries.
2. Assign students the following roles: scriptwriters, editors, cameraman, narrator, exercise leaders, video participants.
3. Students write and self-edit the script, perform and film the video.
4. Show the videos to the class and have the entire class vote on the best one.

GRADING THE PROJECT

The same grade should be given to all group members.

Suggested point distribution (total = 100 points):

Ability to work cooperatively 30
Accuracy of Spanish vocabulary and structures 50
Creativity 20

Capítulo 11: Para vivir bien

On this page you will find suggestions for games in which students practice some of the functions, structures, vocabulary, and cultural features studied in Chapter 11. When planning your lessons for this chapter, remember that games such as these not only make the students' classroom experience more enjoyable, they are also effective in motivating students to practice and review.

JUGAR AL BÉISBOL

With this game students will practice the new chapter vocabulary words and expressions as well as review vocabulary from previous chapters. It may be played at the end of the chapter.

Preparation Develop a list of questions whose answers require the students to use the chapter vocabulary and vocabulary from previous chapters. (Examples: **Para evitar el estrés yo practico ______ . Para tener músculos grandes hay que levantar ______ . Debes dormir para no estar ______ . Antes de hacer ejercicio hay que ______ .**)

Procedure Divide the class into two teams. Ask one student to be the scorekeeper. Draw a baseball diamond with four bases on the board. Set a number of innings or time limit for playing.

The batter is the first player on Team A. You serve as the pitcher and ask the batter a question. If the batter gives a correct answer, he or she moves to first base. The scorekeeper places a mark on first base. If the batter cannot answer, he or she is out. You then ask a question of the second batter on Team A. If the second batter answers correctly, she or he goes to first base. If there is a player on first base, he or she advances to second base and the scorekeeper places a mark on second base.

A team scores a run by advancing a player around the bases to home plate. Team A continues batting until it has three outs. Then Team B goes to bat. When Team B has three outs, the first inning is over. Teams get one point for each run, and the team with the most points wins.

¿QUÉ DIBUJAS?

*This game is good for vocabulary review. It may be played after the **Primer paso.***

Procedure Whisper to one student, or write down on a slip of paper, a word or phrase that the class has recently studied. The student draws a representation of it on the board. This can be a drawing, a symbol, or a hint clarified through mime. The rest of the class guesses the term.

IR DE PESCA

*This game can be used to practice any vocabulary category, the verbs **tener** and **ir**, and direct object pronouns. It may be played after the **Segundo paso.***

Materials Index cards

Procedure This game follows the same basic rules as Go Fish. Divide students into groups of three to five. Give each group 48 index cards. Have them make a card deck by writing one body part on four cards, another body part on four other cards, and so on until they have 12 sets of four cards. (You might have your students draw body parts instead of write them.

The dealer shuffles the cards and deals five cards to each player. The remaining cards are placed face down in the middle of the table. The object of the game is to form as many matching pairs as possible. The dealer asks any of the players for a card that matches one the dealer has. (**¿Tienes una nariz?**) If the player has the card, he or she answers **Sí, tengo una nariz** and gives it to the dealer.

The dealer places the matching pair on the table and asks any of the players for another card. If the player doesn't have the card, he or she says **Ve de pesca** and the dealer must draw a card from the stack. Then it is the next player's turn. The game ends when one of the players has no more cards. The player with the most pairs is the winner.

JUGAR AL GOLF

*This game is good for vocabulary review. It may be played after the **Primer paso.***

Procedure Ask students to write the numbers from one to 18 on separate lines on a piece of paper. These are the 18 **hoyos** (*holes*) of their golf course. After each number they are to write a different letter of the alphabet. Then have students exchange papers with each other.

The object of the game is to make the shortest word possible at each **hoyo**, using the letter beside the number as part of the word. The player with the fewest number of strokes (letters) for the 18 **hoyos** is the winner. You may wish to shorten the game to nine holes.

Capítulo 11: Para vivir bien

pp. 286–311

Using the Chapter Opener

Motivating Activity

Initiate a discussion on physical fitness with students. How much do they believe of what they read concerning diets, exercise, and the dangers of excess. What do they like to do for exercise? Do they play sports? If they are not interested in sports, what do they like to do for fun and exercise?

Building on Previous Skills

Group Work Review the vocabulary for the different sports that the students have worked with in past chapters and the verbs **jugar, mirar, gustar,** and **encantar.** Have students interview each other in Spanish asking which sports they like to play and which ones they like to watch. They should take notes (**tomar apuntes**) on what their partner says, so they can report the conversation to the class.

Photo Flash!

① Roller skating (**patinar sobre ruedas**) is a very popular sport in Puerto Rico. Ice-skating (**patinar sobre hielo**) is also popular. San Juan has ice-skating and rollerskating rinks that are open until late at night.

Culture Notes

• On January 28, 1993, Governor Pedro Rosselló of Puerto Rico declared Spanish and English joint official languages of the island. Spanish had been the official language since 1991 when the Puerto Rican Congress declared it so. Prior to 1991, no official language had been declared for the island.

• At midnight on June 23, the eve of **el día de San Juan Bautista** (*the day of Saint John,* the patron saint of San Juan), **sanjuaneros** (*people from San Juan*) traditionally walk into the sea backwards three times for good luck for the coming year. In San Juan, as well as the rest of the island, there are many festivals that celebrate this event.

Students in Spanish-speaking countries have their own ideas about how to live well. For some, a tropical island might seem like paradise. But, living well also means paying attention to things like diet and exercise. It also includes planning activities that are fun and make one feel good.

In this chapter you will learn

- to make suggestions and express feelings
- to talk about moods and physical condition
- to say what you did and talk about where you went and when

And you will

- listen to people talk about how they feel
- read an article on how to do different exercises
- write a paragraph telling what you did last weekend to live well
- find out what living well means to students in Spanish-speaking countries

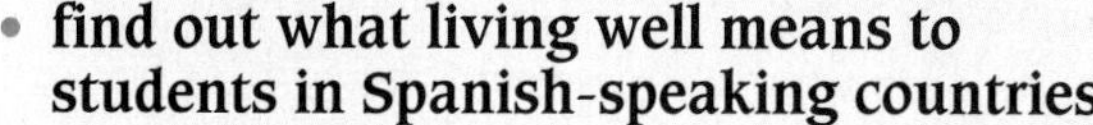

(2) **No puedo correr más. Me duelen los pies.**

(3) **En Puerto Rico fuimos a un gran partido de béisbol.**

Culture Note

In addition to the sporting activities pictured, Puerto Rico has all types of water sports, golf, tennis, hiking, horse racing, basketball, and boxing. With the island's temperate climate, most sports can be enjoyed year round. Other activities that are practiced by many Puerto Ricans are: **jugar a la paleta** (this is a type of sand-tennis) and **escalar El Yunque** (climbing the peaks of El Yunque).

Focusing on Outcomes

- Have students look at the photos on these pages and identify which learner outcomes correspond to which photo. (Photo 1 represents making suggestions; photo 2 represents talking about physical conditions; and photo 3 represents saying where you went.) Perhaps students can suggest other situations in which the outcomes might be used.
- Ask students how they feel about discussing moods, feelings, and physical conditions. How would they feel if they were unable to express such things?

Teacher Note

You may want to use the video to support the chapter objectives. The self-check activities in **A ver si puedo...** on page 310 help students assess their achievement of the learner outcomes.

Photo Flash!

(3) Many Puerto Ricans are very devoted baseball fans. They follow U.S. baseball during the spring-to-fall season, keeping up with their favorite professional teams and their favorite Puerto Rican baseball players. Many U.S. teams have training camps in Puerto Rico. In the winter they watch the Puerto Rican professional league.

Thinking Critically

Analyzing Ask students to discuss the following questions. Do moods and feelings affect one physically? If so, how? Does a smile, frown, or other gesture always mean the same thing? It not, what are possible reasons for differences?

VIDEO PROGRAM OR EXPANDED VIDEO PROGRAM, Videocassette 4

OR VIDEODISC PROGRAM, Videodisc 6A

Video Synopsis

Ben, Carmen, and their mother are New Yorkers visiting family in Puerto Rico. Ben and Carmen's mother drops them off for a day of sightseeing in San Juan and tells them she will pick them up at 3:00 at **la Plaza de Hostos.** After some time sightseeing they stop to rest and meet Pedro, a boy from San Juan. Pedro decides to accompany them to the next site, **el Castillo del Morro.** While the three are exploring **el Castillo,** Pedro asks if they have seen **la Plaza de Hostos.** Ben looks at his watch and sees that it is now 2:55.

Motivating Activity

Ask students how they and their friends decide what to do as a group. What do they do? Where do they go? Are there a few people in their circle of friends who always seem to have good ideas?

Teaching Suggestion

Ask students to estimate the age of Ben, Carmen, and Pedro by completing the expression **Me parece que...**

DE ANTEMANO

Un recorrido por San Juan

Ben and Carmen have taken time to do some exploring in San Juan, Puerto Rico. Read the **fotonovela** to find out what they see and who they meet. Why might Ben and Carmen get into trouble at the end of the episode?

1
Bueno, hijos... a las tres paso por Uds. por la Plaza de Hostos. Y después, vamos al partido de béisbol de tu tío. ¿De acuerdo?
Sí. Te esperamos en la Plaza de Hostos a las tres. ¡Adiós!

2
Vamos, tenemos todo el día para explorar el Viejo San Juan. ¿Tienes ganas de caminar?

3
Dos horas más tarde...
Ben, me duelen los pies... estoy cansada. ¿Podemos descansar? Caminamos mucho. No me siento bien.
Claro, Carmen. A mí me duelen los pies. ¿Por qué no descansamos en esta banca?

4
¡Hola! ¿Eres de San Juan?
¡Somos de Nueva York!
Sí. Y ustedes no son de aquí, ¿verdad?
Estamos en Puerto Rico de vacaciones. Estamos visitando a nuestra familia de aquí.
Me llamo Pedro Méndez.
Yo soy Benjamín, Y ésta es mi hermana Carmen.

288

RESOURCES FOR DE ANTEMANO

Textbook Audiocassette 6A/Audio CD 11
Video Guide
Video Program
Expanded Video Program, Videocassette 4
Videodisc Guide
Videodisc Program, Videodisc 6A
Practice and Activity Book, p. 121

Photo Flash!

You'll notice that Ben is wearing braces on his teeth. The Spanish term for braces is **los frenos.**

5

¿Adónde van ahora?

Bueno, ya fuimos a la Puerta de San Juan y al Museo Pablo Casals.

Yo tengo ganas de ver el Castillo del Morro. ¿Podemos?

¿Qué tal si yo los acompaño?

6

¿Juegan mucho al béisbol en Nueva York?

Sí, pero me gusta más patinar sobre ruedas, como ese muchacho que va por allí.

7

Ah, ¿patinas sobre hielo también?

Yo sí, pero no me gusta el frío. Cuando hace frío me duele la nariz y me duelen las orejas.

8

Oye, Carmen... ¡Estás corriendo mucho! ¿Siempre haces tanto ejercicio?

¡Sí! Mamá y yo hacemos mucho ejercicio. Hago aeróbicas todas las mañanas con mi mamá.

9

Bueno, ¿tienen ganas de ir a otra parte? ¿Ya fueron a la Plaza de Hostos?

No... ¡La Plaza de Hostos! ¡Ay, no! Carmen, si son las tres menos cinco! ¡Mamá nos espera en la Plaza de Hostos a las tres!

289

Presentation

Play the video or audio recording. Then have students form groups of four to practice reading the roles of Sra. Corredor, Ben, Carmen, and Pedro. You might ask one or two groups to read the dialogue aloud for the class prior to answering the questions on page 290.

Background Information

Pablo Casals (1876–1973), one of the world's leading cellists, died in Río Piedras, Puerto Rico. Born in Vendrell, Spain, Casals was an outspoken opponent of Fascism who lived most of his life in exile. He moved to Puerto Rico in 1956, where he continued his personal musical crusade for peace. He revitalized public interest in the works of J. S. Bach, especially the six unaccompanied suites for cello. At the **Museo de Pablo Casals,** one can see his cello and other memorabilia. Casals is honored by Puerto Ricans at an annual festival in mid-June in San Juan.

Language Note

Puerto Rican Spanish has several distinctive characteristics. For example, some speakers of Puerto Rican Spanish pronounce the **s** or **z** at the end of a syllable as an aspiration similar to the English *h, (graciah, arroh con pollo, ¿cómo ehtáh tú?)*. The **d** between vowels often becomes silent *(hablao, pescao, mira'a)*. The **ll** and **y** may be pronounced with a sound like the *s* in *leisure,* so that **El Yunque** is pronounced *El Zhunque.* The **r** at the end of a syllable is often pronounced like an **l**, as in *pol favol.*

Video Integration

- ***Expanded Video Program,* *Videocassette 4,***
- ***Videodisc Program,* *Videodisc 6A***

You may choose to continue with **Un recorrido por San Juan (a continuación)** now or wait until later in the chapter. At this point in the story, the kids hurry to their meeting place with Ben and Carmen's mother, where they find she has not yet arrived. When she arrives, they discover that Pedro is Ben and Carmen's cousin. Later, the family goes to a baseball game in which Pedro, Carmen, and Ben's uncle is playing.

Using the Photograph

Ask students to write a caption for this photo which Sra. Corredor put in the family album after they returned to New York from Puerto Rico.

Teaching Suggestion

3 Ask students to explain how they decided on their answers. What cues did they identify in the **fotonovela**?

For Individual Needs

4 Slower Pace Before students write their answers, have the class give adjectives describing each of the characters. Write their answers in three columns on the board or a transparency.

5 Challenge Have students in small groups revise the **fotonovela** script to reflect their community. You may wish to have the students perform their version of the local **fotonovela** for the class.

Biology Link

In the video, Carmen orders a **batido de guanábana** (*custard apple* or *soursop milkshake*) from a vendor in Old San Juan. The **guanábana** is a sweet, acidic fruit from the **guanábano** tree of the Annona species that is native to the Caribbean. Have students look up information about other trees that are native to the Americas. (guavas, papayas)

1 ¿Comprendes? See answers below.

Contesta las preguntas para ver si entiendes lo que pasa en la fotonovela.

1. Where are Ben and Carmen, and why?
2. What are they doing today?
3. Who do they meet, and where is that person from?
4. What do Ben and Pedro talk about?
5. Why is Ben upset at the end of the story?
6. What do you think they'll do? What would you do?

2 ¿Cómo se dice? See answers below.

¿Qué frases de la fotonovela puedes usar para expresar estos conceptos?

1. to suggest that you go with a friend
2. to say that your feet hurt
3. to ask if someone feels like walking
4. to say you've already been to the museum
5. to say you and a friend exercise a lot
6. to say you do aerobics
7. to say that a friend is waiting for you in the plaza

3 ¿Quién lo diría?

Con base en la fotonovela, ¿quién diría lo siguiente?

1. ¡Patinar sobre ruedas es mi deporte favorito! Ben
2. Son las tres. ¿Qué están haciendo mis hijos? Sra. Corredor
3. A mí me gustaría visitar Nueva York. Pedro
4. ¡No quiero caminar más! Tengo ganas de descansar. Carmen
5. Yo voy con ustedes al Castillo del Morro. Pedro
6. Me encanta hacer ejercicios aeróbicos. Carmen

4 ¡Escribamos! See sample answer below.

¿Qué sabes de *(What do you know about)* Ben, Carmen y Pedro? Escribe tres oraciones sobre cada persona, con base en lo que hace o dice en la fotonovela.

5 ¿Y tu ciudad?

Imagine that this story happened in a tourist spot in or near your hometown. How would the story be different? What places would Ben and Carmen go and what kind of people might they meet?

Answers

1 1. in Puerto Rico on vacation and visiting relatives
2. walking around old San Juan and visiting different places
3. Pedro from Puerto Rico
4. baseball and skating
5. It is almost 3:00 and they are not at the **Plaza de Hostos** where their mother is waiting to meet them.
6. *Answers will vary.*

2 1. ¿Qué tal si yo lo/la acompaño?
2. Me duelen los pies.
3. ¿Tienes ganas de caminar?
4. Ya fuimos al museo.
5. Mi amigo y yo hacemos mucho ejercicio.
6. Hago ejercicio aeróbico.
7. Un amigo me está esperando en la plaza.

4 *Sample answer:*
Ellos son de Nueva York. Son hermanos. Tienen familia en Puerto Rico.

PRIMER PASO

Making suggestions and expressing feelings

ASÍ SE DICE Making suggestions and expressing feelings

To suggest something to a friend, say:

¿Qué tal si vamos al gimnasio?
What if . . .?

¿Por qué no vamos mañana?

Your friend might answer:

Gracias, pero no quiero.

No, en realidad **no tengo ganas.**

To ask how a friend is feeling, say:

¿Qué tienes? ¿Te sientes mal?
What's the matter? Do you feel bad?

No, **me siento bien.** . . . *I feel fine.*

Estoy un poco cansado, **nada más.**
. . . *that's all.*

Nota Gramatical

Sentirse *(to feel)* is a reflexive verb with an **e** → **ie** stem change.

¿Cómo **se siente** Ud.?

Me siento magnífico.

6 Escuchemos: Régimen de salud

Mira los dibujos de estas seis personas. Escucha mientras ellos hablan de su vida diaria. Escoge *(choose)* el nombre de la persona que habla según lo que dice.

Answers on p. 285C.

Adriana

Raúl

Daniel

Fernando

Natalia

Soledad

RESOURCES FOR PRIMER PASO

Textbook Audiocassette 6A/Audio CD 11
Practice and Activity Book, pp. 122–124
Native Speaker Activity Book, pp. 51–55
Videodisc Guide
Videodisc Program, Videodisc 6A

Chapter Teaching Resources, Book 3
- Additional Listening Activities 11-1, 11-2, p. 127
  Audiocassette 10B/Audio CD 11
- Student Response Forms, pp. 136–138
- Realia 11-1, pp. 131, 133
- Situation Cards 11-1, pp. 134–135
- Teaching Transparency Master 11-1, pp. 123, 126
  Teaching Transparency 11-1
- Quiz 11-1, pp. 139–140
  Audiocassette 8B/Audio CD 11

Jump Start!

On the board or a transparency write the following words and ask students to write an antonym (**antónimo**) for each: **hola, bajo, aquí, campo, nada, debajo de, antes, frío, pequeño, viejo.**

MOTIVATE

Ask students to think of as many ways as possible to suggest to a friend in English that they do something. (Would you like to. . .? How about. . .?) Write their suggestions in one column on the board or a transparency. Ask students if they can think of ways to make similar suggestions in Spanish using vocabulary from previous chapters. (**¿Te gustaría...?** or **¿Quieres...?**) You might save this list for future review of material learned in this chapter.

TEACH

Presentation

Nota gramatical Explain to students that **sentirse (ie)** is a reflexive verb that means *to feel,* while **sentir (ie)** (as in **lo siento**) is not reflexive and means *to regret* or *to be sorry about.*

Ask a student **¿Cómo te sientes?** After the student replies, ask another student to report how the first one feels. (**Miguel, ¿cómo se siente Susana?**)

Así se dice After introducing the grammar, model both sides of the conversation to present the phrases for making suggestions and expressing feelings. Next, involve students by having them answer your questions, and finally have students practice the dialogue in pairs.

Presentation

Vocabulario Tell the class a story describing what the people in the gym are doing. **Lina y Felipe se estiran. Mónica y Ricardo hacen yoga. Luisa levanta pesas y Manolo patina sobre ruedas.** As you name the new activities, mime their meanings. Have students repeat your story, pointing to each person in the drawing as they describe him or her. Continue with personalized questions such as **¿Te estiras todas las mañanas? Ana y Luis, ¿levantan pesas Uds. algunas veces por semana?** Have students ask classmates questions using the new vocabulary.

Additional Practice

8 Have students explain to their partner why they like or dislike an activity. If they like it, have them tell each other when and how often they do it.

For Individual Needs

9 Slower Pace Write the answers on the board or a transparency in scrambled order and ask students to match them with the blanks in the text.

Additional Vocabulary

practicar el esquí acuático *to water-ski*
nadar con el esnórquel *to snorkel*
ir de vela *to sail*
ir de windsurfing *to windsurf*
practicar tabla hawaiana *to surf*
jugar al golf *to play golf*

Language Note

The word yoga means *discipline* in Sanskrit, the classical language of India.

7 Consejos See sample answer below.

Mira los dibujos en la Actividad 6. ¿Qué debe hacer cada persona para llevar una vida sana? Dale un consejo a cada uno. Puedes usar las frases de **Así se dice** si necesitas ideas.

VOCABULARIO

Para llevar una vida sana.

8 Y a ti, ¿qué te gusta?

¿Cuáles de las actividades en el dibujo te gustan? Pregúntale a un compañero o una compañera sobre su rutina y compartan *(share)* sus ideas con el resto de la clase.

9 Una nueva rutina See answers below.

You've just joined a health club but you're not sure how to get started. Complete the dialogue between you and Jill, your personal trainer for the day.

TÚ Quiero cambiar mi rutina pero no sé qué hacer. ¿Me ayudas?
JILL Con mucho gusto. Primero, ______ .
TÚ ¿Estirarme? ¿Por cuántos minutos?
JILL ______ . Entonces, ______ .
TÚ Ay, pero no me gusta levantar pesas.
JILL Bueno, ______ .
TÚ Muy bien. ¿A qué hora empieza la clase?
JILL ______ .
TÚ ¡Dios mío! ¿Tan temprano?
JILL ______ .

Multicultural Link

Yoga is a Hindu discipline and system of breathing and stretching exercises to promote control of the body and mind. Many non-Hindus in Western countries practice forms of yoga exercise in hope of improving their physical and mental states. Most athletes work to control and discipline the mind and body. Have students discuss the sports they do or are familiar with. Do they help both mind and body? Why is this good?

Answers

7 *Sample answer:*
Natalia, ¿te sientes cansada? ¿Por qué no das un paseo al aire fresco?

9 *Answers may vary.*
1. Necesitas estirarte.
2. 10 minutos
3. Debes levantar pesas.
4. Puedes asistir a una clase de yoga.
5. Empieza a las 7:00 todos los días.
6. ¡Sí! ¿Quieres empezar hoy?

10 Un cuestionario Answers will vary.

Escribe con qué frecuencia haces lo siguiente.

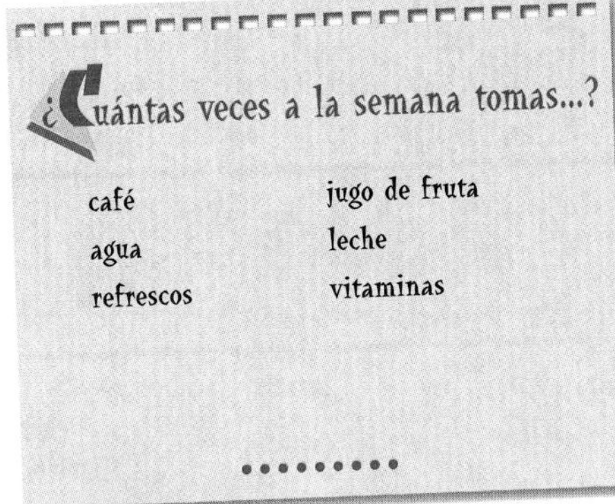

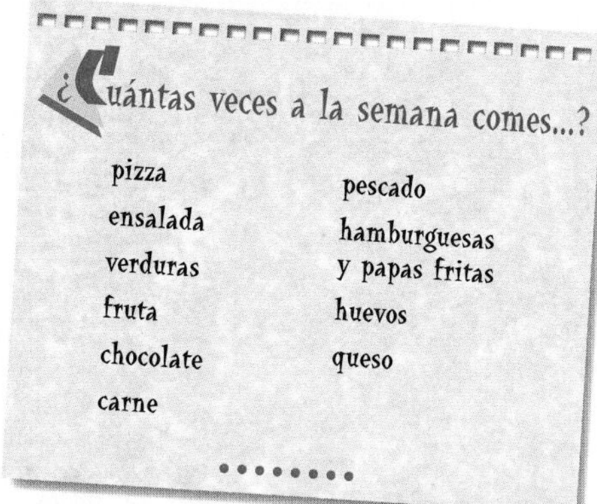

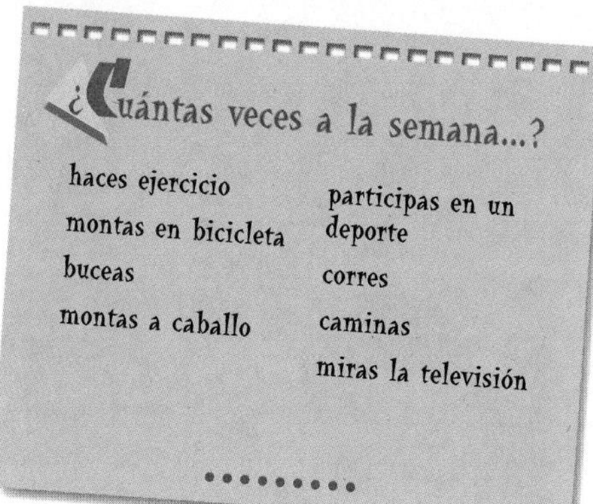

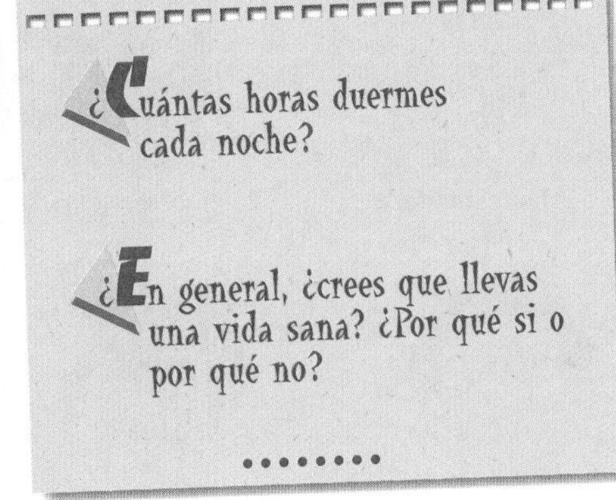

11 Una vida diferente

Get together with three classmates and compare your answers from Activity 10. Make suggestions about how each person in your group can improve her or his weekly routine. Be prepared to share your suggestions with the class.

12 En mi cuaderno Answers will vary.

Based on what you discussed with your partners in Activity 11, write a paragraph in your journal telling what you plan to do for the next week to try to improve your routine.

10 *Sample answer:*
En general, creo que llevo una vida sana. Duermo ocho horas cada noche. Como las verduras y las frutas cada día. Como pescado o un poco de carne de vez en cuando. No como pizza, hamburguesas ni papas fritas mucho porque tienen mucha grasa. Cada día tomo vitaminas. Hago ejercicio tres veces a la semana y tomo ocho vasos de agua al día.

12 *Sample answer:*
Para llevar una vida más sana, voy a hacer ejercicio tres veces a la semana. Voy a beber ocho vasos de agua cada día. No voy a mirar tanta televisión por la noche. Voy a dormir ocho horas cada noche.

Language Note

10 Point out to students that **sano/a** is a false cognate; it means *healthy.* The Spanish word for *sane* is **cuerdo/a.** Ask students what English words related to *healthy* share the root *san–*. (sanitary, sanitation)

Close

Ask several students questions from the **Primer paso** and have them answer using vocabulary and expressions they have learned. (**¿Qué tal si vamos al gimnasio? ¿Crees que llevas una vida sana? ¿Tomas vitaminas?**) Have students answer with their books closed.

Assess

Quiz 11-1, *Chapter Teaching Resources, Book 3,* pp. 139–140

Assessment Items, Audiocassette 8B/Audio CD 11

Performance Assessment

Type the following letter on a hand-out for students or write it on the board or a transparency. Then, have students write a return letter to Pedro.

Querido/a ____,
Vas a llegar para tu visita a Puerto Rico en menos de dos semanas. Tengo muchas ganas de verte. Estoy haciendo planes para las cosas que podemos hacer. ¿Qué tal si todas las mañanas vamos al gimnasio a las seis para levantar pesas y hacer ejercicio? Después podemos hacer las cosas que te gustan. Me haces el favor de escribir una carta para decirme las cosas que te gustaría hacer.
Hasta pronto.
Tu primo, Pedro

Jump Start!

Have students write their answers to these questions. **¿Levantas pesas en el gimnasio? ¿Te gusta hacer yoga? ¿Cuántas veces a la semana te estiras? ¿Te gusta patinar sobre ruedas? ¿Cómo te sientes hoy?**

MOTIVATE

Ask students how they feel after eating. How do they feel after physical education class? after lifting weights or exercising vigorously? after staying up late to finish homework? after hearing some very good news? How many of these feelings can they already express in Spanish?

TEACH

Así se dice, Vocabulario
Present new phrases building backwards upon syllables. (**-pe, -gripe, -er gripe, tener gripe**) Then review spelling, pronunciation, and intonation of question words with students. Ask several students **¿Cómo te sientes?** and **¿Cómo estás?** and **¿Qué tienes?** Students should answer with **Estoy... Tengo...** and a new vocabulary word.

Native Speakers

Encourage native speakers to list and share with the class regional vocabulary variations for expressions related to how one is feeling. (**tener resfrío** *(to have a cold)*; **tener ansias, estar comiendo ansias,** *(to feel anxious)*; **tener calambre** *(to have a cramp)*; **tener náuseas, estar nauseabundo** *(to feel nauseous)*)

SEGUNDO PASO

Talking about moods and physical condition

ASÍ SE DICE Talking about moods and physical condition

To find out what kind of mood or condition a friend is in, ask:

¿Cómo estás?

¿Cómo te sientes?

¿Qué le pasa a Roberto?
What's wrong with . . . ?

Your friend might say:

Estoy nerviosa. Tengo un examen hoy.

Estoy mal. Tengo gripe.

No sé pero me parece que **está preocupado por algo.**

VOCABULARIO

1. estar resfriado/a

2. estar nervioso/a

3. estar enojado/a

4. estar triste

5. estar preocupado/a

6. tener fiebre

7. tener tos

8. tener gripe

13 Escuchemos: ¿Cómo te sientes hoy?

Listen to these people talk about how they feel today. Using the drawings in the vocabulary box above, write the correct number/numbers that corresponds to each description. Answers on p. 285C.

También se puede decir...
Another expression for **estar resfriado** is **tener catarro.** Another way to say **tener fiebre** is **tener calentura.**

RESOURCES FOR SEGUNDO PASO

Textbook Audiocassette 6A/Audio CD 11
Practice and Activity Book, pp. 125–127
Native Speaker Activity Book, pp. 51–55
Video Guide
Video Program
Expanded Video Program, Videocassette 4
Videodisc Guide
Videodisc Program, Videodisc 6A

Chapter Teaching Resources, Book 3
- Communicative Activity 11-1, pp. 119–120
- Additional Listening Activities 11-3, 11-4, p. 128
  Audiocassette 10B/Audio CD 11
- Student Response Forms, pp. 136–138
- Realia 11-1, pp. 131, 133
- Situation Cards 11-2, pp. 134–135
- Teaching Transparency Master 11-2, pp. 124, 126
  Teaching Transparency 11-2
- Quiz 11-2, pp. 141–142
  Audiocassette 8B/Audio CD 11

14 Dificultades

Escribe unas oraciones para explicar cómo te sientes en estas situaciones.

1. Estás en un restaurante con unos amigos y a la hora de pagar la cuenta, no tienes dinero.
2. Tienes tres exámenes muy importantes hoy y necesitas sacar buenas notas.
3. Tu hermanito acaba de romper *(has just broken)* el televisor y no puedes ver tu programa favorito.
4. Estás haciendo la tarea en la computadora cuando se va la electricidad.
5. Tu mejor amigo se va para vivir en otra ciudad.
6. Acabas de recibir la noticia de que tienes un trabajo nuevo.
7. Hace mucho frío y no te sientes bien.
8. Acabas de comer tres hamburguesas, papas fritas, dos helados y un pastel.

VOCABULARIO

El cuerpo humano

la cabeza
el pelo
el oído
la oreja
el ojo
la nariz
la boca
el cuello
la garganta
los dedos
el brazo
el estómago
la espalda
la pierna
los dedos
el pie

15 ¿Para qué sirve?

¿Qué parte o partes del cuerpo usamos en las siguientes situaciones? Cada persona debe mencionar una parte diferente. See possible answers below.

1. para hablar por teléfono
2. para escuchar música rock
3. para correr por el parque
4. para maquillarte o afeitarte
5. para hacer ejercicios aeróbicos
6. para tocar el piano
7. para escribir una carta
8. para levantar *(to lift)* cosas
9. para montar en bicicleta

16 Simón dice...

Work in groups of four to play **Simón dice**. Take turns being leader and practice the words in the **Vocabulario**. Here are some phrases you may need:

Levanta *Lift*	**Cierra** *Close*	**Abre** *Open*
Toca *Touch*	**Indica** *Point*	

A LO NUESTRO

Parts of the body are used in many common expressions in Spanish.

¡Ojo! *Pay attention!* or *Watch out!*

Él es muy **codo.** He's really *stingy*. (**Codo** means *elbow*.)

Cuesta **un ojo de la cara.** It's *very expensive*.

¿Me estás tomando el pelo? *Are you pulling my leg?*

Answers

14 1. Estoy muy preocupado/a.
2. Estoy nervioso/a.
3. Estoy enojado/a.
4. Estoy enojado/a.
5. Estoy triste.
6. Estoy contento/a.
7. Tengo gripe.
8. No me siento bien. Tengo dolor de estómago.

15 *Possible answers:*
1. los oídos, la boca
2. los oídos
3. las piernas, los pies
4. las manos, los dedos de la mano
5. los brazos, las piernas, los pies
6. los dedos de la mano, los oídos, los pies
7. las manos, los ojos
8. la espalda, las piernas, los manos, los brazos
9. las piernas, los brazos

For Individual Needs

14 Slower Pace Go over these sentences orally with the class before having students write their answers. Ask students to give as many alternative answers as possible for each question.

Presentation

Vocabulario Model the new words by pronouncing them as you point to the correct part of the body. Teach parts of the body by using TPR and playing **Simón dice.** (See Preliminary Chapter, page 8.) After a few rounds of play with you calling out the words, have a student be **Simón.**

For Individual Needs

15 Visual Learners Hold up magazine pictures of people doing different activities. Students tell you in Spanish which parts of the body are being used. You might ask them to express this in a sentence. (**Para hablar por teléfono, usas la boca, el oído y la mano.**)

Visual/Auditory Learners Memory devices may help your students to remember the distinction between **oreja** and **oído**. Tell your students to visualize the word **oído** with each **o** as an ear and the **i** as the inner ear. If this technique helps, ask students to make up some more memory devices for other vocabulary.

Language Note

La oreja is the term for the *outer ear* or *ear lobe,* while **el oído** means *inner ear* and refers to the hearing aparatus.

Presentation

Nota gramatical Review the use of **gustar**, a verb that students are comfortable with. Ask several students **¿Te gusta montar en bicicleta?** and other questions with vocabulary from the **Primer paso.** Explain the similar use of **doler(ue).** Have six volunteers come to the front of the class. Hand them each a card with a body part written on it. (**estómago, cabeza**) The students use gestures to pretend that the body part hurts. Use the students as models for the forms of **doler,** asking the class comprehension questions. (**Clase, ¿a Celia le duele la cabeza?**)

Additional Practice

19 Have students tell their partner what they think happened to the people in the pictures. They should use the preterite tense. You might have students create a short dialogue for each of the pictures and ask them to present one to the class. (**¿Qué le pasó? Le duele el estómago. Pues, debe descansar, no comer mucho y luego hacer ejercicio.**)

Native Speakers

Working in small groups, students engage in conversations about how they feel. The object of this exercise to have one student make a statement and have other students paraphrase what he or she has said. **—Estoy agotado. —Entonces te duele la cabeza y estás cansado, ¿no?**

17 Escuchemos: Quejas

Listen to several people tell how they feel. Match each person's complaint with the correct symptom. Answers on p. 285C.

1. Gregorio	**a.** Me duelen los brazos.
2. Flor	**b.** Me duelen los ojos.
3. Félix	**c.** Me duelen los pies.
4. Betty	**d.** Me duelen las piernas.
5. Laura	**e.** Me duele la mano.
6. Roberto	**f.** Me duele la garganta.
7. Cecilia	**g.** Me duele el estómago.

Nota Gramatical

Doler *(to hurt, ache)* is an **o** to **ue** stem-changing verb that follows the same pattern as **gustar.** Do you notice anything special about how you indicate who you're talking about?[1]

Me duele el estómago.
¿**Te duele** la garganta?
Le duele la cabeza.
Me duelen los pies.
Te duelen las piernas.
¿**Le duelen** los brazos?

18 ¿Qué te pasa? See answers below.

Completa las oraciones con la forma apropiada del verbo **doler** y las partes del cuerpo que corresponden.

1. Cuando leo demasiado...
2. Cuando mi papá corre mucho...
3. Si como muy rápido el helado...
4. Cuando voy al dentista...
5. Cuando Brenda levanta pesas...
6. Cuando estoy resfriado/a...

19 ¿Cómo se siente? See sample answer below.

Look at the drawings. With a partner, take turns saying what you think is wrong with each person. Then tell each person what he or she should do to feel better.

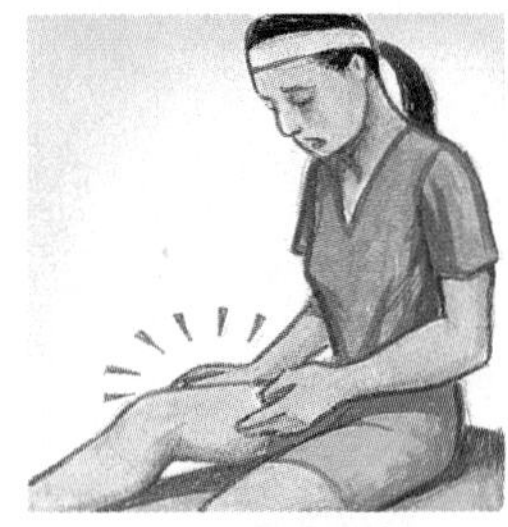
Midori

Linda

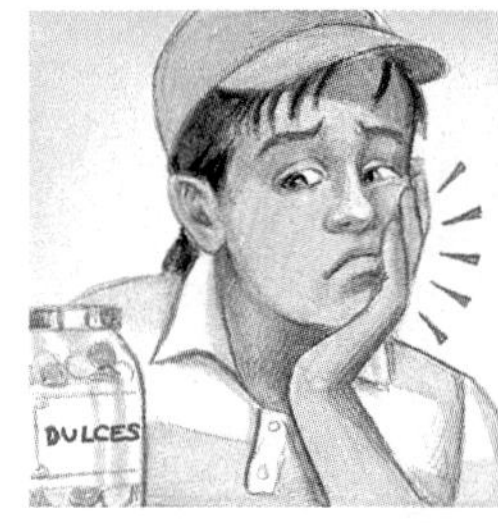

Joe

Deidre

Conchita

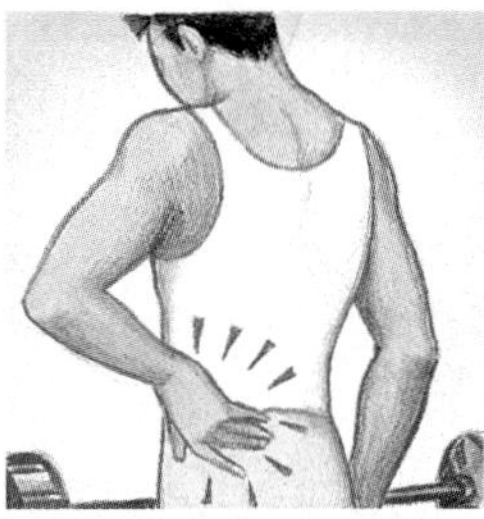
Jeff

Laura

Benito

[1] The definite article, rather than a possessive, is used with body parts in Spanish.

Culture Note

The fishing village of **La Parguera** in the southwest portion of Puerto Rico is the home of one of the world's few phosphorescent bays. Millions of microorganisms illuminate the water. Moonless nights are the best times to witness these underwater "fireworks." The trip to see the phosphorescent portion of the bay takes about one hour by boat from land and is a good way to relax.

Answers

18 1. me duelen los ojos.
2. le duelen las piernas.
3. me duele el estómago.
4. me duelen los dientes.
5. le duelen los brazos.
6. me duele la garganta.

19 *Sample answer:*
A Midori le duele la pierna. Debe sentarse y descansar.

20 ¡Un día fatal!

How do you feel when you have a bad day? With a partner, take turns asking and answering the following questions.

MODELO —¿Cómo te sientes?
—Me duele la cabeza y no tengo ganas de estudiar.

1. ¿Qué te pasa?
2. ¿Cómo te sientes?
3. ¿Te gustaría estudiar conmigo?
4. ¿Qué tal si tomamos un refresco?
5. ¿Te duele la cabeza?
6. ¿Por qué no descansas un poco?

21 Consejos para un mejor vivir

Lee estos consejos para llevar una vida con menos estrés y piensa un poco en tu rutina.

1. Comer por lo menos una comida balanceada al día. La nutrición es esencial para una buena salud y proporciona defensas contra el estrés.

2. Dormir por lo menos 8 horas cada noche. Un sueño apropiado puede añadir años de vida. Trate de acostarse y levantarse a la misma hora.

3. Hacer ejercicio, por lo menos 3 veces por semana. Busque una actividad divertida, como la bicicleta, o como caminar o nadar.

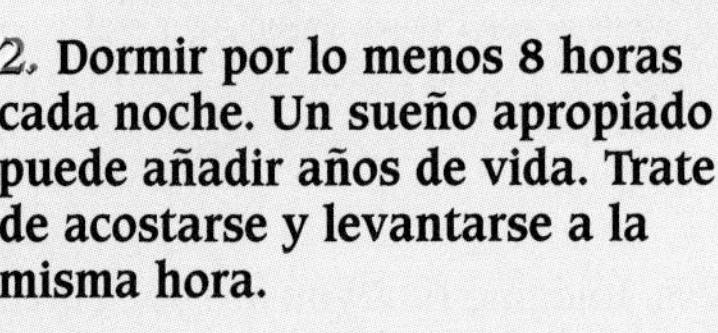

4. No debe tomar demasiada cafeína. Puede producir irritabilidad, dolor de cabeza, ansiedad y depresión.

5. Salir y cultivar sus amistades; un buen amigo es un gran soporte. Tener amigos cercanos es algo valioso; un buen amigo puede subir la moral con sólo estar presente.

6. Organizar su tiempo. Planée su uso y empléelo.

7. Sea optimista: las personas optimistas tienen menos problemas mentales y síquicos.

22 ¿Qué haces para manejar el estrés?

Con base en la Actividad 21, contesta las siguientes preguntas.

1. ¿Comes por lo menos una comida balanceada al día? ¿En qué consiste?
2. ¿Cuántas horas duermes cada noche?
3. ¿Cuántas veces a la semana haces ejercicio? ¿Qué te gusta hacer?
4. ¿Tomas muchos refrescos?
5. ¿Sales con frecuencia con tus amigos?
6. ¿Tienes un buen amigo o una buena amiga a quien puedes contar tus cosas?
7. ¿Organizas bien tu tiempo?
8. ¿Eres optimista o pesimista?

For Individual Needs

Kinesthetic Learners Give each student four index cards. Referring them to Chapter 8, have each person write the word for one food item from each food group on the cards. (See Health Link below.) Collect the cards, shuffle them, and hand out four cards to every student. The object of this activity is for students to collect one card from all four food groups by asking their classmates in Spanish what cards they have. They may trade cards until everyone has a set of four food-group cards. This activity is best accomplished with a small class. If you have a large class, you might consider dividing the class in two and having each half of the class make their own set of cards.

Additional Practice

22 Group Work Ask students to work with people they do not usually work with to discuss stress management. As each person reports what they have written about how they handle each stressful situation, the other students should say what they do and why it works for them. You might then ask groups to tell the class about their most interesting discussion.

Health Link

Ask students to name the six food groups that form the food pyramid. (From top of pyramid down: fats, oils, and sweets; milk, yogurt, and cheese; meat, poultry, fish, dry beans, eggs, and nuts; vegetables; fruits; bread, cereal, rice, and pasta) Ask which of these items they already know how to say in Spanish. **(carne, leche, queso, pollo, pescado, legumbres, huevos, frutas, pan, cereales)** You may want to give students the following words: **grasa** *fat,* **aceite** *oil,* **yogur** *yogurt,* **verduras** *vegetables,* **nueces** *nuts,* **pasta.** With this information, they will be able to make the proper index cards for the Kinesthetic Learners activity above.

For Individual Needs

Auditory Learners Have students role-play the following situation. A local Spanish-speaking television station has a call-in health program that answers the questions of viewers. Ask one student to serve as the television counselor (**consejero/a**) and the others to call in with questions. If a student is able to stump the counselor, or if the class decides that the counselor gives the student an inadequate answer, that student becomes the new counselor.

CLOSE

Review the material from this **Paso** by using *Teaching Transparency 11-2.*

ASSESS

Quiz 11-2, *Chapter Teaching Resources, Book 3*

Assessment Items, Audiocassette 8B/Audio CD 11

Performance Assessment

Ask students to write a dialogue between a doctor and patient using as much of the vocabulary as possible from this **Paso.** When they have completed their dialogues, have students present them to the class. You might grade both the written dialogues and oral presentations.

NOTA CULTURAL

Baseball is the most popular sport in the U.S. But do most people watch or play? Athletes from Spanish-speaking countries are important to the success of U.S. teams in many different sports, but nowhere is this more visible than in baseball. Since 1911, more than 500 Spanish-speaking athletes from Puerto Rico, Colombia, Cuba, the Dominican Republic, Mexico, Nicaragua, Panama, and Venezuela have made it into baseball's major leagues. The Baseball Hall of Fame currently honors five acclaimed Hispanic players: Puerto Rico's Roberto Clemente, Martín Dihigo of Cuba, the Dominican Republic's Juan Marichal, Luis Aparicio of Venezuela, and Rod Carew of Panama.

23 El estrés

Many professional athletes must deal with a lot of stress. Imagine that you are your favorite athlete. With a partner, use the suggestions included in Activity 21 and take turns suggesting to each other what you can do to relieve stress.

24 Una semana sin estrés

See sample answer below.

¿Puedes reducir el estrés por una semana? Escribe un párrafo de seis oraciones en que describes con detalles las cosas que puedes hacer durante la próxima semana para reducir *(reduce)* el estrés.

25 ¡Qué problemas tengo yo!

Form a group of three. For each of the following situations, one of you will role-play the situation and the other two will make suggestions on how the person can relieve stress in his or her life. Take turns acting out these situations, and then, each of you create your own.

1. Quieres ir al gimnasio con tus amigos esta noche, pero tienes dos exámenes mañana y mucha tarea y no tienes tiempo para hacer todo.
2. Pasas todas las tardes y los fines de semana en las actividades del colegio. Nunca tienes tiempo para salir con tus amigos.
3. Trabajas diez horas cada día en una oficina muy ocupada. Muchas veces no tienes tiempo ni para desayunar ni almorzar. Siempre estás muy cansado/a.

Social Studies Link

Ask students to name as many athletes from Spanish-speaking countries as they can who play on major league sports teams. You might have the class write the names as they are called out as an informal dictation exercise. Have students choose a Hispanic athlete, actor, or politician and research his or her life: childhood, choice of profession, where he or she lived, etc.

Answers

24 *Sample answer:*

Para reducir el estrés, necesito dormir 8 horas cada noche. No debo tomar muchos refrescos con cafeína. Debo hacer ejercicio tres veces a la semana y tener una dieta sana con muchas frutas y legumbres. Necesito organizar bien mi tiempo y debo ser optimista.

¿Qué deporte practicas?

Although some sports, like soccer or baseball, are perceived to be more popular in Spanish-speaking countries, there are other sports that many people play. In this chapter, we asked some people what sport they play and why.

Víctor
Ciudad de Mexico
"Yo practico la charrería *(Mexican rodeo)*, que es el deporte nacional, es el deporte mexicano...[Son] suertes a caballo. Es... como en Estados Unidos los "cowboys", aquí son los charros... Mi abuelo fue charro y mi padre fue charro y... por seguir la tradición".

Manoli
Sevilla, España
"Practico piragüismo... Esto es un K-1 [ca-uno]... en inglés, "kayak", por eso le decimos K-1 nosotros. Ésta es una pala... Me gusta porque el agua me encanta y me gusta estar aquí... en el río".

Raquel
Miami, Florida
"Me gusta el voleibol... Es bonito jugarlo, es un deporte muy femenino, no es tan masculino como el "softball" o el fútbol soccer".

Para pensar y hablar

A. With a classmate, make a list of five reasons why you like a particular sport. Present your list to the class.

B. In small groups, make a list of your favorite sports players. Then, choose the two most popular players and discuss why you like them.

Preguntas

1. ¿Qué se necesita para hacer el piragüismo? (un bote y una pala)
2. Según Víctor, ¿cuál es el deporte nacional de México? (la charrería)
3. En tu opinión, ¿para qué deporte necesitas practicar más? (*Answers will vary.*)
4. ¿Por qué practica Víctor la charrería? (para seguir la tradición de su familia)
5. ¿Por qué dice Raquel que el voleibol es un deporte femenino? (Es bonito jugarlo. No es tan masculino como el "softball" o el fútbol.) ¿Estás de acuerdo con ella? (*Answers will vary.*)

VIDEO PROGRAM OR EXPANDED VIDEO PROGRAM, *Videocassette 4*

OR VIDEODISC PROGRAM, *Videodisc 6A*

Teacher Notes

- See *Video Guide* and *Videodisc Guide* for activities related to the **Panorama cultural.**
- Remind students that cultural material may be included in the Chapter Quizzes and Test.

Motivating Activity

Ask students if they have done or viewed any exotic or unusual sports. (**jai alai, el paracaidismo** *parachuting* or *sky diving,* **el rodeo, el surfing, la ascención sobre hielo** *ice climbing*) Which ones would they like to try? Which ones seem too dangerous?

Presentation

View the video. Ask **¿Qué deporte practica Manoli? ¿Raquel?** After you've asked and received answers for several comprehension questions, ask a student **¿Qué deportes practicas tú?** Next, have students ask each other what sports they play and why. Then play the video again and have students answer the **Preguntas.**

Jump Start!

On the board or a transparency, write the following expressions: **estar resfriado/a, estar enojado/a, estar triste, estar preocupado/a, estar bien.** Have students illustrate each with their books closed.

Motivate

Take a poll of the class to find out some of the things they did yesterday. (**¿Cuántas personas estudiaron ayer? ¿Cuántos ayudaron en casa ayer? ¿Cuántos desayunaron ayer? ¿Cuántos llevaron bluejeans ayer? ¿Cuántos compraron ropa ayer?**) Write the number of students who did each thing on the board.

Teach

Presentation

Model the forms of verbs in the preterite tense by asking students personalized questions such as **¿Qué hiciste ayer?** Then, practice the dialogue with a number of students. (**¿Qué hizo ____ anoche?**) Encourage students to answer with an activity that is not mentioned in **Así se dice.** When students seem comfortable with the verb **hacer,** have students read the **Nota gramatical** silently while you put several sentences using **jugar** on the board or on a transparency. (Examples: **Ayer, yo jugué al voleibol** or **Alicia jugó al fútbol.**) Have students practice asking each other questions with **hacer** and answering them with **jugar.** You might wish to introduce the Additional Vocabulary on pages 341–343.

TERCER PASO

Saying what you did; talking about where you went and when

ASÍ SE DICE **Saying what you did**

To find out what a friend did last night, ask:

¿Qué hiciste anoche?
What did you do . . . ?

¿Ganaste?
Did you win?

Your friend might say:

Jugué al tenis.
I played . . .

No. Mi prima **ganó. Jugó** muy bien.
. . . She played . . .

26 Un día en el parque

El sábado pasado Marcela y su familia pasaron un día fabuloso en el parque. Describe a tu compañero/a qué hicieron los miembros de la familia.

27 Escribamos See sample answer below.

Escribe un párrafo sobre lo que hicieron Marcela y su familia el sábado pasado. Incluye también qué hizo cada uno cuando regresaron a casa.

Nota Gramatical

In the preterite, **jugar** *(to play)* has a regular conjugation in all forms except the **yo** form.

jugué	**jugamos**
jugaste	**jugasteis**
jugó	**jugaron**

Resources for TERCER PASO

Textbook Audiocassette 6A/Audio CD 11
Practice and Activity Book, pp. 128–130
Native Speaker Activity Book, pp. 51–55
Videodisc Guide
Videodisc Program, Videodisc 6A

Chapter Teaching Resources, Book 3
- Communicative Activity 11-2, pp. 120–121
- Additional Listening Activities 11-5, 11-6, p. 129
  Audiocassette 10B/Audio CD 11
- Student Response Forms, pp. 136–138
- Realia 11-2, pp. 132–133
- Situation Cards 11-3, pp. 134–135
- Teaching Transparency Master 11-3, pp. 125, 126
  Teaching Transparency 11-3
- Quiz 11-3, pp. 143–144
  Audiocassette 8B/Audio CD 11

28 Una semana llena de actividades

En un grupo de cuatro, describe a tus compañeros lo que hicieron los miembros de tu familia durante la semana pasada. Uno de Uds. debe tomar apuntes *(to take notes)* y todos necesitan describir las actividades de la semana. Incluye los días de la semana, adónde fueron y a qué hora hicieron cada actividad.

NOTA CULTURAL

In general, the majority of the most popular sports in the United States are also very popular in Spanish-speaking countries. The one exception is American football. While it's often played on an informal basis, it's only beginning to gain official status in a few Spanish-speaking countries. When Spanish speakers talk about **el fútbol**, they're referring to the game that Americans call *soccer*. On the other hand, a game that originated in the Basque country of Spain, **jai alai**, (sometimes known as **pelota**) is not widely played in the United States.

29 ¿Qué hiciste durante la semana? Answers will vary.

Escribe un párrafo en español que incluye siete cosas que hiciste durante la semana pasada. Incluye cuándo, con quién y dónde hiciste cada actividad. Aquí hay unas sugerencias:

escuchar música — lavar platos — estudiar para mis clases — preparar la cena — hablar por teléfono — mirar la televisión — jugar al... — levantar pesas — limpiar el cuarto

30 Te toca a ti

Work with a partner and share information from Activity 29 about what you did last week. Be sure to take notes so you can be prepared to report about your partner's activities to the class.

Culture Note

Jai alai is a fast and exciting game that resembles handball. Players use a narrow wicker basket to throw a hard ball against the front wall of a court. The basket, called a **cesta,** has a glove on one end that fits the player's hand. The other end is used for catching and throwing the ball. The **pelota** is slightly smaller than a baseball. **Jai alai** is played on a walled court called a **cancha.** Spectators sit along the open side of the court, watching the game through a clear, protective screen. **Jai alai** originated from a game played in the Basque country of Spain and France during the 1600's. Ask students if they have ever seen or played **jai alai.**

Native Speakers

Engage the class in a debate about a health-related topic and ask native speakers to help moderate. One topic might start off: **Se dice que el fumar es dañoso para la salud. ¿Cree Ud. que el gobierno tiene el derecho de decidir dónde se puede fumar?** Other topics might include the value of exercise, the consumption of sugar or caffeine, or the benefits of bicycle helmets **(cascos)**.

Language Note

The Basque words **jai alai** mean *merry festival.*

Answers

27 *Sample answer:*
En el parque, Marcela jugó al basquetbol. Sus padres jugaron al tenis. Su hermano...

Additional Vocabulary

las cartas *playing cards*
el dominó *dominoes*
el crucigrama *crossword puzzle*
el rompecabezas *jigsaw puzzle*
el ajedrez *chess*
las damas *checkers*

Presentation

Así se dice, Nota gramatical Read the examples from the **Así se dice** aloud to students. Have individual students repeat the sentences. Ask several students **¿Adónde fuiste anoche?** and elicit answers with **Fui...** Then ask several others **¿Adónde fuiste anoche? ¿Adónde fueron Uds. el verano pasado? ¿Adónde fuimos en el capítulo tres de *¡Ven conmigo!*?** Explain that **adónde** implies *movement;* going from one place to another, while **dónde** describes *location.* After you have modeled questions and answers, ask students to practice in small groups. You might also review **¿Cuándo?** and have students ask people in their groups: When did you go to the movies? to a game? to a party? to a restaurant? You might ask several students to tell the class what their group members said about what they did and when.

Native Speakers

Point out to native speakers that the standard **tú** form of **ir** is **fuiste**, not **fuistes.** The final "**-s**" is not necessary in the preterite.

Building on Previous Skills

To review the names of stores (Chapter 9) and practice **ir** in the preterite, write the following on the board or a transparency: **tus hermanos/zapatillas de tenis, tu hermana/aretes, tú y tus amigos/pizza, tu abuela/pastel, tu papá/arroz con pollo, nosotros/flores.** Ask students to write where the various people went to buy each thing. (**Mis hermanos fueron a la zapatería.**)

ASÍ SE DICE Talking about where you went and when

To ask where someone went, say:

¿**Adónde fuiste** anoche?

Your friend might answer:

Anoche **fui** al parque con mi familia.

To talk about different times in the past, you might say:

¿Adónde fuiste anteayer? *(the day before yesterday)*
anteanoche? *(night before last)*
la semana pasada?
antes de regresar a casa?

When you look up a word in a Spanish-English dictionary, make sure you read *all* the meanings and usages listed. Words mean different things depending on the context in which they are used or they may merely sound the same. For example, you cut down trees with a *saw* or talk about the movie you *saw* last night. When you want to know how to say something in Spanish, think about how you're going to use a word when looking it up.

Nota Gramatical

The verb **ir** has an irregular conjugation in the preterite.

fui	**fuimos**
fuiste	**fuisteis**
fue	**fueron**

31 ¿Adónde fueron? See sample answer below.

Look at each of the drawings. Create three sentences for each drawing telling where the people went and what they did there. Add any other details that you might find interesting. Use your imagination.

a. 

b. 

c. 

d. 

e. 

f. 

g. 

h. 

Portfolio

31 Written This activity may be used as a written Portfolio entry. For Portfolio suggestions, see *Assessment Guide,* p. 24.

Answers

31 *Sample answer:*
a. El señor fue al centro comercial. Es el cumpleaños de su hijo. Compró muchos regalos para su hijo.

32 El fin de semana pasado

Get together with two or three classmates and find out where they and their friends went last week. Take notes and be prepared to report to the class. Find out which group was most active.

VOCABULARIO

la cancha de fútbol

la cancha de tenis

el estadio

la pista de correr

33 Escuchemos: ¿Adónde fuiste? Answers on p. 285D.

Listen as people talk about where they went last weekend. When they mention what they did there, write **sí** if it's logical and **no** if it isn't. If it isn't logical, write an activity or two that you might do at the place mentioned.

34 Un día libre en San Juan

Imagine that you spent the day with Ben and his family in San Juan. Using the items in each box, create a story describing the day. Include where each person went and what each person did there. Be creative.

Carmen	fui	el estadio municipal
Pedro y tío Juan	fuiste	la cancha de tenis
Sra. Corredor	fue	la cancha de fútbol
Benjamín	fuimos	la piscina
Abuelo	fueron	el parque
Yo		el centro

Presentation

Vocabulario Point out to students that they already know much of this new vocabulary (**tenis, correr, fútbol**), but in order to describe these sports completely, they need to know how to say where they are played. Model pronunciation and then ask several students **¿Dónde jugaste el tenis? ¿Adónde fueron para jugar al fútbol?**

Additional Practice

34 Ask students to work with a partner to orally create the story. Have them use expressions of time including **por la mañana, por la tarde, por la noche,** and **anoche.**

Group Work

34 In large groups or with the entire class, construct a story using the vocabulary and expressions from this chapter. One student begins by saying a sentence in the preterite. Another student adds to the story by saying another sentence. Other classmates continue in this manner. Once students are comfortable with this format, you might designate a theme to the story and ask that the students use words that go with the theme.

35 Una excursión de los amigos See sample answer below.

Mira las fotos de Ben, Carmen y Pedro. Escribe lo que pasó durante su día en San Juan y comparte tu descripción con la de un compañero o una compañera.

1.

2.

3.

4.

5.

6.

LETRA Y SONIDO

A. In Spanish the vowels **a**, **e**, and **o** are called strong vowels and **i** and **u** weak vowels.

1. Two strong vowels together are pronounced as separate syllables:

   peor **oeste** **rodeo** **correo** **Rafael**

2. A strong vowel and a weak vowel or two weak vowels combine into one syllable called a *diphthong*. When this happens **i** is pronounced like the *y* in *yet* and **u** is pronounced like the *w* in *wet*:

   familia **pie** **adiós** **ciudad**
   cuando **bueno** **Europa** **fui**

3. An accent mark over a weak vowel keeps it from combining into one syllable with another vowel:

   tía **día** **período** **baúl** **aúlla**

B. **Dictado** Script on p. 285D.
You're going to hear Rafael describe a typical day in his life. Write what he says.

C. **Trabalenguas**
Bueno es el aire suave cuando sueño da, pero el fuerte viento despierto nos mantiene ya.

Teaching Suggestion

Letra y sonido Ask the students to look at the **Vocabulario** on page 311 to see if they can find additional examples of diphthongs.

Close

Tell students to imagine that they have taken a Caribbean cruise (**un crucero por el mar Caribe**) together as a class. They were on a huge ship (**barco**) with lots of recreational facilities and activities. (**pista para correr, cancha de tenis, pista de baile, restaurantes, piscina**). They also spent several days in Puerto Rico, sightseeing and visiting friends. You want to know what they did, where they went, and when. Ask the first student **¿Qué hiciste el primer día?** The student should answer with an activity or sport. Ask the second student **¿Adónde fueron Uds. la primera noche?** That person might say **Fuimos a la pista de baile del barco.** When comprehension is high, you might have them embellish their answers by asking **¿Qué hiciste allí?**

Assess

Quiz 11-3, *Chapter Teaching Resources, Book 3,* pp. 143–144

Assessment Items, Audiocassette 8B/Audio CD 11

Performance Assessment

Ask students to write a summary of the **crucero** from CLOSE or of a recent memorable trip or weekend. Have them write five sentences saying what they did, where they went, and when. You might have them present their sentences to the class. Remind them that they may include imaginary information.

Culture Note

Encuentro cultural Many Spanish-speaking countries have extensive public health-care systems. Large private health insurance programs are less common in Europe and Latin America, and it is almost unheard of to sue one's physician. Rules governing the availability and use of prescription drugs vary from country to country, and travelers should be aware that they can be liable for penalties if they are not informed about local laws and practices.

Answers

35 *Sample answer:*
Pedro y tío Juan fueron a la cancha de tenis para jugar al tenis.

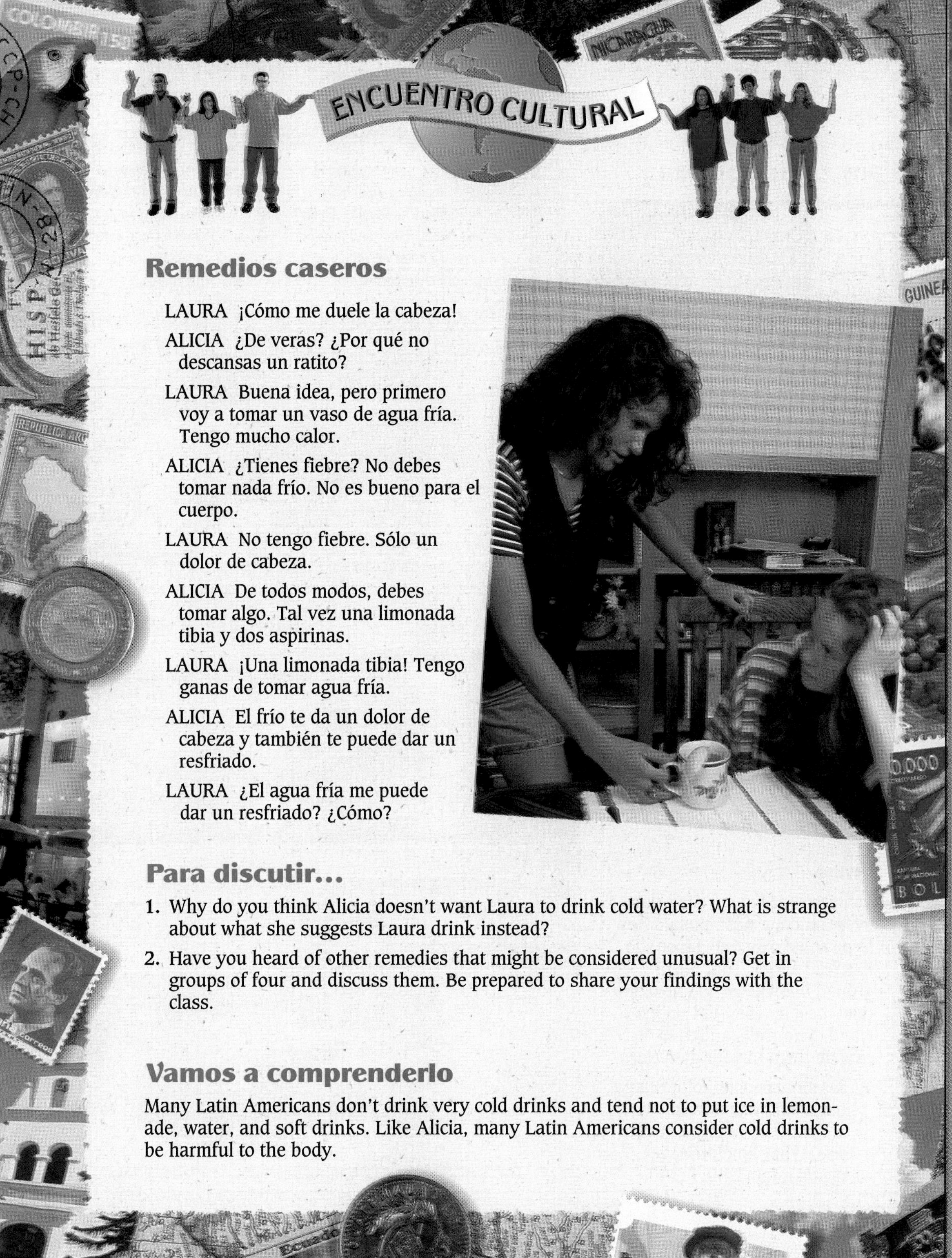

Remedios caseros

LAURA ¡Cómo me duele la cabeza!

ALICIA ¿De veras? ¿Por qué no descansas un ratito?

LAURA Buena idea, pero primero voy a tomar un vaso de agua fría. Tengo mucho calor.

ALICIA ¿Tienes fiebre? No debes tomar nada frío. No es bueno para el cuerpo.

LAURA No tengo fiebre. Sólo un dolor de cabeza.

ALICIA De todos modos, debes tomar algo. Tal vez una limonada tibia y dos aspirinas.

LAURA ¡Una limonada tibia! Tengo ganas de tomar agua fría.

ALICIA El frío te da un dolor de cabeza y también te puede dar un resfriado.

LAURA ¿El agua fría me puede dar un resfriado? ¿Cómo?

Para discutir...

1. Why do you think Alicia doesn't want Laura to drink cold water? What is strange about what she suggests Laura drink instead?
2. Have you heard of other remedies that might be considered unusual? Get in groups of four and discuss them. Be prepared to share your findings with the class.

Vamos a comprenderlo

Many Latin Americans don't drink very cold drinks and tend not to put ice in lemonade, water, and soft drinks. Like Alicia, many Latin Americans consider cold drinks to be harmful to the body.

ENCUENTRO CULTURAL
CAPÍTULO 11

Motivating Activity

Ask students to volunteer if their family uses any home remedies for minor illnesses. What have they heard of for home remedies? (scaring someone to relieve hiccups, chicken soup for a cold, don't drink very cold liquids when body temperature is elevated) Which ones do they think really work? (For example, recent medical studies reported in the media have indicated that chicken soup does, in fact, contain appropriate nutrients to counter colds.) You might volunteer something your family does or something you've heard of.

Presentation

Ask students what cognates or familiar words they recognize. Then ask two volunteers to read the parts of Alicia and Laura. Check pronunciation and comprehension.

Thinking Critically

Drawing Inferences Ask students why they think Laura recommends warm lemonade for her friend's headache. (In very warm weather, it is better to drink fluids that are temperate so as to maintain your body temperature. Cold drinks cool your body momentarily, but will soon make you feel even warmer against the hot air outside.)

Science Link

Ask a science teacher to help you organize a cooperative assignment with Spanish students and students from a science class. Have them research a home remedy. They should find out the origin of the remedy and whether it has been proven effective. Have students report their findings back to the class.

Reading Strategy
Using background knowledge

PREREADING
ACTIVITY A

Motivating Activity

Ask students about their exercise habits. Where do they go to exercise indoors? outdoors? Which activities do they prefer?

Teaching Suggestions

- Before doing the prereading activities, review the parts of the body with students.
- Have students look at the reading to identify words that are similar to English expressions used to describe exercises.
- In small groups, have students compare and discuss their answers to **¡A comenzar!** before you go over the correct answers. Once students have completed this section, remind them of how using background knowledge helped.

READING
ACTIVITIES B AND C

Teaching Suggestion

B. Have students act out the exercises as you read. Or ask for volunteers to read and act out the movements in front of the class.

For Individual Needs

Slower Pace Group students. Before they read the captions, have them work on just one or two of the captions.

Thinking Critically

Observing Ask students which body parts will be toned or relaxed in each of the exercises.

VAMOS A LEER

Para estar en forma

Estrategia

You learned about background knowledge in Chapter 3. Background knowledge is what you already know about a subject. Before you read something, take a minute to remember what you already know about that topic. Doing this will make it easier to guess the meanings of difficult words or phrases.

¡A comenzar! See answers below.

A. Look at pictures, title, and subtitles first. Then, complete the following statements:

1. Both of these readings are about ______.
2. In Reading A, the goal of doing those activities is to ______.
3. In Reading B, the goal of doing those activities is to ______.

Compare your answers with at least two classmates.

Al grano See answers below.

B. Imagine that in your gym class every student must explain how to do some exercises he or she has read about. Your background knowledge will help you read these articles and understand them well enough to explain them to your gym class.

1. For most people, complicated, harsh and fast movements are not the best type of exercise. What kind of movements might be better?

A

MÚSCULOS EN FORMA PARA UNA FIGURA SENSACIONAL

Hacer ejercicio al aire libre es ideal cuando vacacionamos en la playa o en el bosque. Lo importante es comenzar con los ejercicios simples, similares a los que hacemos día a día pero de una manera constante. No se trata de saltar de un lado para otro, sino de hacer movimientos suaves, continuos y lentos, especialmente diseñados para ejercitar todos los músculos del cuerpo.

1. Con los antebrazos y las rodillas en el suelo, levante una pierna, flexionándola con el pie en punta. Repita diez veces con cada pierna y fortalezca sus músculos.

2. Recostada, flexione una pierna hasta que pueda sujetar el pie con la mano; luego, estire la pierna. Repita diez veces con cada pierna.

3. Acostada pero con los hombros levantados, flexione las piernas. Repita diez veces para endurecer el abdomen y las piernas.

Answers

A 1. ejercicios simples
2. mantener los músculos
3. eliminar tensión

B 1 movimientos suaves, continuos y lentos
a. ejercicios simples
b. movimientos suaves
c. continua y lenta

2 la cabeza, la espalda

3 b, a, c

B

DILE ADIOS A LAS TENSIONES... ¡CON EJERCICIOS!

Aprende a eliminar la tensión muscular sin moverte de tu asiento. Las personas que pasan mucho tiempo en sillas – en la escuela o en la oficina – frecuentemente sufren de dolores de cabeza, en el cuello, en la barbilla, en los hombros y en la espalda. Para eliminar esas desagradables tensiones, aquí tienes tres ejercicios sencillos y fáciles de realizar, que te ayudarán muchísimo.

4. Para los hombros y la espalda: Cruza los brazos poniendo las palmas encima de los hombros (como si te estuvieras abrazando). Respira profundamente y ve girando tu cuerpo (de la cintura hacia arriba) todo lo que puedas de izquierda a derecha y en dirección contraria. Suelta el aire cuando estés en el centro. De tu cintura hacia abajo nada debe moverse.

5. Para la espalda y el cuello: Levanta los brazos en forma recta. Luego déjalos caer poco a poco hasta tocar el piso con las manos, doblando también tu cintura, el cuello y la cabeza.

Read: Read the introductory paragraph of Reading A.

Answers: What words from the text mean:

a. simple exercises
b. smooth movements
c. continuous and slow

2. What parts of the body are likely to become tense if you spend a lot of time sitting at a desk?

Read: Read the introductory paragraph of Reading B.

Answer: Five parts of the body are mentioned in the paragraph.

cuello = neck **barbilla** = chin/jaw **hombros** = shoulders. Can you name the other two?

3. If the written directions for a certain exercise have several steps, in what order will the steps be written?

Read: Read Exercise 2 in Reading B.

Answer: Put these three steps in the correct order from one to three.

a. Breathe deeply.
b. Cross your arms.
c. Turn from right to left.

C. Form groups of two or three students. Choose one of the five exercises. While one person reads the description, listen and try to act it out. Try this with all five exercises. Take turns reading and acting out the exercises.

D. Inventa un ejercicio nuevo de tres pasos. Escribe las instrucciones en español. (Tip: ¡A veces es correcto dar indicaciones mediante el uso de infinitivos! Por ejemplo, "Repetir diez veces".) Luego, júntate con un compañero o compañera de clase. Lee tu ejercicio en voz alta y verifica si tu compañero/a puede seguir las instrucciones.

 For Individual Needs

D. Visual/Auditory Learners
Hold up pictures of three different exercises. Give oral directions for one of the three exercises. The class is to guess which one you described.

Native Speakers

Ask native speakers if they have any Spanish-language health magazines or exercise videos at home that they could bring in. If so, read any exercise instructions or play an exercise video and see how much the nonnative speakers understand. If no one has these materials to bring in, you might consider having a native speaker lead the class in a few simple exercises.

Be sure that your students use caution when exercising.

POSTREADING

Teaching Suggestion

Ask students to imagine that they didn't understand the directions for an exercise. Have them work with a partner and write an additional question about each exercise. Then have students exchange questions with a partner and see if they can answer their partner's questions.

Teacher Note

For additional readings, see *Practice and Activity Book,* p. 131 and *Native Speaker Activity Book,* pp. 51–55.

Additional Practice

The "Hokey, Pokey" is a dance in which individual body parts are named as part of the dance (You put your right arm in; you put your right arm out; you put your right arm in, and you shake it all about). The song could be translated and taught in Spanish, or could be sung and danced to in English with only the body parts named in Spanish.

Repaso reviews all four skills and culture in preparation for the Chapter Test.

For Individual Needs

Slower Pace Use pictures clipped from magazines to review the various expressions and vocabulary in this chapter.

For Individual Needs

1 Challenge Ask students to imagine they are Ben or Carmen and that they keep a diary. Have them write the things they did and the places they went on their sightseeing trip around San Juan.

Portfolio

3 Oral Ask students to work in pairs. One partner is to take the role of Dra. Demora and the other student is to be one of her patients. Instruct pairs to develop a conversation between doctor and patient in which 1) the patient complains of an ailment, 2) the doctor inquires about how, when, and where it occurred or began, 3) the patient answers, and 4) the doctor recommends a cure. You might recommend that students include their conversation in the oral Portfolio. For Portfolio suggestions, see *Assessment Guide,* p. 24.

REPASO

1 Look at the photo of Ben, Carmen, and Sra. Corredor. Create a dialogue in which Ben and Carmen tell their mom how they spent their day in San Juan.

2 Get together with two classmates and share your dialogues from Activity 1. Be prepared to take the roles of the characters and role-play your dialogues.

3 Look at the drawing of Dra. Demora's waiting room. How would each patient tell the doctor how he or she feels? See answers below.

Ray Bernardo Lu Bonita Lupita Mickey

4 Listen as Rafi and Sara talk about their last weekend in Puerto Rico. Answer the questions in Spanish. Answers on p. 285D.

1. ¿Cómo se siente Rafi?
2. ¿Cómo se siente Sara?
3. ¿Qué quieren hacer ellos?
4. ¿Qué le gustó a Sara?
5. ¿Qué le gustó a Rafi?

Answers

3
- RAY: No me siento bien. Estoy resfriado y tengo tos.
- BERNARDO: Tengo fiebre muy alta. Me siento horrible.
- LU: Me siento mal. Tengo gripe.
- BONITA: ¡No sé qué me pasa! Me duele mucho el brazo.
- LUPITA: Comí mucho chocolate anoche. Esta mañana me duele mucho el estómago.
- MICKEY: Fui al lago ayer y nadé todo el día. Hoy me duele el oído.

5 Match each Spanish expression with a closely related English phrase.

1. ¿Te puedo dar una mano?	**a.** to give someone the cold shoulder
2. Cuando él habla, todos levantan las orejas.	**b.** to stick your nose in somebody else's business
3. Le gusta meter la nariz en todo.	**c.** to lend a hand
4. ¿Por qué me das la espalda?	**d.** to put your foot in your mouth
5. Cada vez que abres la boca, metes la pata.	**e.** to perk up your ears

6  Imagine you're a reporter for your school newspaper. Benjamín and Carmen have just returned from their vacation in Puerto Rico. Write a story about their trip and what they did. See sample answer below.

7  Spanish-speaking teenagers are interested in sports. Write a short paragraph telling what you learned about Hispanic teenagers and what sports interest them.
Answers will vary.

8 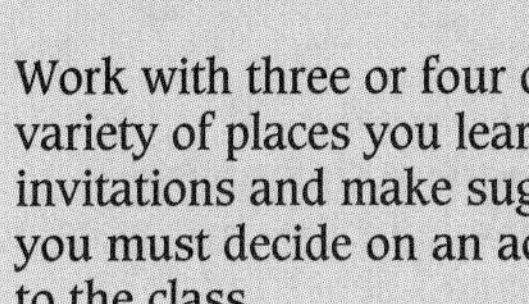

SITUACIÓN

Work with three or four classmates. Invite each other to go to the variety of places you learned about in San Juan. Turn down some invitations and make suggestions of other places to go. In the end, you must decide on an activity. Prepare the scene for presentation to the class.

REPASO
CAPÍTULO 11

Teaching Suggestions

- The Rose technique is a fun, useful way to practice vocabulary. Ask students to draw a monster using the body parts in the **Vocabulario** (with two heads, three arms, etc.). Tell them not to let other students see what they draw. Then have them describe their monster to a partner, holding it so the partner cannot see it. The student draws the monster his or her partner describes. They should then compare the two monsters and evaluate description, comprehension, and creative interpretation. You may wish to display students' artwork.
- Have students look back to the Location Opener on pages 282–285 or to the Chapter Opener on pages 286–287 for ideas to support the **Situación.**

Video Integration

- ***Video Program***
- ***Expanded Video Program, Videocassette 4***
- ***Videodisc Program, Videodisc 6A***

At this time, you might want to use the video resources for additional review and enrichment. See *Video Guide or Videodisc Guide* for suggestions regarding the following:

- **Un recorrido por San Juan** (Dramatic episode)
- **Panorama cultural** (Interviews)
- **Video clips** (Authentic footage)

Answers

5 1. c 2. e 3. b 4. a 5. d

6 *Sample answer:*
Benjamín y Carmen regresaron a Nueva York ayer. Pasaron dos semanas en Puerto Rico con su familia. Visitaron unos museos y el Castillo del Morro en San Juan.

This page is intended to help students prepare for the Chapter Test. It is designed for the students to work on their own initiative and consists of a brief checklist of the major points covered in the chapter. The students should be reminded that this is only a checklist and does not necessarily include everything that will appear on the Chapter Test.

A VER SI PUEDO . . .

Can you make suggestions and express feelings? p. 291

1 Look at the drawings. Can you tell what each person does to lead a healthy life? See answers below.

Cristóbal

Dolores

Adriana

2 What would you suggest to the following people who want to live a healthy life? See sample answer below.

1. tus padres
2. tu mejor amigo/a
3. tu profesor/a
4. tu hermana
5. tu novio/a
6. tu primo/a

Can you talk about moods and physical condition? p. 294

3 Write a sentence telling how you feel in these situations.

1. cuando corres mucho
2. cuando comes muy rápido
3. cuando trabajas demasiado
4. cuando lees mucho
5. cuando estudias seis horas
6. cuando recibes una mala nota
7. cuando tienes tos
8. cuando hace mucho frío
9. cuando escribes exámenes todo el día
10. cuando no estudias para un examen

See sample answer below.

4 What parts of the body do you use in these activities? See answers below.

1. patinar
2. preparar la cena
3. bailar
4. dibujar
5. hablar por teléfono
6. nadar
7. cantar
8. esquiar
9. escuchar música
10. leer

Can you say what you did and talk about where you went and when? pp. 300, 302

5 For each combination below, write a sentence telling what the person or persons did at each location. See answers below.

1. Roberto/la piscina
2. Silvia y Sofía/la cancha de tenis
3. La familia Pérez/la cancha de fútbol
4. Mi hermana y yo/la tienda de discos
5. Tú/el estadio
6. Mónica y Gabi/la biblioteca
7. Federico y sus padres/el parque
8. Yo/el gimnasio

Answers

1 a. Levanta las pesas.
b. Hace yoga.
c. Monta a caballo.

2 *Sample answer:*
1. No deben trabajar tanto.

3 *Sample answer:*
1. Estoy cansada y me duelen las piernas.

4 *Answers may vary.*
1. piernas, pies
2. manos
3. piernas, pies, brazos
4. manos, dedos de mano
5. boca, manos, oídos
6. piernas, brazos, manos
7. boca
8. piernas, pies, brazos, manos
9. oídos
10. ojos

5 *Answers may vary.*
1. Roberto nadó en la piscina.
2. Silvia y Sofía jugaron al tenis en la cancha de tenis.
3. La familia Pérez miró el partido en la cancha de fútbol.
4. Mi hermana y yo compramos cintas en la tienda de discos.
5. Tú jugaste al fútbol americano en el estadio.
6. Mónica y Gabi estudiaron en la biblioteca.
7. Federico y sus padres caminaron en el parque.
8. Yo hice ejercicio en el gimnasio.

PRIMER PASO

Making suggestions and expressing feelings

estirarse *to stretch*
hacer yoga *to do yoga*
levantar pesas *to lift weights*
llevar una vida sana *to lead a healthy life*
magnífico/a *great*
montar a caballo *to ride a horse*
nada más *that's all*
patinar sobre ruedas *to roller skate*
¿Por qué no...? *Why don't . . .?*
¿Qué tal si...? *What if . . .?*
¿Qué tienes? *What's the matter?*
sano/a *healthy*
sentirse (ie) *to feel*
la vida *life*

SEGUNDO PASO

Talking about moods and physical condition

la boca *mouth*
el brazo *arm*
la cabeza *head*
el cuello *neck*
el cuerpo *body*
el dedo *finger, toe*
doler (ue) *to hurt, to ache*
enojado/a *angry*
la espalda *back*
el estómago *stomach*
la garganta *throat*
la nariz *nose*
nervioso/a *nervous*
el oído *ear*
la oreja *earlobe*
el pie *foot*
la pierna *leg*
preocupado/a por algo *worried about something*
¿Qué le pasa a...? *What's wrong with . . .?*
resfriado/a *congested*
tener fiebre *to have a fever*
tener gripe *to have the flu*
tener tos *to have a cough*
triste *sad*

TERCER PASO

Saying what you did and talking about where you went and when

anteanoche *the night before last*
la cancha de (fútbol) *(soccer) field*
la cancha de tenis *tennis court*
el estadio *stadium*
ganar *to win, to earn*
la pista de correr *running track*

Teacher Note

The active vocabulary list in this chapter is intentionally light to allow your class more time for end-of-the-year wrap-up activities, such as oral interviews or completion of long-term projects. The next chapter is a global integration and review of Chapters 1 to 11 and contains no new grammar.

Games

MÍMICA Prior to class write each of the following activities on small sheets of paper: **bailar, jugar al baloncesto, jugar al béisbol, bucear, caminar, correr, hacer ejercicio, esquiar, estirarse, hacer yoga, jugar al fútbol, levantar pesas, montar en bicicleta, nadar, patinar, jugar al voleibol.** Fold the papers and place them in a container. Divide the class into two teams. Ask the first player on Team A to select a paper and to act it out the activity on it. Team A players try to guess their teammate's activity. Once they have guessed correctly, Team B has a turn.

CHAPTER 11 ASSESSMENT

CHAPTER TEST

- *Chapter Teaching Resources, Book 3*
- *Assessment Guide,* Speaking Test, p. 33
- *Assessment Items, Audiocassette 8B Audio CD 11*

TEST GENERATOR, CHAPTER 11

ALTERNATIVE ASSESSMENT

Performance Assessment

You might have students use the **Situación** on page 309 as a cumulative performance assessment activity.

Portfolio Assessment

- **Written:** Activity 31, *Pupil's Edition,* p. 302
  Assessment Guide, p. 24
- **Oral: Repaso** Activity 3, *Pupil's Edition,* p. 308
  Assessment Guide, p. 24

Capítulo 12: Las vacaciones ideales
Chapter Overview

De antemano pp. 314–316	**Unas vacaciones ideales**	*Practice and Activity Book*, p. 133	*Video Guide* OR *Videodisc Guide*	
	FUNCTIONS	**GRAMMAR**	**CULTURE**	**RE-ENTRY**
Primer paso pp. 317–320	• Talking about what you do and like to do every day, p. 317 • Making future plans, p. 318	• Stem-changing verbs **e** to **ie** and **o** to **ue,** p. 318 • Verbs followed by an infinitive, p. 319	**Panorama cultural, ¿Adónde vas y qué haces en las vacaciones?** p. 321	Chapter 12 is a global review of chapters 1–11.
Segundo paso pp. 322–326	Discussing what you would like to do on vacation, p. 323	Uses of **ser** and **estar,** p. 325	• Realia, Ad for Puerto Rican resort, p. 324 • **Nota cultural,** Spain's **paradores,** p. 326	Chapter 12 is a global review of Chapters 1–11.
Tercer paso pp. 327–329	Saying where you went and what you did on vacation, p. 327	The preterite of **-ar** verbs, and **ir,** p. 327	Spanish colloquialisms, p. 328	Chapter 12 is a global review of Chapters 1–11.

Letra y sonido p. 329 — **Pronunciación:** The letters **p, t, k** — **Dictado:** *Textbook Audiocassette 6B/Audio CD 12*

Vamos a leer pp. 330–331 — **¿Cuáles son las vacaciones ideales para ti?** — **Reading Strategy:** Recognizing text organization

Review pp. 332–335 — **Repaso,** pp. 332–333 — **A ver si puedo...,** p. 334 — **Vocabulario,** p. 335

Assessment Options

Quizzes
- *Chapter Teaching Resources, Book 3*
  Primer paso, Quiz 12-1, pp. 197–198
  Segundo paso, Quiz 12-2, pp. 199–200
  Tercer paso, Quiz 12-3, pp. 201–202
- *Assessment Items, Audiocassette 8B/Audio CD 12*

Chapter Test
- *Chapter Teaching Resources, Book 3*, pp. 203–208
- *Assessment Guide*, Speaking Test, p. 33
- *Assessment Items, Audiocassette 8B/Audio CD 12*

Test Generator, Chapter 12

Video Program OR *Expanded Video Program, Videocassette 4* OR *Videodisc Program, Videodisc 6B*	*Textbook Audiocassette 6B/Audio CD 12*

RESOURCES: Print	RESOURCES: Audiovisual
	Textbook Audiocassette 6B/Audio CD 12
Practice and Activity Book, pp. 134–136	
Native Speaker Activity Book, pp. 56–60	
Chapter Teaching Resources, Book 3	
• Additional Listening Activities 12-1, 12-2, p. 185	*Additional Listening Activities, Audiocassette 10B/Audio CD 12*
• Student Response Forms, pp. 194–196	
• Realia 12-1, p. 189, 191	
• Situation Cards 12-1, pp. 192–193	
• Teaching Transparency Master 12-1, pp. 181, 184	*Teaching Transparency 12-1*
• Quiz 12-1, pp. 197–198	*Assessment Items, Audiocassette 8B/Audio CD 12*
Video Guide	*Video Program* OR *Expanded Video Program, Videocassette 4*
Videodisc Guide	*Videodisc Program, Videodisc 6B*
	Textbook Audiocassette 6B/Audio CD 12
Practice and Activity Book, pp. 137–139	
Native Speaker Activity Book, pp. 56–60	
Chapter Teaching Resources, Book 3	
• Communicative Activity 12-1, pp. 177–178	
• Additional Listening Activities 12-3, 12-4, p. 186	*Additional Listening Activities, Audiocassette 10B/Audio CD 12*
• Student Response Forms, pp. 194–196	
• Realia 12-1, pp. 189, 191	
• Situation Cards 12-2, pp. 192–193	
• Teaching Transparency Master 12-2, pp. 182, 184	*Teaching Transparency 12-2*
• Quiz 12-2, pp. 199–200	*Assessment Items, Audiocassette 8B/Audio CD 12*
Videodisc Guide	*Videodisc Program, Videodisc 6B*
	Textbook Audiocassette 6B/Audio CD 12
Practice and Activity Book, pp. 140–142	
Native Speaker Activity Book, pp. 56–60	
Chapter Teaching Resources, Book 3	
• Communicative Activity 12-2, pp. 179–180	
• Additional Listening Activities 12-5, 12-6, p. 187	*Additional Listening Activities, Audiocassette 10B/Audio CD 12*
• Student Response Forms, pp. 194–196	
• Realia 12-2, pp. 190, 191	
• Situation Cards 12-3, pp. 192–193	
• Teaching Transparency Master 12-3, pp. 183, 184	*Teaching Transparency 12-3*
• Quiz 12-3, pp. 201–202	*Assessment Items, Audiocassette 8B/Audio CD 12*
Videodisc Guide	*Videodisc Program, Videodisc 6B*
Video Guide	*Video Program* OR *Expanded Video Program, Videocassette 4*
Videodisc Guide	*Videodisc Program, Videodisc 6B*

Alternative Assessment

- Performance Assessment
  Primer paso, p. 320
  Segundo paso, p. 326
  Tercer paso, p. 329
- Portfolio Assessment
  Written: **Repaso** Activity 6, *Pupil's Edition,* p. 333
  Assessment Guide, p. 25
  Oral: **Repaso** Activity 3, *Pupil's Edition,* p. 332
  Assessment Guide, p. 25

Capítulo 12: Las vacaciones ideales

Textbook Listening Activities Scripts

For Student Response Forms, see *Chapter Teaching Resources, Book 3,* pp. 194–196.

Primer paso

Activity 10, p. 319

1. — ¡Ay, las montañas de Colorado! Me encanta esquiar.
   — Sí, pero debes tener cuidado.
2. — Es el viaje de mis sueños—una semana en Cancún.
   — ¡Qué maravilla! Voy a pasar todos los días en la playa.
3. — ¡Dos semanas en el Caribe! Pensamos acampar, estar lejos de todo, sin trabajar, ni estudiar.
   — Y espero dar muchos paseos. Va a ser fantástico.
   — A propósito, ¿tienes la cámara?

Answers to Activity 10

1. a 2. c 3. b

Segundo paso

Activity 20, p. 324

SARA Me llamo Sara Mercado y vivo en San Juan, Puerto Rico. A mí me gustaría viajar a España porque quiero ver el país de mis abuelos. En España hay muchas cosas interesantes, sobre todo las montañas y los castillos hermosos. Quiero quedarme en España durante todo el verano. Pienso viajar con mis primos que viven en Nueva York.

DAVID Soy David Álvarez Medellín y vivo en Guadalajara. A mí me gustaría ver las Islas Galápagos. Quiero ir de excursión en las Galápagos porque tengo muchas ganas de ver los animales que viven allí. Es que hay muchos que no existen en otras partes del mundo. Me gustaría viajar a las Galápagos en dos años, al terminar mi colegio. Tengo tres amigos que también quieren viajar conmigo.

MARTÍN Me llamo Martín Valerio y vivo en Los Ángeles. Tengo muchas ganas de viajar a la Argentina. Quiero ver la capital, Buenos Aires, y los gauchos y las pampas. También me gustaría esquiar y escalar una montaña en los Andes. La Argentina es un país muy interesante. Espero ir allí con unos amigos, pero no sé cuándo.

Answers to Activity 20

SARA MERCADO: San Juan, Puerto Rico, España, quedarse todo el verano;
DAVID ÁLVAREZ MEDELLÍN: Guadalajara, las Galápagos, ver los animales allí;
MARTÍN VALERIO: Los Ángeles, la Argentina, ver Buenos Aires, los gauchos y las pampas, y esquiar y escalar una montaña

Tercer paso

Activity 29, p. 327

CARLOS	¡Qué divertido el viaje!
YOLANDA	Sí, tienes razón. Me gustó mucho el día en que fuimos a la playa con la prima Mari y preparamos una comida.
CARLOS	Sí, tomamos el sol, hablamos con Mari y luego jugamos al voleibol. ¿Te gustó el partido?
YOLANDA	Sí, muchísimo.
CARLOS	Y a mí me gustó mucho ver El Yunque. Cuando pienso en Puerto Rico, voy a pensar en las flores y la selva.
YOLANDA	Sí, es muy bonito. Caminamos mucho ese día, ¿no?
CARLOS	Sí, y sacamos muchas fotos.
YOLANDA	¿Te acuerdas de la fiesta con los amigos de Miguel?
CARLOS	¡Claro que sí! Lo pasé muy bien. Voy a escribir cartas a todos ellos.
YOLANDA	La visita a los abuelos también fue muy bonita. Su vida es muy diferente de nuestra vida de Nueva York, pero me encantó.
CARLOS	Sí, a mí también.

Answers to Activity 29
1. b 2. a. 3. d. 4. c.

Letra y sonido, p. 329

For the scripts for Parts A and C, see p. 329. The script for Part B is below.

B. Dictado

Hola, Pablo, habla Pedro. Hoy tenemos que preparar la cena para papá. Voy a comprar la comida en la tienda. Tú necesitas poner las papas en el horno a las cinco. Hasta entonces.

Repaso

Activity 1, p. 332

1.	MARTA	Espero ir de vacaciones en julio. Este verano pienso ir con mi mejor amiga al norte de California para saltar en paracaídas.
2.	FRANCISCO	Voy a pasar mis vacaciones en Colorado, en las montañas. Allí pienso acampar, pescar y dar caminatas por el bosque. Por eso necesito comprar una tienda de camping.
3.	JUAN	Yo no voy a ningún lugar. Pienso quedarme en casa y pasar el verano con mi mejor amigo.
4.	ROSARIO	A mí me gusta mucho el océano. Por eso me gustaría ir de vela este verano con mi perro. A él también le gusta.
5.	SILVIO	Para mí no hay nada mejor que tomar el sol con unos buenos libros. Por eso me gustaría pasar una semana en la playa.
6.	LETICIA	Espero ir a México este verano. Quiero escalar unas montañas con mi padre.

Answers to Repaso Activity 1
1. a 2. b 3. f 4. e 5. d 6. c

Capítulo 12: Las vacaciones ideales
Projects

In this activity students will describe their ideal vacation spot to the class. They will develop collages to enhance their presentation.

MATERIALS

Students may need
- Poster board
- Old magazines
- Crayons or markers
- Index cards
- Scissors
- Glue
- Tape

SEQUENCE

1. Depending on class size and time available, assign this activity as individual or group work.
2. Students decide which vacation spot to illustrate.
3. Ask students to do research by looking up information in the school library or local library, using almanacs, world reference books, or travel magazines. Local travel agencies often have a variety of information available.
4. Have students gather materials for their collages such as drawings, photographs, magazine pictures, or small objects such as ribbons. All text is to be in Spanish. You may want to make Spanish-English dictionaries available.
5. Students lay out their collages on a large sheet of paper using paper clips or removable tape. When they decide on a final design, they affix materials to poster board.
6. Have students make a brief written outline of how they plan to present their vacation spot. Provide general feedback and suggestions, if necessary. You may have them exchange outlines with partners.
7. Students practice their presentations with a partner, concentrating on presenting it without reading it.
8. On the day of the presentation, have the students make a short presentation to the rest of the class. After all of the posters have been presented and submitted they may be displayed.

GRADING THE PROJECT

The same grade should be given to all members of each group.

Suggested point distribution (total = 100 points):

Collage

Creativity	20
Labels and explanations	20
Neatness	10

Oral Presentation

Content	20
Vocabulary and grammar	20
Oral presentation skills	10

Capítulo 12: Las vacaciones ideales

Games

LAS VACACIONES IDEALES

In this game, students learn the location and pronunciation of various cities. It can be used at any time.

Materials You will need an index card for each student in your class. Write the names of two Spanish-speaking cities on each card. Tape a large world map (or map of Latin America) on the chalkboard. Cut a piece of string long enough to reach across the map.

Procedure Divide the class into two teams. Give the first player on Team A a card. The player is to say **Vivo en** (first city on card) **y voy a** (second city on card) **para las vacaciones.** If the player can locate and connect the two cities with the string, his or her team gets one point.

The string and a new card then go to the first player on Team B. Follow the same procedure. When all cards have been used, the team with the highest score wins.

Variation Instead of Spanish-speaking cities, write the names in Spanish of any two countries in the world and ask students to connect them. Refer students to the world map on pages xxii–xxiii and tell them that the names of most places will be similar to their English forms.

LOS DIBUJOS

This game is played like Pictionary®. It will allow students to practice the vocabulary from this chapter or from any preceding chapter.

Materials Prepare index cards with a vocabulary word or expression on each.

Procedure Divide the class into two teams. Give the first player on Team A a card. The player is to draw a picture on the board that represents the word or expression on the card. If his or her teammates can guess it within two minutes, they receive one point.

Give the first player on Team B another card and follow the same procedure. The team with the most points wins.

Teacher Note
At this point your students have probably had an opportunity to play several kinds of games. You might offer them an opportunity to invent their own game. Give them a definite goal, such as practicing "telling what happened" or reviewing descriptive adjectives, and set limits on the kind of play that is allowed and the amount of time they can use. Then ask them to write the rules for the game and try it out. You may want to have your students teach successful games they invent to other Spanish classes.

¿QUÉ VOY A NECESITAR PARA MIS VACACIONES?

In this game students will use many of the vocabulary words related to vacations.

Procedure Before beginning, remind students that **llevar** means both *to wear* and *to take with you.* Ask one student to leave the room. The class decides on a place where the absent student is to take a vacation. When the student returns, he or she tries to guess the vacation location by asking questions such as **¿Qué voy a llevar?** Class members are to provide clues with answers such as **Vas a llevar un traje de baño.** Each student should be given a three-minute time limit to try to guess the vacation spot.

BUSCA A ALGUIEN...

Students will enjoy reviewing vocabulary with this game.

Procedure Divide students into groups of four. Tell a group to find someone who fits one of the situations in the list below. **(Busca a alguien que lleva chancletas.)**

The students have a minute to walk around the room asking questions in Spanish to find at least one person who fits your description. If the group succeeds, give it one point. You might choose to give bonus points for some of the more exotic items on the list. Follow the same procedure with the other groups. The group with the highest score wins.

Busca a alguien. Esta persona...

lleva chancletas
quiere viajar a Inglaterra, Francia, Egipto...
quiere saltar en paracaídas
quiere tomar el sol en la China, en...
quiere explorar la selva
usa el bloqueador en el verano
lleva lentes (de sol)
tiene una cámara buena, una bicicleta, ...
tiene un traje de baño verde
bajó un río en canoa
dio una caminata en el bosque
fue de vela el verano pasado

Capítulo 12: Las vacaciones ideales

pp. 312–335

Using the Chapter Opener

Motivating Activity

Hang a large world map on the wall and give each student a small self-stick notepad. Ask students to write their name on a note and stick it next to their ideal vacation spot. They should then explain in Spanish to a partner why they chose their location. Have students report to the class what they found out from their partner.

Building on Previous Skills

Review vocabulary for free-time activities from previous chapters. Have students interview a partner in Spanish asking what he or she likes to do on vacation. They should take notes on what their partner says to report his or her answers to the class.

Geography Link

Puerto Rico's El Yunque rain forest comprises 45 square kilometers of the Caribbean National Forest. It can receive more than 200 inches (510 centimeters) of rain per year, whereas most of the rest of the island averages 70 inches (154 centimeters) annually. Have students locate El Yunque on a map of Puerto Rico.

CAPÍTULO 12

Las vacaciones ideales

1 ¡Qué divertido salir de vacaciones!

Biology Link

At night in El Yunque, one can hear the song of the **coquí**, a tiny tree-frog that is often referred to as **"el mascota nacional"** of Puerto Rico. It cannot be found anywhere else in the world. In addition to having a powerful voice, the **coquí** changes its color from a light beige to black or brown to protect itself from the sun. Suction cups on its toes enable it to climb or walk upside-down on smooth surfaces.

Culture Note

El Yunque is located in the Luquillo mountain range. The name Luquillo comes from the name of the good spirit Yuquiyú. According to Taíno legend, Yuquiyú protected the island and its people from his mountain-top home.

Summer vacation is probably the most exciting time for everyone. School's out and you can do all kinds of fun and interesting things. You might take a trip, visit relatives, get a summer job, or just spend time with your friends.

In this chapter you will

- talk about what you do and like to do every day; make future plans
- discuss what you would like to do on vacation
- say where you went and what you did on vacation

And you will

- listen to students from Spanish-speaking countries tell where they like to travel on their vacations
- read an entry from a travel journal
- write a journal entry of your own about where you would like to go on vacation
- find out about inns in Spanish-speaking countries

2 **¡Cuánto me gustaría explorar un castillo!**

3 **¿Te gustaría ir a Nueva York, Pedro?**

Multicultural Link

Have students investigate what Arabic influences remain in Spain and the rest of the Spanish-speaking world.

Focusing on Outcomes

- Have students identify which learner outcomes correspond to which photo on these pages. (Photo 1 represents talking about what you do and like to do every day; photo 2 represents discussing what you would like to do on vacation; and photo 3 represents saying where you went and what you did on vacation.)
- Ask students what they would consider an ideal vacation day during each season. Ask them to compare their ideas about ideal vacations with those of the **fotonovela** characters as they read this chapter.

Photo Flash!

The castle in the thought bubble is the **Alcázar** in Segovia, Spain, home of the kings of Castile during the 12th and 13th centuries. In the 19th century, the castle served as a military school until some disgruntled cadets set fire to it. Today the castle is a museum housing 14th-century armor and weapons, as well as various pieces of art.

Language Note

The word **alcázar** came to Spanish from Arabic, where it means *castle.* In Spanish it means *fortress.* Ask students if they know why Spanish has many words from Arabic. (Much of Spain was Arabic-speaking for over 700 years.)

Teacher Note

You may want to use the video to support the chapter objectives. The self-check activities in **A ver si puedo...** on page 334 help students assess how well they achieved the learner outcomes.

VIDEO PROGRAM OR EXPANDED VIDEO PROGRAM, Videocassette 4

OR VIDEODISC PROGRAM, Videodisc 6B

Video Synopsis

Ben and Carmen, two New York residents, are visiting their maternal grandfather in Puerto Rico. He is surprised that they are bored and asks what they would like to do on an ideal vacation. Ben would like to go to a tropical forest in South America and travel down the Amazon in a canoe. Carmen would like to cruise around the Pacific in an old-fashioned ship and find a deserted island. While they are talking, their mother comes in and announces they are going to take a short mystery trip.

Motivating Activity

Ask students to discuss where they would have to go to visit their relatives. Would they have to go to another country or state, or would they be able to visit them near their home?

DE ANTEMANO

Unas vacaciones ideales

Can you imagine being bored on a trip to a tropical island? Ben and Carmen were, at least for a while! Read the **fotonovela** to find what their ideal vacations are.

Benjamín

Carmen

Abuelo

Sra. Corredor

1

Aquí las playas son muy bonitas. Carmen está jugando con el abuelo en la arena, y Mamá está leyendo una novela. Pasamos un día maravilloso el sábado — fuimos a un bosque tropical, El Yunque. Todo comenzó por la mañana...

2

¿Qué hacen aquí en la casa? Hace mucho sol. ¿Por qué no juegan afuera? ¿Por qué no dan un paseo?

Ay, abuelo... Carmen y yo dimos un paseo anoche.

3

¿Por qué no visitan a los vecinos?

Yo visité a los vecinos ayer. No hay nada interesante que hacer, abuelo.

¿Cómo que no hay nada interesante que hacer? Están en una isla, hace un tiempo maravilloso y están de vacaciones. Díganme, entonces... ¿qué les gustaría hacer? En su opinión, ¿qué son las vacaciones ideales?

314

RESOURCES FOR DE ANTEMANO

Textbook Audiocassette 6B/Audio CD 12
Video Guide
Video Program
Expanded Video Program, Videocassette 4
Videodisc Guide
Videodisc Program, Videodisc 6B
Practice and Activity Book, p. 133

4

¿Las vacaciones ideales...? ¡Yo sé!

A mí me gustaría viajar a una selva y bajar el río en canoa. Me gustaría acampar en la selva, pescar, y explorar... Sí, algún día espero explorar todo el río Amazonas.

5

A mí me gustaría ir de vela, navegar por el océano Pacífico en un barco de vela antiguo... ¡Pienso descubrir una isla desierta!

6

Los muchachos están aburridos.

¿De qué hablan?

¿Aburridos? ¿En una isla tropical? Muchachos... Puerto Rico es una maravilla. Y hoy vamos a hacer un pequeño viaje.

7

¿Un viaje? ¿Adónde vamos?

¿Y qué hacemos?

Ya verán, ya verán... ¡es una sorpresa!

8

Unas horas después...

VEREDA
EL YUNQUE
EL YUNQUE TRAIL
BOSQUE NACIONAL
DEL CARIBE

315

Presentation

Play the video or audio recording. After students have viewed the video or listened to the audio recording, have them form groups of three or four to practice reading the roles of abuelo, la señora Corredor, Ben, and Carmen. Then have groups prepare written answers to the questions in Activity 1, page 316.

Teaching Suggestion

Ask students to tell a partner in Spanish whether they would prefer Ben's ideal vacation or Carmen's, and why. If any students would like neither, they should explain why not. Have them describe the ideal vacation to their partner.

Background Information

In the second act of the video, the characters visit El Yunque, a tropical rain forest that supports many different trees, vines, and tropical flowers. More than 200 species of birds live there. It is the only tropical rain forest managed by the U.S. Forest Service. For other information, see the notes on page 312.

Video Integration

- ***Expanded Video Program,*** *Videocassette 4*
- ***Videodisc Program,*** *Videodisc 6B*

You may choose to continue with **Unas vacaciones ideales (a continuación)** at this time or wait until later in the chapter. At this point in the story, Ben and Carmen ask their mother questions about where they are going and what they will need. La señora Corredor is still very secretive and just says that they will need their raincoats. The family gets in the car and heads for the mystery destination, El Yunque. They walk around on a self-guided tour, then end the day relaxing on the beach with a picnic supper.

For Individual Needs

1 Slower Pace You might have students work in pairs to help each other with this activity.

Teaching Suggestion

3 Once students have located the Spanish expressions, have them practice saying them with a partner. If they have difficulty identifying the phrases, play the segment of the audio recording or videocassette or videodisc where these expressions are used.

Building on Previous Skills

After students have watched the video and completed Activities 1–5, ask them to make two packing lists in Spanish: one for the things Ben would need to pack for his ideal vacation, and another for Carmen. When students have finished, ask them to compare their list with a partner's to see if they have forgotten anything.

Native Speakers

Ask native speakers to write a journal entry about a trip, real or imaginary, that they made to visit a friend or relative. Or, have them interview an older friend or relative about a trip they have made, and write about it. Review any spelling and writing skills you have targeted with your native speakers over the course of the school year, and ask them to incorporate all of these skills globally in their reports.

1 ¿Comprendes? See answers below.

¿Comprendes lo que pasa en la fotonovela? Contesta las preguntas. Si es necesario, adivina.

1. ¿Dónde están Benjamín y su familia, y por qué?
2. ¿Por qué están tristes Carmen y Benjamín en la segunda foto?
3. ¿Qué les pregunta su abuelo en la tercera foto?
4. ¿Con qué sueñan *(dream)* Benjamín y Carmen?
5. ¿Qué les menciona su mamá que los anima *(cheers them up)*?

2 ¿Cierto o falso? See answers below.

Decide si las oraciones son ciertas o falsas. Si son falsas, corrígelas.

1. Ben escribe en su diario sobre sus vacaciones en Puerto Rico.
2. Ben y Carmen están aburridos porque hace mal tiempo.
3. Las vacaciones ideales de Ben consisten en ir a la playa y nadar.
4. Las vacaciones ideales de Carmen consisten en navegar en barco de vela.
5. Ben y Carmen no van a hacer nada interesante hoy.

3 ¿Cómo se dice? See answers below.

Find the words and phrases in the **fotonovela** that you could use to . . .

1. say that you went to a tropical forest
2. ask what someone is doing in the house
3. say that the weather is great
4. say that you'd like to explore a river in a canoe
5. say that you plan on discovering a deserted island

4 ¿Quién lo diría? See answers below.

Según la fotonovela, ¿quién diría lo siguiente?

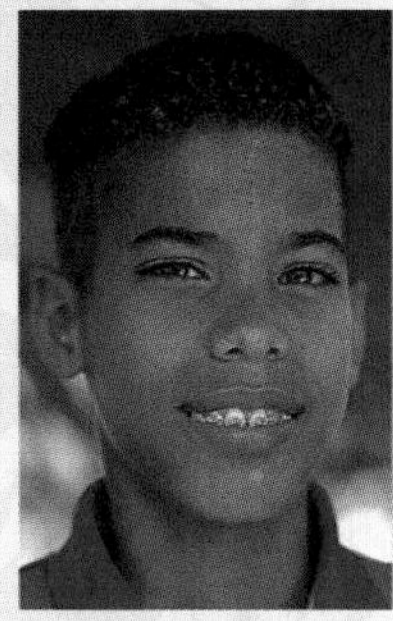
Ben

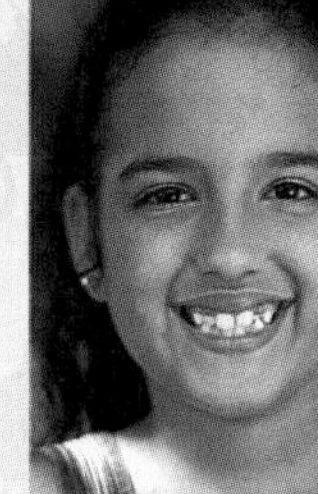
Carmen

Abuelo

La Sra. Corredor

1. Estoy muy aburrido, abuelo.
2. Vamos a ir a un lugar muy interesante, hijos.
3. Los barcos de vela me encantan.
4. ¡Hoy es un día muy bonito!
5. ¡Me gustaría ir a la selva amazónica!

5 ¿Y tú?

Imagine that you're on your dream vacation and you're writing in your journal. Using the **fotonovela** for ideas, write three things that you can do on your vacation.

Possible answers: pasar el día en la playa, nadar y tomar el sol, ir de vela

Answers

1
1. Están en casa del abuelo en Puerto Rico.
2. Porque no hay nada interesante que hacer.
3. ¿Qué les gustaría hacer? ¿Cómo son unas vacaciones ideales?
4. Benjamín sueña con unas vacaciones en la selva amazónica. Carmen sueña con navegar por el océano Pacífico en un barco de vela antiguo.
5. que van a hacer un viaje

2
1. Cierto
2. Falso: Están aburridos porque no hay nada interesante que hacer.
3. Falso: A Ben le gustaría bajar el río Amazonas en canoa, acampar en la selva y explorar.
4. Cierto
5. Falso: Van a hacer un viaje.

3
1. Fui a una selva tropical.
2. ¿Qué hace aquí en la casa?
3. Hace un tiempo maravilloso.
4. Me gustaría explorar un río en canoa.
5. Pienso descubrir una isla desierta.

4
1. Ben or Carmen
2. Sra. Corredor
3. Carmen
4. Abuelo
5. Ben

PRIMER PASO

Talking about what you do and like to do every day; making future plans

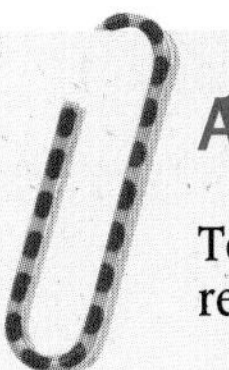

ASÍ SE DICE Talking about what you do and like to do every day

To find out what someone does on a regular basis, ask:

Bueno, ¿qué haces tú **todos los días?**

Your friend might answer:

Primero voy a la escuela, y **después** regreso a casa y hago mi tarea. Ceno con la familia a las seis y **luego** miro la televisión o visito a un amigo.

To ask about someone's routine, say:

¿**Con qué frecuencia** sales con tus amigos?

¿Qué te gusta hacer **después de clases**?

Your friend might answer:

Pues, salgo **todos los viernes.**

Me gusta escuchar música en casa. También me gusta jugar al basquetbol.

6 ¿Qué hacen los demás? See sample answer below.

Describe a las personas en el dibujo. Explica dónde están, cómo son y qué hacen.

Máma Papá Marcos

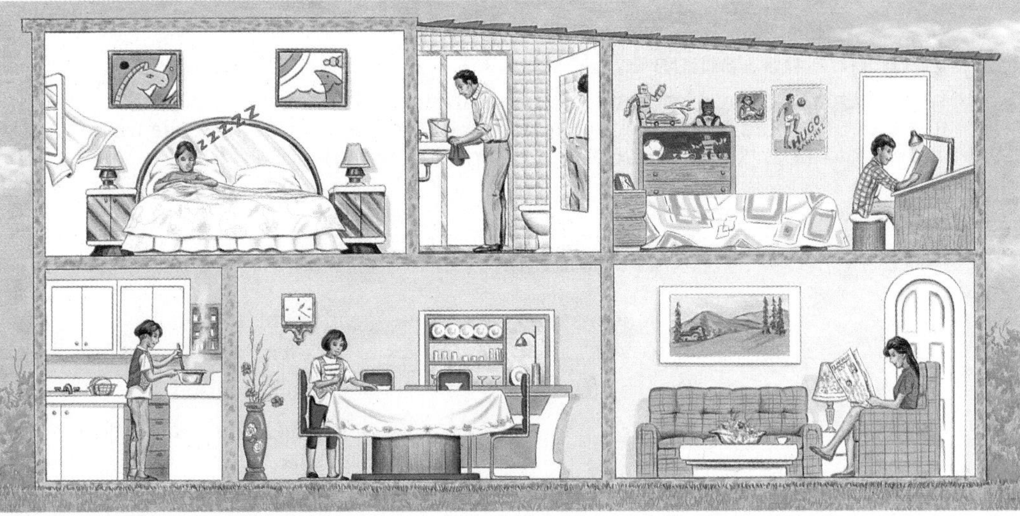

Claudia Marcia María

RESOURCES FOR PRIMER PASO

Textbook Audiocassette 6B/Audio CD 12
Practice and Activity Book, pp. 134–136
Native Speaker Activity Book, pp. 56–60
Videodisc Guide
Videodisc Program, Videodisc 6B

Chapter Teaching Resources, Book 3
- Additional Listening Activities 12-1, 12-2, p. 185
  Audiocassette 10B/Audio CD 12
- Student Response Forms, pp. 194–196
- Realia 12-1, pp. 189, 191
- Situation Cards 12-1, pp. 192–193
- Teaching Transparency Master 12-1, pp. 181, 184
  Teaching Transparency 12-1
- Quiz 12-1, pp. 197–198
  Audiocassette 8B/Audio CD 12

Jump Start!

On the board or a transparency, write the following verbs with their letters scrambled: **jugar, visitar, viajar, acampar, navegar,** and **descubrir.** Ask students to unscramble them and write their answers on paper.

MOTIVATE

Have students list in Spanish things that they have to do every day and things that they like to do every day.

TEACH

Presentation

Así se dice Tell your students a story in Spanish about what you do every day, using the expressions presented in **Así se dice.** Model the questions and answers, then ask students to work with a partner and practice the expressions in this section. After they have done so, ask them to practice answering **¿Qué haces todos los días?**, using the verbs in the list they made for MOTIVATE above. They should include **primero, después,** and **luego** in their responses.

Additional Practice

6 Ask students to tell you how often they or other members of their family do the various activities illustrated in the drawing. (**¿Con qué frecuencia...?**)

Answers

6 *Sample answer:*
Marcos está en su cuarto. Es joven pero inteligente. Está estudiando.

Presentation

Gramática Put several sentences on the board or on a transparency that include the stem-changing verbs from **Gramática: Yo quiero un refresco. Nosotros queremos patinar sobre ruedas. Yo tengo quince años. Ellos no tienen tiempo.** Ask students if they notice differences in the **yo** and **nosotros** forms of the verb **querer.** (The **nosotros** form does not have a stem-change.) How are the **yo** and **ellos** forms of the verb **tener** different? (The **yo** form ends in **-go** and the **ellos** form stem-changes.) Have students write a note to a friend asking three questions with **querer, empezar,** and **preferir.** They are also to ask two questions concerning their friend and another person using **venir** and **tener.** Then have students exchange notes with a partner and answer each other's questions.

Teaching Suggestion

To practice **preferir,** ask students where they prefer to swim. **¿Prefieres nadar en un lago? ¿en un río? ¿en...**

Presentation

Así se dice After modeling the expressions, replay the audio recording of the **fotonovela** on pages 314–315. Ask students to listen carefully to the phrases Ben and Carmen use to describe their dream vacation and future plans. Then, walk around the room and ask the questions of several students. For further practice, modify the questions by using other future time expressions. (**mañana, la semana que viene, el domingo por la tarde**)

Gramática Stem-changing verbs

1. Many verbs have a stem change in the present tense. In verbs such as **querer, empezar,** and **preferir, e** changes to **ie** in all forms except **nosotros** and **vosotros.** The **yo** form of the verbs **venir** and **tener** ends in **-go** and **e** doesn't change to **ie.** (Vengo, tengo. . .)
2. Other verbs, including **poder** and **almorzar,** have **o** to **ue** stem changes. If you've forgotten these forms, see page 210.

7 ¿Qué haces tú? Answers will vary.

Pregúntale a tu compañero o compañera qué hace todos los días a estas horas.

de lunes a viernes a las	los fines de semana a las
1. 8 de la mañana	5. 7 de la mañana
2. 9 de la noche	6. 12 de la tarde
3. 2 de la tarde	7. 10 de la noche
4. ¿?	8. ¿?

¿Se te ha olvidado? **gustar** and **encantar** Consulta la página 208

8 ¿Qué le gusta hacer? Answers will vary.

Pregúntale a tu compañero o compañera si va a estos lugares durante el año escolar o cuando está de vacaciones. Pregúntale también qué hace cuando está en cada lugar.

1. la piscina	5. el colegio
2. la cafetería	6. el centro comercial
3. la playa	7. el gimnasio
4. el cine	8. el parque

9 ¿Por qué no vamos a...?

Work in groups of three. You have some time after school and the three of you would like to get together. Find out what everyone in your group likes so you can decide where to go and what to do. Make a list of your first, second, and third choices.

ASÍ SE DICE Making future plans

To ask what a friend is planning to do, say:	Your friend might answer:
¿Adónde **piensas** viajar algún día?	A Europa, si *(if)* puedo.
¿**Quieres** viajar a México?	No, pero **espero** hacer un viaje a Guatemala.
¿Qué **vas a hacer** este verano?	Voy al Perú.

For Individual Needs

7 Tactile Learners Allow students to use pens and pencils on their desk to represent the hands of a clock. Tell them to rotate them to form the time as they ask each other the questions.

8 Visual Learners Use photos of the indicated places to elicit answers from the entire class or to expand on this activity.

VOCABULARIO

la chaqueta
la bufanda
los esquís

a.

b.

c.

También se puede decir...

En España se dice **el billete** por **el boleto.** En México, por **la chaqueta** muchas personas dicen también **la chamarra.**

10 Escuchemos: De vacaciones

Mira los dibujos y escucha las conversaciones. Decide qué conversación corresponde a cada dibujo. Answers on p. 311C.

11 ¿Qué necesito?

Pick a place where you'd like to travel and make a list of things you'd need to bring with you. Keep in mind the weather and the things you plan to do. Get together with a partner. Take turns asking each other a series of yes/no questions to guess where you're going to go on vacation. You might ask: **¿Traes un/a...? ¿Vas a llevar...?**

Gramática Verbs + infinitives

1. You've learned a number of verbs that may be followed by an infinitive and others that require **a** or **que** before the infinitive.

   querer, necesitar, pensar, deber, esperar, poder } + infinitive

   ir a, tener que } + infinitive

2. Remember that only the first verb changes:

   Pienso pasear en bicicleta.
   ¿Quieres venir conmigo?

12 ¿Qué piensan hacer? See sample answer below.

Mira los dibujos en el **Vocabulario.** Menciona tres cosas que cada persona piensa hacer durante sus vacaciones. ¡Usa tu imaginación!

Answers

12 *Sample answer:*

a. Piensan esquiar en las montañas. Piensan patinar sobre el hielo. Piensan hacer un hombre de nieve.

For Individual Needs

12 Challenge After students have listed the activities of each person in the drawings, have them write a paragraph on one of them, detailing what the person is planning to do, and why.

Presentation

Vocabulario Bring the objects listed in the vocabulary to class in a suitcase. Role-play a vacationer unpacking your bag. Say the name of each object as you remove it from the suitcase, and ask students to repeat after you. At the end of the chapter, the suitcase and its contents can be used to review vocabulary.

Language Note

Point out to students some words that vary regionally. (**espejuelos, anteojos,** or **gafas** for **lentes; sandalias** for **chancletas;** and **bronceador** for **bloqueador**)

TPR As a continuation of the **Vocabulario** presentation, adapt the game HACER LA MALETA, page 335, to use informal command forms.

Presentation

Gramática Say the infinitives aloud, modeling the correct pronunciation of each. Read the example sentences in the **Gramática.** You may want to add some of your own. **Ella espera nadar en el mar Caribe. Usted puede llamarme por teléfono.** Call on individual students to change the subjects in each of the example sentences to the plural. (**Pensamos pasear en bicicleta. ¿Uds. quieren venir conmigo? Ellas esperan nadar en el mar Caribe. Ustedes pueden llamarme por teléfono.)**

Math Link

15 Note that the temperature in the drawing is in degrees Fahrenheit, although Celsius is the standard in many Spanish-speaking countries. Ask students to convert the current temperature from Fahrenheit to Celsius. (subtract 32 degrees, multiply by 5, and divide by 9)

For Individual Needs

16 Challenge Have students develop a follow-up conversation in which the assistant and the customer discuss the date and time the customer could leave, the cost, and what the customer would need to take.

CLOSE

Tell students to imagine they are in San Juan on an exchange program and their host family is making suggestions of what to do and see around town. Using the expressions that they learned in the **Primer paso,** they should respond by telling their host family what they would and would not like to do. (**Quiero ver el Morro. Pienso visitar el Viejo San Juan. Puedo ir de compras en Isla Verde.**)

ASSESS

Quiz 12-1, *Chapter Teaching Resources, Book 3,* pp. 197–198

Assessment Items, Audiocassette 8B/Audio CD 12

Performance Assessment

Have students write a letter to a travel agent requesting information on a place they plan to visit. Each student should ask the cost of the ticket, when the plane will leave, and what he or she will need to take.

13 ¡A viajar!

Planea unas vacaciones ideales con tu compañero/a. Decidan . . .

1. adónde quieren ir
2. cuándo esperan salir
3. cómo quieren viajar (en coche, por avión...)
4. qué necesitan llevar
5. cuánto tiempo piensan quedarse *(to stay)*

Remember your first few weeks in Spanish class? You're probably not as nervous now as you were back then. Learning a new language takes patience and practice. If you still get discouraged from time to time, keep reminding yourself that you can do it!

14 ¿Por qué no te quedas? *Why don't you stay?*

Make a list of five fun things that you can do in your community during vacation. Then try to convince your partner to stay home by telling him or her what you plan to do during vacation. Answers will vary.

15 ¿Qué tiempo hace en...? See answers below.

¿Qué estación del año representan los siguientes dibujos? ¿Qué tiempo hace?

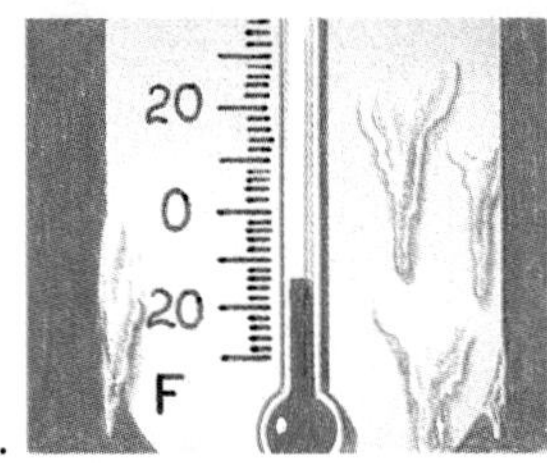

a.

b.

c.

d.

e.

f.

16 Agente de viajes See possible answers below.

In your summer job as an assistant in a travel agency, one task is to give advice to customers. How would you respond to the following questions and comments? Role-play the activity with a partner and take turns playing the assistant and the customer.

1. Tengo vacaciones en julio y quiero esquiar. ¿Adónde puedo viajar?
2. Quiero pasar dos semanas en una playa tropical. ¿Adónde puedo ir?
3. Me gustan las ciudades grandes, el teatro, los museos y los conciertos.
4. No tengo mucho dinero. Quiero viajar con unos amigos a las montañas.
5. Me encantan las ruinas arqueológicas. ¿Adónde puedo viajar?
6. Nos gusta mucho la aventura y ver cosas diferentes.

Answers

15 *Answers may vary.*
a. Hace frío. Es invierno.
b. Hace mucho viento. Es otoño.
c. Hace sol y mucho calor. Es verano.
d. Hace buen tiempo. Es primavera.
e. Llueve. Es primavera.
f. Nieva. Es invierno.

16 *Possible answers:*
1. Nueva Zealanda o la Argentina
2. el Caribe, México, Hawaii
3. Nueva York, San Francisco, Londres, París
4. parques nacionales en Colorado y Nuevo México
5. México, Guatemala, Grecia

PANORAMA CULTURAL

CAPÍTULO 12

¿Adónde vas y qué haces en las vacaciones?

If you lived in a Spanish-speaking country, what would you look forward to doing on your vacation? The answer would depend on where you lived. We asked these teenagers in Spanish-speaking countries what they do and where they go during their vacations.

Camila
Buenos Aires, Argentina
"Voy con mi familia a Pinamar y a Uruguay. Estamos en la playa y recorremos un poco el lugar".

Jaharlyn
Ponce, Puerto Rico
"Me dan dos meses en verano y tres semanas en Navidad. No más lo que hago es que voy a la playa, al río, veo televisión y duermo mucho".

José Luis
Valencia, Venezuela
"Generalmente también voy para la playa, a Puerto Cabello, puede ser desde un mes hasta los dos meses completos de las vacaciones de agosto. Con toda mi familia".

Para pensar y hablar...

A. Which of the interviewee's vacation ideas do you find most appealing? Why?

B. You've won a trip to the Spanish-speaking country of your choice! In small groups, discuss which country you would most like to visit. Why did you choose that particular country? What things do you already know about it? Which places would you most want to see? Why?

VIDEO PROGRAM OR EXPANDED VIDEO PROGRAM, *Videocassette 4*

OR VIDEODISC PROGRAM *Videodisc 6B*

Teacher Notes

- See *Video Guide* or *Videodisc Guide* for activities related to the **Panorama cultural.**
- Remind students that cultural material may be included in the Quizzes and Chapter Test.

Motivating Activity

Ask students what they consider the top tourist attractions in the United States. If a group of students from a Spanish-speaking country came to the United States for the first time, which attractions would they suggest that the group see? Ask students to list their top five recommendations in order.

Presentation

View the video. Ask **¿Adónde va Camila? ¿Jaharlyn?** After you have asked and received answers for several comprehension questions, ask a student **¿Adónde vas tú?** Then have students ask each other where they go and what they do on vacation. Then play the video again and have students answer the **Preguntas.**

Preguntas

1. ¿Con quién viaja Camila? (con su familia)
2. ¿Cuántos meses de vacaciones tiene José Luis? ¿Jaharlyn? (dos meses, dos meses en el verano y tres semanas en Navidad)
3. ¿Quién va a Puerto Cabello? (José Luis)
4. ¿A quién le gusta dormir mucho? (Jaharlyn) ¿Por qué? (*Answers will vary.*)
5. En tu opinión, ¿cuáles son las playas más bonitas de los Estados Unidos? (*Answers will vary.*)

Culture Note

Locations such as **Pinamar** are popular among Argentines who often return to the same vacation spot (some even rent the same **cabaña**) each year. The fostering of a second home leads to a sense of community in each resort.

Geography Link

Using *Map Transparency 2,* have students locate Argentina, Venezuela, and Puerto Rico on the map. Have the students been to any of these places?

Jump Start!

On the board or on a transparency write the following words. Students write as many associated words as they can for each: **playa, cuidad, campo,** and **montaña** (introduced here).

Motivate

Ask students to look at the drawing and discuss the things they would or would not like to do, and why or why not.

Teach

Presentation

Vocabulario Give a "tour" of **La Isla de Paraiso** talking about the activities illustrated, giving details as students point to each activity you mention. Then have students repeat the words after you, using backward buildup for accurate pronunciation. (**-mo, -ismo, turismo**)

Additional Practice

Ask students to make up five true or false statements about what the people in the drawing are doing, ending each with **¿...verdad?** Students are then to respond to a partner's statements, correcting false statements and repeating true ones.

Additional Vocabulary

Alternate expressions used for *surfing* are **montar en tabla de vela** or **tabla hawaiana** and **el surfing.**

SEGUNDO PASO

Discussing what you would like to do on vacation

VOCABULARIO

La Isla del Paraíso

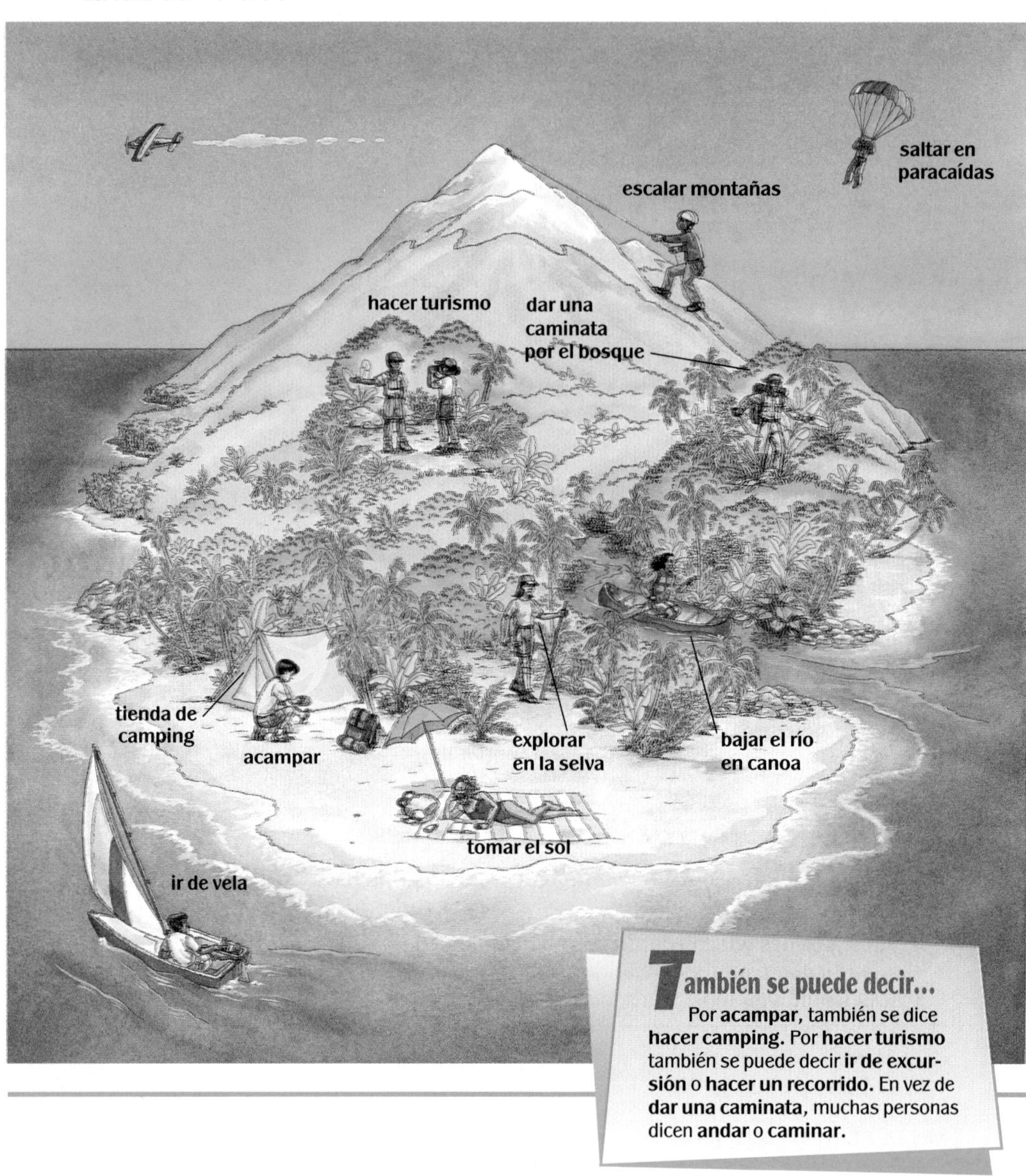

También se puede decir...

Por **acampar,** también se dice **hacer camping.** Por **hacer turismo** también se puede decir **ir de excursión** o **hacer un recorrido.** En vez de **dar una caminata,** muchas personas dicen **andar** o **caminar.**

RESOURCES FOR SEGUNDO PASO

Textbook Audiocassette 6B/Audio CD 12
Practice and Activity Book, pp. 137–139
Native Speaker Activity Book, pp. 56–60
Video Guide
Video Program,
Expanded Video Program, Videocassette 4
Videodisc Guide
Videodisc Program, Videodisc 6B

Chapter Teaching Resources, Book 3
- Communicative Activity 12-1, pp. 177–178
- Additional Listening Activities 12-3, 12-4, p. 186
  Audiocassette 10B/Audio CD 12
- Student Response Forms, pp. 194–196
- Realia 12-1, pp. 189, 191
- Situation Cards 12-2, pp. 192–193
- Teaching Transparency Master 12-2, pp. 182, 184
  Teaching Transparency 12-2
- Quiz 12-2, pp. 199–200
  Audiocassette 8B/Audio CD 12

17 ¿Qué pueden hacer? See answers below.

¿Qué pueden hacer estas personas en sus vacaciones? Completa cada oración con una o más frases del **Vocabulario** en la página 322.

1. Benjamín y Carmen van a pasar sus vacaciones en Texas, en la costa del Golfo de México. Allí pueden ______.
2. Margarita y sus padres piensan ir a los Andes de Chile. Ellos pueden ______.
3. Elizabeth va a pasar una semana en Madrid. Ella quiere ______.
4. Roberto y Carlos esperan ir a Puerto Rico en verano. Ellos van a ______.
5. Voy a Miami, Florida porque quiero ______.
6. Luz María y su familia piensan ir a las montañas en agosto a ______. Por eso necesitan comprar una nueva ______.

18 ¿Qué están haciendo?

Mira el dibujo de la Isla del Paraíso en la página 322.
Escribe lo que está haciendo cada persona en este momento.

ASÍ SE DICE Discussing what you would like to do on vacation

To find out what a friend would like to do, ask:	Your friend might answer:
¿**Qué te gustaría** hacer este verano?	Pues, a mí **me gustaría** ir a las playas en México. Dicen que son fantásticas.
¿**Adónde te gustaría ir** este verano?	A mí **me gustaría** escalar montañas en Colorado porque son muy bonitas.
¡Qué aburrido estoy! Y tú, **¿qué tienes ganas de hacer?**	**Tengo ganas de** dar una caminata en el bosque. ¿Vamos?

19 Destinos

You and your partner look at the list below and each choose three places you'd like to go. Don't tell each other which places you chose. Then, take turns asking each other what you'd like to do in each place. Can you guess each other's **destinos?**

1. Cuenca, Ecuador
2. Madrid, España
3. Cancún, México
4. San Juan, Puerto Rico
5. San Antonio, Texas
6. el Parque Nacional de Yellowstone
7. México, D.F., México
8. el Yunque, Puerto Rico
9. Cuernavaca, México
10. Los Ángeles, California

For Individual Needs

17 Slower Pace If students are having difficulty, ask them to focus first on the topography of the places. (**la costa del Golfo de México, los Andes de Chile**) Then, have them complete the sentences with the new vocabulary.

Portfolio

18 Written This activity may be used as a written Portfolio entry. For Portfolio information, see *Assessment Guide,* pp. 2–13.

Presentation

Así se dice Write the vocabulary words from **Vocabulario** on page 322 on index cards. Then, call on individual students to take a card and, without telling the others what is on the card, act out the activity. When a student knows what activity is being mimed, he or she responds with a phrase from **Así se dice** (affirmative or negative) plus the activity.

Biology Link

Ask students if they know the location of other tropical forests. (Central America, Amazon River Basin of South America, Congo River Basin of Africa, Southeast Asia) Mention that some are located in Spanish-speaking countries. Discuss the environmental consequences of destruction of the world's rain forests. (disruption of weather patterns, permanent loss of plant and animal species, land erosion)

Answers

17
1. tomar el sol y nadar
2. escalar montañas
3. explorar la selva
4. acampar y tomar el sol
5. hacer turismo e ir de vela
6. acampar; tienda de camping

For Individual Needs

19 Slower Pace Have students prepare by looking up three of the locations on the map and listing two activities they might enjoy in each location.

Teaching Suggestion

22 Have students use the maps on pages xxi–xxvii to choose their destination and plan their trip before getting together with their partners.

For Individual Needs

23 Challenge Ask students to select one of the ads and develop a telephone conversation in which one of them is a customer who calls the travel company to get information that is not in the ad. The other student is an employee who provides the information.

Reteaching

Ser y estar Use of anagrams to remember grammar uses may be helpful to some of your students. For the uses of **ser,** suggest the anagram MOPEDTOT. The letters represent: Material, Origin, Possession, Equivalence, Definition, Time, Occupation, and Traits. Uses of **estar** may be remembered by the anagram CLAP: Conditions, Locations, and Present Progressive. Encourage students that are helped by such memory devices to create their own.

Answers on p. 311C.

20 Escuchemos: Me gustaría...

Sara, Davíd y Martín dicen todo lo que les gustaría hacer durante sus vacaciones. Escribe los siguientes datos *(information)* para cada persona:

Nombre
Vive en
Le gustaría ir a
Quiere

21 ¡En la playa... en Puerto Rico! See answers below.

Lee este anuncio *(advertisement)* de un parador puertorriqueño y contesta las preguntas que siguen.

1. ¿Dónde se encuentra *(is located)* el Parador Villa Antonio?
2. Según el anuncio, ¿cómo es el Parador Villa Antonio?
3. ¿Las playas del Parador Villa Antonio son ideales para qué deporte?
4. ¿A ti te gustaría quedarte en este parador? ¿Por qué?
5. ¿Qué te gustaría hacer en este lugar?

22 ¡Pongámonos de acuerdo! *Let's come to an agreement!*

You and your partner have each just won a trip together to anywhere in Latin America. Each of you will choose a different destination. Try to convince each other that your own choice is better. Describe the place and say what you can do if you go there.

23 ¡Ven a la Isla del Paraíso! See sample answer below.

Work with two or three other students to write a short ad convincing people to spend their vacation on **la Isla del Paraíso** on page 322. Describe the setting, say what there is on the island, and tell people what they can do there.

Answers

21
1. Rincón, Puerto Rico
2. tranquilo
3. surfing
4. *Answers will vary.*
5. *Answers will vary.*

23 *Sample answer:*
Deben pasar las vacaciones en la Isla del Paraíso. Es un verdadero paraíso. Hay playas hermosas con arena blanca y fina. Puede nadar, tomar el sol, jugar en la playa e ir de vela. También puede bucear en el mar y ver los peces fantásticos.

Gramática ser and estar

You've learned to use **ser** and **estar,** the two Spanish verbs for *to be.*

Use **ser** . . .

1. to say what someone or something is like:
   ¿Cómo **es** Juanita? **Es** simpática y muy lista.
2. to say where someone or something is from:
   ¿De dónde **son** Uds.? **Somos** de Guadalajara.
3. to define something or someone:
   ¿Quién **es** la chica? **Es** mi amiga Marta. **Es** estudiante.
4. to say what something is made of:
   ¿De qué **son** tus calcetines? **Son** de algodón.
5. to give the date or the time:
   ¿Qué hora **es**? **Son** las dos menos cuarto.

Use **estar** . . .

1. to talk about states and conditions:
   ¿Cómo **está** Rogelio hoy? ¡Uy! **Está** de mal humor.
2. to talk about location:
   ¿Dónde **está** mi libro de álgebra? **Está** debajo de tu cama.

24 ¡Apúrate! See answers below.

Rubén y su hermano Marcos tienen que salir inmediatamente para el aeropuerto. Completa su diálogo con la forma apropiada de **ser** o **estar.**

RUBÉN ¡Marcos! ¿Por qué no __1__ (tú) listo?
MARCOS Es que todavía __2__ haciendo la maleta.
RUBÉN ¡Ay, Marcos! ¡(Tú) __3__ un desastre! No vas a cambiar *(to change)* nunca.
MARCOS Bueno, ¿por qué no me ayudas a encontrar mi camiseta favorita? __4__ roja y __5__ de algodón.
RUBÉN ¿Por qué no sabes dónde __6__?
MARCOS ¿Por qué __7__ (tú) de tan mal humor? Hombre, en tres horas vamos a __8__ en las playas de Puerto Rico. ¡Qué bien!
RUBÉN Ya sé, pero el avión sale a las tres. Mira, ya __9__ las dos.
MARCOS Mira, ¡aquí tengo mi camiseta! Ahora, ¿dónde __10__ mis zapatos de tenis?
RUBÉN ¡Aaayy!

25 ¡Unas vacaciones fantásticas! See sample answer below.

Imagínate que estás de vacaciones en un lugar fantástico. Escribe una tarjeta postal a tu mejor amigo o amiga. Dile dónde estás, cómo estás, cómo es allí y las cosas que te gustaría hacer.

Presentation

Gramática Remind students that they have already learned **ser** and **estar;** what they are learning here is merely the contrast between the two verbs. Read the examples given in **Gramática** and then model the use of both verbs. Walk around the classroom and ask students questions to elicit answers with the correct usage of **ser** and **estar.** (**¿De dónde es Juana? ¿Dónde está Juana?**) Once a student has answered a question correctly, ask another student which condition from **Gramática** the answer represents. (**Juana es de Puerto Rico** represents saying where someone is from. **Juana está en la clase** represents talking about location.)

Additional Practice

Have students write a paragraph about a close friend including the following information: appearance, type of clothing preferred, place of birth, birthday, general disposition, and where he or she is right now.

24 Slower Pace Do the activity with the whole class, having students identify the rule that applies to each usage.

En mi cuaderno

25 You may want to have students do this activity as a journal entry. For additional journal entry suggestion for Chapter 12, see *Practice and Activity Book,* p. 156.

Answers

24
1. estás
2. estoy
3. eres
4. Es
5. es
6. está
7. estás
8. estar
9. son
10. están

25 *Sample answer:*
Querido amigo,
Aquí estoy por fin en España. Todo es fantástico aquí. Estoy bien pero estoy un poco cansada. Pasamos tres días en Madrid y vimos el Escorial, Toledo y el Museo del Prado. Hoy vamos por tren a Granada. Me gustaría ver la Alhambra. Hasta la vista.

Language Note

27 Another way to say **cada cual a su gusto** (*to each his own*) is **cada uno a lo suyo.**

For Individual Needs

28 Slower Pace Before they write the paragraph, ask students to tell a partner what they do during the summer that they don't do during the school year. Partners report one or two things about each other's summer activities to the class.

Teaching Suggestion

Nota cultural Tell students that all over the world, old buildings are sometimes used in ways other than those for which they were built. (e.g., a mansion made into a museum) Have they ever visited a historical building that had been so converted?

Close

Review the material from this **Paso** by using *Teaching Transparency 12-2.* See "Suggestions for using Teaching Transparencies" in *Chapter Teaching Resources, Book 3,* page 184.

Assess

Quiz 12-2, *Chapter Teaching Resources, Book 3,* pp. 199–200

Assessment Items, Audiocassette 8B/Audio CD 12

Performance Assessment

Students in pairs create a dialogue between a travel agent and a client using as much of the vocabulary as possible from this **Paso.** When they have completed their dialogues, students present them to the class. If possible, have props available, such as used airline tickets, a passport, or an itinerary. Consider grading both the written dialogues and oral presentations.

26 Nos gustaría ir a...
See sample answer below.

Look at the photos of different places in Spanish-speaking countries. Work with a partner and choose the location that most appeals to both of you. Write a short paragraph about where you'd like to go **(Nos gustaría...)** and why. Use at least three adjectives. Then tell what you'd like to do there.

México, D.F.

Ponce, Puerto Rico

Toledo, España

Los Andes

27 Cada cual a su gusto
To each his own

Entrevista a un compañero o a una compañera sobre lo que le gustaría hacer en sus vacaciones. Luego sugiere *(suggest)* adónde debe ir de vacaciones con las frases **¿Por qué no vas a...?** y **Debes ir a...**

28 Quedarse en casa
Answers will vary.

Muchas personas pasan las vacaciones en casa. Escribe un párrafo *(paragraph)* que explica qué vas a hacer en casa este verano.

MODELO Me gustaría ir a Barcelona, pero no puedo. Tengo que trabajar. Voy a...

NOTA CULTURAL

Several Spanish-speaking countries offer fascinating **paradores,** or inns, for travelers to stay overnight. Spain has a network of many reasonably priced **paradores,** many of them in old castles, palaces, convents, and monasteries. In the **Parador de Zephra,** for example, you can sleep in the same castle where Hernán Cortés stayed before setting out for the New World. You could stay in a room at the **Parador de Santiago de Compostela,** founded by King Ferdinand and Queen Isabella. And if you get a room at the **Parador de Alarcón,** you'll sleep in a castle built in the eighth century by Moors from North Africa!

Culture Note

Puerto Rico has a number of **paradores** patterned after the **paradores nacionales** in Spain. Some are guest houses, others are tourist villas and small hotels. Operated by the government, the **paradores** in Puerto Rico are situated where the traveler can experience the natural beauty of the island.

Answers

26 *Sample answer:*
Nos gustaría ir a Toledo, España. Parece muy interesante porque es una ciudad muy vieja. Me gustaría ver la muralla alrededor de la ciudad y las iglesias grandes.

TERCER PASO

Saying where you went and what you did on vacation

ASÍ SE DICE — Saying where you went and what you did on vacation

To find out about a friend's vacation, ask:

¿Adónde viajaste el verano pasado?

¿Adónde fueron tú y tu familia durante las vacaciones?

¿Qué hiciste cuando fuiste a Buenos Aires?

Your friend might answer:

Yo **no fui a ningún lugar.**
I didn't go anywhere (lit., nowhere).

Fuimos a Puerto Rico.

En Buenos Aires, **visité** la Plaza de Mayo.

También se puede decir...
Por **ningún lugar** *(nowhere, not anywhere)* también se dice **ninguna parte** o **ningún lado**, como en **No fuimos a ningún lado.**

29 Escuchemos: ¡Qué divertido!

Carlos and Yolanda have just returned from their trip to Puerto Rico. Listen to them tell about it. Place the pictures in the correct order, according to what they say.
Answers on p. 311D.

a.

b.

c.

d.

Gramática — Preterite tense

To talk about what happened in the past, use the preterite tense. All regular **-ar** verbs follow the same pattern as **trabajar.** The verb **ir** is irregular in the preterite.

trabajar		ir	
trabaj**é**	trabaj**amos**	**fui**	**fuimos**
trabaj**aste**	trabaj**asteis**	**fuiste**	**fuisteis**
trabaj**ó**	trabaj**aron**	**fue**	**fueron**

RESOURCES FOR TERCER PASO

Textbook Audiocassette 6B/Audio CD 12
Practice and Activity Book, pp. 140–142
Native Speaker Activity Book, pp. 56–60
Videodisc Guide
Videodisc Program, Videodisc 6B

Chapter Teaching Resources, Book 3
- Communicative Activity 12-2, pp. 179–180
- Additional Listening Activities 12-5, 12-6, p. 187
  Audiocassette 10B/Audio CD 12
- Student Response Forms, pp. 194–196
- Realia 12-2, pp. 190, 191
- Situation Cards 12-3, pp. 192–193
- Teaching Transparency Master 12-3, pp. 183, 184
  Teaching Transparency 12-3
- Quiz 12-3, pp. 201–202
  Audiocassette 8B/Audio CD 12

Jump Start!

Have students copy the following columns and draw lines connecting the verb in column 1 with an appropriate ending in column 2. (column 1. **Viajé, Trabajamos, Estudiaron, Hiciste, Me gustó, Preparó;** column 2. **en casa el sábado, a San Juan por avión, las matemáticas, la maleta para tu viaje, un pastel para el cumpleaños de mi hermana, la película)**

MOTIVATE

Ask students: **¿Cuántos estudiantes viajaron a otra ciudad el verano pasado? ¿Cuántos visitaron a los parientes?...**

TEACH

Presentation

Así se dice Using a wall map of the world or *Map Transparency 2,* point to the locations as you model questions and answers. Have students practice the phrases in pairs. Then ask them to develop some original statements using the expressions and another world location. Have students report their partner's answers to the class, showing the location mentioned on the map.

Gramática After reviewing the preterite forms of **trabajar** and **ir,** write those forms on the board. Ask a student to give an original sentence using one of the forms of **trabajar.** After the student has done so, erase that form. Continue until students have given an original sentence for each form of both verbs.

Family Link

30 Ask students to bring in photos from home of a recent vacation and write captions for them.

Presentation

Vocabulario After students have practiced the pronunciation of the countries, have them consult a world map. They are to list the countries in the order of closest to farthest from where they live. You might also have them list the countries in order from the one they would most like to visit to the one they are least interested in visiting.

Geography Link

Point out to students that the World Map on pages xxii–xxiii shows the names in Spanish of most of this world's countries and capital cities. Consider giving students extra credit on the Chapter Test or Final Exam if they can name in Spanish the cities and countries of origin of their ancestors.

30 Benjamín y Carmen ya regresaron See sample answer below.

Carmen and Benjamín are sorting out their pictures from their trip to Puerto Rico. Help them by writing two sentences for each picture about what they did and where they went.

31 Destino desconocido *Unknown destination*

Escribe una lista de diez cosas que llevaste en un viaje pasado. Tu compañero tiene que hacerte preguntas del tipo sí/no para averiguar *(to find out)* qué llevaste y para adivinar dónde pasaste tus vacaciones.

MODELO —¿Llevaste una cámara?
—Sí, llevé una cámara.

VOCABULARIO

Alemania	*Germany*
China	*China*
Egipto	*Egypt*
Francia	*France*
Inglaterra	*England*
Italia	*Italy*

A LO NUESTRO

A common way to say you had a great time in Spanish is **Lo pasé muy bien** or **fenomenal**. There are different expressions in different countries. In Costa Rica you'll hear **Lo pasé pura vida**. The most common way to say that you had a bad time is **Lo pasé mal**, but you could also say **Lo pasé fatal**.

Answers

30 *Sample answer:*
Fuimos al partido de béisbol. Fue muy divertido porque el equipo favorito de Abuelo ganó.

32 Mi viaje a Puerto Rico See possible answers below.

Julio, un amigo de Ben, le mandó una carta con cinco preguntas sobre su viaje a Puerto Rico. Aquí tienes la carta de Ben con sus respuestas. ¿Puedes adivinar las cinco preguntas de Julio?

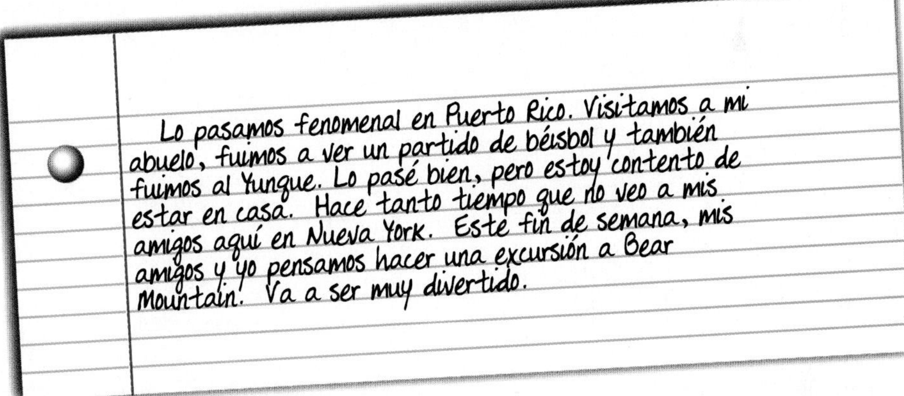

Lo pasamos fenomenal en Puerto Rico. Visitamos a mi abuelo, fuimos a ver un partido de béisbol y también fuimos al Yunque. Lo pasé bien, pero estoy contento de estar en casa. Hace tanto tiempo que no veo a mis amigos aquí en Nueva York. Este fin de semana, mis amigos y yo pensamos hacer una excursión a Bear Mountain. Va a ser muy divertido.

33 Una entrevista

Interview a classmate who has taken a trip. Find out where he or she went, what he or she did, and so on. Ask as many questions as you can. Take notes in order to be able to report to the class.

34 En mi cuaderno See sample answer below.

Escribe un párrafo de cinco oraciones para explicar a qué lugar esperas viajar algún día y por qué. Incluye qué quieres hacer allí y qué tiempo hace típicamente.

LETRA Y SONIDO

A. In English we pronounce *p, t,* and *k* (as in *pin, tin,* and *kin*) with a puff of air. This puff of air does not happen in Spanish. Practice saying these words without releasing that puff of air.

hotel papa paracaídas caminata canoa toalla

In addition, the letter *t* in Spanish is pronounced with the tongue against the upper teeth, not against the area immediately above the teeth known as the alveolar ridge.

tienda carta tiempo hasta tractor tanto

B. Dictado Script on p. 311D.
Listen to the answering machine and take down the message you hear word for word.

C. Trabalenguas

Paco Pérez pone poco papel en el pupitre.
Carla quiere cantar en el coro con Claudia Cortés.

En mi cuaderno

34 Ask students to write a paragraph about what each member of her or his family likes to do and where they like to go on vacation. For an additional journal entry suggestion for Chapter 12, see *Practice and Activity Book,* p. 156.

Close

Give each student a small piece of paper with the name of a country on it and tell them to imagine that they have returned from a trip there. Students are to tell a partner where they went, who they went with, what they took with them, what they did there, and whether they had a good time.

Assess

Quiz 12-3, *Chapter Teaching Resources, Book 3,* pp. 201–202

Assessment Items, Audiocassette 8B/Audio CD 12

Performance Assessment

Ask students to imagine they have just returned from a vacation. They are to create a photo album with pictures clipped from magazines and write a brief description under each picture explaining where they were and what they were doing or seeing when the photo was taken.

Answers

32 *Possible answers:*
1. ¿Quién visitaste?
2. ¿Qué hiciste?
3. ¿Adónde fuiste?
4. ¿Cómo lo pasaste?
5. ¿Qué vas a hacer el fin de semana que viene?

34 *Sample answer:*
Un día espero viajar a Alaska. Me gustaría hacer un viaje en un barco de lujo para ver de cerca los glaciares y las ballenas. Hace mucho frío en invierno y un poco fresco en verano. Quiero ir en verano.

READING STRATEGIES

Recognizing text organization

PREREADING
Activity A

Motivating Activity

Ask students to list five things they would like to do on an ideal vacation. Do they know of an ideal spot where they could do all five things?

Teaching Suggestion

Since this is the last chapter, briefly review the strategies presented throughout the *Pupil's Edition.* Do this by asking students to name and describe as many strategies as they can remember. (using background information, looking at titles and subtitles, using pictures, looking for cognates, making an outline, etc.)

READING
Activities B and C

Thinking Critically

Observing To help them understand as they read, ask students to name as many of the items in the illustration as they can.

Teacher Note

This would be a good time to discuss the locations, especially ones outside of the United States. Ask what students know about these locations, and try to point out some common background knowledge prior to reading in detail.

VAMOS A LEER

¿Cuáles son las vacaciones ideales para ti?

Estrategia Before reading a passage in detail, you should try to recognize how it is organized. This helps you follow along more easily, and can save you time if you need to look only for a certain piece of information.

¡A comenzar!

A. The reading on these pages is about how to choose the vacation that is best for you. Take a minute or two and see if you can determine how it is organized. Doing this will help you enjoy it more. Be sure to look at the following hints.
   1. **¿Te gusta mucho el sol?** is the beginning.
   2. Notice the footprints, and think about their purpose.

   Write your answer, then discuss it with at least two classmates. Make sure that you all agree about how this text is organized.

Al grano

B. Suppose that there will be two Costa Rican exchange students in your school next year, Matías and Berta. You can find out a little about them by seeing what choices they made on the flow chart. Matías' path is blue, and Berta's is red. Read through all their choices, then see how well you know them. Answer *true* or *false*. See answers below.

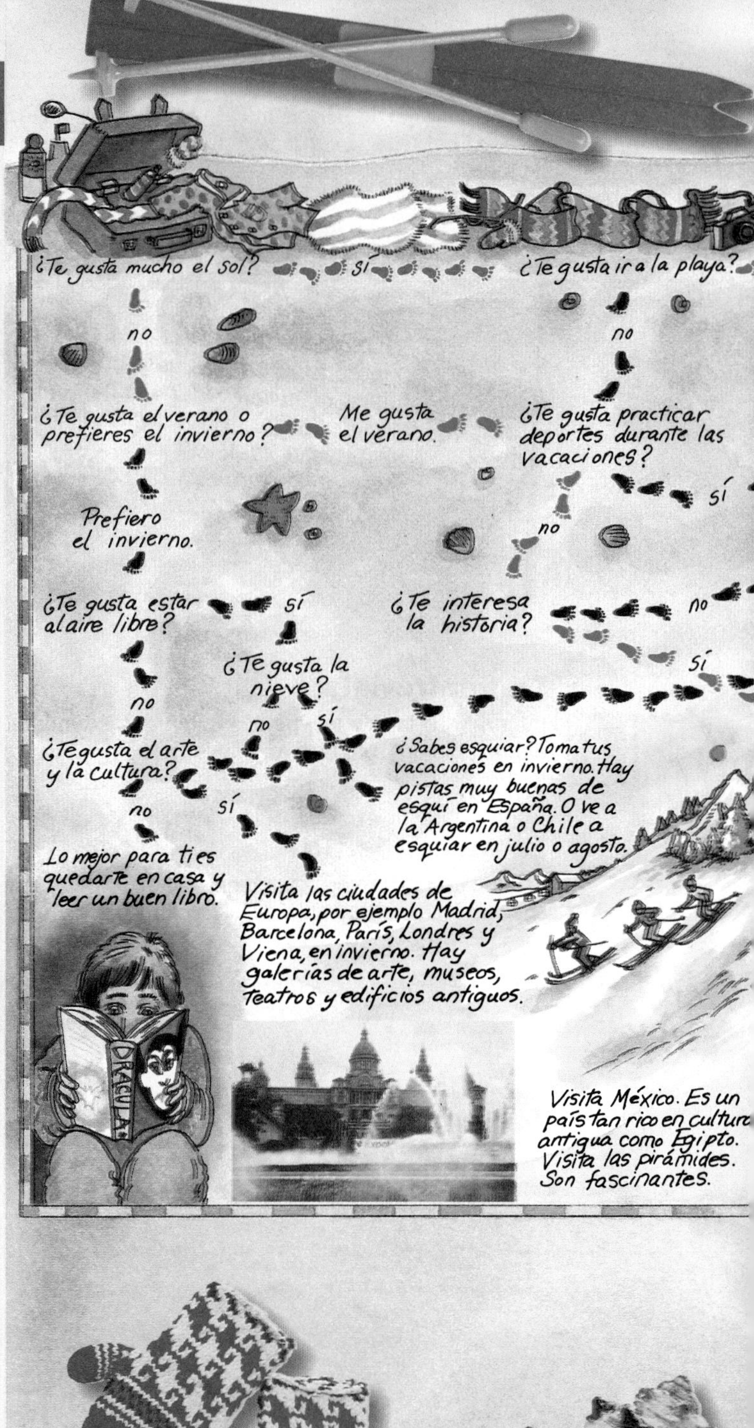

For Individual Needs

Challenge Ask students to invent a country complete with topography, climate, economy, population, and perhaps even history. The description should be detailed enough to convince a tourist it is a good place to visit. Students also could draw a map or create a 3-D model.

Answers

B

Berta:	Matías:
1. falso	1. falso
2. cierto	2. falso
3. cierto	3. cierto
4. falso	4. falso

See answers below.

Berta . . .

1. doesn't like the beach.
2. thinks dancing is fun.
3. likes the sun.
4. is a great swimmer.

Matías . . .

1. loves wintertime.
2. really likes sports.
3. is interested in history.
4. likes the sun.

C. Imagine that you're a travel agent and several people come to you for advice about where to spend their vacation. According to the map, which of the seven destinations would you recommend for a person who . . .?

1. likes the sun, the beach, and learning new things, but can't swim
2. likes being indoors and likes art and culture
3. doesn't like talking with friends, dancing, art, or culture
4. likes the beach, but not swimming or doing new things
5. doesn't like to play sports, but does like history

D. Ahora repasa el mapa por última vez para decidir en dónde debes pasar tus vacaciones. Asegúrate de seguir las indicaciones y de responder verazmente. ¿Adónde recomienda que vayas tú? Escribe un párrafo breve en el cual dices adónde debes ir y por qué. Intenta escribir todo en español. **(Debo ir a... porque...)**

Answers will vary.

POSTREADING
Activity D

Teaching Suggestions

- To extend Activity D, have students make oral presentations. Ask them to choose one place they would like to visit and to prepare a brief oral description of that location. Suggest they use visuals with their talks to facilitate listening comprehension.
- Ask students whether they would be able to do all the things they listed in the Motivating Activity in any of the ideal vacation spots in the reading. Would they need to take more than one vacation to accomplish this?
- In the Chapter Opener, it was suggested that students post a note on a wall map showing their ideal vacation spot. (See Motivating Activity, p. 312.) Based on what they have learned in this chapter, would students change the location of their ideal vacation?
- Have students investigate the cost of their ideal vacation by checking the travel section of their local paper. How expensive is their ideal trip compared to others listed?

Native Speakers

Ask native speakers if they have any photographs of a memorable vacation at home. If so, ask them to bring the photos in and give a short oral report about it. If no one has real photographs to share, you might consider having a native speaker bring a magazine photo of a place where he or she would like to go.

Answers

C 1. un campamento
2. quedarte en casa y leer un buen libro
3. visitar las ciudades de Europa
4. ir a Acapulco, el Caribe, Puerto Rico o la República Dominicana
5. visitar las pirámides de México

Teacher Note

For additional readings, see *Native Speaker Activity Book,* p. 60, and *Practice and Activity Book,* p. 143.

The **Repaso** reviews and integrates all four skills and culture in preparation for the Chapter Test.

For Individual Needs

1 Slower Pace Before they listen to the tape, ask students to identify a specific word or phrase in each picture. By listening for that phrase, they can identify the drawing more easily.

2 Challenge Ask students to imagine that they have just returned from the vacation of their dreams. Have them write a paragraph about what they did based on their answers for this activity.

Portfolio

3 Oral You might recommend that students record their conversation for the oral Portfolio. For Portfolio suggestions, see *Assessment Guide,* p. 25.

Group Work

4 Have each group develop its discussion and itinerary into a skit. Then have them present it to the class. If time permits, ask the class to vote on the trip that they would most like to take.

REPASO

1 Las siguientes personas describen sus planes para las vacaciones. Para cada descripción que oyes, indica el dibujo correspondiente. Answers on p. 311D.

a.

b.

c.

d.

e.

f.

2 ¿Cuáles son las vacaciones de tus sueños? ¿Viajar al Caribe, a España, a la selva amazónica? Explica cómo es tu viaje ideal. Contesta las siguientes preguntas.

1. ¿Adónde te gustaría viajar?
2. ¿Por qué?
3. ¿Qué te gustaría hacer al llegar?
4. ¿Cuándo quieres hacer el viaje?
5. ¿Con quiénes quieres viajar?
6. ¿Por cuánto tiempo piensas quedarte?

3 Work with a partner. One of you will take the role of travel agent, the other will be a customer. The travel agent will ask the customer what he or she would like to do on a vacation. Based upon the customer's responses, the travel agent will suggest some vacation spots from the list in Activity 19 on page 323.

4 Work with two or three classmates to plan a group trip. Decide when and where you will go and what you will need. Talk about the clothing you must take, the weather, and what you will see. Also agree on at least three activities you would like to do and how long you would like to stay. Be ready to present your itinerary to the class.

Cooperative Learning

On the board or a transparency write the following: **Quiero... Necesitan... ¿Piensas...? Debemos... Mi amigo/a espera... Uds. pueden... Vamos a... Tengo que...** Divide the class into groups of three. Ask each group to complete the sentences with an infinitive and any other words necessary. All sentences should relate to a class trip the students are planning. Group members assume the roles of discussion leader, writer, and reporter. The discussion leader guides the discussion as members create the sentences. The writer records the sentences. The reporter reads the completed sentences to the class. Call on different groups until you have two or three completed sentences for each verb. To assist visual learners, you could have a student write the completed sentences on the board or on a transparency as they are read out.

5 Get together in groups of four. Each of you should silently write two sentences about what one of these people did at Manolo's party. The last student will read the details aloud to the class. Answers will vary.

1. Elena
2. tú
3. Carlos y yo
4. Alfredo
5. Berta y Sofía
6. todos los invitados

6 It's December 28, **el Día de los Inocentes** (a kind of April Fool's Day in Spanish-speaking countries). For a joke, write a letter telling a friend everything you did on some imaginary, fantastic vacation. Use your imagination! See sample answer below.

7 Lee las siguientes oraciones. Decide si cada oración es cierta o falsa. Si es falsa, cámbiala para que sea cierta *(change it so that it's true)*. See answers below.

1. Los paradores son un tipo de hotel que hay en muchos países hispanos.
2. Hay paradores en todos los países hispanohablantes, menos *(except)* España.
3. Es posible alquilar una habitación *(to rent a room)* en un parador en un antiguo castillo, palacio, convento o monasterio.
4. Los paradores son bonitos, pero generalmente cuestan demasiado para la mayoría de los turistas.
5. El **Parador de Santiago de Compostela** fue fundado por *(was founded by)* Hernán Cortés hace 500 años.

8 S I T U A C I Ó N

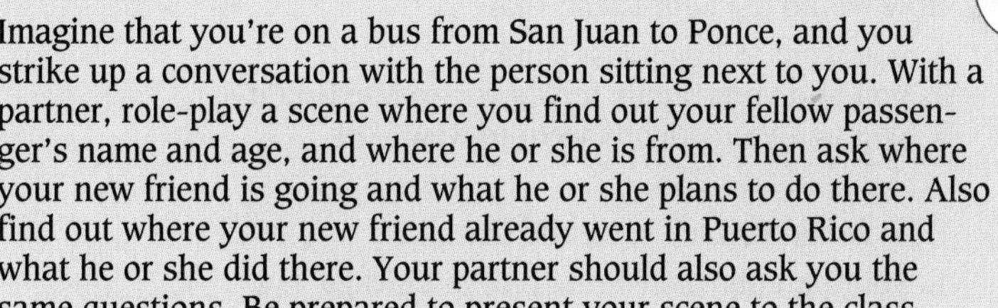

Imagine that you're on a bus from San Juan to Ponce, and you strike up a conversation with the person sitting next to you. With a partner, role-play a scene where you find out your fellow passenger's name and age, and where he or she is from. Then ask where your new friend is going and what he or she plans to do there. Also find out where your new friend already went in Puerto Rico and what he or she did there. Your partner should also ask you the same questions. Be prepared to present your scene to the class.

Additional Practice

5 Have students relate to their partner what each person at their house does to straighten up after a day of normal activity.

Portfolio

6 Written This activity may be used as a Portfolio entry. For Portfolio suggestions, see *Assessment Guide,* p. 25.

Culture Note

6 The Spanish equivalent of April Fool's Day is December 28, **el Día de los Santos Inocentes** (*the Day of the Holy Innocents*), the day on which the Catholic Church commerates the slaughter of the Holy Innocents by Herod. Tricks and pranks played on December 28 are called **inocentadas.** Even newspapers participate in the spirit of the day by publishing retouched photographs and altered news items. It is believed that this day is celebrated with pranks due to the alternative meanings of the word **inocente.** (e.g. *innocent, naïve, blameless,* and *foolish*)

Video Wrap-Up

- **VIDEO PROGRAM**
- **EXPANDED VIDEO PROGRAM, Videocassette 4**
- **VIDEODISC PROGRAM, Videodisc 6B**

At this time, you might want to use the video resources for additional review and enrichment. See *Video Guide or Videodisc Guide* for suggestions regarding:

- **Un recorrido por San Juan** (Dramatic episode)
- **Panorama cultural** (Interviews)
- **Video clips** (Authentic footage)

Answers

6 *Sample answer:*

La semana pasada fui con mi novio de vacaciones a la luna. Fue muy interesante. Viajamos por nave espacial con otras personas. El viaje duró todo el día. Llegamos tarde y fuimos al hotel lunar. Caminamos mucho en la luna. No hay selvas pero hay muchas montañas. El hotel tiene una piscina y nadamos un día. La tierra parece hermosa por la noche. Pasamos cuatro días en la luna y regresamos anteayer.

7
1. Cierto
2. Falso: Hay paradores en España.
3. Cierto
4. Falso: Los paradores son bonitos y generalmente no cuestan demasiado para la mayoría de los turistas.
5. Falso: El Parador de Santiago de Compostela fue fundado por el Rey Fernando y la Reina Isabela.

This page is intended to help prepare students for the Chapter Test. It is a brief checklist of the major points covered in the chapter. The students should be reminded that this is only a checklist and does not necessarily include everything that will appear on the Chapter Test.

Teaching Suggestion

Divide the class into groups of four. Ask each group member to serve as the expert for the skills in two questions. Each expert is responsible for checking with other members of the group to see if they need help with the expert's two questions. If a group member needs help, the expert should provide it.

A VER SI PUEDO . . .

Can you talk about what you do and like to do every day? p. 317

1 How would you ask the following people what they do everyday?

1. your best friend
2. a new student in your class
3. your cousin
4. your brother or sister
5. a group of friends
6. your aunt and uncle

See answers below.

2 How would you ask someone if he or she would like to do the following?

a.

b.

c.

d.

See answers below.

Can you make future plans? p. 318

3 How do you ask someone . . .? See answers below.

1. what he or she is going to do tomorrow
2. what he or she plans to do this summer
3. what he or she hopes to do in the future

4 Tell a friend about a future trip to Mexico. Say what you plan and hope to do. Use these cues:

1. ir a México, D.F. este verano
2. hacer turismo
3. practicar el español

Can you discuss what you would like to do on vacation? p. 323

5 How would you answer if someone asked you the following questions?

1. ¿Qué te gustaría hacer hoy?
2. ¿Adónde te gustaría viajar?

Answers will vary.

6 How would you tell someone that you would like to travel to . . .?

1. Madrid
2. Hong Kong
3. Cancún
4. Moscú

Sample answer: Me gustaría viajar a Madrid.

Can you say where you went and what you did on vacation? p. 327

7 How would tell your friend that . . .?

1. you went to Egypt last summer
2. you and your family took a trip to Mexico City
3. you and your friends went to New York

See answers below.

8 How would you tell someone that . . .?

1. your parents visited relatives in Chicago
2. you and your sister didn't go anywhere and worked all summer

See answers below.

Answers

1 1. ¿Qué haces todos los días?
2. ¿Qué haces todos los días?
3. ¿Qué haces todos los días?
4. ¿Qué haces todos los días?
5. ¿Qué hacen todos los días?
6. ¿Qué hacen todos los días?

2 *Answers may vary.*
1. ¿Te gustaría saltar en paracaídas?
2. ¿Te gustaría bajar el río en canoa?
3. ¿Te gustaría hacer caminatas en la montaña?
4. ¿Te gustaría tomar el sol en la playa?

3 1. ¿Qué vas a hacer mañana?
2. ¿Qué piensas hacer este verano?
3. ¿Qué esperas hacer en el futuro?

7 1. Fui a Indonesia el verano pasado.
2. Mi familia y yo hicimos un viaje a la ciudad de México.
3. Fuimos a Nueva York.

8 1. Mis padres visitaron a familiares en Chicago.
2. Mi hermana y yo no fuimos a ningún lugar y trabajamos todo el verano.

VOCABULARIO

PRIMER PASO

Making future plans

el bloqueador *sunscreen*
el boleto *ticket*
la bufanda *scarf*
la cámara *camera*
las chancletas *sandals, slippers*
los esquís *skis*
hacer la maleta *to pack the suitcase*
los lentes de sol *sunglasses*
quedarse *to stay, to remain*
la toalla *towel*

SEGUNDO PASO

Discussing what you would like to do on vacation

bajar el río en canoa *to go canoeing*
el bosque *forest*
dar una caminata *to go hiking*
escalar montañas *to go mountain climbing*
explorar *to explore*
hacer turismo *to go sightseeing*
ir de vela *to go sailing*
saltar en paracaídas *to go skydiving*
la selva *jungle*
la tienda de camping *camping tent*
tomar el sol *to sunbathe*

TERCER PASO

Saying where you went and what you did on vacation

Alemania *Germany*
China *China*
Egipto *Egypt*
Francia *France*
Inglaterra *England*
Italia *Italy*
ningún lugar *nowhere, not anywhere*

Game

HACER LA MALETA For this game you will need a suitcase and things to put in it. You might use the items you used to teach the vocabulary or objects in the classroom. The first student begins by saying **Voy a poner un/a ___ en la maleta,** and puts the item in the suitcase. You then call a second student. The second student repeats what the first student said, adds a new item at the end of the sentence, and puts the new item in the suitcase. The game continues following this pattern.

VOCABULARIO
CAPÍTULO 12

For Individual Needs

Visual Learners Create scrambled versions of vocabulary to be reviewed. For example, you could make a list of scrambled words for vacation activities, e.g. **rache mosritu** for **hacer turismo.** Give each student a copy of the scrambled activities and have them try to unscramble them.

CHAPTER 12 ASSESSMENT

CHAPTER TEST

- *Chapter Teaching Resources, Book 3*
- *Assessment Guide,* Speaking Test, p. 33
- *Assessment Items, Audiocassette 8B Audio CD 12*

TEST GENERATOR, CHAPTER 12

ALTERNATIVE ASSESSMENT

Performance Assessment

You might have students use the **Situación** on page 333 as a cumulative performance assessment activity.

Portfolio Assessment

- **Written: Repaso** Activity 6, *Pupil's Edition,* p. 333 *Assessment Guide,* p. 25
- **Oral: Repaso** Activity 3, *Pupil's Edition,* p. 332 *Assessment Guide,* p. 25

SUMMARY OF FUNCTIONS

Functions are probably best defined as the ways in which you use a language for specific purposes. When you find yourself in specific situations, such as in a restaurant, in a grocery store, or at a school, you will want to communicate with those around you. In order to do that, you have to "function" in the language so that you can be understood: you place an order, make a purchase, or talk about your class schedule.

Such functions form the core of this book. They are easily identified by the boxes in each chapter that are labeled **Así se dice.** These functions are the building blocks you need to become a speaker of Spanish. All the other features in the chapter—the grammar, the vocabulary, even the culture notes—are there to support the functions you are learning.

Here is a list of the functions presented in this book and the Spanish expressions you will need in order to communicate in a wide range of situations. Following each function is the chapter and page number where it was introduced.

SOCIALIZING

Saying hello **Ch. 1, p. 21**

Buenos días.
Buenas tardes.
Buenas noches.
Hola.

Saying goodbye **Ch. 1, p. 21**

Adiós.
Bueno, tengo clase.
Chao.
Hasta luego.
Hasta mañana.
Tengo que irme.

Introducing people and responding to an introduction **Ch. 1, p. 22**

Me llamo...
Soy...
¿Cómo te llamas?
Éste es mi amigo...
Ésta es mi amiga...
Se llama...
¡Mucho gusto!
Encantado/a.
Igualmente.

Asking how someone is and saying how you are **Ch. 1, p. 24**

¿Cómo estás?
¿Y tú?
¿Qué tal?
Estoy (bastante) bien, gracias.
Yo también.
Estupendo.
Excelente.
Regular.
Más o menos.
(Muy) mal.
¡Horrible!

Talking on the telephone **Ch. 7, p. 183**

Aló.
Diga.
¿Quién habla?
¿Está ..., por favor?
¿De parte de quién?
La línea está ocupada.
¿Puedo dejar un recado?
Un momento...
Llamo más tarde.

Extending and accepting invitations **Ch. 7, p. 184**

¿Te gustaría...?
Sí, me gustaría...
Nos gustan...
¿Quieres...?
Te invito.
¡Claro que sí!

Making plans **Ch. 7, p. 188**

¿Qué piensas hacer hoy?
Pienso...
¿Piensas...?

Talking about getting ready **Ch. 7, p. 190**

¿Estás listo/a?
No, todavía necesito...
No, porque necesito...

Turning down an invitation and making an excuse **Ch. 7, p. 193**

¡Qué lástima!
Ya tengo planes.
Tal vez otro día.
Lo siento, pero no.
Estoy ocupado/a.
Tengo una cita.
Tengo que...
Me gustaría, pero no puedo.
Estoy cansado/a y un poco enfermo/a.

EXCHANGING INFORMATION

Asking and saying how old someone is **Ch. 1, p. 27**

¿Cuántos años tienes?
Tengo ... años
¿Cuántos años tiene?
Tiene ... años

Asking where someone is from and saying where you're from **Ch. 1, p. 28**

¿De dónde eres? ¿De dónde es...?
Soy de... Es de...

Talking about what you want and need ***Ch 2, p. 48***

¿Qué quieres? Necesito...
Quiero... ¿Qué necesita?
Quiere... Ya tengo...
¿Qué necesitas? Necesita...
¿Necesitas...?

Describing the contents of your room **Ch. 2, p. 53**

¿Qué hay en tu cuarto? Hay ... en su cuarto.
Tengo ... en mi cuarto. ¿Tienes...?
¿Qué hay en el cuarto de...? ¿Qué tiene ... en su cuarto?
Tiene ... en su cuarto.

Talking about what you need and want to do **Ch. 2, p. 56**

¿Qué necesitas hacer? ¿Qué quieres hacer?
Necesito... Quiero hacer...
¿Qué necesita hacer...? ¿Qué quiere hacer...?
Necesita... No sé, pero no quiero...
Quiere...

Talking about classes and sequencing events **Ch. 3, p. 76**

¿Qué clases tienes este semestre? Primero tengo..., después... y luego...
Tengo... Por fin...
¿Qué clases tienes hoy? ¿Y mañana?

Telling time **Ch. 3, p. 77**

¿Qué hora es? Son las...
Es la una. Son las ... y cuarto.
Es la una y cuarto. Son las ... y media.
Es la una y media. ¿Ya son las...?
Es tarde.

Telling at what time something happens **Ch. 3, p. 80**

¿A qué hora es...? ¡Es ahora!
(Es) a las ... de la tarde. En punto.

Talking about being late or in a hurry **Ch. 3, p. 82**

Estoy atrasado/a. Tengo prisa.
Está atrasado/a. ¡Date prisa!

Describing people and things **Ch. 3, p. 84**

¿Cómo es...? ¿Cómo son...?
Es... Son...
No es... No son...

Discussing what you and others do during free time **Ch. 4, p. 102**

¿Qué haces después de clases?
Antes de regresar a casa...
En el tiempo libre...

Telling where people and things are **Ch. 4, p. 106**

¿Dónde estás? ¿No está en...?
Estoy en... No, no está aquí. Está en...

Talking about where you and others go during free time **Ch. 4, p. 111**

¿Adónde vas? Va a...
Voy a... Va al...
¿Adónde va...? Va a la...

Discussing how often you do things **Ch. 5, p. 129**

¿Con qué frecuencia...? ¿Todavía...?
Todos los días Durante la semana
Siempre A veces
Nunca Muchas veces
Sólo cuando...

Talking about what you do during a typical week **Ch. 5, p. 135**

¿Qué haces típicamente durante el día?
¿Qué hace ... por la mañana?
¿Qué hacen ... por la tarde?
¿Qué hacen ... por la noche?

Giving today's date **Ch. 5, p. 138**

¿Cuál es la fecha?
¿Qué fecha es hoy?
Hoy es el primero de...
Hoy es el ... de...

Talking about the weather **Ch. 5, p. 140**

¿Qué tiempo hace?
Hace buen tiempo.
Hace muy mal tiempo hoy.

Describing a family **Ch. 6, p. 154**

¿Cuántas personas hay en tu familia? Somos...
Hay ... en mi familia. ¿Cómo es tu familia?
Tenemos...

Describing people **Ch. 6, p. 158**

¿Cómo es...? ¿De qué color es...?
Tiene... ¿De qué color son...?

***Discussing things a family does together* Ch. 6, p. 160**

¿Qué hacen ustedes los fines de semana?
¿Hacen ustedes algo durante el verano?

Talking about meals and food **Ch. 8, p. 207**

¿Qué tomas para el desayuno?
¿Qué tomas para el almuerzo?
A veces tomo...
No me gusta ... para nada.
Tengo sed. ¿Qué hay para tomar?
¿Qué prefieres?

Ordering dinner in a restaurant **Ch. 8, p. 218**

¿Qué vas a pedir? ¿Qué le puedo traer?
Voy a pedir... Yo quisiera...

***Asking for and paying the bill in a restaurant* Ch. 8, p. 218**

¿Nos puede traer la cuenta?
La cuenta, por favor.
¿Desean algo más?
¿Cuánto es?
¿Está incluida la propina?
No, no está incluida. Es aparte.

Discussing gift suggestions **Ch. 9, p. 237**

¿Qué piensas regalarle a...?
Le voy a dar...
¿Para quién es el regalo?
El regalo es para...
¿Qué tipo de regalo buscas?
Busco...

***Asking for and giving directions downtown* Ch. 9, p. 239**

Perdón, ¿dónde está...?
Está a ... cuadras de aquí.
¿Me puede decir dónde queda...?
Queda al lado de...

Making comparisons **Ch. 9, p. 245**

¿Cuál es más barato?
El ... es menos caro que el...
¿Son los ... tan caros como el...?
Son del mismo precio.

***Asking about prices and paying for something* Ch. 9, p. 248**

¿Cuánto cuesta...? ¿Cuánto cuestan...?
Cuesta... Cuestan...

***Talking about what are you doing right now* Ch. 10, p. 262**

¿Qué estás haciendo?
Estoy colgando las decoraciones.
Él está limpiando la sala.
¿Todos están decorando la casa?
Sí, estamos decorando la casa.

Talking about past events **Ch. 10, p. 271**

¿Qué hiciste anoche?
Bailé y hablé con...
¿Qué hizo ... ayer?
¿Lo pasaron bien la semana pasada?
Sí, lo pasamos bien.

Saying what you did **Ch. 11, p. 300**

¿Qué hiciste anoche?
¿Ganaste?
Jugué...
Jugó...

***Talking about where you went and when* Ch. 11, p. 302**

¿Adónde fuiste anteayer?
¿Adónde fuiste anteanoche?
Anoche fui...

Talking about what you do and like to do every day **Ch. 12, p. 317**

¿Qué haces todos los días?
Primero...
Después...
Y luego...
¿Con qué frecuencia...?
¿Qué te gusta hacer después de clases?
Me gusta...

Making future plans **Ch. 12, p. 318**

¿Adónde piensas viajar algún día?
¿Quieres viajar a...?
No, pero espero hacer un viaje a...
¿Qué vas a hacer este verano?

Saying where you went and what you did on vacation **Ch. 12, p. 327**

¿Adónde viajaste el verano pasado?
No fui a ningún lugar.
¿Adónde fueron durante las vacaciones?
Fuimos a...
¿Qué hiciste cuando fuiste a...?

EXPRESSING ATTITUDES AND OPINIONS

Talking about things you like and explaining why **Ch. 3, p. 87**

¿Te gustan...?	Sí, a ella le gustan mucho.
Sí, me gustan.	¿Por qué?
¿Cuál es...?	Porque...
¿A ella le gustan...?	

Talking about what you like to do **Ch. 4, p. 101**

¿Qué te gusta hacer?	¿A quién le gusta...?
Me gusta...	A mí me gusta...
¿A él le gusta...?	Por eso, me gustan...
No, no le gusta..., pero le gusta...	

Talking about what you and your friends like to do together **Ch. 5, p. 132**

¿Qué les gusta hacer?	Nos gusta...
	¿Les gusta ... juntos?

Discussing problems and giving advice **Ch. 6, p. 164**

Tengo un problema.	Debes ... menos.
¿Qué debo hacer?	Debes ... más.

Commenting on food **Ch. 8, p. 212**

¿Cómo está...?	¿Cómo están...?
Está...	Están...

Commenting on clothes **Ch. 9, p. 242**

¿Qué ropa vas a llevar?	¿No tienes algo más formal?
¡Lo de siempre!	Sí, pero prefiero llevar...

Expressing preferences **Ch. 9, p. 247**

¿Cuál de estos ... prefieres?
Prefiero el azul.
¿Qué camisa te gusta más? ¿La verde o la amarilla?
La verde. Además, te queda muy bien.

Asking for and giving an opinion **Ch. 10, p. 264**

¿Crees que...?	Me parece bien.
Creo que sí.	Perfecto.
¿Qué te parece si...?	Buena idea.

Discussing what you would like to do on vacation **Ch. 12, p. 323**

¿Qué te gustaría hacer este verano?
A mí me gustaría...
¿Adónde te gustaría ir este verano?
¿Qué tienes ganas de hacer?
Tengo ganas de...

EXPRESSING FEELINGS AND EMOTIONS

Talking about likes and dislikes **Ch. 1, p. 32**

¿Qué te gusta?	Me gusta (más)...
¿Te gusta...?	No me gusta...

Making suggestions and expressing feelings **Ch. 11, p. 291**

¿Qué tal si...?	¿Qué tienes?
Gracias, pero no quiero.	¿Te sientes mal?
En realidad no tengo ganas.	No me siento bien.
	Estoy un poco cansado/a, nada más.
	Entonces, ¿por qué no...?

Talking about moods and physical condition **Ch. 11, p. 294**

¿Cómo estás?	Tengo gripe.
Estoy...	¿Qué le pasa a...?
¿Cómo te sientes?	Está preocupado/a por algo.

PERSUADING

Making polite requests **Ch. 8, p. 216**

Camarero/a, ¿nos puede traer..., por favor?
¿Me puede traer..., por favor?

Asking for help and responding to requests **Ch. 10, p. 266**

¿Me haces el favor de...?	¡Con mucho gusto!
Claro que sí.	Un momentito.
¿Me ayudas a...?	Me pasas...
Cómo no.	Lo siento, pero en este momento estoy ocupado/a.
¿Me traes...?	Perdóname, pero...

Telling a friend what to do **Ch. 10, p. 268**

Prepara ... y limpia ..., ¿quieres?
De acuerdo.
Por favor, decora ... y llama...
Está bien.

ADDITIONAL VOCABULARY

This list includes additional vocabulary that you may want to use to personalize activities. If you can't find a word you need here, try the Spanish-English and English-Spanish vocabulary sections, beginning on page 348.

ASIGNATURAS
(SCHOOL SUBJECTS)

el cálculo *calculus*
la contabilidad *accounting*
la física *physics*
la geometría *geometry*
el latín *Latin*
la mecanografía *typing*
la química *chemistry*
el ruso *Russian*

CELEBRACIONES
(CELEBRATIONS)

el bautizo *baptism*
la canción *song*
el desfile *parade*
el Día de la Raza *Columbus Day*
el disfraz *costume*
los fuegos artificiales *fire works*
la Pascua Florida *Easter*
la piñata *piñata*
la Semana Santa *Holy Week*
la vela *candle*

COMIDA *(FOOD)*

las arvejas *peas*
el bróculi *broccoli*
la carne asada *roast beef*
la cereza *cherry*
la coliflor *cauliflower*
el champiñón *mushroom*
la chuleta de cerdo *pork chop*
las espinacas *spinach*
los fideos *noodles*
el filete de pescado *fish fillet*
los mariscos *shellfish*
la mayonesa *mayonnaise*
el melón *cantaloupe*
la mostaza *mustard*
la pimienta *pepper*
la sal *salt*
el yogur *yogurt*

DE COMPRAS *(SHOPPING)*

ahorrar *to save*
el/la dependiente *clerk*
el descuento *discount*
dinero en efectivo *cash*
en venta *for sale*
gastar *to spend*
hacer cola *to stand in line*
hacer una pregunta *to ask a question*
la rebaja *discount*
regatear *to bargain*
la tarjeta de crédito *credit card*
el vendedor, la vendedora *salesperson*

DEPORTES Y PASATIEMPOS
(SPORTS AND HOBBIES)

el anuario *yearbook*
las artes marciales *martial arts*
la banda *band*
el boxeo *boxing*
el ciclismo *cycling*
coleccionar sellos *to collect stamps*
el coro *choir*
coser *to sew*
el debate *debate*
el drama *drama*
la fotografía *photography*
la gimnasia *gymnastics*
jugar al ajedrez *to play chess*
jugar a las cartas *to play cards*
jugar a las damas *to play checkers*
la lucha libre *wrestling*
la orquesta *orchestra*
patinar sobre hielo *to ice skate*

EN EL ZOOLÓGICO

(IN THE ZOO)

las aves *birds*
el canguro *kangaroo*
la cebra *zebra*
el cocodrilo *crocodile*
el delfín *dolfin*
el elefante *elephant*
el gorila *gorilla*
el hipopótamo *hippopotamus*
la jirafa *giraffe*
el león *lion*
el lobo marino *seal*
el mono *monkey*
el oso *bear*
el oso blanco *polar bear*
el pingüino *penguin*
la serpiente *snake*
el tigre *tiger*

EN LA CASA

(AROUND THE HOUSE)

la alfombra *rug*
el balcón *balcony*
el comedor *dining room*
las cortinas *curtains*
el cuarto de baño *bathroom*
el despertador *alarm clock*
la escalera *stairs*
el escritorio *desk*
el espejo *mirror*
el estante *bookcase*
el garaje *garage*
la lavadora *washing machine*
la mesita *night stand*
los muebles *furniture*
el patio *patio*
el refrigerador *refrigerator*
la secadora *dryer*
el sillón *easy chair*
el sofá *couch*
el sótano *basement*
el timbre *doorbell*
el tocador *dresser*

EN LA CIUDAD *(IN THE CITY)*

el aeropuerto *airport*
la agencia de viajes *travel agency*
el banco *bank*
el edificio *building*
la esquina *corner*
la fábrica *factory*
la farmacia *pharmacy*
el hospital *hospital*
la iglesia *church*
la mezquita *mosque*
la oficina *office*
la parada de autobuses *bus stop*
la peluquería *barber shop*
el rascacielos *skyscraper*
el salón de belleza *beauty salon*
el semáforo *traffic light*
el templo *temple*

INSTRUMENTOS MUSICALES

(MUSICAL INSTRUMENTS)

la armónica *harmonica*
el bajo *bass*
la batería *drum set*
el clarinete *clarinet*
la mandolina *mandolin*
el oboe *oboe*
el saxofón *saxophone*
el tambor *drum*
el trombón *trombone*
la trompeta *trumpet*
la tuba *tuba*
la viola *viola*
el violín *violin*

NÚMEROS ORDINALES

(ORDINAL NUMBERS)

primero/a *first*
segundo/a *second*
tercero/a *third*
cuarto/a *fourth*
quinto/a *fifth*
sexto/a *sixth*
séptimo/a *seventh*
octavo/a *eighth*
noveno/a *ninth*
décimo/a *tenth*

PALABRAS DESCRIPTIVAS

(DESCRIPTIVE WORDS)

amistoso/a *friendly*
bien educado/a *polite*
gracioso/a *funny*
llevar gafas *to wear glasses*
las pecas *freckles*
el pelo laso *straight hair*
el pelo rizado *curly hair*
ser calvo *to be bald*
tener barba *to have a beard*
tener bigote *to have a moustache*

REFRANES (PROVERBS)

Más vale pájaro en mano que cien volando.
A bird in the hand is worth two in the bush.
Hijo no tenemos y nombre le ponemos.
Don't count your chickens before they're hatched.
Quien primero viene, primero tiene.
The early bird catches the worm.
Más vale tarde que nunca.
Better late than never.
El hábito no hace al monje.
Clothes don't make the man.
Más ven cuatro ojos que dos.
Two heads are better than none.
Querer es poder.
Where there's a will, there's a way.
Ojos que no ven, corazón que no se siente.
Out of sight, out of mind.
No todo lo que brilla es oro.
All that glitters is not gold.
Cara vemos, corazón no sabemos.
Appearances are deceiving.
Donde una puerta se cierra, otra se abre.
Every cloud has a silver lining.
En boca cerrada no entran moscas.
A closed mouth does not catch flies.
Dime con quién andas y te diré quién eres.
You are known by the company you keep.

REGALOS (GIFTS)

la agenda *agenda, daily planner*
el álbum *album*
el anillo *ring*
el animal de peluche *stuffed animal*
el calendario *calendar*
la cámara *camera*
la colonia *cologne*
el llavero *key chain*
el perfume *perfume*
la pulsera *bracelet*
el rompecabezas *puzzle*
las rosas *roses*

ROPA (CLOTHES)

la bata *robe*
el chaleco *vest*
el jersey *sweater*
las medias *stockings, nylons*
el paraguas *umbrella*
el pijama *pajamas*
la ropa interior *underwear*
el saco *blazer*
los tacones *high-heels*

TEMAS DE ACTUALIDAD (CURRENT ISSUES)

el bosque tropical *rain forest*
la contaminación *pollution*
el crimen *crime*
los derechos humanos *human rights*
la educación *education*
el medio ambiente *the environment*
las noticias *news*
la política *politics*
la salud *health*
el sida *AIDS*
la tecnología *technology*
la violencia *violence*

VACACIONES (VACATION)

la aduana *customs*
el aeropuerto *airport*
el avión *airplane*
el equipaje *luggage*
hacer una reservación *to make a reservation*
el hotel *hotel*
la llegada *arrival*
el mar *sea*
el pasaporte *passport*
la salida *departure*
el tren *train*
visitar los lugares de interés *to sightsee*
volar (ue) *to fly*

GRAMMAR SUMMARY

NOUNS AND ARTICLES

GENDER OF NOUNS

In Spanish, nouns (words that name a person, place, or thing) are grouped into two classes or genders: masculine and feminine. All nouns, both persons and objects, fall into one of these groups. Most nouns that end in -**o** are masculine, and most nouns that end in -**a**, -**ción**, -**tad**, and -**dad** are feminine.

MASCULINE NOUNS	FEMININE NOUNS
libro chico cuaderno bolígrafo vestido	casa universidad situación mesa libertad

FORMATION OF PLURAL NOUNS

Add -**s** to nouns that end in a vowel.		Add -**es** to nouns that end in a consonant.		With nouns that end in -**z**, the -**z** changes to -**c**.	
SINGULAR	PLURAL	SINGULAR	PLURAL	SINGULAR	PLURAL
libro	libro**s**	profesor	profesor**es**	vez	ve**ces**
casa	casa**s**	papel	papel**es**	lápiz	lápi**ces**

DEFINITE ARTICLES

There are words that signal the class of the noun. One of these is the definite article. In English there is one definite article: *the.* In Spanish, there are four: **el, la, los, las.**

SUMMARY OF DEFINITE ARTICLES

	MASCULINE	FEMININE
Singular	**el** chico	**la** chica
Plural	**los** chicos	**las** chicas

CONTRACTIONS

a	+	el	→	**al**
de	+	el	→	**del**

INDEFINITE ARTICLES

Another group of words that are used with nouns is the *indefinite article:* **un, una,** (*a* or *an*) and **unas, unos** (*some* or *a few*).

SUMMARY OF INDEFINITE ARTICLES

	MASCULINE	FEMININE
Singular	**un** chico	**una** chica
Plural	**unos** chicos	**unas** chicas

PRONOUNS

SUBJECT PRONOUNS	DIRECT OBJECT PRONOUNS	INDIRECT OBJECT PRONOUNS	OBJECTS OF PREPOSITIONS
yo	**me**	**me**	**mí**
tú	**te**	**te**	**ti**
él, ella, usted	**lo, la**	**le**	**él, ella, usted**
nosotros, nosotras	**nos**	**nos**	**nosotros, nosotras**
vosotros, vosotras	os	os	vosotros, vosotras
ellos, ellas, ustedes	**los, las**	**les**	**ellos, ellas, ustedes**

ADJECTIVES

Adjectives are words that describe nouns. The adjective must agree in gender (masculine or feminine) and number (singular or plural) with the noun it modifies. Adjectives that end in -**e** or a consonant only agree in number.

		MASCULINE	FEMININE
Adjectives that end in -**o**	Singular	chico alt**o**	chica alt**a**
	Plural	chicos alt**os**	chicas alt**as**
Adjectives that end in -**e**	Singular	chico inteligent**e**	chica inteligent**e**
	Plural	chicos inteligent**es**	chicas inteligent**es**
Adjectives that end in a consonant	Singular	examen difícil	examen difícil
	Plural	exámenes difícil**es**	exámenes difícil**es**

DEMONSTRATIVE ADJECTIVES

	MASCULINE	FEMININE		MASCULINE	FEMININE
Singular	**este** chico	**esta** chica	*Singular*	**ese** chico	**esa** chica
Plural	**estos** chicos	**estas** chicas	*Plural*	**esos** chicos	**esas** chicas

When demonstratives are used as pronouns, they match the gender and number of the noun they replace and are written with an accent mark.

POSSESSIVE ADJECTIVES

These words also modify nouns and tell you *whose* object or person is being referred to (*my* car, *his* book, *her* mother).

SINGULAR		PLURAL	
MASCULINE	FEMININE	MASCULINE	FEMININE
mi libro	**mi** casa	**mis** libros	**mis** casas
tu libro	**tu** casa	**tus** libros	**tus** casas
su libro	**su** casa	**sus** libros	**sus** casas
nuestro libro	**nuestra** casa	**nuestros** libros	**nuestras** casas
vuestro libro	vuestra casa	vuestros libros	vuestras casas

AFFIRMATIVE AND NEGATIVE EXPRESSIONS

AFFIRMATIVE	NEGATIVE
algo **alguien** **alguno (algún), -a** **o ... o** **siempre**	**nada** **nadie** **ni ... ni** **ninguno (ningún), -a** **nunca**

INTERROGATIVE WORDS

¿Adónde? **¿Cómo?** **¿Cuál(es)?** **¿Cuándo?**	**¿Cuánto(a)?** **¿Cuántos(as)?** **¿De dónde?** **¿Dónde?**	**¿Por qué?** **¿Qué?** **¿Quién(es)?**

COMPARATIVES

Comparatives are used to compare people or things. With comparisons of inequality, the same structure is used with adjectives, adverbs or nouns. With comparisons of equality, **tan** is used with adjectives and adverbs, and **tanto/a/os/as** with nouns.

COMPARATIVE OF INEQUALITY

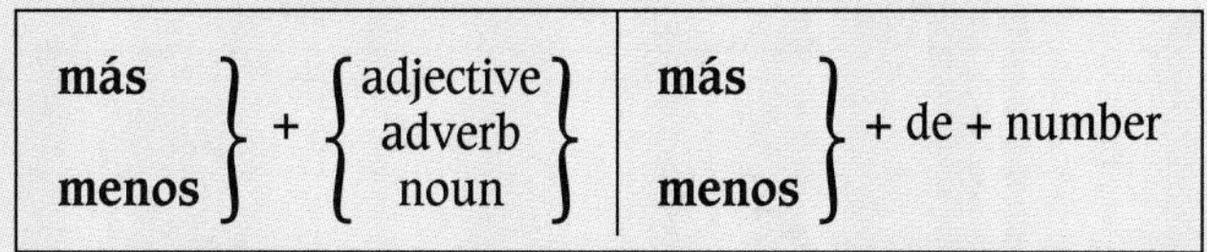

más / **menos** + adjective / adverb / noun	**más** / **menos** + de + number

COMPARATIVE OF EQUALITY

tan	+	adjective or adverb	+	**como**
tanto/a/os/as	+	noun	+	**como**

VERBS

REGULAR VERBS

In Spanish we use a formula to conjugate regular verbs. The endings change in each person, but the stem of the verb remains the same.

PRESENT TENSE OF REGULAR VERBS

INFINITIVE	PRESENT	
habl**ar**	habl**o** habl**as** habl**a**	habl**amos** habl**áis** habl**an**
com**er**	com**o** com**es** com**e**	com**emos** com**éis** com**en**
escrib**ir**	escrib**o** escrib**es** escrib**e**	escrib**imos** escrib**ís** escrib**en**

VERBS WITH IRREGULAR YO FORMS

hacer		poner		saber		salir		traer	
hago	hacemos	**pongo**	ponemos	**sé**	sabemos	**salgo**	salimos	**traigo**	traemos
haces	hacéis	pones	ponéis	sabes	sabéis	sales	salís	traes	traéis
hace	hacen	pone	ponen	sabe	saben	sale	salen	trae	traen

VERBS WITH IRREGULAR FORMS

ser		estar		ir	
soy	somos	estoy	estamos	voy	vamos
eres	sois	estás	estáis	vas	vais
es	son	está	están	va	van

PRESENT PROGRESSIVE

The present progressive in English is formed by using the verb *to be* plus the *-ing* form of another verb. In Spanish, the present progressive is formed by using the verb **estar** plus the -**ndo** form of another verb.

-**ar** verbs	-**er** and -**ir** verbs	For -**er** and -**ir** verbs with a stem that ends in a vowel, the -**iendo** changes to -**yendo**:
hablar → Estoy habl**ando** trabajar → trabaj**ando**	comer → com**iendo** escribir → escrib**iendo**	leer → le**yendo**

STEM-CHANGING VERBS

In Spanish, some verbs have an irregular stem in the present tense. The final vowel of the stem changes from **e** → **ie** and **o** → **ue** in all forms except **nosotros** and **vosotros.**

e → ie		**o → ue**		**u → ue**	
preferir		**poder**		**jugar**	
pref**ie**ro	preferimos	p**ue**do	podemos	**jue**go	jugamos
pref**ie**res	preferís	p**ue**des	podéis	**jue**gas	jugáis
pref**ie**re	pref**ie**ren	p**ue**de	p**ue**den	**jue**ga	**jue**gan

The following is a list of some **e** → **ie** stem-changing verbs:	The following is a list of some **o** → **ue** stem-changing verbs:
empezar **pensar** **querer**	**almorzar** **doler** **encontrar**

THE VERBS GUSTAR AND ENCANTAR

To express likes and dislikes, the verb **gustar** is used in Spanish. The verb **encantar** is used to talk about things you really like or love. The verb endings for **gustar** and **encantar** always agree with what is liked or loved. The indirect object pronouns always precede the verb forms.

gustar		encantar	
If one thing is liked:	If more than one thing is liked:	If one thing is really liked:	If more than one thing is really liked:
me / **te** / **le** / **nos** / **les** } **gusta**	**me** / **te** / **le** / **nos** / **les** } **gustan**	**me** / **te** / **le** / **nos** / **les** } **encanta**	**me** / **te** / **le** / **nos** / **les** } **encantan**

PRETERITE OF REGULAR VERBS

INFINITIVE	PRETERITE OF REGULAR VERBS	
habl**ar**	habl**é** habl**aste** habl**ó**	habl**amos** habl**asteis** habl**aron**
com**er**	com**í** com**iste** com**ió**	com**imos** com**isteis** com**ieron**
escrib**ir**	escrib**í** escrib**iste** escrib**ió**	escrib**imos** escrib**isteis** escrib**ieron**

PRETERITE OF HACER, IR, SER, AND VER

hacer	ir	ser	ver
hice	fui	fui	vi
hiciste	fuiste	fuiste	viste
hizo	fue	fue	vio
hicimos	fuimos	fuimos	vimos
hicisteis	fuisteis	fuisteis	visteis
hicieron	fueron	fueron	vieron

SPANISH-ENGLISH VOCABULARY

This vocabulary includes almost all words in the textbook, both active (for production) and passive (for recognition only). Active words and phrases are practiced in the chapter and are listed on the **Vocabulario** page at the end of each chapter. You are expected to know and be able to use active vocabulary. An entry in black, heavy type indicates that the word or phrase is active. All other words—some in the opening dialogues, in exercises, in optional and visual material, in **Panorama cultural, Encuentro cultural, A lo nuestro, También se puede decir, Vamos a leer,** and **A ver si puedo...**—are for recognition only. The meaning of these words and phrases can usually be understood from the context or may be looked up in this vocabulary index.

Nouns are listed with definite article and plural form, when applicable. The numbers in the entries refer to the chapter where the word or phrase first appears or where it becomes an active vocabulary word. Vocabulary from the preliminary chapter is followed by the letter "P".

Although the **Real Academia** has recently deleted the letters **ch** and **ll** from the alphabet, many dictionaries still have separate entries for these letters. This end-of-book vocabulary follows the new rules, with **ch** and **ll** in the same sequence as in English.

Stem changes are indicated in parentheses after the verb: **poder (ue)**.

A

a *to, at,* 5
a lo largo de *along,* 10
a principios de *at the beginning of,* 10
¿A qué hora...? *At what time . . .?,* 3
¿A quién le gusta...? *Who likes . . .?,* 4
a veces *sometimes,* 5
abajo *down,* 11
el abdomen *abdomen,* 11
abierto *open,* 7
el abril *April,* 5
abrir *to open,* 10; **abrir regalos** *to open gifts,* 10
la abuela *grandmother,* 6
el abuelo *grandfather,* 6
los abuelos *grandparents,* 6
abundar *to abound,* 6
aburrido/a *boring,* 3
acampar *to camp,* 5
el acento *accent mark, P*
el achiote *annatto,* 8
el actor *actor* (male); mi actor favorito es *my favorite actor is,* P
la actriz *actress;* mi actriz favorita es *my favorite actress is,* P
el acuario *aquarium,* 7
acuático *aquatic,* 12
además *besides,* 9
el adiestramiento *teaching, training, instruction,* 2
Adiós. *Goodbye.,* 1
¿adónde? *to where?,* 4
Adonde fueras haz lo que vieras. *Wherever you go do as you see.,* 1
aeróbico *aerobic,* 5; **una clase de ejercicios aeróbicos** *aerobics class,* 5
afeitarse *to shave,* 7
el afiche *poster,* 2
agobiado/a *tired,* 7
el agosto *August,* 5
agotado/a *tired,* 7
agresivo/a *aggressive,* 6
el agua (f.) *water,* 5; **el agua mineral** *mineral water,* 8
ahora *now,* 3
el aire *air;* al aire libre *outdoors,* 11
el ají *spicy condiment made of tomatoes, onions, and hot, red chili peppers,* 8
ajustado/a *tight, tight-fitting,* 9
al (a + el) *to the,* 4
al gusto *to your liking,* 8
al lado de *next to,* 4
la alberca *swimming pool,* 4
el alcalde *mayor,* 10
alcanzar *to reach,* 11
alegre *happy,* 10
el alemán *German,* 3
Alemania *Germany,* 12
el alfabeto *alphabet,* P
la alfombra *rug,* 2
el álgebra *algebra,* 3
algo *something,* 6; **preocupado/a por algo** *worried about something,* 11
algodón *cotton,* 9; **de algodón** (made of) *cotton,* 9
allá *there,* 4
el almacén *department store,* 9
almorzar (ue) *to eat lunch,* 8
el almuerzo *lunch,* 3
Aló. *Hello.,* 7
alquilar *to rent,* 5
alrededor de *around,* 6
alto/a *tall,* 3
amarillo/a *yellow,* 9
americano/a *American;* **el fútbol norteamericano** *football,* 1
la amiga *friend* (female), 1, 4; **Ésta es mi amiga.** *This is my* (female) *friend.,* 1
el amigo *friend* (male), 1, 4; amigo/a por correspondencia *pen pal,* 4; amigos hispanos *Hispanic friends,* 1; **Éste es mi amigo.** *This is my* (male) *friend.,* 1; **nuevos amigos** *new friends,* 2; **pasar el rato con amigos** *to spend time with friends,* 4
anaranjado/a *orange,* 9
andar *to walk,* 12; andar en bicicleta *to ride a bike,* 4
¡Ándale! *Hurry up!,* 3
la anécdota *anecdote,* 7
el anfibio *amphibian,* 2
la anfitriona *host,* 10
el animal *animal,* 2
el aniversario *anniversary;* **la fiesta de aniversario** *anniversary party,* 7; ¡Feliz

aniversario! *Happy anniversary!,* 10
añadir *to add,* 8
el año *year,* 5; **el Año Nuevo** *New Year's Day,* 10; **el año pasado** *last year,* 10; ¡Feliz Año Nuevo! *Happy New Year!,* 10; **¿Cuántos años tiene?** *How old is (she/he)?,* 1; **¿Cuántos años tienes?** *How old are you?,* 1; **Tengo ... años.** *I'm . . . years old.,* 1; **Tiene ... años.** *She/he is . . . years old.,* 1
anoche *last night,* 10
anteanoche *the night before last,* 11
anteayer *day before yesterday,* 10
el antebrazo *forearm,* 11
antes de *before,* 4
antiguo/a *old, ancient,* 12
antipático/a *disagreeable,* 3
los antojitos *appetizers,* 7
la antropología *anthropology,* 7; **el museo de antropología** *anthropology museum,* 7
el anuncio *advertisement,* 12; los anuncios personales *personal ads,* 4
aparte *separate,* 8; **Es aparte.** *It's separate.,* 8
aprender *to learn,* 12
¡Apúrale! *Hurry up!,* 3
aquí *here,* 4
el arete *earring,* 9
el armario *closet,* 2
los aros *earrings,* 9
arriba *up,* 11
arrojar *to throw (out),* 10
el arroz *rice,* 8
el arte *art,* 3
la artesanía *handicrafts,* 9
el artista *artist* (male), 6
la artista *artist* (female), 6
artístico/a *artistic,* 6
el asiento *seat,* 11
la asignatura *subject,* 3
los asistentes *participants,* 7
asistir a *to attend,* 5
la aspiradora *vacuum cleaner;* **pasar la aspiradora** *to vacuum,* 6
atlético/a *athletic,* 6
la atracción *attraction;* **el parque de atracciones** *amusement park,* 7
atrasado/a *delayed, running late;* **Está atrasado/a.** *She/he is late.,* 3 **Estoy atrasado/a.** *I'm late.,* 3;
el atún *tuna,* 8
el auditorio *auditorium,* 10
el auto *car,* 4
el autobús *bus,* 5; **tomar el autobús** *to take the bus,* 5
las aventuras *adventures,* 2
las aves *birds,* 2
el aviso *notice, advertisement,* 6
ayer *yesterday,* 10
ayudar *to help;* **ayudar en casa** *to help at home,* 5; **¿Me ayudas a...?** *Can you help me . . .?,* 10
el azúcar en polvo *powdered sugar,* 8
azul *blue,* 6

B

bailar *to dance,* 4
el baile *dance,* 3
bajar *to descend, to go downstairs;* **bajar el río en canoa** *to go canoeing,* 12
bajo/a *short* (to describe people), 3
la balada *ballad,* 6
el balcón *balcony,* 2
el baloncesto *basketball,* 1
la bandeja *tray,* 8; la bandejita de hielo *ice tray,* 8
barato/a *cheap,* 9; **¡Qué barato/a!** *How cheap!,* 9
la barbilla *chin,* 11
el barco *boat, ship, vessel,* 5
el barrio *district, quarter, neighborhood,* 6
el básquet *basketball,* 1
el básquetbol *basketball,* 1
¡Basta ya! *Enough!,* 7
bastante *quite,* 6
la basura *garbage, trash;* **sacar la basura** *to take out the garbage,* 4
la batería *drum set,* 4
el batido *milkshake,* 8
la batidora *beater,* 10
batir *to beat,* 8
beber *to drink,* 5
la bebida *beverage,* 8
el béisbol *baseball,* 1
las bellas artes *fine arts,* 9
la biblioteca *library,* 4
la bicicleta *bicycle;* andar en bicicleta, dar un paseo en bicicleta *to ride a bicycle,* 4; **montar en bicicleta** *to ride a bike,* 4; pasear en bicicleta *to ride a bicycle,* 3
bien *good, well;* **Está bien.** *All right.,* 2; Lo pasé muy bien. *I had a great time.,* 12; ¡Qué bien te ves! *You look great!,* 9; **Me parece bien.** *It seems fine to me.,* 10
el billete *ticket,* 12
la billetera *wallet,* 9
la biología *biology,* 3
el bistec *steak,* 8
blanco/a *white,* 9
el bloqueador *sunscreen,* 12
los bluejeans *bluejeans,* 9
la blusa *blouse,* 9
la boca *mouth,* 11
el bocadillo *sandwich* (Spain), 8
la boda *wedding,* 7
el boleto *ticket,* 12
el bolígrafo *ballpoint pen,* 2
el bolívar *domestic currency in Venezuela,* 9
la bolsa *bag,* 10; la bolsa de plástico *plastic bag,* 10
bonito/a *pretty,* 3
borrar *to erase;* **goma de borrar** *eraser,* 2
el bosque *forest,* 12
las botas *boots,* 9
el brazo *arm,* 11
bucear *to scuba dive,* 5
Bueno. (telephone greeting in Mexico), 7
Bueno... *Well . . .,* 2; **Bueno, tengo clase.** *Well, I have class (now).,* 1
bueno/a *good,* 3; **Buenos días.** *Good morning.,* 1; **Buena idea.** *Good idea.,* 10; **Buenas noches.** *Good night.,* 1; **Buenas tardes.** *Good afternoon.,* 1
la bufanda *scarf,* 12
buscar *to look for,* 9

C

la cabeza *head,* 11
el cacahuate (cacahuete) *peanut,* 8
caer *to fall,* 11
el café *coffee;* **café con leche** *coffee with milk,* 8; **de color café** *brown,* 6;
la cafetería *cafeteria,* 1
el cafetín *cafeteria,* 6
los calcetines *socks,* 9
la calculadora *calculator,* 2
el caleidoscopio *kaleidoscope,* 7
la calentura *fever;* tener calentura *to have a fever,* 11
caliente *hot,* 8
la calificación *grade,* 3
la calle *lane* (in a swimming pool), 5; *street,* 9

el calor *heat;* **Hace calor.** *It's hot.*, 5; Hace un calor tremendo. *It's really hot.*, 5
la cama *bed*, 2; **hacer la cama** *to make the bed*, 6
la cámara *camera*, 12
la camarera *waitress*, 8
el camarero *waiter*, 8
los camarones *shrimp*, 8
cambiar *to change*, 12
caminar *to walk;* **caminar con el perro** *to walk the dog*, 4
la caminata *stroll, walk*, 12; **dar una caminata** *to go hiking*, 12
la camisa *shirt*, 9
la camiseta *T-shirt*, 9
el camping *camping;* hacer camping *to camp*, 12; **la tienda de camping** *tent*, 12
el campo *country*, 7
las canas *gray hair*, 6; **Tiene canas.** *He/she has gray hair.*, 6
la cancha *playing court*, 11; **la cancha de fútbol** *soccer field*, 11; **la cancha de tenis** *tennis court*, 11
la canoa *canoe*, 12; **bajar el río en canoa** *to go canoeing*, 12
cansado/a *tired*, 7
el cantante *singer* (male), 7
la cantante *singer* (female), 7
cantar *to sing*, 4
la cara *face*, 11; Cuesta un ojo de la cara. *It's very expensive.*, 11
el caramelo *candy*, 9
la caráota *kidney bean*, 8
cariñoso/a *affectionate*, 6
el carnaval *carnival*, 10
la carne *meat*, 8; **la carne de res** *beef*, 8
caro/a *expensive*, 9; **¡Qué caro!** *How expensive!*, 9
la carpeta *folder*, 2
el carro *car;* **lavar el carro** *to wash the car*, 4
la carta *letter*, 5; la carta de amor *love letter*, 5
la carta *menu*, 8
el cartel *poster*, 2
la cartera *wallet, purse*, 9
la cartuchera *pencil case*, 2
la casa *house, home*, 4
casi *almost*, 6; **casi siempre** *almost always*, 6
castaño/a *brown, chestnut-colored*, 6
el castellano *Spanish language*, 2
el catarro *cold;* tener catarro *to have a cold*, 11
la categoría *category*, 1
catorce *fourteen*, 1
el cazador *hunter*, 2
la cazuela *casserole;* cazuela de marisco *Ecuadorean casserole dish with seafood and peanuts*, 8
la cebolla *onion*, 8
la celebración *celebration*, 10
celebrar *to celebrate*, 10
la cena *dinner*, 4; **preparar la cena** *to prepare dinner*, 4
cenar *to eat dinner*, 6
el centro *downtown*, 4
el centro comercial *shopping mall*, 2
cerca de *near*, 4
el cereal *cereal*, 8
cero *zero*, 1
cerrar (ie) *to close*, 11
el césped *grass*, 6; **cortar el césped** *to cut the grass*, 6
la chamarra *jacket*, 12
las chancletas *sandals, slippers*, 12
Chao. *'Bye.*, 1
la chaqueta *jacket*, 12
charlar *to chat*, 12
la charrería *Mexican rodeo*, 11
charro/a *Mexican cowboy or cowgirl*, 11
la chica *girl*, 5
el chico *boy*, 5
China *China*, 12; **la comida china** *Chinese food*, 1
el chocolate *chocolate*, 1; el chocolate *hot chocolate*, 8
cinco *five*, 1
cien, ciento *one hundred*, 2
las ciencias *science*, 3
las ciencias sociales *social sciences*, 3
cierto *true*, 6; **No es cierto.** *It isn't true.*, 6
cincuenta *fifty*, 2
el cine *movie theater*, 4
la cintura *waist*, 11
el cinturón *belt*, 9
el circo *circus*, 7
la cita *date, appointment*, 7
la ciudad *city*, 7
el civismo *civics*, 3
el clarinete *clarinet*, 4
¡Claro que sí! *Of course!*, 7
la clase *class, classroom*, 1; **Bueno, tengo clase.** *Well, I have class* (now)., 1; **la clase de baile** *dance class*, 5; **la clase de inglés** *English class*, 1; **una clase de ejercicios aeróbicos** *aerobics class*, 5
clásica *classical*, 1
el club nocturno *nightclub*, 6
el coche *car*, 4
la cocina *kitchen*, 6; cocina francesa clásica *classical French cooking*, 7; **limpiar la cocina** *to clean the kitchen*, 6
codo/a *stingy;* ser muy codo/a *to be really stingy*, 11
el coco *coconut*, 6
el cognado *cognate*, 1
coleccionar *to collect, to form a collection*, 4
el colegio *high school*, 2
colgar (ue) *to hang*, 10; **colgar (ue) las decoraciones** *to hang decorations*, 10
el collar *necklace*, 9
el colón *currency in Costa Rica*, 9
el color *color*, 6; **de color café** *brown*, 6; **¿De qué color es/son...?** *What color is/are . . .?*, 6
colorido/a *colored*, 10
combinar *to combine*, 8
comenzar (ie) *to begin*, 11
comer *to eat*, 5
cómico/a *comical, funny*, 3
la comida *food, meal*, (Mex.) *lunch;* **la comida italiana/china/mexicana** *Italian/Chinese/Mexican food*, 1
como *like, as*, 9; **tan ... como** *as . . . as*, 9
¿Cómo? *How?, what?;* **¿Cómo es...?** *What's . . . like?*, 3; **¿Cómo estás?** *How are you?* (to ask a friend), 1; **¿Cómo son?** *What are . . . like?*, 3; **¿Cómo te llamas?** *What's your name?*, 1
¡Cómo no! *Of course!*, 7
cómodo/a *comfortable*, 9
el compadrazgo *relationship between parents and godparents of a child*, 6
el compadre *friend* (male), 4
la compañera *friend, pal, companion* (female), 3
el compañero *friend, pal, companion* (male), 3
la compañía de balet *ballet company*, 2
comprar *to buy*, 2
compuesto/a *composed*, 2

la computación *computer science,* 3
la computadora *computer,* 2
con *with;* **conmigo** *with me,* 4; **contigo** *with you,* 4
con frecuencia *often;* **¿Con qué frecuencia?** *How often?,* 5
¡Con mucho gusto! *Gladly!, Sure!,* 10
el concepto *concept,* 7
el concierto *concert,* 3
el confite *candy,* 9
el congelador *freezer,* 8
conmigo *with me,* 4
conocer a *to get to know (someone),* 2; *to be familiar or acquainted with,* 2
la consistencia *consistency,* 8
constante *constant,* 11
contar (ue) *to say, to tell,* 9
contigo *with you,* 4
continuo/a *continuous,* 11
controlar *to control,* 5
convertirse (ie) *to change,* 10
la corbata *tie,* 9
el coro *choir,* 3
la coronación *coronation,* 10
¡Córrele! *Hurry up!, Run along!,* 3
el correo *post office,* 4
correr *to run,* 5; ¡Córrele! *Hurry up!, Run along!,* 3; **la pista de correr** *running track,* 11
la correspondencia *mail,* 4
cortar *to cut,* 6; **cortar el césped** *to cut the grass,* 6
la cosa *thing,* 2
costar (ue) *to cost,* 9; **¿Cuánto cuesta...?** *How much does . . . cost?,* 9; **¿Cuánto cuestan...?** *How much do . . . cost?,* 9
creativo/a *creative,* 6
creer *to believe, to think,* 10; **Creo que sí.** *I think so.,* 10; **Creo que no.** *I don't think so.,* 10
la crema de maní *peanut butter,* 8
Creo que no. *I don't think so.,* 10
cruzar *to cross,* 11
el cuaderno *notebook,* 2
la cuadra *city block,* 9
el cuadro *square,* 9; **de cuadros** *plaid,* 9
¿cuál? *what?, which?;* **¿Cuál es la fecha?** *What is today's date?,* 5
cuando *when,* 5; **sólo cuando** *only when,* 5
¿cuánto/a? *how much?,* 2; **¿Cuánto es?** *How much is it?,* 8; **¿Cuánto cuesta...?** *How much does . . . cost?,* 9; **¿Cuánto cuestan...?** *How much do . . . cost?,* 9;
¿cuántos/ as? *how many?,* 2; **¿Cuántos años tienes?** *How old are you?,* 1; **¿Cuántos años tiene?** *How old is (she/he)?,* 1
cuarenta *forty,* 2
cuarto *quarter, fourth;* **menos cuarto** *quarter to (the hour),* 3
el cuarto *room,* 2
el cuate *friend* (slang), 4
cuatro *four,* 1
cuatrocientos/as *four hundred,* 8
cubano/a *Cuban,* 6
el cubo de hielo *ice cube,* 8
la cuchara *spoon,* 8
la cucharada *tablespoon,* 8
el cuchillo *knife,* 8
el cuello *neck,* 11
la cuenta *bill,* 8
el cuero *leather;* **de cuero** (made of) *leather,* 9
el cuerpo *body,* 11
cuidar *to take care of;* **cuidar al gato** *to take care of the cat,* 6; **cuidar a tu hermano/a** *to take care of your brother/sister,* 4
culinario/a *culinary,* 6
culminar *to culminate,* 10
la cultura *culture,* 12
el cumpleaños *birthday,* 7; ¡Feliz cumpleaños! *Happy birthday!,* 10; **la fiesta de cumpleaños** *birthday party,* 7
curioso/a *curious,* 6

D

dar *to give,* 9; **¿Me das...?** *Can you give me . . .?,* 10
dar un paseo en bicicleta *to ride a bike,* 4
dar una caminata *to go hiking,* 12
¡Date prisa! *Hurry up!,* 3
los datos *information,* 12
de *of, from, made of, in,* 3; **de algodón** (made of) *cotton,* 9; **de color café** *brown,* 6; **de cuadros** (made of) *plaid,* 9; **de cuero** (made of) *leather,* 9; **¿De dónde eres?** *Where are you from?,* 1; **¿De dónde es?** *Where is she/he from?,* 1; **de lana** *wool,* 9; **de la mañana** *in the morning* (A.M.), 3; **de la noche** *in the evening* (P.M.), 3; **de la tarde** *in the afternoon* (P.M.), 3; **¿De parte de quién?** *Who's calling?,* 7; **¿De qué color es/son?** *What color is/are?,* 6; **de rayas** *striped,* 9; **de seda** (made of) *silk,* 9; **de sorpresa** *surprise,* 7
De acuerdo. *Agreed.,* 10
de cuadros *plaid,* 9
debajo de *under, beneath,* 4
deber *should, ought to,* 6
decir *to say,* 6; **Dice que...** *She/he says that . . .,* 6; **Diga.** *Hello.* (to answer the phone), 7; **¿Me puede decir...?** *Can you tell me . . .?,* 9
la decoración *decoration,* 10; **colgar (ue) las decoraciones** *to hang decorations,* 10
decorar *to decorate,* 10
el dedo *finger, toe,* 11
dejar *to leave behind,* 7; **¿Puedo dejar un recado?** *May I leave a message?,* 7
del (de + el) *of the, from the,* 3
delgado/a *thin,* 6
delicioso/a *delicious,* 8
demasiado *too much,* 6
los deportes *sports,* 3
la derecha *right-hand,* 11
desagradable *unpleasant,* 11
desayunar *to eat breakfast,* 5
el desayuno *breakfast,* 8
descansar *to rest,* 4; **descansar en el parque** *to rest in the park,* 4
el descanso *recess, break,* 3
el descendiente *descendant,* 6
el descubrimiento *discovery,* 2
desde *since,* 7
el desfile *parade,* 10
desorganizado/a *disorganized,* 6
después *after,* 3; **después de** *after,* 4
el día *day,* 4; **Buenos días.** *Good morning.;* **el Día de Acción de Gracias** *Thanksgiving Day,* 10; **el Día de la Independencia** *Independence Day,* 10; **el Día de las Madres** *Mother's Day,* 10; **el Día de los Enamorados** *Valentine's Day,* 10; **el Día del Padre** *Father's Day,* 10; **los días**

festivos *holidays,* 10; **un día libre** *a free day,* 3; **todos los días** *every day,* 5; día de santo *saint's day,* 1; cada día *each day,* 5; **tal vez otro día** *perhaps another day,* 7; día a día *day by day,* 11
diariamente *daily,* 6
dibujar *to draw,* 4
el dibujo *drawing;* dibujos animados *animated cartoons,* 2
el diccionario *dictionary,* 2
dice que *he/she says that,* 6
el diciembre *December,* 5
diecinueve *nineteen,* 1
dieciocho *eighteen,* 1
diecisiete *seventeen,* 1
dieciséis *sixteen,* 1
el diente *tooth;* **lavarse los dientes** *to brush one's teeth,* 7
la dieta *diet;* estar a dieta *to be on a diet,* 5
diez *ten,* 1
difícil *difficult,* 3
Diga. *Hello.* (to answer the phone), 7; *Dígame.* (telephone greeting), 7
el dinero *money,* 2
el dinosaurio *dinosaur,* 2
la dirección *address,* 4
el disco *phonograph record;* **el disco compacto** *compact disc,* 9
el diseño *design,* 2
el disfraz *costume,* 10
disfrutar *to enjoy,* 8
el disgusto *distaste,* 1
la distancia *distance;* distancia social *interpersonal distance,* 1
la diversión *diversion, fun,* 10
divertido/a *amusing, fun,* 3
dividido/a *divided,* 5
doblar (una película) *to dub* (a film), 2
doce *twelve,* 1
el dólar *dollar,* 2
doler (ue) *to hurt, to ache,* 11
el dolor de cabeza *headache,* 11; el dolor de espalda *backache,* 11
el domingo *Sunday,* 4
el dominó *dominoes,* 6
donde *where;* **¿Adónde?** *Where (to)?,* 4; **¿De dónde eres?** *Where are you from?,* 1; ¿De dónde es? *Where is he/she from?,* 1; **¿dónde?** *where?,* 4; ¿Dónde te gustaría estudiar? *Where would you like to study?,* 3; **¿De dónde es?** *Where is she/he from?,* 1
dos *two,* 1
doscientos/as *two hundred,* 8
ducharse *to take a shower,* 7
dulce *sweet,* 8; **el pan dulce** *sweet rolls,* 8
la dulcería *candy store,* 9
los dulces *candy,* 9
durante *during,* 5
el durazno *peach,* 8

E

la edad *age,* 1
la ecología *ecology,* 1
el edificio *building,* 12
la educación *education,* 3
la educación física *physical education,* 3
educar *to educate,* 2
Egipto *Egypt,* 12
egoísta *selfish,* 6
el ejercicio *exercise,* 5; **una clase de ejercicios aeróbicos** *aerobics class,* 5; **hacer ejercicio** *to exercise,* 5; hacer ejercicios aeróbicos *to do aerobics,* 4
el (article) *the,* 1
él (pronoun) *he,* 2
eliminar *to eliminate,* 11
ella *she,* 2
ellas *they,* 3; **a ellas** *to them,* 5
ellos *they,* 3; **a ellos** *to them,* 5
empanizado/a *breaded,* 8
empezar (ie) *to begin,* 7
en *in, on,* 3; **en punto** *on the dot,* 3
en seguida *immediately,* 8
Encantado/a. *Delighted to meet you.,* 1
encantar *to really like, to love,* 8
el encanto *delight, pleasure,* 9
la enciclopedia *encyclopedia,* 2
encima de *on top of,* 4
encontrar (ue) *to find,* 2
la encuesta *survey,* 1
endurecer *to strengthen,* 11
el enero *January,* 5
enfermo/a *sick,* 7
enojado/a *angry,* 11
enorme *large,* 8
en punto *on the dot,* 3
la ensalada *salad,* 1
entre *among, between,* 9
el entretenimiento *entertainment,* 10
la entrevista *interview,* 1
el equilibrio *equilibrium,* 5
Es aparte. *It's separate.,* 8
es de... *he/she/it is from . . .,* 1
Es la una. *It's one o'clock.,* 3
Es un robo! *It's a rip-off!,* 9
en voz alta *aloud,* 11
esa, ese *that,* 9
esas, esos *those,* 9
escalar *to climb,* 12; **escalar montañas** *to go mountain climbing,* 12
el esclavo *slave,* 6
escoger *to choose,* 11
el escote *neckline,* 9
escribir *to write,* 5
el escritorio *desk,* 2
escuchar *to listen,* 4; escuchar la radio *listen to the radio,* 4; **escuchar música** *to listen to music,* 4
la escuela *school,* 2; escuela secundaria *secondary school,* 2
la espalda *back,* 11
el español *Spanish,* 1
especialmente *especially,* 5
el espectáculo *show,* 7
espeso/a *thick,* 8
espontáneo/a *spontaneous,* 7
la esposa *wife, spouse,* 6
el esposo *husband, spouse,* 6
esquiar *to ski,* 5
los esquís *skis,* 12
esta, este *this,* 9
las estaciones *seasons,* 5
el estadio *stadium,* 11
las estampillas *stamps,* 4
el estante *bookcase,* 2
estar *to be,* 4; **¿Cómo estás?** *How are you?,* 1; **Está atrasado/a.** *She/he is late.,* 3; **Está bien.** *She/he is okay.,* 7; **Está bien.** *All right.,* 7; estar en forma *to be in shape,* 11; **Ésta es mi amiga.** *This is my friend* (female)., 1; **Éste es mi amigo.** *This is my friend* (male)., 1; **¿Está incluida?** *Is it included?,* 8; **Está lloviendo.** *It's raining.,* 5; **Está nevando.** *It's snowing.,* 5; **Está nublado.** *It's cloudy.,* 5; **estar resfriado/a** *to be congested,* 11; **Estoy atrasado/a.** *I'm late.,* 3; **Estoy (bastante) bien, gracias.** *I'm (quite) well, thanks.,* 1; **La línea está ocupada.** *The line is busy.,* 7
éstas, éstos *these,* 6

estas, estos *these,* 9
el estéreo *stereo,* 2
el estilo *style,* 1; el estilo personal *personal style,* 1
estirarse *to stretch,* 11
el estómago *stomach,* 11
Estoy atrasado/a. *I'm late.,* 3
la estrella *star,* 10
estricto/a *strict,* 3
la estudiante *student* (female), 3
el estudiante *student* (male), 3
la estudiantina *strolling student band,* 10
estudiar *to study,* 4
Estupendo. *Great./Marvelous.,* 1
la etiqueta *etiquette,* 1
étnico/a *ethnic,* 9
el evento *event,* 7
el examen *exam* (pl. **los exámenes**), 3
Excelente. *Great./Excellent.,* 1
la excursión *excursion;* ir de excursión *to go sight-seeing,* 12
la exhibición *exhibition,* 10
la experiencia *experience,* 5
experimentar *to experience,* 8
explicar *to explain,* 12
explorar *to explore,* 12
la expresión *expression,* 6
exprimir *to squeeze,* 8

F

fácil *easy,* 3
la falda *skirt,* 9
las Fallas *spring festival in Valencia, Spain,* 10
la familia *family,* 6
famoso/a *famous,* 10
el fanático *fan,* 5
fantástico/a *fantastic,* 3
fascinante *fascinating,* 12
favor *favor,* 10; **¿Me haces el favor de...?** *Can you do me the favor of . . .?,* 10; **por favor** *please,* 8
favorito/a *favorite,* 3
el febrero *February,* 5
la fecha *date,* 5; **¿Cuál es la fecha?** *What is today's date?,* 5; **¿Qué fecha es hoy?** *What's today's date?,* 5
¡Felicidades! *Congratulations!,* 10
felicitar *to congratulate;* Te felicito. *Congratulations.,* 10
feliz *happy,* 10; ¡Feliz aniversario! *Happy anniversary!,* 10; ¡Feliz Año Nuevo! *Happy New Year!,* 10; ¡Feliz cumpleaños! *Happy birthday!,* 10; ¡Feliz Navidad! *Merry Christmas!,* 10
feo/a *ugly,* 3
la feria *fair,* 10
festejar *to celebrate,* 10
el festival *festival,* 10
festive *festive,* 10; **los días festivos** *holidays,* 10
la fiebre *fever,* 11; **tener fiebre** *to have a fever,* 11
la fiesta *party,* 3; **la fiesta de aniversario** *anniversary party,* 7; **la fiesta de cumpleaños** *birthday party,* 7; **la fiesta de graduación** *graduation party,* 7; **la fiesta de sorpresa** *surprise party,* 7
la figura *figure,* 10
la filosofía *philosophy,* 2
el fin *end,* 4; **el fin de semana** *weekend,* 4
la física *physics,* 3
flamenco *flamenco* (music, singing, dancing), 6
el flan *custard,* 8
la flauta *flute,* 4
flexionar *to flex,* 11
la florería *flower shop,* 9
las flores *flowers,* 9
formal *formal,* 9
fortalecer *to strengthen,* 11
la foto *photo,* 10
la frambuesa *raspberry,* 8
el francés *French,* 3
Francia *France,* 12
la fresa *strawberry,* 8
fresco/a *fresh;* **Hace fresco.** *It's cool.,* 5
los frijoles *beans,* 8
el frío *cold,* 8; **Hace frío.** *It's cold.,* 5; Hace un frío tremendo. *It's really cold.,* 5
la fruta *fruit,* 1
los fuegos artificiales *fireworks,* 10
fuerte *strong, heavy,* 8
el fútbol *soccer,* 1; **el fútbol norteamericano** *football,* 1; **la cancha de fútbol** *soccer field,* 11
el futuro *future,* 2

G

la galería *gallery,* 9
la galleta *cookie,* 8
la gana *desire;* **tener ganas de** (+ infinitive) *to feel like doing something,* 7
ganadero/a *cattle breeder,* 9
ganar *to win, to earn,* 11
la ganga *bargain,* 9; **¡Qué ganga!** *What a bargain!,* 9
la garganta *throat,* 11
gastado/a *tired,* 7
el gato *cat,* 6; **cuidar al gato** *to take care of the cat,* 6
el gazpacho *cold soup served in Spain,* 8
generoso/a *generous,* 6
¡Genial! *Great!,* 2
la gente *people;* gente famosa *famous people,* 1
la geografía *geography,* 3
el gimnasio *gym,* 4
el globo *balloon,* 10; **inflar los globos** *to blow up balloons,* 10
la goma de borrar *eraser,* 2
gordo/a *fat, overweight,* 6; **un poco gordo/a** *a little overweight,* 6
Gracias. *Thanks.,* 1; **el Día de Acción de Gracias** *Thanksgiving Day,* 10
la graduación *graduation;* **la fiesta de graduación** *graduation party,* 7
grande *big,* 3
la gripe *flu;* **tener gripe** *to have the flu,* 11
gris *gray,* 9
el grupo *group,* 1
guapo/a *good-looking, handsome* or *pretty,* 3; ¡Qué guapo/a estás! *You look great!,* 9
el guarapo *sugar-cane juice,* 6
la guía *guide,* 2
el guineo *banana,* 8
la guitarra *guitar,* 4
gustar *to like someone/something;* **¿A quién le gusta...?** *Who likes . . .?,* 4; **Le gustan** *She/he likes,* 3; **Les gusta** *They like,* 5; **Me gusta...** *I like . . .,* 1; **Me gusta más.** *I like it more.,* 1; **Me gustan** *I like,* 3; **Me gustaría** *would like,* 7; **No me gusta...** *No, I don't like . . .,* 1; **Nos gusta** *We like,* 5; **Nos gustan...** *We like . . .,* 5, 7; **¿Qué te gusta?** *What do you like?,* 1; **¿Qué te gusta hacer?** *What do you like to do?,* 4; **Sí, me gusta.** *Yes, I like it.,* 1; **¿Te gusta...?** *Do you like . . .?,* 1; **Te gustan...** *you like . . .,* 3; **¿Te gustaría?** *Would you like . . .?,* 7

el gusto *taste, pleasure;* **¡Con mucho gusto!** *Sure!,* 10
los gustos *likes;* gustos personales *personal likes,* 1

H

hablar *to speak, to talk;* **hablar por teléfono** *to talk on the phone,* 4
hacer *to do, to make,* 2; **Hace buen tiempo.** *The weather is nice.,* 5; **Hace calor.** *It's hot.,* 5; **Hace fresco.** *It's cool.,* 5; **Hace mal tiempo.** *The weather is bad.,* 5; **Hace (mucho) frío.** *It's (very) cold.,* 5; **Hace sol.** *It's sunny.,* 5; **Hace viento.** *It's windy.,* 5; **hacer ejercicio** *to exercise,* 5; **hacer la cama** *to make the bed,* 6; **hacer la maleta** *to pack the suitcase,* 12; **hacer turismo** *to go sightseeing,* 12; **hacer un viaje** *to take a trip,* 6; **hacer yoga** *to do yoga,* 11; **¡Haz!** *Do!, Make!,* 10; **¿Me haces el favor de...?** *Can you do me the favor of . . .?,* 10; **¿Qué tiempo hace?** *What's the weather like?,* 5
el hambre *hunger,* 8; **tener hambre** *to be hungry,* 8
la hamburguesa *hamburger,* 5
hasta *until;* **Hasta luego.** *See you later.,* 1; **Hasta mañana.** *See you tomorrow.,* 1
hay *there is, there are,* 2
¡Haz! *Do!, Make!,* 10
hecho/a a mano *handmade,* 10
el helado *ice cream,* 4; **tomar un helado** *to eat ice cream,* 4
la herencia *heritage,* 9
la hermana *sister,* 6; **la media hermana** *half-sister,* 6
la hermanastra *stepsister,* 6
el hermanastro *stepbrother,* 6
el hermano *brother,* 6; **el medio hermano** *half-brother,* 6
los hermanos *brothers, brothers and sisters,* 6
el hielo *ice,* 8
la hija *daughter,* 6
el hijo *son,* 6
los hijos *children,* 6
la historia *history,* 3
histórico/a *historic,* 10
¡Hola! *Hello!,* 1
el hombre *man,* 10
el hombro *shoulder,* 11
el homenaje *homage,* 6
la hora *hour, time;* **¿A qué hora...?** *At what time. . .?,* 3; la hora latina *Latin time,* 3; **¿Qué hora es?** *What time is it?,* 3
el horario *schedule;* horario escolar *school schedule,* 3
Horrible. *Horrible.,* 1; ¡Qué horrible! *How terrible!,* 2
hoy *today,* 3; **¿Cuál es la fecha hoy?** *What is today's date?,* 5; **¿Qué fecha es hoy?** *What's today's date?,* 5
los huevos *eggs,* 8
el humor *humor,* 1

I

la idea *idea,* 10; **Buena idea.** *Good idea.,* 10
ideal *ideal,* 8
igual *equal,* 6
Igualmente. *Same here.,* 1
ilustrada *illustrated,* 2
el impermeable *raincoat,* 10
imposible *impossible,* 3
incluir *to include,* 8; **¿Está incluida?** *Is it included?,* 8
¡Increíble! *Incredible!,* 2
independencia *independence,* 10; **el Día de la Independencia** *Independence Day,* 10
independiente *independent,* 6
indicar *to point,* 11
la individualidad *individuality,* 10
el infinitivo *infinitive,* 11
inflar *to blow up, to inflate,* 10; **inflar los globos** *to blow up balloons,* 10
la informática *computer science,* 3
la influencia *influence,* 10
Inglaterra *England,* 12
inglés *English,* 1; **la clase de inglés** *English class,* 1
los ingredientes *ingredients,* 8
inocente *innocent,* 10
inolvidable *unforgettable,* 9
las instrucciones *instructions,* 8
el instrumento (musical) *instrument;* **tocar un instrumento** *to play an instrument,* 4
inteligente *intelligent,* 3
intercambiar *to exchange,* 4
interesante *interesting,* 3
interesarse *to interest,* 12
internacional *international,* 7
interrumpirse *to interrupt,* 6
el invierno *winter,* 5
la invitación *invitation,* 10; **mandar las invitaciones** *to send the invitations,* 10
el invitado *guest,* 10; **llamar a los invitados** *to call the guests,* 10
ir *to go,* 2; **ir + a +** infinitive *going to (do something),* 7; **ir al centro comercial** *to go to the mall,* 2; **ir de vela** *to go sailing,* 12; **¡Ve!** *Go!,* 10; **¡Vete!** *Go away!,* 10
la isla *island,* 2
Italia *Italy,* 12
italiano/a *Italian,* 1; **la comida italiana** *Italian food,* 1
izquierdo/a *left,* 11

J

el jai alai *Basque ball game,* 11
el jamón *ham,* 8
el jardín *garden,* 6; **trabajar en el jardín** *to work in the garden,* 6
el jazz *jazz,* 1
joven *young,* 6; **Se ve joven.** *She/he looks young.,* 6
las joyas *jewelry,* 9
la joyería *jewelry store,* 9
el juego *game,* 3; juego de ingenio *guessing game,* 1; **el juego de mesa** *board game,* 9; **el videojuego** *videogame,* 3
el jueves *Thursday,* 4
jugar (ue) *to play,* 4; jugar al tenis *to play tennis,* 4
el jugo *juice,* 5; **jugo de naranja** *orange juice,* 8
la juguetería *toy store,* 9
los juguetes *toys,* 9
el julio *July,* 5
el junio *June,* 5
juntos/as *together,* 5
juvenil *juvenile,* 7

L

la *it/her,* 10
la *the,* 1
el lado *side;* **al lado de** *next to,* 4
el lago *lake,* 7
la lámpara *lamp,* 2
la lana *wool;* **de lana** (made of) *wool,* 9
la lancha *launch, boat,* 5
el lapicero/a *pencil holder,* 2
el lápiz *pencil,* 2; lápiz de color *colored pencil,* 2

largo/a *long,* 5
las *the,* 3
lástima *shame,* 7; **¡Qué lástima!** *What a shame!,* 7
el latín *Latin,* 3
lavar *to wash;* **lavar el carro** *to wash the car,* 4; **lavar la ropa** *to wash the clothes,* 4
lavarse *to wash oneself;* **lavarse los dientes** *to brush one's teeth,* 7
le *to/for him, her, you,* 9
leal *loyal,* 6
las lecciones *lessons,* 5; tomar lecciones *to take lessons,* 5
la leche *milk,* 8; **el café con leche** *coffee with milk,* 8; **un vaso de leche** *a glass of milk,* 8
la lechuga *lettuce,* 8
leer *to read,* 5
legal *legal,* 1
las legumbres *vegetables,* 8
lejos *far, far away;* **lejos de** *far from,* 4
los lentes *contact lenses, glasses;* **los lentes de sol** *sunglasses,* 12
lento/a *slow,* 11
les *to/for them, you,* 9; **Les gusta** *They/you like,* 5
levantar *to lift, to raise,* 11; **levantar pesas** *to lift weights,* 11
libre *free,* 3; **un día libre** *a free day,* 3
la librería *bookstore,* 2
el libro *book,* 2
el liceo *school,* 2
la licuadora *blender,* 8
ligero/a *light,* 8
el limón *lime,* 8
la limonada *lemonade,* 8
limpiar *to clean,* 6; **limpiar la cocina** *to clean the kitchen,* 6
limpio/a *clean,* 8
la línea *line,* 7; **La línea está ocupada.** *The line is busy.,* 7
listo/a *clever, smart* (with **ser**), 6; **estar listo/a** *to be ready* (with **estar**), 7
la literatura *literature,* 3
llamar *to call, name;* Me llamo... *My name is . . .,* P; Mi amigo/a se llama... *My friend's name is . . .,* P
llamar *to call, to phone;* **llamar a los invitados** *to call the guests,* 10; **Llamo más tarde.** *I'll call later.,* 7
llamarse *to be named,* 1; **¿Cómo te llamas?** *What's your name?,* 1; **Me llamo...** *My name is . . .,* 1; **Se llama...** *Her/his name is . . .,* 1
llenar *to fill,* 10
llevar *to wear,* 9; **llevar una vida sana** *to lead a healthy life,* 11
llover (ue) *to rain;* 5; **Está lloviendo.** *It's raining.,* 5; Está lloviendo a cántaros. *It's raining cats and dogs.,* 5; **Llueve.** *It's raining.,* 5
lo *it/him/you,* 10
lo mejor *the best thing,* 12
Lo siento. *I'm sorry.,* 7
los *the,* 3
luego *then, later,* 3; **Hasta luego.** *See you later.,* 1
el lugar *place,* 7
el lunes *Monday,* 4

M

la madrastra *stepmother,* 6
la madre/mamá *mother/mom,* 6; **el Día de las Madres** *Mother's Day,* 10
el madrileño *resident of Madrid,* 1
la madrina *godmother,* 6
magnífico/a *great,* 11
el maíz *corn,* 8
mal *bad,* 1; No está mal. *It's not bad.,* 2; Lo pasé mal. *I had a bad time.,* 12
la maleta *suitcase,* 12; **hacer la maleta** *to pack the suitcase,* 12
malo/a *bad,* 3; **Hace mal tiempo.** *The weather is bad.,* 5
el mamey *mamey* (fruit), 6
el mamífero *mammal,* 2
la mañana *morning,* 3; **de la mañana** *in the morning* (A.M.), 3; **por la mañana** *in the morning,* 5
mañana *tomorrow,* 3; **¡Hasta mañana!** *See you tomorrow!,* 1
mandar *to send, to order,* 10; **mandar las invitaciones** *to send invitations,* 10
la manera *way,* 8
el mango *mango,* 8
el maní *peanut,* 8; **la crema de maní** *peanut butter,* 8
mano *friend* (short for hermano), 4
mantener (ie) *to maintain,* 6
la mantequilla *butter,* 8
la manzana *apple,* 8
maquillarse *to put on makeup,* 7
la máquina del tiempo *time machine,* 2
maravilloso/a *great, marvelous,* 3
el marcador *marker,* 2
el mariachi *mariachi,* 10
la marioneta *marionette,* 7
marrón *brown,* 6
el martes *Tuesday,* 4
el marzo *March,* 5
más *more,* 1; **Llamo más tarde.** *I'll call later.,* 7; **Más o menos.** *So-so.,* 1; **más...que** *more . . . than,* 9; **nada más** *that's all,* 11
la máscara *mask,* 10
las matemáticas *mathematics,* 3
la materia *subject,* 3
el mayo *May,* 5
mayor *older,* 6
me *to/for me,* 9; **¿Me ayudas a...?** *Can you help me . . .?,* 10; **Me das...?** *Can you give me . . .?;* **Me gusta** *I like,* 1; **Me gusta más** *I like more,* 1; **Me gustan...** *I like . . .,* 3; **Me gustaría...** *I would like . . .,* 7; **¿Me haces el favor de...?** *Can you do me the favor of . . .?,* 10; **Me llamo...** *My name is . . .,* 1; **Me parece bien.** *It seems fine with me.,* 10; **¿Me pasas...?** *Can you pass me . . .?,* 10; **¿Me puede decir..?** *Can you tell me . . .?,* 9; **¿Me puede traer...?** *Can you bring me . . .?,* 8; **¿Me traes...?** *Can you bring me . . .?,* 10
el mecanismo *mechanism,* 1
medio/a *half;* **media hermana** *half-sister,* 6; **medio hermano** *half-brother,* 6; **y media** *half past* (the hour), 3
menor *younger,* 6
menos *less,* 6; **Más o menos.** *So-so.,* 1; **menos cuarto** *quarter to* (the hour), 3; **menos...que** *less . . . than,* 9
el menú *menu,* 8
menudo/a *minute, small;* a menudo *often,* 5
la merienda *snack served around 5:00 P.M.,* 8
la mermelada *jam,* 8
el mes *month,* 5

la mesa *table,* 2; **el juego de mesa** *board game,* 9; **poner la mesa** *to set the table,* 6
la mesera *waitress,* 8
el mesero *waiter,* 8
el meteorólogo *weather forecaster,* 5
la mezcla *mixture,* 8
mi/mis *my,* 2, 6
el miércoles *Wednesday,* 4
mil *one thousand,* 8
la milla *mile,* 5
el mimo *mime,* 7
los minerales *minerals,* 8
mirar *to watch, to look at,* 4; **¡Mira!** *Look!,* 3; **mirar la televisión** *to watch television,* 4
la misa *mass,* 9
las misiones *missions,* 9
mismo/a *same,* 9; **Son del mismo precio.** *They're the same price.,* 9
la mochila *book bag, backpack,* 2
el momento *moment,* 7; **Un momentito.** *Just a second.,* 10; **un momento** *one moment,* 7
la montaña *mountain;* **escalar montañas** *to go mountain climbing,* 12
montar *to ride;* **montar en bicicleta** *to ride a bike,* 4
la mora *blackberry,* 8
morado/a *purple,* 9
moreno/a *dark-haired, brunette,* 3
mostrar (ue) *to show, to exhibit,* 10
la moto *moped,* 7
el motoesquí *jet-ski,* 5
moverse (ue) *to move,* 5
el movimiento *movement,* 6
mucho *a lot,* 1
mucho/a *a lot (of),* 2; **¡Con mucho gusto!** *Sure!, Gladly!,* 10; **Mucho gusto.** *Nice to meet you.,* 1
muchos/as *many, a lot of,* 2; **muchas veces** *often,* 5
muerto/a *dead;* completamente muerto/a *dead tired,* 7
la mujer *woman,* 10
multicultural *multicultural,* 10
el mundo *world,* 2
municipal *municipal,* 7
el músculo *muscle,* 11
el museo *museum,* 7; **el museo de antropología** *anthropology museum,* 7
la música *music,* 1; **escuchar música** *to listen to music,* 4; **la música clásica/pop/rock** *classical/pop/rock music,* 1; **la música de...** *music by . . .,* 1; la música folklórica *folkloric music,* 10
muy *very,* 1; **muy bien** *very well,* 1; **(Muy) mal.** *(Very) bad.,* 1

N

nada *nothing,* 5; **nada más** *that's all,* 11; **para nada** *at all,* 8
nadar *to swim,* 4
nadie *nobody,* 5
la naranja *orange,* 8; **el jugo de naranja** *orange juice,* 8
la nariz *nose,* 11
la natación *swimming,* 1
la natura *nature,* 1
naturalmente *naturally,* 5
la Navidad *Christmas,* 10; ¡Feliz Navidad! *Merry Christmas!,* 10
necesitar *to need,* 2; **Necesita** *She/he needs,* 2; **Necesitas** *You need,* 2; **Necesito** *I need,* 2
negro/a *black,* 6
nervioso/a *nervous,* 11
nevar (ie) *to snow;* **Está nevando.** *It's snowing.,* 5; **Nieva.** *It's snowing.,* 5
ni *nor,* 6; ni...ni... *neither . . . nor . . .,* 6
la nieve *snow,* 12
ningún/ninguna *none, not any,* 12; ninguna parte *nowhere, not anywhere,* 12; **ningún lado** *nowhere, not anywhere,* 12; **ningún lugar** *nowhere, not anywhere,* 12
no *no,* 1; **¿no?** *isn't it?,* 3; **No es cierto.** *It isn't true.,* 6; **No me gusta el/la...** *I don't like . . .,* 1; **No, no me gusta.** *No, I don't like it.,* 1; **No puedo.** *I can't.,* 7; **No sé.** *I don't know.,* 2; **No te preocupes.** *Don't worry.,* 3
la noche *night;* **Buenas noches.** *Good night.,* 1; **de la noche** *in the evening* (P.M.), 3; **por la noche** *at night,* 5
la Nochebuena *Christmas Eve,* 10
la Nochevieja *New Year's Eve,* 10
el nombre *name,* P; nombres comunes *common names,* P
normal *normal,* 5
nos *to/for us,* 9; **Nos gusta...** *We like . . .,* 5; **Nos gustan...** *We like . . .,* 7
nosotros/as *we,* 4
novecientos/as *nine hundred,* 8
la novela *novel,* 3
noventa *ninety,* 2
el noviembre *November,* 5
nublado *cloudy,* 5; **Está nublado.** *It's cloudy.,* 5
nuestro/a *our,* 6
nueve *nine,* 1
nuevo/a *new,* 3; **nuevos amigos** *new friends,* 2
los números *numbers,* 1; el número secreto *secret number,* 1
numeroso *numerous,* 6
nunca *never, not ever,* 5
la nutrición *nutrition,* 8

O

la obra *work,* 7
ochenta *eighty,* 2
ocho *eight,* 1
ochocientos/as *eight hundred,* 8
el océano *ocean,* 5
el octubre *October,* 5
ocupado/a *busy,* 7; **La línea está ocupada.** *The line is busy.,* 7
ofrecer *to offer,* 9
el oído *inner ear,* 11
oír *to hear, to listen to,* 4; ¡Oye! *Listen!,* 3
los ojos *eyes,* 6; ¡Ojo! *Pay attention! Watch out!,* 11
la ola *wave,* 5
olímpico/a *Olympic,* 5
once *eleven,* 1
operar *to operate,* 5
la oreja *earlobe, outer ear,* 11
organizar *to organize,* 2
el otoño *fall,* 5
otro/a *other, another,* 8
¡Oye! *Listen!,* 3

P

el pabellón *typical dish of Venezuela,* 8
el padrastro *stepfather,* 6

el padre *father,* 6; **el Día del Padre** *Father's Day,* 10
los padres *parents,* 6
el padrino *godfather,* 6
el país *country,* 4
las palmas *palms,* 11
el pan *bread,* 8; **el pan dulce** *sweet rolls,* 8; **el pan tostado** *toast,* 8
la panadería *bakery,* 9
el panecillo *plain or sweet roll,* 8
los pantalones *pants,* 9; **los pantalones cortos** *shorts,* 9
la pantomima *pantomime,* 10
el papá *dad,* 6
la papa *potato,* 5; **las papas fritas** *french fries,* 5
las papitas *potato chips,* 8
la papaya *papaya,* 8
el papel *paper,* 2
para *for, to,* 4; **para +** infinitive *in order to,* 4; **para nada** *at all,* 8; **¿Para quién...?** *For whom . . .?,* 9
el paracaídas *parachute;* **saltar en paracaídas** *to go sky-diving,* 12
el parador *inn,* 12; *roadside stand,* 6
el paraguas *umbrella,* 10
pardo/a *brown,* 9
parecer *to give the impression of, to seem;* **Me parece bien.** *It seems fine to me.,* 10; **¿Qué te parece si...?** *How do you feel about . . .?,* 10
el pariente *relative,* 6
el parque *park,* 4; **descansar en el parque** *to rest in the park,* 4; **el parque de atracciones** *amusement park,* 7
el párrafo *paragraph,* 12
la parrilla *grill,* 9
la parte *part,* 7; **¿De parte de quién?** *Who's calling?,* 7; ninguna parte *nowhere, not anywhere,* 12
la participación *participation,* 7
el partido de... *game of . . .* (sport), 3
pasado/a *past, last* (with time), 10; **el sábado pasado** *last Saturday,* 10; **el verano pasado** *last summer,* 10; **la semana pasada** *last week,* 10
pasar *to pass, to spend time,* 4; **¿Me pasas...?** *Can you pass me . . .?,* 10; **pasar el rato con amigos** *to spend time with friends,* 4; **pasar la aspiradora** *to vacuum,* 6; **¿Qué le pasa a...?** *What's wrong with . . .?,* 11
el pasatiempo *hobby,* 1
las Pascuas *Easter,* 10
los paseantes *passersby,* 10
pasear *to go for a walk,* 12; pasear en bicicleta *to ride a bicycle,* 4
la pasión *passion,* 6
el pastel *cake,* 8
la pastelería *pastry shop, sweet shop,* 9
patinar *to skate;* **patinar sobre ruedas** *to roller skate,* 11
el patio *patio,* 7
el payaso *clown,* 7
la pecera *fishbowl,* 2
los peces *fish,* 2
el pedacito *small piece,* 8
pedir (i) *to order, to ask for,* 8
peinarse *to comb one's hair,* 7
pelar *to peel,* 8
la película *movie, film,* 4; ver una película *to see a film,* 4
pelirrojo/a *redheaded,* 6
el pelo *hair,* 6
la pena *sorrow, pain, embarrassment;* **Lo pasé de pena.** *I had a bad time.,* 12
la peña *South American musical event or club,* 7
los pendientes *earrings,* 9
pensar (ie) *to think,* 7; **pensar (ie) +** infinitive *to plan, to intend,* 7
pequeño/a *small,* 3
la pera *pear,* 8
Perdón. *Excuse me.,* 9; **Perdóname.** *Excuse me.,* 10
perezoso/a *lazy,* 6
Perfecto. *Perfect.,* 10
el periódico *newspaper,* 5
pero *but,* 1
el perro *dog,* 4; **el perro caliente** *hot dog,* 8
personal *personal,* 2; anuncios personales *personal ads,* 4; estilo personal *personal style,* 2
las pesas *weights,* 11; **levantar pesas** *to lift weights,* 11
el pescado *fish,* 8
pescar *to fish,* 5
la peseta *currency in Spain,* 9
¡Pésimo! *Terrible!,* 2
el peso *currency in Colombia, Argentina, and Mexico,* 9
el pez *fish,* 2
el piano *piano,* 4
picado *chopped, crushed,* 8
picante *spicy,* 8
el pie *foot,* 11
la pierna *leg,* 11
la pileta *swimming pool,* 4
el piloto *pilot,* 5
la piña *pineapple,* 8
la piñata *hanging ornament filled with fruits and candies,* 10
el pincel *paintbrush,* 2
pintar *to paint,* 4
la pintura *paint, painting,* 2
el piragüismo *canoeing,* 11
la pirámide *pyramid,* 12
la piscina *swimming pool,* 4
el piso *apartment,* 2
la pista *track,* 11; **la pista de correr** *running track,* 11; la pista de esquí *ski slope,* 12
la pizza *pizza,* 1
la pizzería *pizzeria,* 1
el plan *plan,* 7; **Ya tengo planes.** *I already have plans.,* 7
planchar *to iron,* 6
la planta *plant,* 9
el plástico *plastic,* 8
el plátano *banana,* 8
el plato *plate, dish,* 8
los platos *dishes,* 6; lavar los platos *to wash the dishes,* 6
la playa *beach,* 5; **por la playa** *along the beach,* 5
la pluma *ballpoint pen,* 2
poco *a little,* 6; **un poco gordo/a** *a little overweight,* 6
poder (ue) *to be able to, can,* 8; **¿Me puede decir...?** *Can you tell me . . .?,* 9; **¿Me puede traer...?** *Can you bring me . . .?,* 8; **No puedo.** *I can't.,* 7; **¿Puedo dejar un recado?** *May I leave a message?,* 7
la poesía *poetry,* 7
la política *politics,* 6
el pollo *chicken,* 8
poner *to put, to place,* 2,; **¡pon!** *put!, place!,* 10; **poner la mesa** *to set the table,* 6
por *at,* 3; *by,* 5; *for,* 12; *in,* 4; por ejemplo *for example,* 12; **por eso** *that's why,* 4; **por favor** *please,* 8; **por fin** *at last,* 3; **por la mañana** *in*

the morning, 5; **por la noche** *at night, in the evening,* 5; **por la playa** *along the beach,* 5; **por la tarde** *in the afternoon,* 5
¿Por qué? *Why?,* 3; **¿Por qué no...?** *Why don't...?,* 3
porque *because,* 3
la portada *cover* (of a book or magazine), 2
el póster *poster,* 2
el postre *dessert,* 8
practicar *to practice,* 4
el precio *price,* 9; **Son del mismo precio.** *They're the same price.,* 9
preferir (ie) *to prefer,* 7
preocupado/a por algo *worried about something,* 11
preocuparse *to worry;* **No te preocupes.** *Don't worry.,* 3
preparar *to prepare,* 4
la presentación *introduction,* 1
la procesión *procession,* 10
el propósito *purpose,* 10
el protagonista *protagonist,* 2
la prima *cousin* (female), 6
la primavera *spring,* 5
el primo *cousin* (male), 6
primero *first,* 3; *the first (of the month),* 5
la prisa *haste;* **tener prisa** *to be in a hurry,* 7; **Tengo prisa.** *I'm in a hurry.,* 3
probar (ue) *to try, to taste,* 6
el problema *problem,* 6
producir *to produce,* 8
el profesor *teacher* (male), 3
la profesora *teacher* (female), 3
profundamente *deeply,* 11
el programa *program,* 3; el programa de televisión *television program,* 3
el pronóstico *forecast,* 5; el pronóstico del tiempo *weather report,* 5
Pronto. (telephone greeting), 7
la propina *tip,* 8; **¿Está incluida la propina?** *Is the tip included?,* 8
la puerta *door,* 2
el puesto *stand,* 10
punto *point, dot,* 3; **en punto** *on the dot,* 3
el pupitre *student desk,* 2
el puré *purée,* 8

Q

que *that, which, who,* 4; **Dice que...** *She/he says that...,* 6
¿Qué? *What?,*
¡Qué barato/a! *How cheap!,* 9
¡Qué caro/a! *How expensive!,* 9
¿Qué fecha es hoy? *What's today's date?,* 5
¡Qué ganga! *What a bargain!,* 9
¿Qué hay en...? *What's in...?,* 2; ¿Qué hay? *What's up?,* 1
¿Qué hiciste? *What did you do?,* 10
¿Qué hizo? *What did he/she/you do?,* 10
¿Qué hora es? *What time is it?,* 3
¿Qué hubo? *What's up?,* 1
¡Qué lástima! *What a shame!,* 7
¿Qué le pasa a...? *What's wrong with...?,* 11
¡Qué lío! *What a mess!,* 3
¿Qué onda? *What's up?,* 1
¡Qué padre! *How cool!,* 2
¿Qué pasa? *What's happening?,* 1
¡Qué pesado/a! *How annoying!,* 2
¿Qué tal? *How's it going?,* 1; ¿Qué tal? *What's up?,* 1
¿Qué tal si...? *What if...?,* 11
¿Qué te gusta hacer? *What do you like to do?,* 4
¿Qué te gusta? *What do you like?,* 1
¿Qué te parece si...? *How do you feel about...?,* 10
¿Qué tiempo hace? *What's the weather like?,* 5
¿Qué tienes? *What's the matter?,* 11
quedar *to be situated,* 9
quedarse *to stay, to remain,* 12
los quehaceres *chores,* 2
quemar *to set on fire,* 10
querer (ie) *to want,* 2; **Quiere...** *He/she wants...,* 2; **Quieres...** *You want...,* 2; **Quiero...** *I want...,* 2; **quisiera** *I would like,* 8
el queso *cheese,* 8
¿quién? *who?,* 4; **¿De parte de quién?** *Who's calling?,* 7; **Para quién?** *For whom?,* 9; **¿quiénes?** *who?,* 5
la química *chemistry,* 3
quince *fifteen,* 1
quinientos/as *five hundred,* 8
quitar *to remove, to take out,* 8
quiteño/a *from Quito,* 7

R

el racismo *racism,* 1
la radio *radio,* 2
la raíz *root,* 10
la raya *stripe;* **de rayas** *striped,* 9
real *royal,* 1
la realeza *royalty,* 10
realizar *to carry out, to perform,* 11
la rebeldía *rebelliousness,* 6
el recado *message,* 7; **¿Puedo dejar un recado?** *May I leave a message?,* 7
la receta *recipe,* 8
recibir *to receive,* 5; **recibir regalos** *to receive gifts,* 10
el recorrido *trip, journey,* 12; hacer un recorrido *to go sightseeing,* 12
recostar (ue) *to recline, to lean back,* 11
el recuerdo *souvenir, remembrance,* 9
refrescante *refreshing,* 8
el refresco *soft drink,* 4; **tomar un refresco** *to drink a soft drink,* 4
regalar *to give (a gift),* 9
el regalo *gift,* 9; **recibir regalos** *to receive gifts,* 10
la regla *ruler,* 2
regresar *to return,* 4
Regular. *Okay.,* 1
la religión *religion,* 3
el reloj *clock, watch,* 2
la remembranza *memory, remembrance,* 10
el remo *paddle, oar,* 5
rendido/a *tired,* 7
renombre *renown,* 6
repetir (i) *to repeat,* 11
los reptiles *reptiles,* 2
la res *head of cattle;* **la carne de res** *beef,* 8
resfriado/a *congested,* 11; **estar resfriado/a** *to be congested,* 11
respirar *to breathe,* 11
responsable *responsible,* 6
el restaurante *restaurant,* 4
reunirse *to gather, to join together,* 6
la revista *magazine,* 2
rico/a *rich, delicious,* 8
el río *river,* 12
el ritmo *rhythm,* 6
el robo *rip-off, robbery,* 9; **¡Es un robo!** *It's a rip-off!,* 9

la rodilla *knee,* 11
rojo/a *red,* 9
romántico/a *romantic,* 4
la ropa *clothing,* 2; **lavar la ropa** *to wash the clothes,* 4
rubio/a *blond(e),* 3
la rutina *routine,* 7

S

el sábado *Saturday,* 4; **el sábado pasado** *last Saturday,* 10
saber *to know (information);* **No sé.** *I don't know.,* 2; **Sé.** *I know.,* 2
el sabor *flavor, taste,* 8
sacar *to take out;* **sacar la basura** *to take out the trash,* 4
la sala *living room,* 6
salado/a *salty,* 8
salir *to go out, to leave,* 6
la salsa *salsa music,* 6
saltar *to jump;* **saltar en paracaídas** *to go skydiving,* 12
salvar *to save,* 2
sano/a *healthy,* 11; **llevar una vida sana** *to lead a healthy life,* 11
el sancocho *soup made of green plantains, corn, and* carne colorada, 8
la sandalia *sandal,* 9
el sándwich *sandwich,* 5
el saxofón *saxophone,* 4
Sé. *I know.,* 2; **No sé.** *I don't know.,* 2
Se llama... *Her/his/your name is . . .,* 1
Se ve joven. *She/he looks young.,* 6
la sed *thirst;* **tener sed** *to be thirsty,* 8
la seda *silk;* **de seda** (made of) *silk,* 9
seguir (i) *to follow,* 8; *to continue,* 12
seis *six,* 1
seiscientos/as *six hundred,* 8
la selva *jungle,* 12
la semana *week,* 4; **la semana pasada** *last week,* 10
el semestre *semester,* 3
las semillas *seeds,* 8
sencillo/a *simple,* 11
señor *sir, Mister,* 1
señora *ma'am, Mrs.,* 1
señorita *miss,* 1
el sentido *sense, faculty of sensation,* 5
sentir (ie) *to regret;* **Lo siento.** *I'm sorry.,* 7; **Lo siento, pero no puedo.** *I'm sorry but I can't.,* 7
sentirse (ie) *to feel,* 11
el septiembre *September,* 5
ser *to be,* 1; **¿Cómo es?** *What's he/she/it like?,* 3; **¿Cómo son?** *What are they like?,* 3; **¿De dónde eres?** *Where are you from?,* 1; **Es de...** *He/she is from . . .,* 1; **Es la una.** *It's one o'clock,* 3; **¡Es un robo!** *It's a rip-off!,* 9; **No es cierto.** *It isn't true.,* 6; **Somos** *We are,* 3; **Son las...** *It's . . . o'clock.,* 3; **Soy de...** *I'm from . . .,* 1; **Soy** *I am,* 1
la servilleta *napkin,* 8
sesenta *sixty,* 2
setecientos/as *seven hundred,* 8
setenta *seventy,* 2
la sevillana *folk dance of Seville,* 10
el sexismo *sexism,* 1
si *if,* 11
sí *yes,* 1
la sicología *psychology,* 1
siempre *always,* 5; **casi siempre** *almost always,* 6
siento *I regret,* 7; **Lo siento.** *I'm sorry.,* 7
siete *seven,* 1
el siglo *century,* 6
la silla *chair,* 2
simpático/a *nice,* 3
sinfónico/a *symphonic,* 7
el sintetizador *synthesizer,* 4
el sistema *system,* 9
social *social,* 1
la sociología *sociology,* 1
sol *sun,* 5; **tomar el sol** *to sunbathe,* 12; **Hace sol.** *It's sunny.,* 5
sólo *only,* 5; **sólo cuando** *only when,* 5
soltar (ue) *to let go, to let out,* 11
somos *we are,* 3
Son las... *It's . . . o'clock.,* 3
la sopa *soup,* 8
el sorbete *sherbet,* 8
la sorbetera *ice cream/sherbet maker,* 8
la sorpresa *surprise,* 7; **la fiesta de sorpresa** *surprise party,* 7
soy *I am,* 1; **Soy de...** *I'm from . . .,* 1
su/sus *your/his/her/their,* 2, 6
suave *soft,* 11
subir *to go up, to move up,* 11
sucio/a *dirty,* 8
el sucre *domestic currency in Ecuador,* 9
el suelo *floor, ground,* 11
el sueño *dream;* **tener sueño** *to be sleepy,* 7
la suerte *skillful maneuver;* suertes a caballo *skillful maneuver riding a horse,* 11
el suéter *sweater,* 9
sugerir *to suggest,* 12
el supermercado *supermarket,* 4

T

el tacón *heel of shoe,* 9
la tajada *slice of meat,* 8
tal vez *maybe, perhaps;* **tal vez otro día** *perhaps another day,* 7
el taller *workshop,* 7
el tamaño *size,* 5
también *too, also,* 1
tan... como... *as . . . as . . .,* 9
la tarde *afternoon,* 3; **Buenas tardes.** *Good afternoon.,* 1; **de la tarde** *in the afternoon* (P.M.), 3; **por la tarde** *in the afternoon,* 5
tarde *late,* 3; **Llamo más tarde.** *I'll call later.,* 7
la tarea *homework,* 1
la tarjeta *greeting card,* 9; **la tarjeta postal** *postcard,* 5
la taza *cup,* 8
el tazón *bowl,* 8; El Tazón de la Naranja *Orange Bowl,* 10
el té *tea;* **el té frío** *iced tea,* 8
te *to/for you,* 9; **¿Te gusta...?** *Do you like . . .?,* 1; **Te gustan...** *You like . . .,* 3; **¿Te gustaría...?** *Would you like . . .?,* 7; **Te invito.** *It's my treat.,* 7; **Te queda muy bien.** *It fits you very well.,* 9
el teatro *theater,* 7
el techo *ceiling, roof,* 6
la tecnología *technology,* 1
el teléfono *telephone,* 7; **hablar por teléfono** *to talk on the phone,* 7; los números de teléfono *telephone numbers,* 10
la televisión *television;* el programa de televisión *television program,* 3; **mirar la televisión** *to watch television,* 4

el televisor *television set,* 2
el tenedor *fork,* 8
tener (ie) *to have,* 2; **Bueno, tengo clase.** *Well, I have class.,* 1; **¿Cuántos años tiene?** *How old is (she/he)?,* 1; **¿Cuántos años tienes?** *How old are you?,* 1; **¿Qué tienes?** *What's the matter?,* 11; **tener fiebre** *to have a fever,* 11; **tener ganas de** + infinitive *to feel like (doing something),* 7; **tener gripe** *to have the flu,* 11; **tener hambre** *to be hungry,* 8; **tener prisa** *to be in a hurry,* 7; **tener sed** *to be thirsty,* 8; **tener sueño** *to be sleepy,* 7; **tener tos** *to have a cough,* 11; **Tengo...** *I have . . .,* 2; **Tengo ... años.** *I'm . . . years old.,* 1; **Tengo prisa.** *I'm in a hurry.,* 3; **Tiene...** *He/she has . . .,* 2; **Tiene ... años.** *She/he is . . . years old.,* 1; **Tiene canas.** *He/she has gray hair.,* 6; **Tienes...** *You have . . .,* 2; **Ya tengo planes.** *I already have plans.,* 7; **tener que** + infinitive *to have to (do something),* 7; **Tengo que irme.** *I have to go.,* 1
el tenis *tennis,* 1; **la cancha de tenis** *tennis court,* 11; **las zapatillas de tenis** *tennis shoes* (Spain), 2
la tensión *tension,* 11
terminar *to end, to finish,* 10
el terror *terror,* 2
los tesoros *treasures,* 9
la tía *aunt,* 6
el tiempo *weather, time,* 5; **el tiempo libre** *free time,* 4; **Hace buen tiempo.** *The weather is nice.,* 5; **Hace mal tiempo.** *The weather is bad.,* 5; Hace un tiempo precioso. *It's a beautiful day.,* 5; pronóstico del tiempo *weather report,* 5; **¿Qué tiempo hace?** *What's the weather like?,* 5
la tienda *store,* 4; **la tienda de camping** *camping tent,* 12; **la tienda de comestibles** *grocery store,* 9
tiene *he/she has,* 2; **Tiene ... años.** *He/she is . . . years old.,* 1; **Tiene canas.** *He/she has gray hair.,* 6
tienes *you have,* 2; **¿Cuántos años tienes?** *How old are you?,* 1; **¿Qué tienes?** *What's the matter?,* 11
la tierra *Earth,* 2
tímido/a *shy,* 6
el tío *uncle,* 6
típicamente *typically,* 5
las tiras cómicas *comics,* 5
la toalla *towel,* 12
el tocador de discos compactos *compact disc player,* 2
tocar *to touch, to play;* **tocar un instrumento** *to play an instrument,* 4
el tocino *bacon,* 8
todavía *still, yet,* 5; todavía no *not yet,* 7
todo/a *all, every;* todo el tiempo *all the time,* 5; **todos los días** *every day,* 5
tomar *to drink, to take,* 4; **tomar el autobús** *to take the bus,* 5; tomarle el pelo *to pull someone's leg,* 11; **tomar el sol** *to sunbathe,* 12
el tomate *tomato,* 8
el tomo *volume, tome,* 2
el toro *bull,* 10
la toronja *grapefruit,* 8
la torta *sandwich,* 8
la tortilla *tortilla, omelet,* 8; tortilla española *omelet with potatoes, onions, and olive oil,* 8
la tos *cough;* **tener tos** *to have a cough,* 11
tostado/a *toasted,* 8; **el pan tostado** *toast,* 8
trabajar *to work,* 4; **trabajar en el jardín** *to work in the garden,* 6
el trabajo *work, job,* 4
trabajador/a *hard-working,* 6
el trabalenguas *tongue twister,* 2
tradicional *traditional,* 6
las tradiciones *traditions,* 6
traer *to bring,* 8; **¿Me puede traer...?** *Can you bring me . . .?,* 8; **¿Me traes...?** *Can you bring me . . .?,* 10
el traje *suit,* 9; **el traje de baño** *bathing suit,* 9
transportado/a *transported, carried away,* 2
tratarse de *to be a question of,* 11
travieso/a *mischievous,* 6
trece *thirteen,* 1
treinta *thirty,* 1
tres *three,* 1
trescientos/as *three hundred,* 8
triste *sad,* 11
el trivia *trivia,* 1
la trompeta *trumpet,* 4
tropical *tropical,* 8
tú *you,* 1
tu/tus *your,* 2, 6; Tu ropa hace juego. *Your clothes go well together.,* 9
el turismo *tourism;* **hacer turismo** *to go sightseeing,* 12
el turista *tourist,* 7

U

último/a *last;* Estás a la última. *You're stylish.,* 9
un *a, an,* 2; **un momento** *one moment,* 7; **Un momentito.** *Just a second.,* 10
una *a, an,* 2
uno *one,* 1
los unicornios *unicorns,* 4
unido/a *close-knit,* 6
el uniforme *school uniform,* 2
unos/as *some, a few,* 2
usted *you,* 4
ustedes *you* (pl.), 4,; **a ustedes** *to you,* 5
la uva *grape,* 8

V

vacacionar *to vacation,* 11
las vacaciones *vacation,* 5
la variedad *variety,* 8
el vaso *glass,* 8; **el vaso de leche** *glass of milk,* 8
¡ve! *go!,* 10
veinte *twenty,* 1
el vejigante *reveler,* 10
la vela *sail,* 12; **ir de vela** *to go sailing,* 12
la velocidad *velocity, speed,* 5
venir *to come,* 7; **¡ven!** *come!,* 10
la ventana *window,* 2
ver *to watch, to see,* 6; ver televisión *to watch television,* 4
el verano *summer,* 5; **el verano pasado** *last summer,* 10
¿verdad? *don't you?, right?,* 3
verde *green,* 6
las verduras *greens, vegetables,* 10

verificar *to verify, to confirm,* 11
el vestido *dress,* 9
¡vete! *go away!,* 10
la vez *time, turn, occasion, occurrence;* de vez en cuando *once in a while,* 5; **muchas veces** *often,* 5; otra vez *again,* 8; **tal vez otro día** *perhaps another day,* 7; una vez *once,* 5
el viaje *trip,* 6; **hacer un viaje** *to take a trip,* 6
la vida *life,* 11; Lo pasé pura vida. *I had a great time.,* 12; la vida nocturna *night life,* 9
el video *video,* 1
el videojuego *videogame,* 3
la videocasetera *VCR,* 2
los videojuegos *videogames,* 2
viejo/a *old,* 6
el viento *wind,* 5; **Hace (mucho) viento.** *It's (very) windy.,* 5
el viernes *Friday,* 4
el violín *violin,* 4
visitar *to visit,* 6
la vista *view,* 12
vivir *to live,* 6
vivo/a *alive,* 6
el voleibol *volleyball,* 1
volver (ue) *to return,* 8
vosotros/as *you,* 4
vuestro/a *your,* 6

Y

y *and,* 1; **y media** *half past* (the hour), 3; **¿Y tú?** *And you?,* 1
ya *already,* 2; **Ya tengo planes.** *I already have plans.,* 7; Ya voy. *I'm on my way.,* 7; ¡Ya, ya! *Enough!,* 7
yo *I,* 1; **Yo también.** *Me too.,* 1
yoga *yoga,* 11; **hacer yoga** *to do yoga,* 11

Z

la zanahoria *carrot,* 8
la zapatería *shoe store,* 9
el zapato *shoe,* 2
las zapatillas de tenis *tennis shoes* (Spain), 2
la zarzamora *blackberry,* 8
la zoología *zoology,* 1
el zoológico *zoo,* 7
el zumo *juice,* 8

ENGLISH-SPANISH VOCABULARY

A

a/an *un, una,* 2
ache, to *doler (ue),* 11
aerobics *los ejercicios aeróbicos,* 5
a few *unos, unas,* 2
affectionate *cariñoso/a* , 6
after *después,* 3; *después de,* 4
afternoon *la tarde,* 3; **in the afternoon** *de la tarde,* 3; *por la tarde,* 5
afterward *después,* 3
agreed *de acuerdo,* 10
a little *un poco,* 6
all *todo/a, todos/as,* 5
a lot *mucho,* 1
a lot of; a lot *mucho/a, muchos/as,* 2
all right *está bien,* 7
almost *casi,* 6; **almost always** *casi siempre,* 6
along *por,* 5; **along the beach** *por la playa,* 5
already *ya,* 2
always *siempre,* 5
American *americano/a,* 1; *norteamericano,* 1; **American football** *el fútbol norteamericano,* 1
amusement park *el parque de atracciones,* 7
amusing *divertido/a,* 3
and *y,* 1; **And you?** *¿Y tú?,* 1
angry *enojado/a,* 11
anniversary *el aniversario,* 7; **anniversary party** *la fiesta de aniversario,* 7
another *otro/a, otros/as,* 8
anthropology *la antropología,* 7
apple *la manzana,* 8
appointment *la cita,* 7
April *abril,* 5
aquarium *el acuario,* 7
arm *el brazo,* 11
art *el arte,* 3; *las artes* (pl.)
as . . . as . . . *tan... como...* , 9
ask for, to *pedir (i)* , 8
at *a, por,* 3; **at all** *para nada,* 8; **at last** *por fin,* 3; **at night** *por la noche, en ia noche,* 5; **At what time . . .?** *¿A qué hora...?,* 3
attend, to *asistir a,* 5
attraction *la atracción,* 7
August *agosto,* 5
aunt *la tía,* 6
autumn *el otoño,* 5

B

back *la espalda,* 11
backpack *la mochila,* 2
bacon *el tocino,* 8
bad *malo/a,* 3
bakery *la panadería,* 9
balloons *los globos,* 10
ballpoint pen *el bolígrafo,* 2
banana *el plátano,* 8
baseball *el béisbol,* 1
basketball *el baloncesto,* 1
bathing suit *el traje de baño,* 9
be, to *ser,* 1; *estar,* 4; **to be able** *poder (ue),* 8; **to be in a hurry,** *tener prisa,* 3; **to be ready** *estar listo/a,* 7; **to be situated** *quedar,* 9; **to be sleepy** *tener sueño,* 7
beach *la playa,* 5
beans *los frijoles,* 8
because *porque,* 3
bed *la cama,* 2
beef *la carne de res,* 8
before *antes de,* 4
begin, to *empezar (ie),* 7
believe, to *creer,* 10
belt *el cinturón,* 9
beneath *debajo de,* 4
besides *además,* 9
beverage *la bebida,* 8
bicycle *la bicicleta,* 4
big *grande,* 3
bill *la cuenta,* 8
birthday *el cumpleaños,* 7; **birthday party** *fiesta de cumpleaños,* 7
black *negro/a,* 6
block, city *la cuadra,* 9
blond *rubio/a,* 3
blouse *la blusa,* 9
blow up balloons, to *inflar los globos,* 10
blue *azul,* 6
bluejeans *los bluejeans,* 9
board game *el juego de mesa,* 9
body *el cuerpo,* 11
book *el libro,* 2
book bag *la mochila,* 2
bookstore *la librería,* 2
boots *las botas,* 9
boring *aburrido/a,* 3
boy *el chico,* 5
bread *el pan,* 8
break *el descanso,* 3
breakfast *el desayuno,* 8
bring, to *traer,* 8
brother *el hermano,* 6; **brothers and sisters** *los hermanos,* 6
brown *de color café,* 6; *pardo,* 9
brunette *moreno/a,* 3
brush one's teeth, to *lavarse los dientes,* 7
bus *el autobús,* 5
busy *ocupado/a,* 7; **the line is busy** *la línea está ocupada,* 7
but *pero,* 1
buy, to *comprar,* 2
by *por,* 5
'bye *chao,* 1

C

cafeteria *la cafetería,* 1
cake *el pastel,* 8
calculator *la calculadora,* 2
call, to *llamar,* 7; **to call the guests** *llamar a los invitados,* 10
camera *la cámara,* 12
camp, to *acampar,* 5
Can you bring me . . .? *¿Me puedes traer...?,* 8; *¿Me traes...?,* 10; **Can you do me the favor of . . .?** *¿Me haces el favor de...?,* 10; **Can you give me . . .?** *¿Me das...?,* 10; **Can you help me . . .?** *¿Me ayudas a...?,* 10; **Can you pass me . . .?** *¿Me pasas...?,* 10; **Can you tell me . . .?** *¿Me puede decir...?,* 9
candy *los dulces,* 9; **candy store** *la dulcería,* 9
canoe *la canoa,* 12
car *el carro,* 4
card *la tarjeta,* 9
carrot *la zanahoria,* 8
cat *el gato,* 6; **to take care of the cat** *cuidar al gato,* 6
cereal *el cereal,* 8
chair *la silla,* 2
cheap *barato/a,* 9
cheese *el queso,* 8
chicken *el pollo,* 8
children *los hijos,* 6
China *(la) China,* 12
Chinese food *la comida china,* 1
chocolate *el chocolate,* 1
Christmas *la Navidad,* 10; **Christmas Eve** *la Nochebuena,* 10
circus *el circo,* 7
city *la ciudad,* 7

city block *la cuadra,* 9
class *la clase,* 1
classical music *la música clásica,* 1
classmate *el compañero* (male), *la compañera* (female) *de clase,* 3
clean *limpio/a,* 8
clean, to *limpiar,* 6; **clean the kitchen, to** *limpiar la cocina,* 6
clever *listo/a,* 6
climb, to *escalar,* 12
clock *el reloj,* 2
close-knit *unido/a,* 6
closet *el armario,* 2
clothing *la ropa,* 2
cloudy *nublado,* 5; **It's cloudy.** *Está nublado.,* 5
coffee *el café,* 8
cold *frío,* 8; **It's cold.** *Hace frío.,* 5
color *el color,* 6
comb one's hair, to *peinarse,* 7
come, to *venir (ie),* 7; **Come!** *¡Ven!,* 10; **Come along!** *¡Ven conmigo!,* P
comfortable *cómodo/a,* 9
comical *cómico/a,* 3
comics *las tiras cómicas,* 5
compact disc *el disco compacto,* 9
companion *el compañero* (male), *la compañera* (female), 3
computer science *la computación,* 3
concert *el concierto,* 3
congested *resfriado/a,* 11
cookie *la galleta,* 8
corn *el maíz,* 8
cotton *el algodón,* 9; **made of cotton** *de algodón,* 9
cough *la tos,* 11
country *el campo,* 7
cousin *el primo* (male), *la prima* (female), 6
custard *el flan,* 8
cut, to *cortar,* 6; **to cut the grass** *cortar el césped,* 6

D

dad *el papá,* 6
dance *el baile,* 3
dance, to *bailar,* 4
date *la fecha,* 5; *la cita,* 7
daughter *la hija,* 6
day *el día,* 4; **day before yesterday** *anteayer,* 10; **every day** *todos los días,* 5; **free day** *día libre,* 3
December *diciembre,* 5
decorate, to *decorar,* 10
decorations *las decoraciones,* 10
delicious *delicioso/a,* 8; *rico/a,* 8
delighted *encantado/a,* 1
department store *el almacén,* 9
desk *el escritorio,* 2
dessert *el postre,* 8
dictionary *el diccionario,* 2
difficult *difícil,* 3
dinner *la cena,* 4
dirty *sucio/a,* 8
disagreeable *antipático/a,* 3
do, to *hacer,* 2; **Do!** *¡Haz!,* 10; **to do yoga** *hacer yoga,* 11; **Do you like . . .?** *¿Te gusta...?,* 1; **Don't worry!** *¡No te preocupes!,* 3
dog *el perro,* 4; **to walk the dog** *caminar con el perro,* 4
dollar *el dólar,* 2
door *la puerta,* 2
downtown *el centro,* 4
draw, to *dibujar,* 4
dress *el vestido,* 9
drink, to *tomar,* 4; *beber,* 5
during *durante,* 5

E

ear *el oído,* 11; **outer ear** *la oreja,* 11
earlobe *la oreja,* 11
earring *el arete,* 9
Easter *las Pascuas,* 10
easy *fácil,* 3
eat, to *comer,* 5; **to eat breakfast** *desayunar,* 5; **to eat dinner** *cenar,* 6; **to eat lunch** *almorzar (ue),* 8
education *la educación,* 3; **physical education** *la educación física,* 3
eggs *los huevos,* 8
Egypt *el Egipto,* 12
eight *ocho,* 1
eighteen *dieciocho,* 1
eight hundred *ochocientos/as,* 8
eighty *ochenta,* 2
eleven *once,* 1
end *el fin,* 4
England *Inglaterra,* 12
English class *la clase de inglés,* 1
eraser *la goma de borrar,* 2
especially *especialmente,* 5
evening *la noche,* 5
event *el evento,* 7
every *todo/a, todos/as;* **every day** *todos los días,* 5
exam *el examen,* 3
excellent *excelente,* 1
Excuse me. *Perdón.,* 9; *Perdóname.,* 10
exercise *el ejercicio,* 5; **to exercise** *hacer ejercicio,* 5
expensive *caro/a,* 9
explore, to *explorar,* 12
eye *el ojo,* 6

F

fall *el otoño,* 5
family *la familia,* 6
fantastic *fantástico/a,* 3
far *lejos,* 4; **far from** *lejos de,* 4
father *el padre,* 6; **Father's Day** *el Día del Padre,* 10
favorite *favorito/a,* 3
February *febrero,* 5
feel, to *sentirse (ie),* 11; **to feel like (doing something)** *tener ganas de* + infinitive, 7
fever *la fiebre,* 11; **to have a fever** *tener fiebre,* 11
few, a *unos/as,* 2
field, playing *la cancha,* 11
fifteen *quince,* 1
fifty *cincuenta,* 2
find, to *encontrar (ue),* 2
finger *el dedo,* 11
first *primero,* 2
fish *el pescado,* 8
fish, to *pescar,* 5
fit, to *quedar,* 9; **It fits you very well.** *Te queda muy bien.,* 9
five *cinco,* 1
five hundred *quinientos/as,* 8
flowers *las flores,* 9
flower shop *la florería,* 9
flu *la gripe,* 11
folder *la carpeta,* 2
food *la comida,* 6; **Chinese food** *la comida china,* 1; **Italian food** *la comida italiana,* 1; **Mexican food** *la comida mexicana,* 1
foot *el pie,* 11
football *el fútbol norteamericano,* 1
for *para,* 9; **For whom?** *¿Para quién?,* 9
forest *el bosque,* 12
fork *el tenedor,* 8
formal *formal,* 9
forty *cuarenta,* 2
four *cuatro,* 1
four hundred *cuatrocientos/as,* 8
fourteen *catorce,* 1
France *Francia,* 12
free time *el tiempo libre,* 4
French *el francés,* 3
french fries *las papas fritas,* 5
Friday *el viernes,* 4
friend *el amigo* (male), *la amiga* (female), 1; *el compañero* (male), *la compañera* (female), 3

fruit *la fruta,* 1
fun *divertido/a,* 3
funny *cómico/a,* 3

G

game *el juego,* 9; **game of . . . (sport)** *el partido de...,* 3
garden *el jardín,* 6
geography *la geografía,* 3
Germany *Alemania,* 12
get to know someone, to *conocer,* 2
gift *el regalo,* 9; **to open gifts** *abrir los regalos,* 10; **to receive gifts** *recibir regalos,* 10
girl *la chica,* 5
give, to *dar, regalar,* 9
Gladly! *¡Con mucho gusto!,* 10
glass *el vaso,* 8
go, to *ir,* 2; **Go!** *¡Ve!,* 10; **Go away!** *¡Vete!,* 10 ; **to go canoeing** *bajar el río en canoa,* 12; **to go hiking** *dar una caminata,* 12; **to go mountain climbing** *escalar montañas,* 12; **to go out** *salir,* 6; **to go sailing** *ir de vela,* 12; **to go sightseeing** *hacer turismo,* 12; **to go skydiving** *saltar en paracaídas,* 12; **to go to the mall** *ir al centro comercial,* 2
good *bueno/a,* 3; **Good afternoon.** *Buenas tardes.,* 1; **Good morning.** *Buenos días.,* 1; **Good evening.** *Buenas noches.,* 1; **Good night.** *Buenas noches.,* 1
Goodbye. *Adiós.,* 1
good-looking *guapo/a,* 3
graduation *la graduación,* 7; **graduation party** *la fiesta de graduación,* 7
grandfather *el abuelo,* 6
grandmother *la abuela,* 6
grandparents *los abuelos,* 6
grapefruit *la toronja,* 8
grapes *las uvas,* 8
grass *el césped,* 6
gray *gris,* 9; **gray hair** *las canas,* 6
great *excelente,* 1; *estupendo,* 1; *magnífico,* 11
green *verde,* 6
greeting card *la tarjeta,* 9
grocery store *la tienda de comestibles,* 9
guests *los invitados,* 10
guitar *la guitarra,* 4
gym *el gimnasio,* 4

H

hair *el pelo,* 6; **He/she has gray hair.** *Tiene canas.,* 6
half past (the hour) *y media,* 3
half-brother *el medio hermano,* 6
half-sister *la media hermana,* 6
ham *el jamón,* 8
hamburger *la hamburguesa,* 5
hang up, to *colgar (ue),* 10
have, to *tener (ie),* 2; **to have a cough** *tener tos,* 11; **to have a fever** *tener fiebre,* 11; **to have breakfast** *desayunar,* 5 **to have the flu** *tener gripe,* 11; **to have to (do something)** *tener que* + infinitive, 7; **to have to go** *tener que irse,* 1
he *él,* 2
head *la cabeza,* 11
healthy *sano/a,* 11
heat *el calor,* 5
heavy *fuerte,* 8
Hello. *Aló.,* 7; *Diga.,* 7; *¡Hola!,* 1 (telephone greetings)
help at home, to *ayudar en casa,* 5
her *la,* 10; **to/for her** *le,* 9
here *aquí,* 4
high school *el colegio,* 2
him *lo,* 10; **to/for him** *le,* 9
holidays *los días festivos,* 10
home *la casa,* 4; **at home** *en casa,* 4
homework *la tarea,* 1
horrible *horrible,* 1
hot *caliente,* 8; **to be hot** *hacer calor,* 4
hot dog *el perro caliente,* 8
hour *la hora,* 3
house *la casa,* 4
How? *¿Cómo?,* 1; **How are you?** *¿Cómo estás?,* 1
How cheap! *¡Qué barato!,* 9
How do you feel about . . .? *¿Que te parece si...?,* 10
How expensive! *¡Qué caro!,* 9
How many? *¿cuántos?, ¿cuántas?,* 2
How much? *¿cuánto/a?,* 2; **How much do . . . cost?** *¿Cuánto cuestan...?,* 9; **How much does . . . cost?** *¿Cuánto cuesta...?,* 9; **How much is it?** *¿Cuánto es?,* 8
How often? *¿Con qué frecuencia?,* 5
How old are you? *¿Cuántos años tienes?,* 1
How's it going? *¿Qué tal?,* 1
hurry *la prisa;* **Hurry up!** *¡Date prisa!,* 3; **I'm in a hurry.** *Tengo prisa.,* 3
hundred *cien, ciento,* 2
hungry, to be *tener hambre,* 8
hurt, to *doler (ue),* 11
husband *el esposo,* 6

I

I *yo,* 1
iced tea *el té frío,* 8
idea *la idea,* 10
if *si,* 10
in *en, por,* 5; **in order to** *para* + infinitive, 4; **in the afternoon (P.M.)** *de la tarde,* 3; **in the evening (P.M.)** *de la noche,* 3; **in the morning (A.M.)** *de la mañana,* 3
included *incluido/a,* 8
Independence Day *el Día de la Independencia,* 10
inflate, to *inflar,* 10
intelligent *inteligente,* 3
intend, to *pensar* + infinitive, 7
interesting *interesante,* 3
invitation *la invitación,* 10
invite, to *invitar,* 7
iron, to *planchar,* 6
Isn't it? *¿No?,* 3
it *la, lo,* 10
It's a rip-off! *¡Es un robo!,* 9
It's cold. *Hace frío.,* 5
It's cool. *Hace fresco.,* 5
It's hot. *Hace calor.,* 5
It's raining. *Está lloviendo.,* 5; *Llueve.,* 5
It's snowing. *Está nevando.,* 5; *Nieva.,* 5
It's sunny. *Hace sol.,* 5
It's windy. *Hace viento.,* 5
Italian food *la comida italiana,* 1
Italy *Italia,* 12

J

jacket *la chaqueta,* 9
January *enero,* 5
jazz *el jazz,* 1
jewelry store *la joyería,* 9
job *el trabajo,* 4
juice *el jugo,* 5; **orange juice** *el jugo de naranja,* 8
July *julio,* 5
June *junio,* 5
jungle *la selva,* 12

K

kitchen *la cocina,* 6
knife *el cuchillo,* 8
know, to *saber,* 2; *conocer,* 2

L

lake *el lago,* 7
lamp *la lámpara,* 2
last *pasado/a,* 10; **last night** *anoche,* 10; **last Saturday** *el sábado pasado,* 10; **last summer** *el verano pasado,* 10; **last week** *la semana pasada,* 10; **last year** *el año pasado,* 10
late *atrasado/a,* 3; **to be late** *estar atrasado/a,* 3
later *más tarde,* 7
lead, to *llevar,* 11; **to lead a healthy life** *llevar una vida sana,* 11
leather (made of) *de cuero,* 9
leave, to *salir,* 6; **to leave a message** *dejar un recado,* 7
leg *la pierna,* 11
lemonade *la limonada,* 8
less *menos,* 6
less . . . than *menos ... que,* 9
letter *la carta,* 5
lettuce *la lechuga,* 8
library *la biblioteca,* 4
life *la vida,* 11
lift, to *levantar,* 11; **to lift weights** *levantar pesas,* 11
light *ligero/a,* 8
like, to *gustar,* 1; **to really like** *encantar,* 8
likewise *igualmente,* 1
listen to, to *escuchar,* 4; **to listen to music** *escuchar música,* 4
little, a *un poco,* 6
live, to *vivir,* 6
living room *la sala,* 6
look for, to *buscar,* 9
look young, to *verse joven,* 6
lot, a *mucho,* 1
love, to *encantar,* 8
lunch *el almuerzo,* 3

M

ma'am *señora,* 1
magazine *la revista,* 2
make the bed, to *hacer la cama,* 6
mall *el centro comercial,* 2
mango *el mango,* 8
many *muchos/as,* 2
March *marzo,* 5
mathematics *las matemáticas,* 3
May *mayo,* 5
maybe *tal vez,* 7
meat *la carne,* 8
menu *el menú,* 8
message *el recado,* 7; **May I leave a message?** *¿Puedo dejar un recado?,* 7
me too *yo también,* 1
Mexican food *la comida mexicana,* 1
mile *la milla,* 5
milk *la leche,* 8
milkshake *el batido,* 8
mineral water *el agua mineral,* 8
mischievous *travieso/a,* 6
miss *señorita,* 1
mister *señor,* 1
moment *el momento,* 7
Monday *el lunes,* 4
money *el dinero,* 2
month *el mes,* 5
more *más,* 1
more . . . than *más ... que,* 9
morning *la mañana,* 5
mother/mom *la madre/mamá,* 6; **Mother's Day** *el Día de las Madres,* 10
mountain *la montaña,* 12; **to go mountain climbing** *escalar montañas,* 12
mouth *la boca,* 11
movie *la película,* 4
movie theater *el cine,* 4
Mrs. *Señora,* 1
museum *el museo,* 7
music *la música,* 1; **classical music** *la música clásica,* 1; **music by...** *la música de...,* 1; **pop music** *la música pop,* 1; **rock music** *la música rock,* 1
my *mi,* 2; *mis,* 6

N

named, to be *llamarse,* 1; **My name is...** *Me llamo . . .,* 1
napkin *la servilleta,* 8
near *cerca de,* 4
neck *el cuello,* 11
necklace *el collar,* 9
need, to *necesitar,* 2
nervous *nervioso/a,* 11
never *nunca,* 5
new *nuevo/a,* 3; **new friends** *los nuevos amigos,* 2; **New Year's Day** *el Año Nuevo,* 10; **New Year's Eve** *la Nochevieja,* 10
newspaper *el periódico,* 5
next to *al lado de,* 4
nice *simpático/a,* 3
Nice to meet you. *Mucho gusto.,* 1
night *la noche,* 1; **Good night.** *Buenas noches.,* 1; **last night** *anoche,* 10; **the night before last** *anteanoche,* 11
nine *nueve,* 1
nine hundred *novecientos/as,* 8
nineteen *diecinueve,* 1
ninety *noventa,* 2
no *no,* 1
nobody *nadie,* 5
nor *ni,* 6
nose *la nariz,* 11
not *no,* 1
notebook *el cuaderno,* 2
nothing *nada,* 5
novel *la novela,* 3
November *noviembre,* 5
now *ahora,* 3
nowhere *ningún lugar,* 12
number *el número,* P

O

October *octubre,* 5
Of course! *¡Claro que sí!,* 7; *¡Cómo no!,* 10
often *muchas veces,* 5
okay *regular,* 1
old *viejo/a,* 6; **older** *mayor,* 6
on *en,* 3; **on the dot** *en punto,* 3; **on top of** *encima de,* 4
one *uno,* 1; **one moment** *un momento,* 7
onion *la cebolla,* 8
only *sólo,* 5
open, to *abrir,* 10; **to open gifts** *abrir regalos,* 10
orange *anaranjado/a,* 9
orange *la naranja,* 8; **orange juice** *el jugo de naranja,* 8
order, to *pedir (i),* 8
organize, to *organizar,* 2
other *otro/a,* 8
ought to, should *deber,* 6
our *nuestro/a,* 6
overweight *gordo/a;* **overweight (a little)** *un poco gordo/a,* 6

P

pack the suitcase, to *hacer la maleta,* 12
paint, to *pintar,* 4
pal *el compañero* (male), *la compañera* (female), 3
pants *los pantalones,* 9
papaya *la papaya,* 8

paper *el papel,* 2
parents *los padres,* 6
park *el parque,* 4; **amusement park** *el parque de atracciones,* 7
party *la fiesta,* 3
pasar *to pass,* 10
pastry shop *la pastelería,* 9
peanut butter *la crema de maní,* 8
pencil *el lápiz,* 2, (pl. *los lápices)*
perfect *perfecto,* 10
perhaps *tal vez,* 7; **perhaps another day** *tal vez otro día,* 7
physical education *la educación física,* 3
piano *el piano,* 4
pineapple *la piña,* 8
pizza *la pizza,* 1
pizzeria *la pizzería,* 2
place *el lugar,* 7
place, to *poner,* 2; **Place!** *¡Pon!,* 10
plaid *de cuadros,* 9
plan *el plan,* 7; **I already have plans.** *Ya tengo planes.,* 7
plan to, to *pensar* + infinitive, 7
plant *la planta,* 9
plate *el plato,* 8
play an instrument, to *tocar un instrumento,* 4
playing court *la cancha,* 11
please *por favor,* 8
pop music *la música pop,* 1
post office *el correo,* 4
postcards *las tarjetas postales,* 5
poster *el cartel,* 2
potato *la papa,* 5
potato chips *las papitas,* 8
practice, to *practicar,* 4
prefer, to *preferir (ie),* 7
prepare, to *preparar,* 4
pretty *bonito/a,* 3
price *el precio,* 9
problem *el problema,* 6
purple *morado/a,* 9
put on makeup, to *maquillarse,* 7
put, to *poner,* 2; **Put!** *¡Pon!,* 10

Q

quarter to (the hour) *menos cuarto,* 3
quite *bastante,* 6

R

radio *la radio,* 2
read, to *leer,* 5
ready *listo/a,* 7
receive, to *recibir,* 5; **to receive gifts** *recibir regalos,* 10; **to receive letters** *recibir cartas,* 5
recess *el descanso,* 3
red *rojo/a,* 9
redheaded *pelirrojo/a,* 6
rest, to *descansar,* 4; **to rest in the park** *descansar en el parque,* 4
restaurant *el restaurante,* 4
return, to *regresar,* 4
rice *el arroz,* 8
ride, to *montar,* 4; **to ride a bike** *montar en bicicleta,* 4
right? *¿verdad?,* 3
rip-off *el robo,* 9
river *el río,* 12
rock music *la música rock,* 1
roller skate, to *patinar sobre ruedas,* 11
room *el cuarto,* 2
ruler *la regla,* 2
run, to *correr,* 5
running track *la pista de correr,* 11

S

sad *triste,* 11
salad *la ensalada,* 1
salty *salado/a,* 8
same *mismo/a,* 9
Same here. *Igualmente.,* 1
sandals *las sandalias,* 9; *las chancletas,* 12
sandwich *el sándwich,* 5
Saturday *el sábado,* 4
say, to *decir,* 6
scarf *la bufanda,* 12
science *las ciencias,* 3
scuba dive, to *bucear,* 5
seasons *las estaciones,* 5
see, to *ver,* 7
See you later. *Hasta luego.,* 1
See you tomorrow. *Hasta mañana.,* 1
semester *el semestre,* 3
send, to *mandar,* 10; **to send invitations** *mandar las invitaciones,* 10
separate *aparte,* 8
September *septiembre,* 5
set the table, to *poner la mesa,* 6
seven *siete,* 1
seven hundred *setecientos/as,* 8
seventeen *diecisiete,* 1
seventy *setenta,* 2
shave, to *afeitarse,* 7
she *ella,* 2
shirt *la camisa,* 9
shoe *el zapato,* 9
shoe store *la zapatería,* 9
shopping mall *el centro comercial,* 2
short (to describe people) *bajo/a,* 3
shorts *los pantalones cortos,* 9
should *deber,* 6
shrimp *los camarones,* 8
sick *enfermo/a,* 7
silk (made of) *de seda,* 9
sing, to *cantar,* 4
sir *señor,* 1
sister *la hermana,* 6
six *seis,* 1
six hundred *seiscientos/as,* 8
sixteen *dieciséis,* 1
sixty *sesenta,* 2
skate, to *patinar,* 11
ski, to *esquiar,* 5
skirt *la falda,* 9
skis *los esquís,* 12
sleepy, to be *tener sueño,* 7
slippers *las chancletas,* 12
small *pequeño/a,* 3
smart *listo/a,* 6
snow *la nieve,* 5; **It's snowing.** *Nieva.,* 5
so-so *más o menos,* 1
soccer *el fútbol,* 1; **soccer field** *la cancha de fútbol,* 11
social sciences *las ciencias sociales,* 3
socks *los calcetines,* 9
soft drink *el refresco,* 4
some *unos/as,* 2
something *algo,* 6
sometimes *a veces,* 5
son *el hijo,* 6
soup *la sopa,* 8
Spanish *el español,* 1
speak, to *hablar,* 4
spend time with friends, to *pasar el rato con amigos,* 4
spicy *picante,* 8
spoon *la cuchara,* 8
sports *los deportes,* 3
spouse *la esposa* (wife), *el esposo* (husband), 6
spring *la primavera,* 5
stadium *el estadio,* 11
stay, to *quedarse,* 12
steak *el bistec,* 8
stepbrother *el hermanastro,* 6
stepfather *el padrastro,* 6
stepmother *la madrastra,* 6

stepsister *la hermanastra,* 6
still *todavía,* 5
stomach *el estómago,* 11
store *la tienda,* 4
strawberry *la fresa,* 8
stretch, to *estirarse,* 11
strict *estricto/a,* 3
striped *de rayas,* 9
stroll *la caminata,* 12; **to go hiking** *dar una caminata,* 12
strong *fuerte,* 8
study, to *estudiar,* 4
subject *la materia,* 3
suit *el traje,* 9; **bathing suit** *el traje de baño,* 9
suitcase *la maleta,* 12; **to pack the suitcase** *hacer la maleta,* 12
summer *el verano,* 5
sunbathe, to *tomar el sol,* 12
Sunday *el domingo,* 4
sunglasses *los lentes de sol,* 12
sunscreen *el bloqueador,* 12
supermarket *el supermercado,* 4
Sure! *¡Con mucho gusto!,* 10
surprise *la sorpresa,* 7; **surprise party** *la fiesta de sorpresa,* 7
sweater *el suéter,* 9
sweet rolls *el pan dulce,* 8
sweet shop *la pastelería,* 9
swim, to *nadar,* 4
swimming *la natación,* 1
swimming pool *la piscina,* 4

T

T-shirt *la camiseta,* 9
table *la mesa,* 2
take, to *tomar,* 4
take a shower, to *ducharse,* 7
take a trip, to *hacer un viaje,* 6
take care of, to *cuidar,* 4; **to take care of your brother/sister** *cuidar a tu hermano/a,* 4
take out the garbage, to *sacar la basura,* 4
take the bus, to *tomar el autobús,* 5
talk, to *hablar,* 4; **to talk on the phone** *hablar por teléfono,* 4
tall *alto/a,* 3
tea *el té,* 8; **iced tea** *el té frío,* 8
teacher *el profesor* (male), *la profesora* (female), 3
teeth *los dientes,* 7; **to brush one's teeth** *lavarse los dientes,* 7
telephone *el teléfono,* 4
television set *el televisor,* 2
tell, to *decir,* 6
ten *diez,* 1
tennis *el tenis,* 1; **tennis court** *la cancha de tenis,* 11; **tennis shoes** (Spain) *las zapatillas de tenis,* 2
tent *la tienda de camping,* 12
Thanks. *Gracias.,* 1
Thanksgiving *el Día de Acción de Gracias,* 10
that *esa, ese,* 9
that *que,* 4
that's why *por eso,* 4
the *el, la,* 1; *los, las,* 3
theater *el teatro,* 7
them *ellas/ellos,* 4; **to/for them** *les,* 9
then *luego,* 3
there *allá,* 4
there is, there are *hay,* 2
these *estas, estos,* 9
these *éstas, éstos,* 6
they *ellas, ellos,* 3
thin *delgado/a,* 6
thing *la cosa,* 2
think, to *creer,* 10; *pensar (ie),* 12
thirsty, to be *tener sed,* 8
thirteen *trece,* 1
thirty *treinta,* 1
this *esta, este,* 9; *ésta, éste,* 1
those *esas, esos,* 9
thousand *mil,* 8
three *tres,* 1
three hundred *trescientos/as,* 8
throat *la garganta,* 11
Thursday *el jueves,* 4
ticket *el boleto,* 12
tie *la corbata,* 9
time *la hora,* 3; **to spend time with friends** *pasar el rato con amigos,* 4
tip *la propina,* 8
tired *cansado/a,* 7
to *a,* 4; **to the** *al (a + el), a la,* 4
to *para,* 9
to/for her, him, you *le,* 9; **to/for me** *me,* 9; **to/for them, you** (pl.) *les,* 9; **to/for us** *nos,* 9; **to/for you** *te,* 9
toast *el pan tostado,* 8
today *hoy,* 3
toe *el dedo,* 11
together *juntos/as,* 5
tomato *el tomate,* 8
tomorrow *mañana,* 3
too *también,* 1
too much *demasiado/a,* 6
towel *la toalla,* 12
toy store *la juguetería,* 9
toys *los juguetes,* 9
trash *la basura,* 4
Tuesday *el martes,* 4
tuna *el atún,* 8
twelve *doce,* 1
twenty *veinte,* 1
two *dos,* 1
two hundred *doscientos/as,* 8
typically *típicamente,* 5

U

ugly *feo/a,* 3
uncle *el tío,* 6
under *debajo de,* 4

V

vacation *las vacaciones,* 5; **on vacation** *de vacaciones,* 12
vacuum, to *pasar la aspiradora,* 6
Valentine's Day *el Día de los Enamorados,* 10
vegetables *las legumbres,* 8
very *muy,* 1; **very bad** *muy mal,* 1; **very well** *muy bien,* 1
videogame *el videojuego,* 3
visit, to *visitar,* 6
volleyball *el voleibol,* 1

W

waiter *el camarero,* 8
waitress *la camarera,* 8
walk *la caminata,* 12
walk, to *caminar,* 4; **to walk the dog** *caminar con el perro,* 4
wallet *la cartera,* 9
want, to *querer (ie),* 2
wash, to *lavar,* 4; **to wash oneself** *lavarse,* 7
watch *el reloj,* 2
watch, to *mirar,* 4; **to watch TV** *mirar la televisión,* 4
water *el agua,* 5; **mineral water** *el agua mineral,* 8
we *nosotros/as,* 4
wear, to *llevar,* 9
weather *el tiempo,* 5; **The weather is bad.** *Hace mal tiempo.,* 5; **The weather is nice.** *Hace buen tiempo.,* 5
Wednesday *el miércoles,* 4
week *la semana,* 4
weekend *el fin de semana,* 4
weights *las pesas,* 11
Well . . . *Bueno...,* 2

what? *¿cuál?,* 3; *¿qué?,* 3
What a bargain! *¡Qué ganga!,* 9
What a shame! *¡Qué lástima!,* 7
What are . . . like? *¿Cómo son...?,* 3
What color is . . .? *¿De qué color es...?,* 6
What did you do? *¿Qué hiciste?,* 10
What do you like? *¿Qué te gusta?,* 1
What do you like to do? *¿Qué te gusta hacer?,* 4
What if . . .? *¿Qué tal si...?,* 11
What is today's date? *¿Cuál es la fecha?,* 5
What time is it? *¿Qué hora es?,* 3
What's . . . like? *¿Cómo es...?,* 3
What's the matter? *¿Qué tienes?,* 11
What's the weather like? *¿Qué tiempo hace?,* 5
What's wrong with . . .? *¿Qué le pasa a...?,* 11
What's your name? *¿Cómo te llamas?,* 1
when *cuando,* 5
When? *¿Cuándo?,* 3
where *donde,* 1
Where? *¿Dónde?,* 4; **Where are you from?** *¿De dónde eres?,* 1
Where (to)? *¿Adónde?,* 4
which *que,* 4
Which? *¿Cuál?,* 3; *¿Qué?,* 1
white *blanco/a,* 9
who *que,* 4
who? *¿quién?,* 4; *¿quiénes?,* 5; **Who likes . . .?** *¿A quién le gusta...?,* 4; **Who's calling?** *¿De parte de quién?,* 7
why? *¿por qué?,* 3; **Why don't you . . .?** *¿Por qué no...?,* 11
wife *la esposa,* 6
win, to *ganar,* 11
window *la ventana,* 2
winter *el invierno,* 5
wish, to *querer (ie),* 2
with *con,* 4; **with me** *conmigo,* 4; **with you** *contigo,* 4
wool (made of) *de lana,* 9
work *el trabajo,* 4
work, to *trabajar,* 4; **to work in the garden** *trabajar en el jardín,* 6
worried about something *preocupado/a por algo,* 11
worry, to *preocuparse,* 3; **Don't worry!** *¡No te preocupes!,* 3
write, to *escribir,* 5

Y

year *el año,* 5; **last year** *el año pasado,* 10
yellow *amarillo/a,* 9
yes *sí,* 1
yesterday *ayer,* 10
yet *todavía,* 5; **not yet** *todavía no,* 5
yoga *la yoga,* 11; **to do yoga** *hacer yoga,* 11
you *tú, vosotros/as,* 4
you *usted, ustedes,* 4
younger *menor,* 6
your *tu,* 2; *tus,* 6; *su,* 2; *sus* 6

Z

zero *cero,* 1
zoo *el zoológico,* 7

GRAMMAR INDEX

NOTE: For a summary of the grammar presented in this book see pages 343–347.

PHOTOGRAPHY CREDITS

Abbreviations used: (t) top, (b) bottom, (c) center, (l) left, (r) right, (i) insert, (bkgd) background.

FRONT COVER: (tr), HRW Photo/Marty Granger/Edge Productions; (c), Cosmo Condina/Tony Stone Images. **BACK COVER:** (tr), Frerck/ Odyssey Productions; (c), D. Hornback/International Stock Photos. **FRONT AND BACK COVER COLLAGE:** HRW Photo/Andrew Yates.

CHAPTER OPENERS, PANORAMA CULTURAL, AND ENCUENTRO CULTURAL PAGES: HRW Photo/Scott Van Osdol.

ENCUENTRO CULTURAL PAGE TITLE PEOPLE: Michelle Bridwell/Frontera Fotos.

All photographs belong to Holt, Rinehart and Winston, Inc., by Marty Granger/Edge Productions except:

TABLE OF CONTENTS: Page vi(bl), (c), (br), HRW Photo/Sam Dudgeon; vii(tl), Stuart Cohen/Comstock; viii(bl), (c), HRW Photo/Sam Dudgeon; ix(tc), HRW Photo/Sam Dudgeon; x(bl), (br), HRW Photo/Sam Dudgeon; xi(tl), xi(tr), David Young-Wolf/Photo Edit; xi(bl), HRW Photo/Sam Dudgeon; xi(br), Franklin J. Viola/ Comstock; xii(bl), HRW Photo/Scott Van Osdol; xiii(tl), HRW Photo/Sam Dudgeon; xiii(tl), (br), HRW Photo/Scott Van Osdol; xiv(tc), Scott Van Osdol; xv(tl), (br), Courtesy of *Texas Highways Magazine;* xv(tr), David Ryan/DDB Stock Photo; xv(bl), Scott Van Osdol; xvi(bl); xvii(tr), (br), HRW Photo/Sam Dudgeon; xvii(bl), David Ryan/DDB Stock Photo.

Preliminary Chapter: Page 2(tr), Robert Frerck/Woodfin Camp; 2(tl), (c), (b), Michelle Bridwell/Frontera Fotos; 4(tl), John Swat/Wide World Photos; 4(tr), Culver Pictures, Inc.; 4(c), (bl), The Bettmann Archive; 4(bc), S. Howell/Gamma Liaison; 4(br), HRW Photo; 6(tl), Stephen Dalten/ Animals Animals; 6(cbl), (cbcl), (tc), (bl), (brc), (br), (ctl), (ctr), (ctc), HRW Photo/Sam Dudgeon; 6(cbcr), Superstock; 6(blc), Guido Alberto Rossi/Image Bank; 6(cbr), Animals Animals; 6(tr), F. Mons/Allsport; 7(ctl), (cbr), (cbl), (blc), (trc), (tlc), (cblc), (tl), (cbrc), (br), HRW Photo/ Sam Dudgeon; 7(ctr), Robert Maier/ Animals Animals; 7(ctrc), C. Prescott-Allen/Animals Animals; 7(tr), Johnny Johnson/Animals Animals; 7(ctlc), Michael Fogden/Animals Animals; 7(bl), Michelle Bridwell/Frontera Fotos; 7(brc), SuperStock; 8(t),(b); 9 (All) Michelle Bridwell/Frontera Fotos.

UNIT ONE: Location Openers: Page 12, 13 Dallas & John Heaton/ Westlight; 14(tr), Leo de Wys, Inc./Danilo Boschung; 14(bc), Steve Vidler/Leo de Wys, Inc.; 14(tl), Dallas & John Heaton/Westlight; 15(br), Mike Busselle/Leo de Wys, Inc.; 15(t), SuperStock; 15(cl), Steve Vidler/Leo de Wys, Inc.. **Chapter One:** Page 26(t), David R. Frazier Photolibrary; 27(tr), (tl), HRW Photo/Sam Dudgeon; 27(blc), (tcl), Mavournea Hay; 27(bcr), Laurie O'Meara; 27(ccl), (cl), (bl), (tcr), (ccr), (cr), HRW Photo/Sam Dudgeon; 29(br), (bl), Michelle Bridwell/ Frontera Fotos; 29(c), Gary M. Prior/Allsport; 39(b), Michelle Bridwell/ Frontera Fotos. **Chapter Two:** Page 53, 54, 55(l), (r), 57(All), Michelle Bridwell/Frontera Fotos; 58(l), HRW Photo/Sam Dudgeon; 60(bkgd), HRW Photo/Sam Dudgeon; 63(All), Michelle Bridwell/ Frontera Fotos.

UNIT TWO: Location Openers: Page 66–67, Peter Gridley/FPG International; 68(tr), Marie Ueda/Leo de Wys, Inc.; 68(cl),(b) Randy Faris/ Westlight; 68(cr), Chip and Rosa Maria Peterson; 69(t), SuperStock; 69(cl), (br), Melinda Berge/Bruce Coleman; 69(cr), Randy J. Faris/ Westlight. **Chapter Three:** Page 77(bl), HRW Photo/Eric Beggs; 77(br), (blc), (tr), (tl), HRW Photo/Sam Dudgeon; 77(bcr), (tlc), HRW Photo/ Richard Haynes; 77(trc), HRW Photo/Ken Lax; 78(t), Chip and Rosa Maria Peterson; 83, Michelle Bridwell/Frontera Fotos; 90(bkgd), HRW Photo/Sam Dudgeon; 94(bcl), HRW Photo/Richard Haynes; 94(br), Animals Animals/Charles Palek; 94(bl), HRW Photo/Sam Dudgeon; 94(bcl), Kent Vinyard/ProFiles West; 94(tr), HRW Photo/Eric Beggs; 94(bl), Michelle Bridwell/Frontera Fotos; 94(tcr), HRW Photo. **Chapter Four:** Page 101(bl), (tr), (br), Michelle Bridwell/Frontera Fotos; 101(tl), David Young-Wolf/Photo Edit; 103 (bl), Bob Daemmrich Photography; 103(tc), David R. Frazier Photolibrary; 103(br),(tr), Michelle Bridwell/Frontera Fotos; 103(tl), Robert Frerck/ Woodfin Camp; 103(bc), HRW Photo/Sam Dudgeon; 114(bkgd), FPG International; 118(t), HRW Photo/Sam Dudgeon.

UNIT THREE: Location Openers: Page 120–121, SuperStock; 122(b), Fritz Polking/Peter Arnold, Inc.; 122(t), Stephen Frink/The Stock Market; 123(t), SuperStock; 123(bl), David Phillips; 123(br), Tony Arruza/Bruce Coleman. **Chapter Five:** Page 125(b), Maratea/International Stock Shop; 131(b), CALVIN AND HOBBES © Watterson. Distributed by Universal Press Syndicate. Reprinted with permission. All rights reserved; 132(All), 133(rlc), (lc), (lrc), (r), (rl), Michelle Bridwell/ Frontera Fotos; 133(l), Mark Richards/Photo Edit; 134, Stuart Cohen/ Comstock; 135(tl), D.L. Baldwin/ProFiles West; 135(tr), (tc), (bc), (br), Michelle Bridwell/Frontera Fotos; 135(bl), HRW Photo; 142(t), Michelle Bridwell/Frontera Fotos; 142-143(bkgd), HRW Photo/Sam Dudgeon; 142(b), Bob Martin/Allsport; 143(t), (c), Comstock; 143(b), Peter Grumann/Image Bank; 144(b), HRW Photo/M.L. Miller/Edge Productions. **Chapter Six** Page 153(br), David Young/Photo Edit; 153(tr), (tl), Michelle Bridwell/ Frontera Fotos; 153 (cl), Bachmann/ProFiles West; 157(l), (r), Michelle Bridwell/Frontera Fotos; 158(l), HRW Photo/ M.L. Miller/Edge Productions; 158(c), HRW Photo/M.L. Miller/Edge Productions; 160(blc), (bl), Michelle Bridwell/Frontera Fotos; 160(br), Robert Frerck/Woodfin Camp; 160(brc), HRW Photo; 161, Franklin J. Viola/Comstock; 162(All), HRW Photo/Sam Dudgeon; 164(All), Michelle Bridwell/Frontera Fotos; 168–169(bkgd), David R. Frazier Photolibrary; 168(bl), (br), Michelle Bridwell/Frontera Fotos; 168(t), HRW Photo/M.L. Miller/Edge Productions; 169(tl), (c), Michelle Bridwell/Frontera Fotos; 169(tr), Bob Thomason/Tony Stone; 170 (b), HRW Photo/M.L. Miller/Edge Productions; 172 (All), Natasha Lane.

UNIT FOUR: Location Opener: Page 174-175, R. Smith/Leo de Wys, Inc.; 176(b), Suzanne L. Murphy/DDB Stock Photo; 176(tr), Tui De Roy/ The Roving Tortoise; 177(tl), (cr), Suzanne L. Murphy/DDB Stock Photo; 177(br), Suzanne L. Murphy/FPG International; 178, David Phillips. **Chapter Seven:** Page 179(b), Michelle Bridwell/Frontera Fotos; 183(br), Stuart Cohen/Comstock; 183(r), Comstock; 189(b), Chip and Rosa Maria Peterson; 189(c), David Phillips; 190(All), HRW Photo/ Sam Dudgeon; 193(t), David Phillips; 196-197(bkgd), Superstock. **Chapter Eight:** Page 207(All), 209(l), (r), HRW Photo/Sam Dudgeon; 211(cl), HRW Photo/ M.L. Miller/Edge Productions; 212, From Mafalda 3 © 1989, Joaquin Salvador Lavado (Quino); 216(All), Michelle Bridwell/Frontera Fotos; 221, 222, HRW Photo/Sam Dudgeon; 226(bl), Michelle Bridwell/Frontera Fotos; 226(tl), (tr), (br), HRW Photo/Sam Dudgeon.

UNIT FIVE: Location Openers: Page 228–229, Sanford/Richard Stockton; 230(t), (br), Courtesy of *Texas Highways Magazine;* 230(bl), C.L. Chryslin/The Image Bank; 231(b), Michael Salas/The Image Bank; 231(cr), Bullaty Lomeo/The Image Bank; 231(tl), Michael Schneps/ The Image Bank. **Chapter Nine:** Page 233(t), (b), Michelle Bridwell/ Frontera Fotos; 237(All), HRW Photo/Sam Dudgeon; 246(tr), (bl), (bc), HRW Photo/Sam Dudgeon; 247, Michelle Bridwell/Frontera Fotos; 248, HRW Photo/Sam Dudgeon; 250–251(All), Courtesy of Atkins Agency, San Antonio, TX; 252(tl), (tcl), (tcr), (tr), HRW Photo/Sam Dudgeon; 252(b), Kevin Morris/AllStock; 253(bl), (blc), (brc), (br), HRW Photo/Sam Dudgeon. **Chapter Ten:** Page 256, David R. Frazier Photolibrary; 257(t), David Ryan/DDB Stock Photo; 261(tl), HRW Photo/David Phillips; 261(tr), (br), Chip and Rosa Maria Peterson; 261(tlc), Steven D. Elmore/The Stock Market; 261(trc), Superstock; 261(bl), Bob Daemmrich/ Tony Stone Images; 261(blc), (brc), Michelle Bridwell/Frontera Fotos; 263(All), David Phillips; 272(br), John Feingersh/The Stock Market; 275 (tr), Michelle Bridwell/ Frontera Fotos; 276(tr), Courtesy of *Texas Highways Magazine;* 276(b), Jack Messler/DDB Stock Photo; 276–277(bkgd), HRW Photo/Sam Dudgeon; 276(c), Daniel Aubry/Odyssey; 277(b), Ric Ergenbright; 277(c), Suzanne Murphy-Larronde/DDB Stock Photo; 277(tl), Hector Mendez Caratini; 278(l), (c), (r), David Phillips.

UNIT SIX: Location Openers: Page 282–283, SuperStock; 284(b), Ron Watts/Westlight; 284(t), SuperStock; 285(bl), Ira Block/The Image Bank; 285(cl), David R. Frazier Photolibrary; 285(tl), (br), Suzanne Murphy Larronde/DDB Stock Photo; 285(cr), David R. Frazier Photolibrary. **Chapter Eleven:** Page 286, 287(t), Michelle Bridwell/Frontera Fotos; 297, Michelle Bridwell/Frontera Fotos; 299(c), HRW Photo/M.L. Miller/Edge Productions; 301(cr), Dave Cannon/Tony Stone Images;

301(l), Josu Sturino/Allsport; 303(tl), (tr), (br), Michelle Bridwell/Frontera Fotos; 303(bl), 306(All), 307, Michelle Bridwell/Frontera Fotos. **Chapter Twelve:** Page 313(bl), Michael J. Howell/ProFiles West; 313(tl), James Martin/AllStock; 324(t), David R. Frazier Photolibrary; 326(tr), Art Wolfe/ AllStock; 326(trc), John Heaton/Westlight; 330–331 (bkgd props), Michelle Bridwell/Frontera Fotos.

ILLUSTRATION AND CARTOGRAPHY CREDITS

Arroyo, Fian: 166, 170, 213, 244, 267, 269, 295, 308
Briseño, Jose Luis: 317, 333
Campos, Edson: 22, 32, 117, 131, 136, 139, 186, 194, 242, 292, 296, 300
Castro, Antonio: 52, 86
Cockrille, Eva Vagretti: 64, 107, 138, 199, 239
Cooper, Holly: 75, 84, 87, 243, 262, 322, 330–331
Garcia, Manuel: 28
Gomez, Ignacio: 25, 34, 106, 109, 165, 266, 302, 319, 320, 327
Griffin, David: 50, 217, 219
Heisel, Neel: 6, 20, 23, 24, 29, 38, 39, 62, 88, 112, 156, 191, 195
Henderson, Meryl: 159, 191, 272, 280, 310, 334
Holladay, Reggie: 155, 188
Kinkel, Julie: 29, 35, 38, 85, 88, 92, 116, 166, 171, 182, 185, 195, 198, 217, 224, 246, 273, 293, 297, 324
Lee, Kanokwalee: 222, 223
Maryland CartoGraphics, Inc.: xxi, xxii–xxiii, xxiv, xxv, xxvi, xxvii, xxviii–1, 13, 31, 51, 67, 79, 110, 121, 137, 163, 175, 192, 229, 241, 265, 283, 299, 321
McMahon, Bob: 294, 297, 332
Mistiano, Mauro: 47, 49, 246, 254, 273
Precision Graphics: 9, 10, 21, 78, 92, 140, 145, 215, 254
Pronto Design & Production, Inc.: 250–251
Tachiera, Andrea: 104
Undercuffler, Gary: 108

ACKNOWLEDGMENTS (continued from page ii)

Editorial América, S.A.: From "Dile adiós a las tensiones...¡Con ejercicios!" from the "Consejos" section from *Tú internacional,* año 11, no. 5, May 1990. Copyright © 1990 by Editorial América, S.A. Header, footer, and adaptation of excerpts from "línea directa" from *Tú internacional,* año 13, no. 11, November 1992. Copyright © 1992 by Editorial América, S.A. Excerpts from "La Chica Sándwich" from *Tú internacional,* año 14, no. 1, January 1993. Copyright © 1993 by Editorial América, S.A. Header, footer, and adaptation of excerpts from "línea directa" from *Tú internacional,* año 14, no. 6, June 1993. Copyright © 1993 by Editorial América, S.A.

Editorial Atlántida, S.A.: Front cover from video, *Billiken presenta: Mundo Marino.* Front cover from *La isla del terror* by Tony Koltz, illustrations by Ron Wing. Excerpt from "Deportes en el agua" by Alejandra Becco from *Billiken,* no. 3762, February 17, 1992. Copyright © 1992 by Editorial Atlántida, S.A.

Editorial de Vecchi, S.A.: Front cover from *Guía completa para el adiestramiento del perro* by Vittoria Rossi.

Editorial Everest, S.A.: Front cover from *Everest enciclopedia ilustrada de los animales, Tomo I: Mamíferos* by Dr. Philip Whitfield. Copyright © by Editorial Everest, S.A.

Editorial Televisión, S.A. de C.V.: Excerpts adapted from *Tele*Guía,* año 42, no. 2159, December 25–31, 1993. Copyright © 1993 by Editorial Televisión, S.A. de C.V.

Emecé Editores, S.A.: Front cover from *50 cosas que los niños pueden hacer para salvar la tierra* by The Earth Works Group.

Fortín Salteño: Restaurant receipt from Fortín Salteño.

G+J España, S.A.: Text that accompanies front covers of books (*Everest enciclopedia ilustrada de los animales, Tomo I: Mamíferos* by Dr. Philip Whitfield, *50 cosas que los niños pueden hacer para salvar la tierra* by The Earth Works Group, *Mi Primer Video de Naturaleza,* and *Guía completa para el adiestramiento del perro* by V. Rossi) from "Libro" section from *Natura,* no. 106, January 1992. Copyright © 1992 by G+J España, S.A.

Gativideo S.A.: Front cover from video, *Las nuevas adventuras de Mofli* by Gativideo.

Gessler Publishing Co., Inc.: From "Holidays" from *Hispanic Culture Capsules* by Gessler Publishing Co., Inc. Copyright © 1992 by Gessler Publishing Co., Inc.

Greater Miami Convention & Visitors Bureau: From "Festival Fever" from brochure, *Destination: Greater Miami & The Beaches,* July 1993–January 1994. Translated into Spanish by Holt, Rinehart and Winston, Inc.

Holt, Rinehart and Winston, Inc.: Map, "Territorial Acquisitions of the United Sates 1783-1853," from *World History: People and Nations,* 1993 Edition, Pupil's Edition, by Anatole G. Mazour and John M. Peoples. Copyright © 1993 by Holt, Rinehart and Winston, Inc.

Hotel Tryp María Pita: Advertisement for "Hotel Tryp María Pita."

Instituto Municipal de Deportes, Ayuntamiento de Madrid: Advertisement for "Piscina Municipal Aluche" from the "En Forma" section from *Guía El País,* no. 57, December 27, 1990.

La Guarida del Coyote: Advertisement for "La Guarida del Coyote" from brochure, *Viajes y entretenimientos: Guía de establecimientos Diners Club del Ecuador.*

Mango: Photographs, descriptive labels, and prices from Suplemento Mango, Summer 1992. Photographs, descriptive labels, and prices from Mango, Winter 1992–1993.

Metro Vídeo Española, S.L.: Front cover from video, *Los dinosaurios. Su descubrimiento.*

Normandie: Advertisement for "Normandie: Cocina Francesca Clásica" from brochure, *Viajes y entretenimientos: Guía de establecimientos Diners Club del Ecuador.*

The Quintus Communications Group: Excerpts from "Diez cosas curiosas para hacer en la Pequeña Habana" (Retitled: "Cinco cosas curiosas para hacer en la Pequeña Habana") from *Miami Mensual,* año 13, no. 3, March 1993. Copyright © 1993 by The Quintus Communications Group.

Rincón la Ronda Restaurante: Advertisement for "Rincón la Ronda Restaurante" from brochure, *Viajes y entretenimientos: Guía de establecimientos Diners Club del Ecuador.*

San Antonio Convention Center and Visitors Bureau: "San Antonio" design, text and photograph from "1: Rio San Antonio," text and photograph from "16: Las Misiones," text from "San Antonio ofrece generosas porciones de su vida cosmopolita,...añaden su sabor propio," text and photographs from "Festivales," text and photographs from "Restaurantes," and text and photographs from "Compras" from *San Antonio...Guía de visitantes y mapa* by the Oficina de Convenciones y Visitantes de San Antonio. From "Fiesta San Antonio 1994" news release by San Antonio Convention and Visitors Bureau.

Scholastic, Inc.: Adapted text, photographs, and illustrations from "¿Cuáles son las vacaciones ideales para ti?" from *¿Qué tal?,* vol. 24, no. 6, April–May 1990. Copyright © 1990 by Scholastic, Inc.

Trade & Travel Publications Ltd.: From "Festivals" from "Ecuador" section from *South American Handbook,* 1989. Copyright © 1988 by Trade & Travel Publications Ltd. Translated into Spanish by Holt, Rinehart and Winston, Inc.